An Information Systems Approach to
Object-Oriented Programming Using Microsoft® Visual C#® .NET

Kyle Lutes

Alka Harriger

Jack Purdum

THOMSON
™
COURSE TECHNOLOGY

Australia • Canada • Mexico • Singapore • Spain • United Kingdom • United States

THOMSON
COURSE TECHNOLOGY

An Information Systems Approach to Object-Oriented Programming Using Microsoft® Visual C#® .NET
by Kyle Lutes, Alka Harriger, and Jack Purdum

Executive Editor:
Mac Mendelsohn

Managing Editor:
William Pitkin III

Senior Acquisitions Editor:
Drew Strawbridge

Senior Product Manager:
Tricia Boyle

Associate Product Manager:
Sarah Santoro

Product Marketing Manager:
Brian Berkeley

Editorial Assistant:
Jennifer Smith

Production Editors:
BobbiJo Frasca, Kelly Robinson

Cover Designer:
Laura Rickenbach

Compositor:
GEX Publishing Services

Senior Manufacturing Coordinator:
Laura Burns

Copy Editor:
Foxxe Editorial Services

Proofreader:
John Bosco

Indexer:
Michael Brackney

To Sally.
– Kyle

To the four most important people in my life—Brad, Josh, Logan, and Amber.
– Alka

In memory of my parents, Jeanette and John.
– Jack

Contents

PREFACE xix

READ THIS BEFORE YOU BEGIN xxvii

CHAPTER ONE
Introduction to Object-Oriented Programming 1

CHAPTER TWO
Creating a Simple Application 17

CHAPTER THREE
Storing Data in Objects 51

CHAPTER FOUR
Manipulating Data in Objects 77

CHAPTER FIVE
Changing the Program Flow with Decisions 115

CHAPTER SIX
Catching Exceptions 157

CHAPTER SEVEN
Adding Methods for Objects 187

CHAPTER EIGHT
Program Loops 223

CHAPTER NINE
Arrays and Collections 261

CHAPTER TEN
Encapsulation 309

CHAPTER ELEVEN
Object Persistence Using Data Files 347

CHAPTER TWELVE
User Interface Objects 393

CHAPTER THIRTEEN
Database Connectivity with ADO.NET 447

CHAPTER FOURTEEN
Inheritance and Polymorphism 493

APPENDIX A
C# Keywords   529

APPENDIX B
C# Coding Standards and Guidelines   531

APPENDIX C
Using the Visual Studio Debugger   541

APPENDIX D
Speed-Coding Tips and Tricks   553

APPENDIX E
Application Deployment   557

INDEX   565

TABLE OF

Contents

PREFACE xix

READ THIS BEFORE YOU BEGIN xxvii

CHAPTER ONE
Introduction to Object-Oriented Programming 1
Brief History of Object-Oriented Programming 2
Using Objects in OOP 3
Using Classes in OOP 3
The OOP Trilogy 4
Encapsulation 4
Polymorphism 5
Inheritance 5
An Example Using Objects 6
Why Learn C#? 7
Using Objects in C# 8
Object Instantiation—Creating Objects from Classes 8
The Dot Operator—Key to Getting Inside the Object 9
The .NET Framework Class Library 12
Summary 13
Key Terms 13
Review Questions 14
Programming Exercises 14

CHAPTER TWO
Creating a Simple Application 17
Essential Topics 18
Terminology 18
Introduction to Visual Studio .NET 19
Analyzing the Problem and Designing the Solution 20
Creating the Visual Studio Project Files 21
Creating the User Interface Using the Form Designer 26
Using Regions 27
Changing Form Properties 27
Placing Controls on a Form 30
Adding the Application Logic 32
Adding the Program Logic Source Code 32
Program Events 34
Code Explanation 35
Initialization 35
Event Methods 35
Constants and Variables 36
Making the Code Easier to Read 36
Getting the User's Input 37
Validating the User Input 37
Performing the Calculations 38
Displaying the Results to the User 38
Testing the Program 39
Program Errors 39
Debugging 40

Bonus Topics   **42**
Source Code Format   42
    Comments   43
    Brace Alignment   43
    Visual Studio .NET Project Files   44
    MSIL, the CLR, and JIT Compiling   45
Summary   46
    Essential Topics   46
    Bonus Topics   47
Key Terms   47
    Essential Terms   47
    Bonus Terms   47
Review Questions   48
    Essential Questions   48
    Bonus Questions   48
Programming Exercises   49
    Essential Exercises   49
    Bonus Exercise   49

CHAPTER THREE
Storing Data in Objects   **51**
Essential Topics   **52**
Types of Data Available in C# Programs   52
Numeric Data Types   52
    Integer Data Types   52
    Monetary Values   56
    Floating-Point Numbers   56
    Additional Data Types   58
Reference Data Types   59
    Storing Textual Data Using the String Data Type   61
Choosing bool or DateTime Types   61
Identifier Naming Rules and Conventions   62
    Defining Variables   63
    Defining Constants   65
    Why Use Constants   66
Bonus Topics   **67**
The char Data Type   67
    What Can a char Store?   67
    Special Characters   67
    Verbatim Character with String Literals 68
How C# Creates Variables   69
    lvalues   70
    Define versus Declare   72
Summary   72
    Essential Topics   72
    Bonus Topics   72
Key Terms   73
    Essential Terms   73
    Bonus Terms   73
Review Questions   73
    Essential Questions   73
    Bonus Questions   74
Programming Exercises   74

CHAPTER FOUR
Manipulating Data in Objects   **77**
    Essential Topics   **78**
    Manipulating Numbers   78
        Arithmetic Operators   78
        Type Casting   82
        Arithmetic Expressions   84
    A Program Example   87
        User Interface for the Restaurant Bill Calculator Application   88
        Restaurant Bill Calculator Logic   89
        Initialization   89
        Obtaining the User's Input 90
        Performing the Calculation 90
        Displaying the Results   91
        Testing the Restaurant Bill Calculator   91
        Improving the Restaurant Bill Calculator   93
        Testing the Improved Restaurant Bill Calculator   94
        Introduce an Error to Test Debugging   94
    Manipulating Strings   95
        Concatenation   95
        IndexOf Method   96
        Length Property   97
    Finding Substrings and Parsing   97
        ToUpper Method   98
        ToLower Method   98
    A Program Example   99
        Contact Info User Interface 99
    Bonus Topics   **101**
    Other Common Tasks Using the .NET Framework Classes   102
        Additional String Methods   102
        Insert Method   102
        Remove Method   103
        Trim Method   103
        Replace Method   103
    DateTime Manipulations   104
        Displaying DateTime Information   104
        Retrieving and Manipulating DateTime Information   106
    Using the Math Class   107
        Math.PI (π)   107
    Methods   108
    Summary   109
        Essential Topics   109
        Bonus Topics   110
    Key Terms   110
        Essential Terms   110
        Bonus Terms   110
    Review Questions   111
        Essential Questions   111
    Bonus Questions   112
    Programming Exercises   112
        Essential Exercises   112
        Bonus Exercises   113

CHAPTER FIVE
Changing the Program Flow with Decisions   **115**
    Essential Topics   **116**
    Boolean Expressions   116
        Comparing Numbers   116
        Operator Precedence   118
        Comparing Non-Numbers   118

Comparing Booleans 119
Comparing Dates and Times 119
Conditional Logical Operators 126
Decision Statements 129
True-Only Conditions 130
True and False Conditions 130
Nested Decisions 131
Cascading Decisions 132
Robust Data Validation 134
A Strategy for Data Validation 134
When Should You Validate Data? 135
What Should You Do When Input Values Are Incorrect? 135
Displaying a Better Message Box 136
Existence Check 138
Data Type Check 138
Range Check 139
Reasonableness Check 139
Code Check 140
Cross-Field Check 141
A Program Example 142
Developing the Application 142
Validating Input Values 144
Testing the Validation Logic 146
Bonus Topics **146**
The Switch Statement 146
Alternative Decision Statement Styles 148
Brace Alignment 148
Comparing Boolean Variables to True and False 148
Omitting Braces 149
Early Returns 150
Using System.Globalization for Improved Data Entry 151
Summary 152
Essential Topics 152
Bonus Topics 152
Key Terms 153
Essential Terms 153
Bonus Terms 153
Review Questions 153
Essential Questions 153
Bonus Questions 154
Programming Exercises 155
Essential Exercises 155
Bonus Exercises 156

CHAPTER SIX
Catching Exceptions **157**
Essential Topics **158**
What Are Exceptions? 158
Types of Errors 160
What Causes Exceptions? 161
Why Catch Exceptions? 163
What to Do When You Catch an Exception 163
Syntax for Exception Handlers 163
Data Type Check 164
A General Exception Handler 169
Syntax for Generalized Exception Handlers 169
When to Catch Exceptions 173
Bonus Topics **176**
Catching Exceptions of a Specific Type 177

Throwing Your Own Exceptions   181
Exceptions and the Call Stack   182
Summary   183
   Essential Topics   183
   Bonus Topics   183
Key Terms   184
   Essential Terms   184
   Bonus Terms   184
Review Questions   184
   Essential Questions   184
   Bonus Questions   185
Programming Exercises   186
   Essential Exercises   186
   Bonus Exercises   186

CHAPTER SEVEN
Adding Methods for Objects   **187**
  Essential Topics   **188**
What Is a Method?   188
Private Helper Methods   190
Communicating between Methods   192
   Scope   192
   Parameters   194
   Return Values   200
What Constitutes a "Good" Method?   201
A Program Example   202
   Passing Reference Data Types   204
   A Method for Data Validation   206
When to Use a Method   208
The Call Stack and Methods   210
  Bonus Topics   **211**
Using out Method Arguments   211
Method Overhead   213
Instance versus Shared Methods   216
Signatures   217
Method Overloading   218
Summary   219
   Essential Topics   219
   Bonus Topics   219
Key Terms   220
   Essential Terms   220
   Bonus Terms   220
Review Questions   220
   Essential Questions   220
   Bonus Questions   221
Programming Exercises   221
   Essential Exercises   221
   Bonus Exercises   222

CHAPTER EIGHT
Program Loops   **223**
  Essential Topics   **224**
ListBoxes   224
   Why Use ListBoxes   224
   How to Add an Item to a ListBox   225
   How to Determine Which Item in a ListBox Is Selected   226
   How to Remove an Item from a ListBox   227
   How to Clear the Contents of a ListBox   228
   How to Count Items in a ListBox   228

How to Sort Items in a ListBox   229
How to Select an Item in a ListBox   229
A ListBox Program Example   230
Constructing Loops   233
Three Conditions of a Well-Behaved Loop   234
The counting Loop   235
The while Loop   235
The for loop   241
The foreach Loop   243
The break Statement   245
When and Why to Use the break Statement   246
Bonus Topics   **247**
Writing while Loops with Compound and Complex Conditions   247
Recursion   249
Nested Loops   251
The continue Keyword   253
Summary   255
Essential Topics   255
Bonus Topics   255
Key Terms   256
Essential Terms   256
Bonus Terms   256
Review Questions   256
Essential Questions   256
Bonus Questions   257
Programming Exercises   257
Essential Exercises   257
Bonus Exercises   259

CHAPTER NINE
Arrays and Collections

                                                                       261
Essential Topics   **262**
How Arrays Resemble ListBoxes   262
Why Use Arrays?   262
Terminology   263
Single-Dimensional Arrays   266
ArrayLists Defined   282
Sorting ArrayLists   286
Bonus Topics   **290**
Multidimensional Arrays   290
Other Collection Types   294
Enumerators   295
Hash Tables   295
Queues   299
Stacks   302
Additional Collection Types   304
Summary   305
Essential Topics   305
Bonus Topics   305
Key Terms   306
Essential Terms   306
Bonus Terms   306
Review Questions   306
Essential Questions   306
Bonus Questions   307
Programming Exercises   308
Essential Exercises   308
Bonus Exercises   308

CHAPTER TEN
Encapsulation — 309

Essential Topics — 310
Encapsulation Review — 310
Creating Your Own Classes — 310
Access Specifiers for Methods and Properties — 312
Which Access Specifier Is Best? — 314
    Class User Interfaces — 314
How to Determine Whether get or set Is Called — 316
Why Not Use the public Keyword for All Class Members? — 317
    Guidelines for Designing Accessor Methods — 317
Setting the Initial State of an Object Variable — 319
    Data Member Initialization — 319
Class Constructors — 321
Why Use an Explicit Constructor? — 322
Overloaded Constructors — 323
Why Method Overloading Is a Good Thing — 325
Removing Objects from a Program — 325
How the Program Works — 335
    Storing the Contacts — 336
Bonus Topics — 337
Memory Management — 337
The Program Stack — 337
    Out of Scope — 338
    Managed Heap — 339
Freeing Object References — 340
    Object Reference Goes out of Scope — 340
    Assigning the Value null — 340
    Using Destructors — 341
Summary — 342
    Essential Topics — 342
    Bonus Topics — 342
Key Terms — 343
    Essential Terms — 343
    Bonus Terms — 343
Review Questions — 343
    Essential Questions — 343
    Bonus Questions — 344
Programming Exercises — 344

CHAPTER ELEVEN
Object Persistence Using Data Files — 347

Essential Topics — 348
Why Is Object Persistence Needed? — 348
The Windows File System — 349
    Disks — 349
    Folders — 349
    Files — 350
The .NET System.IO Namespace — 352
    System.IO.Directory — 353
    System.IO.File — 355
    System.IO.Path — 356
Types of Files — 357
    Text and Binary Files — 357
    Sequential Data Files — 359
Persistence Using Sequential Text Files — 361

A Program Example   366
    Serialization and Persistence   366
    Catching Exceptions   371
Bonus Topics   **373**
File Open and File Save Dialogs   373
Fixed-Width Text Files   377
    Reading Fixed-Width Records   379
    Writing Fixed-Width Records   381
Persistence Using Binary Data Files   381
    Viewing the Contents of a Binary Data File   385
Summary   386
    Essential Topics   386
    Bonus Topics   387
Key Terms   388
    Essential Terms   388
    Bonus Terms   388
Review Questions   389
    Essential Questions   389
    Bonus Questions   389
Programming Exercises   390
    Essential Exercises   390
    Bonus Exercises   391

CHAPTER TWELVE
User Interface Objects   **393**
  Essential Topics   **394**
Common Properties, Events, and Methods   394
    Anchor Property   394
    BackColor and ForeColor Properties   395
    Enabled Property   395
    Font Property   395
    Image Property   396
    Left, Top, Width, and Height Properties   396
    Locked Property   396
    Name Property   396
    TabIndex and TabStop Properties   396
    Text and TextAlign Properties   397
    Visible Property   398
    Click and DoubleClick Events   398
    Enter and Leave Events   398
    KeyDown, KeyPress, and KeyUp Events   399
    Focus Method   400
    Hide and Show Methods   400
    Refresh Method   400
Form Objects   401
    The Form Show and ShowDialog Methods   404
    Properties for Common Form Styles   405
Label Objects   406
TextBox Objects   406
Button Objects   408
CheckBox Objects   409
ComboBox Objects   409
DateTimePicker Objects   411
GroupBox Objects   412
ListView Objects   412
    Adding Columns to a ListView   414
    Adding Rows to a ListView   415
    Determining Which Rows Are Selected   415
    Removing a Row from a ListView   415
    Sorting the Contents of a ListView   416

Menu Objects 418
 Adding Menus to Forms 418
NumericUpDown Objects 419
RadioButton Objects 420
Timer Objects 421
ToolBar Objects 422
 Adding Buttons to a Toolbar 423
StatusBar Objects 424
A Program Example 424
 Summary of Changes 425
 Interform Communication 426
Bonus Topics **429**
User Interface Design Guidelines 429
Special Effects with Forms 431
Printing Reports 432
 Objects Used for Printing Reports 433
 A Report Example 434
Summary 441
 Essential Topics 441
 Bonus Topics 442
Key Terms 443
 Essential Terms 443
 Bonus Terms 443
Review Questions 444
 Essential Questions 444
 Bonus Questions 445
Programming Exercises 445
 Essential Exercises 445
 Bonus Exercises 446

CHAPTER THIRTEEN
Database Connectivity with ADO.NET   447
Essential Topics **448**
Database Management Systems 448
Relational Databases 448
 Relational Database Terminology 449
Introduction to SQL 450
 Retrieving Data 452
 Inserting Rows 455
 Updating Rows 455
 Deleting Rows 455
Formatting SQL Statements in Code 456
Database Connectivity Using ADO.NET 459
 The ADO.NET OLE DB Data Provider Classes 460
 Using ADO.NET with C# 461
 The Impedance Mismatch between OOP and Relational Databases 469
 A Program Example 470
Bonus Topics **475**
Bound Controls 475
 Using Bound Controls to Display the Contents of a Database Table 476
Dynamically Creating a Jet Database 482
 Data Definition Language (DDL) 484
 Adding Tables and Columns to a Table 485
Aggregate Queries 486
Summary 487
 Essential Topics 487
 Bonus Topics 488
Key Terms 488
 Essential Terms 488
 Bonus Terms 488

    Review Questions 489
        Essential Questions 489
        Bonus Questions 490
    Programming Exercises 490
        Essential Exercises 490
        Bonus Exercises 491

CHAPTER FOURTEEN
Inheritance and Polymorphism 493

    Essential Topics **494**
    What Is Inheritance? 494
        Inheritance and "is a" Relationships 495
        Benefits of Inheritance 495
    Using Inheritance 496
    Using Inheritance—Program Analysis and Design 496
    The protected Access Specifier 500
        Composite Formatting of String Data 507
        The frmMain Code 508
        Method Overriding 514
    Using Interfaces 515
        Interfaces with Properties and Methods 519
    Bonus Topics **521**
    Serializing Objects 521
        Writing the Object's State 521
        Reading the Object 522
    Summary 524
        Essential Topics 524
        Bonus Topics 525
    Key Terms 525
        Essential Terms 525
        Bonus Terms 525
    Review Questions 525
        Essential Questions 525
        Bonus Questions 526
    Programming Exercises 527
        Essential Exercises 527
        Bonus Exercise 527

APPENDIX A
C# Keywords 529

APPENDIX B
C# Coding Standards and Guidelines 531

    Introduction 531
    Naming Conventions 531
        Variables 531
        User Interface Objects 532
        Consistency 532
        Methods 533
        Class and Source Code Files 534
    Comments 534
    Method Comments 534
    Predefined Data Types 535
    Format 535
        White Space 535
        One Statement per Line 536
        Indenting 536
        Brace Alignment 537
        Variable-Declaration Placement 538

Type Conversions   538
Decisions   539
Qualified Type Names   540

APPENDIX C
Using the Visual Studio Debugger   541
Types of Program Errors   541
Before You Use the Debugger...   542
Displaying the Debug Toolbar   542
A Sample Program to Debug   543
Setting a Breakpoint   545
The Locals Window   546
The Autos Window   547
Clearing a Breakpoint   548
Single-Stepping a Program   548
Step Into versus Step Over   548
The Watch Window   549
The Command Window   551
Boundary Values   551
Other Windows   552

APPENDIX D
Speed-Coding Tips and Tricks   553
General Tips   553
Using Dynamic Help   554
Code Editor Keyboard Tricks   554

APPENDIX E
Application Deployment   557
Creating a Setup Package Using VS.NET   558
Installing an Application   563

INDEX   565

Preface

An *Information Systems Approach to Object-Oriented Programming Using Microsoft Visual C# .NET* is an introductory computer programming text designed to be used in Information Systems, Information Technology, and other application-oriented curricula. Although thousands of introductory programming texts exist, there are none that combine the four attributes that account for the uniqueness of this book:

- Teaches computer programming from an ***application developer perspective***, rather than focusing on how programming languages and compilers work.
- Teaches object-oriented programming by ***integrating it throughout the text***, rather than "grafting" a chapter on to the end as many other texts will do.
- Teaches object-oriented programming with no prior programming experience assumed.
- Uses ***C#*** as the programming language to develop ***Windows forms-based applications*** (rather than console applications) to teach programming concepts and techniques.

If you want to learn how to develop useful Windows forms-based applications using an object-oriented programming language, this book is for you!

THE CASE FOR C#

Today's market has many programming language alternatives for software development. In the recent past, Java drew considerable interest while Visual Basic held on to a strong constituency. However, C# has quickly become the fastest-growing programming language, and that trend is expected to continue in the coming years based on reports published by Gartner. A recent study by *Visual Studio Magazine* even reported that C# programmers earned higher salaries than Visual Basic programmers.

Although Visual Basic is widely accepted as an easy language for beginners to learn, its opponents label Visual Basic as a "toy" programming language limited to simple programming tasks and not suitable for complex application development. We have found many students share this uninformed opinion and object to having to learn Visual Basic.

On the other hand, C++ and Java have been favorites of professional software developers, but these languages tend to be more challenging for a beginner to learn and use to develop useful applications. Nonetheless, there are many computing curricula that opt to use C++ or Java in their introductory programming courses.

Microsoft advertises C# as a language that combines the elegance of C++ with the productivity enhancements offered by Visual Basic, resulting in significant productivity enhancements for the developer who's building complex software applications. Our experience (and the experience of other software developers) confirms the authenticity of this statement. Further, the similarities of C# to Java and C++ make it easier for students to move to these other C-based programming languages should the need arise.

There are no definitive statistics on the installed base for Visual Studio .NET (VS .NET). However, Microsoft has aggressively marketed VS .NET and has signed numerous licensing agreements with many major institutions that allow students and faculty to use VS .NET for free, or to purchase it at a modest price. These licensing incentives make it easier for an educational institution to consider using VS .NET somewhere in the programming curriculum.

The entire .NET paradigm of a single class framework and integrated development environment (IDE) for all of its languages and tools makes it very difficult for any would-be competitor to duplicate the same development environment. The IDE is also designed to make Web and Pocket PC application development much easier. Indeed, the fact that a single IDE supports not only C#, but also Visual Basic and C++, provides a one-stop-shopping set of tools for the programmer.

All of these facts suggest that academia has strong motivation to use C# in the programming curricula rather than Visual Basic, Java, and C++, particularly at the introductory level. A few notable schools are just now beginning to recognize the value of using C# to teach introductory object-oriented programming to undergraduates. Schools that want to play a leadership role in the IT education community (as well as take advantage of various Microsoft incentives) should consider using C# to teach object-oriented programming in the introductory course.

APPROACH

This book is designed to be used by instructors who are looking for an easy-to-use alternative to Visual Basic, C++, or Java for their introductory computer programming courses in Information Systems, Information Technology, and other application-oriented curricula. The typical audience consists of college students with no prior computer programming experience. Additionally, high school students or anyone wishing to learn C# as a first or subsequent object-oriented programming language will find this book useful.

We believe the approach used in this book makes it easier to teach object-oriented programming to students. Unlike many books on the market, this book applies OOP techniques in a consistent fashion *throughout* the text. We begin with a simple, yet effective, introduction to the fundamental concepts of OOP in a familiar, approachable manner. This approach should remove any perceived barriers or fears that teachers and students may have regarding learning object-oriented programming.

The initial introduction stresses the concept of objects, while the details about the topics of encapsulation, polymorphism, and inheritance are discussed at the appropriate places later in the text. Because we envision this text as serving a one semester introductory course, we think the emphasis at this level should be on the encapsulation aspects of OOP (i.e., "data hiding" as it applies to object properties and methods). This emphasis enables us to (1) provide the novice programmer with the appropriate mindset necessary to successfully use OOP techniques, and 2) "convert" the student with procedural programming experience to the OOP paradigm. We believe this approach provides an effective means by which the student can prepare for the more advanced topics of OOP discussed later in the book.

VS .NET is a powerful tool designed for professional software developers and comes with numerous predefined templates and source code generating wizards. However, we find this predefined source code to be unnecessarily complex, and it often does not follow a consistent coding style. *The approach we present discourages the use of generated source code and instead encourages students to write their own code.* We feel that students learn more about how their programs work if they create their projects from scratch, and this approach enriches the learning experience for the student.

For academic programs that teach multiple languages, C# is a good choice for the introductory course. The IDE of Visual Studio facilitates the learning process for the novice programmer, much like what many novices have experienced when learning Visual Basic. Because of the syntax similarity between C#, C++, and Java, once students complete this book, they should be able to transition easily to C++ and/or Java later in the curriculum. Thus, schools that focus on C++ or Java in upper-division courses, but wish to introduce students to object-oriented programming in an approachable way, can benefit from using C# with this book.

All source code for the examples used in this book is included with the supplementary materials that accompany this text. In addition to applying learned concepts by following the supplementary material as they review these program examples, students may get more programming practice by completing the end-of-chapter programming exercises. Sidebars are used where appropriate to discuss tips, techniques, and common programming mistakes. Finally, boldface Courier font is used to help identify C# terms that appear in the text.

After completing the book, students will be able to both explain OOP concepts and use C# to develop practical and useful Windows applications. Furthermore, students will be equipped with the skills and confidence necessary to continue on to more advanced software development courses.

ORGANIZATION AND COVERAGE

The authors believe that there are many issues to present when covering each core programming topic. Some of these issues are critical to program development, whereas other issues simply allow a programmer to enhance an application further or develop it using different techniques. For this reason, the majority of the book divides each chapter into two sections—Essential and Bonus. The Essential section covers the fundamentals of that chapter's subject. The optional Bonus section delves deeper into that chapter's subject area for students and instructors who wish to learn more detailed information and additional related topics. For example, the Essential section in the chapter on iterations (looping) contains the familiar **while** and **for** constructs, and the Bonus section covers recursion. Similarly, the Essential section in the chapter on persistence using files covers simple, tab-delimited text files, and the Bonus section covers persistence using binary files.

We believe this two-part chapter approach has several benefits. It shortens the length of the topics into more easily digestible portions. It gives the reader a chance to understand the general concepts before delving into the details. And most important, it gives course instructors flexibility in how to use the text to best fit the course audience. For example, one instructor may choose to use only the Essential section of each chapter, whereas another instructor may choose to use the Essential section of some chapters and both the Essential and Bonus sections of others. This approach makes it easy for instructors to tailor a class to their needs and time constraints while still teaching the full gamut of OOP.

The two-part chapter design is also applied to the end of chapter material, which includes a bulleted chapter summary, list of key terms, list of review questions, and programming exercises.

For the Student

All chapters use illustrative examples to convey concepts. The authors believe that the best way to learn how to program is to get a good deal of practice writing as many programs as possible. We suggest that you first read the chapter and all program examples assigned by your teacher and then write the programs by following the steps described in the chapter. If you encounter difficulty, you should review Appendix C, which illustrates how to use the debugging tools to step through your program to see how it works. You can also review the source code supplied with the accompanying materials for this book. Once your program works, try making small changes and use the debugging tools again to see the effect of your changes.

You should also try to develop solutions for several programming exercises at the end of each chapter. Remember, the more practice you get, the better you will understand each programming concept. You should also gauge your comprehension of terminology and basic concepts by defining each of the key terms and answering the review questions. By using all the tools that are part of this book, you will learn how to develop useful Windows programs using C# and object-oriented techniques.

For the Instructor

The Essential and Bonus sections in each chapter along with five appendices gives you the greatest flexibility in defining the content you wish to cover in a semester or term. Although you may be able to cover a few chapters in a different order, the book is best used in the order presented because some chapters build on examples developed in earlier chapters. The following discussion explains the main content of each chapter and how it follows a natural, intuitive order for teaching OOP.

Chapter 1 introduces students to OOP concepts using a familiar example describing a meeting between a recruiter and a job applicant. The Essential section of Chapter 2 walks the students through the process of creating a simple application using C# and VS .NET. It helps overcome the intimidation factor by enabling students to recognize that the C# language used in the program can be read and understood even before studying the details of its syntax. The Bonus section of this chapter shares a few optional topics to make programming with C# and VS .NET easier.

The Essential section of Chapter 3 explains data types and variables, and the Bonus section includes additional information about string variables while also illustrating how variables are stored in memory. Once students understand basic data types, Chapter 4 introduces operators and methods for manipulating numbers and strings. The Bonus section describes extra methods for string manipulation, the `DateTime` data type, and explains how to use methods in the `Math` class.

Now that students can write programs that can manipulate different types of data, Chapter 5 explains how to change the program flow with decisions. A recommended approach for data validation is also shared in the Essential section of this chapter, while the Bonus section describes the case structure, alternative conditional expression syntax, and early returns. Chapter 6 presents how exception handling should be used to prevent a program from crashing due to runtime errors. The Essential section describes a general-purpose approach, while the Bonus section explains how to catch specific exceptions, how to throw your own exceptions, and how to display the call stack.

At this point, students may be finding that their source code is getting rather lengthy, so this is an appropriate time to show students how to modularize their code by adding methods to classes. The Essential section of Chapter 7 provides reasons for doing this and also illustrates the benefits by creating helper methods for previously written programs. The Bonus section shows how to overload methods and explains the benefit of using "out" arguments.

Once students can write their own methods, the Essential section of Chapter 8 shows them how to use `ListBoxes` to hold multiple sets of data. Next, they learn the benefit of writing the processing steps for one set of data within a loop. The `while`, `for`, and `foreach` loop statements are presented. In the Bonus section, students compare loops to recursion and write nested loops.

Now that students are equipped with the skills to use iterative structures in their programs, the Essential section of Chapter 9 introduces the concept of single-dimensional arrays, array methods, searching, sorting, and the `ArrayList` class. The Bonus section supplements this material by presenting multidimensional arrays, hash tables, stacks, and queues.

Chapter 10 illustrates the OOP concept of encapsulation, including public and private data members, constructors, and accessor methods. The Bonus section describes memory management and garbage collection. Chapter 11 applies the encapsulation concepts when introducing object persistence using sequential data files. The Essential section describes object serialization and deserialization as applied to reading and writing text files. The Bonus section covers binary files and the use of the open and save file dialogs.

Thus far, most examples have used four basic user interface objects—forms, labels, text boxes, and buttons. However, many students may want to be able to enhance their forms with other user interface objects. Chapter 12 illustrates how the interface may be improved by using multiple forms and `CheckBox`, `ComboBox`, `DateTimePicker`, `GroupBox`, `ListView`, `Menu`, `NumericUpDown`, `RadioButton`, `Timer`, `ToolBar`, and `StatusBar` objects. The Bonus section recommends user interface design guidelines as well as how to print reports from within an application. Instructors who prefer to use more form objects than text boxes, labels, and command buttons may opt to cover this chapter as early as Chapter 4. During a class testing, one of the authors gave Chapter 12 as a reading assignment, and students were able to pick up how to use many new form objects on their own.

Chapter 13 illustrates object persistence to a relational database. The Essential section presents basic SQL syntax for queries, inserting rows, updating rows, deleting rows, and dealing with the embedded quotes problem. ADO.NET is used to connect to a Microsoft Access database table. The Bonus section shows students how to write code that can dynamically create a Microsoft Access database and illustrates how to quickly build a database-driven application using bound controls.

Chapter 14 sums up the subject of OOP by discussing inheritance and polymorphism. This chapter teaches the concepts using a non-trivial application and avoids the overused examples often found in many introductory programming texts.

The five appendices are resources to be used by students at any point in their studies. Appendix A contains a list of C# keywords. Appendix B documents the coding styles and programming guidelines we suggest. Appendix C provides an overview of the debugging tools found in VS .NET. Appendix D presents tips and tricks to speed up coding. Finally, Appendix E shows how to create a setup package to deploy an application to another computer.

KEY FEATURES

The following pedagogical elements help distinguish this textbook from other titles:

- Each chapter identifies learning objectives for both the Essential topics and Bonus topics, so that the student is aware of what to expect.
- Program examples are illustrated with numerous screen shots to allow a student to follow along with relative ease. The source code for all examples is available for comparison purposes, should the student encounter difficulty.
- Chapter summaries identify the key points in a descriptive, bulleted list format, separated into Essential and Bonus topics. The summaries equip the student with a mechanism to review the chapter's key concepts quickly.
- A list of key terms for both the Essential and Bonus sections helps students quickly identify the new terminology presented in each chapter.
- A combination of true/false, completion, and short answer questions for both the Essential and Bonus sections helps students assess their comprehension of new concepts.
- Programming exercises, also separated into Essential and Bonus sections, provide students with problem statements where they can apply newly learned concepts.

These key features also help to make this textbook distinct:

- It teaches computer programming from an application developer perspective, rather than focusing on how programming languages and compilers work.

- Beginning with Chapter 2, every chapter teaches students how to develop Windows applications rather than console applications.
- Students learn to use C# and VS .NET to develop non-trivial, useful applications.
- Students learn to develop applications by writing their own code rather than relying on project templates, and other generated or predefined source code.
- The organization of each chapter into Essential and Bonus topics gives the course instructor the greatest flexibility to define appropriate course content to meet the specific needs of the academic program.
- The book has been tested in the classroom to insure its effectiveness as a learning tool.
- Chapter 1 introduces OOP concepts using a familiar, non-programming example. OOP concepts and terminology are then integrated into all subsequent chapters.
- Students see a complete program example in Chapter 2 and are able to read and understand it, reducing any fears they may have about learning to write computer programs.
- The details of using the fifteen most common user interface objects, as well as how to print reports from within an application, are covered in Chapter 12.
- Students are taught how to us SQL with ADO.NET for database manipulation in Chapter 13.
- Chapter 14 uses inheritance and polymorphism in a real application to teach these concepts.
- The VS .NET debugging tools are covered in Appendix C. This gives instructors the flexibility to cover this topic at any point in the semester, even as early as Chapter 2.
- Appendix E shows students how to easily create a setup package to distribute their programs to different computers.

TESTING CENTER

Available free with this book, Thomson Course Technology's Testing Center combines challenging assessment with helpful review material to provide students with a robust Web-based learning tool. Utilizing the virtual compiler CodeSaw, students sharpen their programming skills through hands-on exercises, self-assessment, and interactive tutorials, all fully integrated with the text. For instructors, the Testing Center provides a central location for review and detailed feedback on student performance. For more information please visit **www.course.com/testingcenter**.

TEACHING TOOLS

The following supplemental materials are available when this book is used in a classroom setting. All of the teaching tools available with this book are provided to the instructor on a single CD-ROM. Most are also available (password protected) at the Thomson Course Technology Web site, **www.course.com**.

Electronic Instructor's Manual The Instructor's Manual that accompanies this textbook includes additional instructional material to assist in class preparation, including items such as Sample Syllabi, Chapter Outlines, Technical Notes, Lecture Notes, Quick Quizzes, Teaching Tips, Discussion Topics, and Key Terms.

e|v
EXAMVIEW **ExamView®** This textbook is accompanied by ExamView, a powerful testing software package that allows instructors to create and administer printed, computer (LAN-based), and Internet exams. ExamView includes hundreds of questions that correspond to the topics covered in this text, enabling students to generate detailed study guides that include page references for further review. The computer-based and Internet testing components allow students to take exams at their computers, and save the instructor time by grading each exam automatically.

PowerPoint Presentations This book offers Microsoft PowerPoint® slides for each chapter. These are included as a teaching aid for classroom presentation, to make available to students on the network for chapter review, or to be printed for classroom distribution. Instructors can add their own slides for additional topics they introduce to the class.

Student Files Program Files for all examples used in the book have been provided. Students may create the files themselves by following along with the explanations or use the available files. These are provided on the Teaching Tools CD-ROM and may also be found on the Thomson Course Technology Web site at **www.course.com**. Both students and instructors should have access to these, so they are not password protected.

Solution Files Solutions to end-of chapter exercises are provided on the Teaching Tools CD-ROM and may also be found on the Thomson Course Technology Web site at **www.course.com**. The solutions are password protected.

WebCT
Bb
Blackboard
www.blackboard.com

Distance Learning Thomson Course Technology is proud to present online test banks in WebCT and Blackboard to provide the most complete and dynamic learning experience possible. Instructors are encouraged to make the most of the course, both online and offline. For more information on how to access the online test bank, contact your local Thomson Course Technology sales representative.

ACKNOWLEDGMENTS

The authors would like to recognize the contributions by the students who class-tested this book at Purdue University. These students were enrolled in the Introduction to Object-Oriented Programming course offered by the Department of Computer Technology in the Fall 2004 semester. Their usage of the book and subsequent input helped make improvements to the finished copy of the manuscript. The following students provided specific suggestions and deserve an extra big thank you: Ryan Allik, Doug Clements, Jordan Gibson, Adam Golden, Dave Hedge, David Kincaid, Jason Leeke, Daniel Obot, Stacy Price, Aaron Ray, Westley Roberts, Taylor Scott, Ricki Thorpe III, and Brad Violand.

Mikel Berger also deserves special recognition for his help in many parts of this project including reviewing draft documents, and providing answers and solutions to the end of chapter questions and exercises. The following academicians and software developers also assisted in improving the quality of the manuscript by serving as reviewers: Dr. Jagdish C. Agrawal, Ph.D., Florida Metropolitan University; Randal L. Albert, Oregon Institute of Technology; Mikel Berger, DelMar Information Technologies, LLC; Bryan Buus, Adeptive Software; Gil Laware, Purdue University—South Bend/Elkhart; Guity Ravai, Purdue University; Martin Schray, DePaul University; and John Ulmer, software developer (Purdue University).

There were many people at Thomson Course Technology who made an important contribution to this book. Tricia Boyle, Mac Mendelsohn, and Drew Strawbridge all played a valuable role in this project. Betsey Henkels, who served as our conduit with the publisher, helped improve the readability of our writing and helped us stay on schedule. Without Betsey's continued support, this project would not have been finished on time.

Finally, but most importantly, the authors also thank our families for their support and understanding during our many late nights, weekend hours on the computer, and extended meetings that often forced them to assume many of our duties.

In addition to those mentioned above:

Kyle Lutes would like to thank Sally, Kameron, and Stefanie for their support and encouragement. He would also like to officially thank Charles Schramm for urging him nearly 25 years ago to go to college and study computer science. Thanks also go out to Ray Cromer for making his first computer courses enjoyable and rewarding even though he taught computer programming using Cobol.

Alka Harriger would like to thank Brad, Josh, Logan, and Amber for serving as an inspiration to work hard to reach a goal and for their patience at times when this work intruded on their family time. Thanks also go to her parents for instilling a love of learning and for sharing the value of education. Alka also credits Nina and Alba for their friendship, which was crucial to preserving her sanity during many 80+ hour work weeks. Alka is grateful to her coauthors for the opportunity to work together on a challenging project, as well as for their perseverance despite a demanding schedule. Finally, she thanks Deepak for taking the time to stay in touch and showing that if a biochemist Ph.D. can love computers, anyone can!

Jack Purdum would like to thank Katie Mohr, John Purdum, and Joyce Scarfo for their understanding and support during this project. Jack would also like to thank Tom Arnold, Jay Crannell, Don Dudine, Doug Felkins, Bill Jones, Mark Keenan, Jim McAllister, Bob McFaring, John Marsh, Jeff Neely, Jeff Nelson, Steve Plopper, Larry Powers, Jim Rheude, Bill Shaw, Mike Shore, and Jim Spuller who served as sounding boards for many teaching examples and other ideas presented in this book. A special thanks to John Strack for his Sherman Klump-like prodding and John Wilson who still knows how to bend the Laws of Physics in ways man never assumed. Rest assured, all your efforts are remembered…somehow, I hope to get even!

Read This Before You Begin

To the Student

Each chapter is written so you may follow along and write the source code yourself. Additionally, the source code for all examples used in this book is part of the supplementary materials that accompany this text. All files for an individual project are contained in a separate project folder (named descriptively to match the wording in corresponding figures) within a chapter folder (named Chapter XX, where XX represents the number of the chapter).

Using Your Own Computer

Visual C# .NET Standard Edition 2003 is supplied with the student edition of this book on six CDs. In addition, to develop the programs in this book, you will need the following:

- Processor: 450 MHz Pentium II-class processor (minimum)
      600 MHz Pentium III-class processor (recommended)
- Operating System: Windows 2000 or Windows XP
- Software: C# .NET Standard Edition 2003 (supplied)
- Memory: 96 MB RAM (minimum)
- Hard Disk Space: 500 MB of available space on system drive
      1.5 GB available space on installation drive
      1.9 GB additional space for MSDN library documentation
- Drive: CD-ROM or DVD-ROM drive
- Display: Super VGA or higher resolution display with 256 colors
- Mouse or compatible pointing device

To the Instructor

The authors have provided program files for all examples used in the book. Students may create the files themselves by following along with the explanations, or use the available files. These files are included on the Instructor Resources CD-ROM. They may also be obtained electronically through the Thomson Course Technology Web site at **www.course.com**. Follow the instructions in the Help file to copy the files to your server or standalone computer. You can view the Help file using a text editor such as WordPad or Notepad. Once the files are copied, you should instruct your students on how to copy the files to their own computers or workstations.

Visit Our World Wide Web Site

Additional materials might be available for your course on the Web. Visit the Thomson Course Technology Web site, **www.course.com**, and periodically search this site for more details.

Thomson Course Technology Program Files

You are granted a license to copy the program files to any computer or computer network used by individuals who have purchased this book.

INTRODUCTION TO OBJECT-ORIENTED PROGRAMMING

In this chapter you will learn:

- ♦ A brief history of object-oriented programming
- ♦ The object-oriented programming trilogy
- ♦ The definition of an object
- ♦ The definition of a class
- ♦ The definitions of properties and methods and how they are used
- ♦ The meaning of encapsulation, polymorphism, and inheritance
- ♦ The definition of object state
- ♦ The reason that C# is a good programming language for learning object-orient programming techniques
- ♦ The meaning of instantiation
- ♦ Use of the dot operator
- ♦ The benefit of using the .NET Framework class library

This textbook is designed to help you discover that C# is an excellent tool for learning object-oriented programming. Although the immediate goal of the textbook is to teach you C#, the ultimate goal is to teach you the discipline of programming. After all, 10 years from now many of today's programming languages will probably have faded from popularity, much as Pascal, Prolog, Fortran, RPG, and many others have already. However, if you master the *discipline* of programming, your skill set will be such that the programming language used doesn't really matter.

With that in mind, let's begin our journey.

BRIEF HISTORY OF OBJECT-ORIENTED PROGRAMMING

Object-oriented programming, or **OOP**, is a methodology that provides a discipline for writing programs. Knowing that the OOP methodology was developed in the late 1980s, many programmers believe that this methodology is fairly new. Actually, that is not the case. OOP was an outcome of simulation research that was performed in the 1960s. Through the simulation, programmers were attempting to model doctors, nurses, patients, and visitors using a hospital elevator. The programmers quickly became frustrated because each time a different person arrived at the elevator doors, they had to write additional code to represent that person's arrival. The more people they wanted to represent, the more code they had to write.

Unlike many other things in life, more is not always better in programming. The reason for this is obvious: programmers not only have to write code but must also correct errors that the code contains. Correcting these errors involves a process known as program **debugging**, and debugging is often more time-consuming than writing the program. The more code you have, the greater the number of errors it may contain. (These program errors are referred to as program **bugs**, hence the term debugging.) To a programmer, "less is good" because the less code a program contains, the easier it is to catch and fix the bugs. Unfortunately, simulating each new arrival at the elevator meant more code and, hence, more complexity.

Complicating the programmers' task even more was this goal: the simulation should distinguish between the four different types of people. For example, the programmers wanted to use stick figures for graphic representation—a doctor as a stick figure with a stethoscope, a nurse with a clipboard, a patient with a bandaged head, and a visitor carrying a bouquet of flowers. The code quickly became so lengthy and complicated that the simulation seemed impossible.

In a moment of frustration, one of the programmers said, "This problem would be simple if each new arrival at the elevator doors knew how to draw itself." At that moment, the team had an epiphany. They reasoned that instead of adding new code for each person arriving at the elevator, they could program a "`person` object" that was capable of responding to the program command: "Draw yourself on the computer screen." The only remaining task for the programmers would be to tell the program which type of person should be drawn. The concept of object-oriented programming was born.

Programming objects was a huge shift in the way programs were written. In fact, the change was so monumental that new programming languages had to be developed. Two of the earliest languages to embrace the idea of using program objects were **Simula**[1] and **Smalltalk**.[2]

Although extremely useful, Simula and Smalltalk were not adopted on a wide scale, probably because these programming languages represented such a significant shift in the conventional wisdom used by programmers at the time. In addition, relatively few programmers were trained to use those languages. Many of the concepts found in Simula and Smalltalk, however, remain the cornerstones of modern-day OOP languages, including C# and Java.

---

[1] Simula was co-developed by Ole-Johan Dahl and Kristen Nygaard in the 1960s at the Norwegian Computing Center in Oslo.

[2] Smalltalk was developed by Alan Kay, Dan Ingalls, Ted Kaehler, Adele Goldberg, and others during the 1970s at Xerox Palo Alto Research Center (PARC).

USING OBJECTS IN OOP

As mentioned in the discussion of the hospital elevator simulation, the program became manageable because of the concept of a "person object." A programming **object** is simply an abstraction of something seen every day. We see people (person objects), cars (vehicle objects), purchase orders (order objects), plus a host of other common things that we see and categorize each day.

Each object has an associated set of characteristics that helps to further define the exact nature of the object. For example, a car might have a "doors" characteristic that describes how many doors this particular car object has. The car object might also have a long list of other characteristics that help describe the car. This list of characteristics might include horsepower, color, manufacturer, model, cylinders, body style, transmission, manufacturer's ID, and so on. In C#, these characteristics are called **properties**.

In addition to the properties used to describe an object, most objects also have certain behaviors, activities, or actions they can perform. For example, a purchase order object can display itself on the screen, print itself to a printer, and save itself to a database. The behaviors that each object is capable of performing are called the **methods** of the object.

One of the real breakthroughs in the hospital simulation problem was combining the properties and methods into one cohesive programming entity called an object. Prior to OOP, the properties and methods were scattered throughout the program making it difficult to isolate cause and effect in a program. That is, if something went wrong in the program, it wasn't obvious where to start looking for the cause of the problem. Further, because the properties could be in one section of the program and the methods in another, tracking down and isolating program bugs was difficult.

OOP moves the properties and methods into one place and calls it a class. As you will see in later chapters, keeping the properties and methods together into a class makes it much easier to write, test, debug, and maintain program code.

USING CLASSES IN OOP

To this point, this chapter has discussed objects on a broad conceptual level. You now need to understand how objects can exist in a program. In other words, you need to understand how a programmer can take the abstract concept of an object and make it a useful part of a program. To accomplish this, the OOP languages use a class to describe an object. A **class** is a blueprint, or template, that is used to describe an object. A class contains program instructions that define each of the properties and methods associated with an object. Just as a cookie cutter describes the actual shape of a cookie, so a class describes the "look" and behavior of an object. The cookie cutter is like a class, and the actual cookie is like an *object* instance of that class. For example, a doctor is a class, and Dr. Morrison is a specific instance of the doctor class. (A more concrete discussion is presented later in this chapter.)

Figure 1-1 shows a heart-shaped cookie cutter named `clsHeart`. It is the C# code within `clsHeart` that determines the shape of the heart. Stated another way, the shape of the cookie cutter is determined by the cookie cutter's properties: its height, width, depth, and metal thickness; the angles of the metal form; and so on. If you grab this cookie cutter and press it into some cookie dough, you create heart-shaped cookies. In C#, your class code declares the basic properties of a cookie cutter. However, it is the values of these properties that determine the exact shape of the cookie cutter. If you change the angles of the metal form, for example, you could end up with a candy cane cookie cutter instead of a heart-shaped cookie cutter. Taking a cookie cutter and carving out a chunk of memory with it is the same as defining an instance of that class. Instances of a class are called **class objects**.

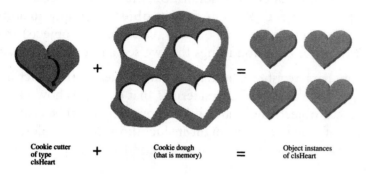

Figure 1-1   Relationship between a class and an instance of a class

THE OOP TRILOGY

As the concepts of object-oriented programming were refined over time, new OOP languages emerged to exploit the advantages offered by the OOP paradigm. One of the first popular OOP languages was C++, spearheaded by the work of Bjarne Stroustrup in the 1980s. He took the C programming language and redesigned it to support the concept of programming with objects. Since that time, other OOP languages have appeared. C#, Visual Basic .NET, and Java are several of the more popular OOP languages.

Although the exact structures of these OOP languages differ, the languages share three common characteristics:

- Encapsulation
- Polymorphism
- Inheritance

Many people believe that a programming language that does not embody these three characteristics is not a true OOP language. For example, although Visual Basic .NET is an OOP language, earlier versions of Visual Basic did not support inheritance, and so it was not considered an OOP language.

This is not the time to delve into the details of encapsulation, polymorphism, and inheritance and the power they bring to the programmer's toolkit, but the sections that follow summarize their main characteristics.

Encapsulation

The primary purpose of encapsulation in an OOP language is data hiding. As mentioned earlier, non-OOP programming methods caused the properties (that is, data) and the methods that operated on that data to be scattered here and there throughout a program, often with little rhyme or reason. This made locating program errors difficult. Program debugging was like grasping a single thread on the right side of a large spider web, pulling on it, and hoping to affect only that single thread as it rippled across the web.

Implementing the concept of encapsulation hides and protects, or encapsulates, the properties and methods of an object inside the object. Using this approach makes it much easier to locate errors because the data and the methods that can operate on that data are located in the same place—inside the object. By inspecting the code that defines the object (which is the code found in the class that defines that object), it becomes much easier to detect and correct program errors.

Simply stated, **encapsulation** refers to the methodology used to hide the data and methods of an object inside the object itself. You can think of encapsulation as hiding the inner workings of a class. It is similar to the use of a lamp and an electrical outlet. Behind the lamp and electrical outlet is wiring as well as things like circuits, fuses, and fuse boxes at work. Lamp designers give you the plug to put into the outlet, while hiding all the details about how the lamp is wired. Encapsulation allows you to hide all the details of how a class works, but allows you to expose the plugs (properties and methods) so that others can use your class without understanding all its inner workings.

Polymorphism

This term literally means "many shapes." In a programming context, however, **polymorphism** refers to the ability of different objects to interpret program commands, or messages, in a way that make sense for the object itself. For example, in the hospital simulation, if the command "Draw Yourself on the Computer Screen" is sent to the doctor, nurse, patient, and visitor objects, each object would have a `Draw` method defined within the class code that is capable of drawing the appropriate stick figure. In this example, of the hospital simulation, a single program message truly can produce objects that have different shapes.

The key to polymorphism is that each object knows how to respond to an outside command or event in its own way. The reason that it can respond in the appropriate manner is that the method for responding to that command or event is encapsulated within the class's code for the object.

Later chapters discuss polymorphism more fully to enhance your understanding of OOP and C#.

Inheritance

Chapter 14 discusses inheritance in more detail. For now, you can simply think of **inheritance** as being similar to the relationship between yourself and your parents. You may have your mother's eyes and your dad's hair color (that is, you inherited those properties). Still, you are different from your parents because other properties and methods (that is, fingerprints) are unique to you.

For the moment, you can think of *inheritance* as the ability of one object to acquire, or inherit, the properties and methods of another object. This ability to inherit properties and methods is an important advantage: For an object to acquire the functionality provided by a parent object, a programmer does not have to write duplicate code for the properties and methods that the child object inherits. Because inheritance reduces the amount of code that must be written, it is faster and easier to develop and maintain the program. Code reuse is often cited as one of the fundamental benefits of OOP.

To this point, the chapter has discussed OOP and its underlying principles in general terms. The next section presents a more realistic example of how properties, methods, classes, and objects relate to each other in an everyday setting.

An Example Using Objects

Suppose that you work for a company as a recruiter, and your company is flying a woman in for a job interview. It is your responsibility to make arrangements to pick her up at the airport, but you have never met. Because you are unknown to each other, you decide to phone the job candidate and tell her the arrangements, such as the flight number and arrival time, the carrier, and so on (see Figure 1-2). What might happen next during the conversation is quite interesting.

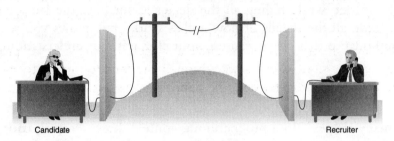

Candidate   Recruiter

Figure 1-2   Chat between recruiter and candidate

During such phone conversations, it is common for each of you to describe yourself. The candidate might say she is 5'2", petite, has blonde hair, wears glasses, and will be wearing a black business suit, white blouse, black shoes, and carrying a leather briefcase. You would describe yourself in the same manner, but add that you will be carrying a sign with her name on it.

Now let's look at this discussion using an object called **Person**. The characteristics that describe the person are listed under Properties. The actions the person can do are listed under Methods. Figure 1-3 shows the **Person** object's properties and the methods for both the candidate and the recruiter.

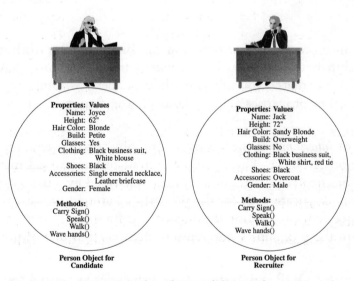

Figure 1-3   Property values for candidate and recruiter
                  person objects

In Figure 1-3, notice that both objects are **Person** objects. Each object has the same properties and the same methods. However, the actual values for the properties and methods differ. Because the properties and methods differ, you can distinguish between the objects. In other words, because the properties and methods use different values, the state of the two objects is different. An object's **state** is the collective values of its properties—basically what an object knows about itself.

Furthermore, the state of the object may change over time. For example, the candidate could change her hair color, start wearing contacts, and change her clothing and accessories. Likewise, the recruiter could start working out, lose weight, wear less conservative clothing, get contacts, and place lifts in his shoes to add some height. Such changes, of course, change the state of the objects. Even though their states may change, however, they are still **Person** objects.

Notice the circle around the properties and methods of each object. Circles are used in the figures to represent the idea of encapsulation. That is, each object protects its current state from contamination that exists outside the circle. At the same time, however, there must be a mechanism that allows programmers to change the values encapsulated within the object in a disciplined and controlled manner. In other words, if you think of the circle as a shell that protects the properties and methods inside the object, there must still be a way through the shell for access to the properties and methods. Later sections of this chapter describe a way of accessing the data of an object.

WHY LEARN C#?

There are many programming languages that you could use to learn OOP. However, C# is the best choice for several reasons. Microsoft advertises **C#** as a simple, yet robust, object-oriented programming language that combines the high productivity of Rapid Application Development (RAD) languages such as Visual Basic with the raw power of C++. Even though the previous sentence sounds like marketing speak (and it is, after all), we believe Microsoft's statements about C# are accurate.

C# truly is an object-oriented programming language. In addition to supporting the OOP trilogy of encapsulation, polymorphism, and inheritance, all data types in C# are derived, or inherit, from a single class type—**System.Object**. This data inheritance is not the case with the other popular OOP languages, such as C++ and Java. Some features found in other languages have purposely been excluded from C#. For example, C# does not support the pointer data type or multiple inheritance like C++ does. While these may be powerful language features, they are frequently the source of obscure program errors and, hence, were not included in C#. Because C# is a fairly new language, its creators benefited from including the best features of those programming languages that preceded it, while avoiding those that are often the source of errors. For these reasons, C# embodies many technical improvements over other languages.

When you use C# with Visual Studio .NET (VS.NET), it facilitates RAD development with its many user interface design tools, integrated language help system, and interactive debugging. You are probably familiar with using Windows applications for such activities as surfing the Web, sending e-mail, and instant messaging with friends. Because of your previous Windows experience and the RAD tools in VS.NET's Integrated Development Environment (IDE), it is relatively easy to create C# Windows applications with graphical user interfaces (GUIs) just like those you already use. On the other hand, creating useful GUI-based Windows applications with C++ or Java is more complex.

With C#, you are not limited to GUI applications. Once you've learned the fundamentals, you can use C# to develop Web applications, programs for Pocket PC personal digital assistants (PDAs) and Smartphones, console applications, and even Windows Services. The only disadvantage of C# is that currently all the applications you develop run only on Windows operating systems, not on Linux, Unix, or Macintosh. However, even this limitation might change in the future if efforts such as the Mono project[3] are successful in porting C# and .NET to alternative platforms.

Visual Basic .NET (VB.NET) is another good choice to learn object-oriented programming for all of the previously mentioned reasons. However, the syntax of the VB.NET programming language is unique. The language syntax of C#, however, is similar to that used by the C and C++ programming languages, and is nearly identical to Java. This syntax similarity makes C# immediately recognizable to millions of existing software developers, and makes learning Java and C++ easier after you've learned C#.

Another advantage C# has over VB.NET is one of perception. Ever since it was introduced, the use of VB has been questioned by many people who don't think of it as a "real" programming langaguage. At first, VB suffered from performance problems because the programs ran more slowly than those written in C. Further, the very name of Visual Basic seemed amateurish to many because its name contained the word "Basic." Finally, VB was never considered a true OOP language because for most of its history it lacked inheritance. All of those criticisms have since been overcome, but the perception that VB is a "toy" language still persists. In fact, salary surveys suggest that software developers who use C# command a higher salary than those who use VB.NET.

For all of these reasons, we believe C# is the best choice to begin your first excursion into object-oriented programming.

USING OBJECTS IN C#

Both objects presented in Figure 1-3 represent individual **Person** objects. Note that the properties and the methods for both objects have the same names. You learned earlier that the **Person** class serves as a template from which you can create multiple **Person** objects. Each object that you create of the **Person** class has the same properties and methods. However, as you can see in Figure 1-3, the values for the properties, or state, in the two objects can be different. In summary, each **Person** object represents a different person. That is, the states for the two objects are different; therefore they must be two different people.

Now that you understand states of objects, you might ask how each of the objects obtained the information that defines its properties and methods. After all, you were told to think of the two circles in the figures as shells that protect the data from the outside world. The data inside the objects is encapsulated for that very purpose—to hide the data from the rest of the program. If that's the case, how can the data be useful if you have no way to reach it?

Object Instantiation—Creating Objects from Classes

The example in Figure 1-3 used two **Person** objects to represent the candidate and the recruiter assigned to pick her up. Let's call these two **Person** objects **candidate** and **recruiter**. You also learned that the **Person** class code serves as a template, or cookie cutter, from which you can create a **Person** object. However, a cookie cutter is of little use without cookie dough.

The same is true in C#. You cannot begin to use any object until you create one. In C#, a class is the cookie cutter, and your computer's memory is the cookie dough. No **Person** objects are available for use in the program until you use the **Person** class template to carve out a **Person** object in memory. The following code snippet shows how to create an object for use in a C#

---

3 See www.mono-project.com for more information.

program. In the following discussion, we have added the prefix "cls" to the Person class to reinforce the idea that Person is a class. You may want to verbalize clsPerson as "class Person" while your read the text.

```
clsPerson candidate = new clsPerson();
clsPerson recruiter = new clsPerson();
```

To fully understand this snippet, you need to understand the exact rules for C# program statements, and you'll learn those rules as you work through this textbook. The end result, however, is that the code has defined two `Person` objects named `candidate` and `recruiter`. To continue the cookie cutter analogy, `clsPerson` in the two statements tells the program which cookie cutter to use. The `new` keyword tells C# to carve out two new pieces of computer memory (cookie dough) using the `clsPerson` class (cookie cutter) and refer to those two (different) places in memory as the two different cookie objects: `candidate` and `recruiter`.

Another way to view these two program statements is to think of them as creating the equivalent of the two circles you saw in Figure 1-3. They now exist in memory with the properties and methods available for you to use as the programmer.

The process of defining the two objects named `candidate` and `recruiter` shown in the code snippet is called **object instantiation**. **Instantiation** is just a formal term that refers to creating a new **instance** of an object from a class. In less formal terms, each statement indicates grabbing a specific class cookie cutter, using it to carve out a chunk of memory called an object, and applying a name to the newly created object.

The Dot Operator—Key to Getting Inside the Object

Obviously, C# must provide a means for setting the values you wish to use for each property and method the class describes. After all, how useful would our two objects be if you couldn't get or set their states? Figure 1-4 shows the C# way of setting the values of an object's properties.

```
candidate.Name = "Joyce";
candidate.Height = 62;
candidate.HairColor = "Blonde";
candidate.Build = "Petite";
candidate.Glasses = True;
candidate.Clothing = "Black business suit, white blouse";
candidate.Shoes = "Black";
candidate.Accessories = "Single emerald necklace, leather briefcase";
candidate.Gender = "Female";
```

Figure 1-4   Assigning values to the object's properties

Note that the general form for each statement is:

```
ObjectName.PropertyName = Value;
```

In the Figure 1-4 example, the `ObjectName` is `candidate` and the `PropertyNames` are the property names presented in Figure 1-3. In each program line, `Value` is the data to be assigned into each specific property of the given object. In the first line of Figure 1-4, the name "Joyce" was assigned to the `candidate` object's `Name` property.

The important thing to notice is how the period, or dot, separates the object name from the property name. You can see this separation in the following statement:

```
candidate.Name = "Joyce";
```

The period is formally called the **dot operator**. In the example, the dot operator is used to specify which property you are going to fill in with the data value of `"Joyce"`. In this example, it is the `Name` property that receives the value `"Joyce"`.

The equal sign (=) is called the **assignment operator** and it simply means:

"Take whatever appears on the right-hand side of the assignment operator (that is, `"Joyce"`) and assign that data into whatever appears on the left-hand side of the assignment operator (that is, `candidate.Name`)."

The effect is that, after the assignment statement has been executed, `candidate.Name` now contains the data `"Joyce"`.

Note this simple line changes the state of the `candidate` object. Before this statement was written, `candidate` was an object with an empty `Name` property hidden away in program memory. Now, at least, you know that the `candidate` object has an explicit value (`"Joyce"`) assigned to this specific property (`Name`). By the time the code in Figure 1-4 finishes executing, you know that the candidate is a petite, stylish blonde businesswoman named Joyce. Note how these statements changed the block of memory from a cold, lifeless state to a state that describes a recognizable human being. All of these changes to the `candidate` object's properties were made because of the recruiter's phone conversation with Joyce.

Note how providing the details about the candidate came from a source (that is, the phone) that is outside the object. In terms of Figure 1-3, the recruiter received the data for the candidate's name from the candidate who might be located hundreds of miles away. In other words, the data for the `Name` property was created outside the circle shown in Figure 1-3.

Consider the following program statement:

```
candidate.Name = "Joyce";
```

This statement can be visualized as taking the data (`"Joyce"`) and moving it from outside the shell surrounding the `candidate` object, through a doorway in the shell, and placing that data into the `Name` property of the object. Figure 1-5 shows this process. Notice in Figure 1-5 how the dot operator is responsible for "creating a doorway" into the `candidate` object.

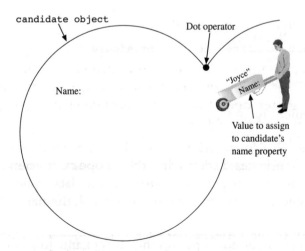

Figure 1-5   Using the dot operator to get inside the object

The process of moving data from outside an object to a property within the object is a **setter operation**. Setter operations, therefore, represent changing the state of an object. (We discuss setter operations in greater detail in Chapter 7.)

So far, you have seen how to use the assignment operator to change the value of a specific property within an object. The actual property that changes is determined by the property name that follows the dot operator. You can also retrieve the value of an object's property.

For example the statement:

```
appointmentName = candidate.Name;
```

performs an operation that reverses the flow of information shown in Figure 1-5. The process now is to go inside the shell of the **candidate** object, go to the property named **Name,** and determine its contents (**"Joyce"**), return to the world outside the object's shell, and copy the data into a variable named **appointmentName**. This process is depicted in Figure 1-6.

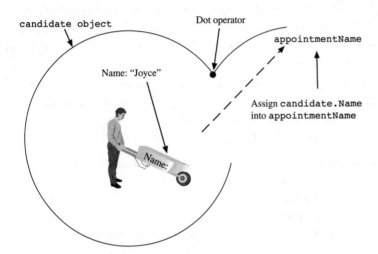

Figure 1-6   Reading the value of a property

Note that in this statement:

```
appointmentName = candidate.Name;
```

you are not changing the state of the object; you are simply reading or getting the data that has already been stored in a specific property of the object. In many OOP languages, the process you are performing in the statement is called a **getter operation**. Getter operations simply copy the data of an object; they do not change the state of the object.

To summarize, a setter operation is used to change the state of an object. Therefore, the object and the appropriate property name always appear on the left side of the assignment operation, as you saw in the statement:

```
candidate.Name = "Joyce";
```

This statement changes the **Name** property of the **candidate** object to **"Joyce"**. Therefore, whatever used to be in the Name property has been replaced with the name **"Joyce"**. The state of the candidate object is changed because one of its properties has been changed.

By contrast, the getter statement:

```
appointmentName = candidate.Name;
```

is used to copy the data that is stored in the `candidate` object's `Name` property into `appointmentName`. Because getter operations only read the data of an object and do not change it, the state of the object after a getter operation remains the same.

As a general rule, setter operations find the object and its property name on the left side of the assignment operator. Getter operations normally find the object and its property name on the right side of the assignment statement. Together, setter and getter methods allow you to change and view any property in the object, unless you specify differently.

The .NET Framework Class Library

If you guess there might be many objects used for a variety of programming tasks, you're right. As you learn to write programs, you will find yourself using many general-purpose objects over and over again. Common examples of such general-purpose objects include labels, text boxes, and button objects found in almost all graphical user interfaces. Other common tasks include saving program data to disk files by using file objects or database objects. The ability to reuse general-purpose objects rather than recreating everything from scratch each time you write a program can save you time, and often money, when developing applications. The companies that develop software development tools know the value of such reusable objects and make available prewritten class libraries from which you can create objects for use in your programs. In the case of Microsoft, these reusable classes are found in the .NET Framework Class Library.

The .NET Framework Class Library is actually a collection of extensible class libraries organized hierarchically into namespaces. As you become familiar with some of the more common namespaces, you can simplify your programming tasks by using the classes and methods in these namespaces. Think about the classes within the framework as the prebuilt and tested cookie cutters for common programming tasks such as reading and writing files, creating graphical applications, and accessing data from a database.

The `System` namespace is at the top of the namespace hierarchy and contains all the types that represent the base data types such as text, numbers, dates, and others. You will learn the C# data types in Chapter 3. The `Systems.Windows.Forms` namespace, on the other hand, allows you to take advantage of the Windows forms engine with all its classes, making it easier for you to create graphical user interface objects for your applications. Chapter 2 contains additional details about namespaces.

The .NET Framework Class Library is the underlying library for all the .NET languages, of which C# and Visual Basic .NET are the most popular. One significant benefit of using the .NET Framework over other vendor class libraries is that the functionality provided by the classes that comprise the .NET Framework are programming-language independent. Therefore, a class that you used in a C# program is available for use in a Visual Basic program, too. Most class libraries from other vendors, such as those used with Java, are designed to be used only with that specific programming language. Although the specific syntax for accessing an object's properties or methods may vary among languages, as a developer you can choose from among a variety of programming languages to develop applications based on the .NET Framework. In this book, C# is used to implement programming concepts, and you will use the C# syntax to access these libraries.

SUMMARY

- Object-oriented programming (OOP) is designed to simplify program development by modeling objects that we observe daily. We do this by observing those properties that describe an object plus the methods that determine the actions that may be associated with the object.

- A class is an abstract model of an object. A class declares the properties and methods that are embodied within the object. A class, therefore, acts like a template or cookie cutter from which we can create objects of the class. The process of creating objects of a class is called object instantiation.

- One goal of OOP is to hide the properties of an object as much as possible. The act of hiding the properties within an object is called encapsulation. Encapsulation helps protect the object and its state from contamination by outside forces.

- OOP promotes code reuse by allowing programmers to extend a class by using inheritance. The basic idea behind inheritance is that one class, often called the base class, can be further refined into a new, more specific class, called a subclass. The OOP concept of polymorphism complements inheritance by allowing each class to respond to various programming events in a way that makes sense for each individual class.

- The dot operator is used with an object to allow access to the object's properties and methods. In general, you can perform two fundamental functions on an object's property. First, you can read the current value of a property, which is often called a get operation. Second, you can change the current value of a property to a new value, which is usually referred to as a set operation. This second operation changes the state of the object because a property value has been changed.

- The .NET Framework Class Libraries provide you with a large number of predefined classes that you can use in your own programs. Most of these classes are language independent, so they may be used with languages other than C#. As you will see in subsequent chapters, these classes serve as building blocks from which you can craft new programs.

KEY TERMS

Define each of the following terms, as it relates to object-oriented programming:

- assignment operator
- bug
- C#
- class
- class object
- debug
- dot operator
- encapsulation
- getter operation
- inheritance
- instantiation
- methods
- object
- object-oriented programming (OOP)
- polymorphism
- property
- setter operation
- Simula
- Smalltalk
- state (of an object)

REVIEW QUESTIONS

1. Object-oriented programming (OOP) is a newly developed programming methodology designed to write programs about people as objects. True or False?

2. C# is known as one of the first OOP languages initially used to write a hospital elevator simulation. True or False?

3. Smalltalk is a popular programming language because it is easy to use for developing OOP applications. True or False?

4. An error in a computer program is known as a bug. True or False?

5. By combining properties and methods into a single unit known as an object, program maintenance is improved. True or False?

6. A class is a specific instance of an object template. True or False?

7. The primary purpose of encapsulation is to allow an object to interpret program commands in a way that makes sense to the object itself. True or False?

8. Inheritance allows programmers to minimize code duplication by creating objects that acquire properties and methods from another object. True or False?

9. Object instantiation is the creation of an object from a class. True or False?

10. A setter operation is used to retrieve the value of an object's property. True or False?

11. List three advantages of an OOP language versus a non-OOP language.

12. _____ are used collectively to describe the _____ of an object.

13. A(n) _____ serves as a blueprint, or template, for an object.

14. A(n) _____ method is used to alter the state of an object whereas a(n) _____ is used to read the state of an object.

15. The process of defining an object in a program is called object _____.

16. The _____ separates the object name from its associated property or method name.

17. A getter operation requires the object to appear on the _____ side of the assignment operator.

18. The _____ is a collection of extensible class libraries.

19. How would you describe the concept of polymorphism to someone who knows nothing about OOP?

20. Of the three OOP trilogy topics, perhaps the concept of _____ helps most to simplify debugging a program.

PROGRAMMING EXERCISES

1. Suppose that you wanted to create a C# program for an automobile manufacturer. Write down a set of properties and methods that could be used to define a vehicle object.

2. Imagine that you want to create a C# program for a landscaping business. Write down a set of properties and methods that could be used to define a plant object, a flower object, and a tree object. How can you describe the relationship of these objects?

3. Suppose that you wanted to create a C# program for simple graphics design. Write down a set of properties and methods that could be used to define a geometric object that you might want to draw.

4. Suppose that you wanted to create a C# program for order processing. Business customers often use a purchase order (PO) to describe the items they wish to purchase from a seller, the price they pay for each item purchased, and the quantity of each item they wish to purchase. Each PO is normally tied to a unique purchase order number so that the company can track what it is buying. Because such purchases are usually made on credit, sellers that allow such POs usually require a customer to have an ID number. Sellers perform credit checks on customers to make sure that they have not gone over their credit limit. Write a set of properties and methods that could be used to define a purchase order (PO) object.

5. Write a code snippet to instantiate a dream car object, and define its property values using the definition of the vehicle object you created in Programming Exercise 1.

6. Write a code snippet to instantiate a peach tree object, and define its property values using the definition of the tree object you created in Programming Exercise 2.

7. Write a code snippet to instantiate the shapes needed for a blue house, and define property values using the definition of the shape object you created in Programming Exercise 3. (At a minimum, your answer should include the following: a triangle for the roof and a square or rectangle for the body.)

8. Write a code snippet to instantiate a purchase order object for a personal digital assistant (PDA) purchase from Rock-Bottom Supply House. Define field values using the definition of the PO object you created in Programming Exercise 4.

9. Draw a diagram similar to that shown in Figure 1-3 for the purchase order object you defined in Programming Exercise 4.

10. Using the vehicle object you described in Programming Exercise 1, show a code snippet that makes the style of the car a sedan, makes the color metallic silver, has an optional polarized windshield, and has the optional James Bond ejector seat installed on the passenger side.

2

CREATING A SIMPLE APPLICATION

In the Essentials section you will learn:

♦ Fundamental computer programming terminology

♦ How to design a solution to a simple programming problem

♦ What Visual Studio .NET is and how to use it to create an object-oriented program

♦ How to use the .NET class libraries to develop a simple Windows Forms application

♦ What namespaces are

♦ What `using` directives are and why to use them

♦ How to use the Form Designer to create a graphical user interface (GUI)

♦ How to set properties for user interface objects

♦ How to use regions to hide chunks of source code

♦ What events are and how to connect an event to a method

♦ How and why to use comments in source code

♦ Three types of errors a program might contain

♦ How to use breakpoints to watch how your programs execute

In the Bonus section you will learn:

♦ The impact of formatting on the compiler and programmer

♦ An alternative notation for comments

♦ What all those files VS.NET creates are used for

♦ The difference between Visual Studio .NET solutions and projects

♦ What the common language runtime (CLR), Microsoft Intermediate Language (MSIL), and Just In Time (JIT) compiling are

In Chapter 1, you learned the concepts and terminology associated with object-oriented programming. The purpose of this chapter is to introduce the concepts and terminology associated with using the Visual Studio .NET Integrated Development Environment (IDE) and C# to create a simple object-oriented program.

Before you can begin to write programs, you should have some computer experience, including working with data files and understanding basic computer terminology. This book assumes that you are familiar with the Windows environment and know how to use the mouse, use menus, perform text editing (typing, copying, pasting, and so on), and manipulate files and folders using the Windows Explorer application.

The application you develop in this chapter is fairly simple, but it does perform a useful function. More importantly, the steps you follow in this chapter are similar to the steps you'll follow in all the remaining programs in this book. If you reach the end of the chapter and are still confused by some of this material, you should not be concerned. Almost everything in this chapter is repeated in detail in the chapters that follow.

ESSENTIAL TOPICS

TERMINOLOGY

In its simplest form, a **computer program**, or **software application**, is a series of instructions, or processing steps, that a computer understands and executes. A computer program consists of data input, processing, and data output. For example, a simple calculator program might allow the user to input two numeric values (input), add them together (processing steps), and display the sum to the user (output). A computer program can be compared to a recipe for baking cookies. A recipe consists of ingredients (input), the instructions for mixing the ingredients and baking (processing steps), and the output (the cookies). The processing steps in a computer program are often referred to as the **program's logic**, the **application logic**, or an **algorithm** the application uses to solve the problem at hand.

The processing steps in a computer program can be generalized as follows:

- **Initialization**—When the program starts, some initialization tasks need to be accomplished. For example, the user interface is constructed and displayed on the computer monitor.

- **Input**—The program waits for the user to request that the program perform an action, for example, by typing in data and clicking a button or menu item. The input values are checked and an error message is displayed if any of the input values are invalid.

- **Processing**—If the input data are acceptable, processing occurs.

- **Output**—Once processing is complete, the results are shown to the user.

- **Termination**—When the user chooses to close the application, termination tasks are performed. Termination tasks, sometimes called clean-up tasks, perform actions that are just the opposite of initialization tasks. For example, the user interface is removed from the computer monitor, and database connections are closed.

The instructions that make up the processing steps of the computer program must be written according to the rules, or **syntax**, of the programming language you are using. Just as the English language has grammatical rules for sentences' structure, programming languages have syntax rules. For example, a typical English sentence should contain a noun, a verb, and end with a period. If you deviate from the grammar rules of English or misspell a word, the reader may still be able to understand your point. Programming languages, on the other hand, are *very, very picky about syntax* and even the tiniest mistake results in a **syntax error**, or, worse yet, your program executes, but produces incorrect results. Each programming language has its own set of syntax rules.

The instructions you type are called the program's **source code**. An application's source code contains many hundreds (or thousands or millions) of instructions. Each instruction is normally typed on a single line and often referred to as a **program statement**, or **statement**. In English, sentences must end with a period or other punctuation mark. In C#, statements must end in a semicolon (;). In English, a group of related sentences might be grouped together in a paragraph with the first sentence indented. In C#, related statements are grouped together in a **statement block** and surrounded by opening and closing curly braces { }.

When your program is finished, you can give it to others to run, but you don't give them your source code. Instead you give them an **executable** file. For example, when you use Microsoft Word, you don't have the source code for it. Instead you run a program named `winword.exe`.

An executable file is sometimes called an .exe because that is its typical file extension. Exes are sometimes referred to as **assemblies** in the .NET documentation.

The job of a **compiler** is to convert source code to an executable file so that it can be run on a computer that doesn't have the compiler or the source code. A compiler is another type of program that takes your source code (input), checks for syntax errors, converts it to executable format (processing steps), and builds an .exe (output). An executable is *compiled* source code. A different compiler is used for each programming language.

INTRODUCTION TO VISUAL STUDIO .NET

The applications you create in this text consist of a graphical user interface (GUI) and C# source code statements. The C# source code instructs the computer on actions to be performed, and the GUI acts as the interface to the user. The user interacts with the GUI to enter input, signal processing by clicking a button or menu item, and viewing the output. You have certainly used GUIs when using a Web browser, word processor, sending e-mail, or instant messaging friends. **Visual Studio .NET (VS.NET)** is the tool you will use to write, test, and debug these GUI applications.

VS.NET is a software development tool from Microsoft used to create applications for the Microsoft Windows operating system. Tools like VS.NET are often referred to as **Integrated Development Environments**, or simply **IDEs**. When you write papers, you probably use a word processor. Similarly, when you write computer programs, you probably use an IDE. In addition to Microsoft, other companies provide development environments for C#. Using an IDE is probably the most effective way to develop applications, but it is not the only way. In fact, you could develop all the applications in this text using a simple text editor such as the Windows Notepad and the C# command-line compiler.

VS.NET can be used to develop software in several programming languages such as C#, Visual Basic .NET, C++, and J#. This allows you to learn one IDE and use it to write applications in multiple languages. The term *integrated* is used because IDEs contain many tools that are useful for writing programs. The tools you use in VS.NET as you complete the exercises in this text include a:

- Text editor with color-coded syntax for typing source code

- Form Designer for developing Windows Form-based GUIs

- Solution Explorer for managing application project files

- Context-sensitive help

- C# compiler that converts source code to an executable file

- Interactive debugging tools to help ensure that programs work correctly

VS.NET contains many other features that are beyond the scope of this text. In fact, one of the early challenges you'll face is learning to use VS.NET effectively. VS.NET is a powerful tool designed for professional software developers and not necessarily for teaching an introductory course in object-oriented programming. But don't be intimidated by all the VS.NET menus, buttons, toolbars, status bars, and various windows. You are not expected to learn all their functions. This text uses only a few, and you'll find you can perform many functions with only the basic features.

The VS.NET user interface is highly customizable, and therefore your screen may not always match the examples shown in this text. VS.NET windows can be hidden, moved, docked, and pinned. Even the keyboard shortcuts can be customized. Like many Windows applications, VS.NET gives you several ways to accomplish a task. For example, you can select a menu item, click a toolbar button, press a function key, or use a keyboard shortcut. Rather than attempt to list all toolbars and keyboard shortcuts, this book lists most instructions using the menus. Of course, you are encouraged to learn the alternatives and use whichever you find easiest. Appendices C and D include additional tips on using VS.NET to the fullest.

ANALYZING THE PROBLEM AND DESIGNING THE SOLUTION

The first step in writing a computer program is to fully understand what the program should accomplish. This chapter presents a rather simple program so that you can concentrate on the process of creating the program rather than understanding complex algorithms.

If you've ever purchased carpet for a room, you know that most carpeting is priced by the square yard. However, when you measure a room, you typically measure the length and width of the room in feet and inches. To know the cost of the carpeting, you must convert the room measurements from feet and inches into square yards. You then multiply the square yards by the cost per square yard and add sales tax.

Listed in more detail, the processing steps for a computer program that determines how much it costs to purchase carpeting for a room are:

1. Initialization: Initialize the form and other objects that make up the program's user interface.

2. Input:

   a. Measure length of the room in feet (ignore inches for the sake of simplicity).

   b. Measure the width of the room in feet.

   c. Learn the price per square yard.

3. Processing:

   a. Multiply the length times the width to calculate the total square feet.

   b. Divide the total square feet by 9 to determine the total square yards.

   c. Multiply the total square yards by the price per square yard to calculate the subtotal cost.

   d. Multiply the subtotal cost by the sales tax rate (5%) to get the tax amount.

   e. Add the subtotal amount to the tax amount to calculate the total cost.

4. Output: Display the calculated values on the user interface.

5. Termination: Allow the user to close the form and terminate the program.

Processing Steps 3.a through 3.e can be written as the following series of mathematical expressions:

- Total Square Feet = Length In Feet * Width in Feet

- Total Square Yards = Total Square Feet / 9

- Subtotal Cost = Total Square Yards * Price per Square Yard

- Tax Amount = Subtotal Cost * .05

- Total Cost = Subtotal Cost + Tax Amount

The challenge for this chapter, therefore, is to convert the processing steps presented in 3.a through 3.e into a C# program. The remainder of this chapter walks you through the steps necessary to create the program shown in Figure 2-1.

Figure 2-1 Carpet Cost user interface

CREATING THE VISUAL STUDIO PROJECT FILES

Start Visual Studio .NET (VS.NET from now on). Using the VS.NET menu bar, choose File→New→Project. You will see that VS.NET contains templates for many different types of programs. Because you are creating a Windows application, you might expect to select the Windows Forms project template. *But don't!*

If you start with a Windows Forms project, VS.NET uses predefined templates to create files for your project that contain a good deal of code. *You will learn more about object-oriented programming if you create your projects from scratch instead of using the automatically generated code.* In addition, the predefined code is unnecessarily complex and does not follow the coding style used throughout this text. Instead, this book shows you how to create a Windows Forms application using your own code. To do so, follow these steps:

1. Instead of selecting a Windows Forms project, choose **Visual C# Projects** from the Project Types pane.

2. Next select **Empty Project** from the Templates pane, type "CarpetCost" for the project name, and specify an appropriate folder location, as shown in Figure 2-2.

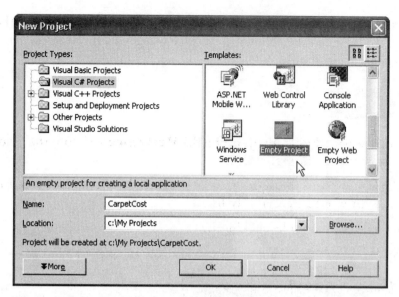

Figure 2-2   VS.NET New Project dialog box

3. Click **OK**.

VS.NET creates a new folder on your computer and writes several project files into this folder. The new folder has the same name you typed as your project name and is located under the folder you chose for Location.

4. Next, mark your new project so that it runs as a Windows Application instead of the default Console application. From the VS.NET menu bar, choose **Project→Properties** to show the Project Property Pages dialog box, as shown in Figure 2-3.

5. In this dialog box, choose **Common Properties→General** and set the Output Type to **Windows Application**. Click **OK** to close the Project Properties window.

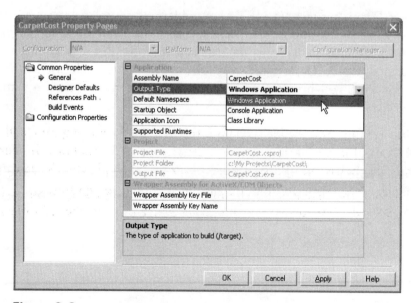

Figure 2-3   Project Property Pages dialog box

In Chapter 1, you learned about class libraries and frameworks. Your C# code can use any of the classes available in the .NET framework but you must first identify for VS.NET which class libraries your project will use. To identify which class libraries, include a reference to them. For this project, reference the class libraries found in the following three Dynamic Link Libraries (DLLs):

- `System.dll`

- `System.Drawing.dll`

- `System.Windows.Forms.dll`

6. From the VS.NET menu bar, choose **Project→Add Reference** to show the Add Reference dialog box displayed in Figure 2-4.

7. Choose the **.NET tab** and scroll through the files listed in the Component Name column until you see the three DLLs previously listed.

8. Add each project reference by double-clicking it.

9. After adding the three DLLs, click **OK** button to close the dialog box.

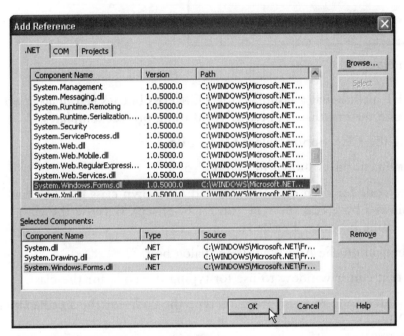

Figure 2-4   Add Reference dialog box

You are now ready to begin typing source code to define the first class your program will use. In Chapter 1, you learned that an object is an instance of a class, and a class contains the code that determines an object's state and behavior. Your first object will be the application's main form.

10. To create a class to code the behavior for the main form, use the VS.NET menu bar, and select **Project→Add New Item**. This menu sequence displays the Add New Item dialog box, as shown in Figure 2-5.

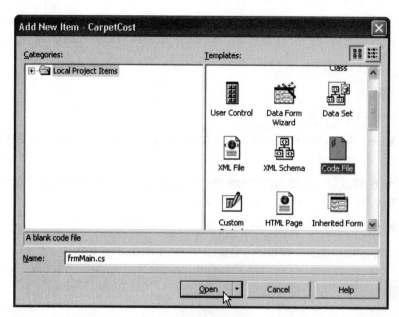

Figure 2-5   Add New Item dialog box

Notice that VS.NET already has a template for a C# class but *it's best to avoid using class templates* for the same reasons that it's best to avoid using project templates.

11. Instead of selecting the Class option, select **Code File**.

12. Name the file `frmMain.cs` as shown in Figure 2-5.

By convention, the code for each class is contained in its own class file. The file-name is the class name followed by a `.cs` file type (`cs` for C-Sharp). Because the class name is `frmMain`, the file name becomes `frmMain.cs`.

13. Click the **Open** button on the Add New Item dialog box.

VS.NET opens a text editor window to use for typing the code for the class.

14. To begin adding source code to your program, type the code for the `frmMain` class as shown in Figure 2-6.

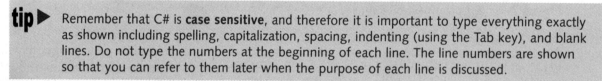

tip ▶ Remember that C# is **case sensitive**, and therefore it is important to type everything exactly as shown including spelling, capitalization, spacing, indenting (using the Tab key), and blank lines. Do not type the numbers at the beginning of each line. The line numbers are shown so that you can refer to them later when the purpose of each line is discussed.

It is best to configure VS.NET to display line numbers in the text editor to make it easier to follow along with the examples. From the VS.NET menu bar, choose Tools→Options→Text Editor→C#→Display→Line numbers.

```
1    using System;
2    using System.Windows.Forms;
3
4    public class frmMain: Form
5    {
6        public static void Main()
7        {
8            frmMain main = new frmMain();
9            Application.Run(main);
10       }
11   }
```

Figure 2-6 frmMain code

tip ▶ As you type, you are likely to notice and be surprised by pop-up windows that appear with code related to your input. This VS.NET feature is known as **Intellisense**. As soon as you type the dot operator, VS.NET shows a pop-up list of properties and methods that may be used in the current context. Intellisense can be a productivity booster that facilitates typing and helps you identify applicable properties and methods.

Let's examine how these lines of code function. As mentioned previously, the Carpet Cost application uses objects that are instantiated from predefined .NET class libraries. These class libraries are grouped into what .NET calls namespaces. A **namespace** is simply a way to organize the class libraries in a hierarchical fashion. Classes that help objects be drawn on the screen are in a namespace called System.Drawing. Classes that are used to create user interface objects are found in **System.Windows.Forms**. Different namespaces are often implemented in separate files, which is why you added references for the System and System.Windows.Forms DLLs to your project. The **using directives** in lines 1 and 2 allow your code to use the classes in these libraries without having to fully qualify the class names with the complete namespace name. For example, instead of typing the **using** directives, the code could be written like this:

```
1    public class frmMain: System.Windows.Forms.Form
2    {
3        public static void Main()
4        {
5            frmMain main = new frmMain();
6            System.Windows.Forms.Application.Run(main);
7        }
8    }
```

Note that the **using** statements have been removed. As a result, you now are forced to prefix each class name with the fully qualified name (shown highlighted) for the specific class you wish to use. Not having to fully qualify a class with its complete namespace name makes your program source code easier to type and easier to read and understand. *It is best to use* **using** *directives rather than fully qualifying class names.* Appendix B contains a complete list of the coding styles and guidelines used in this text.

Line 4 in Figure 2-6 simply indicates that you are defining a new class named **frmMain**. The **:** **Form** text at the end of the statement indicates that the class named **frmMain** is derived, or inherits from, another class named **Form.** The **Form** class is defined in the **System.Windows.Forms** class library. Recall that when one class is derived from another class, it inherits the properties and methods defined in the base class. By defining the **frmMain** class as derived from the **Form** class, you notify C# that the **frmMain** class has all the same properties and methods as **System.Windows.Forms.Form**, plus whatever additional properties and methods you add to the **frmMain** class.

The opening and closing curly braces on lines 5 and 11 are used to delimit the beginning and ending of the content of the `frmMain` class.

Lines 6 through 10 notify C# how to start the application. As your programs become more complex, you add more class files to define the objects the program uses. When Windows starts your program, it needs to identify which statement should be run first. To tell Windows which statement to run first, you code a method named `Main` in one of your classes and prefix it with **public static void** (see line 6 in Figure 2-6). For now, don't worry about what these keywords mean; they are defined in a later chapter. Just accept for now that the `Main` method can be called without first having to instantiate an object from the `frmMain` class. The code in line 8 defines and instantiates a form object from the `frmMain` class. Line 9 starts the application and uses this object as the main user interface, which means that when the user closes this form, the application ends. The opening and closing curly braces on lines 7 and 10 delimit the beginning and ending of the `Main` method.

At this point, you've created the minimal amount of code for a Windows Forms project. In fact you have enough to run your application. To do so, choose Debug→Start from the VS.NET menu bar. If you've done everything correctly, you should see a form like that shown in Figure 2-7. The application doesn't perform many functions yet because you haven't added any application-specific code. However, because the `frmMain` class is derived from `System.Windows.Forms.Form`, the form object has all the functionality of a basic Windows form. The form shows in the Windows taskbar, and it can be minimized, maximized, resized, and closed.

Figure 2-7   Minimal frmMain running

CREATING THE USER INTERFACE USING THE FORM DESIGNER

VS.NET contains a **Form Designer** tool used to easily define the user interface for your application. You could create a user interface yourself by typing all the code to instantiate various user interface objects (such as text boxes and buttons) and then set their properties to make them behave as you want. However, as you will see, this requires hundreds of lines of code for even simple applications. Normally, it's best to avoid using code generators when learning to program. However, user interface code is one exception.

Before you use the Form Designer, you have to add code to your class file to notify the Form Designer of where to insert the generated code. Do this by inserting lines 6 through 12 as shown in Figure 2-8. Also add the code in lines 20 through 23 to execute the generated code when the form is instantiated. Again, be sure to type everything exactly as shown including spelling, capitalization, spacing, indenting, and blank lines (but not the line numbers).

```
1    using System;
2    using System.Windows.Forms;
3
4    public class frmMain: Form
5    {
6        #region Windows Form Designer generated code
7
8        private void InitializeComponent()
9        {
10       }
11
12       #endregion
13
14       public static void Main()
15       {
16           frmMain main = new frmMain();
17           Application.Run(main);
18       }
19
20       public frmMain()
21       {
22           InitializeComponent();
23       }
24   }
```

Figure 2-8 Windows Form designer region

Using Regions

The new lines 6 through 12 in Figure 2-8 define what VS.NET calls a region. A **region** is simply a chunk of code that you want to keep together to increase readability. The VS.NET text editor lets you collapse a region to temporarily hide the chunk of code that is of no concern at the moment. In the text editor window, a small plus sign (+) marks the beginning of the region's name. If you click on the plus sign, the region is expanded to reveal all the code associated with that region. When the code in the region is visible, the plus sign is changed to a minus sign (-), so you can easily identify the state of the region (that is, hidden or expanded). Clicking the minus sign hides the region's code and changes the minus sign back into a plus sign. Therefore, clicking the plus or minus sign toggles the state of the region.

If you don't put this region in your class, it is more difficult to distinguish your code from that generated by the Form Designer. After you see the code the Form Designer generates, you'll understand why it's best to keep it separated and hidden by collapsing the region.

Using regions is purely for making code easier to read in the text editor. Putting code in a region has no effect on the way a program runs or the behavior of the object being coded.

Changing Form Properties

To use the Form Designer, choose View→Designer from the VS.NET menu bar. You should see an empty form similar to that shown in Figure 2-9.

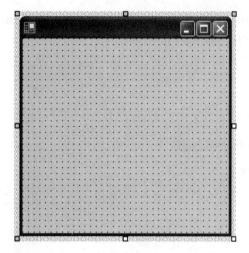

Figure 2-9   Empty form shown in the Form Designer

You change some of the properties on the form to make it behave more like a proper Windows application. The best way to do this is to use the Properties window. Recall from Chapter 1 that changing the property value of an object changes the state of that object. The **Properties window** provides a visual means for changing the state of user interface objects.

You can show the Properties window (see Figure 2-10) by choosing View→Properties Window from the VS.NET menu bar, or by right-clicking the object in the Form Designer and choosing Properties from the pop-up menu.

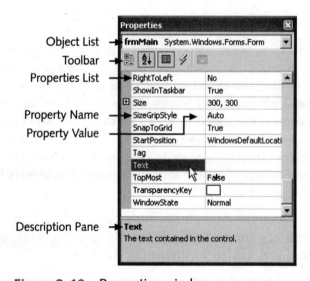

Figure 2-10   Properties window

The Properties window, shown in Figure 2-10, consists of the following elements:

- Object List
- Toolbar
- Properties List
- Description Pane

The Object List contains the user interface objects on the form, as well as the form itself. It also lists the type, or class, of the object. You can select objects from it by choosing them from the list, or by selecting them on the form in the Form Designer. The toolbar has buttons that enable you to change how the list of properties is displayed (either in categories or in alphabetical order), and enables you to view the properties or events for the selected object. We feel that it is easier to locate properties when they are listed alphabetically. If the list of properties does not appear to be alphabetized, click the button.

The Properties List consists of two columns. The left column lists the properties and the right column lists each property's current value for the object selected in the Object List. Because different objects have different sets of properties, the content of this Properties List changes depending on the type of the object selected. To change a property value, first select the property name from the Properties List. Next, click the property value and, depending on the acceptable values for that property, type in a new value or select from the drop-down list. Notice that property values that have been changed from their default value, are shown in boldface. The Description Pane simply shows a short description of the selected property.

To change the behavior of the form so that it works more like a proper Windows application, change the default property values of the form as shown in Table 2-1:

Table 2-1   Setting the values of the properties

Property	Value
(Name)	frmMain
FormBorderStyle	FixedSingle
MaximizeBox	False
StartPosition	CenterScreen
Text	Carpet Cost

tip ▶ The steps you have completed so far will be repeated for every example program presented in this text. It may be handy to use Windows Explorer to copy the folder that contains your project files so that the next time you start a new project you can begin with a copy of these files rather than starting from the beginning.

To create the user interface, you have to place user interface objects, also called **controls**, on the form. A list of the user interface objects that are available is presented in the Toolbox window. You can access the Toolbox window by selecting View➔Toolbox from the VS.NET menu bar. The Toolbox window, shown in Figure 2-11, contains a list of the controls defined in the `System.Windows.Forms` class library that can be used with Windows forms. Notice that the Toolbox contains approximately 50 objects, but don't worry about learning how to use them all. For the Carpet Cost application (and most programs in the first half of this text), you primarily use just three controls: buttons, labels, and text boxes.

Figure 2-11   Toolbox window

Text boxes can be used for either input or output values. When used for input, a text box into which the user types should have a white background. When used for output, the text box into which the user is not allowed to type should have the same background color as the form. In other words, an output-only text box should have its `ReadOnly` property set to `true`.

Labels are used to identify objects on the form, and **buttons** give the user a way to request that an action take place. The Carpet Cost application user interface requires three input values and three output values. Each label identifies an input or output value. One button is for calculation, and another button closes the form and ends the application.

Placing Controls on a Form

Controls can be placed on a form in two ways. The first way is to double-click a control in the Toolbox. When you do this, an instance of that control is placed in a default position on the form. The second way is to select a control in the Toolbox and, while holding down the left mouse button, drag it to the form and release the mouse button. After a control is placed on the form, you can use the mouse to drag it to a new position and to drag its border to resize it. When you set the form's `SnapToGrid` property to `true`, the controls are aligned on the grid dots shown on the form. Using this layout grid makes aligning controls easy.

To complete the user interface, add six labels, six text boxes, and two buttons to the form and set their properties, as shown in Table 2-2. Be sure to change the `Name` property of the controls so that you can refer to them from the code in the form's class file. When finished, your form should look similar to the Form Designer form shown in Figure 2-12.

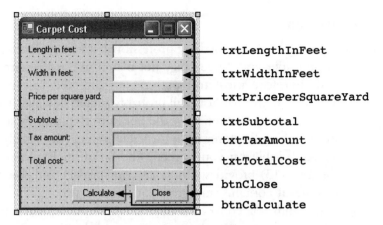

Figure 2-12 Carpet Cost application user interface

The form shown in Figure 2-12 results from the values shown in Table 2-2.

Table 2-2 Values used to produce the Carpet Cost application user interface

Object Type	Name	Property	Value
Label	label1	Text	Length in feet:
	label2	Text	Width in feet:
	label3	Text	Price per square yard:
	label4	Text	Subtotal:
	label5	Text	Tax amount:
	label6	Text	Total cost:
Text box	txtLengthInFeet	Text	empty
	txtWidthInFeet	Text	empty
	txtPricePerSquareYard	Text	empty
	txtSubtotal	Text	empty
		ReadOnly	True
		TabStop	False
	txtTaxAmount	Text	empty
		ReadOnly	True
		TabStop	False
	txtTotalCost	Text	empty
		ReadOnly	True
		TabStop	False
Button	btnCalculate	Text	Calculate
	btnClose	Text	Close

The Solution Explorer—a Handy Tool

As mentioned before, VS.NET is a powerful tool designed for professional software developers. Because its user interface is highly customizable, your screen may not match the text's examples, and therefore most instructions are directed toward the VS.NET menu bar. You will probably prefer, however, to use the Solution Explorer. View the Solution Explorer by selecting Solution Explorer from the View menu. Most likely it is already visible on your screen. The Solution Explorer (see Figure 2-13) provides a view of your project and the various files it contains, and gives you a quick way to access the commands related to each object. For example, you can use it to switch between the code view and the Form Designer for a form. You can add, rename, and remove files from the project. Try experimenting with the Solution Explorer by right-clicking an object to show a pop-up menu of available commands for that object.

Figure 2-13   Solution Explorer

ADDING THE APPLICATION LOGIC

After the project files have been created and the user interface defined, you're ready to begin. Start by typing the code necessary to implement the algorithm for the calculation. Choose View→Code from the VS.NET menu item to switch back to the source code.

tip ▶   You can also switch between code and the Form Designer by clicking the tabs at the top of the Form Designer (frmMain.cs **frmMain.cs [Design]**) or by pressing Ctrl+Tab.

You should now see all the code that the Form Designer has generated. The user interface for this simple application takes almost 200 lines of code. For this reason, you should collapse the region to hide as much of the Form Designer–generated code as possible. As mentioned earlier, regions can be expanded and collapsed by clicking the plus (+) and minus (-) symbols in the left margin of the text editor as shown in Figure 2-14.

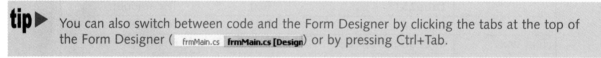

Figure 2-14   Windows Form Designer—generated code—region expanded and collapsed

Adding the Program Logic Source Code

To make your application perform the calculation, add the statements that represent the program logic. The entire code for the **frmMain** class, minus the Form Designer–generated code from lines 6 through 190, is shown in Figure 2-15. Your line numbers may differ slightly. As always, be sure to type your code exactly as shown. For now, don't worry about what each statement means; you'll understand each one shortly. The next section explains how to complete the application by connecting the methods to the button click events.

```
  1    using System;
  2    using System.Windows.Forms;
  3
  4    public class frmMain: Form
  5    {

191        public static void Main()
192        {
193            frmMain main = new frmMain();
194            Application.Run(main);
195        }
196
197        public frmMain()
198        {
199            InitializeComponent();
200        }
201
202        private void btnClose_Click(object sender, System.EventArgs e)
203        {
204            Close();
205        }
206
207        private void btnCalculate_Click(object sender, System.EventArgs e)
208        {
209            const decimal taxRate = .05M;
210
211            decimal lengthInFeet;
212            decimal widthInFeet;
213            decimal pricePerSquareYard;
214            decimal squareFeet;
215            decimal squareYards;
216            decimal subtotal;
217            decimal taxAmount;
218            decimal totalCost;
219
220            // Get the input values from the form.
221
222            lengthInFeet = decimal.Parse(txtLengthInFeet.Text);
223            widthInFeet = decimal.Parse(txtWidthInFeet.Text);
224            pricePerSquareYard = decimal.Parse(txtPricePerSquareYard.Text);
225
226            // Validate that the input is correct.
227
228            if (lengthInFeet <= 0)
229            {
230                MessageBox.Show("Length in Feet must be > zero.");
231                txtLengthInFeet.Focus();
232                return;
233            }
234
235            if (widthInFeet <= 0)
236            {
237                MessageBox.Show("Width in Feet must be > zero.");
238                txtWidthInFeet.Focus();
239                return;
240            }
241
```

Figure 2-15 Completed frmMain code

```
242            if (pricePerSquareYard <= 0)
243            {
244                MessageBox.Show("Price Per Square Yard must be > zero.");
245                txtPricePerSquareYard.Focus();
246                return;
247            }
248
249            // Calculate the amounts.
250
251            squareFeet = lengthInFeet * widthInFeet;
252            squareYards = squareFeet / 9;
253
254            subtotal = squareYards * pricePerSquareYard;
255            subtotal = Math.Round(subtotal, 2);
256
257            taxAmount = subtotal * taxRate;
258            taxAmount = Math.Round(taxAmount, 2);
259
260            totalCost = subtotal + taxAmount;
261
262            // Display the results back to the user.
263
264            txtSubtotal.Text = subtotal.ToString("C");
265            txtTaxAmount.Text = taxAmount.ToString("C");
266            txtTotalCost.Text = totalCost.ToString("C");
267        }
268    }
```

Figure 2-15 Completed frmMain code (continued)

Program Events

When your program begins execution, the user interface is displayed on the computer's monitor. The program waits for a user to indicate that he or she wants the program to perform a function. Typically, the user requests an action by clicking a button with the mouse. Each time the user clicks a button, the Windows operating system generates a button click event message and passes it back to the application.

Clicking an object with the mouse is one example of an event, but there are many others—for example, pressing a key on the keyboard or moving the mouse over an object. Each action causes a specific type of event message to be sent to the application. Each object responds to a specified set of events. To make your application respond to one of these events, you must write code in a method and then connect that method to the event using the Properties window.

The code in Figure 2-15 contains two methods that are executed when the user clicks one of the buttons on the form. You could type in the code that connects each method to a specific button yourself, but it is more efficient to use the Form Designer to establish that connection.

Switch VS.NET back to the Form Designer (View→Designer), and show the Properties window (View→Properties Window). You used the Properties window earlier to set properties for the user interface objects. You can also use the Properties window to connect an object's events to the method associated with that event in the class file. To do so, follow these steps:

1. Select the **btnCalculate** button from the Object List.

2. Click the **Events** toolbar button ⚡ in the Properties window.

3. Find the **Click** event, and select the **btnCalculate_Click** method as shown in Figure 2-16.

4. Repeat the same process for the **Close** button, except connect its click event to the **btnClose_Click** method.

Note you can also double-click the column next to the event name rather than select it from the list. If a method with the appropriate name isn't found, VS.NET creates a method in your code and connects the event to it. Of course, you must add code to the event to make it perform an action.

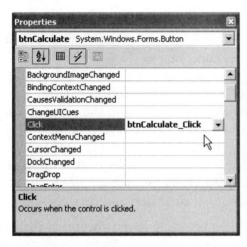

Figure 2-16   Connecting the btnCalculate_Click method to the click event of btnCalculate

CODE EXPLANATION

Initialization

Lines 197 through 200 in Figure 2-15 define a constructor for the **frmMain** class. A **constructor** is simply a method that is executed whenever an object is instantiated from this class. Constructors, which are often used to perform initialization functions, are discussed in detail in Chapter 10.

In the Carpet Cost program, the only initializing required of the form is to instantiate and initialize the controls that make up the form's user interface. The code to accomplish this task is found in the **InitializeComponent** method, which was generated by the Form Designer. This code is hidden in the Windows Form Designer–generated code region.

Event Methods

Lines 202 through 205 in Figure 2-15 define the method that you've indicated should be executed when the user clicks the Close button on the user interface. This method performs only one task—it calls another method, named **Close**. But where is the code for the **Close** method? You didn't type the code into the program, and the Form Designer didn't generate it.

Recall that your **frmMain** class is derived from the **System.Windows.Forms.Form** base class, and when one class is derived from another, the derived class inherits all the properties and methods defined in the base class. The **Close** method is one of the methods inherited from the

`System.Windows.Forms.Form` base class. Although you didn't write code for `Close`, it may be used in your code because it exists through `System.Windows.Forms.Form`. When the `Close` method is called, the form is closed, and because this is the form created in the `Main` method, the application ends.

Lines 207 through 267 define the method that you want executed when the user clicks the Calculate button. As you saw earlier in this chapter, the opening and closing curly braces on lines 208 and 267 indicate where the content of the `btnCalculate_Click` method begins and ends.

Constants and Variables

Lines 209 through 218 in Figure 2-15 define the data items the program needs to perform the calculation. Data items in a computer program are either constants or variables. A **constant** is a value that does not change as the program runs. A constant value of .05 is defined at line 209 that represents the 5% state sales tax rate, because it isn't an input value and is always the same. A **variable** is a value that may change as the program runs. Lines 211 through 218 define the variable data items for the calculation. Both constants and variables are defined in the program using similar syntax, except that constants are prefixed with the **const** keyword to indicate that the value cannot change. The definition for constants and variables includes a C# keyword to indicate the type of data being stored in memory, and a name that you create to refer to that piece of data. In this example, all numbers are defined using the **decimal** data type, which means they can store numbers with fractional values. Chapter 3 covers variables, constants, and data types in detail.

Keywords are reserved identifiers that have been defined previously with meanings that the compiler understands.

Making the Code Easier to Read

Lines 220, 226, 249, and 262 in Figure 2-15 contain source code comments. Unlike most other statements in the source code, **comments** do not give any actual instruction to the computer on how the program should execute. Instead, programmers include comments in their source code to give explanations, or documentation, to anyone who may read the source code. Comments are helpful because the logic represented by program statements can become lengthy and confusing as the program becomes more and more complex. The source code for an application may contain hundreds, thousands, and even millions of lines of code.

All comment lines are preceded with two forward slashes. Any text positioned from the right of the slashes to the end of the line is interpreted as a comment. We recommend that you include comments in your source code to indicate what the code does and to break up large sections into easier-to-understand chunks. Comments may be included almost anywhere in the code. By convention, however, most comments are typed on separate lines before the code they are describing and are indented at the same level as the code being documented. Appendix B contains a complete list of coding style we recommend and includes guidelines for using comments.

Like comments, blank lines increase the readability of your source code, just as white space makes a printed page more inviting. *Your code is easier to read if you include blank lines before and after comments, between methods, and around other statements to group them into logical units of work.*

Getting the User's Input

As the comment indicates, lines 222 through 224 in Figure 2-15 take the user input data and store these values in three variables. These statements all perform approximately the same function, but a few actions occur in each statement, so let's examine line 222 in detail:

```
222                lengthInFeet = decimal.Parse(txtLengthInFeet.Text);
```

This statement is executed from right to left, just as you read algebraic equations from right to left. For example, when you read the following expression in algebra:

```
x = 5 + 2
```

you add 5 and 2 together and then assign the resulting value 7 to the variable **x**.

In line 223, **txtLengthInFeet** is the name given to one of the text box objects on the user interface. Text boxes have a **Text** property that contains the characters shown in the text box on the user interface. When the program is run, the **Text** property should contain the characters the user has typed into the **txtLengthInFeet** text box.

The characters from the **txtLengthInFeet.Text** property are passed, or used as input, to a method named **decimal.Parse**. The **Parse** method converts the characters the user typed into the **txtLengthInFeet** text box to their numerical value equivalent. This conversion is necessary because a text box contains only text characters (even if they are the characters "123"). However, the program needs numeric values to perform its mathematical calculations. Chapter 3 covers type conversions in detail. Finally, the numeric value returned from **decimal.Parse** is stored in the variable **lengthInFeet**.

Validating the User Input

After the input values have been obtained from the user interface, the next step is to validate that the values the user has entered can be used for calculations. To keep things simple, the Carpet Cost application assumes that the user enters only valid digit characters into the input text box. Although C# can ensure that the user enters only numeric characters, the logic for that validation process is too complex for this chapter. Chapters 5 and 6 describe how to incorporate robust data validation into programs. For now, the application only checks that the three input values are positive numbers greater than zero, because it makes no sense to perform the calculations with zero or negative values.

Typically, validating an input value consists of these steps:

- The value of the data item is checked to ensure that the task can be performed.
- If the task can't be performed, a message is displayed to the user notifying him of the error.
- The cursor is placed in the text box containing the erroneous data (that is, the focus is set to that control).
- The method exits. The method is exited using the **return** keyword because code can't continue processing with bad data.

Because each input value is validated using similar logic, only *the validation of the* first input value is explained here. Line 228 in Figure 2-15 contains a **Boolean expression** that uses the less than or equal to (<=) **comparison operator** to check the value of the **lengthInFeet** variable. If the value is negative or equal to zero, the lines of code within the **if** statement block are executed. The opening and closing curly braces on lines 229 and 233 delimit the **if** statement block.

If the value in the `lengthInFeet` variable is greater than zero, the statements on lines 230, 231, and 232 are *not* executed and processing continues at line 235.

Line 230 uses the `Show` method of the `MessageBox` class to display the error message to the user if `lengthInFeet` is negative. The text within the quotes is passed as input to the `Show` method and is displayed in a dialog box (see Figure 2-17). When the user clicks the OK button in the message box dialog box, line 231 is executed. It calls the `Focus` method of the `txtLengthInFeet` text box, which causes the cursor to be placed in the `txtLengthInFeet` text box. Finally the `return` keyword is executed on line 232, which causes the program to exit the `btnCalculate_Click` method and causes all other statements within the method to be skipped. Chapter 5 covers in detail decisions, data validation, and a better way to display a message box.

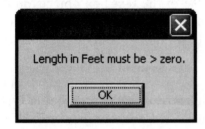

Figure 2-17   An error message shown in a message box

Performing the Calculations

As discussed at the beginning of this chapter, the steps to calculate the cost of carpet are fairly simple, but they require several calculations.

Line 251 in Figure 2-15 uses the multiplication operator (*) to multiply the length in feet by the width in feet to calculate the total number of square feet. The result is then stored in a variable named `squareFeet`.

Line 252 uses the division operator (/) to divide the contents of variable `squareFeet` by a constant value of nine to calculate the total number of square yards. The result of the division operation is stored in a variable named `squareYards`.

Line 254 calculates the subtotal cost by multiplying the contents of variable `squareYards` by the contents of variable `pricePerSquareYard` and stores the result in variable `subtotal`. Line 255 uses the `Round` method found in class `Math` to round the subtotal cost to two decimal positions. This step is necessary because the calculation on line 254 may result in a value with more than two decimal positions. For example, if the total square yards are 29.5 and the price per square yard is $3.99, the subtotal cost is calculated as $117.705. However, in this country dollar amounts are rounded to the nearest cent, and therefore the `Round` method is used to yield the proper value of $117.71.

Line 257 calculates the amount of sales tax to be charged, and line 258 again rounds the amount to two decimal positions (that is, to the nearest cent). Line 260 uses the addition operator (+) to add the subtotal amount to the sales tax amount and stores that sum in the variable `totalCost`.

Displaying the Results to the User

The final step in the program logic is to display the calculated values to the user. Recall that the code that captures the input from the user used the `decimal.Parse` method to convert it from the text characters in the **Text** property of the input text boxes to numeric values. This conversion was done because the mathematical calculations require numeric values. Now that the calculations are completed, you have to reverse the operation. That is, the code must now convert the numeric values back to text characters so they can be displayed in the output text boxes.

All the numbers in the Carpet Cost program are defined with the **decimal** data type, meaning that they can store numbers with fractional values, or decimal positions. The **decimal** data type, and all the other numeric data types for that matter, has a **ToString** method. The **ToString** method returns the text character equivalent of the numeric value of the object. The **ToString** method is named for the common programming language term for a sequence of text characters, which is a **string**. The "C" that is passed as input to the **ToString** method indicates that the string of characters returned from the **ToString** method should be formatted as a money value, or currency. When you run the program you will see the output data formatted with a dollar sign, commas, and a decimal point.

TESTING THE PROGRAM

After you've completed the coding for the application, you must test it to make sure that it will work correctly. The first step in testing is to build the project. This step uses the C# compiler to convert the source code into an executable. You build the application by selecting Build→Build Solution from the VS.NET menu. If you've done everything correctly up to this point, you should see a message indicating that the build was successful in the VS.NET Output window, like that shown in Figure 2-18.

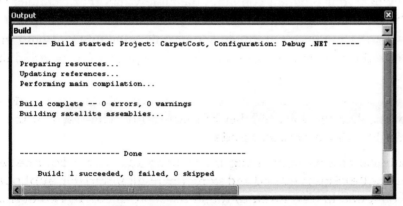

```
Output                                                          [X]
Build                                                            [▼]
 ------ Build started: Project: CarpetCost, Configuration: Debug .NET ------

 Preparing resources...
 Updating references...
 Performing main compilation...

 Build complete -- 0 errors, 0 warnings
 Building satellite assemblies...



 ---------------------- Done ----------------------

     Build: 1 succeeded, 0 failed, 0 skipped
```

Figure 2-18   Output window showing the build was successful

If the Output window shows an error, it is most likely because you've made a typing error in the source code. Programs can contain three general categories of errors.

Program Errors

Compile, or syntax errors occur when the C# compiler can't understand the code you've typed. And as mentioned before, compilers are very picky about syntax. In the C# programming language, code is **case sensitive**. If you define a variable **lengthInFeet** and then later refer to it as **LengthInFeet**, it won't work because the case doesn't match exactly. Variables and keywords must be typed to exactly match the case used in their definition. Compile errors are the easiest errors to find and correct because the compiler reports the exact line of the error. Almost all compile errors are caused by typing errors, so if you have compile errors at this point, compare your code with the code given to find the differences.

tip ▶ VS.NET has a useful feature that is similar to a spell checker in a word processor. Just as a word processor can underline a misspelled word with a red squiggly line, VS.NET underlines a word it doesn't recognize with a squiggly blue line. It is very common to make typing mistakes when coding, so you'll see the dreaded squiggly blue line frequently while coding. If you were lucky enough to type all the sample code without errors, go back and purposefully create a mistake. For example, change a lowercase letter to an uppercase letter. Try to rebuild the project and see how C# shows you what requires correction.

Another category of errors is **run-time errors**. These errors, also called **exceptions**, occur when a program is executing. In this case the C# compiler understands source code and compiles it into an executable. But when the executable runs, it attempts to perform an impossible function. These are examples of run-time errors: your program attempts to divide a value by zero or to convert text such as "abc" into a number using the `decimal.Parse` method. If your program encounters an exception, a message (often cryptic) is displayed to the user and your program terminates, or crashes. Chapter 6 covers catching exceptions to prevent program crashes.

The third type of error is known as a **logic error**. Logic errors occur when source code has been converted to an executable, and it runs without crashing, but it produces incorrect results. These errors are often subtle and hard to find and correct.

Fortunately, VS.NET contains a handy interactive debugger.

Debugging

To test, or **debug**, a program, you first need to create sample input values, perform the calculations yourself by hand, and check that your program computes the same values. For example, Table 2-3 shows some sample input values and correct output values. To thoroughly test a program, try many input values using a wide range of numbers. You should also include some invalid data to make sure your program handles it correctly.

Table 2-3   Test data for the Carpet Cost application

	Test 1	Test 2	Test 3	Test 4
Length in feet	10	12	27	−20
Width in feet	20	16	36	15
Price per square yard	2.50	3.99	4.50	1.99
Subtotal	$55.56	$85.12	$486.00	Error
Tax amount	$2.78	$4.26	$24.30	message
Total cost	$58.34	$89.38	$510.30	displayed

The best way to see how a program executes is to set a breakpoint on the first logic statement in a method and watch it execute line by line. Set a breakpoint in the Carpet Cost program by clicking the left margin next to line 222, as shown in Figure 2-19. Remember your line numbers may vary slightly. It is important to set the breakpoint on the correct statement and not necessarily on line 222.

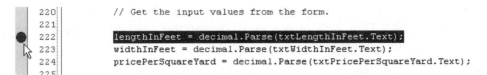

```
220    // Get the input values from the form.
221
222    lengthInFeet = decimal.Parse(txtLengthInFeet.Text);
223    widthInFeet = decimal.Parse(txtWidthInFeet.Text);
224    pricePerSquareYard = decimal.Parse(txtPricePerSquareYard.Text);
225
```

Figure 2-19   Setting a breakpoint

Note that you do not set a breakpoint on the constant and variable declarations on lines 209 through 218 because declarations don't actually execute in sequence when the program runs.

Start up your program by choosing Debug→Start from the VS.NET menu. If the code contains no compile errors, your program will start by executing the code in the **public static void Main** method. A new form object should be instantiated, which executes the constructor method, which in turn causes the user interface objects to be created and drawn on the screen. At this point, your program is waiting for the user to enter data and click the Calculate button.

> **tip ▶**   Choosing Debug→Start from the VS.NET menu will build the application if necessary before executing it in debug mode. This means you don't have to explicitly choose Build→Build Solution from the VS.NET Build menu. You can also build and start the application in debug mode by pressing F5.

Type the input values shown in Test 1 in Table 2-3 into the input text boxes, and click the Calculate button. When the Calculate button is clicked, the **btnCalculate_Click** method executes, and the statements begin to execute. Because you've set a breakpoint on line 223, the debugger stops the program at that statement and highlights it. When the debugger has stopped execution at a statement, it means that statement has not yet been executed, but it will execute whenever you indicate. Choose Step Into from the Debug menu to execute the statement on line 222 and advance the execution point to the statement on line 223. Using interactive debugging is an excellent way to see the order in which program statements execute.

> **tip ▶**   You can also step through your code by clicking F11 or clicking the ▣ toolbar button.

With the execution point set at line 223, hover the mouse pointer over the **widthInFeet** variable. When you hover the mouse pointer over a variable, VS.NET displays a Datatip window that shows you the content of the variable. See Figure 2-20 for an example.

```
220    // Get the input values from the form.
221
222    lengthInFeet = decimal.Parse(txtLengthInFeet.Text);
223    widthInFeet = decimal.Parse(txtWidthInFeet.Text);
224    pricePerSq[widthInFeet = 0]decimal.Parse(txtPricePerSquareYard.Text);
225
```

Figure 2-20   Datatip window

Because the statement on line 222 has not yet been executed, the contents of the **widthInFeet** variable should be zero. Execute line 222 by choosing Step Into from the Debug menu, and then again hover the mouse pointer over the variable. This time you should see that the variable has a value of 20 because you typed the characters "20" in the **txtWidthInFeet** text box. Continue stepping through the code until you reach the end of the method. You should now see the correct output values in the user interface.

Continue entering the test values in the input text boxes and clicking the Calculate button to further test your application. Continue this process of debugging until you are confident the program is producing the correct output.

Setting breakpoints, stepping through code, and examining the contents of variables are the easiest and most commonly used tools for debugging code. The VS.NET debugger contains many other useful debugging tools. See Appendix C for more tips on debugging your applications.

BONUS TOPICS

SOURCE CODE FORMAT

As previously mentioned, the C# compiler is extremely picky about language syntax, but it is *not* picky about the format (appearance) of source code. As long as the syntax is correct, the compiler understands the code. For example, the first group of statements you typed looked like this:

```
1    using System;
2    using System.Windows.Forms;
3
4    public class frmMain: Form
5    {
6        public static void Main()
7        {
8            frmMain main = new frmMain();
9            Application.Run(main);
10       }
11   }
```

But as far as the compiler is concerned, this code could have been typed in this way:

```
1    using System;using System.Windows.Forms;public
2    class frmMain:Form{public static void Main(){
3    frmMain main=new frmMain();Application.Run(main);}}
```

The syntax is the same; only the format has been changed. Remember, the format of the statements does not change the program's behavior.

On the other hand, software developers (and professors) *are* extremely picky about the format of source code. Because compilers have no rules for code formatting, programmers have developed guidelines and styles for formatting source code. Guidelines cover the use of comments, the use of blank lines, spaces for indentation, the naming of variables, and the placement of curly braces. Unfortunately for anyone learning programming, there are about as many styles as there are software developers (and professors), and each person enthusiastically defends his or her method as the best.

Actually, the most important aspect of source code formatting is that the code be easy to read. In addition, the style should be consistent (for example, always indent four spaces rather than four spaces in one place and three spaces in another). The style used in this text is based on the authors' experience using C# and a variety of other programming languages. The style is also based on the C# examples published by Microsoft. See Appendix B for a complete list of the coding styles and guidelines used in this text.

There are at least two common deviations from the style used in this text that you are likely to encounter in other texts, and these are discussed in the next section.

Comments

The first deviation is a method for indicating comments. In all examples used in this text, comments are preceded by two forward slashes. For example:

```
// Get the input values from the form and display
// an error message if anything is invalid.
```

Recall that when you use "//" to indicate the beginning of a comment, everything after, and until the end of the line, is considered comment text.

Another method for indicating comments is by including "/*" before the comment text and "*/" after the comment text. Unlike "//", the comment text doesn't end until "*/" is encountered. This means that comments indicated in this way can span many lines without any markers at the beginning of each line. Here is an example:

```
/* Get the input values from the form and display
    an error message if anything is invalid. */
```

If you happen to type "/*" but forget to type "*/", you can accidentally change large chunks of code into comments. Most modern text editors, including the text editor in VS.NET, display comments in a different color, making your code easier to read and debug. But if your code is printed in black and white, it is next to impossible to notice an accidental "/*" in your code. For this reason, the "//" style of comments is preferable.

Brace Alignment

C# code examples in this text and most others show curly braces on a line by themselves (the so-called Allman style). However, many programmers prefer to include the opening curly brace on the same line as the statement that precedes it (the so-called K&R style). So, instead of this:

```
1    public class frmMain: System.Windows.Forms.Form
2    {
3        public static void Main()
4        {
5            frmMain main = new frmMain();
6            System.Windows.Forms.Application.Run(main);
7        }
8    }
```

they code end-of-line curly braces like this:

```
1    public class frmMain: System.Windows.Forms.Form {
2        public static void Main() {
3            frmMain main = new frmMain();
4            System.Windows.Forms.Application.Run(main);
5        }
6    }
```

This K&R style is popular among C and Java programmers. However, even more styles exist.[1] The Allman style is used in this text because it is most prevalent in C# examples.

---

[1] http://www.encyclopedia4u.com/i/indent-style.html

Visual Studio .NET Project Files

VS.NET creates many files on your computer. This section describes them and explains which files are the most critical. But first, you need to understand how VS.NET projects are organized.

Solutions and Projects

When you start a new application, VS.NET requests a name for your project and a folder location for the project files (see Figure 2-2). You probably didn't notice that VS.NET also created something it calls a solution and gave it the same name as the project name you specified. What's a solution? A **solution** is something that can contain one or more VS.NET projects. Each VS.NET project creates a VS.NET assembly—a program, executable, or .exe.

Each program example in this text is contained in its own VS.NET project, because the concept of a solution isn't useful for simple applications. However, the solution concept could be useful in large systems composed of several programs. You could create a single VS.NET solution and add to it a VS.NET project for each program in the system. Then, when you instruct VS.NET to open the solution, it opens all the projects within the solution, which allows you to work on all the projects within the solution without having to open each project in its own instance of VS.NET.

A VS.NET project contains the files necessary to create a single assembly. Project files typically consist of the class files you code. But projects more advanced than those shown in this text might contain many other types of files. For example, you can include image files, icons, cursors, audio files, and anything else you might need to distribute with your application.

For each example in this text, you should create a single solution and in that solution have a single project with the same name as the solution. Then, keep all solution and project files in a single folder on your computer, and give the folder the same name as the solution and project.

File Types

When you use the Windows Explorer to view the contents of a project folder, you see a group of files you didn't explicitly create. These are files VS.NET creates to store information about your solutions and projects in the project folder. Most of the time, you should keep all these files together in a single folder without deleting any of them. However, if some of the files happen to be deleted or lost, you may still be able to recreate your project by copying and pasting your code from the class files you've created into a new project.

The C# source files are the most critical, because these files contain all the source code you've spent so much time creating. Another important file is any .resx file. These files usually have the same name as form class files and contain further information about the user interface controls on the forms. Table 2-4 lists common file types. Many of the files are stored as Extensible Markup Language (XML) text files. You can open them in a text editor such as Notepad if you are curious about their content. Just be careful not to change them.

Table 2-4   VS.NET project files

File Type	File Extension	Purpose
Microsoft Visual Studio Solution Object	.sln	Defines the project files and other items that compose a solution; this is the file you normally open with VS.NET to work on a project
Visual Studio Solution User Options	.suo	Contains the VS.NET IDE settings for the solution
C# Project File	.csproj	Contains project-specific options
Visual Studio Project User Options	.csproj.user	Contains the VS.NET IDE settings for the project
C# Source File	.cs	Contains the source code for the various class files you create
Resource File	.resx	Contains the non–source code resources that might be included in an application
Application	.exe	Contains the executable (assembly) code that includes your compiled source code; you can copy this file to another PC and run it there, even if it doesn't have VS.NET installed, but it must have the .NET Framework installed

MSIL, the CLR, and JIT Compiling

As mentioned previously, the job of a compiler is to convert your source code to an executable file so that it can be run on another computer that doesn't have the compiler or the source code. Historically, most compilers did just this. That is, they converted source code files into a binary format .exe file that was directly executable by the CPU of the computer. In C# (and any other .NET language) it doesn't work quite that simply.

When the C# compiler is run against your source code, it generates an .exe file, but it doesn't actually contain directly executable instructions. Instead, it contains what Microsoft calls MSIL, or **Microsoft Intermediate Language**. When you run an .exe file that contains MSIL, it doesn't interact with the operating system directly. Instead, it interacts with a component of the .NET Framework called the **common language runtime**, or **CLR**. The CLR performs many services including memory management, exception handling, and code verification. Microsoft calls code that targets the CLR "managed code," to emphasize the fact that the application doesn't interact directly with the operating system and is instead managed by the CLR. The benefit of using MSIL and the CLR is that the .NET platform supports many programming languages, and they all share the same MSIL, CLR, and the .NET class libraries. New languages can be added to .NET by creating a compiler that outputs MSIL.

The Java environment uses a very similar system except that instead of MSIL, Java refers to the intermediate code as **bytecode.** And instead of a CLR, Java uses a Java Virtual Machine (JVM) to manage execution of the bytecode.

Programs compiled to intermediate code typically have poorer performance than code compiled to directly executable instructions. They run more slowly because of the overhead created by the run-time environments (that is, the CLR and JVM). To overcome this poor performance, the CLR performs one task that the JVM does not.

When you first execute a managed code application, the CLR performs a quick compile of the MSIL and creates a directly executable file from it. This process, known as **Just In Time (JIT)** compiling, happens only the first time you execute an MSIL program on a computer. The next time you execute it, the CLR runs the JIT-compiled version. JIT compiling solves the poor performance problem, while still providing the benefits of managed code.

SUMMARY

Essential Topics

- In its simplest form, a computer program is a series of instructions that the computer can understand. Programs consist of data input, processing, and data output.

- The processing steps in a computer program can be generalized as initialization, input, processing, output, and termination.

- Each instruction you type as the program's source code is normally typed on a single line and is often referred to as a program statement.

- The job of a compiler is to convert source code to an executable file .exe so it can be run on another computer that doesn't have the source code.

- Visual Studio .NET (VS.NET) is a tool you can use to write, test, and debug applications. Tools like VS.NET are often referred to as Integrated Development Environments, or simply IDEs. The term *integrated* is used because IDEs contain many tools you use when writing programs.

- The first step in writing a computer program is to make sure you understand what the program should accomplish.

- VS.NET contains templates for many types of applications, but you will learn more about object-oriented programming if you start your programs from scratch.

- The .NET class libraries are contained in a series of DLLs and your project must reference the class libraries that the application will use. This is done using the Add References dialog box.

- A namespace is simply a way to organize class libraries in a hierarchical fashion. *using* directives allow your code to use the classes in class libraries without having to fully qualify the class names with the complete namespace name.

- The **public static void Main** method is used to start a C# program. The examples used in this text are all Windows Form applications, and therefore the **Main** method instantiates and runs a form that is derived from the **System.Windows.Forms.Form** class.

- A region is simply a chunk of code that you want to keep together to increase readability. Regions can be collapsed and expanded when needed by using the plus and minus signs in the text editor window.

- VS.NET contains a Form Designer tool that can be used to easily define the user interface for an application. Using the Form Designer tool to generate code is one exception to our recommendation to write all code from scratch. The Properties window can be used to visually set the properties of the controls you place on forms.

- Clicking an object with the mouse is one example of a program event. Each event indicates a specific type of event message be sent to the application. Each object responds to the specified set of events that it can respond to. You make your application respond to events by writing code in a method and then connecting that method to the event.

- Placing comments in source code can make the source code easier to read. Unlike most other statements in the source code, comments do not give any actual instructions to the computer concerning program execution. In C#, comments are indicated by preceding them with two forward slashes.

- Programs may contain three types of errors: compile or syntax errors, exceptions or run-time errors, and logic errors.

- VS.NET allows you to set a breakpoint in your source code and step through code as it executes, line by line. Using breakpoints is the best way to see how a program executes.

2

Bonus Topics

- The C# compiler is extremely picky about language syntax, but it is generally unaffected by format of source code. To make source code easy for human readers, programmers develop guidelines for formatting source code. The most important aspects of source code formatting are that the code be easy to read and that styles be used consistently.

- A VS.NET application is created from many files including solution files, project files, and most important, the C# class files that contain the code you write.

- In .NET languages, the language compiler doesn't actually convert source code to native machine executable instructions. Instead, it converts source code to an intermediate language called MSIL. When the program is first run, the common language runtime (CLR) converts the MSIL into machine executable instructions in a process known as Just In Time (JIT) compiling.

KEY TERMS

Define each of the following terms, as it relates to software application development using C# and Visual Studio .NET:

Essential Terms

- algorithm
- application logic
- assemblies
- Boolean expression
- button
- case-sensitive
- comment
- comparison operator
- compiler
- computer program
- constant
- constructor
- control
- debugging
- exception
- executable
- Form Designer
- initialization
- input
- Integrated Development Environment (IDE)
- Intellisense
- label
- logic error
- namespace
- output

- program logic
- processing
- program statement (or statement)
- Properties window
- region
- run-time error
- software application
- source code
- statement block
- string
- syntax
- syntax error
- text box
- termination
- **using** directive
- variable
- Visual Studio .NET (VS.NET)

Bonus Terms

- bytecode
- common language runtime (CLR)
- Just In Time (JIT) compiling
- Microsoft Intermediate Language (MSIL)
- project
- solution

REVIEW QUESTIONS

Essential Questions

1. In its simplest form, a computer program, or software application, is just a series of instructions, or processing steps, that a computer can understand and execute. True or false?

2. Each source code statement in a C# program is normally typed on a single line. True or false?

3. In C#, source code statements end in a period. True or false?

4. The job of a compiler is to help you type source code. True or false?

5. The VS.NET IDE includes a tool for helping you design Windows Form–based GUIs. True or false?

6. You will learn more about object-oriented programming if you use the templates that are included with VS.NET when you start a new project. True or false?

7. Hiding chunks of code in **regions** prevents those statements from being executed. True or false?

8. Comment lines are indicated simply by preceding them with two forward slashes. True or false?

9. The `ToString` method returns a text representation of a number value. True or false?

10. The best way to see how a program executes is to use the Form Designer. True or false?

11. The first step in writing a computer program is to _____.

12. _____ allow your code to use classes in class libraries without having to fully qualify the class names with the complete namespace name.

13. The _____ window provides a visual means of changing the state of user interface objects.

14. Another name for user interface objects is _____.

15. The cause of almost all compile errors is _____.

16. What is the purpose of the `public static void Main` method?

17. Define program events.

18. Why are comments included in the source code of a program?

19. Describe the purpose of the `decimal.Parse` method.

20. Describe the purpose of setting breakpoints.

Bonus Questions

1. C# is very picky about the format of source code. True or false?

2. Software developers are very picky about the format of source code. True or false?

3. One alternative for marking source code lines as comments, besides preceding a comment line with two forward slashes (//), is to wrap the comments with /* and */. True or false?

4. The .NET platform supports many programming languages and they all share the same MSIL. True or false?

5. .NET programs are JIT compiled every time they are executed. True or false?

6. The two most common styles of curly brace alignment are the so-called _____ and _____ styles.

7. The Java environment uses a _____ for many of the same purposes as the .NET CLR.

8. Describe the difference between a VS.NET solution and a VS.NET project.

9. Define MSIL.

10. Define CLR.

PROGRAMMING EXERCISES

Essential Exercises

1. Use what you've learned from writing the Carpet Cost example to write other calculation-based programs:

    a. Calculate the circumference of a circle given its radius.

    b. Convert kilograms to pounds using the formula: lbs = kg * 2.204.

    c. Convert a Celsius temperature to Fahrenheit using the formula (C * 1.8) + 32 = F.

    d. Write a calculator application that allows the user to enter two values and click one of four buttons to either add, subtract, multiply, or divide them, depending on which of four buttons is clicked.

2. Modify the Carpet Cost application to include the cost of installation. Allow the user to enter the number of hours of labor and an hourly rate for the installers. Include the code to ensure that these new input values are not less than zero.

3. Write an application that allows the user to change the color of the form. The user interface should allow the user to enter several colors as text, for example, "red," "green," or "blue." When a button is clicked, the program should set the form's background color property according to which value was entered. The color of a form can be changed using statements such as:

```
BackColor = Color.Red;
BackColor = Color.Green;
BackColor = Color.Blue;
```

Display an error message to the user if he or she enters a value you haven't added code for.

Bonus Exercise

To illustrate the importance of source code readability, see how much you can shorten the Carpet Cost application's source code by removing blank lines, comments, and using the K&R style of brace alignment. Ask a friend which version is easier to read.

3

STORING DATA IN OBJECTS

In the Essentials section you will learn:

♦ The types of data that can be used in a computer program

♦ How to store numbers using numeric data types

♦ When to use **bool** and **DateTime** data types

♦ The difference between value types and reference types

♦ How to store text using the **string** data type

♦ When to use each data type

♦ What variables are and how to define them

♦ What constants are and how to define them

In the Bonus section you will learn:

♦ How to store text using the **char** data type

♦ What escape characters are

♦ Verbatim characters and string literals

♦ How the C# compiler creates variables and keeps track of them

♦ What a symbol table is

♦ What **lvalues** and **rvalues** are

♦ The difference between **define** and **declare**

The primary purpose of this chapter is to teach you how to store data in a C# computer program. The topics presented provide the foundation for writing more complex programs that use more advanced data types. In some of the program examples discussed in this chapter, it is necessary to use some C# elements that are covered in later chapters. This approach allows the use of real code to illustrate the data types, and this method provides the most robust learning experience.

ESSENTIAL TOPICS

TYPES OF DATA AVAILABLE IN C# PROGRAMS

When you write a computer program, you need to identify the type of data that are used. Each type of data is represented differently and has its own set of properties and methods so choosing the wrong data type may produce undesirable results.

In Chapter 1 you learned that, in C#, all data types can be treated as objects because they all inherit from the `System.Object` class. C# implements its data types as either *value* types or *reference* types. **Value types** include basic numeric types and a few other special-purpose types. **Reference types** are used with more complex objects, such as forms, text boxes, and textual strings. At this point, it isn't too important for you to understand why the types are implemented differently, except to know that value types execute faster than reference types. However, it is important for you to understand that, because they are implemented differently, they sometimes behave differently. These differences can cause subtle errors in your programs that are costly to find and difficult to debug unless you understand how they work.

The simplest types of data are the numeric types, so they are presented first. The discussion of how value types work differently from reference types is saved for later in the chapter.

NUMERIC DATA TYPES

Two common types of data used in a computer program are numeric data and textual data. Generally, if the data are likely to be used in an arithmetic operation, you should choose to store the data using a numeric data type. If the data are not likely to be used in an arithmetic operation, then you should choose to store the data as text. You store the data as text even if the data consist of numeric characters only. For example, you store exam scores as numbers because you might want to find their average. But you *do not* store part numbers, telephone numbers, zip codes, Canadian postal codes, or student IDs as numbers because it makes no sense to average them or perform other calculations on these kinds of data.

There are various numeric data types that C# makes available to you. Some of the most common are integer, **decimal**, and floating-point data types. You select a numeric type based on the type of data required for the task at hand. For example, you use an **integer data type** to store the number of students in a classroom because you can't have half of a student. The take-home pay of an individual uses a **decimal data type** because **decimal** is used to store monetary amounts. And you use a **floating-point data type** to compute the average student exam score because the result is likely to contain a fractional value. Each of these data types is discussed in detail in the following sections.

Integer Data Types

Integer data types are used to store whole numbers (numbers without any digits after the decimal point). This means that integer data types cannot be used to store numeric values that have fractional values, such as 1.25 tons of steel or 2.5 yards of fabric. C# supplies several choices of integer data types. Table 3-1 lists the available integer data types in C#, their corresponding ranges, and a **data suffix** that may be used on numbers to denote the particular type.

Table 3-1   Integer data types

Data type specifier	Bits	Numeric range	Data suffix
byte	8	0 to 255	
sbyte	8	–128 to 127	
short	16	–32,768 to 32,767	
ushort	16	0 to 65,535	
int	32	–2,147,483,648 to 2,147,483,647	
uint	32	0 to 4,294,967,295	U, u
long	64	–9,223,372,036,854,775,808 to 9,223,372,036,854,775,807	L, l
ulong	64	0 to 18,446,744,073,709,551,615	UL, ul

3

Range of Values of Data Types

Each data type can store a different range of values depending on its representation in memory. The smallest unit of storage in computer memory is a **bit**. The range of values that can be represented by any data type is closely linked to the number of bits associated with the data type. A bit can only assume one of two values: On (1), or Off (0). Because a bit has only two states, digital computers use binary (that is, base 2) arithmetic. The range of values shown in Table 3-1 is determined by raising 2 to a power that equals the number of bits used by the data type. For example, a **byte** data type uses 8 bits. If you raise 2 to the 8th power, the result is 256 ($2^8 = 256$). Because zero is a perfectly legal value in arithmetic operations, the range of values that can be represented in 8 bits (or 1 byte) is 0 through 255. As you can see in Table 3-1, a **byte** data type, therefore, can assume only values from 0 through 255.

If your numeric calculations need to be sensitive to the sign of a number (that is, whether it is a positive or negative number), the highest bit is reserved to keep track of the sign of the number. Because the leftmost bit (the 8th bit) records the sign of the number, there are only 7 bits remaining for the number itself. In that case, the range of values is approximately plus or minus 2 raised to the number of bits minus the 1 bit that is used for the sign bit. For example, an **sbyte** data type would be used when you need to pay attention to the sign of a single data byte. The range of values becomes 2^7, or 128. Again, because 0 is a valid value, the range for an **sbyte** data type is from 0 through 127 for positive numbers, and –128 to –1 for negative numbers. As a general guideline, the sign bit cuts the range of positive values approximately in half, but makes up for that decrease by adding negative values to the range.

The following table shows how binary values are determined. The value associated with any given bit is its bit position expressed as a power of 2. Therefore, if bit 7 is turned on (that is, has a binary value of 1), its value is 2^7 or 128. The final row in the table shows

Bit position	7	6	5	4	3	2	1	0
Power	2^7	2^6	2^5	2^4	2^3	2^2	2^1	2^0
Decimal value	128	64	32	16	8	4	2	1
Sign bit	Yes							
Example = 138	1	0	0	0	1	0	1	0

that binary $10001010 = 128 + 0 + 0 + 0 + 8 + 0 + 2 + 0 = 138$. Note that if the sign bit is used, the largest number for a byte is $0 + 64 + 32 + 16 + 8 + 4 + 2 + 1 = 127$.

When you are not concerned with the sign of a number, you can use the unsigned version of th
data type. In C#, most unsigned data types begin with the letter "u", such as **ushort** and **ulong**
The exception is the **byte** data type, which uses the unsigned range of values by default, but use
the prefix letter "s" for the signed version. The advantage of an unsigned integer data type is tha
it approximately doubles the range of positive values that can be expressed.

Notice in the last column of Table 3-1 that some of the integer data types have suffixes that ma
be used to indicate the type of data being used. For example, if you read the statement

```
myNumber = 3UL;
```

you would know that **myNumber** is being assigned an **unsigned long** data type. If the "UL"
suffix is absent, it is less obvious that the variable is receiving an **unsigned long** data type
Although it is syntactically correct, you should avoid using a lowercase "l" (ell) for the **long** dat
type suffix. The "l" is too easily confused with the digit "1." Although the use of data suffixes i
optional, their use does help document the code and can save time because you can determin
the data type of a variable without having to look for the variable's data definition.

Sample Program Using Integers

Chapter 2 illustrated a general process for creating a form-based C# program. You need to repea
the steps from Chapter 2 starting with the section labeled "Creating the Visual Studio Project Files"
up to the section labeled "Placing Controls on a Form." Now look at the form in Figure 3-1 for an
idea of the user interface that is needed for your next program. This program accepts two number
in text boxes from the user and then divides **operand1** by **operand2**. The result of the division
is displayed in a third text box. The major code difference between the program in Chapter 2 and
this program is the **btnCalc_Click** method, which is presented in Figure 3-2.

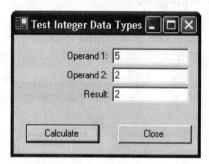

Figure 3-1   Sample run of the Division program

```
1      using System;
2      using System.Windows.Forms;
3
4      public class frmMain: Form
5      {

123        public static void Main()
124        {
125            frmMain main = new frmMain();
126
127            Application.Run(main);
128        }
129
```

Figure 3-2   Dividing two integer numbers

```
130        public frmMain()
131        {
132            InitializeComponent();
133        }
134
135        private void btnCalc_Click(object sender, System.EventArgs e)
136        {
137            int operand1;
138            int operand2;
139            int result;
140
141            operand1 = int.Parse(txtOperand1.Text);
142            operand2 = int.Parse(txtOperand2.Text);
143
144            result = (operand1 / operand2);
145
146            txtResult.Text = result.ToString();
147        }
148
149        private void btnExit_Click(object sender, System.EventArgs e)
150        {
151            Close();
152        }
153    }
```

Figure 3-2 Dividing two integer numbers (continued)

Let's examine the code in the **btnCalc_Click** method. Lines 137–139 define three **int** variables named **operand1**, **operand2**, and **result**. To keep the code as simple as possible, the user entries into the two text boxes are not validated. (A more robust program would ensure that the user typed only numeric characters into each text box.) In addition, the code sample does not show the Windows-generated code that appears between lines 6 and 122, a practice followed throughout this text.

As discussed in Chapter 2, anything the user types into a text box is textual data. Because you want to manipulate the content of the text box as numeric data, you must convert these textual representations of the numbers to integer numeric values. The statement:

```
operand1 = int.Parse(txtOperand1.Text);
```

takes the textual data being held in the text box named **txtOperand1** and converts it to an **int** value using the **int.Parse()** method and assigns the result to **operand1**. The outcome of the statement is that variable **operand1** now contains the integer value of the textual representation entered by the user into the **txtOperand1** text box. Line 142 performs the same type of conversion for **operand2**.

The next two statements:

```
result = (operand1 / operand2);

txtResult.Text = result.ToString();
```

take **operand1**, divide it by **operand2**, and assign the result into **result**. Note, however, that **result** is a numeric value, but the result should be displayed in a text box named **txtResult**. Once again, you have the problem of a numeric data type (the result of the division) being displayed in a textual context (that is, placing the numeric result in a text box). To resolve this conflict, you simply use the `ToString` method of `result` to get a string representation of the number and assign to the `Text` property of `txtResult`. Figure 3-1 shows a sample run of the program.

As shown in Figure 3-1, the sample program that was run takes the numeric value 5 and divide it by 2. Obviously the result of such division is 2.5. However, as explained earlier, integer dat types do not permit fractional values. Because fractional values are not permitted with intege data types, the result of the calculation is 2, not 2.5. Note that integer division does *not* round th result; it truncates the result. That is, if the program rounded 2.5 to the nearest integer value, th result would be 3 instead of 2. Always remember that integer division truncates the result; an fractional remainder is discarded.

If your program needs to keep track of fractional values, you need to use either the **decimal** dat type or one of the floating-point data types introduced in the next sections.

Monetary Values

The **decimal** data type is used to store monetary values (that is, money or currency) for financial cal culations. The **decimal** type uses 16 bytes of memory and can store positive and negative values. I can accurately represent up to 28 significant digits of precision (the number of digits that make u the base number) without any rounding errors ($\pm 1.0 \times 10^{-28}$ to $\pm 7.9 \times 10^{28}$). Of those 28 digit four appear to the right of the decimal point. (The four decimal positions of the **decimal** data typ are needed when developing applications for countries that use more than two digits after the deci mal point.) Because there are always four digits after the decimal point, you might hear someone refe to the **decimal** data type as a **fixed-point numeric format**.

Experimenting with Decimal Types

To experiment with the **decimal** type, modify the code in Figure 3-2 to use **decimal** instead of **int** types. Be sure to change the variable definition statements and use `decimal.Parse` instead of `int.Parse`. You might also change the calculation statement to use the addition (+), subtraction (−), or multiplication (*) operators rather than the division (/) operator.

You can use the suffix "M" or "m" to help document that you are using the **decimal** data type For example,

```
decimal myDebt;

// perhaps several dozen lines of code

myDebt = 150000M;
```

Because you used the "M" in the assignment statement, you save the reader from having to scrol back to the definition of **myDebt** to determine its data type.

The **decimal** data type should only be used with calculations that involve money because ther is a small performance penalty when compared with other data types.

Floating-Point Numbers

Floating-point data types are used for numeric values that may contain fractional values, but tha are not monetary values. **Floating-point numbers** are numbers in which the decimal point i free to "float" as needed by the numbers being manipulated. C# has two types of floating-poin number data types: **float** and **double**. The range for the two floating-point data types is shown in Table 3-2.

To better understand how floating-point numbers are expressed, think about how scientific notation can be used to represent a number. The number 1234.567 can also be written as 1.234567×10^3 using scientific notation by moving the decimal point three places to the left. Because base 10 numbers are being used, if you are given a base value of 1.234567 and an exponent of 3, you know the number being discussed is 1234.567. In other words, the decimal point is moved to the right by an amount that equals the base 10 exponent, which is 3 in this example. In our example, the number has seven digits of precision.

Table 3-2   Floating-point data types

Type	Bits	Numeric range	Data suffix	Precision
float	32	$\pm 1.5 \times 10^{-45}$ to $\pm 3.4 \times 10^{38}$	F, f	7
double	64	$\pm 5.0 \times 10^{-324}$ to $\pm 1.7 \times 10^{308}$	D,d	15

Of the two floating-point types, the **double** data type is more commonly used. There are several reasons why you should use the **double** data type in most cases.

First, because a **double** uses 64 bits, it has approximately 15 digits of precision, and therefore can store fractional values more accurately. *The **precision** of a number is the number of digits that are correctly represented by the numeric value being stored.* Even though a **double** can show more than 15 digits, only the first 15 digits are significant. The rest of the digits are understood to be the computer's best estimate of the actual numbers. For the **float** data type, the number of digits of precision is limited to seven.

A second reason for using a **double** is because calculations execute more efficiently than a **float**. It might seem counterintuitive that a data type that uses more memory is more efficient, but there is a good explanation for this. Most PCs have a floating-point math coprocessor chip built into the central processing unit (CPU) of the computer. These math coprocessors are better suited to processing 64-bit floating-point numbers (**double**) than they are 32-bit floating-point numbers (**float**). As a result, there is a small processing speed advantage to using a **double** data type for floating-point numbers even though they use more bits than **float** data types.

A third reason for using the **double** data type is because many methods of the .NET **System.Math** class use the **double** data type. For example, the **Math.Sqrt** method can calculate the square root value of a **double.**

Experimenting with Double and Float Data Types

You should experiment with the **double** and **float** data types by again modifying the code in Figure 3-2 to use **double** and **float** instead of **int**. Change the variable definition statements and use either **double.Parse** or **float.Parse** to convert the text box values to numbers. Be sure to perform some division calculations that result in values with many decimal positions (for example, 11 divided by 3 as shown in Figure 3-3). And change the calculation statement to use the addition (+), subtraction (−), or multiplication (*) operators rather than the division (/) operator.

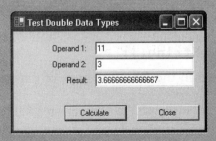

Figure 3-3   Using the double
data type

Additional Data Types

This section discusses two additional value types used in C# programs: **bool** and **DateTime**.

Boolean Types

Boolean[1] types store information that can only have a value of either logical true or logical false. C# uses the keyword **bool** to denote Boolean types, and uses the keywords **true** and **false** to denote the values a **bool** might contain.

A Boolean data type is useful in programs that track the state of a condition, such as whether an item is in stock or not. For example:

```
bool itemInStock;

itemInStock = true;
```

Because **bool** variables are limited to only two values, it doesn't make sense to perform mathematical calculations with them. Trying to do so results in a compile error.

Booleans are often used in decision statements. For example:

```
if (itemInStock == false)
{
    // Perform logic to order more of this item.
}
```

A complete discussion of decisions can be found in Chapter 5.

Dates and Times

The final value type discussed in this section is **DateTime**. As you might guess, **DateTime** is used to store a value that represents a moment in time—for example, the date an order was placed, someone's birthdate, or an employee's hire date. You can store a date-only value, such as "December 3, 1961" or a date/time pair such as "December 3, 1961 5:46 p.m." **DateTime**s can store values ranging from "January 1, 0001 midnight" to "December 31, 9999 11:59:59 p.m."

It is important to know that **DateTime**s values are not stored as text, but are actually stored as the number of ticks (100 nanoseconds) since "January 1, 0001 midnight." So, to manipulate the values, **DateTime** exposes a rich set of properties and methods. For example, the **Year** property lets you capture just the year portion of a date, and the **Hour** property captures just the hour portion of the time. Many methods perform calculations on dates and times. For example, you can use the **Subtract** method to determine how many days exist between two dates. Just as with the other C# value types, **DateTime** has **Parse** and **ToString** methods that allow you to convert a text string to a date and time value, and back to a text string. For example:

```
DateTime dateOrdered;
dateOrdered = DateTime.Parse(txtDateOrdered.Text);
...
txtDateOrdered.Text = dateOrdered.ToString();
```

Other **DateTime** properties and methods are discussed in the Bonus section of Chapter 4.

---

[1] Boolean types get their name from Charles Boole, the nineteenth-century English mathematician who invented symbolic logic.

REFERENCE DATA TYPES

So far, this chapter has described the most commonly used C# value types. These types consist mainly of the numeric, **bool**, and **DateTime** data types. You should consider everything else to be a reference type. In general, value types are simple numeric types and reference types are for more complex objects.

The distinction between simple types and reference types is largely determined by the way each is stored in memory. When you define a variable using one of the value data types described previously, C# directly reserves space in memory for it. But a reference type variable *never* contains the actual object value. Consider this example:

```
1    int nbrStudents;
2    nbrStudents = 500;
3
4    clsPerson jobCandidate;
5    jobCandidate = new clsPerson();
6    jobCandidate.Glasses = false;
```

Because the variable definition for **nbrStudents** in line 1 uses an **int** data type, the C# compiler reserves 4 bytes (64 bits) of memory for it. Then, in line 2, the value 500 is copied into this memory space.

The statement in line 5 defines a reference variable named **jobCandidate**. C# reserves 4 bytes of memory for it, but the variable doesn't contain a **clsPerson** object. Because **jobCandidate** is a reference type, these 4 bytes of memory are reserved to hold a memory reference to an object. (Think of a memory reference as a memory address where an object is actually stored). When line 5 is executed, a **clsPerson** object is instantiated in memory, and the value of variable **jobCandidate** is assigned a memory reference to it. In other words, **jobCandidate** is assigned the memory address where the actual **clsPerson** object is stored in the computer's memory. (See Figure 3-4.) The statement in line 6 uses the memory reference to the **clsPerson** object contained in variable **jobCandidate** to find the **clsPerson** object in memory, and then assigns **false** to its **Glasses** property. A graphic depiction of this sample is shown in Figure 3-4.

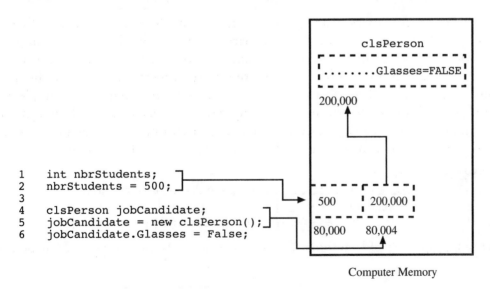

Computer Memory

Figure 3-4   A value type and a reference type

In Figure 3-4, **nbrStudents** is defined as an **int**, and it is assumed that the compiler gave it th_ location in memory of 80,000. Each time you change the value of **nbrStudents**, the 4 bytes o_ memory at memory address 80,000 change. Because the second statement line assigns the valu_ of 500 to **nbrStudents**, the block of computer memory is shown on the right with the valu_ of 500 at memory address 80,000.

The third statement defines a reference variable named **jobCandidate** of type **clsPerson**. I_ is assumed that the memory address for **jobCandidate** is 80,004. However, the compiler doe_ *not* store a **clsPerson** object at memory address 80,004. Instead, it stores a new memory addres_ at 80,004 that tells the program where to find the **clsPerson** object in memory. In Figure 3-4_ it is assumed that the compiler located all of the properties and methods associated wit_ **jobCandidate** at memory address 200,000. In other words, the reference variable name_ **jobCandidate** refers to a **clsPerson** object that resides in memory starting at memory addres_ 200,000. The assignment statement that changes the **Glasses** property of **jobCandidate** t_ **false** actually changes the state of the object somewhere around memory address 200,000. A_ you can see in Figure 3-4, the **jobCandidate.Glasses** property is changed after memor_ address 200,000. It is important to remember, however, that the content of a reference variable i_ actually a memory address, and the compiler uses that memory address to find the object.

The difference between value types and reference types becomes extremely important to under_ stand when you assign the value of one variable to another. When you assign the value of on_ value type to another value type, the value of the variable is copied. The assignment is easier t_ understand when depicted graphically, as shown in Figure 3-5. The definition statements in line_ 1 and 2 create two value type variables named **nbrStudents** and **nbrGoodStudents** and plac_ them at memory addresses 80,000 and 80,008, respectively. Line 3 assigns the value 500 int_ **nbrStudents**, so the 4 bytes of memory starting at memory address 80,000 now contain th_ value 500. Line 4 copies the value of **nbrStudents** into **nbrGoodStudents**. Line 4 really goe_ to memory address 80,000, fetches the 4 bytes stored there, and copies those bytes into memor_ location 80,008. In Figure 3-5, you can see that both variables now contain the integer value 500_ All value types work this way.

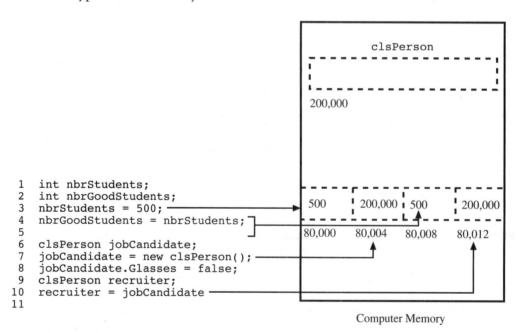

Figure 3-5   Two value types and two reference types

Reference variables do not work the same way as value types. In Figure 3-5, we showed how lines 6 and 7 performed three actions: created a reference variable named `jobCandidate`, placed it at memory address 80,004, and set its value to point to a chunk of computer memory that actually holds the `clsPerson` (starting at memory address 200,000). Line 9 also created a new reference variable named `recruiter` and stored it at memory address 80,012. However, `recruiter` is not associated with its own `clsPerson` object (that is, it's missing the **new clsPerson( )** code). Line 10 assigns the contents of reference variable `jobCandidate` into reference variable `recruiter`. Now note what has happened: both reference variables refer to the same `clsPerson` object stored at memory address 200,000. This is a very important distinction: *when you assign the value of a reference type to another reference type, only the memory address where the object is stored is copied, not the values associated with the object itself.* Note that the code in Figure 3-5 defines two reference types (`jobCandidate` and `recruiter`) but only one **person** object. Both reference type variables refer to the same object because only the reference (that is, the memory address 200,000) was copied in line 10.

Also note that you don't have to use the **new** operator to explicitly instantiate value types as you do with reference types.

The syntax for using value types is very similar to that used for reference types, but the preceding example shows that the behaviors differ significantly. The difference in the way value and reference types work can cause subtle bugs in your program if accidentally used incorrectly. It would be extremely helpful to spend enough time with this section so that you fully understand the difference between value types and reference types.

Storing Textual Data Using the String Data Type

As stated previously, when storing data that are likely to be used in arithmetic operations, you should store the data as numeric data types. If the data aren't likely to be used in an arithmetic operation, you should store the data as text. The most commonly used data type for storing textual data is the **string type.**

 tip ▶ Actually, **string** is a class and not a value type, whereas number data types are value types. Therefore, variables defined as type **string** contain references to string objects that contain text and not to the textual data themselves.

Because strings are used so frequently in programs, C# syntax has some shortcuts that allow you to use syntax similar to value types, rather than the syntax you have to use with other reference types. For example, the statement:

```
string user = "Katherine";
```

is equivalent to:

```
string user;
user = new string();
user = "Katherine";
```

CHOOSING **bool** OR **DATETIME** TYPES

The process of writing computer programs involves making many choices. One of the first decisions is choosing the appropriate data type to store a piece of information. The guidelines in this section are designed to help you make the right choice.

If it makes sense for the data item to contain only a **true** or **false** value (that is, yes or no) use type **bool**. For example, use a **bool** to track whether an instant messaging application should show you as online or not.

If the information indicates a moment in time as a date, a date and time, or just a time, use **DateTime**. For example, all of the following should be stored as **DateTime** data: a birthdate, the time and day an order was processed, and the time a class starts each day.

If the data item is not likely to be used in calculations, even if it normally contains numeric characters only, use **string**. For example, use **string**s to store names, street addresses, telephone numbers, and catalog item descriptions.

In all other cases, use one of the number types. To decide which number type to use, consider the following:

- If the data item is a monetary value used in financial calculations, use **decimal**. For example, the balance of your account at the bank, or the cost of a product in a store should use a **decimal** data type. The extended precision of the **decimal** data type means that you can have very large numbers and still keep track of the pennies accurately.

- If the piece of data needs to contain fractional values but is not a monetary amount, use either **float** or **double**. The earlier discussion on the **double** type provided several reasons for using a **double** to store nonmonetary, fractional data. For example, the financial ratios used in business planning should use a **double** data type. However, if memory or disk space is extremely scarce, you might use a **float** because it requires fewer bytes of storage.

- If the data item doesn't need fractional values, use one of the integer data types. If the value might be negative, you must use one of the signed integer types. To select a specific type, consider the range of values you might need. However, if you have access to a large body of C# code, you will likely find that the **int** data type is the most-often-used integer data type, regardless of the range of values to be represented. Because it is popular, this text uses the **int** data type in most of its examples.

IDENTIFIER NAMING RULES AND CONVENTIONS

C# has certain naming rules you must follow whenever you define your own variables, constants, methods, classes, or any other user-defined program element. The term **identifier** simply refers to the name that you give to the variable or other item you are defining in your program.

The identifier naming rules are:

- An identifier must start with an alphabetic letter or an underscore.

- After the first character, an identifier may contain letters, digits characters, or an underscore.

- Punctuation characters are not allowed (for example, a period, comma, question mark, and so on are illegal).

- An identifier cannot be a C# keyword. (Appendix A contains the list of C# keywords that cannot be used as identifiers.)

In addition to these rules, it is important to remember that C# is case-sensitive. That is, **myNewCar** and **mynewCar** are two different variable names. While this is not a rule, most C# programmers have adopted the convention of using a lowercase letter for the first character in an identifier and then capitalizing the beginning of each word thereafter. For example, most C# programmers prefer the identifier name **myNewCar** to **mynewcar**.

Keep in mind that the purpose of a variable identifier is to give an easy-to-read name to data in a program. For that reason, short, cryptic names do little to help document or allow users to understand the identity or purpose of a variable in a program. As a general rule, try to create names that suggest the purpose of the variable, but are not so long that they make the source code harder to read. Using between 5 and 20 characters is usually good. Table 3-3 presents a number of valid and invalid C# identifier names.

Table 3-3   Sample C# identifier names

Identifier name	State	Comment
Size12	Valid	Acceptable, but should start with a lowercase letter
7Sins	Invalid	Must start with an alphabetic letter
_interestRate	Valid	Uses a leading underscore character, but that does not follow the recommended conventions of this text
propertyLine	Valid	Follows the convention of beginning with a lowercase letter and capitalizing words within the name
your.PropertyLine	Invalid	Punctuation characters not allowed
T_4_2	Valid	Cute name but not very informative.
10SNE1	Invalid	Starts with a digit character. Tennis anyone?
Volatile	Invalid	A C# keyword

Appendix B contains the recommended coding style conventions.

Defining Variables

From Chapter 2 on, you have seen variables defined and used. It's time to formalize the C# rules associated with defining and using variables in programs. The syntax for defining a variable is simple:

```
TypeSpecifier Identifier;
```

where **TypeSpecifier** is a data type and **Identifier** is a valid identifier name that follows the naming rules discussed earlier. **TypeSpecifier** can be one of the value types (**int**, **double**, and so on) discussed earlier in the chapter, a class declared in the .NET Framework, or a class you declare somewhere else in your project.

Sample data definitions include:

```
int distanceTraveled;
decimal weeklyWage;
string lastName;
```

Figure 3-6 lists the **btnCalc_Click** code from the previous example (Figure 3-2):

```
135        private void btnCalc_Click(object sender, System.EventArgs e)
136        {
137            int operand1;
138            int operand2;
139            int result;
140
```

Figure 3-6   The btnCalc_Click method

```
141            operand1 = int.Parse(txtOperand1.Text);
142            operand2 = int.Parse(txtOperand2.Text);
143
144            result = (operand1 / operand2);
145
146            txtResult.Text = result.ToString();
147        }
```

Figure 3-6 The btnCalc_Click method (continued)

Lines 137–139 define three variables, which are subsequently used to perform the division of two numbers. (Figure 3-1 shows the results of the program when run.) In the code snippet, it is not obvious that the variables **operand1**, **operand2**, and **result** "come to life" in statements 137–139, perform their assignments in lines 141–146, and then "die" when the closing brace of the **btnCalc_Click()** event code is reached (line 147). In other words, variables have a lifetime in a C# program. **Lifetime** refers to the length of time a variable is available for use in a program. The lifetime of a variable varies according to where that variable is defined. Variables defined within a method, like **operand1** in the **btnCalc_Click** event method, are called **local scope variables**, and their lifetime extends from the point of their definition (that is, line 137 for **operand1**) to the closing brace of the statement block in which they are defined (line 147 in our example). When the closing brace in line 147 is reached, all local variables defined within that statement block are destroyed and are no longer available for use in the program. Chapter 7 supplies additional information on this topic.

When you define variables in C#, the compiler gives the variables initial values. The initial value for numeric types is zero; the initial value for Booleans is **false**; **DateTime**s get an initial value of midnight on January 1, 0001; and **string** variables are set to **null** (empty). You can also set the initial value of a variable as part of its definition:

```
int hitCounter = 0;
int stackDepth = 100;
```

These statements initialize their variables, so they are created with a known value. C# insists that you set the initial value of a local variable if you use it as part of an assignment statement. For example:

```
decimal amountDue;
decimal amountBilled;

amountDue = amountBilled;
```

produces the error message: "Use of unassigned local variable **amountBilled**." The compiler is complaining because you have used **amountBilled** in an assignment statement before initializing it with a value. Although **amountBilled** assumes the value of zero when it is defined, the C# compiler still complains because you have not explicitly given it a value. To fix the problem, you must explicitly assign a value into **amountBilled** before you use it in the assignment statement:

```
decimal amountDue;
decimal amountBilled;

amountBilled = 29.95M;
amountDue = amountBilled;
```

The code compiles without error after **amountBilled** has been assigned a value. (Recall the "M" suffix is used with the **decimal** data type as a form of documentation.) Although variable initialization before use may seem like a nuisance in some cases, it does stop you from using variables that might otherwise exist with an unknown state. Because many languages do not give variables initial values upon definition, good programming practice dictates that the programmer explicitly assign an initial value to a variable before attempting to use it.

> ### Define Each Variable on a Separate Line
>
> The C# syntax also allows you to define several variables of the same data type with a single statement. For example:
>
> ```
> decimal totalBooks, totalFood, totalHousing;
> ```
>
> Although some C# programmers may use this type of single statement, multivariable definition, this textbook strongly discourages it. It is included here only because you might see it in other examples. Defining each variable on separate lines makes it easier to locate variable definitions and to specify an initial value.

Defining Constants

Sometimes when writing programs, you use a value that you know will not change during program execution. Unlike variables with values that are likely to change as the program executes, **constants** are not allowed to change. Two types of constants are used in programming: literal constants and symbolic constants.

Literal constants, sometimes simply called **literals**, refer to values that are fixed at the time the source code for the program is written. For example, you might want to assign the literal name "Jennifer" to the variable **yourName**:

```
string yourName;
yourName = "Jennifer";
```

Everything that appears between the two double quotation marks (that is, Jennifer) is a literal constant. Sometimes it's convenient to initialize a variable with a literal constant, as in:

```
string defaultCity = "Indianapolis";
```

At some later point in the program, perhaps a text box is filled with the value of the default city.

Symbolic constants, also called **named constants**, are used to help make the code in a program more readable. Symbolic constants are defined using the **const** keyword and must include the value of the constant as part of the definition. For example, perhaps your program performs investment calculations that require the use of the company's (planning) cost of capital. In the short run, chances are pretty good that the value of the cost of capital will not change soon, so you might define a constant for it as follows:

```
const double planningCostOfCapital = 0.125;
```

and use it in a calculation as follows:

```
discountFactor = 1.0 / Math.Pow(1.0 + planningCostOfCapital, years);
```

This statement could have been written as:

```
discountFactor = 1.0 / Math.Pow(1.125, years);
```

However, using the named constant `planningCostOfCapital` makes the calculation in th
first version more understandable to someone reading your code.

As a general rule, you can create constants by placing the keyword **const** before the data typ
in most data definitions. That is, the definitions:

```
const int inchesPerFoot = 12;
const long speedOfLight = 186000;
```

are valid constant definitions. Obviously, you must initialize the value of the constant at the tim
you define the constant.

Why Use Constants

There are several reasons for using constants in programs. First, experienced programmers hate wh
are called "magic numbers." **Magic numbers** *are simply numeric values that appear in a program state
ment, usually with no clue to their meaning.* If you saw an area/circumference calculation with the li
eral value 3.1416, it might take you a moment or two longer to recognize the statement's functio
than if you use the statement with a constant named `Math.PI` instead of the magic number 3.141€

Consider another example:

```
time = d / 65;
```

If you were trying to figure out what a program does, would you rather read the preceding state
ment, or the statement that follows?

```
tripTime = distanceTraveled / averageSpeed;
```

In this statement, `averageSpeed` is a constant that's been defined earlier in the program. Magi
numbers simply lead to unnecessary head scratching that could be avoided by simply defining
constant. Magic numbers often force you to pause to figure out the meaning of a particular valu
These delays can be avoided by using constants to help document code.

When using constants, remember that you cannot change the value of a constant in code. Fc
example, if you define `averageSpeed` to be a constant and then try to change the value of th
`averageSpeed` constant with a statement like:

```
averageSpeed = 70;
```

the compiler issues an error message telling you that the left-hand side of an assignment must b
a variable, and `averageSpeed` is not a variable.

A second reason for using constants is because some "constants" do change over time. For exam
ple, before 1972, the maximum speed on most interstate highways was 65 miles per hour. Th
was later reduced to 55 miles per hour. Now suppose you had used the magic number 65 in you
code instead of a constant. When the law changed, you would have to go through all of your pro
gram code looking for each occurrence of 65 to manually change it—a very time-consuming an
potentially error-prone process. On the other hand, if you had used a named constant, you woul
simply change the constant's definition from:

```
const int maxSpeed = 65;
```

to:

```
const int maxSpeed = 55;
```

and recompile the program. The compiler would automatically use the new value everywhere th
named constant is used in the source code.

You should always use constants whenever you see a magic number in your code. After all, some constants do change eventually, and thoughtfully named constants can help document the purpose of a program statement much better than a magic number.

BONUS TOPICS

This section explores several topics that are related to earlier chapter topics, but in greater detail. Specifically, you gain a better understanding of how C# creates variables, how they are stored in memory, and how they are removed from memory. Although you can write good C# code without reading this section of the chapter, an understanding of the concepts presented here will help you understand what a program does when it executes, and to the extent that is true, help you debug and maintain your code.

THE char DATA TYPE

The **char** data type may be used each time you wish to store a single character in a program. Each **char** data type requires 2 bytes (16 bits) for storage. For example, the statements:

```
char vowel;

vowel = 'A';
```

define a character variable named **vowel** and assign the capital letter 'A' into it. Note the single quotation marks that surround the letter A. The single quotation marks are necessary whenever you wish to assign a specific character into a **char** variable. (String data use double quotes.)

What Can a char Store?

Look at your keyboard. The **char** data type is capable of storing just about any key you see. In fact, in many countries, such as the United States, virtually every character ever used in normal writing could be stored in a single byte. As a result, the American Standard Code for Information Interchange (ASCII) character set became the standard way to store character data many years ago. The ASCII character set uses only 2^7, or 128 different characters.

The ASCII character set works fine for languages like English. However, the programs we write today are not necessarily restricted to English-speaking users. With the widespread use of the Internet, programs need to recognize character sets that are much more extensive than the ASCII character set. Some languages, such as Chinese, use more than 128 characters and would require a keyboard the size of a card table! Clearly, the ASCII character set is simply too small to contain all the characters used worldwide.

The **Unicode** character set was created to accommodate the need for an extended character set. Each character in the Unicode character set takes two bytes, or 16 bits, of memory for storage. Therefore, there are 65,536 (that is, 2^{16}) possible characters in the Unicode character set. It is important to remember that, unlike many other programming languages, each **char** in C# requires 2 bytes of storage. Other than differences in storage requirements, however, use of the Unicode character set in C# is just like use of the ASCII character set in most other programming languages.

Special Characters

Sometimes you need to use nonprinting characters in your programs. In other cases, you need to use characters that already have special meaning in a C# program. For example, you've already learned that a single quote is used to surround a character that's being assigned into a **char** variable. Given that use for single quotes, how can you print a single quote as a character? You use an **escape sequence** to accomplish this. Each escape sequence is formed by a backslash followed by the escape sequence character. For example, to assign a single quote into a **char** variable named ch, you would use the following statement:

```
ch = '\'';
```

Placing a backslash before the single quote lets the C# compiler know that you wish to use an escape sequence rather than a simple Unicode character.

If you want to surround Nicky's greeting in the statement that follows with quotation marks, you do it this way:

```
string greeting = "Nicky said \"Hello!\"";
```

The value of the variable `greeting` is a reference to a string containing:

```
Nicky said "Hello!"
```

The leading backslash tells the compiler that the next character is to be treated in a special way. Although double quotation marks also mark the beginning and end of a string, preceding the double quotation mark with a backslash allows you to actually display the double quotation mark as part of the output.

Table 3-4 presents a complete list of the C# escape sequences.

Table 3-4   C# escape sequences

Escape sequence	Description
\a	Alarm (bell)
\b	Backspace
\f	Form feed
\n	Linefeed (newline)
\r	Carriage return
\t	Tab
\v	Vertical tab
\0	Null
\'	Single quote
\"	Double quote
\\	Backslash

Not all the escape sequences listed in Table 3-4 produce visible results on the screen. The Null escape sequence, for example, is not directly observable and the Alarm escape sequence only produces an audible beep.

Verbatim Character with String Literals

Sometimes you need to use special characters in a string literal. A common example is the backslash when describing a disk file path name. As shown in Table 3-4, the backslash character in string literals is used to indicate so-called escape characters (\n indicates a new line, \t indicates a horizontal tab, \\ indicates a backslash, and so on). To avoid backslashes being interpreted as escape characters in string literals, use verbatim string literals. A **verbatim string literal** tells

C# to treat a string literal exactly the way it appears within the quotes. You create a verbatim string literal by placing an **at** symbol (@) before the string literal:

```
string path = @"C:\My Projects\Carpet Cost";
```

If you didn't use the string literal symbol in the preceding statement, you would have to write the string literal as:

```
string path = "C:\\My Projects\\Carpet Cost";
```

to prevent the C# compiler from misinterpreting the meaning of the backslashes.

How C# Creates Variables

Consider the following programming statement:

```
int miles = 0;
```

Immediately after you type the preceding statement, the compiler checks to see if the statement follows the C# syntax rules for defining an integer variable. If there is a syntax error in the statement, the IntelliSense component of VS.NET displays a red squiggly line under the offending section of the statement, thus calling your attention to the error. If you place the program cursor on the red line, IntelliSense displays a relevant error message to help you correct the error.

Because our statement contains no syntax errors, the compiler checks to see if you have already defined a variable named **miles** in the program. It performs this check by examining the program's symbol table. Maintained by the compiler, *a **symbol table** is a table of information about all the data items that are defined in the program.* Table 3-5 is a hypothetical symbol table.

Table 3-5   Hypothetical symbol table (Step 1)

ID	Type	lvalue	Scope level	Other
i	int	3500000	0	
loanAmount	double	3500100	0	

The C# compiler examines the symbol table to see if a variable named **miles** is already in the table. If a variable named **miles** is already in the symbol table (and has the same value for the scope level), the compiler issues a duplicate definition error. The complete discussion of scope is deferred until Chapter 7. For the moment, think of each scope value as a room number. If you look into room number 5 and see two variables with the same name, an error exists. If two variables have the same name, but are in different rooms, no error exists.

On the other hand, because **miles** does not appear in the symbol table, the compiler then sends a message to the Windows Memory Manager asking for enough memory to store one integer variable (that is, 4 bytes). If the Windows Memory Manager has enough free memory available to satisfy the compiler's request, it sends back the memory address of those bytes. For example, the Windows Memory Manager might send back the address 3,500,200 for variable **miles**. The compiler then records that memory address in the symbol table under the **lvalue** column. The symbol table would now look like that shown in Table 3-6.

Table 3-6 Hypothetical symbol table (Step 2)

ID	Type	lvalue	Scope level	Other
i	int	3500000	0	
loanAmount	double	3500100	0	
miles	int	3500200	0	

The Other column in Table 3-6 is used to represent other details that are likely to be maintained in the symbol table by the compiler. It is not unusual for a symbol table to have 30 or more columns of information about each data item. The Other column, therefore, is used to represent the missing columns you are likely to find in a real symbol table.

lvalues

Notice the purpose of the `lvalue` column. *The* **lvalue** *of a data item is the memory address of that item.* The `lvalue` permits the compiler to locate an item in memory. Let's consider what this means.

Suppose that you write the following statement later in the program:

```
miles = 300;
```

When you assign the value 300 into the variable `miles`, the compiler must do three things to process the assignment statement.

First, the compiler checks whether a variable named `miles` has been defined. From Table 3-6 you can determine that the compiler will find `miles` defined in the symbol table. If `miles` were not defined in the symbol table, the compiler would issue an error message stating that `miles` does not exist. However, because `miles` is defined in the symbol table, the compiler proceeds to the next task.

Second, the compiler must now locate where `miles` is stored in memory. It accomplishes this task by getting the memory address where `miles` is stored from the `lvalue` column of the symbol table.

Third, the compiler must know how many bytes to use when forming the value 300. The compiler can figure this out from the Type column in the symbol table. Because the **int** data type requires 4 bytes for storage, the compiler generates a 4-byte integer with the value 300. (The binary representation of 300 is: 0000 0000 0000 0000 0000 0001 0010 1100.) The compiler then takes those 4 bytes and moves them into memory starting at memory location 3,500,200.

Let's review this process in a different way, starting with the data definition for `miles`. After the statement:

```
int miles = 0;
```

the variable miles appears in the symbol table with an lvalue of 3,500,200. The definition of miles is shown in Figure 3-7.

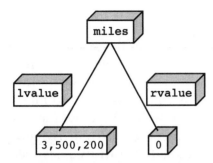

Figure 3-7   After defining miles

The `lvalue` is the memory address for the data item named `miles`. *The* **rvalue** *is the current value of the data item.* (The terms `lvalue`, or location value, and `rvalue`, or register value, are terms that evolved from assembly language programming many years ago.) The value zero has been shown for the `rvalue` of `miles` because the compiler initializes integer variables to 0 when they are defined.

Now consider what happens after the compiler processes the assignment statement:

```
miles = 300;
```

The compiler looks up the `lvalue` for miles in the symbol table (3,500,200), notes how many bytes are associated with that variable (4 for an **int**), forms the appropriate value (300) using the proper number of bytes, and moves those bytes to the `lvalue` memory address. Figure 3-8 depicts `miles` after the assignment statement is processed.

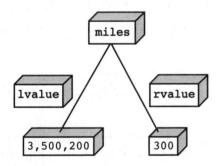

Figure 3-8   After assigning miles

Notice that the `rvalue` has been changed to 300 because of the assignment statement. As you can see, the information in the symbol table enables the compiler to manipulate the variable named `miles`. Also note that, because the `rvalue` has changed, the state of `miles` is changed. Therefore, any time the `rvalue` of a variable is changed, the state of the variable is also changed.

If you want a memory jogger to help you remember the relationship between `lvalues` and `rvalues`, think of a bucket. The `lvalue` tells you where the bucket is located in memory, the `rvalue` is the bucket's contents, and the **Type** column in the symbol table tells you the size of the bucket (in bytes).

Understanding `lvalues` and `rvalues` will help you in later chapters, especially when it becomes necessary to debug more complex programs. A little time spent now understanding these concepts will pay huge benefits later on.

Define versus Declare

Programmers often use the terms define and declare as if they mean the same thing. They don't. The rules for using the two terms are quite simple. If a program statement causes a new entry to be created in the `lvalue` column of the symbol table, the statement is a **data definition**. Data definitions always result in a call to the operating system's Memory Manager to find a memory address where the data item can be stored. That memory address then becomes the `lvalue` that is used to find the data item in memory. If a statement causes new entries in the symbol table, but does not make an entry in the `lvalue` column, it is a **data declaration**. A data declaration, therefore, does not cause a call to be made to the operating system's Memory Manager for data storage. To this point, the chapter has used only examples of data definitions. Later chapters present examples of data declarations.

For the moment, try to use the term data definition when you are defining a new data item. Alas, even the online help for C# confuses the two terms. However, with a little thought and effort, you should be able to use the two terms correctly. Understanding the difference between define and declare now will help you to better understand other terms that are introduced later in the book.

SUMMARY

Essential Topics

◻ The data used in C# programs are either value types (**int**, **double**, **float**, and so on) or reference types (variables that reference objects). You learned that value types are usually associated with numeric data. Each value type has its own range of values that it can represent, and each has its own advantages and disadvantages. Reference type variables are normally used with objects.

◻ Value types directly store data values at their associated memory addresses. Reference types, however, always take 4 bytes for the storage of a memory address that points to where the object is actually stored in memory.

◻ You learned the rules for creating a valid variable name, or identifier, for a data item. Variable names should be long enough to document what the variable does, but short enough that it's not a burden to type the variable name into the program.

◻ You also learned how to define variables and constants for use in a program. You saw how literal constants are defined and how symbolic constants can be used to make a program easier to understand.

Bonus Topics

◻ The **char** data type was discussed, and you learned that the Unicode character set is used to express character data in C# programs. Escape sequences are special characters that may be used to display characters that may have multiple interpretations in a C# program.

◻ You also learned how C# creates and stores data in memory. The terms `lvalue` and `rvalue` were discussed. Understanding these terms will help you understand other topics covered in later chapters more completely. This understanding will also help you understand program code better and make program debugging easier.

KEY TERMS

Define each of the following terms, as they relate to object-oriented programming:

Essential Terms

3

- **bool**
- **byte**
- constant
- **Datetime**
- Data suffix
- **decimal** data type
- **double**
- Fixed-point numeric format
- **float**
- Floating-point data type
- Floating-point numbers
- Integer data type
- Identifier
- **int**
- Lifetime
- Literal
- Literal constant
- Local scope variable
- **long**
- Magic number
- Named constant

- object
- Precision (of a number)
- **sbyte**
- **short**
- **string**
- Symbolic constant
- **ulong**
- Unit (of storage)
- **ushort**

Bonus Terms

- **char**
- Data declaration
- Data definition
- Escape sequences
- **lvalue**
- **rvalue**
- Symbol table
- Unicode
- Verbatim character

REVIEW QUESTIONS

Essential Questions

1. If you do not explicitly define a variable in C#, the variable is automatically created as a **double** data type. True or false?

2. There are several different integer data types in C# covering a wide range of data values. True or false?

3. Unsigned integer data types allow for larger positive values than do signed data types. True or false?

4. Signed integer data types have approximately half the range of positive values as do their unsigned counterparts. True or false?

5. The two basic value types of data used in C# programs are numeric and objects. True or false?

6. If you divide two integer numbers and a fractional value results, the compiler generates an error message. True or false?

7. If you try to assign textual data into an **int**, the C# compiler does not issue an error message. True or false?

8. Integer division rounds the fractional value to the next largest number. True or false?

9. Fixed-point numbers always have the same number of digits to the right of the decimal point. True or false?

10. A reference variable contains the value of the object's properties. True or false?

11. Magic numbers in a program make it easier to understand the program's intent. True or false?

12. A string variable is for textual data and cannot contain digit characters. True or false?

13. What is the purpose of data suffixes?

14. The letter _____ is the data suffix used for unsigned integer values

15. The _____ data type has up to 28 digits of precision.

16. If you were writing a statistics software package, what data type would you use for data storage and why?

17. The term _____ is used to indicate the number of significant digits associated with a given data type.

18. Because a _____ data type only has two permissible values, they are not used in arithmetic expressions.

19. Explain the difference between value data types and reference data types.

20. What is the C# style convention for naming variables?

Bonus Questions

1. A program's symbol table is used by the compiler to locate variables in memory. True or false?

2. The `lvalue` of a variable is the memory address where that variable resides in memory. True or false?

3. Changing the `rvalue` of a variable also changes the state of that variable. True or false?

4. When you declare a variable, you are allocating memory space for that variable. True or false?

5. How does C# store character data?

6. The _____ causes the terminal's bell (or buzzer) to sound.

7. Write the statements necessary to display the following on the screen:

    Never forget: "Wherever you go, there you are."

8. Write the statements necessary to display an operating system path name.

9. You're at a party and one of the guests has never heard of `lvalues` or `rvalues`. How would you explain those concepts to someone who is not a programmer?

PROGRAMMING EXERCISES

1. Write definitions of variables for the following:
   - Your street address
   - The number of students majoring in CPT at Purdue University
   - The number of students attending Purdue University
   - Someone's birthdate

❑ Your account number at the bank

❑ The balance of your checking account at the bank

❑ Something to indicate whether your PC has a soundcard installed or not

❑ Hourly pay rate

❑ Credit card interest rate

❑ Zip code

❑ The number of days in the week

❑ Class start time

❑ A person's gender

2. The concept of the Time Value of Money suggests that a dollar today is worth more than a dollar in the future. Conversely, future sums of money must be discounted to determine their present value. The formula for the discount factor is:

```
discountFactor = 1.0 / (1.0 + interestRate) ^ yearsInTheFuture
```

For example, if the interest rate is 5% and you want to consider a future sum of $100, its present value is $95.24. Stated another way, $95.24 placed in the bank today would have a value of $100 a year from now if it earns 5% interest. Write a program that allows the user to type in a future sum of money, an interest rate, and the number of years in the future the payment is made, and have the program display the present value of the future sum.

3. Write a program that accepts a number entered into a text box and then displays that number as a dollar amount. For example, 1210.94 would be displayed as $1,210.94. (Hint: check the Format topic in the online help to see if that might be of some help to you. In fact, whenever you have a small task like this, the Format topic should be the first place you look to check if something already exists in the C# collection of methods that might make things easier for you.)

4. Write a program that has five text boxes numbered 1 through 4 and Result. After the user types something into each of the four text boxes, display whatever was typed into each in a 4-3-2-1 order in the Result text box

5. Drag a groupbox control from the toolbox and place it on a form. Next, drag four radio buttons onto the groupbox, labeling each radio button "A", "B", "C", and "D". Now run the program and click on each of the radio buttons. What happens? How might this behavior be useful in a program?

6. The average total cost of a good is equal to the sum of the variable costs plus the fixed costs of production divided by the number of units. Write a program that has text boxes for Variable Costs, Fixed Costs, and the number of units produced and then displays the Average Total Cost in a text box. The program should have functioning Calculate and Close buttons.

7. Write a program that has a text box that allows the user to enter his or her birthday. The program should then display the number of days between the user's birthday and New Year's Day in a read-only text box. Use the online help to find the appropriate **DateTime** method(s) to use.

4

MANIPULATING DATA IN OBJECTS

In the Essentials section you will learn:

♦ How to manipulate numbers using basic arithmetic operators

♦ How implicit type conversion occurs

♦ When to use explicit type casting

♦ How to write and evaluate arithmetic expressions

♦ How to manipulate strings using concatenation and common string methods

♦ How to format results for display to the user

In the Bonus section you will learn:

♦ How to handle other common tasks using .NET Framework classes and methods

♦ How to use additional string methods

♦ How to manipulate date/time values

♦ How to use the Math class

The ability to perform numerous mathematical computations very quickly makes computers an essential tool for solving business problems. This chapter shows you how to write and evaluate arithmetic expressions in C# so you can write programs that solve business problems. This chapter also shows you how to manipulate textual data to gain better control of the presentation of results to the user.

ESSENTIAL TOPICS

MANIPULATING NUMBERS

The business world is full of problems that require mathematical operations on different types of numbers. Although you can solve such problems with a calculator, as the computations become more involved, using a computer simplifies the task considerably. You can even check your intermediate results and control how the results are displayed. Before getting started, let's discuss the basic arithmetic operators used to solve most problems.

Arithmetic Operators

In elementary school, you learned about basic arithmetic operators for addition, subtraction, multiplication, and division. As a child, you represented these operations in several ways. For example, to indicate that you wanted to multiply 2 by 5, you could use any of the following styles to represent the mathematical expression:

(2)(5)
2 · 5
2*5
2 × 5

These styles illustrate how you might write a **mathematical expression,** which consists of two **operands** (the numbers you are operating on) and a symbol between the two operands called the **operator** to identify the type of operation to perform. In each of these expressions, the two operands are the 2 and the 5, but the operator is different. Although people can easily recognize that all four expressions are synonymous, when you use a computer program to perform any basic arithmetic operation, the compiler is not that smart! To indicate the type of operation you need to perform, you generally have one choice for the operator. You therefore need to know which operators to use in various operations.

Figure 4-1 shows a simple calculator that computes each of the basic math operations discussed in this section. The top version uses the `int` data type for everything, whereas the versions on the bottom use the `double` data type. Notice that the data type for each result matches the data type of the operands.

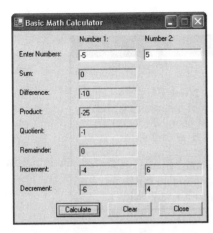

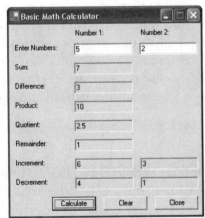
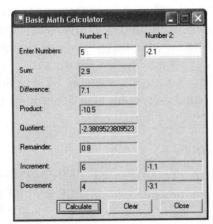

Figure 4-1 Basic math calculator

Table 4-1 summarizes the basic arithmetic operators for addition, subtraction, multiplication, division, and remainder. You should review the table and notes carefully. You may also wish to run the basic math calculator from the accompanying CD with different sets of numbers and compare the results.

Table 4-1   Basic arithmetic operators

Name	Symbol	Usage in expression	Notes
Addition operator	+	oper1 + oper2	Returns the sum of oper1 and oper2. For example, 5 + 2 yields 7.
Subtraction operator	–	oper1 – oper2	Returns the difference of oper2 from oper1. For example, 5 – 2 yields 3. If oper2 is bigger than oper1, the result is a negative number. So 2 – 5 yields –3.
Multiplication operator	*	oper1 * oper2	Returns the product of oper1 and oper2. For example, 5 * 2 yields 10.
Division operator	/	oper1 / oper2	Returns the quotient of oper1 (numerator) divided by oper2 (denominator). For example, 5 / 2 yields 2½, but that's not the final answer. Recall from Chapter 3 that if the data type of oper1 and oper2 is int, then the actual result is 2 (also an int); however, if the data type is double, then the fractional part of the answer is preserved and gives an answer of 2.5.

Table 4-1   Basic arithmetic operators (continued)

Name	Symbol	Usage in expression	Notes
Modulus operator	%	oper1 % oper2	Returns the remainder after dividing oper1 by oper2. For example, 5 % 2 yields 1. Note that the sign of the result matches the sign of the first operand (oper1), so 5 % –2 yields 1 and –5 % 2 yields –1. If the operands are non-integers, modulus still returns the residual amount after performing the division to find the largest integer quotient, so 5.1 % 2 yields 1.1.

All the operators in Table 4-1 are called **binary operators** because they operate on two operands. Further, one or both operands could be numbers or expressions. There are two other basic operators called **unary operators**, which use only one operand. Unlike the binary operators just discussed, the operand for these basic unary operators is a variable and not a constant. These operators are used to increment or decrement a variable by one and are discussed in the next section. You should note that the need to increment and decrement is so common that other languages such as C++ and Java also have these unary operators.

Increment Operator (++)

The increment operator is two successive plus signs (++). It's a shortcut for adding one to the value of the variable operand. For example, if a variable named `count` has the value 5, then `count++` increments the value in `count` by 1, resulting in 6 being stored in `count`. You can think of this notation as shorthand for writing `count = count + 1;`

The increment operator can appear either before or after its operand, with slightly different results. When the ++ is placed before the operand, it is called a **prefix increment expression**. The operand is increased by 1 for the result of the operation. When the ++ is placed after the operand, it is called a **postfix increment expression**. The result of the operation is the original value of the operand, but after the statement is executed, the operand is increased by 1.

For example, let's assume that your program has two variables named `myNbr1` and `myNbr2`, both containing the value 5. If you display a message box using the prefix and postfix operations on these variables, as shown in Figure 4-2, the displayed results are different, but both `myNbr1` and `myNbr2` contain the value 6 after the statement has been processed, as illustrated by the second message box.

```
MessageBox.Show("Prefix:" + ++myNbr1 + " Postfix:" + myNbr2++);
if (myNbr1 == myNbr2)
{
     MessageBox.Show("Same");
}
else
{
     MessageBox.Show("Different");
}
```

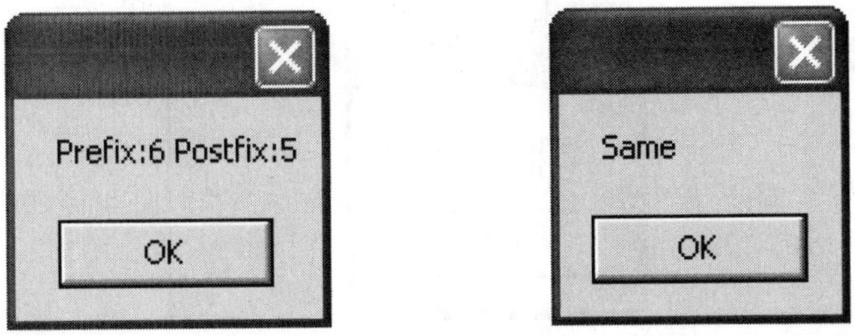

Figure 4-2 Prefix and postfix increment operator

These examples use the postfix increment operator; however, you should be aware of both alternatives. If you observe results different from the examples, it would be a good idea to double-check your code to make sure that you didn't mistype the statement using the prefix notation.

Decrement Operator (--)

The decrement operator is two successive minus signs (--). It's a shortcut for subtracting one from the value of the variable operand. For example, if a variable named `count` has the value 5, then `count--` decrements `count` by 1, resulting in 4 being stored in `count`. This notation can be thought of as shorthand for writing `count = count - 1;`

Like the increment operator, the decrement operator can appear either before or after its operand, with slightly different results. When the (--) is placed before the operand, it is called a **prefix decrement expression**. The operand is decreased by 1 for the result of the operation. When the (--) is placed after the operand, it is called a **postfix decrement expression**. The result of the operation is the original value of the operand, but after the operation, the operand is decreased by 1.

For example, let's assume that your program has two variables named `myNbr1` and `myNbr2`, both containing the value 5. If you displayed a message box using the prefix and postfix operations on these variables, as shown in Figure 4-3, the displayed results are different, but both `myNbr1` and `myNbr2` contain 4 after the statement has been processed, as depicted by the second message box that is displayed.

```
MessageBox.Show("Prefix:" + --myNbr1 + " Postfix:" + myNbr2--);
if (myNbr1 == myNbr2)
{
        MessageBox.Show("Same");
}
else
{
        MessageBox.Show("Different");
}
```

Figure 4-3 Prefix and postfix decrement operator

Type Casting

You need to know one more thing about writing expressions. Let's assume that you were multiplying 2.5 (a floating point number) and 5 (an integer). It makes no difference to you that the operands are of different types—you know that the product is 12.5 (a floating point number). If you needed to provide the answer as whole number, you would say 12 or 13. If you needed to provide the result as a floating point number, you would say 12.5.

When you write an arithmetic expression in a computer program and the operands are of different data types, one of the operand's data type must change so both operands are of the same data type. A similar situation arises when you assign data of one type to a variable of another type. In some cases, the compiler automatically performs the type conversion for you. When the data type conversion happens without the code having a specific instruction to make the change, it is called **implicit type conversion** or **silent cast**.

As a general rule, C# permits implicit type conversion from a smaller data type to a larger data type—a process called **data widening**. The terms "smaller" and "larger" mean that one data type requires fewer bytes of storage (smaller) than does the other data type (larger). For example, if you assign a **byte** data type (one byte of memory) into an **int** data type (four bytes of memory), C# converts the **byte** value into a 4-byte value before assigning that value into the **int**.

If you attempt to assign a larger data type value into a smaller data type variable, you see an error message that states that the compiler "cannot implicitly convert type xx to xy" to let you know why the program won't compile. Attempting to change one numeric data type to another data type with a smaller range is known as **data narrowing**. To understand the difference between data widening and data narrowing, think about having 16 ounces of your favorite beverage, which you need to pour into a glass. You have an 8-ounce glass and a 32-ounce glass. You could easily pour the drink into the 32-ounce glass (data widening) without problems; however, pouring it into the 8-ounce glass (data narrowing) would cause a spill. That's what happens in computer memory. Placing a smaller value into a space larger than required works, but attempting to put it inside a smaller space would cause the loss of some valuable data and is not permitted.

Although implicit type conversion can be accomplished in some cases, it can still be the source of rather obscure program bugs. Therefore, good programming practice dictates that you explicitly convert data types when the operands are of different types. You should never rely on implicit type conversion even when the code correctly performs the task you intend. Explicitly performing the data conversion using one of the C# conversion methods or the cast operator tells all who read your code exactly what your intentions are. Avoid implicit type conversion!

You have already used **explicit type conversion** in Chapters 2 and 3. Recall that the **Text** property of a text box represents the textual (string) data in the text box. When you assigned the (textual) data in a text box to a numeric variable or displayed the contents of a numeric variable in a text box, you used methods to explicitly convert the value to another data type. The following two statements illustrate each of these conversions:

```
lengthInFeet = decimal.Parse(txtLengthInFeet.Text);

txtTotalCost.Text = totalCost.ToString("C");
```

When the user enters data in the **txtLengthInFeet** text box, the data is type **string**. To store it inside the **decimal** variable **lengthInFeet**, you needed to convert the **string** data entered by the user to its **decimal** equivalent using the **decimal.Parse** method. When you were ready to display the computed answer stored in the **decimal** variable named **totalCost**, you converted it to a **string** by using the **ToString** method. There are several other methods that allow you to convert data from one type to another. Other languages, such as C and C++, refer to type conversion as a cast. In C#, you can also use a cast operator to perform explicit type conversion.

When you write expressions involving data of different numeric types, you should convert the smaller data type to the larger data type using explicit casting. **Explicit casting** is performed by prefixing the smaller operand with the cast operator that matches the larger operand. The **cast operator** is written as a data type inside parentheses. For example, if **interestRate** is a **double** type and **accountBalance** is a **decimal**, you might try to use the following expression to compute the interest earned:

```
interestRate * accountBalance
```

Because the two multiplication operands are different types, and implicit conversion cannot be done, your program will not compile. The recommended solution in this type of situation is to force the operands to be of the same type by using some type of conversion method on the operands. To fix the expression so that it can be compiled, you should cast the **interestRate** to a **decimal** type (because a **double** is a smaller data type than decimal), as shown in the following statement:

```
(decimal) interestRate * accountBalance
```

Note that if you had written the operation with the operands switched, the expression with casting would look like this:

```
accountBalance * (decimal) interestRate;
```

Because there are a few alternatives for explicit type conversions, we suggest you follow these three guidelines:

1. When you retrieve data entered on a form by the user, use the **Parse** method to convert the textual data to the appropriate numeric data type before the assignment.

2. When you display numeric data on a form, use the **ToString** method to convert it to a string first.

3. When you perform arithmetic operations between operands of different types, you should use explicit type casting to convert the smaller operand to the type of the other (larger) operand.

Arithmetic Expressions

As stated earlier, an arithmetic expression consists of one or two operands and an operator, which is a symbol representing the type of operation to perform. As previously stated, both operands should be of the same data type, but how do you decide which type to use? In Chapter 3, you learned that each data type has a limited range of values that can be stored. The chapter provided guidelines for selecting the best data type for a particular situation. In the event that an arithmetic operation yields a result outside the range for the selected data type, you get undesirable results. For example, suppose that bookCount is type **short** and contains the value 30000. If you try to multiply bookCount by 2 and store the result back in bookCount, you get an overflow exception error, and your program terminates abnormally (that is, it crashes). The **overflow error** indicates that the result cannot be represented within the range limits of the specific data type. Likewise, you can get an **underflow error** if a negative value falls outside the specified range for a negative number.

One way to correct an overflow or underflow problem is to convert the data to a type that has a larger range of values. Another solution is to anticipate the problem by validating the input data and preventing the program from attempting the operation if the data is unreasonable. You will learn how to do this in Chapter 5. Possibly the best approach is to include code designed to catch exceptions to prevent your code from crashing. You will learn about exception handling in Chapter 6. For now, you should use the first approach and assume that the user's data will be reasonable.

All of the previous examples described simple expressions that involved only one operation. However, most business problems involve multiple mathematical operations. Therefore, you need to know how to write and evaluate expressions using multiple operations.

 tip ▶ When writing expressions, surround the operator with a space on both sides to make your code more readable.

Operator Precedence

When a single expression has many operators, the **precedence** of the operators determines the order in which the operations are performed. For example, 2 + 3 * 4 results in 14 because multiplication has a higher precedence than addition. If addition had the highest precedence, the result would be 20. Table 4-2 shows the order of precedence for the basic operators discussed thus far.

Table 4-2 Operator precedence

Precedence order	Operator type	Operator symbol
1	Increment and decrement	++ --
2	Multiplication, division, and modulus	* / %
3	Addition and subtraction	+ −

When an expression contains multiple operators with the same precedence, the **associativity** of the operators controls the order in which the operations are performed. The basic math operators are left-associative. **Left-associative** means that the operations are performed from left to right, much as one reads a book in the English language.

For example, suppose that you wanted to write an expression to calculate how much money you had in coins. The coins could include quarters (25¢), dimes (10¢), nickels (5¢), and pennies (1¢). An expression to compute the result may look like this:

```
0.25 * quarters + 0.1 * dimes + 0.05 * nickels + 0.01 * pennies
```

To illustrate what happens, let's assume that you have 5 quarters, 3 dimes, 2 nickels, and 8 pennies. To find the value of money in your pocket, you would go through the following progression of calculations:

1. Write the original equation:

   <u>0.25 * quarters + 0.1 * dimes + 0.05 * nickels + 0.01 * pennies</u>

2. Substitute the number of each type of coin in your pocket:

   <u>0.25 * 5</u>   + 0.1 * 3   + 0.05 * 2   + 0.01 * 8

3. Find the first product:

   1.25   + <u>0.1 * 3</u>   + 0.05 * 2   + 0.01 * 8

4. Find the second product (multiplication has higher precedence than addition):

   1.25   +   0.3   + <u>0.05 * 2</u>   + 0.01 * 8

5. Find the third product (multiplication has higher precedence than addition):

   1.25   +   0.3   + 0.10   + <u>0.01 * 8</u>

6. Find the fourth product (multiplication has higher precedence than addition):

   <u>1.25   +   0.3</u>   + 0.10   + 0.08

7. Find the first sum (perform operations at same precedence from left to right):

   <u>1.55   + 0.10</u>   + 0.08

8. Find the second sum:

   <u>1.65   + 0.08</u>

9. Find the final sum:

   1.73

Generically, you might write the rules to compute the money-in-your-pocket algorithm as follows:

1. Compute value of quarters (0.25 * quarters)

2. Compute value of dimes (0.1 * dimes)

3. Compute value of nickels (0.05 * nickels)

4. Compute value of pennies (0.01 * pennies)

5. Sum of value of quarters and dimes (#1 & #2 above)

6. Sum of above and value of nickels (#5 & #3 above)

7. Sum of above and value of pennies (#6 & #4 above)

Notice that all the multiplication expressions (Steps 1 through 4) are evaluated first. Their resulting values then become the operands used in the remaining addition operations (Steps 5 through 7). Thus, each addition computation could be considered a **binary operation** between expressions, each of which is a multiplication operation. The complex expression is resolved in this order because of the operator precedence and associativity rules explained earlier.

Overriding with Parentheses ( )

An expression with many operations on a single line may look confusing. To avoid confusion, place parentheses around parts of the expression to clarify or emphasize the order of operations.

 tip ▶ When writing complex expressions, it is acceptable to use more parentheses than you need, to make the expression more understandable.

For example, you could rewrite the coin calculator equation using either of the following expressions to yield the same result:

```
(0.25 * quarters) + (0.1 * dimes) + (0.05 * nickels) + (0.01 * pennies)
```

```
(((0.25 * quarters) + (0.1 * dimes)) + (0.05 * nickels)) + (0.01 * pennies)
```

People often use parentheses extensively to help clarify equations. An even more important reason for using parentheses is for writing a complex expression in which the precedence and associativity rules would yield an incorrect result. Because parentheses override the inherent order that is determined by precedence and associativity rules, parentheses allow you to write complex expressions in a manner that solves the problem as you want. For example, let's suppose that you regularly go to dinner with three friends and split the bill equally. The computation for the average bill is:

$$\frac{myBill + myPal1 + myPal2 + myPal3}{4}$$

However, if you write out the expression as:

```
myBill + myPal1 + myPal2 + myPal3 / 4
```

the answer will be incorrect, because only **myPal3** is divided by **4**! You must place parentheses around the four addition operands before dividing their sum by 4 as follows:

```
(myBill + myPal1 + myPal2 + myPal3) / 4
```

The parentheses override the higher division operator precedence and perform all additions before dividing the sum by 4. You now get the correct answer.

Storing Intermediate Results

It is important to recognize that writing the fewest lines of program code is not always the best programming practice. As the arithmetic expressions in your program increase in complexity, the source code's readability also increases in complexity. In general, you should avoid writing statements that exceed the visible line width of the source code editor. Another alternative to using parentheses is to compute part of the computation, store it in an intermediate variable, and then perform the rest of the computation using the intermediate result. This is particularly appropriate when the subexpression itself carries meaning.

For example, the coin calculator previously discussed could store the intermediate results for **valueOfQuarters**, **valueOfDimes**, **valueOfNickels**, and **valueOfPennies**, and then add all four subexpressions together to determine the total money in your pocket. Similarly, if you reconsider the average bill calculator, you could store the sum of the four bills in `totalBill` and then divide `totalBill` by 4 for the `averageBill`.

> **tip** ▶ Storing intermediate results in variables leads to programs that are easier to read and debug.

4

Assignment Operators

To store intermediate and final results, use the **assignment operator** that you've studied and used in Chapters 2 and 3. There are a few additional assignment operators that combine an arithmetic operation with an assignment operation. These combined operators effectively allow you to write less code. Keep in mind that getting carried away with program code brevity can sometimes make understanding the code more difficult.

Table 4-3 illustrates some assignment operators that you may find useful.

Table 4-3   Assignment operators

Operator	Example	Description
=	`costOfMilk = 2.79;`	The value 2.79 is stored in the variable `costOfMilk`.
+=	`totMoney += tax;`	The same as: `totMoney = totMoney + tax;` The value in variable `tax` is added to the current value in `totMoney`, and the resulting total that includes the tax is stored back into `totMoney`.
*=	`totBill *= tipPercent;`	The same as: `totBill = totBill * tipPercent;` The current value in `totBill` is multiplied by the value in `tipPercent` and the total tip result is stored back into `totBill`.
-=	`total -= coupon;`	The same as: `total = total - coupon;` The value in variable `coupon` is subtracted from the current value in `total`, and the discounted result is stored back into `total`.
/=	`total /= count;`	The same as `total = total / count;` The value in variable `total` is divided by the value in `count`, and the average result is stored back into `total`.

These assignment operators are right-associative. **Right-associative** means that the expression on the right side is evaluated first, and then the result is stored in the variable on the left side. Assignment operators also have the lowest precedence (assignments are performed after all the other arithmetic operations are completed).

A PROGRAM EXAMPLE

To make sure you understand how arithmetic expressions should be used in a program, let's write a C# program to calculate your restaurant bill and split it equally among all diners. The user provides the cost of all meals, the cost of drinks, the value of any discount, and the number of diners. The application assumes a sales tax rate of 6% and tip of 15%. It finds and displays the total bill (without discount, tax, and tip), the total taxes, the tip amount, the meal total (with discount, taxes, and tip), and the amount each diner must pay. This example uses the addition, subtraction, multiplication, and division arithmetic operators. The first version that you create displays only the final result. The next version also saves and displays intermediate results. You will see how the shorter version looks more complex but, by adding a few more lines of code, you can make it more readable.

User Interface for the Restaurant Bill Calculator Application

To start, repeat the steps from Chapter 2 starting with the section titled "Creating the Visual Studio Project Files" and going to the section titled "Placing Controls on a Form." Name the project *RestaurantBillCalc*, and change the text property of *frmMain* to Restaurant Bill Calculator.

This application's user interface requires four input values, five output values, labels to identify the input and output values, one button for the calculation, and one button to close the form and end the application. When the design of the form is finished, it should include nine labels, nine text boxes, and two buttons, and look similar to the form in Figure 4-4. You will use this same design for both versions of the Restaurant Bill Calculator. The first version of this application ignores the first four output text boxes. The improved version of this application uses intermediate calculations and displays those results in the first four output text boxes.

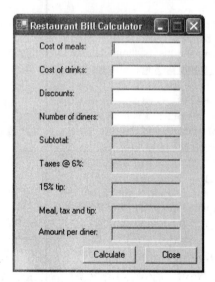

Figure 4-4 Restaurant Bill Calculator user interface

To complete the form, set the properties of the labels, text boxes, and buttons as shown in Table 4-4. Be sure to change the **Name** property of the controls so that you can refer to them in the code of the form's class file.

4

Table 4-4 Properties of the user interface for the Restaurant Bill Calculator application

Object type	Name	Property	Value
Label	label1	Text	Cost of meals:
	label2	Text	Cost of drinks:
	label3	Text	Discounts:
	label4	Text	Number of diners:
	label5	Text	Subtotal:
	label6	Text	Taxes @ 6%:
	label7	Text	15% tip:
	label8	Text	Meal, tax, tip:
	label9	Text	Amount per diner:
Text box	txtMealCost	Text	empty
	txtDrinkCost	Text	empty
	txtDiscounts	Text	empty
	txtNbrDiners	Text	empty
	txtSubtotal	Text	empty
		ReadOnly	True
		TabStop	False
	txtTaxRate	Text	empty
		ReadOnly	True
		TabStop	False
	txtTipPct	Text	empty
		ReadOnly	True
		TabStop	False
	txtTotalCost	Text	empty
		ReadOnly	True
		TabStop	False
	txtCostPerDiner	Text	empty
		ReadOnly	True
		TabStop	False
Button	btnCalculate	Text	Calculate
	btnClose	Text	Close

Restaurant Bill Calculator Logic

Figure 4-6 shows the program code that you need to write for version 1. Before looking at this listing, review the explanation that follows to make sure you understand how the application logic is organized and try to write it yourself as you review it. If you encounter problems, compare your code against the complete listing. The best way to learn how to program is to practice writing programs on your own. Always try to code a sample program on your own before looking at the solution.

Initialization

The only initializing the program needs to do is limited to instantiating and initializing the controls that make up the form's user interface. The initialization code appears in the method named **InitializeComponent**, which was generated by the Form Designer and is hidden in the Windows Form Designer–generated code region. Write the code that follows immediately after this region:

```
1    public static void Main()
2    {
3        frmMain main = new frmMain();
4        Application.Run(main);
```

```
 5    }
 6
 7    public frmMain()
 8    {
 9        InitializeComponent();
10    }
```

Obtaining the User's Input

This application requires the user to enter four different values, and you've already created four input text box objects for this purpose. To handle the user's input, you write code to retrieve the data entered by the user and store them in corresponding variables. Because **mealCost**, **drinkCost**, and **discounts** represent monetary values, they should be defined as **decimal** data types. Because **nbrDiners** is a whole number, it should be an **int** data type.

Write definitions for each of these four variables. Write four more lines of code to convert the string data in each of the input text boxes to the correct data type using the **Parse** method and make an assignment to its corresponding variable. For example, to assign **nbrDiners** the **string** data held in the **txtNbrDiners** text box, use:

```
nbrDiners = int.Parse(txtNbrDiners.Text);
```

In the processing steps, you add code to find the cost per diner by dividing the total cost by the number of diners. Whenever you write code to perform a division operation, it is a good idea to make sure that the denominator is not zero. We suggest using a simple decision (like that used in Chapter 2) to check the value of **nbrDiners** just after the assignment statement shown previously. If the value is negative or zero, show a descriptive message, position the cursor in this text box, and bypass the remaining processing steps. The code snippet below shows sample code to accomplish this task:

```
if (nbrDiners <= 0)
  {
    MessageBox.Show("The number of diners must be a positive number.");
    txtNbrDiners.Focus();
    return;
  }
```

Performing the Calculation

To find the total cost per diner, you find the meal and drinks subtotal and use this subtotal to find the 6% taxes due and the 15% tip. After you have the total bill, including taxes and tip, to find how much each diner should pay, divide the total bill by the number of diners. Define two constants to hold the fixed tax rate and tip percent:

```
const double taxRate = .06;
const double tipPct = .15;
```

In addition, define variables to hold the total cost as well as the cost per diner:

```
decimal totalCost;
decimal costPerDiner;
```

In this version, you are attempting to minimize the amount of code you write. Therefore, you should write the calculation for the total cost as a single expression. Because the subtotal is not stored separately, the total cost calculation should use the sum of the meals and drinks three times: first, to calculate the meal subtotal; second, to calculate the taxes; and third, to calculate the tip amount. Because **taxRate** and **tipPct** are **double** data types, you need to cast these values to **decimal** before multiplying them with the subtotal. After you have the **totalCost**, you can find the **costPerDiner** by dividing **totalCost** by **nbrDiners**. Although this compiles without casting to **decimal**, we recommend that you cast explicitly. You should also round the results to two decimal positions using the same **Math.Round** method used in Chapter 2. The following code snippet shows the assignment statements for **totalCost** and **costPerDiner**. Notice how the indentation used on the assignment statement for **totalCost** makes it easier to recognize that lines 1 through 4 make up a single C# statement.

```
1    totalCost = Math.Round((mealCost + drinkCost)
2         + ((decimal) taxRate * (mealCost + drinkCost))
3         + ((decimal) tipPct * (mealCost + drinkCost))
4         - discounts, 2);
5    costPerDiner = Math.Round(totalCost / (decimal) nbrDiners, 2);
```

Displaying the Results

In version 1, the only result being displayed is the amount each diner pays. To display this value in the **txtCostPerDiner** text box, you need to convert the **decimal** value in **costPerDiner** to a **string** and display in currency format. Chapter 2 explained that typing "C" between the parentheses of the **ToString** method displays the result as currency:

```
txtPerDiner.Text = costPerDiner.ToString("C");
```

Recall that you must perform this conversion because you need to assign a **decimal** data type into a **string** data type.

Testing the Restaurant Bill Calculator

You can run the application and enter any set of numbers, but to have any confidence in the accuracy of your solution, you need to test values for which you know the correct answers. Let's assume the following input values:

```
Meals: 28.25 Drinks: 10 Discounts: 1.25 Diners: 3
```

Using these values, the subtotal should be 38.25 (28.25 + 10). The 6% tax on the subtotal is 2.295 (38.25 * 0.06). A 15% tip on the subtotal is 5.7375 (38.25 * 0.15). The total cost is 45.0325: the subtotal + tax + tip − discount (38.25 + 2.295 + 5.7375 - 1.25). This means that each diner should pay $15.01 (45.0325 / 3). Test the program by using this set of input values, and compare the result to your manual calculation. (See Figure 4-5.)

Attempting to calculate an answer when there are zero diners causes problems. When you execute the program, you should see a message box explaining that you need to enter a value for the number of diners. For any program you write, your sample test data should always include values for problematic cases, such as checking for zero diners in this program.

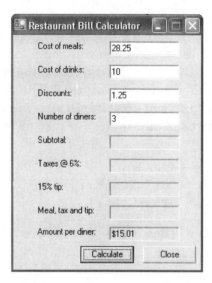

Figure 4-5 Sample execution of Restaurant Bill Calculator application

tip ▶ Program errors or bugs lurk in cases that push the boundaries of a program. Always test your code using extreme values such as 0, no data, and so on, to help uncover bugs.

Now that you understand how the program is designed, you should review the complete code listing in Figure 4-6 to see how all of the code fits together. Notice how the use of indentation and line spacing between blocks of code helps improve the readability of the program.

```
1    using System;
2    using System.Windows.Forms;
3
4    public class frmMain: Form
5    {

244      public static void Main()
245      {
246          frmMain main = new frmMain();
247          Application.Run(main);
248      }
249
250      public frmMain()
251      {
252          InitializeComponent();
253      }
254
255      private void btnClose_Click(object sender, System.EventArgs e)
256      {
257          Close();
258      }
259
260      private void btnCalculate_Click(object sender, System.EventArgs e)
261      {
262          const double taxRate = .06;
263          const double tipPct = .15;
264          decimal mealCost;
265          decimal drinkCost;
```

Figure 4-6 Code listing of Restaurant Bill Calculator application

```
266            decimal discounts;
267            int nbrDiners;
268            decimal totalCost;
269            decimal costPerDiner;
270
271            // Get the input values from the form.
272
273            mealCost = decimal.Parse(txtMealCost.Text);
274            drinkCost = decimal.Parse(txtDrinkCost.Text);
275            discounts = decimal.Parse(txtDiscounts.Text);
276            nbrDiners = int.Parse(txtNbrDiners.Text);
277
278            // Validate that nbrDiners is not zero to avoid divide by zero error.
279
280            if (nbrDiners <= 0)
281            {
282                MessageBox.Show("The number of diners must be a positive number.");
283                txtNbrDiners.Focus();
284                return;
285            }
286
287            // Calculate the total per diner.
288
289            totalCost = Math.Round((mealCost + drinkCost)
290                + ((decimal) taxRate * (mealCost + drinkCost))
291                + ((decimal) tipPct * (mealCost + drinkCost))
292                - discounts, 2);
293            costPerDiner = Math.Round(totalCost / (decimal) nbrDiners, 2);
294
295            // Display the results back to the user.
296
297            txtCostPerDiner.Text = costPerDiner.ToString("C");
298        }
299    }
300
```

Figure 4-6 Code listing of Restaurant Bill Calculator application (continued)

Improving the Restaurant Bill Calculator

The expression used to calculate total cost is unnecessarily complex. Furthermore, it would be helpful to be able to show the results of the intermediate calculations, particularly the tip amount in case some of the diners want to increase it. Therefore, you will now update the restaurant bill calculator to find, store, use, and display some intermediate calculations.

Figure 4-7 shows an updated version of the restaurant bill calculator program. Only the new lines and updated sections of code are included with the figures, so use the line numbers to determine where to make these changes. First, add definitions for three new variables to hold the intermediate results for subtotal, taxes, and tip (see new lines 268 through 270). In addition, add statements to compute these values (see new lines 292 through 294). Because you have intermediate results stored in variables, you can revise the computation for `totalCost` so that it uses these values (revised line 295). As a final step, display the values in these intermediate variables in their corresponding text boxes (see new lines 300 through 303).

```
268             decimal subtotal;
269             decimal taxAmount;
270             decimal tipAmount;

290             // Calculate the subtotal, taxAmount, tipAmount, totalCost and costPerDiner.
291
292             subtotal = mealCost + drinkCost;
293             taxAmount = Math.Round((decimal) taxRate * subtotal, 2);
294             tipAmount = Math.Round((decimal) tipPct * subtotal, 2);
295             totalCost = subtotal + taxAmount + tipAmount - discounts;
296             costPerDiner = Math.Round(totalCost / (decimal) nbrDiners, 2);
297
298             // Display the results back to the user.
299
300             txtSubtotal.Text = subtotal.ToString("C");
301             txtTaxAmount.Text = taxAmount.ToString("C");
302             txtTipAmount.Text = tipAmount.ToString("C");
303             txtTotalCost.Text = totalCost.ToString("C");
304             txtCostPerDiner.Text = costPerDiner.ToString("C");
305         }
306     }
307
```

Figure 4-7 Partial code listing of New Restaurant Bill Calculator

Testing the Improved Restaurant Bill Calculator

Once the improved application is complete, save everything and then build the solution. Now you can run the application and enter the same set of numbers you used before. Figure 4-8 shows a screen shot of a sample solution. Note that the final result is the same because of rounding, but now you have additional, valuable information because the intermediate results are also displayed.

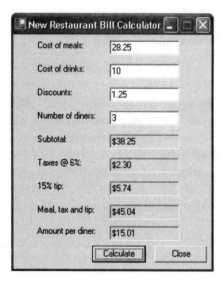

Figure 4-8 Sample execution of New Restaurant Bill Calculator

Introduce an Error to Test Debugging

Now that you have a working version of the improved application, you will introduce a trivial-looking error in the code and use the debugger to walk through the steps necessary to trace the problems you observe. This process helps you better understand how to find and correct errors (debug your program). To begin the experiment, you need to introduce a logic error. Change the text box referenced in the **discounts** assignment (line 275 in Figure 4-6) to **txtDrinkCost**, and rebuild the project:

```
275        discounts = decimal.Parse(txtDrinkCost.Text);
```

Now forget that you introduced this error to get a feel for how you can use the debugger to troubleshoot your program. When you run the program with the same input data, none of the answers after tip amount looks correct.

The best way to trace what is happening is to set a breakpoint on the **tipAmount** assignment (line 294). (See Appendix C for tips on using the Debugger.) Run the program again and enter the same data. When you click Calculate, the Code window appears on top of your form with the **tipAmount** calculation statement line highlighted. You can hover the mouse pointer over the variables whose values you'd like to verify.

At this point, **subtotal** and **taxAmount** have the correct values, but **tipAmount** is zero (because the statement to compute it has not yet executed). Step through the statements one at a time by selecting Debug➔Step Into from the menu bar, by clicking the 🖅 toolbar button, or by pressing F11.

You should see that **tipAmount** now has the correct value. If you look at the individual values for the variables that make up the **totalCost** computation, you should see that **discounts** shows the value of 10 instead of 1.25, which you typed into the form. Because the expression to compute **totalCost** is correct but one of the values used in the computation is wrong, look up through the program code to locate the line where **discounts** is assigned. Hovering the mouse on the right side of the assignment operator shows that **discounts** is 10. Hovering on the left shows that the text box from which **discounts** receives its value is also 10. Because you know you entered 1.25 into the text box, let's hope you would realize that the wrong text box was used in the assignment. From the menu, select Debug➔Stop Debugging to stop debugging. (You can also stop debugging by clicking the ■ toolbar button.) Now you can correct the code, rebuild the project, and test your program again.

There are many other valuable debugging features in VS.NET, which we recommend you explore further by reviewing Appendix C.

MANIPULATING STRINGS

Everything you did in the preceding sections dealt exclusively with numeric data, but you will also frequently need to manipulate textual data. People are usually adept at dealing with textual information, probably due to all of the reading and writing they do. To solve business problems that require you to handle character data, you need to learn about a few more operators and methods that can be applied to **string** objects. You've already used the **ToString** method to convert a number to a **string** in order to display it in an output text box. There are many more **string** methods available, the most common of which are discussed in the following sections.

Concatenation

Sometimes you may have a couple pieces of **string** data that you want to combine or concatenate into a single value. This can be accomplished using the concatenate operator, which is the plus sign (+). Because this is the same symbol that is used for addition, how do you know when the operation is adding or concatenating? Recall that the (+) operator is a binary operator because it has two operands. If one or both of the operands is a **string** data type, the operation being performed is **concatenation**. If both operands are numeric, the operation is addition. For example, if the variable `firstName` is "Amber" and `lastName` is "Lucas," the expression `firstName + lastName` is equal to "AmberLucas." Note that there is no space between the first and last name. To add the space, use the expression:

```
firstName + " " + lastName
```

If `lastName` is an **int** data type with the value 123, then you might expect an error to occur. However, the number 123 is converted to the **string** "123", so the concatenated result becomes "Amber123". This fact is important to remember, because sometimes when you want your program to produce errors due to bad data, it doesn't!

Another alternative for concatenating strings is by using the **String** class's. `Concat` method. For example, to combine the first and last names, use the following expression:

```
String.Concat(firstName, " ", lastName)
```

You may wish to use this alternative to make the operation clearer in your program code, because `Concat` can only mean concatenation, but (+) could mean addition or subtraction. However, this alternative also concatenates strings and numbers. The examples in this book use the (+) sign for both operations. If the context of the type of operation is unclear, explanations are provided,

IndexOf Method

Sometimes you need to determine whether a string value contains a partial string. In this case, you can use the String class's `IndexOf` method. For example, if `myString` contains `"The quick brown fox"`, and you want to find out if the substring `"k b"` is in `myString`, you could use the following expression: `myString.IndexOf("k b")`. In this example, the result is 8, which is the character position where the first match of "k b" occurs, assuming that the first character is at position 0. (All string methods start their character counts with 0, not 1. In other words, string methods are *zero-based*, not one-based.) Note that if you would have used `myString.IndexOf("K B")` or `myString.IndexOf("kb")`, the result would be −1, indicating that there is no occurrence of the substring in `myString`. These examples show that when you use the IndexOf method, you must use the correct case and spacing. Refer to Figure 4-9 for sample executions to verify that the `IndexOf` method works as described.

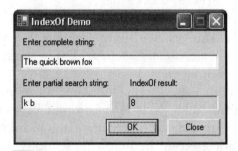 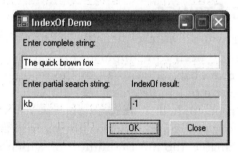

Figure 4-9 Sample executions of IndexOf Demo program

In many situations the `IndexOf` method is useful. For example, an application that asks the user for a filename (that may include a path) may need to look for special characters, for example a colon (:), to determine if a drive letter is provided. Another example is an application that obtains a telephone number from the user and determines if the format is International (+1.765.494.2560) or in the United States (765−494−2560) and whether an area code is provided or not.

Length Property

The **Length** property returns the number of characters in a string. This is often useful when a program manipulates string data, and you need to know how much textual data was given. For example, if **user** has the value **"Rupert Jones"**, then **user.Length** is 12. Refer to Figure 4-10 for a sample execution that uses the **Length** property.

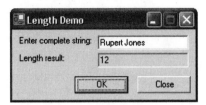

Figure 4-10 Sample execution of Length Demo program

FINDING SUBSTRINGS AND PARSING

Although concatenating puts many strings together, the **Substring** method allows you to break a long string into smaller strings. You must provide the long string with the starting position and the number of characters to be used. For example, if a variable **user** had the user's first name, a space, and a last name, and you wanted to separate the first name and last name into separate string variables, you could use the following code:

```
1    string user;
2    string userFName;
3    string userLName;
4    int spacePosition;
5    int lastPosition;
6
7    user = txtUser.Text;
8
9    spacePosition = user.IndexOf(" ");
10   lastPosition = user.Length;
11   userFName = user.Substring(0, spacePosition);
12   userLName = user.Substring(spacePosition + 1,
13       lastPosition - spacePosition - 1);
14
15   txtFName.Text = userFName;
16   txtLName.Text = userLName;
```

To better understand how this works, let's walk through some sample code and write down what you expect will happen. Assume that the name Jerry Maxwell was entered in the text box. First, note the position number of each character, keeping in mind that strings are zero-order (that is, the first position is zero):

```
                1111111111222222222223
      0123456789012345678901234567890
      Jerry Maxwell
```

On line 7, the variable **user** receives the value **"Jerry Maxwell"**. On line 9, **spacePosition** is assigned 5 (the position number of the space). On line 10, **lastPosition** is set to 13 (there are 13 characters in the name Jerry Maxwell). On line 11, **userFName** is set to **user.Substring(0,5)**. This assigns the value **"Jerry"** to **userFName** (starting at position 0, count five characters). Finally, on line 12, `userLName` is assigned `user.Substring(5+1 13-5-1)`, which is `user.Substring(6, 7)`, which is `"Maxwell"` (starting at position 6, count seven characters). Figure 4-11 shows a sample execution of this example, which confirms the walk-through just performed.

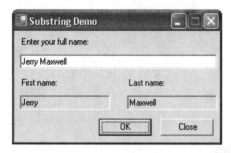

Figure 4-11   Sample execution of Substring Demo program

ToUpper Method

If you have an alphabetic string value, and you want to display it using only uppercase letters, you can use a **string** object's `ToUpper` method. For example, if `user` contains `"Season Wilcox"`, then `user.ToUpper()` will yield `"SEASON WILCOX"`. This method is useful for situations in which you want to provide the user with more flexibility on user input without adding considerable code to handle the processing of every possible input. For example, if you ask the user for her name to find out if her record is in your files, keep in mind that she may enter `"Mary"`, `"mary"`, `"MARY"`, or other combinations of upper- and lowercase letters. The data in your files may have the name saved as `"Mary"`. To make sure you find the name, you should convert the data she entered and the data in your files to uppercase to handle all combinations. In a similar fashion, if a user wants to look up a product in inventory using a product code but enters a mixture of upper- and lowercase characters, `ToUpper` could be applied to ensure that the value being compared matches the values in the database, which may be stored in uppercase. Refer to the sample execution in Figure 4-12 to see the effect of applying `ToUpper` to input provided by the user. Notice that numbers and special characters are not affected by the `ToUpper` method.

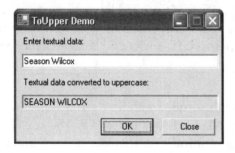 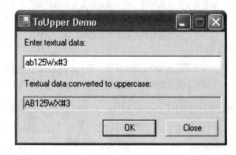

Figure 4-12   Sample execution of ToUpper Demo program

ToLower Method

As you might expect, the `ToLower` method converts an alphabetic string with the result that only lowercase characters are used. In the previous example, to show the user's name using only lowercase letters (as in "jerry maxwell"), use `myUser.ToLower()`. Like the `ToUpper` method, the `ToLower` method is useful for situations in which you want to provide the user with more flexibility for user input without adding considerable code to handle the processing of every possibility. As with **ToUpper**, numbers and special characters are not affected by the **ToLower** method. Figure 4-13 shows a sample execution of this method.

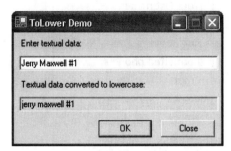

Figure 4-13 Sample execution of ToLower Demo program

A PROGRAM EXAMPLE

To make sure that you understand how to manipulate strings, let's write a C# program to obtain the user's first and last name and phone number (digits only), and display the full name and telephone number in a more readable format. In addition to a Show and Close button, add a Clear button to allow the user to erase all input and output values and continue to test the program with new data.

Contact Info User Interface

To start, follow the steps you've used before to create a new project. Name the project **ContactInfo**. You should also change the **Text** property of **frmMain** to User Contact Information. Refer to Figure 4-14 for the user interface design. Table 4-5 lists the properties of the form elements that must be changed to match our solution. Figure 4-15 shows a sample execution of this application. After you've designed the form, try to develop the code for the **btnShow_Click** event procedure by reviewing the **string** methods discussed in this section and determining which to apply.

You should also be able to write the **btnClear_Click** event procedure, which clears all input and output text boxes by setting their **Text** property to an empty string (**""**) and positions the cursor in the first input text box using the **Focus** method. If you encounter difficulty, you may want to refer to the code listing in Figure 4-16.

Figure 4-14 Contact Info application user interface

Table 4-5   Contact Info Application user interface properties

Object type	Name	Property	Value
Label	label1	Text	Your first name:
	label2	Text	Your last name:
	label3	Text	Your 10-digit phone #:
	label4	Text	Full name:
	label5	Text	Formatted phone #:
Text box	txtFirstName	Text	empty
	txtLastName	Text	empty
	txtPhoneDigits	Text	empty
	txtFullName	Text	empty
		ReadOnly	True
		TabStop	False
	txtFormattedPhone	Text	empty
		ReadOnly	True
		TabStop	False
Button	btnShow	Text	Show
	btnClear	Text	Clear
	btnClose	Text	Close

Figure 4-15   Contact Info application sample execution

```
189        private void btnClear_Click(object sender, System.EventArgs e)
190        {
191            txtFirstName.Text = "";
192            txtLastName.Text = "";
193            txtPhoneDigits.Text = "";
194            txtFullName.Text = "";
195            txtFormattedPhone.Text = "";
196            txtFirstName.Focus();
197        }
198
199        private void btnShow_Click(object sender, System.EventArgs e)
200        {
201            string tempName;
202            string firstName;
203            string lastName;
204            string phoneDigits;
205            string areaCode;
206            string exchange;
207            string number;
208            string fullName;
209            string formattedPhone;
210
211            // Get the input values from the form.
212
213            tempName = txtFirstName.Text;
214            firstName = tempName.Substring(0,1).ToUpper() +
                   tempName.Substring(1,tempName.Length-1).ToLower();
215            tempName = txtLastName.Text;
216            lastName = tempName.Substring(0,1).ToUpper() +
                   tempName.Substring(1,tempName.Length-1).ToLower();
217            phoneDigits = txtPhoneDigits.Text;
218
219            // Reformat the name and create the display message
220
221            fullName = firstName + " " + lastName;
222            areaCode = "(" + phoneDigits.Substring(0, 3) + ") ";
223            exchange = phoneDigits.Substring(3, 3) + "-";
224            number = phoneDigits.Substring(6, 4);
225            txtFullName.Text = fullName;
226            txtFormattedPhone.Text = areaCode + exchange + number;
227        }
228
229    }
230
```

Figure 4-16 Partial listing of Contact Info application

BONUS TOPICS

The "Essential Topics" section described several useful operators and methods, which are used throughout the remainder of this book. There are, however, many more operators, methods, and properties that you may need to use when writing a business application. This bonus section describes some of these useful operators and methods and also demonstrates their use in simple programs. The inclusion of these operators and methods, however, is simply for reference purposes. They can help you with your own application development projects. None of the core sections of this book require their use.

OTHER COMMON TASKS USING THE .NET FRAMEWORK CLASSES

As you learned from Chapter 1, the .NET Framework is the underlying library for all .NET programming languages. The "Essential Topics" section of this chapter presented the most commonly used arithmetic operators and methods for manipulating strings. This section discusses some of the less common, but handy, string methods and other classes.

Additional String Methods

You have already learned many practical string methods for use in programs that you write. This section describes additional string methods that can help you fine-tune applications that use strings.

LastIndexOf Method

Remember the `IndexOf` method? It allows you to locate a substring that occurs within another string. The `LastIndexOf` method is similar, but returns the location of the last match of the substring within the string. Assume that `myString` has the value "How much wood could a woodchuck chuck, if a woodchuck could chuck wood?" You know from the previous discussion that `myString.IndexOf("wood")` returns 9, but what does the expression `myString.LastIndexOf("wood")` return? If you look at the sample execution in Figure 4-17, you see that the answer is 67.

Just as the `IndexOf` method could be useful for determining if a filename and path entered by the user contained a drive letter, the `LastIndexOf` method could be useful for finding a file type by locating the last period (.) just before the extension suffix.

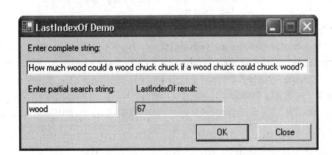

Figure 4-17   Sample execution of LastIndexOf Demo program

Insert Method

The "Essential Topics" section discussed string concatenation for joining multiple strings and the substring method for obtaining a portion of a string. The `Insert` method allows you to place a portion of a string inside another string at a specified position. Consider the following example:

```
1    myName = "Georgia Brown";
2    maidenName = "Wilson ";
3    spacePosition = myName.IndexOf(" ") + 1;
4    result = myName.Insert(spacePosition, maidenName);
```

After executing these statements, the value in **maidenName** is inserted between the first and last names in the original **myName** to yield the new value "Georgia Wilson Brown" now stored in **myName**. A variation of this example that allows the user to enter any name and maiden name is illustrated in Figure 4-18.

Figure 4-18 Sample execution of Insert Demo program

Remove Method

Instead of inserting a string inside another string, you might need to remove part of a string. The **Remove** method makes this possible. To use the **Remove** method, specify the position where the removal should begin and the total number of characters to be removed. For example, to revert to the original value in **myName**, you can apply the **Remove** method as follows:

```
myName.Remove(spacePosition, maidenName.Length);
```

Note how you have used a variable name and the **Length** method in the statement to decide how the substring is to be removed and from what location.

Trim Method

Trim allows you to remove all spaces that might be present at the beginning and ending of a string. For example, if the **string** user contained " Joey Davis ", user.Trim() would yield just the name **"Joey Davis"** without the leading and ending spaces. You might use **Trim** if you stored textual data provided by user in a file or database and later searched the file or database for this data. For example, if you stored the user value as originally entered with the extraneous spaces, and the user later entered his name as **"Joey Davis"**, looking up his data in the files, you would find no match. The search would fail because of the leading and trailing spaces surrounding the name. You could use **Trim** on the data after reading it from the data files, but then you would have unnecessarily wasted storage space in the data file. You might be better off applying **Trim** before storing the data, thus discarding the unnecessary spaces surrounding the name.

Replace Method

The **Replace** method is handy when you try to foolproof your programs by "fixing" typos introduced by the user's input. It allows you to replace all occurrences of one substring with another substring. For example, assume that **myString** has the value: "How much wood cood a wood chuck chuck if a wood chuck cood chuck wood?" Figure 4-19 illustrates how the program should look. To correct the misspelled "cood" to "could," use the following code:

```
myString.Replace("cood","could");
```

Figure 4-19 Sample execution of Replace Demo program

`Replace` is also useful when you know that the input supplied from the user is an abbreviation, but you wish to store the fully expanded data in the database. For example, if you know that a user is taking orders in Indianapolis and that's the most frequently used city, you might accept "indy" in the text box, and, if you find that as the city, simply use `Replace` to expand the input to "Indianapolis."

DateTime Manipulations

Often in business applications, you need to work with date and time information. The `DateTime` data type is useful for this purpose. You can define a `DateTime` variable (myDateTime) as follows:

```
DateTime myDateTime;
```

To assign a specific date and time to the variable, you can provide the year (yyyy), month number (MM), date (dd), hours (HH), minutes (mm), seconds (ss), and milliseconds (xx) using the general format shown in the code segment that follows. To assign the `DateTime` value for 2:45 p.m. on April 5, 2010, use the specific statement shown immediately after the general format.

```
myDateTime = new DateTime(yyyy, MM, dd, HH, mm, ss, xx);

myDateTime = new DateTime(2010, 4, 5, 14, 45, 0, 0);
```

If you only wanted to assign a date, you could use the assignment:

```
myDateTime = new DateTime(2010, 4, 5);
```

If the `DateTime` value is provided on a form in a text box named `txtUserDate`, you could use:

```
myDateTime = DateTime.Parse(txtUserDate.Text);
```

You might also want to have your program get the current date from the system. To store the current date in a variable named `today`, you should use the `Now DateTime` property as follows:

```
DateTime today;
today = DateTime.Now;
```

Displaying DateTime Information

When dealing with `DateTime` information, it is useful to be able to control how the information is displayed. Table 4-6 lists some of the standard formats used to display `DateTime` information.

Table 4-6 Standard DateTime patterns

Description	Pattern	ToString character	Specific pattern method
ShortDatePattern	MM/dd/yyyy	d	ToShortDateString
LongDatePattern	dddd, MMMM dd, yy	D	ToLongDateString
FullDateTimePattern	dddd, MMMM dd, YYYY HH:mm:ss	F	
General	MM/dd/yyyy HH:mm	g	
ShortTimePattern	HH:mm	t	ToShortTimeString
LongTimePattern	HH:mm:ss	T	ToLongTimeString

Keep in mind that the patterns are based on the regional settings, and therefore, if your settings are not US English, your dates will appear in a format appropriate to your settings. To display the date using a particular pattern, apply the **ToString** method to the **DateTime** variable, and supply the **ToString** character listed in Table 4-6. Alternatively, use the specific method listed in the last column of Table 4-6. For example, to display the variable **today** using the short date pattern, either of the following may be used:

```
txtDate.Text = today.ToString("d");
txtDate.Text = today.ToShortDateString();
```

To perform a quick test, create a form to display a given date using each of these patterns. Figure 4-20 shows the code for the **btnShow_Click** event, and Figure 4-21 shows a sample run in which the regional settings were for US English. On line 5, the **date/time** value of January 1, 2006, 9:35 a.m. is assigned through the argument list by providing the year, month number, date, hour, minute, second, and millisecond values in order. You could modify this program to allow the user to provide a **date** value in a text box and then display it using each of these patterns.

```
1    private void btnShow_Click(object sender, System.EventArgs e)
2    {
3        DateTime myDate;
4        string myDateString;
5        myDate = new DateTime(2006, 1,  1, 9, 35, 0, 0);
6        myDateString = myDate.ToString("d");
7        txtShortDate.Text = myDateString;
8        myDateString = myDate.ToString("D");
9        txtLongDate.Text = myDateString;
10       myDateString = myDate.ToString("F");
11       txtFullDate.Text = myDateString;
12       myDateString = myDate.ToString("g");
13       txtGeneral.Text = myDateString;
14       myDateString = myDate.ToString("t");
15       txtShortTime.Text = myDateString;
16       myDateString = myDate.ToString("T");
17       txtLongTime.Text = myDateString;
18   }
```

Figure 4-20 btnShow_Click code for DateTime Pattern application

Figure 4-21 Sample run of DateTime Pattern application

Retrieving and Manipulating DateTime Information

You may also find it useful to refer to individual pieces of the date and time information by using `DateTime` properties: `Year`, `Month`, `Date`, `DayOfWeek`, `DayOfYear`, `Hour`, `Minute`, `Second`, `Millisecond`, and `Now`. To demonstrate this, create a small application to ask the user for a special date. The program finds and displays both how many years have passed since that date and the day of week for the special date. Refer to Figure 4-22 to view a sample execution of this program.

Figure 4-22 Sample execution of DateTime Demo program

You need to define two `DateTime` variables, one to hold the special date and the other to hold the current date:

```
DateTime specialDate;
DateTime today;
```

You can parse the textual date entered by the user as a `DateTime` value and assign it to `specialDate`. To assign the current local date and time to the computer on which the application is being executed, you can use the `Now` property of the `DateTime` type using the syntax `DateTime.Now`:

```
specialDate = DateTime.Parse(txtSpecialDate.Text);
today = DateTime.Now;
```

To keep it simple, you can find the `yearsSince` by subtracting the `Year` property of both dates:

```
yearsSince = today.Year - specialDate.Year;
```

Finally, to find the day of the week of the special date, you can use the `DayOfWeek` property. If you assign it to a `string` variable, you need to convert it to a `string`:

```
specialDay = specialDate.DayOfWeek.ToString();
```

Now all that remains is to display the results in their corresponding text boxes. When displaying a date value, you can use several methods to convert the date in a variety of formats. For example, if you want to see only the long date for the current date, use:

```
txtToday.Text = today.ToLongDateString();
```

which displays the date as "Monday, May 24, 2005" (assuming that today is 5/24/2005.)

In addition to capturing parts of a date, you might find it useful to manipulate a date or parts of a date. Table 4-7 lists some useful `DateTime` methods that allow you to change the date using different increments, figure out if a given year is a leap year, and figure out the number of days in a given month and year. You may wish to refer to the Help documentation to view examples of these and other `DateTime` methods and properties.

Table 4-7   Other useful DateTime methods

Method	Description	Example
AddDays	Adds the given number of days to the date	myDate.AddDays(7);
AddHours	Adds the given number of hours to the time	myDate.AddHours(3);
AddMinutes	Adds the given number of minutes to the time	myDate.AddMinutes(35);
AddMonths	Adds the given number of months to the date	myDate.AddMonths(2);
AddYears	Adds the given number of years to the date	myDate.AddYears(10);
DaysInMonth	Returns the number of days in the given month and year	x = myDate.DaysInMonth(2004, 9);
IsLeapYear	Returns whether the given year is a leap year	if (myDate.IsLeapYear()) {

USING THE MATH CLASS

The `Math` class provides constants and methods for trigonometric, logarithmic, and other common mathematical functions. Let's first consider a useful mathematical constant.

Math.PI (π)

You might recall from geometry that π is an important constant used in calculating areas and circumferences of circles, as well as inner angles of other geometric shapes. If you needed to modify the carpet cost program in Chapter 2 to compute the area of a circular room in an old Victorian home, you would need to reference the `Math` class's `PI` property whose value is 3.14159265358979323846. Sample code for finding the area of a circle (πr^2) follows:

```
area = Math.PI * radius * radius;
```

METHODS

Although **Math.PI** is needed on occasion, the greater benefit from the **Math** class lies in an abundance of other useful math methods. Table 4-8 lists a select sampling of these methods, which are sometimes useful when writing business applications. Some of the bonus exercises use these methods as well.

After reviewing each method in Table 4-8, try to create an application that accepts two numbers from the user and then performs all the math operations in Table 4-8 using the values entered by the user. All answers should be stored in variables and then converted to strings for display in separate text boxes. You may wish to refer to the sample execution in Figure 4-23 for help in designing the user interface and checking the behavior of the application.

Table 4-8　Select Sampling of Useful Math Class Methods

Mathematical task	Description	C# notation
Absolute value	Returns the magnitude of the given decimal	`Math.Abs(number)`
Minimum	Returns the smaller of two decimal numbers	`Math.Min(number1, number2)`
Maximum	Returns the larger of two decimal numbers	`Math.Max(number1, number2)`
Square root	Returns the square root of the given double number	`Math.Sqrt(number)`
Ceiling	Returns the smallest whole number greater than or equal to the given number	`Math.Ceiling(number)`
Floor	Returns the largest whole number less than or equal to the given number	`Math.Floor(number)`
Round	Returns the whole number nearest the given decimal number	`Math.Round(number)`
Round	Returns a value nearest the given decimal number and rounded to the nearest decimal position indicated by the second argument	`Math.Round(number, decimalPosition)`
Power	Returns the result of the number raised to the specified power	`Math.Pow(number,power)`

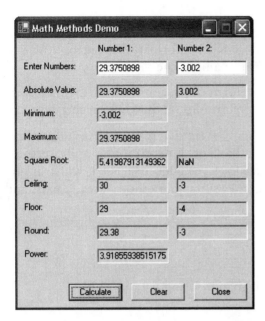

Figure 4-23 Sample execution of Math Methods Demo program

You might be wondering about the **"NaN"** answer for the square root of –3.002. Recall from your algebra classes that the square root of a negative number is undefined. If you attempt to perform such an operation in your program, a result of **"NaN"**, which literally translates to "not a number," is displayed.

SUMMARY

Essential Topics

- Most business problems require manipulating numeric and string data. This chapter showed you how to write C# programs that obtained numeric and string data from the user, manipulated the data using the appropriate operators and methods to obtain the desired results, and then displayed the results to the user.

- The basic binary math operators include addition (+), subtraction (-), multiplication (*), division (/), and modulus (%). The basic unary operators include increment (++) and decrement (--). These unary operators may be used in prefix or postfix notation, with a subtle difference.

- When performing binary operations, the operands should be of the same type. In some cases, implicit type conversion may allow data widening to take place. An attempt to convert a larger type to a smaller type is called data narrowing and is not allowed.

- Explicit type casting may be performed using the cast operator—a data type name in parentheses that precedes an operand.

- Using a single expression with many operators requires knowing the precedence rules that dictate the order by which mathematical operations are performed. The unary operators have the highest precedence, followed by multiplication, division, and modulus, followed by addition and subtraction. Assignments are performed last. Parentheses should be used to enhance the meaning of a complex expression as well as to override precedence rules when necessary.

- The concatenate (+) operator or **Concat** method may be used to join strings end to end. Additional methods allow you to locate the position of a substring in a string, extract a portion of a string, find the number of characters in a string, replace all occurrences of one substring in a string with another substring, and force all alphabetic characters to be uppercase or lowercase.

Bonus Topics

❑ DateTime methods allow you to store date and/or time information, control how dates are displayed, and retrieve specific parts of a date (for example, the year or month).

❑ Additional methods exist in the **Math** class to perform other common mathematical operations such as absolute value, rounding, ceiling, floor, minimum, maximum, and exponentiation.

You should note that this chapter has barely touched the surface regarding useful methods available through the .NET Framework. When you embark on a new programming project, if you have to perform a mathematical operation that has not yet been discussed, we strongly suggest you use VS.NET's dynamic help to determine whether suitable methods already exist and can be used to simplify your programming tasks.

KEY TERMS

Define each of the following terms, as it relates to manipulating data in objects:

Essential Terms

❑ addition operator
❑ assignment operators
❑ associativity
❑ binary operations
❑ binary operator
❑ casting
❑ cast operator
❑ concatenation
❑ data narrowing
❑ data widening
❑ division operator
❑ explicit type conversion
❑ explicit casting
❑ expression
❑ implicit type conversion
❑ **IndexOf** method
❑ left-associative
❑ **length** method
❑ mathematical expression
❑ modulus operator
❑ multiplication operator
❑ operand
❑ operator
❑ operator precedence
❑ overflow error
❑ overriding with parentheses
❑ precedence
❑ prefix decrement expression
❑ prefix increment expression

❑ postfix decrement expression
❑ postfix increment expression
❑ right-associative
❑ silent cast
❑ **substring** method
❑ subtraction operator
❑ **ToLower** method
❑ **ToString** method
❑ **ToUpper** method
❑ unary operator
❑ underflow error

Bonus Terms

❑ **Abs** method
❑ **Ceiling** method
❑ **DateTime** method
❑ **Floor** method
❑ **Insert** method
❑ **LastIndexOf** method
❑ **Max** method
❑ **Min** method
❑ **Now** property
❑ **PI** property
❑ **Pow** method
❑ **Remove** method
❑ **Replace** method
❑ **Round** method
❑ **Sqrt** method
❑ **Trim** method

REVIEW QUESTIONS

Essential Questions

1. The C# statement that follows is used to assign the product of `taxRate` and `subTotal` to `totalBill` (all data types are decimal). True or false?

   ```
   totalBill = taxRate × subTotal;
   ```

2. The modulus operator is used to find the remainder of an integer division. True or false?

3. If you have two `int` variables in which `nbr1` is 10 and `nbr2` is 6, then `nbr1/nbr2` yields 1.67. True or false?

4. True or false? The increment unary operator is equivalent to adding one to the operand and storing the result back in the operand. For example,

   ```
   nbrChairs++;
   ```

   is equivalent to

   ```
   nbrChairs = nbrChairs + 1;
   ```

5. True or false? To find the average pay of three employees, the formula:

   $$\frac{pay1 + pay2 + pay3}{3}$$

   should be written as the C# statement:

   ```
   averagePay = pay1 + pay2 + pay3 / 3;
   ```

6. True or false? Assuming that `total` contains the base cost of all purchases (100.00) and `taxRate` is the sales tax rate (0.06), the following C# statements places the total with tax inside the variable `total`:

   ```
   taxRate++;
   total *= taxRate;
   ```

7. When multiplying `taxRate` (a **double**) by `totalBill` (a **decimal**), the resulting product is converted to a **double-decimal** to preserve the precision of the answer. True or false?

8. Assuming that myName contains the string `"Mary Jane Williams"` and **middle** contains the string `"jane"`, then `myName.IndexOf(middle)` will return 0. True or false?

9. Assuming that `myName` contains the **string** `"Mary Jane"`, then `myName.Length` will return 9. True or false?

10. The `ToUpper` method is recommended when comparing user-provided input to data previously stored in a database or file to account for any variations in case. True or false?

11. A binary expression consists of two _____ and a(n) _____ between them that defines the function to be performed.

12. The _____ symbol denotes the modulus (or remainder) operation.

13. The prefix increment operator provides a shortcut notation for writing _____.

14. To perform explicit type casting the _____ operator is used.

15. Of the operators +, −, *, /, %, and ++, the _____ has the highest precedence.

16. When the division operator is applied to integer data types, what is the type of the result? What else can be said about the accuracy of the answer when dividing integers?

4

17. Assume that a = 5, b = 7, c = 0.5, and d = −2. Evaluate the expression below using precedence rules:

    a + d * c − b * d / c % 2

18. What is the difference between the prefix and postfix decrement operator?

19. Assume that `nbr` is an integer, `rate` is a **double**, and answer is a **decimal**. Rewrite the statement that follows to perform explicit type casting:

    ```
    answer = nbr * rate;
    ```

20. What are the two alternatives for concatenating strings?

Bonus Questions

1. The `StrDelete` **string** method deletes part of a string. True or false?

2. The `Add` **string** method places a string inside another string. True or false?

3. The `LastIndexOf` **string** method returns the location of the last occurrence of a substring inside another string. True or false?

4. The `Replace` **string** method replaces all occurrences of one substring with another substring inside another string. True or false?

5. The `DateTime.Now` property obtains the current time, whereas the `DateTime.Today` property obtains the current date. True or false?

6. The _____ method places one string inside another string.

7. The _____ property of the `DateTime` type returns the current local date and time on the computer.

8. The _____ method of the `Math` class returns the smallest whole number greater than or equal to the given number.

9. Write statements to define a variable named `today` and assign it the current date.

10. Write an expression to round the value in the double variable `grandTotal` to the fourth decimal position. (The number 123.456789 should be rounded to 123.4568.)

Programming Exercises

Essential Exercises

1. Write a C# program that collects the number of each type of coin that the user has and then finds and displays the total amount of money in coins.

> Refer to the discussion in the "Operator Precedence" section.

2. Write a C# program that can be used as a simple calculator to find and display the square or cube of a given number.

> 4^2 is the same as 4*4 and 5^3 is the same as 5*5*5.

3. Write a C# phone formatter program to obtain the area code, exchange, and four-digit number in separate text boxes. Then, concatenate and format the strings so that the phone number is displayed in the format used in the United States (xxx) xxx-xxxx or the International format +1.xxx.xxx.xxxx.

4. Write a C# program to determine if a phone number provided in the format (xxx) xxx-xxxx is a local call on the user's cell phone. For the sake of simplicity, assume that the user also provides his area code and if it matches the area code of the phone number, it is a local call. Otherwise, it is long distance.

5. Write a C# program that accepts a filename with path in a single text box and displays whether the file can be found on the computer's hard drive (c:\file, C:\file), floppy drive (a:\file or A:\file), or is located elsewhere.

Use the `IndexOf` method to locate the colon; the Substring method to get the character before the colon for the drive letter; and the `ToUpper` method to compare the letter against A, C, or anything else to determine whether the file is on a floppy disk, the hard drive, or elsewhere.

Bonus Exercises

6. Write a C# program that accepts a filename and path in a single text box and displays the file type based upon the extension of the filename.

7. Write a C# program that collects a paragraph of text from the user and filters it so that all references to "dead," "hate," and "kick" are replaced with the alternate text provided in another text box.

Your teacher may assign a different set of outlawed words to be filtered and a specific replacement string.

8. Write a C# program that obtains a product's name and expiration date and then finds and displays the number of weeks until it expires.

tip▶ When you subtract two dates, the result is a `TimeSpan` data type. The `TimeSpan`'s `TotalDays` property will yield the number of days (positive or negative) between two dates. Because every week has exactly seven days, you can compute the number of weeks (past or future) between the current date and the expiration date.

9. Revise the program you created in Chapter 2 to calculate the area of a circular room in an old, Victorian house (using the radius of the circular room rather than the length and width of a rectangular room), and display the cost to carpet the room. Recall that the area of a circle is (πr^2).

10. Write a C# program to help you decide which route to take. Route 1 requires traveling on two perpendicular interstates (a and b) at a speed of 65 miles per hour. Route 2 requires traveling on a third county road, c, (which forms a right triangle with a and b) at a speed of 55 miles per hour. The user provides the distance of a and b. Your program should compute the distance c. It should also compute the time required to travel route 1 on the interstate and route 2 on the county road. Minimally, the two times should be displayed. Ideally, the faster route number should be displayed.

Recall that the sum of the squares of the two sides of a right triangle is equal to the square of the hypotenuse: $a^2 + b^2 = c^2$.

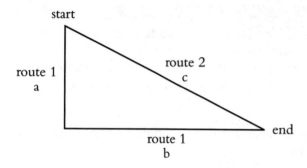

5

CHANGING THE PROGRAM FLOW WITH DECISIONS

In the Essentials section you will learn:

♦ What Boolean expressions are and how they are evaluated

♦ How to use relational operators to compare values

♦ How the time portion of a **DateTime** affects comparisons

♦ How to perform case-sensitive string compares

♦ How **string** values are compared

♦ How to use the **string.Compare** method to perform a case-insensitive compare

♦ What conditional logical operators are and how to use them to form complex Boolean expressions

♦ The syntax for several forms of decision (if) statements

♦ A strategy for robust data validation

♦ How to code six types of data validation statements

In the Bonus section you will learn:

♦ How to code a case structure using **switch** statements

♦ Alternative coding styles of decision statements

♦ Alternatives to using early returns

♦ How to use number styles for improved data entry

All but the very simplest computer programs require many levels of decisions. The software that makes up an information system models the processing steps an organization uses when it conducts business, and these steps cannot be automated by just a few sequential calculation statements. Even the simple Carpet Cost application presented in Chapter 2 used decision statements to validate input data. (If the input values contain zero or a negative number, an error message is displayed.) Thus, the decision statement is one of the key features of a programming language that enables you to write powerful applications.

Essential Topics

When used in decision statements, Boolean expressions exhibit their real value. Because you can't code a decision without a Boolean expression, Boolean expressions are covered first in this chapter. After you understand Boolean expressions, you will find writing decision statements relatively easy. A good way to practice coding decision statements is by writing data validation code. Proper data validation makes your applications more usable.

Boolean Expressions

The core of a decision statement is the Boolean expression. In earlier chapters, you learned about arithmetic expressions. An arithmetic expression typically consists of two operands separated by an arithmetic operator. When executed, the arithmetic expression is evaluated to a single arithmetic value and then an operation is performed with that value, such as storing it in a variable.

For example, in the statement:

```
squareFeet = lengthInFeet * widthInFeet;
```

the arithmetic expression `lengthInFeet * widthInFeet` is evaluated by multiplying the contents of the variable `lengthInFeet` by the contents of the variable `widthInFeet`, and the resulting arithmetic value is stored in the variable `squareFeet`.

Boolean expressions work in a similar manner. Instead of operands being separated by arithmetic operators, however, the operands in Boolean expressions are separated by **relational operators**. (Relational operators are also sometimes called **comparison operators**). Instead of evaluating to a numeric value, however, Boolean expressions yield a Boolean data type result, which must be either **true** or **false**, as discussed in Chapter 3.

For example, in the statements:

```
bool inStock;
inStock = quantityOnHand > 0;
```

the Boolean expression `quantityOnHand > 0` is evaluated by comparing the contents of the variable `quantityOnHand` to zero. If the value of `quantityOnHand` is greater than zero, the value **true** is stored in the variable `inStock`. If the value of `quantityOnHand` is not greater than zero (that is, less than or equal to zero), the value **false** is stored in the variable `inStock`.

The operands in Boolean expressions can be variables (`quantityOnHand`) and constants (`0`) (as shown in the previous examples), but they may also be properties of an object, a return value from a method, and even other Boolean expressions. Operands in Boolean expressions must also be of compatible data types. You can compare numbers to other numbers, even if they don't have the same type specifier. For example, you can compare the value of a **double** to the value of an **int**. You cannot, however, directly compare a value type to a reference type. For example, attempting to compare a **double** to a **string** results in a compile error.

Comparing Numbers

Just as C# uses symbols for arithmetic operators, C# also uses symbols for *relational operators*. In Chapter 3, you learned that C# has many types of data items: numbers, **DateTime**s, Booleans, object references, and strings. When comparing operands that are numbers, the relational operators behave just as you might guess. Comparing **DateTime**s, Booleans, object references, and strings is a little messier, and therefore that discussion is deferred until later in this chapter.

Greater Than Operator (>)

The *greater than* operator is represented by the greater than symbol (>). When this symbol is placed between two operands, the expression is evaluated as **true** if the value of the operand on the left side of the relational operator is greater than the value of the operand on the right of the relational operator. The expression evaluates to **false** if the value of the operand on the left side of the relational operator is less than, or equal to, the value of the operand on the right side of the relational operator. For example, the relational expression 2 > 5 evaluates to **false**.

Less Than Operator (<)

The *less than* operator is represented by the less than symbol (<). Less than works much like greater than, except that the expression is evaluated as **true** if the value of the operand on the left of the relational operator is less than the value of the operand on the right side of the expression. The result is **false** if the value of the operand on the left side of the relational operator is greater than, or equal to, the value of the operand on the right side of the expression. For example, the relational expression 5 < 10 evaluates to **true**.

Greater Than Or Equal To Operator (>=)

The *greater than or equal to* operator uses the greater than symbol (>) followed by the equal symbol (=) with no spaces between. When these symbols are combined and placed between two operands, the expression is evaluated as **true** if the value of the operand on the left side of the relational expression is greater than, or equal to, the value of the operand on the right side of the expression. The expression is **false** if the value of the operand on the left side of the relational expression is less than the value of the operand on the right side of the expression. For example, the expression 3 >= 5 evaluates to **false**, whereas 3 >= 3 is **true**.

Less Than Or Equal To Operator (<=)

The *less than or equal to* operator is the less than symbol (<) followed by the equal symbol (=) with no spaces between. It behaves in a manner similar to the (>=) symbol, except the expression is evaluated as **true** if the value of the operand on the left of the relational expression is less than, or equal to, the value of the operand on the right. The expression evaluates to **false** if the value of the operand on the left side of the expression is greater than the value of the operand on the right of the expression. For example, 3 <= 5 evaluates to **true**, but 5 <= 5 also evaluates to **true**.

Equal To Operator (==)

You might guess that the *equal to* relational operator is the equal (=) sign, and in some programming languages it is. However, because the equal sign symbol is already used to indicate an assignment operation, C# uses two consecutive equal signs (==) for the *equal to* relational operator. (This is also the case for other programming languages, such as C++ and Java, which also have syntax derived from the C programming language.) If the values of both operands are the same, the relational expression is evaluated as **true**. If the values of the operands in the relational expression are not identical, the expression is **false**. For example, 3 == 3 evaluates to **true**, 3 == 5 evaluates to **false**, but 3 = 5 results in a compile error. (Note that the last expression uses a single equal sign.)

Not Equal To Operator (!=)

The *not equal to* operator is the exclamation point symbol (!) followed by the equal symbol (=) with no spaces between. If both operands *do not* have the same value, the expression is evaluated as **true.** The expression is **false** if both operands *do* have the same value. For example, 3 != 3 evaluates to **false**, and 3 != 5 evaluates to **true**.

Operator Precedence

In Chapter 4, you learned that operator precedence exists when evaluating expressions containing multiple arithmetic operators. For example, multiplication is evaluated before addition because multiplication has a higher precedence. These precedence rules also include the relational operators so that you can determine how an expression is evaluated if the expression contains both arithmetic and relational operators. Table 5-1 shows the precedence table from Chapter 4 with new additions for the relational operators listed in rows 4 through 8.

Table 5-1   Precedence of arithmetic and relational operators

Increment and Decrement	++	--	
Multiplication, Division, Modulus	*	/	%
Addition, Subtraction	+	-	
Equal To (Equality)	==		
Not Equal To (Inequality)	!=		
Less Than, Greater Than	<	>	
Greater Than or Equal To	>=		
Less Than or Equal To	<=		

As with arithmetic expressions, we suggest that you use parentheses to control and clarify how an expression is evaluated, as shown in Table 5-2. In an attempt to make the evaluation more clear, we have shown only numeric constants in Table 5-2. In normal programming situations, expressions containing only numeric constants are usually not coded into a program. (You wouldn't need such constant expressions, because you could evaluate their state at the time you were writing the code.) Instead, arithmetic and relational expressions normally contain a mix of constants, variables, property values, and return values from methods.

Table 5-2   Examples of relational expressions

Expression	Evaluates to
5 < 10	true
5 + 5 < 10	false
5 + 5 < 10 * 2	true
5 + 5 * 2 < 10 * 2	true
(5 + 5) * 2 < 10 * 2	false
((5 + 5) * 2) == (10 * 2)	true

Comparing Non-Numbers

The following sections describe how the relational operators can be used to compare non-number data types.

Comparing Booleans

Like the number data types, Booleans are value types. Unlike numbers, however, a **bool** can have only one of two possible values—**true** or **false**. Because Booleans can have only one of two values, writing code that uses the relational operators (<), (>), (<=), and (>=) with Booleans doesn't make sense, and therefore C# doesn't allow it. Instead, Boolean variables are compared to each other using only the (==) and (!=) operators. As you can see from Table 5-3, if both operands have a value of **true**, the expression evaluates to **true**. If both operands have a value of **false**, the expression evaluates to **true**. Otherwise, the expression evaluates to **false**.

Table 5-3   Comparing Booleans

A	B	A == B	A != B
true	true	true	false
true	false	false	true
false	true	false	true
false	false	true	false

It is important to note that when comparing Boolean values using the *equal to* operator, programmers commonly make the mistake of typing the assignment operator (=) rather than the *equal to* operator (==). If you make this mistake in a Boolean expression and the operands are not Boolean operands, you'll get a compile error because the compiler expects the result of the expression to be a Boolean value. However, if you type the expression using Boolean operands, you don't get a compile error, and this kind of error can be very difficult to catch. Consider this example:

```
1    bool operand1;
2    bool operand2;
3    bool result1;
4    bool result2;
5
6    operand1 = false;
7    operand2 = true;
8    result1 = (operand1 == operand2);
9    result2 = (operand1 = operand2);
```

If you ran this code, what would you guess the values for **result1** and **result2** are? The value of **result1** is obviously **false** because the values of **operand1** and **operand2** are not equal. However, would you believe the value of **result2** is actually **true**? It is, but why? **Result2** has a value of **true** because the expression in line 9 isn't a Boolean expression. Instead, the **true** value of **operand2** is *assigned* into the value **operand1**. The value of **operand1** is then assigned to **result2**. Because **operand2** is **true** and that value is then assigned into **operand1**, **result2** must also be assigned the value of **true**. This forest-for-the-trees kind of problem can be difficult to find because your mind reads what it wants to see, not necessarily what is actually in the expression.

You begin using Boolean expressions in decision statements later in this chapter. If your program's logic doesn't execute as you think it should, make sure to check that you are using the equal to operator (==) in the Boolean expressions and not the assignment operator (=).

Comparing Dates and Times

In Chapter 3, you learned that the .NET Framework contains the **DateTime** data type you can use to hold values that represent dates, times, or both a date and time. As with the numeric types, you can use the (<), (>), (<=), or (>=) operators to compare the value of **DateTime**s. The relational operators work just as you might expect—a recent date is greater than an older date. Consider this example:

```
1    DateTime myBirthDate;
2    DateTime mySistersBirthDate;
3    DateTime myDadsBirthDate;
4
5    myBirthDate = DateTime.Parse("1981-12-3");
6    mySistersBirthDate = DateTime.Parse("1978-12-19");
7    myDadsBirthDate = DateTime.Parse("1954-11-17");
```

Lines 1 through 3 define three variables of type **DateTime**. Lines 5 through 7 use the **DateTime.Parse** method to give year, month, and day values to the three variables. You can now compare two dates using relational operators, as shown in Table 5-4.

Table 5-4 Comparing dates that have no times

myBirthDate < DateTime.Now	evaluates to **true**
myBirthDate > mySistersBirthDate	evaluates to **true**
myDadsBirthDate < mySistersBirthDate	evaluates to **true**
myBirthDate == myDadsBirthDate	evaluates to **false**
myBirthDate == DateTime.Parse("Dec 3, 1981");	evaluates to **true**

The preceding examples are relatively straightforward because all the values contain dates only. What happens when you compare them with date and time objects? Let's try some examples.

```
1    DateTime partyStartTime;
2    DateTime partyEndTime;
3    DateTime pizzaDeliveryTime;
4
5    partyStartTime = DateTime.Parse("Friday, July 16, 2004 8:00 PM");
6    partyEndTime = DateTime.Parse("Saturday, July 17, 2004 1:00 AM");
7    pizzaDeliveryTime = DateTime.Parse("Friday, July 16");
```

Lines 1 through 3 define three variables of type **DateTime**. Lines 5 through 7 use the **Parse** method to initialize their values. Note that **pizzaDeliveryTime** on line 7 is initialized to a date value only. Just as before, you can compare the variables using the normal comparison operators, as shown in Table 5-5.

Table 5-5 Comparing dates that include times

partyStartTime < partyEndTime	evaluates to **true**
partyEndTime > partyStartTime	evaluates to **true**
partyEndTime == partyStartTime	evaluates to **false**

What happens if you compare a **DateTime** value that has only date information to one that contains date and time values? The expression **pizzaDeliveryTime > partyStartTime** evaluates to **false** because a **DateTime** object with no time values is less than a **DateTime** object with time values, even if they have the same year, month, and day values. Time causes the comparison to yield a larger comparison value.

Comparing Reference Types

If you compare one object reference variable to another, you are checking that those variables refer to the same object—not checking that the objects have the same value. (Recall from Chapter 3 that the value of a reference variable is always a memory address.) As with Booleans, using the relational operators (<), (>), (<=), or (>=) doesn't make sense with object references, and C# gives a compile error if you try comparisons using these relational operators with reference types. You can, however, use the (==) and (!=) operators with reference types. In such a comparison, always remember that you are checking to see if those variables refer to the same object (that is, the same memory address). You are not comparing them to see if their values are logically equal.

Consider the following example:

```
1    clsPerson mySister;
2    clsPerson myMom;
3    clsPerson myFriend;
4
5    mySister = new clsPerson();
6    myMom = new clsPerson();
7    myFriend = mySister;
```

As shown in Figure 5-1, only two **Person** objects are created even though there are three reference variables of type **clsPerson**. Lines 5 and 6 create new **clsPerson** objects, but line 7 just copies a reference variable named **mySister** into **myFriend**. A relational expression such as **mySister == myFriend** evaluates to **true** because both variables refer to the same object. An expression such as **mySister != myMom** evaluates to **true** because the two variables contain references to two separate and distinct person objects.

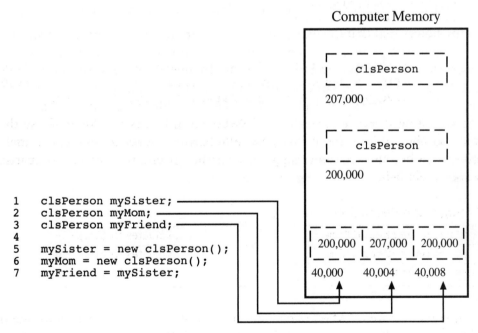

Figure 5-1 Comparing object references

The need to compare object references to each other is rather uncommon. However, because the C# syntax allows comparison of reference variables and such comparisons do not generate compile errors, they can be a source of bugs if you aren't careful.

Comparing Strings

Recall from Chapter 3 that a variable of type **string** is actually an object reference and not a value type like **int** or **decimal**. If you define two variables like this:

```
string momsName = "Janet";
string dadsName = "Keith";
```

the variable **momsName** doesn't actually contain the characters for the name **"Janet"** and the variable **dadsName** doesn't actually contain the characters for the name **"Keith"**. Rather, these variables contain references, or memory addresses, that indicate where the **string** objects were created in memory, and those **string** objects are what contain the characters. If you try to compare a **string** object reference to another object reference using the (<), (>), (<=), or (>=) operators, you receive a compile error because C# doesn't allow you to compare object references in this way.

Although you can't use the (<), (>), (<=), or (>=) operators to compare the value of **string** objects, you can use the (==) and (!=) operators. Consider this example:

```
1    string mySistersName;
2    string myMomsName;
3    string myFriendsName;
4
5    mySistersName = "Jodi";
6    myMomsName = "Janet";
7    myFriendsName = "Jodi";
```

Given the code in this example, it should be obvious that **mySistersName != myMomsName** evaluates to **true** and **myMomsName == myFriendsName** evaluates to **false**, because the variables being compared contain references to two different **string** objects.

What isn't obvious, however, is that the expression **mySistersName == myFriendsName** evaluates to **true.** As with the previous examples, this expression contains two variables that appear to have references to two different **string** objects. In reality, because the code creates two **string** variables that contain the same set of characters, C# creates only one **string** object containing the characters **"Jodi"** and places the memory address of that **string** object into both **mySistersName** and **myFriendsName,** as shown in Figure 5-2. So, when you compare **string** variables to see if they are equal, you are comparing the object references, but because the two variables reference the same **string** object if they have the same set of characters, the comparison works as if it were comparing the characters.

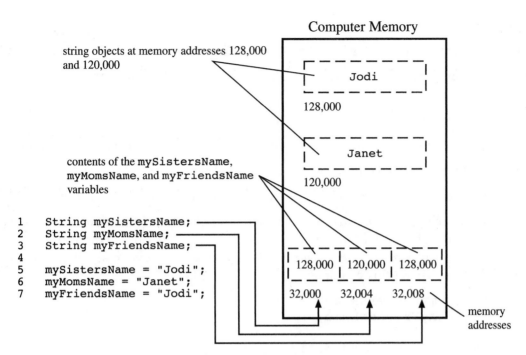

Computer Memory

string objects at memory addresses 128,000 and 120,000

Jodi

128,000

Janet

120,000

contents of the mySistersName, myMomsName, and myFriendsName variables

```
1   String mySistersName;
2   String myMomsName;
3   String myFriendsName;
4
5   mySistersName = "Jodi";
6   myMomsName = "Janet";
7   myFriendsName = "Jodi";
```

| 128,000 | 120,000 | 128,000 |

32,000   32,004   32,008

memory addresses

Figure 5-2 Comparing string object references

If you then execute a statement like:

```
myFriendsName = "Jesi";
```

C# creates a new **string** object containing the characters **"Jesi"** and changes the reference in **myFriendsName** to have the address of this new **string** object.

Sometimes you may need to check if one string is logically greater than another. Comparing strings this way is needed when sorting a list of text into alphabetical order, or validating that a string input value is within an acceptable range. For example, if you need to be sure an input value is numeric, you might check each character to make sure it is **>= "0"** and **<= "9"**. As mentioned earlier, you can't use the (**<**), (**>**), (**<=**) or (**>=**) operators to compare the value of **string** objects. Instead, you can use the **string** class's **Compare** method.

The **Compare** method compares the value of one **string** object to the value of another **string** object. **Compare** returns an integer value that indicates if one string is logically less than, equal to, or greater than the value of the other. If **Compare** returns the value zero, the two strings are equal to each other. If **Compare** returns a value greater than zero, the first string is logically greater than the second string. Finally, if **Compare** returns a value less than zero, the first string is logically less than the second string. Let's look at some examples.

Assume that the following code is executed:

```
1   string myGrade;
2   string excellentGrade;
3   string goodGrade;
4   string averageGrade;
5
6   myGrade = "B";
7   excellentGrade = "A";
8   goodGrade = "B";
9   averageGrade = "C";
```

The expression:

```
string.Compare(myGrade, excellentGrade)
```

evaluates to a value greater than zero (normally a value of 1) because **"B"** is greater than **"A"**. The expression:

```
string.Compare(myGrade, goodGrade)
```

evaluates to zero because both arguments evaluate to **"B"** in the preceding expression, and

```
string.Compare(myGrade, averageGrade)
```

evaluates to a value less than zero (normally a value of –1) because **"B"** is less than **"C"**.

When comparing strings of more than one character, C# compares them character by character, moving from left to right until a difference is found. Also note that the **Compare** method examples as shown perform a *case-sensitive compare*. This means that lowercase letters do not equal uppercase characters. Given this example:

```
1    string mySistersName;
2    string myFriendsName;
3
4    mySistersName = "Jodi";
5    myFriendsName = "jodi";
```

the expression

```
string.Compare(mySistersName, myFriendsName)
```

is not evaluated to a value of zero because the two string values aren't equal. In fact, the expression is evaluated to a value greater than zero because, by default, uppercase characters are greater than lowercase characters. So **"Jodi"** is greater than **"jodi"**. If you are trying to check for the equality of two strings, and you want to do a **case-insensitive compare** (that is, you don't care about case), the **Compare** method allows you to pass a **true** Boolean as a third argument to tell the **Compare** method to ignore the case of the characters when comparing them. So the expression:

```
string.Compare(mySistersName, myFriendsName, true)
```

evaluates to zero.

What happens when you compare two strings of unequal length? For example, the expression:

```
string.Compare("Bobby", "Bob")
```

evaluates to 1, indicating that **"Bobby"** is greater than **"Bob"**. If the two strings compared are equal to the end of the shorter string, and the other string has characters remaining, then the longer string is considered greater.

Rule for Comparing Characters

When comparing characters, how do you know which characters are greater than or less than other characters? A quick rule of thumb to remember is:

special characters < **"0"** < **"9"** < **"a"** < **"z"** < **"A"** < **"Z"**

where special characters are periods, semicolons, commas, and so on.

You should know that this is the default for comparing characters. The way strings are compared can actually be changed using the **System.Globalization.CompareOptions** class.

String Compare Example

To see for yourself how strings are compared, create a small test application. The user interface is shown in Figure 5-3. The application accepts two strings as input and compares them using the `string.Compare` method. The result is shown in a third text box. Create the test application using the same steps you've used in previous chapters. The source code for the `btnCompare_Click` event is shown in Figure 5-4.

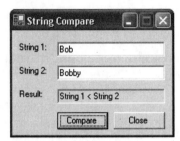

Figure 5-3   Sample run of the String Compare program

```
1    private void btnCompare_Click(object sender, System.EventArgs e)
2    {
3        string string1;
4        string string2;
5        int result;
6
7        // Get the input values.
8
9        string1 = txtString1.Text;
10       string2 = txtString2.Text;
11
12       // Do a case-sensitive compare.
13
14       result = string.Compare(string1, string2);
15
16       // Display the results to the user.
17
18       if (result == 0)
19       {
20           txtResult.Text = "String 1 equals String 2";
21       }
22       else if (result < 0)
23       {
24           txtResult.Text = "String 1 < String 2";
25       }
26       else
27       {
28           txtResult.Text = "String 1 > String 2";
29       }
30   }
```

Figure 5-4   Source code for comparing two strings

Note that the statement on line 14 performs a case-sensitive compare. You should also test the program by changing line 14 to:

```
14        result = string.Compare(string1, string2, true);
```

to compare the input strings using a case-insensitive compare.

Conditional Logical Operators

Often, you need to code a decision that involves more than one simple condition. For example, you can eat pizza *if* you attend the party *and* the pizza is delivered after you arrive.

Boolean expressions can be combined with other Boolean expressions using **conditional logical operators** to create a new, more complex, Boolean expression.

Conditional *Logical And* Operator (&&)

When two Boolean expressions are combined with the conditional *logical And* operator (written as two ampersands, &&), it forms a new Boolean expression that is evaluated to **true** *only if both* the original expressions evaluate to **true**. If either Boolean expression is **false**, the complex expression evaluates to **false**. Table 5-6 summarizes the various combinations involving the (&&) operator.

Table 5-6   *And* truth table

exp1	exp2	exp1 && exp2
true	true	true
true	false	false
false	true	false
false	false	false

For example, consider the following complex expression:

```
6 < 20 && "A" < "C"
```

has two expressions: 6 < 20 and "A" < "C". Obviously, 6 is less than 20, so that expression is **true**. You already know that the "A" is less than "C", so that expression is also **true**. You can then substitute these comparison results as:

```
true && true
```

Because both expressions evaluated to **true**, the *And* truth table, Table 5-6, shows that the resulting expression must also be **true**. If you change the two expressions to:

```
6 > 20 && "A" < "C"
```

the comparison evaluates to:

```
false && true
```

Because one expression evaluated as **false**, the overall result is **false** even though the second expression remains **true**. (See the *And* truth table, Table 5-6.)

Some additional sample complex expressions include those shown in Table 5-7:

Table 5-7   Sample complex expressions using (&&)

`5 < 10 && "B" < "C"`	evaluates to **true**
`5 > 10 && "B" < "C"`	evaluates to **false**
`5 < 10 && "B" > "C"`	evaluates to **false**
`5 > 10 && "B" > "C"`	evaluates to **false**

Conditional *Logical Or* Operator (||)

Two Boolean expressions that are combined with the conditional *logical Or* operator (written as two vertical bars, ||) form a new Boolean expression that is evaluated to **true** if *either or both* of the original expressions evaluate to **true**. Only when both expressions in the complex expression evaluate to **false** does the overall expression evaluate to **false**. Table 5-8 summarizes the various combinations involving the (||) operator.

Table 5-8   *Or* truth table

exp1	exp2	exp1 || exp2
true	true	true
true	false	true
false	true	true
false	false	false

The expressions in Table 5-9 are examples of complex expressions using conditional *logical Or*:

Table 5-9   Sample complex expressions using (||)

`5 < 10 || "B" < "C"`	evaluates to **true**
`5 > 10 || "B" < "C"`	evaluates to **true**
`5 < 10 || "B" > "C"`	evaluates to **true**
`5 > 10 || "B" > "C"`	evaluates to **false**

Logical Not Operator (!)

The *logical Not* operator (written as a single exclamation point, !) is a *unary operator* (that is, an operator that uses only one operand). *Not* reverses the logical value of its Boolean operand. If the expression has a value of **true**, the *Not* operator reverses its logical value to evaluate to **false**. If the expression has a value of **false**, the *Not* operator reverses the state of the expression to evaluate to **true**. Table 5-10 summarizes the various combinations involving the (!) operator.

Table 5-10   *Not* truth table

exp1	! exp1
true	false
false	true

The expressions in Table 5-11 are examples of complex expressions using logical *Not*:

Table 5-11   Sample complex expressions using (!)

`!(5 < 10)`	evaluates to **false**
`!(5 > 10 && "B" < "C")`	evaluates to **true**
`!(5 < 10 || "B" > "C")`	evaluates to **false**

Avoid Using the *logical Not* (!) operator

Because the *logical Not* operator in C# is a small, single character, it can be a source of logic errors in your program because (!) is easy to miss when you are reading code. All the relational operators have an "opposite" operator. For example, (==) is opposite to (!=), and (<=) is opposite to (>). In most cases, you can make your code more readable by coding expressions without using the *logical Not* (!) operator.

In Table 5-1, the operator precedence table was modified to include the relational operators. Now that you understand the conditional logical operators, the operator precedence table can be expanded one more time, as shown in Table 5-12 (rows 3, 10, and 11 contain operators that have not been presented in previous tables.). As usual, we suggest that you use parentheses to control and clarify how an expression is evaluated.

Table 5-12   Precedence of arithmetic and relational operators

Increment and Decrement	++	--	
Multiplication, Division, Modulus	*	/	%
Logical Not	!		
Addition, Subtraction	+	-	
Equal To (Equality)	==		
Not Equal To (Inequality)	!=		
Less Than, Greater Than	<	>	
Greater Than or Equal To	>=		
Less Than or Equal To	<=		
Conditional Logical And	&&		
Conditional Logical Or	||		

Even if parentheses are used, complex Boolean expressions can be difficult to understand. For example, given the code fragment that follows, can you determine the value of **canAttendParty**?

```
1    DateTime birthDate;
2    string major;
3    string firstName;
4    int numberSnacks;
5    bool canAttendParty;
6
7    birthDate = DateTime.Parse("March 15, 1984");
8    major = "EE";
9    firstName = "Bob";
10   numberSnacks = 10;
11
```

```
12   canAttendParty =
13       (birthDate < DateTime.Parse("July 19, 1986")
14       && numberSnacks > 0
15       && (major == "IT" || major == "CS" || major == "LA"))
16       || (firstName == "Claire")
17       || (numberSnacks > 10);
```

Whenever you are presented with such a confusing expression, we suggest that you solve it by using the same substitution technique you probably use when solving algebraic equations. It might take several steps as shown in Table 5-13.

Table 5-13   Solving a complex Boolean expression using substitution

First, replace all variables with their known values.	```canAttendParty = ("3/15/1984" < "7/19/1986" && 10 > 0 && ("EE" == "IT" || "EE" == "CS" || "EE" == "LA")) || ("Bob" == "Claire") || (10 > 10);```
Next, solve the Boolean expressions and replace them with **true** and **false**.	```canAttendParty = (true && true && (false || false || false)) || (false) || (false);```
	```canAttendParty = (true && true && false) || false || false;```
Finally, put all the resolved expressions on a single line to make the statement more readable.	```canAttendParty = (true && true && false) || false || false;```
	```canAttendParty = false || false || false;```
	```canAttendParty = false;```

DECISION STATEMENTS

Most statements in a computer program execute in sequential order. Statements are executed one at a time, one after the other, until the end of a method, or a **return** statement is reached. Decision statements allow your code to execute different **statement blocks** depending on the value of a Boolean expression. Previous chapters have presented examples in which decision statements were used to validate input values, but decision statements are used each time your program executes instructions as the result of a specific condition being met. Often, the condition being met involves comparing the value of one variable to another variable. After you understand how Boolean expressions are evaluated, coding decision statements is easy.

Most programming languages use the same keywords for *decision statements*—**if** and **else.** Decision statements are also called *conditional statements*, and because they use the keyword **if,** they are frequently called by the informal name of *if statements*.

Decision statements in C# typically use one of the two syntax formats.

True-Only Conditions

To execute one or more statements when a condition is **true**, you use:

```
if (Boolean expression)
{
    Statement block to execute if Boolean expression is true
}
```

If the Boolean expression evaluates to **true**, the statement block is executed. If the Boolean expression evaluates to **false**, the statement block is not executed. Curly braces are used as statement block delimiters. The next statement to be executed is whatever statement is coded after the closing statement block delimiter. For example:

```
1        if (perfectAttendance == true && passingScore == true)
2        {
3            bonusPoints = 10;
4            examScore += bonusPoints;
5        }
6
7        semesterScore += examScore;
```

If the expression on line 1 evaluates to **true**, the statements on line 3, 4, and 7 are executed in sequence. But if the expression on line 1 evaluates to **false**, only the statement on line 7 is executed.

 It should be noted that by convention, the statements in the statement block are indented four spaces (or one tab stop) to make the code more readable. Indention doesn't change the sequence of how statements are executed.

True and False Conditions

To execute one or more statements when a condition is **true**, and a different set of instructions when a condition is **false**, you use the **else** keyword:

```
if (Boolean expression)
{
    Statement Block A
}
else
{
    Statement Block B
}

Statement Block C
```

If the Boolean expression evaluates to **true**, Statement Block A is executed and then control passes to Statement Block C. If the Boolean expression evaluates to **false**, Statement Block A is bypassed and program control is transferred to Statement Block B. Either way, program control ultimately executes Statement Block C.

Because the Boolean expression controls which statement block is executed, the program is capable of executing different code based on the outcome of the Boolean expression. In other words, your program can decide to do different things based upon whatever test you code for the Boolean expression—it can make a decision.

Here is an example:

```
1          if (examScore > 60)
2          {
3               passingScore = true;
4          }
5          else
6          {
7               passingScore = false;
8          }
```

This code assigns a Boolean value to **passingScore** based on the value of **examScore**. If the Boolean expression evaluates to **true**, **passingScore** is set to **true**. If the Boolean expression evaluates to **false, passingScore** is set to **false**. After **passingScore** is set to either **true** or **false**, the next statement to be executed is whatever statement is coded after the closing statement block's curly brace.

Strictly speaking, you could possibly code a **false**-only condition, as shown in this example:

```
1          if (perfectAttendance != true || passingScore != true)
2          {
3               // Do nothing.
4          }
5          else
6          {
7               bonusPoints = 10;
8               totalScore += bonusPoints;
9          }
```

Although the code is syntactically correct, and it executes correctly, a **false**-only condition isn't generally coded. Instead, the Boolean expression is changed to make it in the same style a **true**-only condition. The change is simple, as shown here:

```
1          if (perfectAttendance == true && passingScore == true)
2          {
3               bonusPoints = 10;
4               totalScore += bonusPoints;
5          }
```

Notice how the code has been simplified (that is, there are fewer program statements) merely by rewriting the logic of the two test expressions.

Nested Decisions

Decisions in most real programs aren't always as straightforward as the previous examples. In many cases, decisions can become quite complex. To handle these types of complex decisions, you can use nested decisions. A **nested decision** occurs when one decision is coded inside another, either as part of the statements that execute if the original Boolean expression evaluates to **true**, or as part of the statements that execute if the original expression evaluates to **false**. Nested decisions can also be used to make complex Boolean expressions more readable. Here is an example:

```
1          if (birthDate < DateTime.Parse("July 19, 1986")
2              && numberSnacks > 0
3              && (major == "IT" || major == "CS" || major == "LA"))
4          {
5               canAttendParty = true;
6          }
```

```
 7          else
 8          {
 9              if (firstName == "Claire")
10              {
11                  canAttendParty = true;
12              }
13              else
14              {
15                  if (numberSnacks > 10)
16                  {
17                      canAttendParty = true;
18                  }
19              }
20          }
```

Example of Statement Indentation

Again notice the statement blocks are indented to make the code more readable, and indention doesn't change the sequence of statement execution. Notice that if the indentation is removed from the preceding example, it becomes much more difficult to determine the final result:

```
 1          if (birthDate < DateTime.Parse("July 19, 1986")
 2          && numberSnacks > 0
 3          && (major == "IT" || major == "CS" || major == "LA"))
 4          {
 5          canAttendParty = true;
 6          }
 7          else
 8          {
 9          if (firstName == "Claire")
10          {
11          canAttendParty = true;
12          }
13          else
14          {
15          if (numberSnacks > 10)
16          {
17          canAttendParty = true;
18          }
19          }
20          }
```

For all practical purposes, decision statements can be nested for as many levels as you want. Experience has shown, however, that you should try to keep nesting to three levels or fewer. Using more than three levels of nesting confuses the reader. You should try to rework your logic to avoid too many levels of nesting.

Cascading Decisions

Sometimes you find yourself coding a nested decision statement that is testing the value of one variable for many value possibilities. For example, suppose that you have a program that assigns a letter grade based on an exam score. A score of 90 or above earns an A, a score equal to or above 80 but below 90 earns a B, and so on. You might use code like that shown in Figure 5-5 to assign the letter grade.

```
 1          if (examScore >= 90)
 2          {
 3              letterGrade = "A";
 4          }
 5          else
 6          {
 7              if (examScore >= 80)
 8              {
 9                  letterGrade = "B";
10              }
11              else
12              {
13                  if (examScore >= 70)
14                  {
15                      letterGrade = "C";
16                  }
17                  else
18                  {
19                      if (examScore >= 60)
20                      {
21                          letterGrade = "D";
22                      }
23                      else
24                      {
25                          letterGrade = "F";
26                      }
27                  }
28              }
29          }
```

Figure 5-5 Assigning a letter grade using a cascading decision

Statements like those shown in Figure 5-5 are sometimes referred to as **cascading decisions** because of their indentation. (The code looks like water cascading down a staircase-shaped fountain.) The code in Figure 5-5 produces the desired results, but it is difficult to read because there are so many levels of indention. When you have such highly nested decisions—that is, decisions that test the contents of a single variable over and over—it is generally accepted practice to code them without indenting each statement block. Figure 5-6 shows an alternative style for coding indention. We think you'll agree that the second version is much easier to understand.

```
 1          if (examScore >= 90)
 2          {
 3              letterGrade = "A";
 4          }
 5          else if (examScore >= 80)
 6          {
 7              letterGrade = "B";
 8          }
 9          else if (examScore >= 70)
10          {
11              letterGrade = "C";
12          }
13          else if (examScore >= 60)
14          {
15              letterGrade = "D";
16          }
17          else
18          {
19              letterGrade = "F";
20          }
```

Figure 5-6 Alternative indention for assigning a letter grade

The idea of testing one variable for many values occurs so often in programming that it has its own name. This **case structure** of decision typically has special syntax to make writing and understanding the code even easier. In C#, case structures can be coded using the **switch** keyword. The use of the **switch** keyword is discussed in the Bonus Topics section of this chapter.

ROBUST DATA VALIDATION

Robust data validation improves the user friendliness of your application. If a user can crash your program by entering incorrect data, or even worse, if your program produces incorrect results when bad input is provided, users soon lose confidence in the program. A good measurement for the quality of an application is how it handles data validation. If a program crashes when it receives bad input data, it probably isn't written very well. Therefore, real programs need robust data validation. Chapter 2 introduced the concept of data validation because we wanted to accustom you to checking input values before processing them. The next section covers the topic of data validation in greater detail.

A Strategy for Data Validation

There are generally two strategies for validating data. With the first strategy, your code inspects the input values, tries to predict if the values will work, and warns the user if the values seem unlikely to produce the desired results. With the second strategy, your code uses the values and warns the user if something goes wrong as a result of using the values. We feel that the best strategy is to use a mixture of both. In other words, write code that does a good job of checking the input values for correctness before trying to process with them. However, you should also include code to prevent your program from crashing should an error occur (that is, an exception, or runtime error) while the data is being processed. Chapter 6 covers preventing your program from crashing by catching exceptions.

A third strategy you might consider using is simply not to allow invalid data to be entered by the user. For some types of data, user interface objects can be used that limit the user's input to only valid choices. For example, a check box can be used to limit a Boolean input value to two choices. Radio buttons can be used to limit a selection to one of a set of choices. In addition, text boxes can sometimes have properties set to limit which characters can be typed in. Chapter 12 covers many of these GUI objects.

Even if you do use GUI objects that restrict input values, there are still cases where you need to do your own data validation because you can't completely eliminate invalid input values using control properties and methods alone. For example, suppose that a user must enter a valid currency amount that your program needs to store in a **decimal** type. You might try to prevent the user from entering an invalid value by changing the text box to accept numbers only. What if the user prefers to enter the currency symbol ($), decimal points, and commas? Further, if you do allow users to enter commas and decimal points, how can you make them enter these symbols in the correct positions? To make your program as user-friendly as possible, you should avoid strict input rules. For example, a user may prefer to enter a date as `December 3, 1961` or `12-3-61` rather than `12/03/1961`. Most of the time, you are better off allowing users to input data the way they like and then later checking the input to see if it is in a format your program can use.

Additionally, some environments, such as a Web browser–based application, have a limited set of input controls and events, and you need to do your own validation should you develop that kind of application. Knowing how to code proper data validation without relying on GUI objects will serve you well in the long run. Besides, coding validation logic is a great way to practice coding decision statements.

When Should You Validate Data?

Text boxes have several events that you might consider using for data validation. These events include `KeyPress`, `LostFocus`, `TextChanged`, and even a `Validating` event. The problem with coding validation in these events is that they don't always work. One thing to remember in a GUI environment such as Windows is that you really can't force users to enter valid values. You can limit the choices, but at any time, a user should be able to stop entering data into your program and switch to another application or even close your program. Another problem with using these events is that your validation logic becomes scattered over scores of event methods associated with the controls, making debugging more difficult. Still another reason not to rely on these events is that these events may not be available in all programming languages and application environments.

We suggest that you start with the style of allowing the users to enter input values in whatever ways they want, and validate the values just before you process them. For example, validate the input values when the user clicks a button or menu item. After all, who cares if the input values are incorrect if you aren't going to process them anyway? This style of "checking before use" produces excellent results and works no matter what programming language and application environment you are using.

Data validation logic can be quite long, and most of the time users never notice it because they enter correct input values. Chapter 7 shows you how to simplify data validation even further by moving the data validation logic to a separate method.

What Should You Do When Input Values Are Incorrect?

Some applications substitute a valid value when an invalid value is entered. We don't recommend this data-substitution technique. For example, suppose that a clerk is entering the number of hours you worked for the week into a payroll program. Further, suppose that this was a particularly busy week and you worked 60 hours. Finally, assume that the developer of the payroll program felt any hours greater than 40 was an invalid input value and just defaulted to a value of 40 hours for anything over 40. Wouldn't you prefer that the program warn the data entry clerk that 60 hours seemed like too many hours and ask her to confirm the input value before continuing?

Chapter 2 introduced basic data validation. Recall that this decision statement:

```
1        if (lengthInFeet <= 0)
2        {
3            MessageBox.Show("Length in Feet must be > zero.");
4            txtLengthInFeet.Focus();
5            return;
6        }
```

validates that an input value is a positive number greater than zero. If the input data is incorrect, a message is shown to the user telling him what is wrong, the cursor is placed in the text box containing the erroneous data (that is, the program's focus is set to that control), and the method is exited because your code can't continue processing with bad data. We suggest that you use this strategy whenever an invalid input value is found. That is, validate each input value and, when a bad value is found, display a message to the user for that one input item only. We don't suggest that your code attempt to validate everything on the form and show one message box with everything that is wrong. When in doubt, try some of your favorite commercial applications and see what they do with unexpected input values and emulate their behavior.

Error messages should be written as a complete sentence using good grammar. Avoid jargon and abbreviations. Error messages should inform the user of which input value is bad, and what the expected input value should be. Error messages shouldn't try to inform users of what they did wrong. For example, display "Quantity must be a numeric integer value" rather than "Quantity cannot contain alphabetic characters." The first message politely informs the user of the problem, whereas the second message seems more like finger-pointing. Good error messages provide a type of documentation to help users quickly learn how to use your application.

Using the Focus Method Correctly

You should make note of the purpose of the **Focus** method. Sometimes students who are new to programming mistakenly think the **Focus** method moves the cursor to the text box and then causes the application to wait until they've corrected the input values. It doesn't work that way. The sole purpose of calling a text box's **Focus** method is for user convenience. The **Focus** method simply causes the cursor to move to that text box so that the user doesn't have to tab to the text box, or click it with the mouse. Processing immediately continues with whatever statement follows the statement that calls the **Focus** method.

Displaying a Better Message Box

The examples used to this point have shown how to display a message to the user using the **MessageBox.Show** method. To keep things simple, we have used the most basic **MessageBox** style. Although the basic style is simple to code, it doesn't have the appearance of a proper Windows message box dialog because it lacks an icon and a caption in its title bar. The basic style is also limited to displaying a single OK button.

As you might guess, the **Show** method has options that allow you to customize the appearance of the message box dialog. In fact, there are 12 ways to call the **Show** method, and there are a variety of argument values that can be passed to it. Fortunately, in almost all cases, your applications can use one of two styles of message boxes: (1) an OK version to display a message, and (2) a Yes or No question version. Figure 5-7 shows examples of both.

 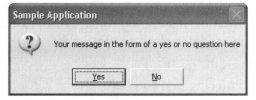

Figure 5-7   The two most useful styles of the message box dialog

To show the OK version, use code like this:

```
MessageBox.Show("Your message here.",
    Text, MessageBoxButtons.OK, MessageBoxIcon.Information);
```

To ask the user to answer a Yes or No question, use code like this:

```
1    DialogResult answer = MessageBox.Show(
         "Your message in the form of a yes or no question here",
2        Text, MessageBoxButtons.YesNo, MessageBoxIcon.Question);
3    if (answer == DialogResult.Yes)
4    {
5        // The user clicked yes.
6    }
7    else
8    {
9        // The user clicked no.
10   }
```

Or a simpler version like this:

```
1    if (MessageBox.Show(
         "Your message in the form of a yes or no question here",
2        Text, MessageBoxButtons.YesNo, MessageBoxIcon.Question)
         == DialogResult.Yes)
3    {
4        // The user clicked yes.
5    }
6    else
7    {
8        // The user clicked no.
9    }
```

Note that in the examples, when **Text** is used as the second argument it causes the **Text** property of the form to be displayed in the caption of the message box dialog. In the examples shown in Figure 5-7, the form's **Text** property has a value of **Sample Application**.

For the Yes or No question style, a value reflecting the button the user presses is returned from the **Show** method. You can compare the value returned from the message box dialog to **DialogResult.Yes** and **DialogResult.No** to determine which button the user clicked. Note that this style shows the message box as part of a decision statement in which the return value is compared to **DialogResult.Yes**.

You can see that it takes a fair amount code to display a proper message box dialog. Chapter 7 shows you techniques that you can use to simplify the code in these examples by moving it to a method that can be called whenever needed.

Existence Check

Sometimes input values are optional. For example, a program that collects contact information for a person might have a text box to collect a fax number. However, not everyone has a fax machine, so this piece of information may be optional. For optional text information like this, it is very likely that no validation is required on the input data.

At other times, it is necessary only to check that the user made an entry. This is common for information stored as strings. Entering first and last names is a common example of simply checking that something was entered—an **existence check**. There really are no rules for what a name must, or cannot, contain. Can a name contain a number or a special character? Maybe. A name might contain a comma or period as in the case of Charles, Jr. The same could be said for an address or city. Although it might be possible to check a city name against a list of all known cities, it really isn't practical to do so.

To perform an existence check on a text box, you have only to compare the object's **Text** property to an empty string. Look at this example:

```
1        if (txtFirstName.Text == "")
2        {
3            MessageBox.Show("First Name is required.",
4                Text, MessageBoxButtons.OK, MessageBoxIcon.Information);
5            txtFirstName.Focus();
6            return;
7        }
```

If **txtFirstName** has no value in it, the error message is displayed and the cursor is placed inside the text box.

Data Type Check

The next simple validation, a **data type check**, ensures that the data type is correct. Numbers and dates are typical examples. If you are expecting to make calculations on an integer value, you have to ensure that the user entered a string that can be converted and stored as an **int** data type. Note that strings don't have to be checked because the **Text** property of a text box is already of type **string**.

Unfortunately, C# currently has no good way to determine if a string can be converted to a certain data type. Instead, the simplest technique is to try to convert the string and see what happens. If it can't be converted, a run-time error occurs. Or, more formally, an *exception* is *thrown*. Recall from the Carpet Cost example in Chapter 2 that, if the user enters an input value that can't be converted to a decimal, the program crashes. The program crashes when the **decimal.Parse** method throws an exception. The program crashes because you didn't include code to *catch*, or process, the exception. Chapter 6 covers performing data type checks and catching thrown exceptions in detail. For now, just continue to use **Parse** methods and be sure to enter the correct data types when testing.

Using the TryParse Method

Visual C# 2005 (and the .NET Framework 2.0) adds a new **TryParse** method to most value types. The **TryParse** method returns **true** or **false** depending on whether a string can be converted to the indicated type or not. With `TryParse`, you will be able to perform data validation like this:

```
if (int.TryParse(txtQuantity.Text, quantity) == false)
{
    MessageBox.Show("Quantity must be an integer value. ",
        Text, MessageBoxButtons.OK, MessageBoxIcon.Information);
    txtQuantity.Focus();
    return;
}
```

Oddly, the current version of C# already has the `TryParse` method, but only for the **double** type. Because `TryParse` isn't available for all data types, this text doesn't use it, for consistency sake. If you are using Visual C# 2005 or later, we recommend that you use `TryParse` to determine if a string can be converted to a value type.

Range Check

Even if the user has entered a string that can be converted to the correct data type, she might have entered a value that isn't within an acceptable range of values. For example, a graphics drawing program might have an option for the percentage to be used to zoom in on a graphic, and the valid values might range from 10 to 500, inclusively. Such a validation is called a **range check**.

Before you can compare the input value against a range, you must first convert the input value to a numeric data type, such as an **int**. If the input string can be converted to an **int**, you've validated only that the string is an integer value that can be stored in the range an **int** supports. The converted value might fall outside the acceptable range of 10 to 500. As a result, you must code a decision statement that displays an error to the user if the zoom percent value is outside of the range 10 through 500. The conditional *logical Or* operator (||) is frequently used in range checks. For example:

```
1      int zoomPercent;
2      zoomPercent = int.Parse(txtZoomPercent.Text);
3
4      if (zoomPercent < 10 || zoomPercent > 500)
5      {
6          MessageBox.Show("Zoom Percent must be an integer value between 10 and 500.",
7              Text, MessageBoxButtons.OK, MessageBoxIcon.Information);
8          txtZoomPercent.Focus();
9          return;
10     }
```

Note that you can't simply use the `Text` property of a text box to check for a numeric range because the `Text` property is a string.

Reasonableness Check

Sometimes applications have an input value that doesn't require a specific range, but it does have a range that seems reasonable. If the value is outside of the reasonable range, the value might be valid but you still want to warn users before processing it, just in case they typed the value incorrectly.

For example, a payroll program might accept the number of hours an employee has worked in a week. A week has an absolute maximum number of hours of 168, but employees rarely work more than 40 hours in a week. If an employee does work more than 40 hours, the program should accept the value, but it should also ask the user to confirm that he entered the correct value. The code to perform a **reasonableness check** for this example might look like this:

```
1        if (hoursWorked > 40)
2        {
3            if (MessageBox.Show("You've entered a value > 40 hours. Is this correct?",
4                Text, MessageBoxButtons.YesNo, MessageBoxIcon.Question) != DialogResult.Yes)
5            {
6                txtHoursWorked.Focus();
7                return;
8            }
9        }
10
```

If the number of hours worked is greater than 40, a confirmation message is displayed to the user in a message box with Yes and No buttons. If the user answers No, focus is set to the text box, and the method is exited. If the user answers Yes, processing continues as normal.

Code Check

Some input values consist of a choice from a predefined set of allowed values. These choices are called "codes" because organizations frequently use a two- or three-character code as an abbreviation, and validating against a list of valid values is therefore known as a **code check**. For example, a university might use codes to represent majors (for example, CS, IT, and EE). Airports are given a three-character code (for example, LIT, IND, and MDW). Every state in the United States has a two-character code (for example, IN, IL, OH) that serves as the state's abbreviation. Using codes like these has the added benefit of making automated processing easier.

Codes typically are validated using the *not equal to* (!=) comparison operator and the conditional *logical And* (&&) operator. For example, suppose that your application allows the user to enter a unit of purchase (UOP) and can accept values of BB for Barrel, BG for bag, BX for box, PK for package, and SP for spool. You might validate a UOP code using the following code:

```
1        if (txtUOP.Text != "BB"
2            && txtUOP.Text != "BG"
3            && txtUOP.Text != "BX"
4            && txtUOP.Text != "PK"
5            && txtUOP.Text != "SP")
6        {
7            MessageBox.Show("UOP must be either BB, BG, BX, PK, or SP.",
8                Text, MessageBoxButtons.OK, MessageBoxIcon.Information);
9            txtUOP.Focus();
10           return;
11       }
```

Note that the preceding code makes case-sensitive comparisons and so requires the user to enter the values as uppercase letters. A more user-friendly approach would be to convert the input values for **txtUOP** to uppercase characters using the string **ToUpper** method, store that result in a local variable, and then compare that local variable against the set of valid values. Or you might use the **String.Compare** method to perform a **case-insensitive compare**.

A common mistake that students make when writing validation code is to use a conditional *logical Or* rather than a conditional *logical And*. If you code (||) instead of (&&), invalid values are rejected, but so are all valid values. Consider what would happen if this Boolean expression were used in a data validation decision statement:

```
stateCode != "IN" || stateCode != "IL" || stateCode != "OH"
```

If the value of `stateCode` contains an invalid value such as `"MI"`, you can use substitution to see the expression evaluates to **true,** which would cause an error message to be displayed:

```
"MI" != "IN" || "MI" != "IL" || "MI" != "OH"

    true      ||     true     ||      true

                   true
```

But now perform the same test using a valid value of `"IN"` and again use substitution:

```
"IN" != "IN" || "IN" != "IL" || "IN" != "OH"

   false   ||      true     ||      true

                   true
```

The expression again evaluates to **true,** which would again cause an error message to be displayed even though a valid value had been entered!

To test your validation statements, pick a set of both valid and invalid values and use the substitution technique covered earlier in this chapter to ensure that your validation statements work correctly.

If the list of allowed values is very large, like airport codes or zip codes, it would be unlikely that you would code a giant decision statement to validate these input values. Instead, you would compare the input values against a lookup table in a data file or database. Chapters 11 and 13 discuss files and connections to databases.

The **switch** statement, covered in the Bonus Topics section of this chapter, can also be used to simplify validating an input value against a set of codes.

Cross-Field Check

Cross-field checks, sometimes called *consistency checks*, occur when the valid values for one input item depend on the value of one or more other input values. For example, if gender indicates male, then maiden name must not be entered. Or, if an employee has a payment code that indicates that she is paid hourly, the weekly payroll amount might use a different range check than that used for an employee who is paid a salary.

Let's create an example that attempts to perform a cross-field check in an inventory application. Suppose that the application has a validation rule that specifies the following: if quantity on hand equals zero, then the reorder date must be a valid date greater than, or equal to, today's date; however, if quantity on hand is greater than zero, then a reorder date must not be entered. You could validate this rule using statements as shown in Figure 5-8. Note that this code assumes that quantity on hand has already been validated as an integer value that is not less than zero.

```
 1  if (quantityOnHand == 0)
 2  {
 3      reorderDate = DateTime.Parse(txtReorderDate.Text);
 4
 5      if (reorderDate < DateTime.Now)
 6      {
 7          MessageBox.Show("Reorder date must be a valid date >= today's date.",
 8              Text, MessageBoxButtons.OK, MessageBoxIcon.Information);
 9          txtReorderDate.Focus();
10          return;
11      }
12  }
13  else
14  {
15      if (txtReorderDate.Text != "")
16      {
17          MessageBox.Show("Reorder Date should not be entered when quantity > zero.",
18              Text, MessageBoxButtons.OK, MessageBoxIcon.Information);
19          txtReorderDate.Focus();
20          return;
21      }
22  }
```

Figure 5-8   A cross-field check data validation example

A PROGRAM EXAMPLE

To make sure that you understand how decisions and data validation can be used in an application, let's write a simple program that lets the user enter information about students. Figure 5-9 shows the user interface. When the Validate button is clicked, the application verifies the input values for each of the input controls using the techniques described in this chapter. For the purpose of this example, no further processing will be performed on the data.

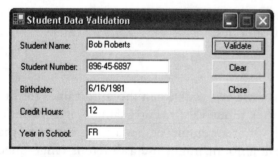

Figure 5-9   Student Data Validation user interface

DEVELOPING THE APPLICATION

Create the application by using Visual Studio to create the project files and a main form just as you've done in previous chapters. Design a user interface similar to that shown in Figure 5-9, and set the control properties as shown in Table 5-14.

Table 5-14   Student Data Validation user interface properties

Object type	Name	Property	Value
Label	label1	Text	Student Name:
	label2	Text	Student Number:
	label3	Text	Birth Date:
	label4	Text	Credit Hours:
	label5	Text	Year in School:
Text box	txtStudentName	Text	empty
	txtStudentNumber	Text	empty
	txtBirthDate	Text	empty
	txtCreditHours	Text	empty
	txtYearInSchool	Text	empty
Button	btnValidate	Text	Validate
	btnClear	Text	Clear
	btnClose	Text	Close

Program initialization is the same as in previous examples. The only initializing the form is required to perform is to instantiate and initialize the controls that make up the form's user interface. In addition, as was done in previous examples, clicking the Close button should close the form and cause the user to exit the application. Clicking the Clear button should reset the input text boxes back to empty strings and set the focus to the first input text box. Figure 5-10 shows the source code for these steps.

```
177        public static void Main()
178        {
179            frmMain main = new frmMain();
180            Application.Run(main);
181        }
182
183        public frmMain()
184        {
185            InitializeComponent();
186        }
187
188        // Clears input text boxes.
189        private void btnClear_Click(object sender, System.EventArgs e)
190        {
191            txtStudentName.Text = "";
192            txtStudentNumber.Text = "";
193            txtBirthDate.Text = "";
194            txtCreditHours.Text = "";
195            txtYearInSchool.Text = "";
196            txtStudentName.Focus();
197        }
198
199        // Close the form to end the application.
200        private void btnClose_Click(object sender, System.EventArgs e)
201        {
202            Close();
203        }
```

Figure 5-10   Student Data Validation secondary source code

In this example, you encounter interesting logic when the Validate button is clicked. The source code for this method first defines variables to hold the input values. The method then obtains the input values from the form. Figure 5-11 shows this code. Student Name, Student Number, and Year in School are stored as `strings`, so only a simple assignment is needed to obtain those values. Birth Date and Credit Hours both use `Parse` methods to convert the input string to the proper data type. Recall that there is no way to perform a proper data type check until you reach Chapter 6, so be sure to enter valid dates and integers for these values when testing.

```
205        private void btnValidate_Click(object sender, System.EventArgs e)
206        {
207            string studentName;
208            string  studentNumber;
209            DateTime birthDate;
210            int creditHours;
211            string yearInSchool;
212
213            // Get the input values from the form.
214
215            studentName = txtStudentName.Text;
216            studentNumber = txtStudentNumber.Text;
217            birthDate = DateTime.Parse(txtBirthDate.Text);
218            creditHours = int.Parse(txtCreditHours.Text);
219            yearInSchool = txtYearInSchool.Text;
220
```

Figure 5-11 Defining variables and getting input values

VALIDATING INPUT VALUES

The validation rules for the input values for this example are somewhat arbitrary but are meant to exercise each validation technique discussed earlier in the chapter. Input data is validated as follows:

- An *existence check* ensures that a value has been entered for the Student Name.

- Student Number is validated to ensure that it is in the format xxx-xx-xxxx, where x is any character. The `Length` property of the **string** object is used to check that the length of the Student Number is 11, and the `Substring` method is used to make sure that the characters at positions 4 and 7 are dashes (recall that the positions used for `Substring` are zero-based, and so the code uses position values of 3 and 6.)

- A range check is used to make sure that Birth Date is not greater than the current date (`DateTime.Today`).

- A range check is used to make sure that the value for Credit Hours is between 3 and 21 hours.

- A code check is used to validate that Year in School is either freshman, sophomore, junior, senior, or graduate student (`"FR"`, `"SO"`, `"JR"`, `"SR"`, or `"GR"`). Note that a case-sensitive compare is used so that the user must enter the values in uppercase.

- If the Year in School indicates a graduate student, a cross-field check is combined with a reasonableness check to get confirmation from the user if the value for Credit Hours is more than 9 hours.

If an invalid value is found for any of the input values, a proper error message is displayed, the focus is set to the appropriate text box, and the method is exited. If all input values are correct, a simple acknowledgment message is displayed to the user. In a real application, information such as this would be saved to a file or database. Chapters 11 and 13 cover storing information in files and databases. Figure 5-12 shows the remaining code for the **btnValidate_Click** event.

```
221        // Check to make sure a name has been entered.
222
223        if (studentName == "")
224        {
225            MessageBox.Show("Name is required.",
226                Text, MessageBoxButtons.OK, MessageBoxIcon.Information);
227            txtStudentName.Focus();
228            return;
229        }
230
231        // Validate student number.
232
233        if (studentNumber.Length != 11
234            || studentNumber.Substring(3, 1) != "-"
235            || studentNumber.Substring(6, 1) != "-")
236        {
237            MessageBox.Show("Student number is required in xxx-xx-xxxx format.",
238                Text, MessageBoxButtons.OK, MessageBoxIcon.Information);
239            txtStudentNumber.Focus();
240            return;
241        }
242
243        // Validate birthdate.
244
245        if (birthDate > DateTime.Today)
246        {
247            MessageBox.Show("Birthdate cannot be > today's date.",
248                Text, MessageBoxButtons.OK, MessageBoxIcon.Information);
249            txtBirthDate.Focus();
250            return;
251        }
252
253        // Validate credit hours.
254
255        if (creditHours < 3 || creditHours > 21)
256        {
257            MessageBox.Show("Credit hours must be an integer value between 3 and 21.",
258                Text, MessageBoxButtons.OK, MessageBoxIcon.Information);
259            txtCreditHours.Focus();
260            return;
261        }
262
263        // Validate year in school.
264
265        if (yearInSchool != "FR"
266            && yearInSchool != "SO"
267            && yearInSchool != "JR"
268            && yearInSchool != "SR"
269            && yearInSchool != "GR")
270        {
```

Figure 5-12 Student Data Validation logic

```
271              MessageBox.Show("Year in school must be FR, SO, JR, SR, or GR.",
272                  Text, MessageBoxButtons.OK, MessageBoxIcon.Information);
273              txtYearInSchool.Focus();
274              return;
275          }
276
277          // Graduate students shouldn't normally have more than 9 credit hours, so
278          // ask for confirmation if credit hours is > 9.
279
280          if (yearInSchool == "GR" && creditHours > 9)
281          {
282              if (MessageBox.Show(
283                  "Credit Hours for graduate students isn't normally > 9. Is this correct?",
284                  Text , MessageBoxButtons.YesNo, MessageBoxIcon.Question) !=
                     DialogResult.Yes)
285              {
286                  txtCreditHours.Focus();
287                  return;
288              }
289          }
290
291          // Display a confirmation message to the user.
292
293          MessageBox.Show("All input values are valid.",
294              Text, MessageBoxButtons.OK, MessageBoxIcon.Information);
295
```

Figure 5-12   Student Data Validation logic (continued)

TESTING THE VALIDATION LOGIC

After you've developed the user interface and written the source code, the next step is to build the application and test it. Trying valid and invalid values for one input control at a time is a good way to test data validation logic. When you are confident that the data validation for one input control is correct, try valid and invalid values for the next input control. For example in this program, test first to make sure the Student Name validation works. Next, test valid and invalid values for Student Number, and so on.

We also recommend that you set breakpoints and step through your code so that you can watch your code execute statement by statement. You haven't done a thorough job of testing until you see each statement executed at least once. This requires you to execute the code many times using many different sets of test data.

BONUS TOPICS

THE SWITCH STATEMENT

An early section of this chapter stated that the *case structure* can be used when testing the value of one variable for many values. In C#, case structures can be coded using the **switch** keyword. Because **switch** statements are simply a different style of decision statement (that is, you can do everything using **if-else** statements that you can do with the **switch** statement), it is included here in the Bonus section.

The general format of the **switch** statement is:

```
switch (expression)
{
    case constant-expression:
        statements to execute;
        break;
    case constant-expression:
        statements to execute;
        break;
    default:
        statements to execute;
        break;
}
```

where **expression** is an expression that evaluates to an integer (for example, **byte, int, long**) or **string** value (a variable is normally used), and **constant-expression** is an integer or **string** value that **expression** is compared to.

The **switch** statement is executed by first evaluating **expression**. The value from **expression** is compared to the first **constant-expression** associated with each **case** statement. If the two values are equal, the *statements to execute* are executed, and processing jumps to whatever statement follows the **switch** statement by executing the related **break** statement. If the two values are not equal, the value from **expression** is compared to the second **constant-expression**, and so on. If the value in **expression** does not equal any of the **constant-expressions**, the statements in the **default** block are executed. Note that you can include as many **case** conditions as you want, and the **default** block is optional.

Figure 5-13 shows examples of using the **switch** statement.

```
1    switch (pizzaSize)              1    switch (pizzaInches)
2    {                              2    {
3        case "small":              3        case 9:
4            pizzaCost = 4.99M;     4            pizzaCost = 4.99M;
5            break;                 5            totalSmalls++;
6        case "medium":             6            break;
7            pizzaCost = 7.99M;     7        case 12:
8            break;                 8            pizzaCost = 7.99M;
9        case "large":              9            totalMediums++;
10           pizzaCost = 11.99M;   10            break;
11           break;                11        default:
12   }                            12            pizzaCost = 11.99M;
                                   13            totalLarges++;
                                   14            break;
                                   15    }
```

Figure 5-13 Switch statement examples

The first example in Figure 5-13 uses **string** expressions and does not use a **default** block. You can omit the **default** block only if you ensure that the **switch** expression in your code has a discrete set of values. The second example is similar except that it compares using an integer value, and *does* include a **default** block.

Although the **switch** statement can be used to make some decision statements easier to read, it isn't as flexible as using **if** statements because it can only test one integer or **string** variable to see if it equals a value.

ALTERNATIVE DECISION STATEMENT STYLES

As mentioned before, most programming languages give you many ways to format the statements that make up your source code. Because style consistency makes source code easier to read and understand, programmers develop specific styles when writing code. We believe that the style used for decisions in this text produces easy-to-read code. Not everyone writes decision statements using the same style, so this section introduces you to several variations you might see while reading someone else's code.

Brace Alignment

The Bonus Topics section of Chapter 2 stated that most C# code examples show curly braces on a line by themselves (the so-called Allman style). Chapter 2 also stated that many programmers prefer the so-called K&R style, which places the opening curly brace on the same line as the statement that precedes the statement block. In Chapter 2, the context of this discussion was for the statement blocks that make up a class and a method. However, the same style is often applied to decision statements.

For example, we prefer the Allman style:

```
1        if (pizzaSize == "small")
2        {
3            pizzaCost = 4.99M;
4        }
5        else if (pizzaSize == "medium")
6        {
7            pizzaCost = 7.99M;
8        }
9        else
10       {
11           pizzaCost = 11.99M;
12       }
```

The same decision, however, could be written as:

```
1        if (pizzaSize == "small") {
3            pizzaCost = 4.99M;
4        }
5        else if (pizzaSize == "medium") {
7            pizzaCost = 7.99M;
8        }
9        else {
11           pizzaCost = 11.99M;
12       }
```

which uses the K&R style of placing the opening curly brace on the same line as the Boolean expression. We think that the Allman style produces a more readable code. Whichever style you select, use it consistently.

Comparing Boolean Variables to True and False

Another variation you might find in other texts is an alternate form of Boolean expression in an **if** statement. Because a Boolean variable can be used as a Boolean expression, some programmers don't bother adding the *equal to* (==) relational operator and the **true** keyword when comparing the value of a Boolean variable. For example, this statement:

```
if (perfectAttendance == true && passingScore == true)
```

could be written as:

```
if (perfectAttendance && passingScore)
```

Both versions function in exactly the same way. Likewise, some programmers use the logical *Not* operator (!) instead of comparing a Boolean variable to **false**.

For example, this statement:

```
if (itemInStock == false)
```

could be written as:

```
if (!itemInStock)
```

In general, less code is usually easier to understand than more code. However, we also believe that the more explicit the code is, the easier it is to understand. For this reason, we recommend including the code to explicitly compare Boolean variables to **true** and **false** when using them in decision statements.

Omitting Braces

A third variation you might see occurs when only a single statement should be executed as the result of a **true**-only decision statement. In this situation, C# allows the curly braces that define the omission of a statement block. (This is also the case for other programming languages, such as C++ and Java, which also have syntax derived from the C programming language.) For example, this decision:

```
1          if (perfectAttendance == true)
2          {
3              bonusPoints = 10;
4          }
```

can be written as:

```
1          if (perfectAttendance == true)
2              bonusPoints = 10;
```

or as:

```
1          if (perfectAttendance == true) bonusPoints = 10;
```

The curly braces that define a statement block after the **else** clause of a decision statement can also be omitted if the result is to execute only a single statement. For example, this decision:

```
1          if (examScore > 60)
2          {
3              passingScore = true;
4          }
5          else
6          {
7              passingScore = false;
8          }
```

can be written as:

```
1          if (examScore > 60)
2              passingScore = true;
3          else
4              passingScore = false;
```

We recommend that you always use curly braces in decision statements even when the C# syntax doesn't require it. The curly braces add white space to make the code easier to read, and if you ever have to change the decision to execute more than one statement as the result of a decision, the curly braces are already present.

EARLY RETURNS

Recall the strategy presented for robust data validation: When the user indicates that she is ready for your program to process the input data, validate each item one at a time. If an invalid value is found, display a message to the user, set the focus to the control in error, and exit the method using the **return** keyword. This style of exiting a method when a condition occurs that prevents anything else in the method from executing is called an **early return**.

However, some programmers believe that a method should *never* contain more than one **return** statement. This belief is based on a style of programming (so-called *structured programming*) that was popular long before OOP became popular. Now that you've learned the variety of decision statements you can code using **if** and **else**, you should understand that it is indeed often possible to write most methods to have only one **return**. Instead of coding an early return, you put any code following the decision into an **else** statement block. Figure 5-14 shows a section of code from the calculate button click event in the Carpet Cost application from Chapter 2. However, this version doesn't use early returns.

```
// Validate that we have correct input.

if (lengthInFeet <= 0)
{
    MessageBox.Show("Length in Feet must be > zero.");
    txtLengthInFeet.Focus();
}
else
{
    if (widthInFeet <= 0)
    {
        MessageBox.Show("Width in Feet must be > zero.");
        txtWidthInFeet.Focus();
    }
    else
    {
        if (pricePerSquareYard <= 0)
        {
            MessageBox.Show("Price Per Square Yard must be > zero.");
            txtPricePerSquareYard.Focus();
        }
        else
        {
```

Figure 5-14   A cross-field check data validation example

```
            // Calculate the amounts.

            squareFeet = lengthInFeet * widthInFeet;
            squareYards = squareFeet / 9;

            subtotal = squareYards * pricePerSquareYard;
            subtotal = Math.Round(subtotal, 2);

            taxAmount = subtotal * taxRate;
            taxAmount = Math.Round(taxAmount, 2);

            totalCost = subtotal + taxAmount;

            // Display the results back to the user.

            txtSubtotal.Text = subtotal.ToString("C");
            txtTaxAmount.Text = taxAmount.ToString("C");
            txtTotalCost.Text = totalCost.ToString("C");
        }
    }
}
```

Figure 5-14 A cross-field check data validation example (continued)

We think you can see that, even though you can write a method without using early returns, the result is code that appears more complex and is harder to understand because it often results in one large complex decision statement. Ironically, the goal of structured programming was to produce source code that was easier to read, understand, and maintain. For this reason, we are firm believers of using early returns to simplify program logic.

USING SYSTEM.GLOBALIZATION FOR IMPROVED DATA ENTRY

You've learned that when the user enters characters into a text box, they are always entering text characters, even if the characters are the digit characters "0" through "9". You've also learned that to process these **strings** in calculations, you must first convert them to numeric data types using the **Parse** methods. For example:

```
        itemCost = decimal.Parse(txtItemCost.Text);
```

While entering statements such as this, you might notice that the **Parse** methods can be passed other arguments in addition to the **string** to be converted. These other arguments allow you to provide additional information to the **Parse** methods that control which characters are allowed to be included in the **string**. Normally if the user enters a currency sign ($) in the text box, the **decimal.Parse** method throws an exception. However, what if you want to give the user the ability to enter a currency sign if he wants to? That's when the **System.Globalization** namespace and **NumberStyles** are used.

The **NumberStyles** are defined in the **System.Globalization** namespace and can be passed to the **Parse** methods to control how characters such as the currency symbol, the thousands character (,), decimal points, parentheses, and spaces are processed.

A complete discussion of all **NumberStyles** variations is beyond the scope of this text, but as an example, this variation of calling the **decimal.Parse** method:

```
        itemCost = decimal.Parse(txtItemCost.Text, NumberStyles.Currency);
```

gives the user the option of entering the currency sign. Similar number styles exist for floating-point and integer numbers. If you try these styles, be sure to include a `using SystemGlobalization` statement at the top of your class file. C#'s Help system provides additional details.

SUMMARY

Essential Topics

❑ All but the very simplest computer programs require many levels of decisions. The core of a decision statement is the Boolean expression. Boolean expressions work like arithmetic expressions, except that the expression always evalutes to a **true** or **false** value.

❑ Numbers are compared using the greater than (>), less than (<), greater than or equal to (>=), less than or equal to (<=), equal to (==), and not equal to (!=) relational operators. Relational operators have a lower operator precedence than the arithmetic operators.

❑ Boolean types can only be compared using the equal to (==), and not equal to (!=) relational operators. You must be careful when comparing Boolean values for equality. Be sure to use the equal to (==) relational operator and not the assignment operator (=).

❑ **DateTime** types can be compared using the greater than (>), less than (<), greater than or equal to (>=), less than or equal to (<=), equal to (==), and not equal to (!=) relational operators. A more recent date is greater than an older date. The time portion of a **DateTime** affects comparisons. If two **DateTime** values have the same year, month, and day, the value with the time latest in the day is greater.

❑ Reference types can only be compared using the equal to (==), and not equal to (!=) relational operators. When reference types are compared, you are evaluating the contents of the reference and not the value of the object they refer to. In other words, you are comparing to see if the variables refer to the same object or not.

❑ **Strings** are compared using the **String.Compare** method. A quick rule of thumb for remembering how characters compare is: special characters < "0" < "9" < "a" < "z" < "A" < "Z".

❑ The conditional logical operators *And* (&&) and *Or* (||) can be used to write complex Boolean expressions. Truth tables are useful for understanding how such expressions are evaluated.

❑ Decision statements allow your program to execute different statement blocks depending on the value of a Boolean expression. **if** and **else** keywords are used to write decision statements. Decision statements can be nested to make complex expressions more readable.

❑ A good strategy for data validation is to check the input values for correctness just before trying to process them. If an input value is invalid, display a message to the user stating what is wrong, place the cursor in the text box containing the error, and exit the method.

❑ Data validation statements can be categorized as existence checks, data type checks, range checks, reasonableness checks, code checks, and cross-field checks.

Bonus Topics

❑ The **switch** statement can be used in place of nested **if** statements.

❑ Programmers use several alternative styles for brace alignment, comparing Boolean values to true and false, and for omitting braces in decision statements.

□ Although some programmers frown on the practice, early returns can be used in place of many levels of nested decision statements.

□ You can use `System.Globalization` to allow more flexible data input. For example, you can use it to allow the user to enter currency symbols ($) when entering monetary values.

5

KEY TERMS

Define each of the following terms, as they relate to changing program flow with decisions:

Essential Terms

□ Boolean expression
□ cascading decision
□ case-insensitive compare
□ case-sensitive compare
□ code check
□ comparison operator
□ conditional logical operator
□ cross-field check
□ data type check
□ existence check
□ focus
□ nested decision

□ range check
□ reasonableness check
□ relational operator
□ statement block

Bonus Terms

□ case structure
□ early return
□ `numberStyles`
□ **switch** statement
□ `System.Globalization`

REVIEW QUESTIONS

Essential Questions

1. In Boolean expressions the operands you compare must be of compatible data types. True or false?

2. Relational operators have a lower precedence then the arithmetic operators. True or false?

3. When comparing reference types, you are comparing the values of the objects. True or false?

4. You can use the *equal to* operator when comparing `strings` for equality, even though `strings` are reference types. True or false?

5. The purpose of calling a control's `Focus` method is to pause program execution while the user corrects an input value. True or false?

6. A data validation existence check occurs when you check only to see if a value has been entered. True or false?

7. A data validation data type check has to be done only on **int** and **decimal** values. True or false?

8. A data validation range check typically uses the *less than* and *greater than* relational operators. True or false?

9. A data validation cross-field check should be done in the `LostFocus` event of a text box. True or false?

10. In almost all cases, your applications use one of three styles of message boxes. True or false?

11. The operands in Boolean expressions are separated by _____ operators.

12. The **string.**_____ method can be used to determine if one **string** is less than or greater than another **string**.

13. When one decision is coded inside another, it is a called a _____ decision.

14. After a data validation statement has determined an input value is not fit for processing, you should display a message to the user, set the focus to the control in error, and _____ the method.

15. A data validation reasonableness check often displays a message box with _____ and _____ buttons.

16. List the six relational operator symbols.

17. Assume that two **DateTime** variables contain the same values for month, day, and year. If one has a time value, and one does not, which of the two is larger?

18. List a quick rule of thumb to remember which characters are less than, or greater than other characters.

19. When is the best time to perform data validation?

20. A data validation decision that checks an input value against a set of valid values is which kind of data validation?

Bonus Questions

1. In C#, case structures can be coded using the **switch** keyword. True or false?

2. In a **switch** statement, the **default** block is required. True or false?

3. In a **switch** statement, you can include as many **case** conditions as you want. True or false?

4. When only a single statement requires execution, C# allows the curly braces that define a statement block to be omitted. True or false?

5. If you want to allow the user to enter a currency sign for a decimal amount, you use the **System.NumberStyles** namespace. True or false?

6. Rewrite the following decision statement using the coding style and message box recommended by this text:

```
1          if (!networkConnectionAvailable) {
2              MessageBox.Show("A network connection does not exist.";
3          }
```

7. Rewrite the following decision statement using the coding style recommended by this text:

```
1          if (todayIsSeniorDiscountDay || customerIsAStudent)
2              discountPercent = 10;
3          else
4              discountPercent = 0;
```

8. Describe why using the "early return" style of exiting a method can help improve source code readability.

PROGRAMMING EXERCISES

Essential Exercises

1. Write a Date Compare program that functions in a manner similar to the String Compare program shown earlier in this chapter. Be sure to test using values that contain both dates only, and dates and times.

2. Modify the Carpet Cost application developed in Chapter 2 to improve data validation. Add range checks for Length in Feet and Width in Feet to make sure each is not greater than 150 feet. Add a reasonableness check to ask the user to confirm any Price per Square Yard that is greater than $25.00. Display all message boxes using the proper style.

3. Modify the Restaurant Bill Calculator application developed in Chapter 4. Improve data validation by requiring Meal Cost to be a positive value between $1.00 and $30.00, Drink Cost to be a positive value between $.50 and $20.00, and Discounts to be between $0.00 and $5.00. Additionally, make sure that the Discount amount is less than the subtotal cost (meal + drinks) of the meal. If the number of diners is seven or more, use a tip percent of 20% rather than 15%. Display all message boxes using the proper style.

4. Write a program that calculates the cost of a pizza. The user interface should contain three text boxes that allow the user to enter:

   - Size of small, medium, or large
   - **integer** value for the number of additional toppings
   - Whether the pizza should be delivered or not

   After the input values have been validated, display the total cost using the following criteria:

   - A small pizza costs $4.99, a medium is $7.99, and a large is $11.99
   - Additional toppings are 99 cents each
   - Delivery charge is $3.00

5. Write a program that allows users to enter their names, phone numbers, graduation dates, and majors. After the information has been entered, the user should click a button to validate the information. Provide a Clear button to reset all text boxes to empty **string**s and a Close button to close the form. Data validation must include the following:

   - Student Name should not be blank.
   - Phone number must be in the format "(xxx) xxx-xxxx" where x is any character.
   - Graduation Date must be a valid date and greater than the current system date.
   - Major must be one of the following: CS, EE, LA, or CPT. Note this should be a *case-sensitive* compare.

6. Write a program that allows the user to enter the following product information: UPC, Product Description, Quantity on Hand, Reorder Date, and Unit of Purchase (UOP). After the information has been entered, the user should click a button to validate the information. The user interface should also include a Clear button, a Close button, and *Your Name's* Product Information in the title bar. When the Close button is clicked, close the form to end the program. When the Clear button is clicked, clear the contents of the input text boxes, and set the focus to the UPC text box. Input the values and data validation rules described in the following list. Use constants to declare the text for data validation error messages.

▫ Verify that the UPC is entered and is of the format mmmppp-c, where mmm is the manufacturer ID, ppp is the product ID, and c is the check digit. All characters of the manufacturer ID and product ID must be numeric digits (a character between 0 and 9, inclusive.) The user must enter all eight characters, including the check digit. Validate the check digit entered by using the following algorithm:

   ▫ Calculate the sum of the odd-spaced digits (the 1st, 3rd, and 5th). Save the result as **Answer1**. Multiply **Answer1** by 5. Calculate the sum of the even-spaced digits (the 2nd, 4th, and 6th) and add this to **Answer1**. The check digit should be whatever number you have to add to your last answer to make it reach the next multiple of 10.

   ▫ Examples of valid UPCs include: 123456-3
   (1 + 3 + 5 = 9; 9 * 5 = 45; 2 + 4 + 6 = 12; 12 + 45 = 57;
   therefore, the check digit should equal 3 (60 − 57 = 3));

   111111-2
   (1 + 1 + 1 = 3; 3 * 5 = 15; 1 + 1 + 1 = 3; 3 +15 = 18;
   therefore, the check digit should equal 2 (20 − 18 = 2));
   333888-1; and 777999-0.

▫ Product Description has to be entered.

▫ Quantity on Hand must be a valid **integer** value >= zero.

▫ If Quantity on Hand is zero, Reorder Date must be entered as a valid date >= today's date. If Quantity on Hand is not zero, Reorder Date must not be entered.

▫ UOP must be one of the following two-character codes: BG (bag), BX (box), CA (case), CT (carton), GL (gallon), or GR (gross). Accept either uppercase or lowercase characters.

Bonus Exercises

1. Write a program that allows the user to enter a zip code, and displays the corresponding city and state when a Lookup button is clicked. Include at least five of your favorite zip codes and use a **switch** statement to display the correct city and state. Use a **default** block to display an error message to the user if the zip code isn't found in your list.

2. Modify the Student Data Validation program shown at the end of the Essentials section of this chapter to use a **switch** statement when validating Year in School. Also make data entry easier by not requiring Year in School to be entered in uppercase.

6

CATCHING EXCEPTIONS

In the Essentials section you will learn:

♦ The definition of exceptions
♦ The difference between syntax and logic errors
♦ The relationship of exception handling to debugging
♦ The causes of exceptions
♦ How to write a general exception handler using `try` and `catch`

In the Bonus section you will learn:

♦ How to catch specific types of exceptions
♦ How to throw your own exceptions
♦ How to display the call stack

In the last chapter, you learned how to use decisions to direct processing down divergent paths, depending on the situation. Sometimes, decisions were used to bypass processing steps when the input data provided by the user would cause an error. This pretest prevented your program from processing a statement that would produce an error. In this chapter, you will learn another way to deal with error conditions that occur during program execution. This posttest approach attempts to correct the problem during program execution, after it is discovered, in an attempt to return the program to a working state.

ESSENTIAL TOPICS

As you've already learned, a program can terminate for many reasons other than by the user clicking the Close button. The programmer should anticipate situations that could cause abnormal program termination. Writing programs that are prepared to deal with such error conditions results in more reliable programs. To create more reliable programs, you may write general code to deal with any unexpected situation or write specific code to deal with each unique situation. This section of the chapter describes how to use general exception handling to deal with any situation. The Bonus section describes how to write specific exception handlers to deal with specific errors.

WHAT ARE EXCEPTIONS?

An **exception** is an error condition that is unexpectedly encountered during program execution. Programmers often refer to this situation as an exception being **thrown**. The .NET Framework provides the `Exception` class, which is a base class for all exceptions. All specialized exceptions are derived from this base class. When an error occurs, the system reports the problem by throwing an exception that contains information about the error. At this point, your programs do not have code to handle exceptions, so the system displays an error message and the program terminates. However, you can make your program more robust by adding code to allow it to recover from some of these error conditions.

For example, if you write a program that performs a division operation, and the denominator happens to be zero, a `DivideByZeroException` occurs during program execution, as shown in Figure 6-1. If you used a decision to compare the value of the denominator against zero before you performed the division, you could prevent the exception from occurring. However, if you don't expect this situation to happen often, there is another alternative to deal with this situation if and when it occurs.

An **exception handler**, or an **error handler**, is a block of program code that you write to identify alternative processing that is executed when an error occurs in lieu of any default error messages displayed by the system, such as illustrated in Figure 6-1. Programmers refer to this notion of bypassing the default error messaging with the code in your exception handler as **catching** exceptions. It is important for you to recognize that exceptions do not reflect a normal situation, but rather an exceptional circumstance. Therefore, writing exception handlers should not be a substitute for handling predictable situations that are easily corrected by other means (such as performing data validation on a denominator to prevent a division by zero exception).

Nonetheless, it may not be possible for you to predict everything that could go wrong, so it is a good idea to include at least a general exception handler that will bypass the display of the sometimes cryptic system messages. Consequently, we recommend that you catch exceptions using an exception handler that displays a friendly error message, rather than allow the exception to be caught by the system, which displays an obscure message.

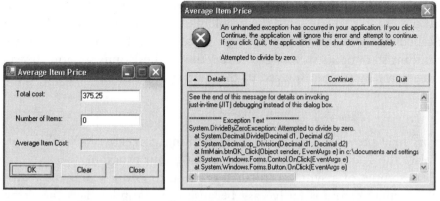

Figure 6-1 Error message for DivideByZeroException

After an exception is thrown, you can actually trace how, when, and where it happened through use of the **call stack**. The **execution call stack** keeps track of all methods that are in execution and the line numbers in the source code where each method was called. To examine all these details, you can view the **stack trace**. Figure 6-2 shows some of the details from the stack trace for the `DivideByZeroException` just discussed. Reviewing this text allows you to see that there are many objects in play and that line 167 in the event method `frmMain.btnOK_Click` is where there was an attempt to divide by zero.

Viewing the Execution Call Stack

Visual Studio provides an option from the Debug menu to view the execution call stack. To try this out, set a breakpoint in the code window and then start executing the program. When the breakpoint is reached, you can access the option as follows: from the Debug menu→Windows→Call Stack. If you step through the code, you will be able to watch the call stack change as the program executes.

```
See the end of this message for details on invoking
just-in-time (JIT) debugging instead of this dialog box.

************** Exception Text **************
System.DivideByZeroException: Attempted to divide by zero.
   at System.Decimal.Divide(Decimal d1, Decimal d2)
   at System.Decimal.op_Division(Decimal d1, Decimal d2)
   at frmMain.btnOK_Click(Object sender, EventArgs e) in c:\avgitemprice\frmmain.cs:line 167
   at System.Windows.Forms.Control.OnClick(EventArgs e)
   at System.Windows.Forms.Button.OnClick(EventArgs e)
   at System.Windows.Forms.Button.PerformClick()
   at System.Windows.Forms.Form.ProcessDialogKey(Keys keyData)
   at System.Windows.Forms.Control.ProcessDialogKey(Keys keyData)
   at System.Windows.Forms.Control.PreProcessMessage(Message& msg)
   at System.Windows.Forms.ThreadContext.System.Windows.Forms.UnsafeNativeMethods+IMso
    Component.FPreTranslateMessage(MSG& msg)
```

Figure 6-2 Stack trace for DivideByZeroException

Thus far, you have only been writing event methods. In Chapter 7, you will begin to separate some of the processing steps into their own methods and initiate them by calling them when and where needed. For example, you might move all of the data validation processing into a `dataValidate` method and call it just before you start performing any computations. If an exception occurs in the middle of the `dataValidate` method, the stack trace identifies the line in the `dataValidate` method that triggered the problem, as well as the line in the `btnOK_Click` event method that called `dataValidate` in the first place. Thus, the stack trace provides a way for you to better pinpoint statements that trigger exceptions. The Bonus section shows you how you can customize the error message displayed to the user by including the stack trace details.

Types of Errors

Several types of errors may prevent a program from working correctly. As you've learned from Chapter 2, if you violate the grammar or syntax rules of C#, your program does not compile due to **syntax errors**. An example of a syntax error is forgetting to end a statement with the semicolon (;). Debugging syntax errors is fairly easy because the compiler flags the errors for you when you attempt to compile the program.

A **semantic error** occurs when the syntax of your code is correct, but what you want the code to do is not. For example, the sentence: "The dog meowed." obeys the rules of English grammar in that the sentence has a noun and a verb. However, the sentence is semantically incorrect because it is used out of context. A program with semantic errors may terminate abnormally, with or without an error message.

If a program with semantic errors is able to complete execution but displays (incorrect) results, then the program has **logic errors**. For example, to find the tax owed, if your program's expression uses `taxRate + total` (instead of `taxRate * total`), you get an answer, but the answer is wrong! Because a program with logic errors may produce results, but not the right results, debugging the program to find the problem becomes more difficult. To illustrate, take a look at the code listing in Figure 6-3. This is a slight revision of the Restaurant Bill Calculator in Chapter 4 in which the statements for performing the calculation and displaying the results were replaced with the code shown in Figure 6-3. How quickly would you be able to find the logic error in this code snippet? (Hint: Take a close look at line 293.)

```
287            // Calculate the total per diner.
288
289            totalCost = Math.Round((mealCost + drinkCost)
290                + ((decimal) taxRate * (mealCost + drinkCost))
291                + ((decimal) tipPct * (mealCost + drinkCost))
292                - discounts, 2);
293            costPerDiner = Math.Round(totalCost % (decimal) nbrDiners, 2);
294
295            // Display the results back to the user.
296
297            txtCostPerDiner.Text = costPerDiner.ToString("C");
```

Figure 6-3 Revised code snippet from the Restaurant Bill Calculator application of Chapter 4

You should always make sure that your program is free of logic errors. Achieving this goal requires a two-pronged approach. First, set breakpoints in your code and use the Debugger to step through the source code statements and watch what happens along the way. At each step, verify that the values in each variable and expression are correct. Second, you should develop a set of test data and calculate the expected answers with a calculator. Make sure that the test data includes valid, extreme, and invalid test cases. Use the same test data when you execute the program to see if you get the same results. If the program's results match the results you worked out with the calculator, you can be fairly confident that the program is free of logic errors.

An exception, or **run–time error**, is an error that is triggered during execution of your program. An exception may be caused by factors such as faulty program logic, bad input provided by the user, or limited system resources. Methods for finding and fixing logic errors have already been discussed. It is possible for your program to recover from some exceptions, but only if you anticipate such problems and add code to handle those potential problems.

You can recognize a run-time error through a message that appears with the words "unhandled exception" and the name of the type of exception. The remainder of this chapter describes how you can write code to anticipate these exceptions and provide alternative processing to replace the default error messages that appear. It's important to keep in mind that exception handling is a supplement to debugging, but it is not the same as debugging. You include exception handlers in your program to augment .NET's built-in exception handling. You go through the debugging process to determine what caused your program to produce incorrect results. Sometimes the information provided by the exception can help you pinpoint the error in the program and fix the logic. However, if the user caused the problem by providing bad data, all your program can do is display a friendly error message and allow the user to reenter the input data.

What Causes Exceptions?

Several situations can trigger exceptions. If you don't add code to handle these errors, your program will terminate abnormally. You may have encountered some of these situations already in testing the programs from Chapters 2 through 5. For example, if you enter alphabetic characters for the input numbers in the Basic Math Calculator from Chapter 4, a `FormatException` is thrown, as shown in Figure 6-4.

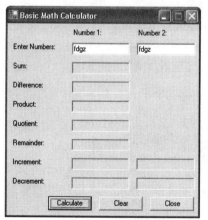
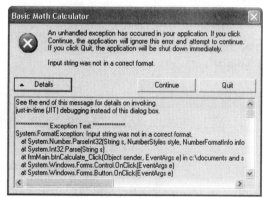

Figure 6-4 Exception thrown by entering alphabetic characters into the Basic Math Calculator

Although the case of providing textual data for numeric input is an obvious error, there are other cases in which a user may provide values that look as if they should work, but throw an exception because of the way the program is set up. Let's consider three cases in which we provide input to the Basic Math Calculator that uses only int data types. Figure 6-5 shows that if you enter a zero value for the second number, a `DivideByZeroException` is thrown. Figure 6-6 shows that if you enter a real number for one or both numbers, a `FormatException` is thrown. Figure 6-7 shows that if you provide a number larger than an `int` can hold, an `OverflowException` is thrown.

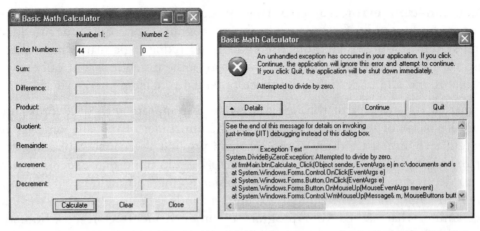

Figure 6-5   Error triggered by providing 0 denominator to the Basic Math Calculator

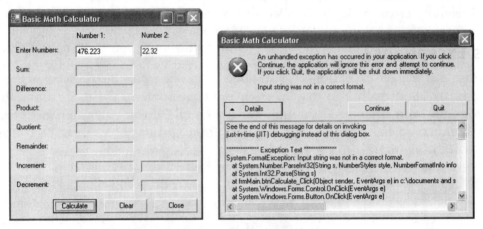

Figure 6-6   Error triggered by providing a non-integer number to the Basic Math Calculator

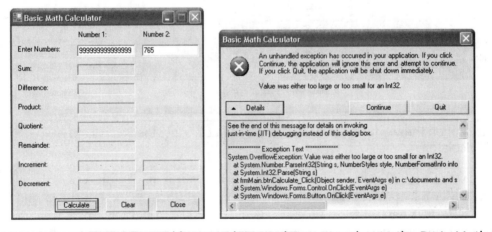

Figure 6-7   Error triggered by providing too large a number to the Basic Math Calculator

Many other situations can cause an exception to be thrown. In later chapters, you will learn about program loops, arrays, reading from, or writing to, text files, and connecting to a database. When you write programs that apply concepts learned in these later chapters, you may find that exceptions are thrown in the following cases:

- You try to loop through an array and go past a valid location.

- Your program uses up considerable system resources.

- Your program specifies the wrong location for the text file or database.

- Your file doesn't have enough data, and your program attempts to read from it.

Why Catch Exceptions?

Many things could go wrong when you execute your program. The factors that you can control have likely been handled through data validation processing. However, there are some potential problems that you simply cannot check using data validation. If you can anticipate where runtime errors might occur, you should incorporate exception handlers in your program to catch the exceptions to prevent the program from crashing. An obvious place to start is by anticipating bad data entered by the user. Another area to consider is any computations that involve division operations. If the expression in the denominator could be zero, your program should be ready to handle the problem.

What to Do When You Catch an Exception

Chapter 5 discussed several options you could use when you detect a problem with the data provided by the user. The recommendation was to display a friendly error message and position the cursor in the text box that contained the bad data. A similar strategy is appropriate for exception handling. If an exception is thrown, inform the user of what happened. Be sure to use proper grammar and complete sentences. Although you could attempt to recover from the error, it's best to follow the advice from Chapter 5—display a friendly message and position the cursor back on the form to allow the user to reenter the data.

In some cases, it is not possible to recover from an exception. For example, if a disk is full, your program may not be able to continue execution. Your program can't remedy this situation, so all you should do is inform the user of what happened.

Syntax for Exception Handlers

The syntax for writing an exception handler introduces three new keywords: **try**, **catch**, and *finally*. Each of these keywords identifies blocks of code that make up part of an exception handler:

- The **try block** surrounds the regular processing code that may throw an exception.

- The **catch block** contains code that provides alternative processing steps in the event that an exception is thrown.

- The **finally block** is an optional statement block used to identify processing steps that are always executed after the **try** or **catch** blocks, whether an exception is thrown or not.

Exception handlers are used in many languages. In fact, if you have seen programs with exception handlers in other languages such as Java, even the syntax for writing exception handlers using **try**, **catch**, and **finally** is the same! The .NET Framework provides ample support to programmers who wish to incorporate exception handlers in their programs.

Figure 6-8 shows the general syntax for writing an exception handler in C#. The program examples used in this chapter use only the **try** and **catch** blocks, but beginning with Chapter 11, there will be good reasons to include a **finally** block.

```
try
{
    normal program statements that may trigger an error
}
catch
{
    exception processing statement block if exception thrown in try block
}
finally
{
    clean-up processing statement block in all cases (error or no error)
}
```

Figure 6-8 General syntax for an exception handler

Valid Combinations for Exception Handlers

When writing an exception handler, there are three valid combinations of **try**, **catch**, and **finally** blocks:

1. Single **try** block, followed by one or more **catch** blocks
2. Single **try** block, followed by a single **finally** block
3. Single **try** block, followed by one or more **catch** blocks, followed by a single **finally** block

For now, this chapter uses combination one, but in later chapters, there will be a need for you to use the other two combinations.

To introduce the code for exception handlers, this chapter uses an example of performing a **data type check**. Recall from Chapter 5 that C# currently has no good way to determine if a string can be converted to a certain data type. Instead, the approach to use is to try to convert the string, but if a problem arises (that is, an exception is thrown), you know that there must have been a problem with the conversion step. If you don't include code to catch the exception, the program crashes. However, if you identify the program statements that have the potential to throw an exception, and you add code to handle that exception, the program will not crash. Thus, you can use an exception handler to deal with data type input errors.

Data Type Check

When the user provides the wrong type of data, you have already seen that a **FormatException** is thrown. Because programs often perform computations on numbers and dates, it is important to verify that the data you are processing are the correct types. If you perform calculations on an integer value, you have to make sure that the user entered a string that can be converted and stored as an **int** data type. Note that strings don't have to be checked because the **Text** property of a text box is already of type **string**. Figure 6-9 shows the syntax for performing a data type check using an exception handler. This particular exception handler provides alternative processing if the value in the quantity input field is not an integer. It should look familiar, because the steps are the same as those used for the other data validation checks discussed in Chapter 5—display a friendly message, position the cursor in the offending text box, and return control back to the form so that the user can reenter corrected data.

```
 1      try
 2      {
 3          quantity = int.Parse(txtQuantity.Text);
 4      }
 5      catch
 6      {
 7          MessageBox.Show("Quantity must be an integer value.",
 8              Text, MessageBoxButtons.OK, MessageBoxIcon.Information);
 9          txtQuantity.Focus();
10          return;
11      }
```

Figure 6-9 Exception handler for quantity input field

In this example, the user is expected to enter an integer value in the **txtQuantity** text box. If the user enters a non-integer value (such as alphabetic characters, a fractional value, or a date), a **FormatException** is thrown, causing control to be passed to the **catch** block. Because the **catch** block is processed when the user enters non-integer data, the message displayed describes the problem and provides guidelines for acceptable input values. The cursor is repositioned in the offending text box using the **Focus** method, and the event is terminated. This code allows the user to see the message and then reenter acceptable data to try again.

You should know that the **Parse** method also acts as an existence check. In other words, if you require the user to enter a numeric value, you don't have to code an existence check for it. The **Parse** method throws an exception if it is passed an empty string. This might also cause a problem if you have an optional input field that is not a string. For example, suppose that your application can accept a birthdate as an input value, but you don't want to require that this information be entered. This means that you need to use a decision statement that validates the data type only if the data is entered. Validation of this type would look similar to Figure 6-10.

```
 1      if (txtBirthDate.Text != "")
 2      {
 3          try
 4          {
 5              birthDate = DateTime.Parse(txtBirthDate.Text);
 6          }
 7          catch
 8          {
 9              MessageBox.Show(("Birthdate must be a valid date.",
10                  Text, MessageBoxButtons.OK, MessageBoxIcon.Information);
11              txtBirthDate.Focus();
12              return;
13          }
14      }
```

Figure 6-10 Data type exception handler for optional input field

The statement in line 1 checks to see if anything has been entered into the birthdate text box. If so, the statements in lines 3 through 14 are executed. Lines 3 through 6 use the

`DateTime.Parse` method to attempt to convert the input string from the text box into a `DateTime`. If the string can't be converted to a `DateTime`, the statements in lines 9 through 12 are executed to tell the user what is wrong.

> **Using the TryParse Method**
>
> Recall from Chapter 5 that waiting for an exception to be thrown and then catching it to display an error message is an inefficient way to handle data type input errors. When you upgrade to Visual C# 2005 (and the .NET Framework 2.0), the authors recommend that you replace your data type check exception handlers with the `TryParse` method to improve program efficiency.

A Program Example with Data Type Checks

To illustrate the use of exception handling for data type checks, let's return to the New Restaurant Bill Calculator from Chapter 4. You may open and review the supplied solution named **NewRestaurantBillCalcDataTypeChecks**; however, we believe that it would be better for you to start with a copy of the Chapter 4 program folder and follow along with us. When you are finished, you can compare your solution with the solution file that can be found with the supplemental files that accompany this book. To get started, rename the new copy of the folder to help you remember that this version implements data type checks. When you open the application in Visual Studio, revise the `btnCalculate_Click` event method so that the new version adds an exception handler for each of the four input fields. The new version actually has four separate **try-catch blocks**. Figure 6-11 includes a partial code listing that replaces lines 271 to 279 from Figure 4-10 in Chapter 4.

```
271    // Get the input values from the form and make sure each is the correct type
272
273    try
274    {
275        mealCost = decimal.Parse(txtMealCost.Text);
276    }
277    catch
278    {
279        MessageBox.Show("Meal cost is required and must be numeric.", Text,
280            MessageBoxButtons.OK, MessageBoxIcon.Information);
281        txtMealCost.Focus();
282        return;
283    }
284
285    try
286    {
287        drinkCost = decimal.Parse(txtDrinkCost.Text);
288    }
289    catch
290    {
291        MessageBox.Show("Drink cost is required and must be numeric.", Text,
292            MessageBoxButtons.OK, MessageBoxIcon.Information);
293        txtDrinkCost.Focus();
294        return;
295    }
```

Figure 6-11   Code listing from Restaurant Bill Calculator with data type checks

```
296
297    try
298    {
299        discounts = decimal.Parse(txtDiscounts.Text);
300    }
301    catch
302    {
303        MessageBox.Show("Discount amount is required and must be numeric. " +
304            "Enter 0 if there are no discounts", Text,
305            MessageBoxButtons.OK, MessageBoxIcon.Information);
306        txtDiscounts.Focus();
307        return;
308    }
309
310    try
311    {
312        nbrDiners = int.Parse(txtNbrDiners.Text);
313    }
314    catch
315    {
316        MessageBox.Show("The number of diners is required and must be " +
317            "a positive integer.", Text,
318            MessageBoxButtons.OK, MessageBoxIcon.Information);
319        txtNbrDiners.Focus();
320        return;
321    }
322
323    // Validate that nbrDiners is not zero to avoid divide by zero error.
324
```

Figure 6-11   Code listing from Restaurant Bill Calculator with data type checks (continued)

Recall that the **Parse** method also performs an existence check. Therefore, Lines 273 to 283 describe a data type exception handler that displays a message if **txtMealCost** has no value or if **txtMealCost** has a value that cannot be converted to a **decimal** data type, as shown in Figure 6–12.

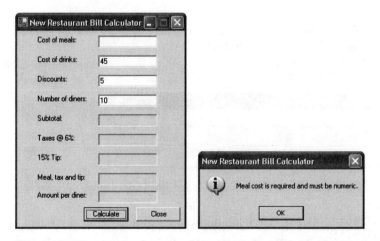

Figure 6-12   Cost of meals data type check from Restaurant Bill Calculator

Lines 285 to 295 perform a data type check on `txtDrinkCost`. Although a **decimal** data type is used to represent monetary data, you can see in Figure 6-13 that including the "$" in the input field throws an exception.

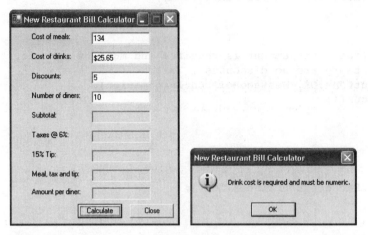

Figure 6-13   Cost of drinks data type check from Restaurant Bill Calculator

Lines 297 to 308 perform a data type check on `txtDiscounts`. Figure 6-14 illustrates the error message that is displayed if nothing is entered in the text box. Notice that the error message not only explains that the field is required, but also indicates that a number is expected. It further advises the user that if there are no discounts, a 0 value should be entered. You may want to note that `txtDiscounts` could be considered an optional input value. In this case, if nothing is entered in `txtDiscounts`, it may be reasonable to assume that the value is 0. To do this, you must add a decision above these lines to perform an existence check on `txtDiscounts` and assign the variable discounts a value of 0 if the field is empty. Otherwise, the program should process the code in lines 297 to 308.

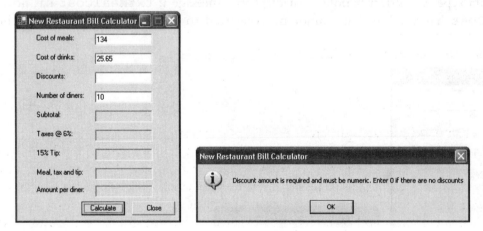

Figure 6-14   Discount amount data type check from Restaurant Bill Calculator

Lines 310 to 321 perform a data type check on `txtNbrDiners`. Figure 6-15 illustrates that if you spell out the number (for example, "ten" rather than "10"), an exception is thrown and the error message is displayed.

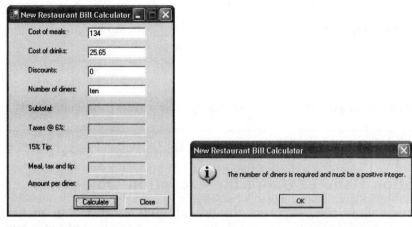

Figure 6-15   Number of diners data type check from Restaurant Bill Calculator

The statements in this event method are ordered in such a way that the computations to find the answers to be displayed are executed only after all data type checks pass. Figure 6-16 illustrates a successful execution of the program in which all data type checks have passed.

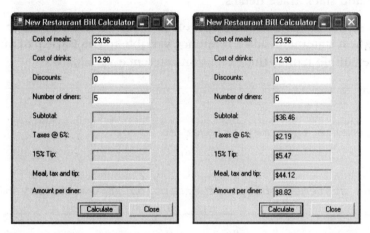

Figure 6-16   Correct results from Restaurant Bill Calculator when no errors occur

A GENERAL EXCEPTION HANDLER

The previous examples illustrated different types of exceptions that were thrown because of bad data entered by the user. You learned how to use an exception handler to perform data type checks for individual input fields and stop the program from crashing due to bad input data. However, you can further enhance the usability of your program by writing a generalized exception handler to deal with any type of exception that could be thrown. This section illustrates a generalized exception handler that catches any type of exception that is thrown. In the Bonus section, you will learn how to write code to catch specific exceptions.

Syntax for Generalized Exception Handlers

Figure 6-8 showed the syntax for adding an exception handler to your code. Remember that you won't be using the **finally** block until later chapters, so Figure 6-17 shows the revised syntax for writing a general exception handler.

```
try
{
    normal program statements that may trigger an error
}
catch
{
    exception processing statement block if exception thrown in try block
}
```

Figure 6-17 Syntax for general exception handler without the `finally` block

Generalized Exception Handler Using the Exception Object

As stated earlier, the details about the exception that was thrown are stored in an `Exception` object. You can make use of these details through properties and methods of the `Exception` object. For example, the **Message property** gets an English description of the current exception. You might want to display this information when an exception is caught. You can use the **StackTrace property** to help locate where the exception was thrown. More details about the `StackTrace` property are provided in the Bonus section. The `ToString` method returns a string that contains both the message and stack trace details.

Let's expand the general syntax so that you can make use of the rich information available through an Exception object. On the **catch** statement, add a reference variable to the `Exception` object, as shown in Figure 6-18. This example names the exception reference variable **ex**.

```
try
{
    normal program statements that may trigger an error
}
catch (Exception ex)
{
    exception processing statement block if exception thrown in try block
}
```

Figure 6-18 Syntax for the general exception handler to use the Exception object

To display the message that the system would have displayed if you didn't have an exception handler, use the **Message** property of the **Exception** object (which you named **ex**), as shown in Figure 6-19. Note that this approach shows only the message in a friendlier message box. It doesn't show the stack trace, which is of little value to the user.

```
catch (Exception ex)
{
    MessageBox.Show("Error: " + ex.Message,
        Text, MessageBoxButtons.OK, MessageBoxIcon.Information);
    return;
}
```

Figure 6-19 Using the Message property of the Exception object

To better understand how to incorporate a generalized exception handler into your program, enhance the Average Item Price program that was presented at the start of this chapter. Review the original code for the **btnOK_Click** event method (shown in Figure 6-20).

```
1   private void btnOK_Click(object sender, System.EventArgs e)
2   {
3       // Define variables to hold values in corresponding text boxes.
4
5       decimal total;
6       int number;
7       decimal average;
8
9       // If txtTotal has a value, convert it to decimal and make sure it is positive.
10
11      if (txtTotal.Text == "")
12      {
13          MessageBox.Show("The total cost is required.", Text, MessageBoxButtons.OK,
14              MessageBoxIcon.Information);
15          txtTotal.Focus();
16          return;
17      }
18      total = decimal.Parse(txtTotal.Text);
19      if (total < 0)
20      {
21          MessageBox.Show("The total cost must be a positive number.", Text,
22              MessageBoxButtons.OK, MessageBoxIcon.Information);
23          txtTotal.Focus();
24          return;
25      }
26
27      // If txtNumber has a value, convert it to int and make sure it is positive.
28
29      if (txtNumber.Text == "")
30      {
31          MessageBox.Show("The number of items is required.", Text, MessageBoxButtons.OK,
32              MessageBoxIcon.Information);
33          txtNumber.Focus();
34          return;
35      }
36      number = int.Parse(txtNumber.Text);
37      if (number < 0)
38      {
39          MessageBox.Show("The number of items must be a whole number.", Text,
40              MessageBoxButtons.OK, MessageBoxIcon.Information);
41          txtNumber.Focus();
42          return;
43      }
44
45      // Compute and display the average.
46
47      average = total / (decimal) number;
48
49      txtAverage.Text = average.ToString("C2");
50  }
```

Figure 6-20 btnOK_Click event method for Average Item Price Program

The first step when writing an exception handler is to write the program without any exception handling. Next, review the code to identify the statements that may potentially cause problems. In general, any statement (excluding variable definitions and comments) may throw exceptions. To add a generalized exception handler to catch any exception that is thrown, encompass these statements within a **try** block. Now add a **catch** block (as shown in Figure 6-18) after the **try** block's closing curly brace. Figure 6-21 shows the revised code for the event method.

```
1    private void btnOK_Click(object sender, System.EventArgs e)
2    {
3        // Define variables to hold values in corresponding text boxes.
4
5        decimal total;
6        int number;
7        decimal average;
8
9        try
10       {
11
12           // If txtTotal has a value, convert it to decimal and make sure it is positive.
13
14           if (txtTotal.Text == "")
15           {
16               MessageBox.Show("The total cost is required.", Text, MessageBoxButtons.OK,
17                   MessageBoxIcon.Information);
18               txtTotal.Focus();
19               return;
20           }
21           total = decimal.Parse(txtTotal.Text);
22           if (total < 0)
23           {
24               MessageBox.Show("The total cost must be a positive number.", Text,
25                   MessageBoxButtons.OK, MessageBoxIcon.Information);
26               txtTotal.Focus();
27               return;
28           }
29
30           // If txtNumber has a value, convert it to int and make sure it is positive.
31
32           if (txtNumber.Text == "")
33           {
34               MessageBox.Show("The number of items is required.", Text,
35                   MessageBoxButtons.OK, MessageBoxIcon.Information);
36               txtNumber.Focus();
37               return;
38           }
39           number = int.Parse(txtNumber.Text);
40           if (number < 0)
41           {
42               MessageBox.Show("The number of items must be a whole number.", Text,
43                   MessageBoxButtons.OK, MessageBoxIcon.Information);
44               txtNumber.Focus();
45               return;
46           }
47
48           // Compute and display the average.
49
50           average = total / (decimal) number;
51
52           txtAverage.Text = average.ToString("C2");
53       }
54       catch (Exception ex)
55       {
56           MessageBox.Show("Error: " + ex.Message,
57               Text, MessageBoxButtons.OK, MessageBoxIcon.Information);
58           return;
59       }
60   }
```

Figure 6-21 General exception handler for Average Item Price Program

The **try** block informs the system that it should be prepared to perform alternative processing in the event of an exception. If an exception occurs, any remaining steps in the **try** block are ignored and control passes to the **try** block. For example, if **txtTotal** contains **"five"**, then an exception will be thrown on line 21. Because this line is inside a **try** block, all remaining code in the **try** block is skipped and control passes to the **catch** statement on line 54. The exception details are passed to the variable **ex** so that when the message box is displayed, the **Message** property of the exception will appear. The **return** statement then causes the **btnOK_Click event** method to terminate. Note that because there are no other processing steps at this point, you could achieve the same result without the **return** statement.

The statements in the **catch** block identify alternative processing steps that are executed when any exception is thrown. These steps cause the system's exception message to be displayed, and then the event method terminates and the user is able to edit the input data and try again. After you compile the program and begin testing, try to enter invalid data to see what the error messages show. Figure 6-22 shows a few sample screen shots to illustrate a format exception and a DivideByZeroException, both of which are handled by the general exception handler you just added.

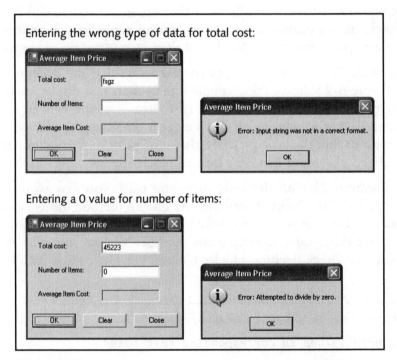

Figure 6-22   Screen shots for Average Item Price Program with a general exception handler

WHEN TO CATCH EXCEPTIONS

As an application developer, your goal should be to make your programs as foolproof as possible. This goal means that you should add exception handlers in all nontrivial event methods. After you identify the types of problems that may be encountered and the statements that trigger the errors, you can follow the steps described in the previous section to include a generalized exception handler for each problem statement or set of statements. Although you used one generalized exception handler in the Average Item Price program, you should have used separate exception handlers around blocks of statements. When you include multiple exception handlers in a single event, make sure that each **try** block has its own **catch** or **finally** block.

Another approach you may want to use is to keep the general exception handler as shown in the last example, but then nest individual exception handlers for individual or sets of program statements. This approach allows you to have customized error processing, for example for data type checks for each input field, as well as a general handler that manages any other problem that you may not have anticipated. Figure 6-23 shows a revised version of the Average Item Price program that uses one generalized exception handler, but nests smaller exception handlers that perform data type checks for each input text box. You should notice that each of the nested **try-catch** blocks is fully enclosed by the outer **try** block of the generalized exception.

When you nest **try-catch** blocks, if an exception is triggered within a nested **try** block (as in lines 14 to 17), control passes to the associated **catch** block (lines 18 to 24). The approach used in this example includes a **return** statement in each **catch** block. Therefore, each time an exception is found, the last step in the associated **catch** block terminates the event method. Now take a closer look at line 56. Notice that the calculation of **average** is not inside a nested **try** block. What do you think happens if **number** is equal to zero? Everything will still work because the outer **try** block (beginning on line 9) will handle any other problem not handled by any of the inner **try-catch** blocks. Thus, if **number** is zero, then control passes to the **catch** block on line 60, which displays the exception **Message** details and then terminates the event method.

You should run this program with different sets of input to make sure that the exception handlers are processed correctly. Figure 6-24 shows a few sample screen shots that display each of the unique messages displayed by different exception handlers. In the cases of the data type errors, only the message that is defined in that exception handler's **catch** block appears. In the case of any other problem, such as trying to find the average when the number of diners is zero, only the message defined in the generalized exception handler's **catch** block appears.

If you compare the code in Figure 6-23 with the code in Figure 6-21, you may wonder what happened to the existence check decision blocks. Recall that the **Parse** method throws an exception if the wrong type of data is entered or no value is given. Because **Parse** performs an existence check on numeric input fields, you can reduce the number of lines in your code by removing the unnecessary existence check decision blocks. Remember, less code is usually easier to debug and maintain.

```
1    private void btnOK_Click(object sender, System.EventArgs e)
2    {
3        // Define variables to hold values in corresponding text boxes.
4
5        decimal total;
6        int number;
7        decimal average;
8
9        try
10       {
11
12           // If txtTotal has a numeric value, convert it to decimal and verify range.
13
14           try
15           {
16               total = decimal.Parse(txtTotal.Text);
17           }
```

Figure 6-23 Nested exception handlers in Average Item Price program

```
18          catch
19          {
20              MessageBox.Show("A numeric value for total cost is required.", Text,
21                  MessageBoxButtons.OK, MessageBoxIcon.Information);
22              txtTotal.Focus();
23              return;
24          }
25          if (total < 0)
26          {
27              MessageBox.Show("The total cost must be a positive number.", Text,
28                  MessageBoxButtons.OK, MessageBoxIcon.Information);
29              txtTotal.Focus();
30              return;
31          }
32
33          // If txtNumber has a value, convert it to int and make sure it is positive.
34
35          try
36          {
37              number = int.Parse(txtNumber.Text);
38          }
39          catch
40          {
41              MessageBox.Show("An integer value for number of items is required.", Text,
42                  MessageBoxButtons.OK, MessageBoxIcon.Information);
43              txtNumber.Focus();
44              return;
45          }
46          if (number < 0)
47          {
48              MessageBox.Show("The number of items must be a whole number.", Text,
49                  MessageBoxButtons.OK, MessageBoxIcon.Information);
50              txtNumber.Focus();
51              return;
52          }
53
54          // Compute and display the average.
55
56          average = total / (decimal) number;
57
58          txtAverage.Text = average.ToString("C2");
59      }
60      catch (Exception ex)
61      {
62          MessageBox.Show("Error: " + ex.Message,
63              Text, MessageBoxButtons.OK, MessageBoxIcon.Information);
64          return;
65      }
66  }
67
```

Figure 6-23 Nested exception handlers in Average Item Price program (continued)

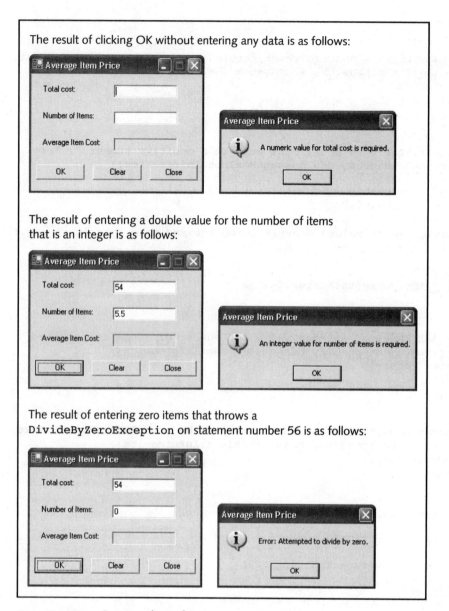

The result of clicking OK without entering any data is as follows:

The result of entering a double value for the number of items that is an integer is as follows:

The result of entering zero items that throws a `DivideByZeroException` on statement number 56 is as follows:

Figure 6-24   Screen shots for Average Item Price program with nested exception handlers

Bonus Topics

The Essential Topics section showed you how to implement generalized exception handling in your programs. This approach works for every type of exception that may be thrown. However, sometimes you may want to treat specific types of errors in different ways. This section discusses how to catch specific types of errors as well as how to throw your own exceptions.

CATCHING EXCEPTIONS OF A SPECIFIC TYPE

As you gain more experience in developing C# programs, you will be able to view code and identify the statements that are likely to trigger exceptions. However, to write specific exception handlers, you need to know what specific exceptions will be thrown. When these have been identified, you incorporate exception handling by writing a **try** block for the statements that may trigger an exception. Next, you add multiple **catch** blocks for each of the specialized exceptions, followed by one final **catch** block that uses the exception base class. Recall that the base class is **Exception**, and all other exception classes are derived from this base class. All these derived exceptions are named descriptively and end with "Exception." Some of the specific exceptions that have already been discussed follow:

- Performing division in which the denominator is zero throws a **DivideByZeroException**.

- Attempting to convert "ten" to a numeric data type using **Parse** triggers a **FormatException**.

- Attempting to store a value larger than the range limit for a particular numeric data type throws the **OverflowException**.

Thus, if you wanted to catch these specific exceptions, you would need to encompass the statements that would throw these exceptions in a **try** block, and then write a specific exception handler to deal with the specific exception thrown by the statements in the try block. As other concepts are presented, you will learn about additional situations that trigger other exceptions. Figure 6-25 shows how you can use Visual Studio to identify specific exceptions.

Another way to discover the specific exceptions that may be thrown by a given program is to start with a program without any exception handlers. Then, try to provide input that you believe may throw exceptions. That is, provide data to the program that doesn't make sense and see what happens. If you see errors from the system, try to pinpoint which lines of code triggered the error. Look carefully at the error message that appears for the names of specific exceptions. You can recognize the errors by the fact that they always end with the word "Exception" and are preceded by words that describe the nature of the problem, as shown in the three examples just described. Once you've completed exhaustive tests, you should have a list of statements that could potentially trigger errors. These statements become your target for including specific exception handlers in your program.

As just stated, once you have identified the specific exceptions that may be thrown by your program, you can add multiple **catch** blocks to handle those specific exceptions. This approach allows you to group several processing steps in one **try** block and display a more generalized error message based on the type of exception that is detected. You should order the **catch** blocks from the specific to the general, because each **catch** block is checked in order of appearance, until a relevant **catch** block is found. Once a **catch** block is processed, no other **catch** blocks for the same **try** block are checked.

When using this ordering scheme, it is a good idea to include a generalized **catch** block to handle anything else that you didn't anticipate. Be sure to position the generalized **catch** block after the last specific **catch** block. If you make the general **catch** block the first **catch** block, it will catch every exception that is thrown, rendering all other **catch** blocks that follow useless. Each **catch** block should display a message, position the cursor in the offending field (if you can determine which field caused the problem), and terminate the event method using **return**.

Identifying Exceptions with Visual Studio

You can use Visual Studio to help you identify the different types of exceptions that may be appropriate for a particular program. To view these specific exceptions, select Exceptions from the Debug menu:

Expand the Common Language Runtime Exceptions list:

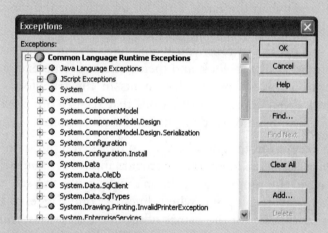

Expand the System list:

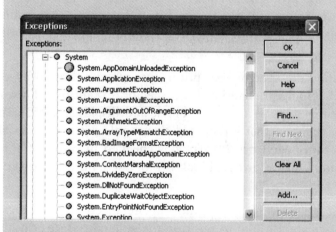

Scroll through the list to view the names of the different types of exceptions for which you may want to add specific exception handlers.

Figure 6-25 Viewing specific exceptions

To better understand how this works, you can open and review the code in the provided program **NewRestaurantBillCalcSpecificExceptions**; however, to get more practice, we recommend that you create another version of the original Restaurant Bill calculator from Chapter 4 and follow along with us. When you finish, you can compare your solution to the provided solution.

To get started, remove the decision that checks to make sure that the number of diners is not zero. If you examine the code listing in Figure 4-6, you can see that you would need to delete lines 278 to 286. Next, the statements that obtain the values from the form (lines 271 to 277) and calculate the values to be displayed (lines 287 to 294) should be grouped in a single try block. Next, add **catch** blocks to handle the **FormatException** and **DivideByZeroException**. Finally, add a generalized exception handler. Be sure to include an exception variable of type **Exception**, so that you can display the default error information using the **Message** property. Figure 6-26 displays a partial code listing that includes these revisions.

6

```
271    try
272    {
273          // Get the input values from the form and make sure each is the correct type
274
275          mealCost = decimal.Parse(txtMealCost.Text);
276          drinkCost = decimal.Parse(txtDrinkCost.Text);
277          discounts = decimal.Parse(txtDiscounts.Text);
278          nbrDiners = int.Parse(txtNbrDiners.Text);
279
280          // Calculate the subtotal, taxAmount, tipAmount, totalCost and costPerDiner.
281
282          subtotal = mealCost + drinkCost;
283          taxAmount = Math.Round((decimal) taxRate * subtotal, 2);
284          tipAmount = Math.Round((decimal) tipPct * subtotal, 2);
285          totalCost = subtotal + taxAmount + tipAmount - discounts;
286          costPerDiner = Math.Round(totalCost / (decimal) nbrDiners, 2);
287    }
288    catch (FormatException)
289    {
290          MessageBox.Show("All input fields are required and must be numeric.",
291               Text, MessageBoxButtons.OK, MessageBoxIcon.Information);
292          return;
293    }
294    catch (DivideByZeroException)
295    {
296          MessageBox.Show("The number of diners must be a positive integer. ",
297               Text, MessageBoxButtons.OK, MessageBoxIcon.Information);
298          txtNbrDiners.Focus();
299          return;
300    }
301    catch (Exception ex)
302    {
303          MessageBox.Show("Error: " + ex.Message, Text,
304               MessageBoxButtons.OK, MessageBoxIcon.Information);
305          return;
306    }
307
```

Figure 6-26 Revised New Restaurant Bill Calculator with specific error handlers

If you enter a non-numeric value in any of the four input text boxes, a **FormatException** is thrown. Figure 6-27 illustrates this with a dollar sign entered in the cost of drinks text box. Note that it doesn't make sense to position the cursor in any text box, because entering the wrong data type in any of the text boxes triggers the same exception.

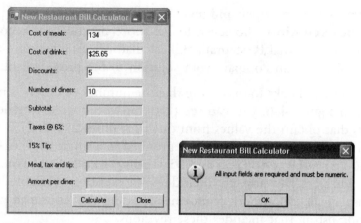

Figure 6-27   FormatException handler shows general error message

If valid numbers are entered for all text boxes, but the number of diners happens to be zero, then attempting to execute line 286 would trigger the `DivideByZeroException`. Because line 286 is the only program statement that could throw this exception, it makes sense to position the cursor in `txtNbrDiners`. (See Figure 6-28.)

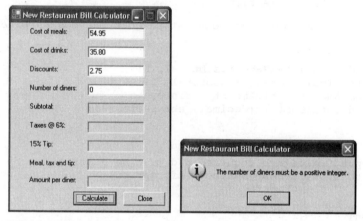

Figure 6-28   DivideByZeroException handler shows specific error message

To test the general exception handler, enter an extremely large value for the number of diners. Look at Figure 6-29 to verify that the general error message uses the **Message** property of the **Exception** object to explain any other exception that may have been thrown. The inclusion of this generalized exception handler, which catches any other exception that you may not have predicted, makes your program a bit less error-prone.

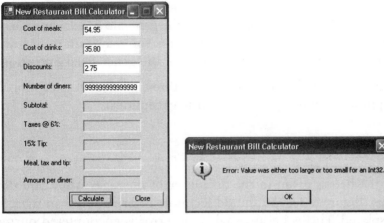

Figure 6-29   General exception handler shows system error message in a friendly manner

After you've verified that all the exception handlers work correctly, it is a good idea to make sure that the program still works when there are no problems. Figure 6-30 illustrates that this version of the Restaurant Bill Calculator still works.

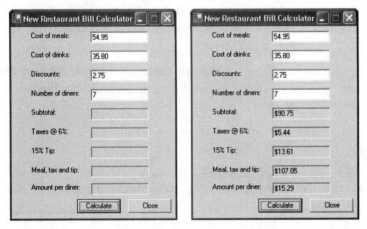

Figure 6-30   Revised Restaurant Bill Calculator with no exceptions thrown

THROWING YOUR OWN EXCEPTIONS

In addition to writing specific exception handlers, C# permits you to create your own exceptions. For example, instead of performing range checks using decision statements in the Restaurant Bill Calculator, you might want to throw your own exception. To accomplish this, you need to define an `ApplicationException` variable and assign it a descriptive message as a **string** value. To trigger or generate the exception, you then use the **throw** keyword followed by the name of the `ApplicationException` object you created. When programmers use the **throw** statement to generate an exception, they often say that an exception was **raised**.

The syntax for throwing your own custom exception looks like:

```
if (BooleanExpression)
{
    ApplicationException exVar = new ApplicationException("Message String");
    throw exVar;
}
```

Remember that all exceptions are derived from the base **Exception** class. Therefore, even though the exception thrown was type **ApplicationException**, the generalized exception handler that you included as the last **catch** block still handles this exception. You may wish to review the code shown on lines 301 to 306 in Figure 6-26 to see the details of the generalized exception handler.

Later chapters present situations in which it makes sense to throw your own exception. For now, you should limit your exception handling to C#'s intrinsic exceptions.

EXCEPTIONS AND THE CALL STACK

If you take a closer look at the details given in the default error messages when you don't write your own exception handlers (Figure 6-1), you should see more information than what your own exception handlers have displayed. This is because, when an error is encountered during execution, the error causes not just the current method to terminate, but all other methods that were in the execution that led up to this method being called. Thus, an error in the current method causes a trickle effect back through all other methods that led to this point. There is an *execution call stack* that keeps track of all the methods that are in execution currently. As previously discussed, a trace of all the method calls is referred to as a *stack trace*. All the information that was displayed in the default error message was really a listing of the stack trace. The stack trace listing gives you a way to follow the call sequence to the line number in the method where the exception occurred. The stack trace may not show as many method calls as expected, but it provides plenty of information to help you pinpoint the problem.

To illustrate a stack trace, copy the Substring Demo program from Chapter 4. Add an OK-Stack button, and write code for its event method so that a general exception handler displays the result of the **ex.StackTrace**, as shown in Figure 6-31.

```
192    catch (Exception ex)
193    {
194        MessageBox.Show("Error: " + ex.StackTrace, Text,
195            MessageBoxButtons.OK, MessageBoxIcon.Information);
196        txtUser.Focus();
197        return;
198    }
```

Figure 6-31 Revised general exception handler to show stack trace

Figure 6-32 shows the message that appears if you click the OK-Stack button without entering a string in the text box.

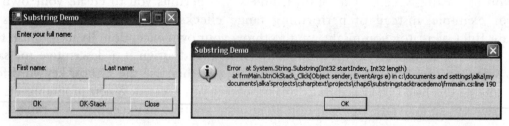

Figure 6-32 Screen shots from revised general exception handler to show stack trace

Showing the **StackTrace** property is often helpful when you are trying to debug your program and determine where the error might be. However, be sure to replace the **StackTrace** property with the **Message** property when you are ready to release the program to the user.

SUMMARY

Essential Topics

- Chapters 5 and 6 showed you that a program may terminate for many reasons other than that the user clicked the Close button. To create more robust programs, you should use data validation as well as exception handling as a first line of defense to prevent a program from crashing.

- Syntax errors occur when you violate the grammar rules of the C# language. A program with syntax errors does not compile, but luckily, syntax errors are the easiest errors to find and correct.

- Logic errors occur when you apply the wrong reasoning in your program logic. A program with logic errors may or may not produce results; however, if any results are displayed, they should not be trusted.

- An exception is an error condition that is triggered when your program is executing. Many situations can cause exceptions to be thrown. Parsing a string to assign to a numeric input field throws a **NumberFormatException**. Attempting to divide by zero throws a **DivideByZeroException**. Assigning a value larger than can be represented by a given data type throws an **OverflowException**.

- Information about the exception is stored in an **Exception** object. You can create a reference variable to the **Exception** object to get to this information.

- A generalized exception handler includes a **try** block, which encompasses the statements that have the potential to throw an exception, and a **catch** block that lists alternative processing when exceptions are thrown. The recommended alternative processing should display a message if any type of problem is detected, and skip execution of any remaining statements in the current event.

Bonus Topics

- A specific exception handler looks similar to the generalized one, but the **catch** block identifies the specific type of exception (such as, **NumberFormatException**) for which it has alternative processing.

- Exception handlers may be nested as long as each **try** block has a corresponding **catch** or **finally** block. A recommended approach is to write a generalized exception handler that surrounds the majority of an event method's program statements, and to write specialized exception handlers for individual statements that may throw specific exceptions, such applying the **Parse** method to data in a text box to convert it to a number.

- The call stack keeps track of all methods in execution and current line numbers. When exceptions are thrown, the stack trace may be used to help identify the statement that threw the exception.

- Controlling the exception handling programmatically, following our recommendations, leads to programs that are more user-friendly and reliable—an important goal for all developers.

KEY TERMS

Define each of the following terms, as they relate to object-oriented programming:

Essential Terms

- call stack
- catch (an exception)
- **catch** block
- data type check
- **DivideByZeroException**
- error handler
- exception
- execution call stack
- exception handler
- exception class
- **finally** block
- **FormatException**
- logic error
- Message property

- **OverflowException**
- raise (an exception)
- run-time error
- semantic error
- stack trace
- syntax error
- throw (an exception)
- **try** block
- **try-catch** block

Bonus Terms

- **ApplicationException**
- **StackTrace** property

REVIEW QUESTIONS

Essential Questions

1. An exception is a block of code that is used to bypass the system's default error handling. True or false?

2. A semantic error occurs when the syntax of your code is correct, but what you want the code to do is not. True or false?

3. When the user provides textual input data for a numeric input field, converting the user's input to a number throws a **FormatException** error. True or false?

4. If a mathematical expression produces an answer that is larger than the range allowed by the data type, a **FormatException** error is thrown. True or false?

5. When adding an exception handler to your code, place the potentially problem-causing statements inside a **catch** block. True or false?

6. The **finally** block of an exception handler is used to define the processing steps for a general exception. True or false?

7. True or false? An **ArgumentOutOfRangeException** is thrown when the following statement is executed:

```
streetAddress = .address.Substring(0,-1);
```

8. True or false? A generalized exception handler takes the form:

```
catch (FormatException ex)
{
    // processing steps if an error is found
}
```

9. The **StackTrace** is used to list the progression of exceptions in all methods that are currently executing. True or false?

10. The best way to implement a data type check for integers with the current version of C# is to use the **TryParse** method. True or false?

11. A(n) _____ _____ is a block of program code that is processed when an exception occurs in lieu of the default error messages displayed by the system.

12. A(n) _____ error violates the grammar rules of C#.

13. When a semantic error is able to complete execution, but displays incorrect results, the program has a(n) _____ error.

14. An attempt to perform division where the denominator is zero results in a(n) _____ being thrown.

15. The _____ block is used to identify remaining processing steps to be completed in an exception handler whether an error is triggered or not.

16. What are the three parts of an exception handler?

17. Write the syntax for a generalized exception handler.

18. How can you display the call stack in an error message displayed by an exception handler?

19. If an error can be detected with a decision statement, when would you use an exception handler instead?

20. How do you use exception handling to perform data type checks?

Bonus Questions

1. When writing multiple **catch** blocks in an exception handler, the generalized **catch** block should be listed first. True or false?

2. A specialized **catch** block should include steps to display an informative message, position the cursor in the offending text box, and terminate execution of the event. True or false?

3. Visual Studio can be used to identify exceptions simply by selecting Exceptions from the Debug menu, expanding the Common Language Runtime Exceptions list, and then expanding the Systems list. True or false?

4. True or false? To throw your own exceptions, define an **ApplicationException** variable, assign it a descriptive string message, and then **raise** the exception as follows:

```
if (BooleanExpression)
{

    ApplicationException exVar = new ApplicationException("MessageString");
    raise exVar;

}
```

5. To display the contents of the call stack, use the **ShowStack** method. True or false?

6. When writing a specialized exception handler to catch the wrong data type, the **catch** statement block should look like _____.

7. To define your own exception named **exBadFit** to display the string, "This does not fit the requirements", use the statement _____.

6

8. Write the statements needed to raise your own exception if the value in nbr is not between 5 and 10.

9. Write the statements needed to define a general-purpose exception handler that displays the call stack.

10. Explain under what condition(s) or for what purpose(s) you might want to include code that displays the call stack in a program.

PROGRAMMING EXERCISES

Essential Exercises

1. Add a generalized exception handler to the Carpet Cost calculator program in Chapter 2.

2. Revise the pizza cost calculator (refer to Essential Exercise 2 in Chapter 5) so that a generalized error handler prevents the program from terminating abnormally.

3. Add a generalized exception handler to the Date Time demo in Chapter 4 (see Figure 4-22).

4. Write a C# program that collects the number of each type of coin that the user has, and then finds and displays the total amount of money in coins. (Refer to Essential Programming Exercise 1 in Chapter 4.) Include a generalized exception handler to prevent the program from crashing when the user enters invalid data.

5. Write a C# program that can be used as a simple calculator to find and display the square or cube of a given number. (Refer to Essential Programming Exercise 2 in Chapter 4.) Include a generalized exception handler to prevent the program from crashing when the user enters invalid data.

6. Write a C# program that accepts a filename with path in a single text box and displays whether the file can be found on the computer's hard drive (`c:\file` or `C:\file`) or floppy drive (`a:\file` or `A:\file`) or is located elsewhere. (Refer to Essential Programming Exercise 5 in Chapter 4.) Include a generalized exception handler to prevent the program from crashing when invalid data are entered by the user.

Bonus Exercises

1. Revise the Contact Info Application from Chapter 4 (see Figure 4-14) so that it has a single **try** block and multiple **catch** blocks to handle the wrong data type for phone number (all digits), and insufficient digits entered for phone number. Be sure to include the generalized **catch** block.

2. Revise the Math Methods demo from Chapter 4 (see Figure 4-23) so that it includes handlers for data type checks. Be sure to include the generalized **catch** block.

3. Write a C# program that gets the user's birthdate and then finds and displays the user's current age. Include a specialized exception handler to perform a **DateTime** type check as well as a generalized exception handler to prevent the program from crashing when other problems occur.

4. Write a C# program to calculate the cost to carpet a circular room. (Refer to Bonus Programming Exercise 9 in Chapter 4.) Include appropriate specialized and generalized **catch** blocks to make the program foolproof.

7

ADDING METHODS FOR OBJECTS

In the Essentials section you will learn:

♦ What a method is

♦ When and why to use methods

♦ How to code methods

♦ The difference between block, local, and class scope

♦ How to communicate between methods by passing arguments and returning values

♦ The difference between passing arguments by value and by reference

In the Bonus section you will learn:

♦ Details on method overhead

♦ What method signatures are

♦ The difference between instance methods and shared methods

♦ How to overload methods

We have stated from the outset of this book that, as a general rule, less code is preferable to more code. After all, the fewer lines of code you have to write, debug, and maintain, the better. In this chapter, we examine a fundamental element of programming that promotes modularity and reduced program size: the method. Understanding methods is a critical element in writing efficient and easily maintained programs.

ESSENTIAL TOPICS

In Chapter 1 you learned that an object might be visualized as a shell that contains the properties and methods of the object. You saw how the dot operator is used to gain access to the properties and methods that are defined within the object. In previous chapters, you have used methods for some of the classes defined in the .NET class library. In this chapter you will learn how and why to add your own methods for objects. Before you can appreciate the usefulness of a method, you need to understand what a method is.

WHAT IS A METHOD?

A **method** is a group of one or more program statements designed to perform a single task. In other programming languages, methods are sometimes called functions, **procedures**, or **subroutines**. You have already used several methods in programs. For example, when you code a statement like:

```
txtName.Focus();
```

the **Focus** method of the text box object named **txtName** is executed to place the cursor in that text box. You can call the **Focus** method because it has already been defined as part of the .NET **TextBox** class. There are also times when you need to define your own methods. For example, in previous chapters you have coded event methods to respond to user actions such as clicking a button on a form. As your programs become more complex, you will find additional reasons for adding methods to classes. Once you have defined a method, other parts of your program can access the method by calling it by name.

Methods are added to class files for several reasons:

- To add behavior to an object

- To reduce redundant code

- To break up large blocks of code into smaller, easier to manage, blocks

The general syntax for defining a method in C# is:

```
[accessSpecifier] returnDataType methodName([paramType paramName [, …]])
{
    Method statement block or body
}
```

Square brackets around a syntax element mean that element is optional. The **accessSpecifier** is usually defined as **public** or **private** and determines what other elements of your program have access to this method. The examples in this chapter use the **private** access specifier. Methods defined as **public** can be called from other classes and are described in more detail in Chapter 10. The **returnDataType** refers to the type of data this method returns to the caller of the method. Methods can return a single value of any data type including the C# value types, or a reference to an object.

Using the accessSpecifier to Define Methods

You can see from the method syntax that the `accessSpecifier` for defining a method is optional. This means if you omit the `accessSpecifier`, C# uses the **private** access specifier. Because the `accessSpecifier` is optional, you might be tempted to let C# use the default value. However, we recommend that you always include **public** or **private** for the `accessSpecifier` when defining methods to help document your intentions. The reason is that, although less code is generally easier to understand than more code, explicit code is better than ambiguous code.

The `methodName` is the name that you've given to a method. The naming rules for methods are the same as the identifier naming rules presented in Chapter 3:

- An identifier must start with an alphabetic letter or an underscore.

- After the first character, an identifier may contain letters, digits, characters, or an underscore.

- Punctuation characters are not allowed (that is, punctuation marks such as a period, comma, and question mark are illegal).

- An identifier cannot be a C# keyword. (Appendix A contains the list of C# keywords that cannot be used as an identifier.)

In addition, method names frequently begin with a verb to indicate that the method performs some task or action. Methods defined as **private** begin with a lowercase letter, and those marked **public** begin with an uppercase letter. These beginning-letter practices are simply a style convention and not a C# rule; many C# programmers use this convention.

Immediately following the method name is an opening parenthesis, followed by zero or more method parameters. A **method parameter** holds a piece of data that is passed to the method to help it perform its designed task. If a method can complete its task without any additional data from other parts of the program, the method needs no parameters. In other cases, a method may need one, two, or perhaps more parameters passed to it to accomplish its task. If a parameter is used, each parameter that is passed to the method must list its data type and its name. Parameters can be of any data type, including the C# value types, or a reference to an object. The group of parameters that appears between the two parentheses is called the method's **parameter list**.

The parameter list is followed by a closing parenthesis and an opening curly brace. Between the opening and closing curly braces for the method are the statements that determine what the method does. The method statements that appear between the curly braces form what is called the **method statement block**, or the **method body**.

All methods in C# follow the syntax rules described in this section. Methods defined as **public** can be called from other classes, and are used to add behavior to an object (Chapter 10 covers this topic in detail). However, all the programs you have written thus far contain a single class— `frmMain`. You've already learned to write methods that respond to events. You can also write methods that are designed to be called only from within the class in which they are defined. That's the subject of the next section.

PRIVATE HELPER METHODS

Methods that are defined as **private** can only be called from within the class in which they are defined. Such methods are called **private helper methods**, or simply **helper methods**. Helper methods are often used to help reduce redundant code, or to break up large blocks of code into smaller, easier to manage, blocks. Helper methods are called from other code in the class, such as from the code in event methods.

Chapter 5 explained how to display a proper message box by calling the `Show` method of the `MessageBox` class using a statement similar to:

```
MessageBox.Show("Your message here.",
    Text, MessageBoxButton.OK, MessageBoxIcon.Information);
```

In both Chapters 5 and 6, this code was repeated many times because message boxes were displayed from various places throughout the programs. The only difference among all the message boxes was the actual message that was displayed. Let's build upon that message box task and create a private helper method that handles all message needs without having to write the duplicate code every time you need to display this style of a message box. Figure 7-1 presents the code for a method that displays such a message box.

```
1    // Purpose: Display a proper message box with only an OK button.
2    //
3    // Parameter list:
4    //      string msg      the message to display
5    //
6    // Return value:
7    //      void
8    //
9    private void messageBoxOK(string msg)
10   {
11        MessageBox.Show(msg, Text, MessageBoxButtons.OK,
12            MessageBoxIcon.Information);
13   }
```

Figure 7-1   The messageBoxOK helper method

From the code presented in Figure 7-1, you can see that the access specifier for the **messageBoxOK** method is **private**. The **private** keyword means that the **messageBoxOK** method can be called only from within the class in which it is defined. Limiting **messageBoxOK** to being called from within its own class is not a problem because so far the simple program uses only one class—**frmMain**. The **void** keyword immediately before the method name indicates that the **messageBoxOK** method does not return a value to its caller.

Finally, for the method **messageBoxOK** to perform its task, it must know the message to be displayed. Therefore, **messageBoxOK** has one parameter named **msg**, which is passed to the method as a **string**. The **msg** parameter is then passed to the **Show** method of the **MessageBox** class, which displays the message text in a modal dialog box.

With the new **messageBoxOK** method defined, the task of displaying a message box is now much simpler. For example, this data validation code:

```
1    // Check to make sure a name has been entered.
2
3    if (studentName == "")
4    {
5         MessageBox.Show("Name is required.",
6             Text, MessageBoxButtons.OK, MessageBoxIcon.Information);
7         txtStudentName.Focus();
8         return;
9    }
10
11   // Validate birthdate.
12
13   if (birthDate > DateTime.Today)
14   {
15        MessageBox.Show("Birthdate cannot be > today's date.",
16            Text, MessageBoxButtons.OK, MessageBoxIcon.Information);
17        txtBirthDate.Focus();
18        return;
19   }
```

can be modified as:

```
1    // Check to make sure a name has been entered.
2
3    if (studentName == "")
4    {
5         messageBoxOK("Name is required.");
6         txtStudentName.Focus();
7         return;
8    }
9
10   // Validate birthdate.
11
12   if (birthDate > DateTime.Today)
13   {
14        messageBoxOK("Birthdate cannot be > today's date.");
15        txtBirthDate.Focus();
16        return;
17   }
```

The new version is simplified by calling the new **messageBoxOK** method, as shown on statements 5 and 14, because the redundant code is contained within the **messageBoxOK** method and not repeated each time you need to display a message to the user. The statements on lines 5 and 14 are examples of **calling a method**. Each of these statements causes the code in Figure 7-1 to be executed using the appropriate string message as the parameter (that is, "Name is required." as the string parameter for line 5 and "Birthday cannot be > today's date." for line 14). After the **messageBoxOK** method performs its task using the string it was passed, control returns to the statement following the call to the **messageBoxOK** method (that is, either line 6 or line 15).

COMMUNICATING BETWEEN METHODS

When you start breaking up a program's logic into several methods, you need a way to communicate information between these methods. A means to communicate is necessary because a variable defined in one method cannot be directly used in another. How to communicate between methods is the focus of this section.

Scope

The term **scope** is used to refer to a variable's visibility in a program. A variable's **visibility** refers to the location in which it can be used in the program. Three levels of scope are discussed in this section. Listed from smallest to largest, the three levels of scope are block scope, local scope, and class scope. Consider the class and method definition in Figure 7-2.

```
1    public class frmMain : Form
2    {
3        private int k;
4
5        private int myMethodA(int number)
6        {
7            int i;
8            if (number < 10)
9            {
10               int j;
11               j = number * 1000;
12           }
13           return j;      // Compile Error!
14       }
15
16       private void myMethodB()
17       {
18           k++;
19       }
20   }
```

Figure 7-2   Example to illustrate scope

Block Scope

In Figure 7-2, variable j is defined on line 10. Because j is defined within a statement block (that is, the **if** statement block), it is said to have block scope. A variable with **block scope** is visible from the point of its definition (line 10) to the closing brace of the statement block in which it is defined (line 12). When the closing brace of its statement block is reached, a variable with block scope ceases to exist. This means that variable j can be used only in the statements between line 10 and line 12. At line 12, variable j can no longer be accessed. Programmers often refer to a variable that has reached its closing brace as "going out of scope." In other words, after line 12 is reached, variable j is "out of scope" and no longer visible to other parts of the program. That is why we have shown line 13 to be a compile error. Variable j is no longer in scope at line 13, and the compiler issues an error message.

Local Scope

Local scope refers to a variable that has been defined within a method, but not within some other statement block. In Figure 7-2, variable i is a variable that has been defined with local scope because its definition appears within **myMethodA**. Variable **i** can be used from its definition in line 7 to its associated closing brace in line 14. If you try to use variable **i** outside the **myMethodA** method, the compiler issues an error message because variable **i** is out of scope. We recommend you define all local scope variables at the beginning of the method in which they are used. By convention, local scope variable names begin with a lowercase letter.

Class Scope

Class scope refers to a variable that has been defined within a class definition, but not within a method in the class. In Figure 7-2, variable **k** is defined on line 3. Because it is defined within the class, but not within any methods, variable **k** has class scope. Variables defined as class scope can be used within any methods defined in the class. We recommend you define all class scope variables at the beginning of the class in which they are used. You might have noticed that the code the Form Designer generates places all UI controls as class scope so they can be accessed by any method within the form class. By convention, **private** class scope variable names begin with a lowercase "m" to indicate they are a private "member" of the class.

Which Scope to Use

Here is a general guideline for choosing which scope to use: If a variable is used within one method, it should be defined with local scope. We recommend you avoid the use of block scope variables (see the sidebar, "Shadowing"). Class scope variables should be reserved to hold data values that make up the state of the object. In other words, class scope variables are the variables that describe the properties of the class. Further, the values of these properties define the state of an object of the class.

Shadowing

What would happen if a method contained two variables with the same name, as shown in this snippet?

```
1    private void myMethod()
2    {
3        int i;
4        if (i < 10)
5        {
6            int i;
7            i++;
8        }
9    }
```

A variable named **i** is defined on line 3 *and* on line 6. It seems that variable definitions like these might cause a compiler error, but they don't. Because the variable **i** defined on line 3 is defined with local scope and the other variable **i** defined on line 6 is defined with block scope, there is no problem. Variables defined using the same name but at different scope levels are perfectly acceptable to the compiler.

However, which variable **i** is used in the calculation on line 7? For situations in which two variables share the same name, but have different scope levels, the most-recently defined variable that is in scope takes precedence. In the example discussed here, the variable **i** defined on line 6 is used.

The variable **i** defined on line 6 is said to **shadow** the definition of variable **i** on line 3. **Shadowing** occurs whenever the definition of one variable is encompassed by the definition of another variable and they both share the same name. In most cases, there is little or no good reason for shadowing to occur. After all, variables should be defined using descriptive names, and so you should never need two variables that serve the same purpose.

Parameters

Here is a general guideline for choosing scope: Define variables as local to the method in which they are used, unless they make up part of the object's state. If the variables make up part of the object's state, define the variables at class scope. After all, variables with class scope should define the properties of the class. But what if two methods need to share information, and that information isn't part of the object's state? The answer is to pass this information from one method to another as an argument. For example, the **messageBoxOK** method presented earlier in this chapter allows the calling method to communicate the message to display by passing an argument to the **messageBoxOK** method.

In this section you learn about method parameters in greater detail. The short program presented in Figure 7-3 illustrates some interesting details about method parameters.

```
1    using System;
2    using System.Windows.Forms;
3
4    public class frmMain : Form
5    {
6        private int mTestValue;

120      static void Main()
121      {
122          frmMain main = new frmMain();
123          Application.Run(main);
124      }
125
126      public frmMain()
127      {
128          InitializeComponent();
129          mTestValue = 10;
130          txtBefore.Text = mTestValue.ToString();
131      }
132
133      public void btnCall_Click(object sender, System.EventArgs e)
134      {
135          SquareParameter(mTestValue);
136          txtAfter.Text = mTestValue.ToString();
137      }
138
139      //Purpose: This method simply squares the number passed to it.
140      //
141      //Parameter list:
142      //    int number      the number to be squared
143      //
144      //Return value:
145      //    n/a
146      //
147      private void SquareParameter(int number)
148      {
149          number *= number;
150          txtInMethod.Text = number.ToString();
151      }
```

Figure 7-3   Test program for parameter details

```
152
153        private void btnClose_Click(object sender, System.EventArgs e)
154        {
155            Close();
156        }
157  }
```

Figure 7-3 Test program for parameter details (continued)

Notice that the constructor method (lines 126 to 131) assigns an initial value of 10 to variable **mTestValue** at line 129 and then displays this value in the text box **txtBefore** at line 130. Because the constructor is automatically called when the program first starts, the value seen in the **txtBefore** text box is 10.

When you click on the button labeled Call Method, the **btnCall_Click** event is executed and the program calls the method named **SquareParameter** at line 135. This means that **mTestValue** is an argument to the **SquareParameter** method before the method is called. Once program control is transferred to **SquareParameter**, the value of the parameter supplied to it (that is, 10) is squared at line 149. The squared value is then displayed in the **txtInMethod** text box at line 150. Because **number** is the square of the parameter (10), the value displayed is 100. When program control returns to the caller at line 136, the program copies **mTestValue** into a text box named **txtAfter**.

Figure 7-4 shows a sample run of the program.

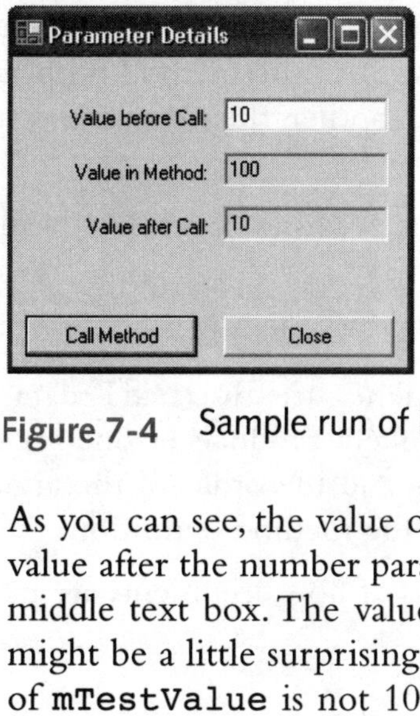

Figure 7-4 Sample run of Parameter Details program

As you can see, the value of **mTestValue** before you clicked the Call Method button is 10. The value after the number parameter in the **SquareParameter** method is squared, as shown in the middle text box. The value in the **SquareParameter** method code is 100, as expected. What might be a little surprising is that, when program control returns from the method call, the value of **mTestValue** is not 100 but is still 10, as shown in the third text box. How is this possible? After all, we squared **mTestValue** in the **SquareParameter** method. Well, not really.

Parameters versus Arguments

It's not uncommon for programmers to use terms interchangeably when they really should not. We have already alluded to the distinction between the terms "define" and "declare." (See the Bonus Topics section in Chapter 3.) Unfortunately, the distinction between parameters and arguments is equally blurred in many cases.

When you are writing the statements that compose an **object method**, for example, you might write a method similar to:

```
private decimal calculatePresentValueFactor(decimal interest, decimal value)
{
    // Method body statements
}
```

As you saw earlier in this chapter, each data item found between the opening and closing parentheses of the method is a parameter. Collectively, these parameters form the parameter list for the `calculatePresentValueFactor` method. Now consider the following statements:

```
decimal rate = .05;
decimal val = 10000;
decimal pvFactor;

pvFactor = calculatePresentValueFactor(rate, val);
```

In this code snippet, the variables `rate` and `val` represent arguments that are being passed to the `calculatePresentValueFactor` method. An **argument**, therefore, represents a data value that is being passed to a method. In more colorful terms, arguments have meaningful values associated with them, while **parameters** are appropriately sized empty buckets capable of holding the arguments. As you might guess, if you pass the wrong data type to a method, problems may occur. For example, if you had defined the `rate` variable in the snippet above to be a **float** instead of a **decimal** data type, and then tried to pass that value to the method, the compiler would issue an error message. The compiler would complain because you are filling a 4-byte argument bucket (a **float**) with the content of the `rate` variable, and then trying to fill a 12-byte bucket (a **decimal**) in the method with its contents. For arguments and parameters to be happy with one another, their data types (that is, bucket sizes) must match.

Another problem can occur when you pass arguments in the wrong order. For example, if you incorrectly write the call in the snippet above as:

```
pvFactor = calculatePresentValueFactor(val, rate);
```

the compiler detects no problems because both arguments are **decimal** data types. Unfortunately, your reversal of the arguments will quite likely produce erroneous results. Therefore, argument and parameter data types must match, and the order of the arguments used in the method call must align with the parameters in the method definition.

The Bonus section of this chapter presents additional details of how arguments are passed to a method.

Pass by Value

Let's examine the statement that calls the `SquareParameter` method:

```
SquareParameter(mTestValue);
```

Suppose that the Windows Memory Manager (WMM) found 4 bytes of memory for `mTestValue` at memory address 500,000. You know that the statement:

```
mTestValue = 10;
```

in the constructor initialized the value of *mTestValue* to 10. It follows then that the 4 bytes beginning at memory address 500,000 now contain the value 10. (Using terms from the Bonus section of Chapter 3, the `lvalue` of `mTestValue` is 500,000 and its rvalue is 10.)

The statement that calls the `SquareParameter` method:

```
SquareParameter(mTestValue);
```

can be visualized as though it were written:

```
SquareParameter(10);
```

Now look at the first line of the `SquareParameter` code:

```
private void SquareParameter(int number)
```

The C# compiler views the statement as though it has to take the argument that is passed to `SquareParameter`, which has a value of 10, and assign that value into a temporary variable named `number`. To use `number` in the `SquareParameter` method, the program code must call the WMM to get 4 bytes of storage for `number`. Let's suppose WMM returns a memory address of 800,000 for `number`. Next, the program code copies the value 10 into the 4 bytes of memory starting at memory address 800,000.

The next two statements in the `SquareParameter` method square the value of `number` and display the new value of 100 in the text box named `txtInMethod`.

```
number *= number;
txtInMethod.Text = number.ToString();
```

The result of these two statements can be seen in the middle text box (Value in Method) in Figure 7-4. Figure 7-5 shows how memory for these variables might look.

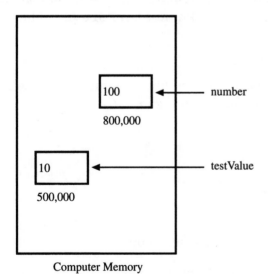

Computer Memory

Figure 7-5   Memory locations for various variables

Upon return from the `SquareParameter` method, the statement:

```
txtAfter.Text = mTestValue.ToString();
```

displays the value of `mTestValue` in the third text box, named `txtAfter`. However, `mTestValue` is still 10, not 100.

If you followed the previous discussion closely, you understand that the reason **mTestValue** remains unchanged is that a copy of the value of **mTestValue** was sent as the parameter to the **SquareParameter** method, not the memory address of where **mTestValue** is located. Because the **SquareParameter** method has no clue where **mTestValue** is located in memory, there is no way for **SquareParameter** to change its value. Indeed, it is variable **number** that is squared, and it resides at memory address 800,000. In other words, the **SquareParameter** method squares the 4-byte integer value stored at memory address 800,000, not memory address 500,000 where **mTestValue** is located.

By default, C# copies the value of arguments that are used in a method call. This process of using copies of argument values in a method call is referred to as **pass by value**. Because pass by value uses only the values of the arguments, not their memory addresses, there is no way for a called method to change the value of the argument being passed to the method. Pass by value is actually a type of safety net in that it does not allow you to change the value of an argument in one part of a program by **calling a method** in another part of the program.

But what if you really need to have a method change the value of an argument in a program?

Pass by Reference

A situation may arise in which you want the value of a variable to be permanently changed by the method call that uses the variable as an argument in a method call. You can permanently alter a variable's value only by letting the method know the address where the variable resides in memory. C# provides a mechanism by which you can pass the actual memory address of a variable to a method.

Let's use the code from Figure 7-3 and modify it for the purposes discussed in this section. First, you must modify the way that you call the method in the **btnCalc_Click** event code. Suppose you rename **SquareParameter** to be named **SquareParameterForever**. The modified method call now becomes:

```
SquareParameterForever(ref mTestValue);
```

Because the method call is modified, you must rename and modify the **SquareParameter** code from Figure 7-3 as well. The necessary changes are shown in Figure 7-6.

```
private void SquareParameterForever(ref int number)
{
    number *= number;
    txtInMethod.Text = number.ToString();
}
```

Figure 7-6 Modified code to permanently change a parameter value

Notice that the two code changes both involve the **ref** keyword. Figure 7-6 shows that the parameter list for the **SquareParameterForever** method now has the **ref** keyword placed before **int number**. The purpose of the **ref** keyword in a method's parameter list is to tell the C# compiler that the memory address of an argument is being passed to the method, not the value of the argument. (Using the terms from the Bonus Topics section of Chapter 3, the method is receiving the **lvalue** of the argument, not the **rvalue**.) In other words, if **mTestValue** does reside at memory address 500,000, as shown in Figure 7-5, the statement:

```
SquareParameterForever(ref mTestValue);
```

behaves as though it were written:

```
SquareParameterForever(500,000);
```

After this memory reference reaches the `SquareParameterForever` code, the **ref** keyword completely changes the way **number** is generated in the program. The **ref** keyword tells the C# compiler to generate code that goes to memory address 500,000 and use that memory address for variable **number**! Unlike the earlier version, no memory is allocated by the WMM for **number**. That is, the expression:

```
ref int number
```

in the method's parameter list is a data declaration, not a data definition. This is a subtle, but extremely important, difference. Because **number** has the same memory address in the program as does **mTestValue**, they are effectively the same variable! Because `SquareParameterForever` now knows where **mTestValue** resides in memory, and that is the same memory address for **number**, any changes to **number** produce exactly the same changes in **mTestValue**. After all, they are the same variable because they share the same memory address!

If you run the modified program, the result looks like that shown in Figure 7-7.

Figure 7-7   Sample program run using ref keyword

You can see by the value in the "Value after Call" text box in Figure 7-7 that the value of **mTestValue** is permanently altered following the call to `SquareParameterForever`. Also notice that it does not matter that the memory address of **mTestValue** is referred to using a different name (that is, **number**) in the `SquareParameterForever` method. Because **number** has the same memory address as **mTestValue**, the C# compiler doesn't care what name you associate with that memory address. It is the memory address that matters, not the name that appears in the `SquareParameterForever` parameter list.

It should be clear now that **pass by reference** means that the memory address of a variable is being sent to a method instead of a copy of its value. You should also know that you must initialize a **ref** argument before you can use it. If you fail to properly initialize a **ref** argument, an error message similar to:

```
Use of unassigned local variable 'varname'
```

is issued, where **varname** is the name of the offending variable.

By default, C# uses pass by value for the parameters used in a method call. Pass by value is more in line with the OOP goal of data hiding, in that the called method cannot alter the original value of the argument. Pass by value is a little safer in that the method receiving the data cannot directly change the value of that data. The method can use the data, but it cannot permanently change the data. Still, an occasion may arise when you need to bend the spirit of the OOP laws and use pass by reference. As a general rule, however, pass by value should be the norm for most of your C# method parameters.

Return Values

The previous section showed that a called method can communicate information back to the calling method if the calling method passes an argument by reference. Another way for a called method to communicate a single piece of information back to the calling method is through a return value.

Many times, there is no need for the calling method to communicate anything back to the caller. For example, the **messageBoxOK** method presented at the beginning of this chapter has no need to communicate anything back to the caller. Methods that do not return a value are defined using the **void** keyword as the return data type.

It is also common, however, to have methods that do return a value to the caller. Methods that do return a value are defined with a type other than **void** as the return type, and return a value using the **return** statement. The benefit of communicating a value back to the calling method through a return value, rather than through an argument passed by reference, is that the statement that calls the method can be used in an expression. To illustrate, let's create another helper method.

At the beginning of this chapter, we created the **messageBoxOK** private helper method that was based on the code for displaying a message box presented in Chapter 5. In Chapter 5 we also showed how to display a proper message box that asks the user a Yes or No question, using a statement similar to:

```
MessageBox.Show("Your message in the form of a yes or no question here",
     Text, MessageBoxButtons.YesNo, MessageBoxIcon.Question)
```

In this example, the **Show** method of the **MessageBox** class returns a value that indicates whether the user clicked the Yes or No button. Just as we simplified the task of displaying a message with an OK button, we can do the same to display a Yes or No question. Figure 7-8 presents the code for a method that displays a Yes or No message box and returns a value that indicates which button was clicked by the user. Note that **DialogResult** is a data type defined in the .NET framework.

```
1    // Purpose: Display a proper message box with Yes and No buttons.
2    //
3    // Parameter list:
4    //      string msg     the message to display
5    //
6    // Return value:
7    //      DialogResult   DialogResult.Yes or DialogResult.No
8    //
9    private DialogResult messageBoxYesNo(string msg)
10   {
11       DialogResult button;
12       button = MessageBox.Show(msg, Text, MessageBoxButtons.OK, MessageBoxIcon.Information);
13       return button;
14   }
```

Figure 7-8 The messageBoxYesNo helper method

Figure 7-9 shows the `messageBoxYesNo` helper method in use.

```
1    DialogResult result;
2    if (hoursWorked > 40)
3    {
4        result = messageBoxYesNo("You've entered a value > 40 hours.  Is this correct?");
5        if (result != DialogResult.Yes)
6        {
7            txtHoursWorked.Focus();
8            return;
9        }
10   }
```

Figure 7-9 Calling the messageBoxYesNo helper method

But Figure 7-10 shows a shorter approach with a different coding style.

```
1    if (hoursWorked > 40)
2    {
3        if (messageBoxYesNo("You've entered a value > 40 hours.  Is this correct?")
4            != DialogResult.Yes)
5        {
6            txtHoursWorked.Focus();
7            return;
8        }
9    }
```

Figure 7-10 Shorter call to the messageBoxYesNo helper method

In this second style, the call to method `messageBoxYesNo` and the comparison of its return value compose the Boolean expression in the **if** statement. There is no need to define the **result** variable to hold the return value.

WHAT CONSTITUTES A "GOOD" METHOD?

The private helper methods shown thus far are well-designed methods for several reasons. First, they perform a single task and do it efficiently and simply. Too often, beginning programmers want to make a method a "multitasker"—that is, they try to perform multiple tasks within the method code. This is almost never a good idea. Limit each method to a single task. Limiting methods to a single task makes it easier to test, debug, and maintain the method. Furthermore, it is easier to reuse code that does one single task than code that tries to do many things.

Second, the method is documented. The style used in this chapter is one that has served us well over the years, but the style is not etched in stone. However, if you do prefer some other style, make sure it:

- Contains a brief description of what the method does
- Lists and explains the parameters passed to the method
- Describes what the method returns and the interpretation of that value
- Lists assumptions or other details the method may expect in order to perform its task. (For example, the method might expect a disk file to already be open.)

Regardless of the documentation style you select, make sure it is complete, and use it consistently with each method you write.

A PROGRAM EXAMPLE

To illustrate more reasons for using helper methods, let's take another look at the Restaurant Bill Calculator from Chapter 6 (Figure 6-11). Recall that you used an exception handler to perform a data type check on each of the four input text boxes. Figure 7-11 shows a revised code listing for the Restaurant Bill Calculator that uses new helper methods to perform the data type checks—**decimalTypeCheck** and **intTypeCheck**. Notice that because of the name given to these new methods, the purpose of the code is clearer. Thus, in addition to saving space by reducing redundant code, using methods can make the code more understandable. In the case of the **inline code**, the **try-catch** blocks are used repeatedly, but unless you understand what they really do, it may not be obvious that you are simply performing a data type check. However, when you use the **decimalTypeCheck** and **intTypeCheck** methods, the name of the method explains its purpose. Furthermore, you have to look at only one place (the method definition itself) to see how the method works. When you call the method by name, you don't have to worry about how the code accomplishes its task.

```
274        // Make sure each of the input values is of the correct type.
275
276        if (decimalTypeCheck(txtMealCost.Text) == false)
277        {
278            messageBoxOK("Meal cost is required and must be numeric.");
279            txtMealCost.Focus();
280            return;
281        }
282
283        if (decimalTypeCheck(txtDrinkCost.Text) == false)
284        {
285            messageBoxOK("Drink cost is required and must be numeric.");
286            txtDrinkCost.Focus();
287            return;
288        }
289
290        if (decimalTypeCheck(txtDiscounts.Text) == false)
291        {
292            messageBoxOK("Discount amount is required and must be numeric. " +
293                "Enter 0 if there are no discounts");
294            txtDiscounts.Focus();
295            return;
296        }
297
298        if (intTypeCheck(txtNbrDiners.Text) == false)
299        {
300            messageBoxOK("The number of diners is required and must be a positive integer.");
301            txtNbrDiners.Focus();
302            return;
303        }
304
305        // Get the input values from the form.
```

Figure 7-11   Restaurant Bill Calculator using helper methods for data type checks

```
306
307         mealCost = decimal.Parse(txtMealCost.Text);
308         drinkCost = decimal.Parse(txtDrinkCost.Text);
309         discounts = decimal.Parse(txtDiscounts.Text);
310         nbrDiners = int.Parse(txtNbrDiners.Text);
311
312         // Validate that nbrDiners is not zero to avoid divide by zero error.
313
314         if (nbrDiners <= 0)
315         {
316             messageBoxOK("The number of diners must be a positive number.");
317             txtNbrDiners.Focus();
318             return;
319         }
```

Figure 7-11   Restaurant Bill Calculator using helper methods for data type checks (continued)

You might be wondering about the code for the new data type check methods used in the Restaurant Bill Calculator. These methods illustrate a few new things that should be explained before reviewing their code. The parameter list in the new methods contains a single string that is tested to see if it can be converted. Remember that converting a string to a number using a **Parse** method might throw an exception, and when an exception occurs, your code needs to catch the exception to prevent your program from terminating. The new type check methods contain these **try** and **catch** blocks. (See lines 351 through 359 in Figure 7-12.) If the string can be converted, the method returns a Boolean value of **true**. Otherwise it returns **false**. The caller can use this return value to decide whether to continue processing or to display an error message. Refer to Figure 7-12 to view the code for the **decimalTypeCheck** method. The **intTypeCheck** method's code is very similar and is left as an exercise for you.

```
339         // Purpose: Determine if given string can be converted to a decimal.
340         //
341         // Parameter list:
342         //     string inputString    the string to check to see if it can be converted
343         //
344         // Return value:
345         //     bool                  true if the string can be converted to a decimal
346         //                           and false otherwise
347         //
348         private bool decimalTypeCheck(string inputString)
349         {
350             decimal tempNbr;
351             try
352             {
353                 tempNbr = decimal.Parse(inputString);
354                 return true;
355             }
356             catch
357             {
358                 return false;
359             }
360         }
```

Figure 7-12   The decimalTypeCheck method

Passing Reference Data Types

The difference between passing arguments by value and passing them by reference was discussed earlier in this chapter. That previous discussion applied to value data types. In Figure 7-12, the argument in the method call is a string. In Chapter 3, you learned that a string is a reference type, not a value type. Given this, you might be wondering what would happen if you inserted the following line between lines 352 and 353 in Figure 7-12:

```
inputString = "abcd";
```

Because the parameter is a string, is the original value of the parameter changed to "abcd" or not? It is not. When strings are used as method arguments, the passing behaves as if it were done by value, so the original values of arguments are not affected. What actually happens is that the reference to the string is passed by value. When the string is changed, the reference points to a new string with that value. And because the reference was passed by value, the change isn't reflected in the calling method.

What if you added the **ref** keyword prefix on the argument in the call and on the parameter in the method's parameter list? The compiler does not allow you to write code like this. Because the argument in the call is a property of a text box, you are not allowed to send property values by reference.

You can, however, use another reference type as a method parameter without the **ref** keyword, and the original value *is* changed. Consider the variation of the Restaurant Bill Calculator shown in Figure 7-13. The revised **decimalTypeCheck** method is shown in lines 1 to 17, and relevant parts of the **btnCalculate_Click** event method are shown in lines 42 to 103. There are three separate calls to the **decimalTypeCheck** method in the **btnCalculate_Click** event method (see lines 58, 67, and 76). Instead of sending just the **Text** property of the input text box, the three calls to the **decimalTypeCheck** method now send a reference to the text box object to be checked.

Look at line 13 in the **decimalTypeCheck** method to see that code was added to change the **Text** property of the **TextBox** parameter in the method. This was done so that you could determine if the original argument's **Text** property is changed. You should note that this example is for illustration purposes only. As stated in Chapter 5, when performing data validation, it is better to simply notify the user than to change a user's invalid input value.

```
1    private bool decimalTypeCheck(TextBox txtInput)
2    {
3        decimal tempNbr;
4        try
5        {
6            tempNbr = decimal.Parse(txtInput.Text);
7            return true;
8        }
9        catch
10        {
11            messageBoxOK(txtInput.Name + " is required and must be numeric.");
12            txtInput.Focus();
13            txtInput.Text = "abcd";
14            return false;
15        }
16    }
17
```

Figure 7-13   Revised decimalTypeCheckMethod with TextBox parameter

```
42    private void btnCalculate_Click(object sender, System.EventArgs e)
43    {

56        // Get the input values from the form and make sure each is the correct type
57
58        if (decimalTypeCheck(txtMealCost) == true)
59        {
60            mealCost = decimal.Parse(txtMealCost.Text);
61        }
62        else
63        {
64            return;
65        }
66
67        if (decimalTypeCheck(txtDrinkCost) == true)
68        {
69            drinkCost = decimal.Parse(txtDrinkCost.Text);
70        }
71        else
72        {
73            return;
74        }
75
76        if (decimalTypeCheck(txtDiscounts) == true)
77        {
78            discounts = decimal.Parse(txtDiscounts.Text);
79        }
80        else
81        {
82            return;
83        }
84
85        if (intTypeCheck(txtNbrDiners) == true)
86        {
87            nbrDiners = int.Parse(txtNbrDiners.Text);
88        }
89        else
90        {
91            return;
92        }
93
94        // Validate that nbrDiners is not zero to avoid divide by zero error.
95
96        if (nbrDiners <= 0)
97        {
98            MessageBox.Show("The number of diners must be a positive number.", Text,
99                MessageBoxButtons.OK, MessageBoxIcon.Information);
100           txtNbrDiners.Focus();
101           return;
102       }
103
```

Figure 7-13   Revised decimalTypeCheckMethod with TextBox parameter (continued)

The screen shots in Figure 7-14 show what happens as a consequence of sending the text box object (instead of just the Text property of a text box). After providing invalid input data, the method displays the message box to explain that the value in **txtMealCost** is required and must be numeric. When program control returns to the caller and terminates the **btnCalculate_Click** event, you can see that the form now shows "abcd" in **txtMealCost**. When the **decimalTypeCheck** method was called by the following statement:

```
58        if (decimalTypeCheck(txtMealCost) == true)
```

the argument **txtMealCost** in the call and the parameter **txtInput** in the method definition referred to the same memory location. Therefore, when the **Text** property of **txtInput** is changed, the **Text** property of **txtMealCost** is changed. This change is reflected in the final screen shot, which shows the "abcd" in **txtMealCost**. You can test this example further to verify that the same thing happens in the other calls that send different text boxes to the same method.

From this example, you can see that when methods use reference data types, such as text box objects, the original argument is changed as if the call were pass by reference. If you included the **ref** keyword, the result would be the same—that is, the original argument would still be changed.

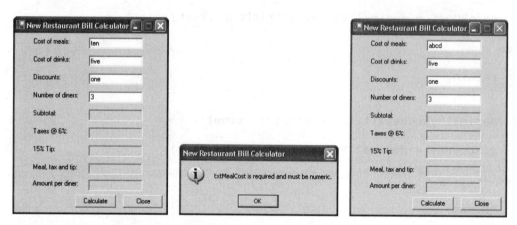

Figure 7-14   Sample run to show change to argument with TextBox parameter

A Method for Data Validation

Many programmers use methods to subdivide large blocks of code into smaller units that serve a distinctive purpose, such as data validation. For example, if you review Figure 7-13, you will see that the data validation processing takes up 45 lines of code. Including all of that code along with the other steps to perform the computations and display the results makes the **btnCalculate_Click** event method rather long. Because the 45 lines of code serve a distinctive purpose—validating the input before performing any computations—you could create a method to handle all of the data validation, and then replace the 45 lines of code with a single call to the validation method in **btnCalculate_Click**. Figure 7-15 presents the code for the **dataIsValid** method. The code consists of several checks, some of which use the other methods previously discussed. If a problem with the data is discovered, a **false** value is returned. If after checking every possible problem, nothing is found, a **true** value is returned on line 46. You should note that this line is executed only if all checks for invalid data pass, that is, no problems are found.

```
1    // Purpose: Determine if the user's input is acceptable or not.
2    //
3    // Parameter list:
4    //none
5    //
6    // Return value:
7    //bool             true if all input okay and false otherwise
8    //
9    private bool dataIsValid()
10   {
11       int nbrDiners;
12
13       // Get the input values from the form and make sure each is the correct type
14
15       if (decimalTypeCheck(txtMealCost) != true)
16       {
17           return false;
18       }
19
20       if (decimalTypeCheck(txtDrinkCost) != true)
21       {
22           return false;
23       }
24
25       if (decimalTypeCheck(txtDiscounts) != true)
26       {
27           return false;
28       }
29
30       if (intTypeCheck(txtNbrDiners) != true)
31       {
32           return false;
33       }
34
35       nbrDiners = int.Parse(txtNbrDiners.Text);
36
37       // Validate that nbrDiners is positive.
38
39       if (nbrDiners <= 0)
40       {
41           MessageBox.Show("The number of diners must be a positive number.", Text,
42               MessageBoxButtons.OK, MessageBoxIcon.Information);
43           txtNbrDiners.Focus();
44           return false;
45       }
46       return true;
47   }
```

Figure 7-15   Definition of dataIsValid method

Figure 7-16 presents the code for the revised **btnCalculate_Click** event method. Line 17 makes a call to the **dataIsValid** method. If the method doesn't return a **true** value, the event method terminates on line 19. However, if the **dataIsValid** method returns a **true** value, the decision fails and control passes to line 21, allowing the rest of the event method to be processed. Notice how the use of the method significantly reduces the lines of code in **btnCalculate_Click**. Being able to read an entire method on a page or less makes it easier for people to understand.

```
1    private void btnCalculate_Click(object sender, System.EventArgs e)
2    {
3        const double taxRate = .06;
4        const double tipPct = .15;
5        decimal mealCost;
6        decimal drinkCost;
7        decimal discounts;
8        int nbrDiners;
9        decimal subtotal;
10       decimal taxAmount;
11       decimal tipAmount;
12       decimal totalCost;
13       decimal costPerDiner;
14
15       // Make sure input is the correct type
16
17       if (dataIsValid() != true)
18       {
19           return;
20       }
21
22       // Assign the input to variables
23
24       mealCost = decimal.Parse(txtMealCost.Text);
25       drinkCost = decimal.Parse(txtDrinkCost.Text);
26       discounts = decimal.Parse(txtDiscounts.Text);
27       nbrDiners = int.Parse(txtNbrDiners.Text);
28
29       // Calculate the subtotal, taxAmount, tipAmount, totalCost and costPerDiner.
30
31       subtotal = mealCost + drinkCost;
32       taxAmount = Math.Round((decimal) taxRate * subtotal, 2);
33       tipAmount = Math.Round((decimal) tipPct * subtotal, 2);
34       totalCost = subtotal + taxAmount + tipAmount - discounts;
35       costPerDiner = Math.Round(totalCost / (decimal) nbrDiners, 2);
36
37       // Display the results back to the user.
38
39       txtSubtotal.Text = subtotal.ToString("C");
40       txtTaxAmount.Text = taxAmount.ToString("C");
41       txtTipAmount.Text = tipAmount.ToString("C");
42       txtTotalCost.Text = totalCost.ToString("C");
43       txtCostPerDiner.Text = costPerDiner.ToString("C");
44   }
```

Figure 7-16 Revised btnCalculate_Click event method

WHEN TO USE A METHOD

What determines whether you should write a method or simply write the code at the point where it is needed? After all, you could use the inline code shown in Chapter 6 to determine if a **string** can be converted to a **decimal** and not even worry about writing a helper method. But remember our general rule of: "The less code there is in a program, the better." In the previous example, the data validation logic has been simplified and contains two fewer statements. However, to make this possible, 22 new statements were added to define the **decimalTypeCheck** helper method. Is the new version actually simpler?

What if your program needs to validate a **decimal** value at 10 different places in the program? Now instead of repeating the inline **decimal** type check, only one line of code is required to call the `decimalTypeCheck method`.

The `decimalTypeCheck` method is a fairly small method. Other methods may contain more complex logic and therefore will contain more statements. In that case, the reduction of duplicate code is even greater. Figure 7-17 illustrates the effect this redundant inline code has on overall program size.

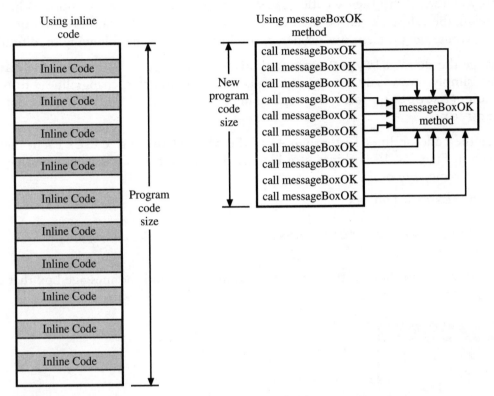

Figure 7-17   Inline code versus using a method

Figure 7-17 shows the difference between inline code and using a method. On the left side of Figure 7-17 is a depiction of writing the message code at 10 different places in a program. On the right side of Figure 7-17 are the same 10 calls, but using a method instead of inline code. As you can see, program size decreases because we have removed the duplicate message code from the program. Now the **decimal** type check code appears only once in the program. Ten values are checked for **decimal** type, but the work is all done in the `decimalTypeCheck` method rather than being scattered throughout the program.

The `decimalTypeCheck`, `intTypeCheck`, and `dataIsValid` methods illustrate another benefit of using methods in your programs—locating and testing the code. With a method, there is only one block of code to test and debug, regardless of how many different places the method is called in the program. By placing the code within a method, you have encapsulated its functionality at one location. Methods make code more modular, insulating it from other elements of the program. Having the code in one location simplifies testing and debugging.

Finally, if in the future the method code must be changed, the code change has to be made only at one place in the program. If you use inline code instead of calling a method, you have to search the entire program to find all the places where the equivalent code appears and make the code changes. Such code changes are very error-prone. Methods make code changes easier because there is only one place where the changes must be typed. Likewise, after you do make the new code change, you only have to test the new version at a single location in the program. Program maintenance becomes easier when you use methods.

THE CALL STACK AND METHODS

In Chapter 6, you learned that the execution call stack tracks all methods in execution. When exceptions are thrown, the call stack can be used to trace the problem and locate the lines of code and method name where the problem was triggered. To illustrate, make the following modifications:

1. Change the **decimalTypeCheck** method shown in Figure 7-13 so that the **catch** block simply throws any exception found. To accomplish this, change line 9 to read `catch (Exception ex)`, and replace lines 11 through 14 with the statement: `throw ex;`

2. Place the code on lines 15 through 43 in the **btnCalculate_Click** event method shown in Figure 7-16 within a **try** block. Add a **catch** block that displays the call stack in a message box:

```
catch (Exception ex)
{
    messageBoxOK("Call Stack: " + ex.StackTrace);
}
```

Figure 7-18 shows screen shots of the form with invalid input and the message box that displays the call stack.

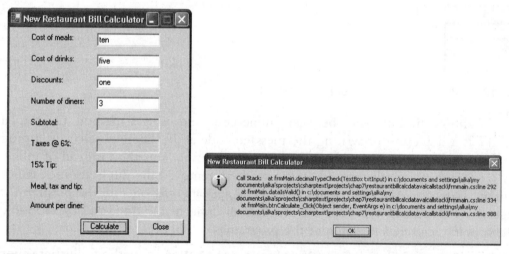

Figure 7-18   Displaying an execution call stack to locate method with error

The line numbers of the code listings displayed in this book don't always perfectly match the actual line numbers of the code as seen by the C# compiler. If you change the Text Editor options to show line numbers in the code window, you can locate the lines that are identified in the stack trace message and determine how the exception was passed through the series of methods in execution. In the sample screen shot in Figure 7-18, the sequence of messages indicates that the initial problem occurred at line 292 at **frmMain.decimalTypeCheck(TextBox txtInput)**—this is the statement that you just added to the `decimalTypeCheck` method that rethrows the exception. After that, the next line indicates that the exception was passed to line 334 in `frmMain.dataIsValid()`. The initial call is made in this line to the `decimalTypeCheck` method: `if (decimalTypeCheck(txtMealCost) != true)`. Because the last action in the `decimalTypeCheck` method was throwing an exception, when that method terminated and control returned to the `dataIsValid` method, the state of having an exception caused the `dataIsValid` method to terminate, sending the same exception up the call stack to the method that initiated it. The last line in the stack trace identifies line 388 in `frmMain.btnCalculate_Click` as the final source of the exception. This statement is the actual call to the `dataIsValid` method: `if (dataIsValid() != true)`. Because this statement is now inside a **try** block, the exception causes control to be passed to the **catch** block. The **catch** block calls the `messagBoxOK` method to display the stack trace shown in Figure 7-18.

This example illustrates how you can use the stack trace to locate problems in programs that employ multiple helper methods. After you locate the problem, if you think about what caused the problem, you can add or change code to handle the problem appropriately.

Bonus Topics

Using *out* Method Arguments

Earlier in this chapter you saw how the keyword **ref** could be used to pass arguments into a method. Passing by reference is useful when you need to send information to a method, allow the method to modify the argument, and get the modified value after the method returns. You also saw how a method could return a single value to the calling method using the **return** keyword. Sometimes a situation arises when a method needs to return more than a single value to the calling method. In this situation, you could pass the arguments by reference, but recall that passing an argument by reference requires the argument to be initialized with some value. In addition to pass by value and pass by reference, C# allows parameters to be defined as **out** parameters. Parameters defined as **out** work very much like those defined as **ref**, except that arguments passed as **out** parameters do not have to be initialized. But just as **ref** parameters must be initialized in the calling method before you can pass them to the other method, **out** variables must have values assigned to them before they go out of scope in the called method.

To illustrate, let's revisit the revision to the Restaurant Bill Calculator shown in Figure 7-11 and Figure 7-12. Notice that if valid values are entered in the input text boxes, each number is converted to a string using a `Parse` method twice—once in the `decimalTypeCheck` or `intTypeCheck` method, and again to get the input values from the form (lines 307 to 310). We can make the program execute a bit more efficiently if each input value is converted to a number only once. This can be accomplished by enhancing the `decimalTypeCheck` and `intTypeCheck` methods to return two values—a Boolean value that indicates if the string argument can be converted to the appropriate number type, and another for the actual number value itself. Figure 7-19 shows a version of the `decimalTypeCheck` method that returns two values. The `intTypeCheck` method is modified in a similar manner.

7

```
1    // Purpose: Determine if given string can be converted to a decimal.
2    //
3    // Parameter list:
4    //      string inputString  the string to check to see if it can be converted
5    //      decimal outValue     the decimal value of the string if it was converted
6    //
7    // Return value:
8    //      bool                 true if the string can be converted to a decimal
9    //                           and false otherwise
10   //
11   private bool decimalTypeCheck(string inputString, out decimal outValue)
12   {
13       outValue = 0;
14       try
15       {
16           outValue = decimal.Parse(inputString);
17           return true;
18       }
19       catch
20       {
21           return false;
22       }
23   }
```

Figure 7-19 The decimalTypeCheck method that returns two values

Notice how the second parameter in line 11 is defined as **out**. Also notice that the variable **outValue** is assigned a value of zero at line 13. This statement is necessary because the **Parse** method on line 16 could fail if the contents of the variable **inputString** can't be converted to a **decimal** type. If line 13 were omitted and if the **Parse** method failed, variable **outValue** would never have a value assigned to it, which would cause a compile error. Figure 7-20 shows how the new **decimalTypeCheck** method can be used to further reduce the number of statements needed.

```
274          // Get the input values and make sure each is of the correct type.
275
276          if (decimalTypeCheck(txtMealCost.Text, mealCost) == false)
277          {
278              messageBoxOK("Meal cost is required and must be numeric.");
279              txtMealCost.Focus();
280              return;
281          }
282
283          if (decimalTypeCheck(txtDrinkCost.Text, drinkCost) == false)
284          {
285              messageBoxOK("Drink cost is required and must be numeric.");
286              txtDrinkCost.Focus();
287              return;
288          }
289
290          if (decimalTypeCheck(txtDiscounts.Text, discounts) == false)
291          {
292              messageBoxOK("Discount amount is required and must be numeric. " +
293                  "Enter 0 if there are no discounts");
294              txtDiscounts.Focus();
295              return;
296          }
297
298          if (intTypeCheck(txtNbrDiners.Text, nbrDiners) == false)
299          {
300              messageBoxOK("The number of diners is required and must be a positive integer.");
301              txtNbrDiners.Focus();
302              return;
303          }
304
305          // Validate that nbrDiners is not zero to avoid divide by zero error.
306
307          if (nbrDiners <= 0)
308          {
309              messageBoxOK("The number of diners must be a positive number.");
310              txtNbrDiners.Focus();
311              return;
312          }
```

Figure 7-20   Restaurant Bill Calculator using revised data type check methods

METHOD OVERHEAD

There is a small price to pay for all the nice things that methods do for you. That price is execution speed. Each time you call a method, the computer must perform work that isn't present for inline code; this is called **method overhead**. Calling a method requires copying any arguments that might be passed to the method, generating the code that performs the call to the method, perhaps creating one or more temporary variables to hold the arguments that are passed in, executing the code, and finally returning a value to a precise point in the program. All these setup tasks are collectively referred to as method overhead, and refer to the extra time it takes to process a method call instead of using inline code. Inline code, on the other hand, avoids almost all the method overhead associated with a method call and, hence, results in slightly faster execution speeds.

The time penalty associated with method overhead is usually miniscule. If a method call is buried in a highly repetitive code loop, however, the time delay might be noticeable. If the method overhead time penalty is significant, using inline code for the method call may be warranted. Such changes can sometimes make significant differences in program performance.

(The following paragraphs make a few simplifying assumptions about the actual process used to call an object method. However, those simplifying assumptions are not sufficiently important to detract from the general discussion of the method-calling process that follows.)

Figure 7-21 presents a sequence of program statements that might be used to call a fictional **LeapYear** method. Assume this method is passed an argument containing a year, and that it returns the integer value 1 if the year is a leap year, and 0 otherwise. (Note that you can use the **DateTime.IsLeapYear** method in the .NET framework to determine if a year is a leap year, but we are writing our own method to illustrate an important point.)

The sequence begins with the definition of a variable named **i**. We have assumed that the compiler has placed **i** at memory location 400,000, and it has an initial value of 0. We have also assumed that a **myDate** object of the **clsCalendar** class has been defined elsewhere and holds the **LeapYear** method. Because we are assuming that **i** is not allocated on the stack (see Chapter 3 Bonus Topics for a discussion of the stack), we show the **top of stack** (TOS) as empty. (Recall that the stack is located in high memory and grows downward as data are pushed onto the stack.)

The next statement shows the value 2004 being assigned into **i**. The assignment statement changes the rvalue of **i**, but nothing else. Next, we call the **LeapYear** method of object **myDate**. The first thing that happens is that the memory address of the program statement following the current statement is pushed onto the stack. Because we assume that the statement following the call to **LeapYear** is located at memory address 123,456, the memory address of that statement is pushed onto the stack. All memory addresses are assumed to require 4 bytes of memory for storage. Immediately after the memory address is pushed onto the stack, the value of **i** (rvalue = 2004) is pushed onto the stack. The result is the stack picture you see at the extreme right of the call to **LeapYear** in Figure 7-21.

Next, the Instruction Register (that is, the CPU register that holds the memory address of the next instruction to be executed) is set to the memory address where the **LeapYear** method of **myDate** is located, and program execution resumes at that memory location. When execution resumes at the statement currently being processed, or:

```
public int LeapYear(int year)
```

the compiler knows that there are 4 bytes of data sitting on the stack and that those (4) bytes should be assigned into a variable named **year**. (The compiler knows there are 4 bytes of data because of the **int** keyword.) Therefore, the code pops off 4 bytes from the stack and moves them into the memory address for **year**. Note that this process is why we refer to such method calls as call-by-value—the value of the argument (**i**) in the caller is copied onto the stack and subsequently copied into a temporary parameter variable (**year**) by the object method's code. Using the bucket analogy, the 4-byte bucket associated with variable **i** and holding the value **2004** is now emptied into the temporary bucket created by the **LeapYear** method for the variable named **year**.

Next, the **LeapYear** method body is executed to determine whether the year is a leap year or not. Because the value of **year** is 2004, which is a leap year, the statement:

```
return 1;
```

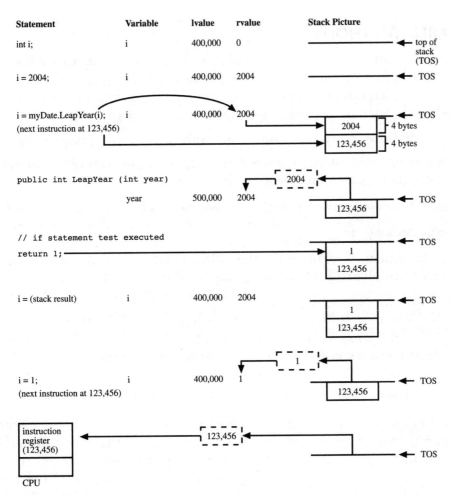

Figure 7-21   Calling an object method

is executed. This statement causes an integer value of 1 (because the return type of the **LeapYear** method is **int**) to be pushed onto the stack. Notice how the TOS holds the integer value 1.

The Instruction Register of the CPU is reset to the memory address of the caller who made the call to the **LeapYear** method, and the code prepares to assign the return value from the call into variable **i**. The integer value returned from the call to **LeapYear** is then popped off the stack and assigned into variable **i**.

Finally, the last 4 bytes on the stack (123,456) are popped into the CPU's Instruction Register, and program execution resumes at the memory address 123,456. Recall that the number 123,456 is the memory address of the next program statement to be executed after the call to the **LeapYear** method.

As you can see, there is a lot of work being done to call an object method. Most of the work shown in Figure 7-21 represents tasks necessary to set up a call to an object method and return to the next program statement. This setup work represents the method overhead we spoke of earlier in the chapter. Although it is true that inline code avoids the overhead of a method call, the benefits of modular code and the avoidance of duplicate code usually far outweigh the performance penalty associated with method overhead. Also, inline code carries its own penalty of duplicate lines of code if the code is used multiple times in a program.

INSTANCE VERSUS SHARED METHODS

If you've been paying close attention to how methods have been used in the examples shown in this and previous chapters, you should have noticed that methods are called in three different ways. Because **private** helper methods are defined in the same class where they are used, they are called simply by coding the method name and passing any required arguments. In this example:

```
messageBoxOK("Drink cost is required and must be numeric.");
```

the **messageBoxOK** method is called. You can tell that it is defined within this same class because you don't have to supply an object variable name.

At other times a method is called using an object variable name. This example:

```
txtDrinkCost.Focus();
```

calls the **Focus** method that is defined in the .NET **TextBox** class, and the variable **txtDrinkCost** refers to an object that has been instantiated from the **TextBox** class. You also know that the **Focus** method must be defined as **public** because it can be called from outside the **TextBox** class. In this example, the **Focus** method is called an **instance method** because to call it, you must use an object that is instantiated from the class in which the method is defined.

A third way of calling methods is using the class name, rather than an instance name. For example, this statement:

```
decimal.Parse(txtDrinkCost.Text);
```

calls a method named **Parse** that is defined in the **decimal** class. Again we know **Parse** must be declared as **public** because it can be called from outside the **decimal** class. But in this case, we didn't have to instantiate an object and then use that object reference to call the **Parse** method. We only had to supply the class name. Methods of this type are called **shared methods** because they are not associated with an instance of an object and are instead shared by all instances of the class in which they are defined. (C# uses the **static** keyword to define shared methods, so sometimes shared methods are referred to as **static methods**.)

How do you know if a method should be defined as an instance method or a shared method? Most of the time, methods should be defined as instance methods. But when writing a method, if you find the parameter list contains everything the method needs to complete its task (the method doesn't rely on any object state information), and you feel you might use this same method in another program, you should consider making the method a shared method. For example, the **messageBoxOK** method shown in this chapter can't be made a shared method because it uses the **Text** property of the current form when calling the **MessageBox.Show** method. However, the **decimalTypeCheck** method could indeed be defined as a shared method. Everything **decimalTypeCheck** needs to perform its assigned task is passed as an argument, and it is likely that you might use this same functionality in other programs.

To define a method as a shared method, you include the **static** keyword in its definition. The **decimalTypeCheck** method shown in Figure 7-12 can be changed from an instance method to a shared method simply by changing line 348 from:

```
348        private bool decimalTypeCheck(string inputString)
```

to:

```
348        private static bool decimalTypeCheck(string inputString)
```

When used from within the class in which it is defined, the **decimalTypeCheck** method is called in the same way as when it is defined as an instance method. A more likely scenario would be to move the **decimalTypeCheck** and **intTypeCheck** methods, along with other related methods, to another class (for example, **clsTypeCheck**) and define them as **public static**. This would make them easier to reuse in other applications. Just include this new class in the VS.NET project and call the method using a statement similar to:

```
if (clsTypeCheck.DecimalTypeCheck(txtBeginningBalance.Text) == false)
    ...
```

Chapter 10 covers more examples of encapsulation and object reuse.

SIGNATURES

7

The **signature** of a method begins with the method's name and continues through to the closing parenthesis of the parameter list. This means that a method signature includes the method name and the method's parameter list, if any. Figure 7–22 shows the signature for several methods.

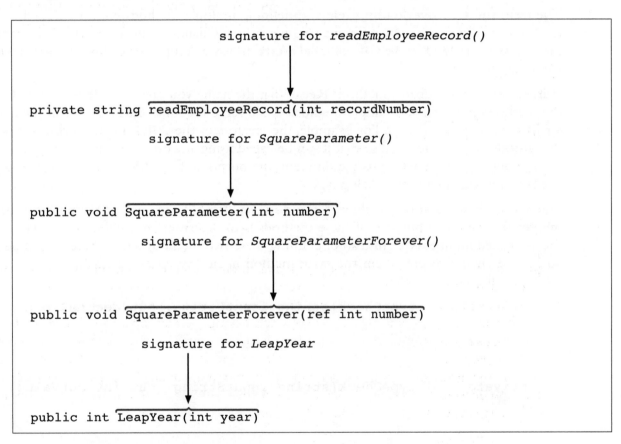

signature for *readEmployeeRecord()*

private string readEmployeeRecord(int recordNumber)

signature for *SquareParameter()*

public void SquareParameter(int number)

signature for *SquareParameterForever()*

public void SquareParameterForever(ref int number)

signature for *LeapYear*

public int LeapYear(int year)

Figure 7-22   Signatures for various methods

No two methods in the same class can have exactly the same signature. If you did try to compile a class with two identical signatures, the compiler would complain about a method being multiply defined. The message would be similar to:

```
Class 'clsCalendar' already defines a member called LeapYear with
the same parameter types
```

The real issue that causes this type of error message is identical signatures. Notice that changing a method's access specifier does not solve the problem. The reason is that the access specifier is not part of the signature, and any meaningful difference between methods must appear in the method signatures.

You can have methods that share a common name as long as the parameter lists are different. This process of sharing the same method name but having different parameter lists is called method **overloading**.

METHOD OVERLOADING

The term **method overloading** refers to defining multiple methods within a class that all have the same method name but different parameter lists. Changing the parameter list changes the method signature, and so the C# compiler won't display a compile error just because the method names are the same.

Why should you overload a method? Recall that the name you give to a method should describe the method's purpose. So multiple methods could serve the same purpose even if their parameter lists are slightly different. For example, the creators of the .NET Framework overloaded the **MessageBox.Show** method so that it can be called using any one of 12 different parameter lists. Even though the parameter lists are different, the purpose of the **Show** method is the same—to display a message in a modal dialog box.

You can apply method overloading to the **decimalTypeCheck** and **intTypeCheck** methods presented earlier. The purpose of these methods is to determine if a string can be converted to the associated number type. Instead of defining these two methods with different method names, you could choose to give them the same method name (**typeCheck**) and give each a unique parameter list. For example:

```
private bool typeCheck(string inputString, out decimal outValue)
{
    ...
}

private bool typeCheck(string inputString, out int outValue)
{
    ...
}
```

Note that the only difference in the two method signatures is the data type of the second parameter. You might then choose to overload the **typeCheck** method for each of the many other number types (for example, **byte**, **double**, and so on).

When the compiler finds two methods with the same name, how does it know which one to call? The answer is simple. The compiler checks the data type of the arguments you are passing, finds the method implementation that has a matching signature, and calls that method. If a method cannot be found with a matching signature, a compile error results. Method overloading makes the compiler locate the correct method so you don't have to.

 You should know that not all programming languages support overloading methods. If a programming language doesn't support method overloading, each method must be given a unique name. Fortunately, C# gives you the versatility of method overloading.

SUMMARY

Essential Topics

- ❑ A method is a block of code designed to perform a specific task. Methods can be used to add behavior to an object, reduce redundant code, or decompose large blocks of code into smaller, more manageable units.

- ❑ Private helper methods are used within the same class, such as `frmMain`, and can enhance the readability and maintainability of your programs.

- ❑ Variables can be defined at three different levels of scope. Block scope variables are defined within the curly braces of a block of program statements. Local scope variables are defined within a method, usually at the beginning of the method. Class scope variables are defined within a class, but outside a method. The lifetime of a variable is determined by the scope of the variable and the location of the definition. When a variable goes out of scope, it ceases to exist.

- ❑ There are several ways to communicate information between methods. Class scope variables, which make up part of the object's state, may be used by methods within that class. Method parameters can be used to receive values from corresponding arguments in method calls. Methods can also return values to the caller.

- ❑ Passing numeric and string arguments "by value" is a safe approach for sending copies of an argument's value to its corresponding parameter. Passing numeric and string arguments "by reference" causes a change to the original value if the corresponding parameter is changed within the method's code. Passing non-string reference data types by value or by reference does change the original argument's source.

- ❑ The execution call stack keeps track of all methods in execution. To locate problematic code, you can display the stack trace to see how an exception is passed from one method to the next up the call stack.

Bonus Topics

- ❑ The **out** method argument is useful when a method needs to return more than one value. An example illustrated how a type check method could return a Boolean value along with the corresponding numeric equivalent value of the string argument.

- ❑ Methods that may be used by different programs should be defined as shared methods or static methods and moved to a separate class using the **public static** keywords in the definition.

- ❑ A method's signature includes the method name and its parameter list. No two methods in the same class may have the same signature; however, you may use method overloading to create similar methods that return the same value, but have different signatures (different parameter lists). A good candidate for an overloaded method would be a method used for performing type checking on different numeric data types.

KEY TERMS

Define each of the following terms, as it relates to adding methods to objects:

Essential Terms

- access specifier
- argument
- block scope
- calling a method
- class scope
- helper methods
- inline code
- local scope
- method
- method parameter
- method statement block
- object method
- parameter
- parameter list
- pass by reference
- pass by value
- procedures
- **ref**
- scope
- shadowing
- subroutines
- user interface
- **void**

Bonus Terms

- instance method
- method overloading
- method overhead
- **out**
- overloading
- shared method
- signature
- **static**
- static method
- top of stack

REVIEW QUESTIONS

Essential Questions

1. An object method is a group of statements designed to perform a single task. True or false?
2. Methods must be defined using the **public** access specifier. True or false?
3. The default access specifier for a method is **private**. True or false?
4. If a method returns a value, it must use a method parameter. True or false?
5. You should use methods wherever possible because they produce faster-running programs. True or false?
6. The dot operator must be used to access methods that are called from outside the class in which they are declared. True or false?
7. Scope refers to the visibility of a data item within a program. True or false?
8. Methods that are declared in a class using the **public** access specifier become part of the user interface for the class. True or false?
9. How do you know if a method should be defined as an instance method or a shared method?
10. A method's signature extends from the return data type specifier to the closing parenthesis of the parameter list. True or false?

11. A _____ method is one that does not require you to rewrite the source code if you wish to use it in another program.

12. The common term used to refer to the process of invoking a method is _____.

13. When a copy of an argument's value is used as a method parameter, it is referred to as pass by _____.

14. When the memory address of a variable is passed to a method, it is referred to as pass by _____.

15. _____ are methods that are not available outside the class in which they are declared.

16. When two data items share the same name and have overlapping scopes, it is said that one variable _____ the other variable.

17. What is meant by the term block scope?

18. What is "shadowing" and how can it be avoided?

19. What is the difference, if any, between arguments and parameters?

20. How do pass by value and pass by reference differ?

Bonus Questions

1. An **out** parameter and a **ref** parameter are actually the same thing. True or false?

2. An **out** parameter must be initialized before it goes out of scope. True or false?

3. Much of the time associated with method overhead includes the time it takes to push data onto the stack prior to the call and then pop it off the stack in the method. True or false?

4. Shared methods are not associated with an instance of an object. True or false?

5. As a general rule, parameters are passed to the method using a special section of memory called the _____.

6. _____ is a process whereby you examine your code and look for ways to make it more efficient and easier to maintain.

7. The **static** keyword is often associated with _____ methods.

8. The _____ keyword allows you to define reference variables that may be initialized at run time.

9. When should a **ref** parameter be used in a method?

10. How do signatures play a part in method overloading?

PROGRAMMING EXERCISES

Essential Exercises

1. Revise the Carpet Cost calculator program from Chapter 2 to include a method that performs data validation. Add separate methods to perform data type checks and call these methods in the data validation method when necessary.

2. Revise the pizza cost calculator program so that it uses a data validation method to simplify the code in the **btnCalculate_Click** event method.

3. Write a program to calculate the change in your pocket. Use a data validation method to ensure that the input values are acceptable. Write a method that computes the total **decimal** value in change given the number of pennies, nickels, dimes, and quarters (these are parameters for the method).

4. Suppose you need a program that converts inches to centimeters, yards to meters, and miles to kilometers, and vice versa. Design the program, always keeping in mind that code reuse is a real benefit in OOP.

5. C# provides a **substring** method that searches one string for a substring. Write your own version of the **substring** method.

6. Write a method that takes a string as a parameter and returns the string, but in an encrypted format. The encryption method used takes the Unicode value of each letter and adds 3 to it to form its encrypted equivalent. You may assume all letters are uppercase. Using this method, the word "ME" becomes "PH." You should also provide a method that "decrypts" an encrypted string and a program to test that your methods work. By the way, how will you encrypt the letters "XYZ"?

7. Write a method that receives the month as a parameter (that is, January = 1, February = 2, and so on) and returns the number of days in that month. Do leap years add a complication you forgot about at first blush?

8. A bank pays a 2% annual interest rate to all bank accounts that have balances greater than $10,000. The interest is paid on the last day of each month. Write a method that calculates how much interest is paid on an account and returns that amount to the caller. A design question: Should the $10,000 cutoff be part of the method? Why or why not?

Bonus Exercises

1. Write a **static** leap year method that returns the value 1 if it is a leap year, and 0 if it is not a leap year. The algorithm is: If the year can be evenly divided by 4, but not by 100, it is a leap year. However, years that are evenly divisible by 400 are also leap years.

2. Write an overloaded method that calculates the discount factor used in present value calculations. The formula is:

$$\text{discountFactor} = 1.0 / (1.0 + \text{interestRate})^{\text{years}}$$

3. Write one method that accepts both the interest rate and the number of years, and a second version that accepts only the number of years. The second method uses an assumed interest rate equal to 5%. All data should be **doubles**.

8

PROGRAM LOOPS

In the Essentials section you will learn:

♦ How to use `ListBox`es

♦ How to construct a well-behaved loop

♦ How to use **while**, **for**, and **foreach** loops

♦ When to **break** out of a loop

In the Bonus section you will learn:

♦ How to write **while** loops with compound and complex conditions

♦ How to use recursion

♦ How to write nested loops

♦ When to use **continue**

Some business problems require you to repeat a sequential (complex) process on multiple sets of data, whereas other problems involve using a repetitive process to get the desired result. As you've already learned, the computer can process complex computations very quickly. This chapter shows how the computer can be an even more useful tool when you have to perform a complex process repeatedly. You will learn the benefit of writing a complex process once and placing it inside a loop, so that the loop applies the process to all sets of data. You will also use `ListBox`es to allow the user to store, display, and interact with lists of data.

ESSENTIAL TOPICS

You know by now that writing a computer program to solve a problem involves some effort. If you need to solve that problem again with different input, you simply run the program again. However, if you need to solve fifteen such problems, running the program fifteen times would seem somewhat tedious. There is a better way. If you could gather all fifteen sets of input data, you could run the program once and solve the problem for all sets of input through the use of a loop. To make this solution possible, you need to have a way to hold multiple input data. In this chapter, we use a **ListBox** on a Windows Form for this purpose. In later chapters, you will learn to use arrays, collections, text files, and databases for storing and retrieving lists of data.

LISTBOXES

The **ListBox** is a Windows Forms control that allows you to store and display multiple pieces of data in a list format. After values are displayed in a list, the user may select one or more items. If the amount of space in the **ListBox** is not big enough to display all of the list items at once, the **ListBox** automatically displays a vertical scrollbar that allows you to scroll up and down through the list items. If the width of the **ListBox** is too small, however, you should assign the **HorizontalScrollbar** property of the **ListBox** the value **true** to scroll left and right.

You have probably used **ListBox**es in several common Windows applications. For example, Figure 8-1 shows the Paste Special dialog box from Microsoft Word. Notice that it contains a **ListBox** labeled "As:" to identify the various types of formats that may be used to paste the data contained in the clipboard.

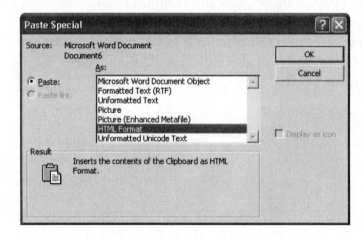

Figure 8-1 ListBox from Paste Special dialog in Microsoft Word

Why Use ListBoxes

When you place a **ListBox** on a form, you are creating an object instance of the .NET **ListBox** class. Your **ListBox** object can take advantage of several properties and methods of the **ListBox** class to simplify programming. For example, by simply setting the **Sorted** property to **true** or **false**, you can control whether the items in the list appear in the order in which they were added to the list or sorted alphabetically.

The **ListBox** class has an **Items** property that is of type **ObjectCollection**, which means that each **ListBox** instance contains a collection of items, usually strings. A **collection** is a group of related objects that share the same name. Grouping items together as a collection gives you a convenient way to refer to the group as if it were a single object with its own methods and properties. Collections are discussed in more detail in Chapter 9. In this chapter, we use the `Items` property of the `ListBox.ObjectCollection` class to gain access to some useful methods that control the contents of the `ListBox`'s collection. The general syntax for getting access to the `ListBox` collection through the `Items` property is as follows:

```
ListBoxName.Items.methodName();
```

Notice that this notation uses multiple dot operators. Remember that the dot operator is the key to getting inside the object. An object instance appears before the dot, and a property or method appears after the dot. In the preceding example, the first dot (in `ListBoxName.Items`) allows you to gain access to a specific `ListBox` object's collection through the `Items` property. This collection is also an object to which you can apply a method. Therefore, the second dot (just before `methodName()`) applies the method's action to the collection object referenced as `ListBoxName.Items`. Some of the methods that allow you to control what you see inside a `ListBox` are discussed in the following sections.

How to Add an Item to a ListBox

Before you can actually use the `ListBox`, you must first place data inside its collection. At this point, this data can come from either computing values programmatically or from asking the user to provide input. In later chapters, you will retrieve data from text files and database tables to populate the `ListBox`.

After you know the source of the data, you can place a copy of the data value inside the `ListBox`'s collection. If the `Sorted` property is **false**, then each newly added value appears after the last item in the list. If `Sorted` is **true**, the value appears in the proper place to preserve alphabetical order. Keep in mind that if you are adding numbers to a sorted `ListBox`, the alphabetical ordering will place 57 after 123541, because these values are being compared as strings, not numbers.

For the purpose of discussion, let's assume that the user provides the input data through a text box called `txtName`. To place the content of `txtName` inside the `ListBox` named `lstNames`, use the **Add method** of the `ListBox.ObjectCollection` class using the `Items` property:

```
lstNames.Items.Add(txtName.Text);
```

If you want to control where to add an item in an unsorted `ListBox`, you may use the **`Items.Insert` method** instead of the **`Items.Add` method**. In addition to specifying the value to be added, you need to include the location where it should be placed. The location is referred to as the item's **index** within the list. Figure 8-2 shows a `ListBox` containing five values and the corresponding index of each value. The indexing for a `ListBox` is referred to as **zero-based** because the first item's index location is 0 and not 1.

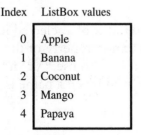

Index	ListBox values
0	Apple
1	Banana
2	Coconut
3	Mango
4	Papaya

Figure 8-2 Index locations for items in a ListBox

If you have a list of ten names, the first name's index is 0, the second name's index is 1, and the last name's index is 9. If you want to add an eleventh name to the middle of the list, you need to specify an index of 5 using the following code:

```
lstNames.Items.Insert(5, "Logan");
```

Figure 8-3 illustrates the addition of an eleventh name (Logan) to the middle of an original list of five girls' names and five boys' names.

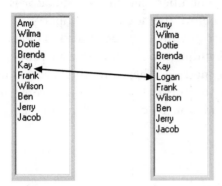

Figure 8-3 Adding a name to the middle of an unsorted list through the Items.Insert method

How to Determine Which Item in a ListBox Is Selected

A user may select one or more items in a **ListBox**. When this happens, it is sometimes helpful to know which item the user selected. To get the value of the selected item, use the **SelectedItem** property. The **SelectedItem** property returns a reference of type **System.Object**, so you must cast the returned value to the appropriate data type:

```
string selectedName;
selectedName = (string) lstNames.SelectedItem;
```

To get the index of the item, use the SelectedIndex property, which returns an **int**:

```
int selectedNameIndex;
selectedNameIndex = lstNames.SelectedIndex;
```

Remember that the indexing is zero-based, so if the first item is selected, the **SelectedIndex** property returns the value 0. If nothing is selected, the value –1 is returned. If you write code that uses the selected value in a **ListBox**, it is a good idea to add checks to ensure that the user indeed made a selection:

```
if (selectedNameIndex == -1)
{
    // display a "nothing was selected" error message
}
```

The example in Figure 8-4 illustrates how to get both the value and index of a selected item. This information is displayed in a **MultiLine** text box. (Set the **MultiLine** property of the text box to **true** using the Properties Window.) When we create the message, we also use "**\r\n**" to force a line break between the name and the index of the text that is displayed when a name is selected.

```
 1    int selectedIndex;
 2    string selectedName;
 3    selectedIndex = lstNames.SelectedIndex;
 4    selectedName = (string) lstNames.SelectedItem;
 5    if (selectedIndex != -1)
 6    {
 7        txtMsg.Text = "Selected Name: " + selectedName + "\r\n" +
 8            "Index: " + selectedIndex.ToString();
 9    }
10    else
11    {
12        txtMsg.Text = "Please select a name and try again.";
13    }
```

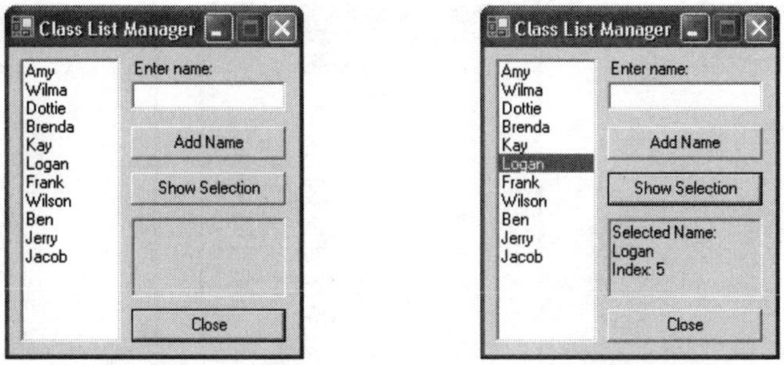

Figure 8-4 Displaying the value and index of a selected ListBox item

8

Using the Environment NewLine for Readability

Because it may not be obvious when reading the code that "\r\n" causes a new line to be added to a string, you may wish to use the longer alternative of Environment.NewLine to make the code more readable. Look at the revised code for line 7 from Figure 8-3 and decide for yourself whether you prefer the abbreviated "\r\n" or more descriptive Environment.NewLine:

```
 7        txtMsg.Text = "Selected Name: " + selectedName +
                Environment.NewLine +
```

How to Remove an Item from a ListBox

After you have added many items to a **ListBox**'s **Items** collection, you may have a need to remove a particular item from the list. The **Items.Remove** and **Items.RemoveAt** methods are used for this purpose. You identify the item to be removed by providing its index value or providing a reference to the object that was added that you now want to delete. Figure 8-5 shows sample code that uses **lstNames** from the above example to progressively remove three names from the **ListBox**.

```
1    // Remove the currently selected item
2    lstNames.Items.Remove(lstNames.SelectedItem);
3
4    // Remove the third item (index is 2)
5    lstNames.Items.RemoveAt(2);
6
7    // Remove the item with value "Wilson")
8    lstNames.Items.Remove("Wilson");
9
```

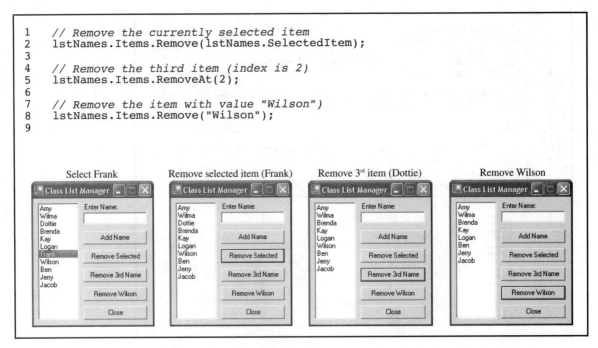

Figure 8-5 Removing items through the Items.Remove and Items.RemoveAt methods

How to Clear the Contents of a ListBox

If you decide that you need to remove everything from the list, you could use the preceding steps until all items had been removed, but there is an easier way. The **Items.Clear method** removes all items at once (see Figure 8-6):

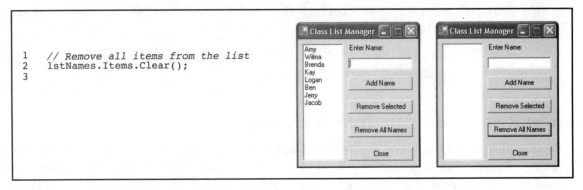

```
1    // Remove all items from the list
2    lstNames.Items.Clear();
3
```

Figure 8-6 Removing all items from a list through the Items.Clear method

How to Count Items in a ListBox

Sometimes when working with data in a `ListBox`'s `Items` collection, it is useful to know how many items there are. This is accomplished using the **Items.Count** property of the `Listbox.Items` object. Refer to Figure 8-7 for an example that counts items in a list.

```
1   {
2       int nameCount;
3       nameCount = lstNames.Items.Count;
4       txtMsg.Text = "Your class has " +
5           nameCount.ToString() + " students";
6   }
```

Figure 8-7 Counting all items in a list through the Items.Count property

How to Sort Items in a ListBox

At the beginning of this section, we described how you can sort **ListBox** items alphabetically using the **Sorted** property. If you try to control the order programmatically, you need to keep in mind that once you sort the list, if you change the **Sorted** property back to **false**, the current contents of the **ListBox** remain sorted, but any newly added items are placed at the bottom of the list. Figure 8-8 illustrates the effect of starting with an unsorted list, sorting it, adding a name, then stopping the sort and adding another name. As you can see, when the **Sorted** property is **true**, names are placed in the list in the correct location to preserve alphabetical order. After the **Sorted** property is changed, the current list items are left as is and all newly added items are placed at the end of the list.

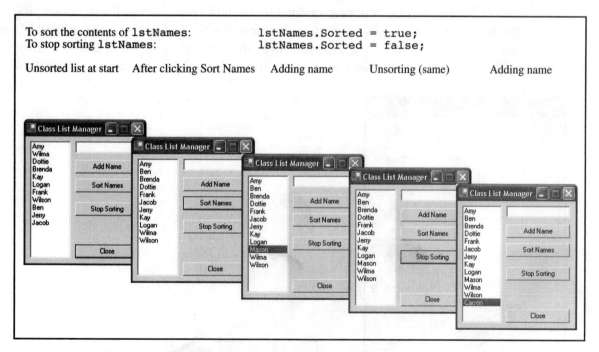

Figure 8-8 ListBox contents based on changing the Sorted property

How to Select an Item in a ListBox

Although the user can select one or more items in a **ListBox** using the mouse or keyboard, your program can also control the selection of list items. The **SelectionMode property** determines both how many items may be selected simultaneously and how to do multiple selections. By default, the `ListBox`'s `SelectionMode` property is set to `One`, so only one item may be selected at a time. However, the `SelectionMode` property may be changed to either `MultiExtended` or `MultiSimple`. Using `MultiSimple` allows the user to select or deselect individual items in the list by using a mouse click or by pressing the Spacebar. Using `MultiExtended` allows the user to select a contiguous group of items by holding down the Shift key and using the mouse or arrow keys to identify the end of the block of items to be selected. If the group of items to be selected is not contiguous, the user can hold down the CTRL key to select all desired items in the list individually.

You have already used the `SelectedIndex` property in a preceding section to find out which item was selected by the user. However, you can change or set an item's selection by assigning a value to this property. For example, if the `ListBox` had ten items and you wanted the fourth item to be selected, you would need to assign the value 3 to the `SelectedIndex` property (because index locations start at 0, so the fourth item's index is 3):

```
lstNames.SelectedIndex = 3;
```

You can also get the value of a particular list item if you know its index value. For example, if you want to display a particular name (from the `lstNames ListBox`) in the text box `txtNameOfInterest` and the location of that name is stored in the variable `indexOfInterest`, then use the following code:

```
txtNameOfInterest.Text = (string) lstNames.Items[indexOfInterest];
```

A ListBox Program Example

To practice using everything you have learned so far, let's create a class list manager program that allows the teacher to add names, remove names, sort the list, count the students, and identify the middle name in the list. The design for the form should look something like the sample shown in Figure 8-9. The properties that you need to change at design time are shown in Table 8-1.

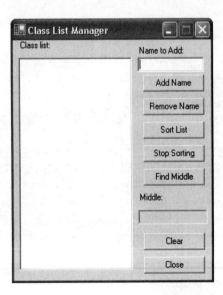

Figure 8-9 Design for a sample Class List Manager form

Table 8-1 Objects properties of a sample Class List Manager form

Object type	Name	Property	Value
ListBox	lstNames	TabStop	False
Label	label1	Text	Class List:
	label2	Text	Name to Add:
	label3	Text	Middle:
TextBox	txtName	Text	empty
	txtMiddleName	Text	empty
		ReadOnly	True
		TabStop	False
Button	btnAdd	Text	Add Name
	btnRemove	Text	Remove Name
	btnSort	Text	Sort List
	btnUnsort	Text	Stop Sorting
	btnMiddle	Text	Find Middle
	btnClear	Text	Clear
	btnClose	Text	Close

8

In order to make it easier for the teacher to keep adding names, after processing any add, remove, clear, sort, or stop sort request, you should erase the contents of **txtName** and place the cursor in that text box. To find the middle name in the list, use the **Count** property to determine how many names are in the list. Once you know how many names are in the list, divide the count by two, then find the largest whole number that is less than or equal to the resulting quotient. To get this result, you can use the **Math.Floor** method, which was discussed in Chapter 4. This value is the index of the middle name you need to display.

To make sure this algorithm for finding the middle name works correctly, consider the following example. Our find-the-middle-name algorithm works perfectly for lists that contain an odd number of items, but when the list contains an even number of items, there are actually two middle names. As long as one of these two names is displayed, the algorithm is acceptable for our needs. For example, if you have five names, the middle name that you want to display is the third name in the list, which has an index of 2. Following the logic we just reviewed, 5 divided by 2 is 2.5. Using the **Floor** method with an argument of 2.5 returns the value 2. If you have ten names, then you have 2 middle names. The fifth and sixth names have indices 4 and 5 respectively. Using the algorithm, you would divide 10 by 2 to get 5, and the **Floor** of 5 is 5. Because that is one of the two middle names, it is acceptable to display that value. You should test this logic on different list sizes to verify for yourself that it works correctly. After you are satisfied that it does work, go ahead and try to write the program. (You will learn much more as you read this text if you try to write your own code for the solution to a problem before reading our solution.) When you finish writing your version, compare it to our sample code shown in Figure 8-10.

```
1    private void btnClear_Click(object sender, System.EventArgs e)
2    {
3        lstNames.Items.Clear();
4        txtName.Text = "";
5        txtMiddleName.Text = "";
6        txtName.Focus();
7    }
8
9    private void btnAdd_Click(object sender, System.EventArgs e)
10   {
11       // Make sure there is a name to be added.
12
13       if (txtName.Text == "")
14       {
15           messageBoxOK("Please enter a name to add it to the class list.");
16           txtName.Focus();
17           return;
18       }
19       lstNames.Items.Add(txtName.Text);
20       txtMiddleName.Text = "";
21       txtName.Text = "";
22       txtName.Focus();
23   }
24
25   private void btnRemove_Click(object sender, System.EventArgs e)
26   {
27       // Make sure that a name has been selected.
28
29       if (lstNames.SelectedIndex == -1)
30       {
31           messageBoxOK("Please select a name to remove it from the class list.");
32           lstNames.Focus();
33           return;
34       }
35       lstNames.Items.Remove(lstNames.SelectedItem);
36       txtMiddleName.Text = "";
37       txtName.Focus();
38   }
39
40   private void btnMiddle_Click(object sender, System.EventArgs e)
41   {
42       int nbrItems;
43       int midLocation;
44
45       // Find out how many names are in the list
46
47       nbrItems = lstNames.Items.Count;
48
49       // Make sure there is at least one name.
50
51       if (nbrItems == 0)
52       {
53           messageBoxOK("There is no middle name in an empty class list.");
54           return;
55       }
56
```

Figure 8-10   Sample Class List Manager program code listing

```
57          // Find the index of the middle name.
58
59          midLocation = (int) Math.Floor(nbrItems/2);
60          txtMiddleName.Text = lstNames.Items[midLocation].ToString();
61          txtName.Focus();
62      }
63
64      private void btnSort_Click(object sender, System.EventArgs e)
65      {
66          lstNames.Sorted = true;
67      }
68
69      private void btnUnsort_Click(object sender, System.EventArgs e)
70      {
71          lstNames.Sorted = false;
72      }
```

Figure 8-10   Sample Class List Manager program code listing (continued)

8

CONSTRUCTING LOOPS

Now that you have a way of keeping a collection of items in a **ListBox**, you are ready to begin using program loops. **Loops** are program structures that represent a set of program statements that are usually processed one or more times. When you have written a program to perform a complex computation for one piece of data, and then discover that you have several more pieces of data that need to be processed in the same manner, you can modify your program by embedding the processing steps you already wrote inside a loop. Using a loop enables you to run the program once for all the data, saving you time.

For example, below is an algorithm for computing a person's final restaurant bill after adding a 6% sales tax and 15% tip:

1. Get the base food/drink price.

2. Find the sales tax by multiplying the base price by 6%.

3. Find the tip by multiplying the base price by 15%.

4. Find the sum of the base price, sales tax, and tip.

5. Pay your server.

If you went out to dinner with nine of your friends, you would repeat the above process for each person to get the total amount your party owed. Because there are ten people, the algorithm would involve fifty steps! However, if you recognize that all of you are doing the same thing, you could embed the similar steps inside a loop and use the following shorthand for a loop-based algorithm:

1. For each diner:

   a. Get the base food/drink price.

   b. Find the sales tax by multiplying the base price by 6%.

   c. Find the tip by multiplying the base price by 15%.

   d. Find the sum of the base price, sales tax, and tip.

   e. Add this to your party's total.

2. Pay your server the final party total.

The preceding algorithm repeats Steps 1a to 1e ten times. Each cycle through the loop is also known as an **iteration**. When you write loops in your programs, you use one of the available iteration statements. However, be careful when using loops. If you create a loop carelessly, your program could continue looping forever. (Loops that get stuck and fail to terminate are called **infinite loops** or **continuous loops**.) One way to avoid this problem is to write well-behaved loops, which are discussed in the next section.

Three Conditions of a Well-Behaved Loop

If you have a way of determining the number of iterations your program needs to complete, you can write a well-behaved loop that counts each loop cycle. A well-behaved loop has three basic conditions:

1. There is an initial state of the data before the start of the loop.

2. During each iteration, some data item must change its state.

3. Before the next iteration begins, the state of the data is checked to determine whether another iteration of the loop is necessary.

If a loop violates any of these three conditions, it is considered an ill-behaved loop and could cause your program to crash or produce incorrect results.

In the case of the restaurant example, the state could be keeping track of the diner by number. After each diner's total bill is processed, the number of diners is increased by one. You keep repeating the process until all ten diners' total bills have been processed. To relate this to the three conditions of a well-behaved loop, you follow these steps:

1. Start with the first diner (initial state is `dinerCount = 1`).

2. After completing the processing for the current diner, prepare for the next diner (change state by adding 1 to `dinerCount`).

3. Before the next iteration begins, check the value of the `dinerCount` to make sure it does not exceed 10.

If you wrote the loop starting with `dinerCount` = 10, you would process only the last diner's bill, resulting in insufficient money to pay off the bill. This ill-behaved loop violates the first condition.

If you forgot to change `dinerCount` after handling the first diner's bill, you would end up processing the first diner's bill a second time, then a third time, and so on, forever! Forgetting to change the state of the data violates the second condition and results in a never-ending or infinite loop.

Using Visual Studio to Terminate an Infinite Loop

During the program development process, you might accidentally write code that creates an infinite loop. When your program executes, it gives the appearance that the program is stuck and you can't get control back; however, Visual Studio provides a way to terminate program execution when you suspect there is a problem, such as an infinite loop. Simply select the Break All or Stop Debugging option from the Debug menu.

To locate the problem, you should use the Break All option and then step through program execution one statement at a time to help pinpoint the error.

If your test compared `dinerCount` against 9 instead of 10, your total would still be too low. If you compared it to 100, the program would produce an error as soon as it tried to process the eleventh diner. If you checked something other than `dinerCount`, you could potentially have another infinite loop. All of these problems violate the third condition.

If you structure the loop correctly, you have a well-behaved loop that should produce the correct results. The restaurant bill example also illustrates a counting loop, which is discussed in the next section.

THE counting LOOP

The **counting loop** is a well-behaved loop that uses a loop counter variable to manage its state. Counting loops are used when your program can determine how many iterations of the loop should be executed. We can define the three conditions of a well-behaved counting loop as follows:

- *Initialize the loop counter*—The loop counter receives an initial value.
- *Change the state of the loop counter*—The loop counter is always incremented or decremented by a fixed amount.
- *Check the state of the loop counter for the next iteration*—After the value of the loop counter is beyond the final value, the loop is terminated.

The next three sections discuss three different C# iteration keywords that may be used to create counting loops: **while**, **for**, and **foreach**. These unique keywords identify the type of program loop, and **curly braces** { } are used to surround the statement(s) that are to be repeated in the loop's statement block. The left curly brace { identifies the start of the loop statement block, whereas the right curly brace } identifies the end of the loop statement block. The statements inside the curly braces are referred to as the **loop body** or **loop statement block**. As you review the following sections that cover writing each of these loop structures, pay careful attention to how you can ensure that all three conditions to make the loop well-behaved have been considered.

The while Loop

The **while** loop is a conditional loop that takes the general form shown in Figure 8-11:

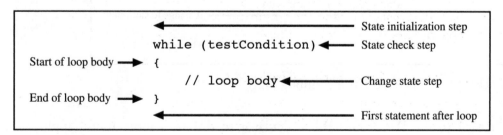

Figure 8-11 General form of a while loop

The `testCondition` on the **while** statement is any Boolean expression. The loop body is executed repeatedly until the given `testCondition` evaluates to **false**. Although the **while** loop can do more than count (as you will see in later chapters), in this section we describe only how to use the **while** loop as a counting loop to allow you to compare it to the **for** and **foreach** loops. The state initialization step occurs before the **while** statement, often the statement immediately before the **while** statement. It frequently looks like an assignment of an initial value to a variable that is used in the **testCondition** of the loop such as:

```
loopCounter = startingValue;
```

When the **while** statement is encountered, and before the loop begins execution, the **testCondition** is checked. The **testCondition** typically looks like a comparison of a variable (assigned in the initial value) to an ending value such as:

```
while (loopCounter <= endingValue)
```

If the result of the **testCondition** is **true**, an iteration of the loop body is executed. If the **testCondition** is **false**, the loop terminates and control passes to the statement after the right curly brace (end of the loop). If the condition is **false** the very first time, based on the state initialization step, the loop executes zero times.

In most cases, the initialization step makes the **testCondition** **true** at the start of the first pass through the loop. This means that somewhere in the loop body, you must have a statement that potentially changes the state in each iteration so the **testCondition** expression becomes **false**. For our **testCondition** using the **loopCounter** variable, the change step may look like:

```
loopCounter++;
```

If you omit the step to change the state, you have an (ill-behaved) infinite loop! After the loop body has been processed and the right curly brace is reached, signifying the end of one loop iteration, program control loops back to the **testCondition** where its state is checked again. If the result is **true**, another iteration of the loop is made; otherwise, it terminates and passes control to the first statement after the loop.

To illustrate how you might use a **while** loop as a counting loop, consider the code snippet shown in Figure 8-12 that displays a message box with the words "Howdy" ten times:

Is this loop well behaved? Can you identify the three conditions that make it well behaved?

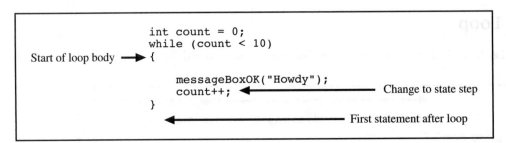

Figure 8-12 Using the while loop as a counting loop

Next, let's return to the Restaurant Bill Calculator to discuss a more useful application of the **while** loop. Writing this generically, the algorithm might look like:

1. Set **totalBill** to 0.

2. Set **dinerCount** to 1.

3. Repeat while the **dinerCount** is no more than 10:

   a. Get this diner's **base food/drink price.**

   b. Find the **sales tax** by multiplying the base price by 6%.

   c. Find the **tip** by multiplying the base price by 15%.

   d. Find the **sum** of the base price, sales tax, and tip.

   e. Add this diner's bill to your **totalBill.**

   f. Add 1 to **dinerCount.**

4. Pay your server the final **totalBill.**

To develop a program to handle this, place all of the individual diners' totals into a **ListBox** named **lstDinerBill.** You need a way to reference the ten individual items in the list, so create an index variable, which would start at 0 and end at 9. Since the index is always one less than the **dinerCount,** you could simply use (**dinerCount-1**) to serve as the index location for the desired item in the list. There is one more thing to consider. This algorithm uses an accumulator to keep track of the party's total bill. Each time you use an accumulator in a program, you need to initialize it to zero before any repetitive processing, then add each individual amount in each iteration, and after all loop processing is complete, the total may be displayed. In the case of the restaurant bill total, you need to accumulate the **totalBill** as you process each diner's individual bill. For the total processing to work correctly, you need to initialize **totalBill** to 0 in Step 1, outside the loop before the loop begins.

Translating the algorithm, the code should look similar to Figure 8-13. The three statements that make this loop well behaved are identified with callouts. The statements that compose the loop body are between the curly braces and have been shaded to help you identify them easily. Figure 8-14 shows a sample execution of a program to process a table of ten diners' bills.

```
1    const double taxRate = .06;
2    const double tipPct = .15;
3    int dinerCount;
4    decimal totalBill;
5    int dinerIndex;
6    decimal dinerBaseCost;
7    decimal dinerTax;
8    decimal dinerTip;
9
10   totalBill = 0;                                              State initialization step
11   dinerCount = 1;                                             State check step
12   while (dinerCount <= 10)
13   {
14       dinerIndex = dinerCount - 1;
15       dinerBaseCost = decimal.Parse(lstDinerBill.Items[dinerIndex].ToString());
16       dinerTax = (decimal) taxRate * dinerBaseCost;
17       dinerTip = (decimal) tipPct * dinerBaseCost;
18       totalBill += dinerBaseCost + dinerTax + dinerTip;
19       dinerCount++;                                           Change state step
20   }
21   txtServerTotal.Text = totalBill.ToString("C");
```

Figure 8-13 Using the while loop to handle a restaurant bill for ten diners

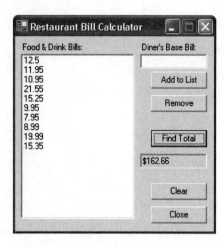

Figure 8-14 Sample execution of Restaurant Bill Calculator for ten diners

What if the number of diners was not exactly 10? Because you are using a **ListBox**, you can use the **Items.Count** property to determine how many times to repeat the loop. This means that you could easily make the program much more generic by simply changing the state check statement as follows:

```
12    while (dinerCount <= lstDinerBill.Items.Count)
```

This example used a **while** loop to count each loop cycle, but what if you don't know how many times to repeat the processing steps? That's exactly the situation for which a **while** loop was designed. We illustrate with another example.

Example Using the while Loop

Suppose you made up a prioritized wish list of things you would like to purchase. After entering all the items you want and their respective costs, you also need to enter your total budget. You could then use a **while** loop to cycle through each of the wish list items from most important to least important until your budget ran out. A message could be displayed stating how many items could be purchased, the total cost, and the money remaining. A suggested form design for this program is shown in Figure 8-15. Notice that the design uses two **ListBoxes** to hold the costs and item descriptions side by side. To remove an item, the user selects the item, and both the item and its corresponding cost are removed from their respective **ListBox**es.

Figure 8-15 Sample form design for wish list program

The algorithm for processing the wish list with the given budget should look something like:

1. Set **currentIndex** to 0.

2. Set **lastIndex** to one less than the number of items in the wish list.

3. Set **spending** to 0.

4. Set **nbrWishItems** to 0.

5. Set **maxBudget** to the budget given by the user.

6. Repeat while **spending** is no more than **maxBudget**.

    a. If **currentIndex** is NOT past the **lastIndex**, then do the following:

        1) Add the cost of the item at **currentIndex** to **spending**.

        2) If **spending** is within the budget, then do the following:

            a)   Add 1 to **nbrWishItems**.

            b)   Add 1 to **currentIndex**.

        3) Otherwise, do the following:

            (1)   Subtract the cost of the item at **currentIndex** from **spending** (since there's not enough money).

            (2)   Reset **maxBudget** to -1 (so the **while** condition will cause the loop to terminate).

    b. Otherwise, do the following:

        1) Add the cost of the item at **currentIndex** to **spending**.

7. Reset **maxBudget** to the budget given by the user minus **spending**.

8. Display a message that includes the user's budget, **nbrWishItems**, **spending**, **maxBudget**.

The code for the **btnProcess_Click** event is shown in Figure 8-16, and sample executions are shown in Figure 8-17. We will return to this example in later sections of this chapter.

```
1    private void btnProcess_Click(object sender, System.EventArgs e)
2    {
3        decimal maxBudget;
4        decimal spending;
5        int currentIndex;
6        int lastIndex;
7        int nbrWishItems;
8
9        currentIndex = 0;
10       lastIndex = lstItems.Items.Count - 1;
11       spending = 0;
12       nbrWishItems = 0;
13       maxBudget = decimal.Parse(txtBudget.Text);
14       while (spending <= maxBudget)
15       {
16           if (currentIndex <= lastIndex)
17           {
18               spending += decimal.Parse(lstCosts.Items[currentIndex].ToString());
19               if (spending <= maxBudget)
20               {
21                   nbrWishItems++;
22                   currentIndex++;
23               }
24               else
25               {
26                   spending -= decimal.Parse(lstCosts.Items[currentIndex].ToString());
27                   maxBudget = -1;
28               }
29           }
30           else
31           {
32               maxBudget = -1;
33           }
34       }
35       maxBudget = decimal.Parse(txtBudget.Text) - spending;
36       messageBoxOK("Your wish budget of " + decimal.Parse(txtBudget.Text).ToString("C") +
37           " will allow you to buy the \r\nfirst" + nbrWishItems.ToString() +
38           " items on your wish list for a total cost of " + spending.ToString("C") +
39           ". \r\nAfter the purchase, you will have " + maxBudget.ToString("C") + " left.");
40   }
```

Figure 8-16 Sample code for wish list program's btnProcess_Click event

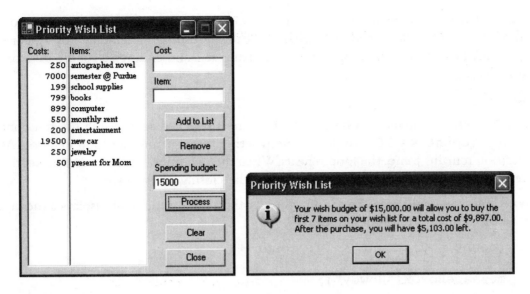

Figure 8-17 Sample executions of wish list program

The for loop

The **for** iteration statement is used to code a counting loop. The **for** loop takes the general form shown in Figure 8-18:

```
                State initialization step(s)              State check step

for (initializer; testCondition; iterator)
{
// loop body
}
// statement after loop terminates
                                              Change state step(s)
```

Figure 8-18 General form of a for loop

As you can see, all three conditions for constructing a well-behaved loop are included in the **for** statement. Generally, a loop counter variable is used to keep track of each loop iteration. When the **for** statement is first encountered during execution, the state initialization step occurs, which assigns an initial value to the loop counter variable. For example, the initializer step may look like the following:

```
count = 1;
```

After initialization, the state check step is processed next. As with the **while** loop, if the result of the test condition in the state check step is **true**, the loop body (set of statements between the curly braces) is processed. If the test condition is **false**, the loop terminates and control passes to the statement after the right curly brace (end of the loop). For example, to indicate that the last valid loop cycle occurs when the loop counter variable is 10, use the following code for the expression:

```
count <= 10;
```

When you constructed the **while** loop, you had to add a separate line of code to make sure that the state changed in each loop iteration. With a **for** statement, the change step is included as part of the **for** statement itself through the iterator. Once the loop body has been processed and the right curly brace is reached, signifying the end of one loop cycle, the iterator statement is processed. Usually, this means that the loop counter variable is changed (usually incremented by 1). For example, if you wanted to execute the loop ten times starting at 1 and ending at 10, the iterator statement would look like:

```
count++
```

As soon as the iterator statement is processed, the state is checked again using the test condition (in this example, `count <= 10;`) to determine whether to begin another loop iteration. As long as the condition remains **true**, the loop repeats. When the condition evaluates to **false**, the loop terminates and control passes to the statement after the closing curly brace.

To illustrate how you could use a **for** loop, consider the code snippet that displays a message box with the words "Howdy" ten times as follows:

```
for (count = 0; count < 10; count++)
{
    messageBoxOK("Howdy");
}
```

Is this loop well behaved? Can you identify the three conditions that make it well behaved?

The **for** loop may be considered a variation of a **while** loop—each time you can write a **while** loop with a loop counter, you can replace it with a **for** loop. To demonstrate this fact, refer to Figure 8-19 to see how we revised the code from the Restaurant Bill Calculator program to use a **for** loop. Figure 8-20 shows a sample execution of this updated program.

```
 1    private void btnTotal_Click(object sender, System.EventArgs e)
 2    {
 3        const double taxRate = .06;
 4        const double tipPct = .15;
 5        int dinerCount;
 6        decimal totalBill;                    State initialization step
 7        int dinerIndex;
 8        decimal dinerBaseCost;                      State check step            change state step
 9        decimal dinerTax;
10        decimal dinerTip;
11
12        totalBill = 0;
13        for (dinerCount = 1; dinerCount <= lstDinerBill.Items.Count; dinerCount++)
14            {
15            dinerIndex = dinerCount - 1;
16            dinerBaseCost = decimal. Parse(lstDinerBill.Items[dinerIndex].ToString());
17            dinerTax = (decimal) taxRate * dinerBaseCost;
18            dinerTip = (decimal) tipPct * dinerBaseCost;
19            totalBill += dinerBaseCost + dinerTax + dinerTip;
20            }
21         txtServerTotal.Text = totalBill.ToString("C");
```

Figure 8-19 Using the for loop to handle a restaurant bill for ten diners

Figure 8-20 Sample execution of Restaurant Bill Calculator using for loop

Because all three conditions of a well-behaved loop appear in the **for** statement, it is easier to construct well-behaved **for** loops. Therefore, if you know the number of iterations needed for a loop-based problem, you should use a **for** loop instead of a **while** loop. That said, do you remember why and when a **while** construct is necessary? If you know you need to perform a process repeatedly, and you know when to quit (terminal state is known), but you don't know how many times you must repeat the process (unknown number of iterations), a **while** loop should be used.

The foreach Loop

The **foreach** iteration statement is used to code a loop that is repeated for every element of an array (explained in Chapter 9) or object collection (for example, **ListBox.ObjectCollection**). The **foreach** loop construct takes the general form shown in Figure 8-21:

```
                                    State initialization step
                                    State check step
                                    Change state step

foreach (type iterationVariable in expression)
{
// loop body
}
```

Figure 8-21 General form of a foreach loop

A major benefit of the **foreach** statement is that it encapsulates the **for** loop without the extra steps needed to identify the three conditions of a well-behaved loop. These steps are implied within the statement through the **iterationVariable** and **expression** shown on the **foreach** line in Figure 8-21. Because you are familiar with how a **ListBox** works, assume that **expression** refers to a **ListBox**, and **iterationVariable** refers to a string variable that is used to reference each item in the **ListBox**. When the **foreach** statement is first encountered during execution, the **iterationVariable** refers to the first item in the **ListBox** (state initialization step). As long as there is a list item (the **ListBox** is not empty), the loop body is processed. When the loop body has been processed and the right curly brace is reached, signifying the end of one loop iteration, the **iterationVariable** refers to the next item in the

ListBox (the state is changed). As long as there is another list item to be processed (state check), another iteration is repeated. This processing continues until all items in the ListBox have been processed.

To illustrate how you could use a **foreach** loop, take another look at the ListBox in Figure 8-4. The code snippet below displays a separate message box with "Hello, name" for each name in the list:

```
foreach (string student in lstNames)
{
      messageBoxOK("Hello, " + student);
}
```

Is this loop well behaved? Can you identify the three conditions that make it well behaved?

The **foreach** loop may be considered a variation of a **for** loop, because you can manually write code to handle each of the three steps of initialization, state change, and state check. However, when you need to process all elements of an object collection, such as for a ListBox, it is much easier to use a **foreach** statement. To demonstrate this fact, refer to Figure 8-22 to see how we revised the code from the Restaurant Bill Calculator program to use a **foreach** loop to process every item in the ListBox. You should notice that the amount of code is reduced, making it easier to understand. Thus, when you need to process all items in a collection or array, the **foreach** loop is preferred to the **for** loop. Figure 8-23 shows a sample execution of this updated program.

```
1     private void btnTotal_Click(object sender, System.EventArgse)
2     {
3          const double taxRate = .06;
4          const double tipPct = .15;
5          decimal dinerBaseCost;
6          decimal totalBill;
7          decimal dinerTax;                   State initialization step
8          decimal dinerTip;                   State check step
9                                              Change state step
10         totalBill = 0;
11         foreach (string itemInList in lstDinerBill.Items)
12         {
13             dinerBaseCost = decimal.Parse(itemInList);
14             dinerTax = (decimal) taxRate * dinerBaseCost;
15             dinerTip = (decimal) tipPct * dinerBaseCost;
16             totalBill += dinerBaseCost + dinerTax + dinerTip;
17         }
18         txtServerTotal.Text = totalBill.ToString("C");
19    }
20
```

Figure 8-22   Using a foreach loop to handle a restaurant bill for ten diners

Figure 8-23 Sample execution of Restaurant Bill Calculator using a foreach loop

8

THE break STATEMENT

The **break** statement is used to terminate a loop before the last loop iteration has been processed. When the **break** keyword is encountered, control passes to the statement following the end of the closest enclosing loop. This statement would have been useful in the wish list program, because there are two places where there is a need to exit the loop. In the original algorithm, one of the variables used in the **while** condition was set to a value that forced the loop to terminate. Using the **break** is a more straightforward and understandable approach. Figure 8-24 shows the revised code using a **break** to simplify the processing. When either **break** statement is encountered, control passes to line 35, the first statement after the closest enclosing loop. Figure 8-25 shows a sample execution. Compare this code with the code in Figure 8-16 to verify this conclusion for yourself.

```
1    private void btnProcess_Click(object sender, System.EventArgs e)
2    {
3        decimal maxBudget;
4        decimal spending;
5        int currentIndex;
6        int lastIndex;
7        int nbrWishItems;
8
9        currentIndex = 0;
10       lastIndex = lstItems.Items.Count - 1;
11       spending = 0;
12       nbrWishItems = 0;
13       maxBudget = decimal.Parse(txtBudget.Text);
```

Figure 8-24   Revised btnProcess_Click event using break in wish list program

```
14        while (spending <= maxBudget)
15        {
16            if (currentIndex <= lastIndex)
17            {
18                spending += decimal.Parse(lstCosts.Items[currentIndex].ToString());
19                if (spending <= maxBudget)
20                {
21                    nbrWishItems++;
22                    currentIndex++;
23                }
24                else
25                {
26                    spending -= decimal.Parse(lstCosts.Items[currentIndex].ToString());
27                    break;
28                }
29            }
30            else
31            {
32                break;
33            }
34        }
35        messageBoxOK("Your wish budget of " + maxBudget.ToString("C") +
36            " will allow you to buy the \r\nfirst" + nbrWishItems.ToString() +
37            " items on your wish list for a total cost of " + spending.ToString("C") +
38            ". \r\nAfter the purchase, you will have " + (maxBudget-spending).ToString("C") +
            " left.");
39    }
40
```

Figure 8-24 Revised btnProcess_Click event using break in wish list program (continued)

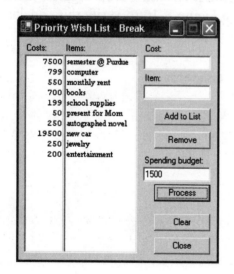

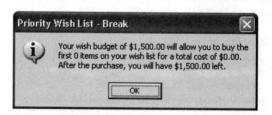

Figure 8-25 Sample executions of wish list program with break

When and Why to Use the break Statement

In general, anytime you write a loop in your program in which the majority of loop iterations
may not be processed, you may need to stop the loop because a certain condition has been met.
In this situation, it is clearer to use a **break** statement rather than artificially forcing the loop

condition's termination rule to be triggered by changing a variable's value (as we did in the first version of the wish list program). For example, if you are searching for a specific name (`targetName`) from a list of 100 names in a `ListBox` (`lstNames`), use a `break` statement to terminate the search when you find what you're looking for:

```
1   while (counter < 100)
2   {
3       if (targetName == lstNames.Items[counter].ToString())
4       {
5           foundItIndex = counter;
6           break;
7       }
8       counter++;
9   }
10
```

If the name you are looking for happens to be the third name in the `ListBox`, the `break` statement allows you to exit from the `while` loop in a simple manner.

BONUS TOPICS

The Essentials section introduced you to the `ListBox` and basic loops, which will continue to be used in the remaining chapters of this book. The Bonus section expands on this discussion by illustrating **while** loops with compound and complex conditions, nested loops, and using recursion as an alternative to looping in certain situations.

WRITING while LOOPS WITH COMPOUND AND COMPLEX CONDITIONS

Take another look at the wish list programs presented in Figures 8-16 and 8-24. The **else** branches of both **if** statements within the **while** loop are there to force the loop to end: spending has exceeded the budget, or there are no more items in the list. Another alternative to the approaches used in these programs is to handle the role of the **else** branches using a compound condition in the **while** statement. As you learned in Chapter 5, you can form a compound condition by joining two relational expressions with a conditional operator. In this case, the **while** condition needs to include all situations in which the loop should be processed. For example, as long as spending has not surpassed the budget and unprocessed items remain in the list, you might use the statement:

```
while (spending <= maxBudget && currentIndex <= lastIndex)
```

Comparing the revised code in Figure 8-26 to the earlier versions, you can see that the resulting code is shorter and more understandable. Figure 8-27 shows a sample execution of the code presented in Figure 8-26.

8

```
1    private void btnProcess_Click(object sender, System.EventArgs e)
2    {
3        decimal maxBudget;
4        decimal spending;
5        int currentIndex;
6        int lastIndex;
7        int nbrWishItems;
8
9        currentIndex = 0;
10       lastIndex = lstItems.Items.Count - 1;
11       spending = 0;
12       nbrWishItems = 0;
13       maxBudget = decimal.Parse(txtBudget.Text);
14       while (spending <= maxBudget && currentIndex <= lastIndex)
15       {
16           if (currentIndex <= lastIndex)
17           {
18               spending += decimal.Parse(lstCosts.Items[currentIndex].ToString());
19               if (spending <= maxBudget)
20               {
21                   nbrWishItems++;
22                   currentIndex++;
23               }
24           }
25       }
26       if (spending > maxBudget)
27       {
28           spending -= decimal.Parse(lstCosts.Items[currentIndex].ToString());
29       }
30       messageBoxOK("Your wish budget of " + maxBudget.ToString("C") + " will allow you to " +
31           "buy the \r\nfirst" + nbrWishItems.ToString() + " items on your wish list for a " +
32           "total cost of " + spending.ToString("C") + ". \r\nAfter the purchase, you will have " +
33           (maxBudget-spending).ToString("C") + " left.");
34   }
```

Figure 8-26 Sample code for wish list program with compound condition

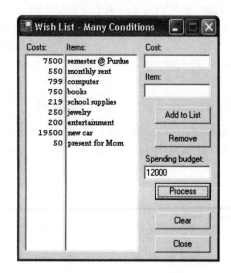
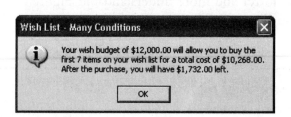

Figure 8-27 Sample execution of wish list program with compound condition

RECURSION

Sometimes, it is easier to write the solution to a problem using **recursion** rather than loops. Recursion involves writing a method that solves a problem by calling itself repeatedly until some specific condition terminates the self-calling process. To explain this, let's consider how to compute the factorial of a number. A factorial of a number is the product of all numbers between the given number and 1. Zero factorial by definition is 1. Table 8-2 lists the first eight factorials, so you can see the pattern. (Note that the exclamation mark is used in Table 8-2 as a mathematical symbol for factorial.)

Table 8-2   The first eight factorials

Number	Product computation	Recursive computation	Result
0!	1	1	1
1!	1	1	1
2!	1*2	2 * 1!	2
3!	1*2*3	3 * 2!	6
4!	1*2*3*4	4 * 3!	24
5!	1*2*3*4*5	5 * 4!	120
6!	1*2*3*4*5*6	6 * 5!	720
7!	1*2*3*4*5*6*7	7 * 6!	5040

After considering the third column, it should be clear that the factorial of a given number is that number times the factorial of the number before it. This rule holds true for all non-negative integers except for 0, which is treated as a special case. Figure 8-28 presents the code that uses the recursive factorial method. The number input by the user has been limited to a **short** data type. Twenty factorial has 19 digits, so the amount of precision required warrants that a **double** data type be used for the return data type.

```
1    private double FindFactorial(short number)
2    {
3        if (number <= 1)
4        {
5            return 1;
6        }
7        else
8        {
9            return FindFactorial((short) (number - 1)) * number;
10       }
11   }
12
```

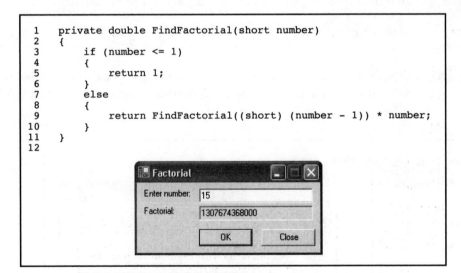

Figure 8-28   FindFactorial recursive method

When you write a recursive method, it is important for you to think about how the repeated calls finally end. An improperly constructed recursive method could result in an infinite loop! To show that the **FindFactorial** method does end properly, let's test the **FindFactorial** method to compute **5!**. Refer to Table 8-3 to view the details of how the process works when computing **5!** recursively.

Table 8-3   Computing 5! recursively

Caller	FindFactorial method processing
FindFactorial(5)	Because number (5) > 1, the **else** branch is processed. The value returned is FindFactorial(4) * 5, which calls FindFactorial for 4.
FindFactorial(4) * 5	Because number (4) > 1, the **else** branch is processed. The value returned is FindFactorial(3) * 4, which calls FindFactorial for 3.
FindFactorial(3) * 4 * 5	Because number (3) > 1, the **else** branch is processed. The value returned is FindFactorial(2) * 3, which calls FindFactorial for 2.
FindFactorial(2) * 3 * 4 * 5	Because number (2) > 1, the **else** branch is processed. The value returned is FindFactorial(1) * 2, which calls FindFactorial for 1.
FindFactorial(1) * 2 * 3 * 4 * 5	Because number (1) <= 1, the **true** branch is processed, returning a value for FindFactorial(1) rather than making another call to FindFactorial.
1 * 2 * 3 * 4 * 5	The computed value is 120.

What would have happened if you removed the decision that tests the value of **number** against 1? In addition to using the wrong algorithm, you would have created an infinite loop! In our test of **5!**, we stopped making recursive calls to **FindFactorial** only after we reached 1. If there was no test to tell us when to stop, the program would make repeated calls to **FindFactorial** forever! You would probably notice that the computer appeared to have locked up, and you would have to terminate the process through Windows Task Manager or by using Stop Debugging from the Debug menu.

An improperly written recursive method often results in a stack overflow condition.

The **FindFactorial** method could also have been written using a **for** loop rather than a recursive method. Figure 8-29 illustrates a looping factorial method that uses a **short** data type for the number and a **double** data type for the return value.

```
1    private double FindFactorial(short number)
2    {
3        double result;
4        result = 1;
5        for (int nbr = 1; nbr <= number; nbr++)
6            {
7                result *= nbr;
8            }
9        return result;
10   }
11
```

Factorial - Loop

Enter number: 15

Factorial: 1307674368000

OK   Close

Figure 8-29   FindFactorial looping method

If you compare the two approaches, you might find the recursive method to be clearer. Although a recursive method directly reflects the abstract solution algorithm, and is likely to be clearer, simpler, shorter, and easier to understand, it is also more likely to result in a less efficient (slower) program. If efficiency is important for a particular application, you may want to look for an iterative equivalent to the recursive algorithm. Thus, if efficiency was important in a program that used the factorial computation, you should employ the `FindFactorial` looping method in favor of the recursive method.

NESTED LOOPS

Sometimes a problem may involve repetitive processes embedded within other repetitive processes. For example, you might have a class with a hundred students, each of whom has five test grades. You might have one loop to examine all students and a loop inside of that loop to add up each student's grades to produce an average grade for each student. To implement a solution for such a problem, you would need to use nested loops. A program with **nested loops** has one loop completely enclosed within the statement block of another loop. When you are coding a nested loop, the inner loop's opening and closing curly braces must appear within the opening and closing curly braces of the outer loop.

You might recall the process you went through to memorize the multiplication tables. First, you learned the 1s tables, then the 2s, then the 3s, and so on. Later on, you learned that multiplication is commutative, which means you can switch the order of the two operands and the result remains the same (a*b is the same as b*a). You may even have used a printed table to help learn these basic math facts.

We illustrate nested loops by sharing a program to display a multiplication table inside a `ListBox`. To produce a multiplication table, you need to know where to start and end. Let's assume that you start at 1 and continue to a number provided by the user. The table has the same number of rows and columns. Row headings display the multiplication operator and every number from 1 to the given number, all across a single line. Column headings do the same, but the values are listed vertically. For a given cell in the table, the row header defines the first operand, and the column defines the second operand. Because printing is done across each line, you need to write the steps to find all of the products for a given column heading value. The logic looks something like the following:

1. Place row headers on the list.

2. For each row from 1 to the given number, do the following:

    a. Set the output line to the column header (=row).

    b. For each column from 1 to the given number, do the following:

    ▪ Find the product of the current row and column.

    ▪ Concatenate the product to the end of the output line.

    c. Copy the output line to the list.

Figure 8-30 lists the code for a program that displays a multiplication table in a `ListBox`. The nested loops have been highlighted to emphasize that one loop is completely enclosed inside another. Keep in mind that, even if your indentation is different, placement of the curly braces relative to the other statements determines the nesting. However, consistent use of indentation helps you more easily identify loop structures and locate problems faster if you happen to forget an opening or closing curly brace. Figure 8-31 shows a sample execution of the program. Note that if you use a number larger than 15, you should change the **HorizontalScrollbar** property of **lstMultTable** to **true** so that you can see the entire table.

```
1    private void btnOkay_Click(object sender, System.EventArgs e)
2    {
3        short number;
4        int answer;
5        string rowLine;
6        lstMultTable.Items.Clear();
7
8        number = short.Parse(txtNumber.Text);
9
10       // print headings
11
12       rowLine = "    *";
13       for (int row = 1; row <= number; row++)
14       {
15           rowLine += row.ToString().PadLeft(4);
16       }
17       lstMultTable.Items.Add(rowLine);
18
19       // process a row in the multiplication table
20
21       for (int row = 1; row <= number; row++)           // outer loop
22       {
23           rowLine = row.ToString().PadLeft(4);
24
25           // process all values from 1 to the number for a row in the multiplication table
26
27           for (int col = 1; col <= number; col++)       // inner, nested loop
28           {
29               answer = row * col;
30               rowLine += answer.ToString().PadLeft(4);
31           }
32
33           // add the row to the listbox
34
35           lstMultTable.Items.Add(rowLine);
36       }
37   }
38
```

Figure 8-30   Multiplication table program code

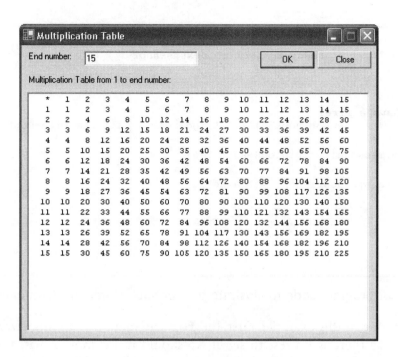

Figure 8-31 Sample execution of the multiplication table program

THE continue KEYWORD

The last optional topic for this chapter is the **continue** statement, which is useful when you have a fairly long loop and encounter a situation in which the remaining statements in the loop should be skipped. For example, suppose you have a building with 100 fire sensors (**fireSensors = 100**). Assume each sensor returns **false** if there is no fire present and **true** if the sensor is tripped. You have written a program that monitors these sensors continually, check-ing to see if a sensor has been tripped due to a fire condition. If a sensor is tripped, an alarm is sounded and a phone call is automatically placed to the fire department. If no fire is sensed, the program examines the next fire sensor in the list. The code might look something like that shown in Figure 8-32.

```
1    private void btnStart_Click(object sender, System.EventArgs e)
2    {
3        int sensorIndex;
4        bool alarmState;
5        string message;
6        sensorIndex = 0;
7        for (; ; )
8        {
9            alarmState = bool.Parse(lstFireSensor.Items[sensorIndex].ToString());
10           if (alarmState == false)
11           {
12               if (sensorIndex == 99)
13               {
14                   sensorIndex = 0;    // reset for another pass
15               }
16               else
```

Figure 8-32 Fire Alarm Sensor program code to illustrate the continue statement

```
17                     {
18                         sensorIndex++;      // ready to look at next sensor
19                     }
20                 continue;
21             }
22         // Not good -- we have a fire!
23         message = "Alarm #: " + (sensorIndex+1) + " triggered -- call the Fire Dept." +
24             " Reset sensor?";
25         if (messageBoxYesNo(message) == DialogResult.Yes)
26         {
27             lstFireSensor.Items[sensorIndex] = "false";
28             sensorIndex++;
29         }
30     }
31 }
32
```

Figure 8-32 Fire Alarm Sensor program code to illustrate the continue statement (continued)

There are several things to notice in this example. First, the **for** statement has no initializers, test conditions, or iterators. Because there is no test to see if we should make another pass through the loop, and there is no loop control variable in the statement, the C# compiler generates code that treats the test condition for the loop as though it were always **true**. Therefore, the statement

```
7            for (; ;)
```

is a useful idiom for creating an infinite loop. Although infinite loops are normally something we wish to avoid, in this application an infinite loop is exactly what we need. After all, we want the fire alarm system to constantly monitor all of the fire alarms—forever!

The **if** statement checks the fire sensor (that is, **alarmState**, which was assigned the value in **lstFireSensor.Items[sensorIndex]**) to see if there is a fire. If the sensor returns **false** (that is, no fire at that sensor), we check the value of the **sensorIndex** variable to see if it is 99. If it is, all 100 sensors (that is, 0 through 99) have been checked and we're ready to reinspect all of them again. Therefore, we set **sensorIndex** to 0 if its current value is 99. If **sensorIndex** is less than 99, we simply increment **sensorIndex** and execute the **continue** statement.

Note that the **continue** statement transfers program control back to the innermost loop control statement. In our example, this means that program control is immediately sent to the **for** statement near the top of the code listing. This means that we bypass the code that handles the steps when we realize there is a fire.

A **continue** statement, therefore, can be used to ignore code that is contained within the loop body. To be more precise, the **continue** statement transfers control to whatever test expression is being used to control the next iteration of the loop. In a **for** loop, control would be sent to the middle expression (expression2). In our fire example, an empty test expression defaults to **true**, so another pass through the loop is made.

SUMMARY

Essential Topics

❑ When you go through the trouble of writing a computer program, you probably intend to use it to solve several problems. If you can gather multiple data sets at one time, the program can employ loops to find solutions for all of those problems in one execution of the program. When you know how many sets of data need to be processed, you can use a counting loop to keep track of each data set being processed.

❑ **ListBoxes** *may be used to* collect and display multiple sets of data for use in repetitive operations. Later chapters show how to obtain these data sets from text files and databases.

❑ Regardless of the source of data, if you can write a program to find a solution for one piece of data, embedding these statements inside a loop statement block allows you to apply the same logic to every piece of data in the same way and solve for all data sets. The key to making the loop work well lies in following the three conditions of a well-behaved loop:

1. There is an initial state before the start of the loop.

2. The state will change inside the loop.

3. The state is checked before another iteration is executed.

Breaking one of these rules often results in a program that crashes, wastes computing resources, or, even worse, produces incorrect results. Using well-behaved loops in programs can save you considerable time and effort when processing multiple sets of data.

❑ The **for**, **while**, and **foreach** iteration statements may be used to construct well-behaved loops. The **while** loop is used when the number of iterations is not known. The **for** loop is used when the iterations will be counted from a starting value to an ending value, with a specific increment value. The **foreach** loop is used to simplify this processing when it is applied to all elements of a ListBox.

❑ In some circumstances, a **break** statement can simplify the logic used to define loop termination condition(s). When a **break** statement is encountered, all loop processing terminates and control passes to the statement immediately after the closing curly brace that signifies the end of the loop.

Bonus Topics

❑ When you write conditional loops, if there are multiple conditions under which the loop should terminate, a compound or complex condition should be used on the **while** statement's condition. Without this approach, the code within the loop body will require extra steps to reset the loop condition in circumstances that are outside the loop condition.

❑ In some cases, recursion may be viewed as a clearer, simpler, shorter, and easier to understand alternative to iterative loops. However, recursive methods are also likely to be less efficient than their iterative counterparts and should be used only when program speed is not an issue.

❑ When one repetitive process involves another repetitive process, nested loops are used. When you code nested loops, indentation should be used to visually identify the beginning and ending of the inner loop, which is entirely contained within the outer loop.

❑ In certain applications, there may be a need to bypass the remaining processing steps in a loop. The **continue** statement is used for such a purpose.

8

KEY TERMS

Define each of the following terms, as it relates to object-oriented programming:

Essential Terms

- **Add** method
- **break**
- collection
- counting loop
- curly braces { }
- **for** loop
- **foreach** loop
- index
- **Items.Clear** method
- **Items.Insert** method
- **Items** property
- **Items.Count** property
- **Items.Remove** method
- **Items.RemoveAt** method
- iteration

- **ListBox**
- loop
- **SelectedIndex** property
- **SelectedItem** property
- **SelectionMode** property
- **Sorted** property
- well-behaved loop
- **while** loop
- zero-based

Bonus Terms

- **continue**
- nested loops
- recursion

REVIEW QUESTIONS

Essential Questions

1. A **ListBox** is not used much in Windows applications, so a C# programmer should avoid using them in C# programs. True or false?

2. When you add an item to a sorted **ListBox**, the new item appears at the bottom of the list. True or false?

3. To access the items in the **ListBox** collection, the **Items** property should be used. True or false?

4. The **Insert** method may be used to add items to a **ListBox**. True or false?

5. To determine the position of the selected item in a **ListBox**, use **lstName.SelectedItem**. True or false?

6. A well-behaved loop should always use a loop counter variable. True or false?

7. A **while** loop should be used when the number of iterations is not known. True or false?

8. A **for** loop can always be rewritten as a **while** loop. True or false?

9. A **foritem** loop should be used when processing every item in a **ListBox**. True or false?

10. The **break** keyword is used to terminate a loop before the last loop iteration has been processed. True or false?

11. The _____ method is used to delete the fifth item in a **ListBox**.

12. The _____ method is used to erase the entire contents of a **ListBox**.

13. The _____ loop is used to process items in a **ListBox**.

14. The _____ statement is used to terminate loop processing before the last loop iteration has been processed.

15. To write a **for** loop that begins at 2, ends at 17, and skips every other cycle, use the following **for** statement:

    for (count = _____; _____; _____)

16. What are the three conditions of a well-behaved loop?

17. What characterizes an ill-behaved loop?

18. What are the three components of a **for** loop statement?

19. What is the role of the iteration variable in a **foreach** loop statement?

20. How do you decide whether to use a **for** iteration statement or **while** iteration statement to construct a loop?

Bonus Questions

1. A repetitive method is a method that solves a problem by calling itself repeatedly. True or false?

2. A recursive method is more efficient than its equivalent iterative method. True or false?

3. When writing nested loops, a single closing curly brace signifies the end of both currently executing loops. True or false?

4. When writing nested loops, using consistent indentation helps improve the readability of the code. True or false?

5. The **quit** statement is used to bypass remaining statements in the loop body to start the next loop iteration. True or false?

6. Write the **while** condition for a loop that processes the loop body only if the **bankBalance** is above the **minimumBalance** or the **checkNumber** is above the **lastCheck**:
    while (_____)

7. A _____ often results from an improperly written recursive method.

8. A program with nested loops places the curly braces of the inner loop _____ the curly braces of the outer loop.

9. Write a nested loop to find the total score (sum of ten quizzes) for each of 100 students in a class.

10. Explain when it makes sense to create an infinite loop as in **for (; ;)**.

PROGRAMMING EXERCISES

Essential Exercises

1. A prime number is defined as a positive integer that only has exactly two positive integer divisors—itself and 1. Since every even integer is divisible by 2, 2 is the only even prime number. To determine if a number is a prime number, try to divide the number by all integers between 2 and half the number. If any divide evenly (no remainder), then the number is not prime. Otherwise, it is a prime number. Write a C# program to determine if a given number is a prime number. Figure 8-33 shows a suggested form.

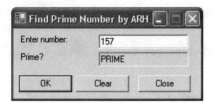

Figure 8-33 Suggested form for Find Prime Number program

2. Write a C# program to get a number from the user and then find the next prime number, starting with the given number. Figure 8–34 shows a suggested form.

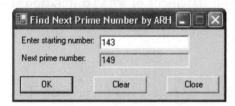

Figure 8-34 Suggested form for Find Next Prime Number program

3. Write a C# program that reverses the items in one **ListBox** and displays the results in another ListBox. Figure 8-35 shows a suggested form.

Figure 8-35 Suggested form for reverse list program

4. Write a C# program to get a starting and ending Fahrenheit temperature from the user, and then print a temperature conversion table that includes all temperatures between the two given temperatures in 3-degree increments and the equivalent temperatures on the Celsius scale. (Celsius = (Fahrenheit – 32) / 1.8)

5. Write a C# program to display a metric conversion table that shows distances in miles and equivalent distances in kilometers in 10-mile increments. Get the starting and ending values (in miles) from the user. (One mile is equivalent to 1.6093 kilometers.)

6. Write a C# program to display a metric conversion table that shows weights in pounds and equivalent weights in kilograms in 10-pound increments. Get the starting and ending values (in pounds) from the user. (One pound is equivalent to 0.4536 kilograms.)

7. Write a C# program to generate a retirement projection, given the amount of money you have to invest today, the current interest rate, the current year, and the year you plan to retire. The projection should display the year, starting balance in that year, interest earned that year based on the starting balance, and ending balance. The ending balance of a given year is equal to the starting balance of the subsequent year. Use a **ListBox** to display the information in a tabular format such as that shown in Figure 8-36.

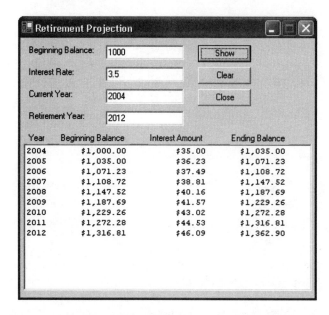

Figure 8-36 Suggested form for retirement projection program

8. Write a C# program to collect exam scores and generate statistics about the exam that include the high score, low score, and average. Figure 8-37 shows a suggested form. Note that integer division was used in the sample, and therefore produced an average of 76; however, if your solution rounds the result, your program would show 77. You should verify with your instructor whether the average should be rounded or truncated.

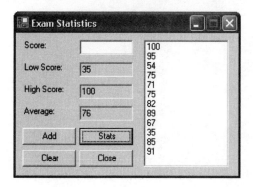

Figure 8-37 Suggested form for exam statistics program

Bonus Exercises

1. Write a variation of the multiplication table program shown in Figures 8-29 and 8-30, but add buttons to display an addition table or a subtraction table.

2. Write a variation of the multiplication table program shown in Figures 8-29 and 8-30, but display a division table. Keep in mind that division by zero is undefined, so instead of doing the division, simply display an * (asterisk).

ARRAYS AND COLLECTIONS

In the Essentials section you will learn:

♦ How arrays are like `ListBoxes`
♦ Why to use arrays
♦ How to use single-dimensional arrays
♦ How to manually search an array
♦ How to manually sort an array
♦ How to use methods to sort an array
♦ What `ArrayLists` are
♦ How to use `ArrayList` properties and methods

In the Bonus section you will learn:

♦ How to use multidimensional arrays
♦ How to use an enumerator to iterate through a collection
♦ How to use hash tables, queues, and stacks

Chapter 8 introduced the concept of using loops to simplify coding of repetitive processes. You can write a single set of process steps once and place them inside a loop to repeat the steps over and over. This option is preferred over having to write the same code every time you need to repeat the process. Often, loops are used to process similar sets of data that are stored collectively. For example, assume that you have a group of ten employees for whom you need to compute the weekly pay. You could write a program to compute the weekly pay for one employee and simply run the program ten times to process all ten employees. Alternatively, you could collect the wage data for all ten employees at once and then use a counting loop to handle each employee's pay calculation. In order to process similar sets of data the same way, you need some type of a structure to hold the related data and take advantage of a loop to repeat the processing. This chapter explains how arrays and collections can be used in this manner.

ESSENTIAL TOPICS

The real value of loops becomes apparent when you have a list of data and you want to process each item in the list in the same way. You've already seen this benefit in Chapter 8 when `ListBoxes` were presented. As you recall, a `ListBox` is a `Windows.Forms` control that allows you to display a list of similar values to the user in a list format. Arrays and `ArrayLists` may be used to store lists of related data that can be accessed by program code, but have no visible presence on a form. The Essentials Topics section shows you how to use loops and methods to process the data in arrays and `ArrayLists`.

HOW ARRAYS RESEMBLE LISTBOXES

An **array** is a group of contiguous memory locations of the same data type that share the same name. You've already seen and used a type of visual array in Chapter 8 when you used a `ListBox` on your form. Recall that a `ListBox` allowed you to keep the same type of information (names of contacts, wish list items, and so on) together under the same name. To get a specific item in the `ListBox`, you used the name of the `ListBox` and the index location within the list. For example, `lstContact.Items[3]` gave you the value of the fourth contact in the `ListBox` named `lstContact`.

Why Use Arrays?

To understand why you should use an array, think about any situation in which you had to handle many sets of similar data in the same way. For example, consider what happens at the cash register when you go shopping. As each product goes across the bar code scanner, the item's price is added to a list, which you see when the receipt is printed. All the items in your shopping cart are processed the same way: each item is added to your list of purchased items, and the item's price is added to a running bill total. Once all items have been processed, they are bagged and you pay the clerk the amount owed. With the receipt, you can review the name of each purchased item as well as its price, as depicted in Figure 9-1. This receipt can be viewed as a picture of the contents of your purchased items array. Every entry on the receipt represents an item you purchased for a specific price. All items were processed in the same manner to be displayed on the receipt and added to the total bill until no items remained. When you were finished, you knew how many items you had purchased and the total amount owed. If you had a question about an item's price (for example, the can of chicken was supposed to be on sale for $1.50), the receipt could be used to identify the item in question (#4 of the customer receipt in Figure 9-1).

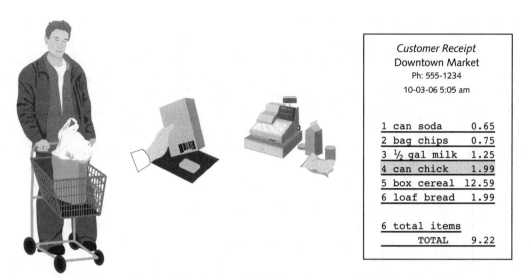

Customer Receipt
Downtown Market
Ph: 555-1234
10-03-06 5:05 am

1	can soda	0.65
2	bag chips	0.75
3	½ gal milk	1.25
4	can chick	1.99
5	box cereal	12.59
6	loaf bread	1.99

6 total items
TOTAL   9.22

Figure 9-1   Customer receipt as an array of purchased items

9

Whenever you have many sets of data of the same type to be processed in the same way, arrays may be used to store the related data as one unit, in much the same way as the receipt stored the items purchased by the customer. When arrays are used in conjunction with loops, your programming task can be simplified considerably. In Chapter 8, you learned how the **ListBox** simplified your programming task. The Restaurant Bill Calculator allowed you to enter multiple food and drink bills and then calculate the total bill. The Wish List program allowed you to enter items on your wish list and the cost of each, and then it determined how many of those items could be purchased based on your budget. Because the values were referenced using the same name, the processing was written once and placed inside a loop. A loop counter variable kept track of the index location in each iteration, so that all values in the list were processed the same way. The rest of this chapter shows how arrays may be used in a similar fashion to yield the same benefit from repetitive processing.

Terminology

Before beginning to use arrays, let's review a few important terms. An array, like a **ListBox**, is zero-based. Many other languages, such as C++ and Java, also use zero-based arrays. The second column in Table 9-1 depicts an array named **hoursWorked**, which contains five items. Each of these items is referred to as an array **element**.

Table 9-1   Array named hoursWorked with five items

index	hoursWorked	To access in code
0	10.5	hoursWorked[0]
1	21.5	hoursWorked[1]
2	45	hoursWorked[2]
3	37	hoursWorked[3]
4	40	hoursWorked[4]

Note that these elements are stored in contiguous locations in computer memory, as depicted in Figure 9-2. If the first array element of type **double** is stored at memory address 200,000, then the next element is at memory address 200,008 (the next contiguous memory location for a **double**, which is 8 bytes after the first memory location). However, you don't have to worry about the specific memory locations to access the data in an array. To identify a specific element, you need to know its distance from the beginning of the array. The first location has an index of 0 because it is at the start, and the last location has an index of 4 because it is four locations past the start. This **index** is sometimes called the **subscript** and is used to identify a specific element in the array. When writing code that references an array element, you supply the array name and subscript or index location. Therefore, using the array name with a specific index uniquely identifies a specific element in the array. For example, `hoursWorked[3]` refers to the fourth array element, which currently contains the value 37 and resides at memory location 200,024.

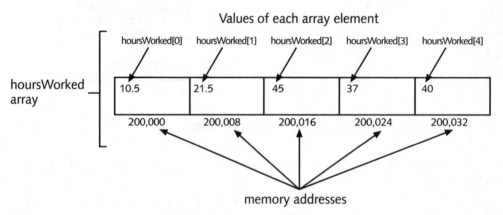

Figure 9-2   How the hoursWorked array of type double may look in computer memory

To illustrate the benefits of using arrays with loops, consider the code shown in Figure 9–3.

```
1          for (hrsIndex = 0; hrsIndex < 5; hrsIndex++)
2          {
3                pay = hoursWorked[hrsIndex] * 12.50M;
4                totalPay += pay;
5          }
```

Figure 9-3   The for loop used to process every element of the hrsWorked array

Line 1 depicts a **for** loop that uses a loop counter variable which also serves as an array index. It starts at 0 (the index of the first element), ends at 4 (the index of the last element), and increments the count by 1 on each pass through the loop to get to every element in the array. Line 3 depicts an assignment statement that calculates the pay using the current element's **hoursWorked** value and a fixed wage rate of $12.50 per hour. The calculated income value is then added to the variable **totalPay** on line 4. You might be wondering why we didn't combine lines 3 and 4 to read:

```
totalPay += hoursWorked[hrsIndex] * 12.50M;
```

By calculating pay separately, it is more obvious that you are computing an individual pay in each iteration. Further, you allow for the option to display the individual pay in a **ListBox** by adding the following line of code before the closing curly brace of the **for** loop:

```
lstResult.Items.Add(pay.ToString("C2"));
```

Remember that the "C2" argument supplied to the **ToString** method signifies that the output style should use the currency format with two positions after the decimal point, to show dollars and cents. The benefit of placing these statements inside a loop is that there is some reduction in lines of code. If you don't use a loop to calculate `totalPay`, you need to repeat lines 3 and 4 for each array element, as shown in Figure 9-4.

```
1          pay = hoursWorked[0] * 12.50M;
2          totalPay += pay;
3          pay = hoursWorked[1] * 12.50M;
4          totalPay += pay;
5          pay = hoursWorked[2] * 12.50M;
6          totalPay += pay;
7          pay = hoursWorked[3] * 12.50M;
8          totalPay += pay;
9          pay = hoursWorked[4] * 12.50M;
10          totalPay += pay;
```

Figure 9-4 Code to process every element of the hoursWorked array without a loop

Using the current array, you would replace the five lines of code with five copies of these two statements for a total of ten lines of code. That may not seem tedious, but what would happen if you had an array with 100 elements? Without the loop, you would need to use 200 lines of code to compute each individual **pay** and add it to **totalPay**. With the loop shown in Figure 9-3, if the array had 100 elements, the only change would be the state check step on line 1 (**hrsIndex < 5** would change to **hrsIndex < 100**). Thus, the combination of arrays and loops can significantly reduce the amount of code you have to write!

tip ▶ When arrays are used, you know how many iterations are needed based on the number of elements, so a counting loop is appropriate. Use a **for** loop when you need to know both the array element value and the index value in each iteration. Use a **foreach** loop when you need to process just the array element value in each iteration.

In Chapter 8, you also learned about the **foreach** loop, which may be used to iterate through an array or collection. Because the **foreach** loop ensures that all elements of the array are processed regardless of the size of the array, you may prefer to use it instead of the **for** loop. Figure 9-5 shows the **foreach** alternative to the **for** loop in Figure 9-3. Notice that line 1 defines the **foreach** variable **hours** to refer to each element in the **hoursWorked** array, and line 3 now uses **hours** in the computation of **pay** during each loop iteration.

```
1          foreach (double hours in hoursWorked)
2          {
3              pay = hours * 12.50M;
4              totalPay += pay;
5          }
```

Figure 9-5 The foreach loop used to process every element of the hrsWorked array

The preceding discussion referred to arrays as a list. However, arrays may also look like a table or groups of tables. The nature of an array's organization is dictated by the array's **dimension**. To identify a specific array element, you need to specify an index for each dimension. For example, to pick an item in a list, you specify one number that represents its position in the list. Because you need to provide only one position number, the array is said to be a single-dimensional array. If the array were more like a table, you would need to specify a row index and a column index to identify an individual element in the table. Such an array is said to be two-dimensional and has a **dimensionality**, or **rank**, of 2. The Bonus Topics section discusses multidimensional arrays in more detail, but let's focus on single-dimensional arrays for now, because they are the most common.

Single-Dimensional Arrays

A **single-dimensional array** (also called a one-dimensional array) is an array that requires one subscript to identify a specific array element. A single-dimensional array looks like a list, such as a shopping list or to do list. Arrays are derived from the .NET `System.Array` class, which means that there are a number of useful methods and properties automatically available to you when you use arrays.

You define an array using the syntax:

```
dataType[] arrayName;
```

To define the `hoursWorked` array discussed earlier, you might use:

```
double[] hoursWorked;
```

An array in C# has static size, which means that after you **initialize** it (state the number of elements in the array), that number is fixed and can't change. Arrays are instantiated and initialized using the **new** keyword. To create an array on the same line where you define it, the syntax is:

```
dataType[] arrayName = new dataType[size];
```

In this example, size refers to the number of elements in the array. Because an array is zero-based, when you specify the size of the array, the valid subscripts are 0 to size − 1. For example, to define and initialize the `hoursWorked` array, you would use:

```
double[] hoursWorked = new double[5]; // valid subscripts are 0 to 4
```

Note that in the definition of the `hoursWorked` array just shown, the size of the array is 5 and represents the number of elements in the array; however, the valid indexes of the array elements are 0 through 4. This relationship between the array size and array indexes means that the largest valid index for the array is always size − 1.

You may also assign the initial values of the array on the same line used to define the array. To assign the array elements initial values, list the element values separated by commas within curly braces. For example, the following line shows how you could assign the five elements in `hoursWorked`, which are the values shown earlier in Table 9-1:

```
double[] hoursWorked = new double[5] {10.5, 21.5, 45, 37, 40};
```

Useful Properties and Methods

Figure 9-3 depicted a **for** loop that was used to process all elements of an array. The state check step (`hrsIndex < 5`) used a literal value of 5 to identify when the loop should terminate. In the discussion, we stated that the state check step is the only part of the code to change if the array size changes from 10 to 100 elements (you would use either a 10 or 100 in place of the 5). However, there is a better approach—use the **Length property** of the array. For example, instead of using:

```
1          for (hrsIndex = 0; hrsIndex < 5; hrsIndex++)
```

you could use:

```
1          for (hrsIndex = 0; hrsIndex < hoursWorked.Length; hrsIndex++)
```

Then, regardless of the size of the array, you would not need to change the code at all! Figure 9-6 shows the screen shot for a program that uses the **Length** property.

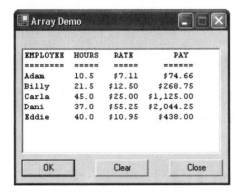

Figure 9-6   Array Demo program using the Length property

The Array Demo program illustrates the definition and initialization of three types of arrays (employee, hours, and rate). Because these arrays are related to each other and have the same number of elements (5), they are called **parallel arrays**. Table 9-2 illustrates the content and indexes of the elements of these three parallel arrays. Notice that the related items in all three arrays have the same index. For example, Carla worked 45 hours and earned $25/hour. These three pieces of information are located in the third element (with index 2) in each of the three arrays.

Table 9-2   Three parallel arrays with five elements each

index	employee	index	hours	index	rate
0	Adam	0	10.5	0	$7.11
1	Billy	1	21.5	1	$12.50
2	Carla	2	45	2	$25.00
3	Dani	3	37	3	$55.25
4	Eddie	4	40	4	$10.95

 tip ▶ When parallel arrays are processed in a loop, use a **for** loop. This type of loop allows you to use the loop counter variable as the index or subscript for each of the parallel arrays in every iteration. Note that a **foreach** loop does not provide a way to handle the elements in parallel arrays in the same iteration unless you separately keep track of an array index variable. Because a **for** loop's loop counter variable also serves as the array index variable, no extra work is required to access all related elements of parallel arrays in the same iteration.

The definition statements in the Array Demo program (lines 101 to 103) initialize the array elements' values. A **ListBox** is used to display the results in a tabular format. A two-line column header is added to the **ListBox** to identify the data in each column. A **for** loop is used to iterate through every array element. A monospace font, Courier, is used to line the display text up by counting characters. The **PadRight** and **PadLeft** string methods are used to left-align or right-align the data. The numeric width of the display field is listed as an argument to these alignment methods. Refer to the code listing in Figure 9-7 for more details. Note that line 116 shows the C# statement that uses the **Length** property of the employee array to identify the state check step.

```
93    private void btnOK_Click(object sender, System.EventArgs e)
94    {
95       int arrayIndex;
96       string display;
97       decimal pay;
98
99       // Define and initialize arrays to hold data.
100
101      string[] employee = new string[5] {"Adam", "Billy", "Carla", "Dani", "Eddie"};
102      double[] hours = new double[5] {10.5, 21.5, 45, 37, 40};
103      decimal[] rate = new decimal[5] {7.11M, 12.50M, 25M, 55.25M, 10.95M};
104
105      // Display column headers in ListBox.
106
107      display = "EMPLOYEE  HOURS    RATE           PAY";
108      lstResult.Items.Add(display);
109      display = "========  =====    =====       ======";
110      lstResult.Items.Add(display);
111
112      // Process all elements in a loop and send results to ListBox.
113
116      for (arrayIndex = 0; arrayIndex < employee.Length; arrayIndex++)
117      {
118         pay = (decimal) hours[arrayIndex] * rate[arrayIndex];
119         display = employee[arrayIndex].PadRight(9) +
120            hours[arrayIndex].ToString("F1").PadLeft(5) + "   " +
121            rate[arrayIndex].ToString("C2").PadLeft(6) + "   " +
122            pay.ToString("C2").PadLeft(9);
123         lstResult.Items.Add(display);
124      }
125   }
```

Figure 9-7   Code listing for the Array Demo program

When processing data in arrays, it is important to access only valid indexes. A common mistake that beginning programmers make is using **Length** to reference the last element in an array. If your program attempts to access an array element using an invalid subscript, an **IndexOutOfRangeException** is thrown. To illustrate this error, change line 116 shown in Figure 9-7 to read:

```
116          for (arrayIndex = 0; arrayIndex <= employee.Length; arrayIndex++)
```

If you execute the program and click the OK button, you will see the error message shown in Figure 9-8. The provided sample solution named ArrayDemoOutOfBounds illustrates this error

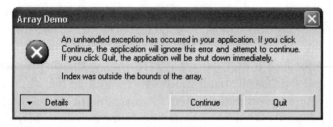

Figure 9-8   Array Demo program which attempts to access a nonexistent array

Thus, it is important to remember that the **Length** property gives the size of the array, which is the number of elements in the array; however, because an array is zero-based, **Length** is always one more than the last valid index.

If you need to know the last valid index of an array, you should use the **GetUpperBound method**. This method takes a single argument that represents the dimension of the array for which you want the last valid subscript. Because you are working with single-dimensional arrays for now, there is only one dimension. Because the array dimension is also referenced using zero-order, you would specify a 0 for the argument to signify the first (and only) dimension. The result of **GetUpperBound(0)** is equal to **Length - 1**. Therefore, to revise the code shown in Figure 9-7 using the **GetUpperBound** method, change line 116 to the following:

```
22      for (arrayIndex = 0; arrayIndex <= employee.GetUpperBound(0); arrayIndex++)
```

Note that in addition to replacing the **Length** property with the **GetUpperBound** method, you also need to change the relational operator from (<) to (<=) to process the element at the last valid subscript. If you keep the (<) operator, the last element in the array is skipped.

Searching an Array Manually

When you use an array to hold a large list of data, it is sometimes useful to look up a specific value. Because the values in the array may not be in any particular order, you find what you are searching for by using a sequential process. You start at the beginning of the array and keep checking each element in sequence until you find what you are searching for or you reach the end of the array without finding a match. Such a process is called a **sequential search**. The screen shots in Figure 9-9 show what happens when you search for a match on name, hours, or rate. When a match is found, the corresponding information is displayed in the **ListBox**. When no match is found, a **MessageBox** is used to explain that the provided lookup value was not found in the array.

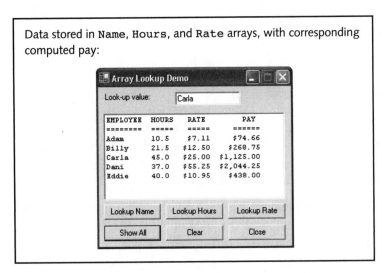

Figure 9-9 Array Lookup Demo program

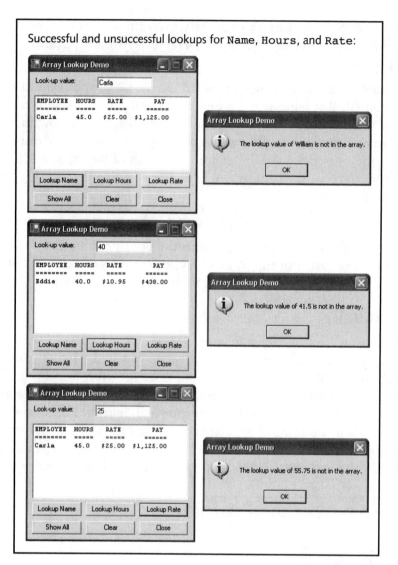

Successful and unsuccessful lookups for Name, Hours, and Rate:

Figure 9-9   Array Lookup Demo program (continued)

Although the current example has just five elements, even if the arrays were larger, the search process should work the same way. Therefore, the program logic should not use literal values or "magic numbers" to identify the end location of the array. Instead, the method to identify the end (< Length or <= GetUpperBound) should be used.

To perform a sequential search, you also need to use two important variables: one to hold the lookup value and another to keep track of whether the lookup value has been found or not. The general logic for performing a sequential search of any type of array is:

1. Get the lookup value entered by the user (such as data entered in a text box on the form).

2. Assign found the value of false (because there is no match before you begin).

3. Repeat for all elements of the array

    a. Compare the **lookup** value against the value at the current element.

        ■ If there is a match, assign **found** a value of **true** and **break** out of the loop

4. Compare the value of **found**.

    a. If **found** is **true**, then show the information for the array at location **arrayIndex**.

    b. If **found** is **false**, then display a message explaining that the **lookup** value was not found.

In step 4a of the general logic, notice that the **arrayIndex** variable is used to identify which element of the array had the match. When you use parallel arrays, as previously shown in Table 9-2, this same index variable identifies the corresponding elements in each of the arrays. Assume that you used the lookup logic to locate a specific name in the **employee** array (Dani). If the match was found at an **arrayIndex** of 3, then you know that the name you were looking for (Dani) is at index 3. Further, you know that Dani's hours worked is in the **hours** array at index 3 (Dani worked 37 hours) and that her hourly wage rate is in the **rate** array at index 3 (Dani's wage rate is $55.25). Therefore, when the match is found, the **arrayIndex** value is used to display the contents of all related arrays at that particular index.

Figure 9-10 shows the code for the **btnLookupHours_Click** event method. The array definitions have been moved outside any event method to give the three arrays class scope. Recall from Chapter 7 that class-scope variables can be accessed from within any method in the form class, and by convention we prefix class-scope variable names with a lowercase "m" to indicate that they are private members of the class. Therefore, defining them with class scope allows all three of the searching event methods to reference the arrays.

```
private string[] mEmployee = new string[5] {"Adam", "Billy", "Carla", "Dani", "Eddie"};
private double[] mHours = new double[5] {10.5, 21.5, 45, 37, 40};
private decimal[] mRate = new decimal[5] {7.11M, 12.50M, 25M, 55.25M, 10.95M};
```

Notice that the **GetUpperBound** method (line 225 in Figure 9-10) is used to identify the last subscript. To verify that this code works with different array sizes, try adding more elements to the three arrays and run the program again. Be sure to add the same number of elements to all three arrays, because they are related to each other in this program. If you add five new values to **hours** and **rate**, but only three **employee**s, then if you happen to look up the last two elements in the **hours** array, an **IndexOutOfRangeException** is thrown. You should include a **try-catch** block to enhance the error message that is displayed in the event of an unexpected error due to this problem. We leave this as an exercise.

9

```
204    private void btnLookupHours_Click(object sender, System.EventArgs e)
205    {
206        // Define variables to hold data.
207
208        double lookup;
209        bool found;
210        int arrayIndex;
211        string display;
212        decimal pay;
213
214        // Get lookup value and search the mEmployee array for a match.
215
216        lookup = double.Parse(txtLookup.Text);
217
218        // Note that a match has not been found yet.
219
220        found = false;
221
222        // Search all elements in order until a match is found or there
223        // are no elements left to search.
224
225        for (arrayIndex=0; arrayIndex <= mHours.GetUpperBound(0); arrayIndex++)
226        {
227            if (mHours[arrayIndex] == lookup)
228            {
229                found = true;
230                break;
231            }
232        }
233
234        if (found == true)
235        {
236            // Erase the ListBox and then display column headers.
237
238            lstResult.Items.Clear();
239            display = "EMPLOYEE  HOURS    RATE          PAY";
240            lstResult.Items.Add(display);
241            display = "========  =====    =====       ======";
242            lstResult.Items.Add(display);
243
244            // Show matching results in ListBox.
245
246            pay = (decimal) mHours[arrayIndex] * mRate[arrayIndex];
247            display = mEmployee[arrayIndex].PadRight(9) +
248                mHours[arrayIndex].ToString("F1").PadLeft(5) + "    " +
249                mRate[arrayIndex].ToString("C2").PadLeft(6) + "    " +
250                pay.ToString("C2").PadLeft(9);
251            lstResult.Items.Add(display);
252        }
253        else
254        {
255            display = "The lookup value of " + lookup + " is not in the array.";
256            messageBoxOK(display);
257        }
258    }
```

Figure 9-10 Code listing for the btnLookupHours_Click event method

What happens if you have two people with the same name or hours or rate? Will you find the one you need? Right now, the sequential search is set up so that you will find only the first match of the lookup value. Can you think of a simple change that would allow you to find the last match? You can apply the same logic, but reverse the order. Thus, you start with the last element and keep checking the previous element (decrement by 1) until you reach the start. The following code change is required to make this work:

```
225        for (arrayIndex = mHours.GetUpperBound(0); arrayIndex >= 0; arrayIndex--)
```

Even with the code change to find the last match, this approach won't always give you the match that you are looking for. For example, if three people have the same name in the array, neither approach finds the "middle" person. The best solution is to search the entire array and show all matches rather than showing just the first match or just the last match. This version is an exercise for you to try on your own.

Sorting an Array Manually

The previous examples showed that the array contents are displayed in their original order; however, when people review a list of data, particularly a long list of data, it is helpful to present the list in an organized fashion. It just so happens that the names are stored alphabetically, but if they were stored randomly instead, it would be a bit more difficult to locate a specific name, especially if the list contained a larger number of names. However, if the list is sorted alphabetically, you could easily find a specific name. Alternatively, you might want to view the data ordered by the hours worked or the wage rate.

The process of arranging the data in an array in an ordered fashion is called **sorting**. There are many different algorithms that may be used to sort an array, and each of them has pros and cons. Because the bubble sort algorithm is fairly easy to understand, it is often used to explain the process for sorting lists.

Most sorting algorithms, including the bubble sort, use nested loops. The bubble sort uses an outer loop to keep track of the top of a smaller and smaller list. The inner loop keeps track of all elements below the top element. Within the inner loop, you compare the element at the top of the list to an element below it. If relative to each other, they are out of order, you swap them. After you've made a complete pass through one list, the inner loop terminates and the outer loop should now have the desired element at the top of the list. Thus, the inner loop functions much like the algorithm for finding the minimum value in a list, but in this case, you actually swap items. To sort the list, you simply repeat this process over and over again for an increasingly smaller list (the top of the list moves down one element each time).

The general logic for performing a **bubble sort** can be applied to any type of array:

1. Repeat using `topIndex` to iterate from the start of the array (0) to one before the end.

    a. Repeat using `nextIndex` to iterate from one past `topIndex` to the end of the list.

        1) Compare the values at `topIndex` and `nextIndex`. If they are not in sorted order, swap them (and all elements in related arrays at the same locations).

To illustrate how the bubble sort works, let's apply it to an array of test data. The following statement may be used to define and initialize the elements of the test array used in the illustration:

```
private double[] test = new double[5] {10.5, 21.5, 4.5, 3.7, 14};
```

The outer loop uses `topIndex` to point to the top of the list and the inner loop uses `nextIndex` to point to every element below the top element. Tables 9-3 through 9-6 show how the contents of this test array change with each iteration of the `topIndex` loop. Each time a smaller element is found, the element at the top is swapped with the current element being compared. Note that if you have multiple, parallel arrays, you need to also swap the items in the related arrays at the same locations to preserve the integrity of the original data. After all next elements have been checked (and a `topIndex` iteration is finished), the smallest element in the current list that was checked has floated to the top like a bubble in a glass of water.

Swapping the Contents of Two Memory Locations

To swap the contents of two memory locations, think about how you would swap the contents of two containers of different beverages. Suppose that you had accidentally filled a mug with iced tea and a glass with hot coffee. To switch the contents, you would need a third container, say a Styrofoam cup. First, you might pour the coffee from the glass into the Styrofoam cup. Next, you could pour the iced tea into the empty glass. Finally, you could pour the coffee from the temporary container into the now empty mug.

Swapping the contents of two memory locations works in a similar fashion. You need to create a temporary variable of the same type as the two memory locations to be swapped. Then you can begin the three-step process:

temp = firstLocation;
firstLocation = secondLocation;
secondLocation = temp;

Make sure that the data type of the temporary variable is the same as the values being swapped.

Table 9-3 First iteration of the topIndex loop

At START   Complete outer loop iteration for topIndex=0

Compare value at test[0] with every value that follows and swap if a larger value is found

topIndex		0			
nextIndex		1	2	3	4
compare		10.5 > 21.5	10.5 > 4.5	4.5 > 3.7	3.7 > 14
		no swap	swap	swap	no swap

index	test	test	test	test	test
0	10.5	←0 10.5	←0 4.5	←0 3.7	←0 3.7
1	21.5	←1 21.5	1 21.5	1 21.5	1 21.5
2	4.5	2 4.5	←2 10.5	2 10.5	2 10.5
3	3.7	3 3.7	3 3.7	←3 4.5	3 4.5
4	14	4 14	4 14	4 14	←4 14

Smallest value at top of list [0–4]

Now that you know that the smallest value is in `test[0]`, you don't need to look at that element again. To sort the rest, you simply repeat the process again, but look at the list starting at element `test[1]`.

Table 9-4 Second iteration of the topIndex loop

At START	Complete outer loop iteration for topIndex=1

Compare value at test[1] with every value that follows and swap if needed

topIndex		1		
nextIndex		2	3	4
compare		21.5 > 10.5	10.5 > 4.5	4.5 > 14
		swap	swap	no swap

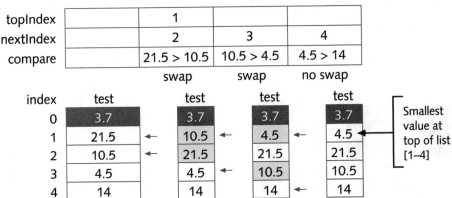

index	test	test	test	test	
0	3.7	3.7	3.7	3.7	Smallest value at top of list [1–4]
1	21.5	10.5	4.5	4.5	
2	10.5	21.5	21.5	21.5	
3	4.5	4.5	10.5	10.5	
4	14	14	14	14	

After the second iteration for `topIndex=1`, `test[1]` has the second smallest value, so you won't need to check it again. Repeat the process again; the list to be checked now begins at element `test[2]`.

Table 9-5 Third iteration of the topIndex loop

At START	Complete outer loop iteration for topIndex=2

Compare value at test[2] with every value that follows and swap if needed

topIndex		2	
nextIndex		3	4
compare		21.5 > 10.5	10.5 > 14
		swap	no swap

index	test	test	test	
0	3.7	3.7	3.7	Smallest value at top of list [2–4]
1	4.5	4.5	4.5	
2	21.5	10.5	10.5	
3	10.5	21.5	21.5	
4	14	14	14	

After the third iteration for `topIndex=2`, `test[2]` has the third smallest value, so you won't need to check it again. Repeat the process one last time, viewing the list starting at element `test[3]`.

9

Table 9-6   Fourth iteration of the topIndex loop

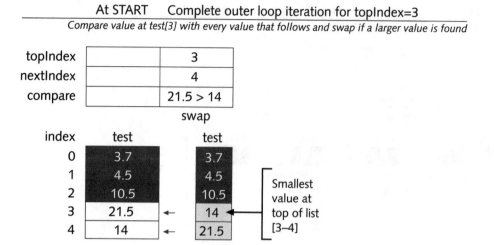

At START	Complete outer loop iteration for topIndex=3

Compare value at test[3] with every value that follows and swap if a larger value is found

After the fourth iteration for `topIndex=3`, `test[3]` has the fourth smallest value, so you won't need to check it again. Since there is only one element remaining, it is also in the correct order, and there is no need to repeat the process. The entire list is finally sorted!

Figure 9-11 contains the code to sort the names in the employees array alphabetically. The provided solution named ArraySortDemo illustrates how this program works. Recall that you need to use the `CompareTo` method to compare string values. If you sorted by `hours` or `rate`, then you would use the relational operator directly to compare the values (for example, `hours[topIndex] > hours[nextIndex]`). Notice that when you discover that two names are out of order, you swap not only the names (lines 202 to 204), but also the hours (lines 206 to 208) and rate (lines 210 to 212). If you forget to include the important step to also swap elements in related parallel arrays, your names will be alphabetized, but the hours and rate will no longer correspond to the same employees!

The array examples used thus far already have the employee array elements in alphabetical order (see the code in Figure 9-7). In order to show a difference between the original list and the one sorted by name, let's revise the array definition and initialization statements to assign values in unsorted order as follows:

```
string[] employee = new string[10] {"Adam", "Max", "Billy", "Mary",
    "Carla", "Charlie", "Dani", "Jane", "Eddie", "Sally"};
double[] hours = new double[10] {10.5, 9.5, 21.5, 10.9,
    45, 38.1, 37, 30, 40, 51};
decimal[] rate = new decimal[10] {7.11M, 9.99M, 12.50M, 13.11M,
    25M, 35.10M, 55.25M, 29.99M, 10.95M, 11.95M};
```

```
190    // Sort the arrays by name.
191
192    for (topIndex = employee.GetLowerBound(0);
193    topIndex < employee.GetUpperBound(0); topIndex++)
194    {
195        for (nextIndex = topIndex + 1;
196        nextIndex <= employee.GetUpperBound(0); nextIndex++)
197        {
198            if (employee[topIndex].CompareTo(employee[nextIndex]) > 0)
199            {
200                // Swap the elements of all arrays.
201
202                tempEmployee = employee[topIndex];
203                employee[topIndex] = employee[nextIndex];
204                employee[nextIndex] = tempEmployee;
205
206                tempHours = hours[topIndex];
207                hours[topIndex] = hours[nextIndex];
208                hours[nextIndex] = tempHours;
209
210                tempRate = rate[topIndex];
211                rate[topIndex] = rate[nextIndex];
212                rate[nextIndex] = tempRate;
213            }
214        }
215    }
```

Figure 9-11 Code for sorting names alphabetically

The screen shots in Figure 9-12 show the Array Sort Demo program, which allows you to show the array data sorted by names, hours, rates, or using the original order. All these examples illustrate how to sort data in ascending order (the smallest value is at the first index and the largest value is at the last index). How difficult would it be to sort the data in descending order? Actually, it requires the change of just a single character! Simply replace the > relational operator on line 198 of Figure 9-11 with the < operator. This is left as an exercise for you to try on your own.

Caution Regarding Sorted ListBoxes

Our current solution places column headers inside the ListBox; however, an alternative would be to remove the headers from inside the ListBox and add labels above the ListBox to identify each column. If the only values in the ListBox are the data elements from the arrays, you might wonder why we don't simply use the Sort property of the ListBox to handle the sorting process. Recall that when you set the Sort property of a ListBox to **true**, the result is not what you might expect when numbers are in the list. The reason is that the data in the list are treated as string values rather than numbers. However, there is still a way to show a list of numbers sorted numerically. If you have the data in numeric arrays and then sort the arrays as we've discussed, then all you have to do is copy the array data to a ListBox that has the Sort property set to **false**. That is effectively what was done in these examples after the headers were displayed. We used a **for** loop after the arrays were sorted to iterate through the array in order, adding an item to the ListBox in each iteration.

Original list

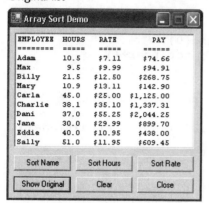

List sorted by name

List sorted by hours

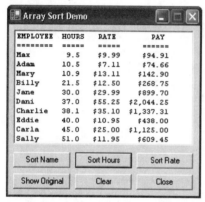

List sorted by rate

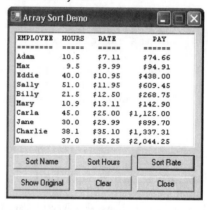

Figure 9-12 Array Sort Demo program

Using the Array.Sort Method

Although writing your own sort is an option, there is an alternative that uses much less code! The **Array.Sort method** allows you to sort a single array or to sort two parallel arrays using one of the arrays for the sort criteria to preserve the integrity of the data in parallel arrays. When sorting two parallel arrays, the **Array.Sort** method takes four arguments:

- The array used for the sort criteria
- A related parallel array
- The starting index for the element where the sorting should begin
- The number of elements to be sorted (use the **Length** property to sort all elements)

The general format of the statement takes the form:

```
Array.Sort(sortArray, relatedArray, 0, sortArray.Length);
```

Because the current example uses three related, parallel arrays but the **Array.Sort** method can handle at most two arrays at a time, you need to create a copy of the **sortArray** so that you can sort all three arrays. It's not enough to simply assign the employee array to another array as in:

```
string[] newEmployee = employee;          // this will not work!
```

Recall that this approach does not work because **newEmployee** references the same array as **employee**. Therefore, when you change the order of the employee array to sort the hours, you've lost the original order of the **employee** array despite having defined the **newEmployee** array. Because **employee** and **newEmployee** both reference the same memory locations, you need to find another solution. You need to create a duplicate copy of the original array. To accomplish this, use the **Array.Copy method**. This method takes five arguments:

- The source array

- The starting subscript of the source array (use 0 to start with the first element)

- The name of the duplicate array to which values are being copied from the source array

- The starting subscript of the duplicate array (usually the same as the starting subscript of the source array)

- The number of elements to be copied (use the **Length** property to copy all elements of the source array to the duplicate array)

Using a combination of the **Array.Copy** method and the **Array.Sort** method, you can replace all 26 lines from Figure 9-11 with the six lines of code shown in Figure 9-13. The provided solution named ArraySortMethod lists the complete code for this program.

```
190    // Sort the arrays by name.
191
192    string[] newEmployee = new string[10];
193    Array.Copy(employee, 0, newEmployee, 0, employee.Length);
194    Array.Sort(employee, hours);
195    Array.Sort(newEmployee, rate);
```

Figure 9-13 Sorting three related arrays by name using Array.Copy and Array.Sort methods

You should note that, if you viewed the **newEmployee** array, you would see that it is also sorted after executing line 195. This means that if you had four or more related arrays, you would need to create additional copies of the original **employee** array before sorting. As the number of related arrays increases, this approach may seem a bit more tedious and less efficient due to the need to create additional arrays for the sole purpose of applying the **Sort** method. If this is an issue, you can always write your own code to sort related arrays as previously discussed and illustrated in Figure 9-11.

Using the Array.Reverse Method

Earlier, you learned that if you write your own sort, you could easily change the sort order from ascending to descending simply by switching a relational operator. Now that you are using the **Array.Sort** method, you may wish to use the **Array.Reverse method** to reverse the order of all three arrays after sorting. Sorting the array in ascending order, and then reversing it results in the array being sorted in descending order.

The three arguments for the **Array.Reverse** method are:

- The source array
- The starting index of the element where the reversing should begin (use 0 to start with the first element)
- The number of elements to be reversed (use the **Length** property to reverse all elements of the array)

The general form of the statement looks like:

```
Array.Reverse(sourceArray, startIndex, numberOfElements);
```

If **startIndex** is 0 and **numberOfElements** is **sourceArray.Length**, then all of the elements of the source array are reversed; however, you could choose to use just a subset of the array for the reversal by varying the values of **startIndex** and **numberOfElements**.

 tip ▶ If you wish to reverse all elements of an array, you can use the shortcut notation:

```
Array.Reverse(sourceArray);
```

This statement is equivalent to the general form with three arguments where the starting index is assumed to be 0 and the number of elements is assumed to be all elements in the array.

To sort our employee, hours, and rate arrays in descending order, you use a two-step process. First, use the **Array.Sort** method described in the last section to sort the arrays in ascending order. Next, reverse all three arrays when the ascending sort is completed. Figure 9-14 shows the specific code that should be placed after the ascending sort has been done (using the code in Figure 9-13).

```
196    // Reverse the arrays.
197
198    Array.Reverse(employee, 0, employee.Length);
199    Array.Reverse(hours, 0, hours.Length);
200    Array.Reverse(rate, 0, rate.Length);
201
```

Figure 9-14   Code to reverse arrays using Array.Reverse method

Figure 9-15 shows screen shots of the Array Reverse Demo program.

Original list

Sorted by reverse-alphabetical names

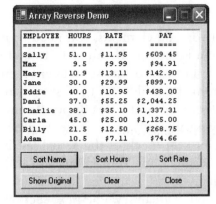

Sorted by descending hours

Sorted by descending rate

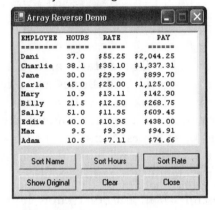

Figure 9-15   The Array Reverse Demo program

tip   When using class scope, static arrays in which you add elements to the array one at a time through user input on a form, it is recommended that you define a class-scope variable to track the current last used location in the array. In any repetitive processing, you need to use this class-scope variable in place of the Length property or the GetUpperBound method so that the unused elements of the array are ignored.

Adjusting the Size of Static Arrays

We stated earlier that the number of elements in a static array is fixed throughout program execution. Nonetheless, you could give the illusion of a growing or shrinking static array, but additional processing would be required to make the illusion work. To add elements to a static array, you need to allow room for extra elements when the array is first created. This means that you need to make the array larger than what you might really need. You also need to do extra processing to figure out the index of the last valid element, so you know where you can start adding more elements. This value would need to be maintained in a class-scope variable, so you could access it in any method in the form class. As you add elements to the array, you need to increment this variable, and as you remove elements from the array, you need to decrement this variable.

When you learned how to process static arrays for searching, manually sorting, and method-based sorting, you used the Length property to identify the number of elements to be processed or the GetUpperBound method to identify the last index; however, if you made the array larger than what you really needed, these would yield undesirable results. Instead, you would need to use the class-scope variable (last valid index) to identify the number of elements (last valid index +1).

Furthermore, when you add elements, you need to make sure you don't go beyond the last valid index or an exception is thrown. If you want to add the value to the middle of the list, you need to add extra code to move all of the subsequent elements to the next index location. To remove an array element from the middle of the list, you need to shift the subsequent elements to the previous index location. Using the `GetUpperBound` method or `Length` property in these cases would result in having unused array elements processed rather than being ignored. Defining a class-scope variable to keep track of the actual last index location used gives you a way to make static arrays appear to grow and shrink, but you should keep in mind that you had to allow for more space than what you really needed for this approach to work. The unused elements become wasted space in computer memory. The next section describes a type of array that allows you to use only the space that you really need.

ARRAYLISTS DEFINED

The arrays you have used so far are **static arrays**. This means that after you initialize the size of the array, you can't change it. `ListBox`es are a type of visual array, but unlike static arrays, `ListBox`es can grow or shrink in size. If you need to use **dynamic arrays** that can grow and shrink like `ListBox`es, .NET provides a useful alternative to static arrays called **ArrayList**s. Like static arrays and `ListBox`es, `ArrayList`s are zero-based and allow access to individual elements through an index reference. Unlike static arrays, however, you can grow or shrink the size of an `ArrayList` throughout program execution.

`ArrayList`s are useful when you don't know how many related data items you need to store. When you consider all the extra processing you have to do to add or remove elements from static arrays, `ArrayList`s become an even more attractive option. Furthermore, `ArrayList`s provide useful methods to manipulate the contents of the list. However, the flexibility of `ArrayList`s comes with a performance penalty when compared to static arrays, so use `ArrayList`s only when you need their flexibility.

The `ArrayList` class is a type of collection. A **collection** is a group of objects with the same characteristics, such as the group of items in a `ListBox`. A collection object includes specialized methods to manage the objects in its collection. The .NET Framework has many collection classes that you can use. You can even create your own collection classes.

The `ArrayList` class is defined in the .NET `System.Collections` namespace. As you learned in Chapter 2, you can add `using` directives at the top of your code to avoid having to fully qualify the class names using the complete namespace. To be able to write `ArrayList` instead of spelling out `Systems.Collections.ArrayList`, add the following statement to the top of your code window with the other `using` statements:

```
using System.Collections;
```

Once you have included the using directive, you can write an `ArrayList` definition with the following statement:

```
ArrayList arrayListName = new ArrayList();
```

To access an element at location `indexAL` in an `ArrayList`, use the following:

```
selectedName = arrayListName[indexAL];
```

Table 9-7 lists some practical **ArrayList** methods that are used in the next program example.

Table 9-7   ArrayList methods

Method name	C# syntax	Purpose
Add	arrayListName.Add(object);	Add elements to the end of an **ArrayList** one at a time.
Insert	arrayListName.Insert(index, object);	Add elements to a specific index location in an **ArrayList**.
Clear	arrayListName.Clear();	Erase all contents of an **ArrayList**.
RemoveAt	arrayListName.RemoveAt(indexAL);	Remove an element at location **indexAL** in an **ArrayList**.
Remove	arrayListName.Remove(objectToRemove);	Remove an element by matching the object in an **ArrayList**.

To better understand **ArrayList**s, let's create an example to manage a list of employee names in an **ArrayList** and display the contents in a **ListBox**. To simplify testing, a static array with ten names is used to fill the **ArrayList**. The static array is called **mEmployee** and the **ArrayList** is called **mEmployeeAL**. Both are defined at class scope, so that they may be used by any method in the form class. Clicking the Test Fill button causes the contents of the static **mEmployee** array to be added to the **mEmployeeAL ArrayList**. The **btnTestFill_Click** method code to accomplish this is shown in Figure 9-16.

```
214   private void btnTestFill_Click(object sender, System.EventArgs e)
215   {
216       // Make sure the ArrayLists start out empty.
217
218       mEmployeeAL.Clear();
219
220       // Fill the mEmployeeAL ArrayList with values in the mEmployee static array.
221
222       foreach (string tempEmployeeAL in mEmployee)
223       {
224           mEmployeeAL.Add(tempEmployeeAL);
225       }
226       showList();
227   }
```

Figure 9-16   The ArrayList Index program's btnTestFill_Click method code

Notice that, once the **ArrayList** has been filled completely using the static array, a private helper method named **showList** is used to display the contents of the **ArrayList** in a **ListBox**. This method is used in several event methods because we need to refresh the **ListBox** each time a change is made to the **ArrayList**. Following the guidelines you learned in Chapter 7, using a private helper method allows you to reuse the code anytime you need it. This method's code is shown in Figure 9-17. Lines 279 to 282 show that this method used a **for** loop to iterate through all elements in the **ArrayList**, starting at 0 and using the **Count** property to identify the number of elements; however, we could have just as easily used the **foreach** loop as follows:

```
279       foreach (string employee in mEmployeeAL)
280       {
281           lstResult.Items.Add(employee);
282       }
```

You should also note that the `ListBox` includes a two-line header (lines 274 to 275) to identify the data that follows the header. This two-line header impacts the processing in other event methods of this program. For example, when the user identifies where to add a particular element to the `ArrayList` by clicking on an item in the `ListBox`, the `SelectedIndex` property of the `ListBox` will be two greater than the corresponding location of that value in the `ArrayList`. For this reason, the code to process the addition of an `ArrayList` item will use `SelectedIndex - 2` to identify the index location of the element to be added.

```
265    private void showList()
266    {
267        // Define loop counter variable to iterate through array list.
268
269        int indexAL;
270
271        // Erase the ListBox and then display column headers.
272
273        lstResult.Items.Clear();
274        lstResult.Items.Add("EMPLOYEE");
275        lstResult.Items.Add("========");
276
277        // Process all elements in a loop and send results to ListBox.
278
279        for (indexAL = 0; indexAL < mEmployeeAL.Count; indexAL++)
280        {
281            lstResult.Items.Add(mEmployeeAL[indexAL]);
282        }
283    }
```

Figure 9-17   The ArrayList Index program's showList method code

The user may type a name and add it to the end of the list or highlight a name in the list to signify where the new name should be added. Figure 9-18 illustrates how the name George is added to the fourth location (`index=3`). Figure 9-19 shows the code for the class-scope definitions and the `btnAddName_Click` event method.

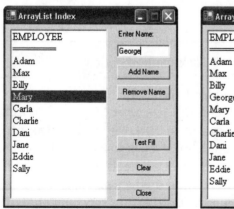

Figure 9-18   The ArrayList Index program used to manage a list of employees

```
  7     // Define static array to hold test values for mEmployees.
  8
  9     private string[] mEmployee = new string[] {"Adam", "Max", "Billy", "Mary", "Carla",
 10                                                "Charlie", "Dani", "Jane", "Eddie",
 11                                                "Sally"};
 12
 13     // Define class-scope ArrayLists to hold mEmployee names.
 14
 15     private ArrayList mEmployeeAL = new ArrayList();
 16
142     private void btnAddName_Click(object sender, System.EventArgs e)
143     {
144         // Make sure that the user provided a name to be added.
145
146         if (txtName.Text == "")
147         {
148             messageBoxOK("Please type a name to add it to the list.");
149             txtName.Focus();
150             return;
151         }
152
153         // Copy the current value in txtName to the mEmployeeAL ArrayList.
154
155         if (lstResult.SelectedIndex > 1)
156         {
157             // If a name in ListBox is selected, to add name in AL in correct
158             // location, subtract 2 since list has a 2-line heading.
159
160             mEmployeeAL.Insert(lstResult.SelectedIndex-2,txtName.Text);
161         }
162         else
163         {
164             mEmployeeAL.Add(txtName.Text);
165         }
166
167         // Show the current list.
168
169         showList();
170
171         // Position the cursor in a blank txtName to allow the user to enter more names.
172
173         txtName.Text = "";
174         txtName.Focus();
175     }
```

Figure 9-19   The ArrayList Index program's class-scope definitions and btnAddName_Click
method code

To remove a name, the user may select the name from the list and click Remove Name. If no
name is selected in the list, the user may also type a name and then click Remove Name. If the
name in the text box is not in the list, an appropriate message is displayed. Figure 9-20 shows the
btnRemove_Click method code.

```
176    private void btnRemove_Click(object sender, System.EventArgs e)
177    {
178        // Make sure this is a valid remove request.
179
180        if (lstResult.SelectedIndex <= 1 && txtName.Text == "")
181        {
182            messageBoxOK("Please type a name to be removed or select it from the list.");
183            txtName.Focus();
184            return;
185        }
186        if (txtName.Text != "" && lstResult.Items.Contains(txtName.Text) == false)
187        {
188            messageBoxOK(txtName.Text + " is not in the list.");
189            txtName.Focus();
190            return;
191        }
192
193        // If a name in the list is selected, remove it and show the new list.
194
195        if (lstResult.SelectedIndex > 1)
196        {
197            mEmployeeAL.RemoveAt(lstResult.SelectedIndex-2);
198            showList();
199        }
200
201        // Since no name was selected, there must be a valid name in the
202        // text box to be removed from the list. Remove the name, erase the
203        // text box, and show the updated list.
204
205        else
206        {
207            mEmployeeAL.Remove(txtName.Text);
208            txtName.Text = "";
209            txtName.Focus();
210            showList();
211        }
212    }
```

Figure 9-20   The ArrayList Index program's btnRemove_Click method code

Sorting ArrayLists

When static arrays were discussed, you learned that you could write code to manually sort the array or use the **Sort** method to arrange the array items in ascending order. You could combine the **Sort** method with the **Reverse** method to arrange the items in descending order. **ArrayLists** also provide **Sort** and **Reverse** methods to control the order of the items in the **ArrayList**. To demonstrate that the sort works correctly for both strings and numbers, let's create a new example that allows you to manage two unrelated ArrayLists—names (**string**s) or grades (**int**s).

To aid testing, define two, class-scope static arrays, one with student names and another with numeric grades, as follows:

```
private string[] mStudent = new string[] {"Adam", "Max", "Billy", "Mary",
                                          "Carla", "Charlie", "Dani",
                                          "Jane", "Eddie", "Sally"};

private int[] mGrades = new int[] {95, 56, 77, 87, 89, 91, 100, 75, 82, 69};
```

To design the form, place a Test Fill button on the form that, when clicked, copies the items in the static arrays into the corresponding **ArrayLists**. The code for accomplishing this is shown in Figure 9-21. Notice that the **ArrayLists** are first emptied using the **Clear** method before adding the values in the static arrays. What do you think happens if you don't start with an empty ArrayList? If a user accidentlly clicks the Test Fill button two (or more) times, then the **ArrayList** will have two (or more) copies of the static array's values. Next, a **foreach** loop is used to iterate through every element in the **student** static array, so it can be added to the **studentAL ArrayList**. Likewise, another **foreach** loop is used to iterate through every element in the **grades** static array to copy the values to the gradesAL **ArrayList**.

9

```
366    private void btnTestFill_Click(object sender, System.EventArgs e)
367    {
368        // Make sure the ArrayLists start out empty.
369
370        mStudentAL.Clear();
371        mGradesAL.Clear();
372
373        // Fill the mStudentAL ArrayList with values in the mStudent static array.
374
375        foreach (string tempStudentAL in mStudent)
376        {
377            mStudentAL.Add(tempStudentAL);
378        }
379
380        // Fill the mGradesAL ArrayList with values in the mGrades static array.
381
382        foreach (int tempGradesAL in mGrades)
383        {
384            mGradesAL.Add(tempGradesAL);
385        }
386
387        messageBoxOK("Test data has been added to mStudent names and mGrades.");
388    }
```

Figure 9-21 The btnTestFill_Click event method in ArrayList Sort program

It would be nice to allow the user to enter the values you want in the **ArrayLists**, so you need to add more controls on the form. Place two text boxes on the form to allow a user to add names or grades for later processing. Add buttons to view the original list, the sorted lists, or the reverse sorted lists for names or grades. Finally, add a **ListBox** to display the contents of the selected **ArrayList**. Figure 9-22 shows a sample form design for this example program.

Figure 9-22   Form design for ArrayList Sort program

Figure 9-23 shows the code for the **btnAddNbr_Click** event method. After making sure that the user's input is a valid number, the **Add ArrayList** method (line 271) is used to add the numeric value entered by the user to the **gradesAL ArrayList**. Recall that this is the same method used in the **foreach** loops shown in Figure 9-21 to copy the values from the corresponding static arrays to the **ArrayLists**. As in the last **ArrayList** example, a private helper method to show the grades is used to display in the **ListBox** the current grades in the **ArrayList** (see Figure 9-24).

```
254    private void btnAddNbr_Click(object sender, System.EventArgs e)
255    {
256        // Copy the current value in txtNumber to the mGradesAL ArrayList.
257
258        int nbr;
259
260        // Make sure the user gave a numeric value.
261
262        if (intTypeCheck(txtNumber.Text, out nbr) == false)
263        {
264            messageBoxOK("Grade must be entered as an integer.");
265            txtNumber.Focus();
266            return;
267        }
268
269        // Since the user's input was okay, add it to the mGradesAL ArrayList.
270
271        mGradesAL.Add(nbr);
272
273        // Position the cursor in a blank txtNumber to allow the user to enter more mGrades.
274
275        txtNumber.Text = "";
276        txtNumber.Focus();
277
278        // Show the mGrades ArrayList in the ListBox.
279
280        showGrades(mGradesAL);
281    }
```

Figure 9-23   The btnAddNbr_Click event method code of ArrayList Sort program

The **btnAddName_Click** event looks very similar, but there is no need to perform a type check on the user input. Nonetheless, you may want to perform an existence check to avoid adding a blank employee name to the **studentAL ArrayList**. This is left as an exercise for you.

```
468    // Purpose: Display the list of grades in the list box.
469    //
470    // Parameter list:
471    //     ArrayList    gradesList    The ArrayList with the student grades
472    //
473    // Return value:
474    //     void
475    //
476    private void showGrades(ArrayList gradesList)
477    {
478        // Erase the ListBox and then display column headers.
479
480        lstResult.Items.Clear();
481        lstResult.Items.Add("GRADES");
482        lstResult.Items.Add("======");
483
484        // Process all elements in a loop and send results to ListBox.
485
486        foreach (int grade in gradesList)
487        {
488            lstResult.Items.Add(grade);
489        }
490    }
491
```

Figure 9-24   The ShowGrades method code of ArrayList Sort program

The remaining methods used in the ArrayList Sort program are used to control the order of elements in the **ArrayList**. The **Sort** method is used to order the elements in ascending order. The **Reverse** method is used to reverse the current order of the elements. If you need to be able to revert to the original (input) order, you need to make a copy of the **ArrayList** as follows:

```
ArrayList newArrayListName = new ArrayList(originalAL);
```

In the sample line of code to make a copy of an **ArrayList**, **newArrayListName** is the copy of the **ArrayList** that you use to sort or reverse the elements, and **originalAL** is the original **ArrayList** that remains unchanged.

The ArrayList Sort Method

When you sorted static arrays using the **Sort** method, you could include both the sort array and a related parallel array as arguments to allow you to preserve the data integrity of the two parallel arrays; however, our **ArrayList** examples have been limited to sorting just numbers or just strings. The **Sort** method for **ArrayList**s provides an even more powerful way to preserve the integrity of related data using an **IComparable Interface**. Interfaces are covered in Chapter 10. After you understand interfaces, you will be ready to define an **IComparable Interface** that can be used to sort **ArrayList**s of objects. Visual Studio's Help system provides examples that illustrate how to do this.

Figure 9-25 shows how these methods are used in the **btnReverseSortNbr_Click** event method to display the **ArrayList** values in descending order.

```
347    private void btnReverseSortNbr_Click(object sender, System.EventArgs e)
348    {
349        // Create newGradesAL array for mGrades
350
351        ArrayList newGradesAL = new ArrayList(mGradesAL);
352
353        // Sort the arrays by mGrades.
354
355        newGradesAL.Sort();
356
357        // Reverse the arrays.
358
359        newGradesAL.Reverse();
360
361        // Show the mGrades ArrayList in the ListBox.
362
363        showGrades(newGradesAL);
364    }
```

Figure 9-25   The btnReverseSortNbr_Click event method code of ArrayList Sort program

The code for the remaining methods is left as an exercise for you. Once you've had time to practice writing the code on your own, you may wish to compare your solution to the sample code provided with this book.

There are many more properties and methods for **ArrayList**s that you may find useful in later programming. Chapter 10 shows you how to create your own classes. Once you've learned how to do this, you can create **ArrayList**s of your own objects (rather than just **int**s and **string**s as in the examples in this chapter). Creating **ArrayList**s of custom objects lends even more flexibility to your programming.

BONUS TOPICS

All of the examples in the Essentials section described lists of data that are stored in single-dimensional arrays. However, some sets of data might be better represented in a tabular format. The .NET Framework provides a wealth of collection types for handling arbitrary sets of data in an organized fashion. The use of multidimensional arrays and other collection types is described in this section.

MULTIDIMENSIONAL ARRAYS

Although single-dimensional arrays may be used in many situations, sometimes a multidimensional array better suits a given situation. Both rectangular and jagged arrays are supported in C#. A **jagged array** may be thought of as an array of different lengths. Because jagged arrays are not used very often, we focus on rectangular arrays in this section. Suppose that you teach a class for which you have assigned seats. The seat arrangement has a total of four rows and six columns. You might wish to create a program to define two 4x6 parallel arrays for the student names and student grades. To define a two-dimensional, 4x6 rectangular array of **string**s to store student names, use the following code:

```
string[,] students = new string[4,6];
```

To define a two-dimensional, 4x6 rectangular array of **int**s to store grades, use the following code:

```
int[,] grades = new int[4,6];
```

Figure 9-26 depicts how you might view the two parallel arrays. To look up a student's name, you need to provide a seat location by the row and column indexes of the seat's location.

students							grades					
0	**1**	**2**	**3**	**4**	**5**		**0**	**1**	**2**	**3**	**4**	**5**
0 Amy	Bill	Carl	Dave	Eddie	Fran	**0** 100	90	56	72	85	91
1 Max	Angel	Billie	Jane	Sam	Mary	**1** 75	68	92	79	83	89
2 Will	Jan	Harry	Henry	Hallie	Joe	**2** 69	98	95	91	67	72
3 Jenna	Amber	Kylie	Manny	Danny	Fred	**3** 77	88	99	52	32	90

Figure 9-26   Two-dimensional parallel arrays used to hold names and grades of students

To match the grades with the individual students in the room, you would provide the same row and column index locations. For example, to get Amber's grade, you would specify the fourth row index (3) and second column index (1). Thus, **students[3,1]** has the value Amber and **grades[3,1]** has the value 88 (Amber's current grade). Note that if the teacher taught several classes, you could add a third dimension (thus forming a data cube) to the array and use the additional dimension to represent the specific class taught.

Regardless of the number of dimensions used, all data elements in a **multidimensional array** are of the same data type. When you processed all the elements in a single-dimensional array, you used a counting loop that iterated through all elements. To process elements of a multidimensional array, you use nested loops, in which each loop counter iterates through all indexes of a given dimension. In the case of the two-dimensional grades array just described, you might use the following nested loops:

```
for (rowIndex = 0; rowIndex <= grades.GetUpperBound(0); rowIndex++)
{
    for (colIndex = 0; colIndex <= grades.GetUpperBound(1); colIndex++)
    {
        // reference specific element as grades[rowIndex, colIndex]
    }
}
```

Can you explain why the outer **rowIndex** loop uses **GetUpperBound(0)**, while the inner **colIndex** loop uses **GetUpperBound(1)**? Recall that the **GetUpperBound** method requires one argument that represents the dimension. Because the dimension is zero-order, an argument of 0 refers to the first dimension (row), and an argument of 1 refers to the second dimension (column).

9

To illustrate multidimensional arrays, let's create a simple program that has a 4x6 array to hold student names and another 4x6 array to hold grades for the corresponding students. The **students** array may be defined and initialized in a single statement as follows:

```
101        string[,] students = new string[4,6] {
102            {"Amy", "Bill", "Carl", "Dave", "Eddie", "Fran"},
103            {"Max", "Angel", "Billie", "Jane", "Same", "Mary"},
104            {"Will", "Jan", "Harry", "Henry", "Hallie", "Joe"},
105            {"Jenna", "Amber", "Kylie", "Manny", "Danny", "Fred"}};
```

Notice that all the data for the student array is contained within the outer curly braces { }, but each set of row data is contained within another set of curly braces { }. Because the data type is **string**, each value is delimited by double quotes.

Can you write the definition and initialization statement for the **grades** array? It looks similar to the student array definition statement, but the data type is **int** and the values are numbers. Therefore, do not use the double quote delimiters.

To design the form, add a large **ListBox** to display the data in a tabular fashion, and three buttons— OK, Clear, and Close. When the OK button is clicked, a two-line header followed by the student names and their corresponding grades appear in the **ListBox**. A nested loop is where the outer loop iterates through each row index and the inner loop iterates through each column index within a given row index (defined in the outer loop). Figure 9-27 shows a screen shot for this sample program, and Figure 9-28 shows the code for the **btnOK_Click** method. The provided solution named MultiArrayDemo lists the complete code for this program.

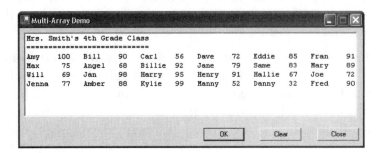

Figure 9-27   Screen shot of multidimensional array program

```
93     private void btnOK_Click(object sender, System.EventArgs e)
94     {
95         int rowIndex;
96         int colIndex;
97         string display;
98
99         // Define and initialize arrays to hold data.
100
101        string[,] students = new string[4,6] {
102            {"Amy", "Bill", "Carl", "Dave", "Eddie", "Fran"},
103            {"Max", "Angel", "Billie", "Jane", "Same", "Mary"},
104            {"Will", "Jan", "Harry", "Henry", "Hallie", "Joe"},
105            {"Jenna", "Amber", "Kylie", "Manny", "Danny", "Fred"}};
106        int[,] grades = new int[4,6] {
107            {100, 90, 56, 72, 85, 91},
```

Figure 9-28   The btnOK_Click event method code of multidimensional array program

```
108                 {75, 68, 92, 79, 83, 89},
109                 {69, 98, 95, 91, 67, 72},
110                 {77, 88, 99, 52, 32, 90}};
111
112         // Display column headers in ListBox.
113
114         display = "Mrs. Smith's 4th Grade Class";
115         lstResult.Items.Add(display);
116         display = "============================";
117         lstResult.Items.Add(display);
118
119         // Process all elements in a nested loop and send results to ListBox.
120
121         for (rowIndex = 0; rowIndex <= students.GetUpperBound(0); rowIndex++)
122         {
123             display = "";
124             for (colIndex = 0; colIndex <= students.GetUpperBound(1); colIndex++)
125             {
126                 display += students[rowIndex,colIndex].PadRight(7) +
127                         grades[rowIndex,colIndex].ToString("F0").PadLeft(3) + "   ";
128                 }
128             lstResult.Items.Add(display);
129         }
130     }
131 }
```

Figure 9-28 The btnOK_Click event method code of multidimensional array program (continued)

Multidimensional arrays may be useful when displaying tables of information such as sales tax tables, mileage tables, discount rate tables, and so on. The next example defines a two-dimensional array that finds and then displays a table to show tip amounts based on the total food bill for various desired tip percentages. Figure 9-29 shows a screen shot of this program.

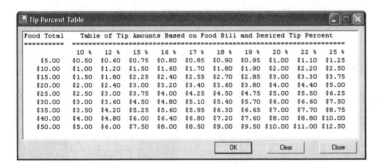

Figure 9-29 Tip Percent Table multidimensional array program

The program uses two single-dimensional arrays: one to hold the bill amounts and the other to hold the tip percentages. A two-dimensional array is created to hold a tip amount for each bill amount (row) and tip percentage (column). A **for** loop (lines 117 to 120) is used to generate the Tip Percent column headings. This code is followed by a **for** loop (lines 125 to 134) that iterates through every row (bill amount). Within each row, a nested **for** loop (lines 128 to 132) is used to iterate through every column (tip percent). Inside the nested loop, the actual tip amount is computed and stored in the corresponding location of the two-dimensional **tipTable** array. This value is then added to the display line. Figure 9-30 shows the code for the **btnOK_Click** event method.

```
93      private void btnOK_Click(object sender, System.EventArgs e)
94      {
95
96          int rowIndex;
97          int colIndex;
98          string display;
99
100         // Define and initialize arrays to hold data and clear the ListBox.
101
102         decimal[] bill = new decimal[] {5, 10, 15, 20, 25, 30, 35, 40, 50};
103         double[] tipPct = new double[] {.10, .12, .15, .16, .17, .18, .19, .20, .22, .25};
104         decimal[,] tipTable = new decimal[9,10];
105         lstResult.Items.Clear();
106
107         // Display column headers in ListBox.
108
109         display = "Food Total    Table of Tip Amounts ";
110         lstResult.Items.Add(display);
111         display = "==========   =========================";
112         lstResult.Items.Add(display);
113
114         // Display the percents across the ListBox.
115
116         display = "              ";
117         for (rowIndex = 0; rowIndex <= tipPct.GetUpperBound(0); rowIndex++)
118         {
119             display += tipPct[rowIndex].ToString("P0").PadLeft(7);
120         }
121         lstResult.Items.Add(display);
122
123         // Process all elements in a nested loop and send results to ListBox.
124
125         for (rowIndex = 0; rowIndex <= tipTable.GetUpperBound(0); rowIndex++)
126         {
127             display = bill[rowIndex].ToString("C2").PadLeft(9) + " ";
128             for (colIndex = 0; colIndex <= tipTable.GetUpperBound(1); colIndex++)
129             {
130                 tipTable[rowIndex,colIndex] = bill[rowIndex] * (decimal) tipPct[colIndex];
131                 display += tipTable[rowIndex,colIndex].ToString("C2").PadLeft(7);
132             }
133             lstResult.Items.Add(display);
134         }
135     }
136
```

Figure 9-30   The btnOK_Click event method code of Tip Percent Table program

OTHER COLLECTION TYPES

In the Essentials section, you learned that the **ArrayList** is a type of collection, specifically a dynamic array that can grow or shrink as needed. The .NET Framework provides additional built-in, generic collections within the **Systems.Collections** namespace. These collections may be classified in three ways:

- Items in indexed collections can be retrieved through a zero-based index value. The **ArrayList** class falls into this category.

- Items in keyed collections can be retrieved through an associated key value. The **Hashtable** class falls into this category.

- Items in ordered collections can be retrieved based on the insertion order. The **Stack** and **Queue** classes are examples of ordered collections.

After you add the **using Systems.Collections** directive to your program, you can use the abbreviated notation when writing code that uses any of the collections in this namespace.

More specialized collections may be found in the **Systems.Collections.Specialized** namespace. However, these specialized collections are quite similar to the generic collections. Therefore, our discussion focuses on the more common collections in the **Systems.Collections** namespace.

Enumerators

The examples you've seen so far have iterated through the collection items using indexes associated with the collection. The last two types of collections (keyed and ordered) don't have a way to access an item in the collection through an index value. Instead, the .NET Framework provides **enumerators**, which are objects that are associated with a specific collection and used as a way to iterate through the elements in that collection. Enumerators can only read the data in their collection but cannot change the data. Several of the following sections illustrate how enumerators may be used to iterate through items in a collection. After you define an enumerator, you may use the following enumerator property and methods:

- The **Current** property is used to refer to the current item in the collection.

- The **MoveNext** method moves the enumerator to the next item in the collection.

- The **Reset** method moves the enumerator to a position that is before the beginning of the collection.

Initially, the enumerator is positioned before the start of the collection. Therefore, you must use **MoveNext** after you create an enumerator or **Reset** it. An exception is thrown if you try to get the **Current** item when the enumerator is either before the start of the collection or after the end of the collection.

When you access the items in a collection sequentially using an enumerator, the order of the items is dictated by the type of collection. For example, because an **ArrayList** is an indexed collection, the items are ordered by the index values. A **hash table**, however, has items ordered by their associated key values. As these other collection types are discussed, you can see the difference in the sequences using enumerators. Keep in mind that our purpose in using the examples in this section is to introduce you to the type of collection and to illustrate how the data are stored and retrieved. The examples are not representative of business programs in which these types of collections would be required.

Hash Tables

You've already learned about the **ArrayList** collection in the Essentials section of this chapter. You saw how easy it was to add, remove, and iterate through items in an **ArrayList**. Using an **ArrayList**, you accessed elements using an index value. Sometimes, it is useful to access an element using a unique identifier, which is often called a key value. For example, if you store student data, a student ID could be a key value. However, you cannot reference an item in an **ArrayList** by using a key value.

Hash tables are ideal for situations in which a large amount of relatively static data needs to be accessed quickly using a unique key. Storing employee data and being able to look up an employee by an ID, such as a Social Security number, is a common business need. Hash tables work well to address such a need.

Each element in a hash table is a key and value pair that is stored in a `DictionaryEntry` object. Therefore, when you add an item to a `Hashtable` collection, you provide a unique key and item value. For example, you might provide an employee's ID as a key value because it is unique and an employee's name as the item value to be stored in the collection. When you try to retrieve an item in the hash table, you provide the key value. The hash table handles the details of locating the item through the provided key. This process can be done very quickly, making hash tables a good option when you need the ability to perform fast lookups based on a key value.

To better understand hash tables, let's consider a program example that manages employee data in a hash table. For now, just store the employee name and use the employee ID as the key. Later, when you create your own objects, you can store the entire employee object rather than just a name. To begin, define a hash table named **mEmployeeHT** at class scope:

```
13      private Hashtable mEmployeeHT = new Hashtable();
```

Write a **showList** helper method that may be called by other event methods after making a change to the contents of the hash table. Figure 9-31 shows sample code for this method. Notice that, in order to iterate through the hash table in which each element is stored as a `DictionaryEntry` object, an `IDictionaryEnumerator` is created. A `while` loop is used to cycle through the items in the hash table. Each iteration adds the item's value and corresponding key to the `ListBox`.

```
327    // Purpose: Display all elements of the hash table in the ListBox
328    //
329    // Parameter list:
330    //     none
331    //
332    // Return value:
333    //     void
334    //
335    private void showList()
336    {
337        // Define enumerator variable and assign value from hash table.
338
339        IDictionaryEnumerator myEnum;
340        myEnum = mEmployeeHT.GetEnumerator();
341
342        // Erase the ListBox and then display column headers.
343
344        lstResult.Items.Clear();
345        lstResult.Items.Add("EMPLOYEE");
346        lstResult.Items.Add("========");
347
348        // Process all elements in a loop and send results to ListBox.
349
350        while (myEnum.MoveNext() == true)
351        {
352            lstResult.Items.Add(myEnum.Value + "   " + myEnum.Key);
353        }
354    }
```

Figure 9-31   Hash Table program's showList helper method

The program should allow a user to add a name (and ID). After validating the user input and assigning the ID in the text box to the variable keyValue, the btnAddName_Click method uses the following code to add the name and ID to the hash table:

```
194            mEmployeeHT.Add(keyValue, txtName.Text);
```

A remove request can be made by selecting an employee name in a ListBox, typing a name in a text box, or typing the ID in a text box. However, you can only access values in a hash table by using the key value. To use the Remove method, you supply the key value. This means that you need another helper method to determine the key value for an item, given the employee name. The getKey method also needs to use an IDictionaryEnumerator to iterate through the items in the hash table collection. A while loop is used to control the loop iterations. In each cycle, the lookup value is compared to the current value in the collection. If there is a match, the corresponding key for the current value is returned. After checking every item in the collection and finding no match, -1 is returned to indicate that there is no matching item in the hash table collection. Refer to Figure 9-32 to see the sample code for the getKey helper method.

9

```
356    // Purpose: Locate the key for a given value in the hash table
357    //
358    // Parameter list:
359    //      Hashtable     myHashTable      hash table to be checked for lookup value
360    //      string        lookup           value to be found in hash table
361    //
362    // Return value:
363    //      int                the corresponding key value for hash table item
364    //
365    private int getKey(Hashtable myHashTable, string lookup)
366    {
367        // Define enumerator and assign value from hash table
368
369        IDictionaryEnumerator myEnum;
370        myEnum = mEmployeeHT.GetEnumerator();
371
372        while (myEnum.MoveNext())
373        {
374            if ((string) myEnum.Value == lookup)
375            {
376                return (int) myEnum.Key;
377            }
378        }
379
380        // No match found, so return invalid value.
381
382        return -1;
383    }
384
```

Figure 9-32   The getKey helper method code of Hash Table program

Now that you have the getKey helper method, you can write the btnRemove_Click event method to remove a selected item from the list. (See Figure 9-33.) After defining variables for hashKey and lookup and performing data validation, the remaining processing depends on how the user identified the item to be deleted. If the user selected an item in the ListBox or typed a name in the text box, the getKey helper method is called to get the key that corresponds to the given name. If an ID is entered in txtID, then that value is used as the key. On line 245, the

ContainsKey method is used to ensure that the key is actually valid. If so, the item is finally removed. Otherwise, a suitable message is displayed.

```
207    private void btnRemove_Click(object sender, System.EventArgs e)
208    {
209        int hashKey;
210        string lookup = "";
211
212        // Make sure this is a valid remove request.
213
214        if (lstResult.SelectedIndex <= 1 && txtName.Text == "" && txtID.Text == "")
215        {
216            messageBoxOK("Please type a name or ID to be removed or select from the list.");
217            txtName.Focus();
218            return;
219        }
220
221        // If a name in the list is selected, remove it and show the new list.
222
223        if (lstResult.SelectedIndex > 1)
224        {
225            lookup = (string) lstResult.Items[lstResult.SelectedIndex];
226            lookup = lookup.Substring(0,lookup.IndexOf(" "));
227            hashKey = getKey(mEmployeeHT, lookup);
228        }
229
230        // Since no name was selected, there may be a valid name to remove.
231
232        else if (txtName.Text != "")
233        {
234            lookup = txtName.Text;
235            hashKey = getKey(mEmployeeHT, lookup);
236        }
237
238        // User must have given ID, so use it to remove mEmployee.
239
240        else
241        {
242            hashKey = int.Parse(txtID.Text);
243        }
244
245        if (mEmployeeHT.ContainsKey(hashKey))
246        {
247            mEmployeeHT.Remove(hashKey);
248        }
249        else
250        {
251            messageBoxOK("There is no mEmployee with a name of " + lookup +
252                " and an ID of " + hashKey.ToString());
253        }
254        txtName.Text = "";
255        txtID.Text = "";
256        txtName.Focus();
257        showList();
258    }
```

Figure 9-33   The btnRemove_Click method code of Hash Table program

Figure 9-34 shows sample screen shots to illustrate how the hash table's contents change as you add and remove list items.

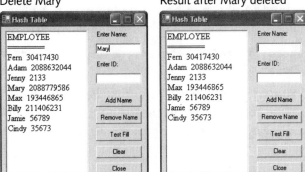

Figure 9-34   The Hash Table program

Queues

If you have ever waited in line to buy something or get something done, you are familiar with the idea of a queue. If you've used a shared computing facility, then you should be familiar with a print queue. **Queues** are data structures that are commonly used to temporarily hold data items for processing. Items are stored in the order they were added to the queue, and they can be retrieved only in that same order. Figure 9-35 illustrates a queue in which Bo's request came in first, followed by Al's request, followed by Xu's request. Because this represents a queue, Bo's request will be processed first, followed by Al's request, and then Xu's request. This processing order is known as first-in, first-out (**FIFO**). Therefore, a queue is appropriate in situations in which the order that items are received and processed is important, you can discard an item after processing it, and you don't need to access arbitrary items in the queue.

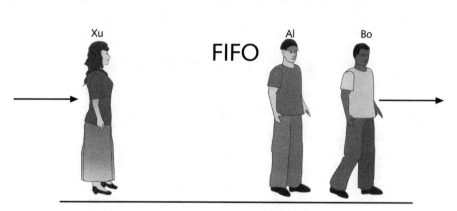

Figure 9-35   Processing order of items in a queue

A variation of the hash table program is used to illustrate how a queue works. A class-scope static array of employees is used to add items to a queue, which is also defined at class scope:

```
private string[] mEmployee = new string[] {"Adam", "Max", "Billy", "Mary", "Carla"};
private Queue mEmployeeQ = new Queue();
```

To add items to a queue, use the **Enqueue method**. To take the first item off of the queue for processing, use the **Dequeue method**. Note that after using Dequeue, the item is no longer in the queue. Figure 9-36 shows the **btnAddName_Click** and **btnRemove_Click** event methods.

```
140    private void btnAddName_Click(object sender, System.EventArgs e)
141    {
142        // Make sure that the user provided a name to be added.
143
144        if (txtName.Text == "")
145        {
146            messageBoxOK("Please type a name to add it to the list.");
147            txtName.Focus();
148            return;
149        }
150
151        // Copy the current value in txtName to the mEmployeeQ Queue.
152
153        mEmployeeQ.Enqueue(txtName.Text);
154
155        // Show the current list.
156
157        showList();
158
159        // Position the cursor in a blank txtName to allow the user to enter more names.
160
161        txtName.Text = "";
162        txtName.Focus();
163    }
164
165    private void btnRemove_Click(object sender, System.EventArgs e)
166    {
```

Figure 9-36   Add and Remove event methods in queue program

```
167        mEmployeeQ.Dequeue();
168        txtName.Text = "";
169        txtName.Focus();
170        showList();
171    }
```

Figure 9-36 Add and Remove event methods in queue program (continued)

To iterate through the items in a queue, use an **IEnumerator** object as shown in Figure 9–37.

```
224    private void showList()
225    {
226        // Define enumerator variable and assign based on queue.
227
228        IEnumerator myEnum;
229        myEnum = mEmployeeQ.GetEnumerator();
230
231        // Erase the ListBox and then display column headers.
232
233        lstResult.Items.Clear();
234        lstResult.Items.Add("EMPLOYEE");
235        lstResult.Items.Add("========");
236
237        // Process all elements in a loop and send results to ListBox.
238
239        while (myEnum.MoveNext())
240        {
241            lstResult.Items.Add(myEnum.Current);
242        }
243    }
```

Figure 9-37 The ShowList helper method to show items in a queue

To see how the contents of a queue change as you add and remove items, review the screen shots in Figure 9–38.

9

Fill with five test values, then get ready to add Marilyn. Next, add Wilson. See the result.

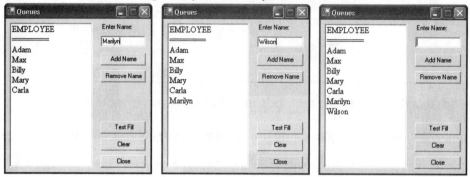

Now start removing names one-by-one in the order they were added.

Figure 9-38   How a queue's content changes

Stacks

If you've eaten at a restaurant with a salad bar, then you probably have some experience using a **stack**. Think about how salad plates are added to stacks of plates in a salad plate dispenser and how consumers take a plate off of the stack for their salad. As a new stack of plates is added (pushed) to the dispenser one by one, the stack is pushed down by the weight of the plates. After all the plates have been added to the stack, the last plate added is the first one to be removed (popped) from the stack of plates. When items are stored in the order they were added to the stack, but they are retrieved in the reverse order, it is referred to as last-in, first-out (**LIFO**) processing. Figure 9–39 illustrates how LIFO stacks are much like the salad plate dispensers you find in a restaurant.

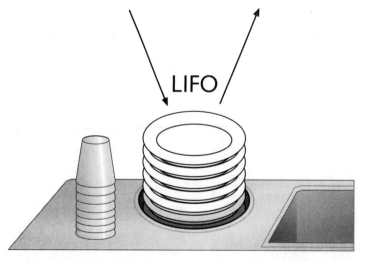

Figure 9-39   Processing order of items in a stack

A variation of the queue program is used to illustrate how a stack works. A class-scope static array of employees is used to add items to a stack, which is also defined at class scope:

```
string[] mEmployee = new string[] {"Adam", "Max", "Billy", "Mary", "Carla"};
Stack mEmployeeS = new Stack();
```

To add items to a stack, use the **Push method**. To remove items from the stack, use the **Pop method**. Figure 9-40 shows the `btnAddName_Click` and `btnRemove_Click` event methods.

```
140    private void btnAddName_Click(object sender, System.EventArgs e)
141    {
142        // Make sure that the user provided a name to be added.
143
144        if (txtName.Text == "")
145        {
146            messageBoxOK("Please type a name to add it to the list.");
147            txtName.Focus();
148            return;
149        }
150
151        // Copy the current value in txtName to the mEmployeeS Stack.
152
153        mEmployeeS.Push(txtName.Text);
154
155        // Show the current list.
156
157        showList();
158
159        // Position the cursor in a blank txtName to allow the user to enter more names.
160
161        txtName.Text = "";
162        txtName.Focus();
163    }
164
165    private void btnRemove_Click(object sender, System.EventArgs e)
166    {
167        mEmployeeS.Pop();
168        txtName.Text = "";
169        txtName.Focus();
170        showList();
171    }
```

Figure 9-40 The btnAdd_Click and btnRemove_Click event methods in the stack program

To iterate through the items in a stack, use an **IEnumerator** object the same way as in the Queue program's **showList** helper method (see Figure 9-37). To see how the contents of a stack change as you add and remove items, review the screen shots in Figure 9-41.

Like queues, stacks are appropriate when the order in which items are received and processed is important, you can discard an item after processing it, and you don't need to access arbitrary items in the stack.

Fill with five test values, then get ready to add Marilyn. Next, add Wilson. See the result.

Now begin removing names one-by-one starting with the last name added.

Figure 9-41   How a stack's content changes

Additional Collection Types

You may want to investigate another collection type—the **SortedList**—which stores objects and sorts them based on an associated key. **SortedList**s are the only built-in .NET collection to support retrieval of objects by both index number and key. This means that **SortedList**s may be used like **ArrayList**s and **Hashtable**s. However, because they involve more overhead than either **ArrayList**s or **Hashtable**s, you should use **SortedList**s only when you need to use the features of both. We leave it to the reader to investigate this collection type further.

As a programmer, you should be aware that using collections can cause problems. The majority of .NET's built-in collections store items internally as type **System.Object**, which is a super-class of all classes. Although this approach gives maximum flexibility, it does result in some per-formance issues on very large collections. Additionally, any time you access an item in a generic collection, it is returned as type **System.Object**, so you have to cast it back to its true type to do anything meaningful with it. This requires greater responsibility on the part of the program-mer to ensure that the collection is populated with objects of the correct type, and that necessary checks are performed while retrieving objects from the collection. The examples in this section were meant to illustrate how the data in each type of collection are stored and retrieved. Real business programs that use these collections would need to incorporate data validation and excep-tion handling to prevent problems during program execution.

Summary

Essential Topics

- To process similar sets of data the same way, it is helpful to have a structure to hold the related data together and then take advantage of a loop to repeat the processing on all items. Arrays and collections provide alternatives for storing related data together.

- Arrays are contiguous memory locations that are of the same type and share a single name. `ListBoxes` provide a way to visualize arrays.

- Arrays should be used whenever you have a group of related data that needs to be processed the same way. By storing the data collectively, you can take advantage of loops to write the processing steps once, and use the loop to iterate through the array elements using the loop counter variable as the array index.

- Single-dimensional arrays are like lists and require a single index value to identify a specific element. To process all the elements in a single-dimensional array, a `for` or `foreach` loop is recommended.

- After an array has been populated with data, a sequential search may be used to locate a specific element. When multiple parallel arrays are used, the index location of the found item may be used to get the corresponding values in the associated parallel arrays.

- When an array becomes lengthy, it is helpful to arrange the values in ascending or descending order before displaying the items. A bubble sort may be used to manually sort an array.

- The Sort and Reverse methods are efficient ways for ordering the elements in an array.

- Static arrays have a fixed size, but by keeping track of a last-used index variable at class scope, you can give the illusion of a static array that can grow and shrink.

- `ArrayLists` are a type of collection that serve as dynamic arrays. To use `ArrayLists` without fully qualifying the class name, the `using Systems.Collections` directive should be used.

- `ArrayLists` have many useful properties and methods to manage the items in the collection. The `Add` and `Insert` methods are used to add items to an `ArrayList`. The `Remove` and `RemoveAt` methods are used to delete items. The `Clear` method is used to erase the entire `ArrayList`.

- To sort `ArrayLists`, the `Sort` and `Reverse` methods should be used.

Bonus Topics

- Although single-dimensional arrays are more commonly used, multidimensional arrays are sometimes required. Each added dimension requires an additional index value to be specified in order to access a specific element in the multidimensional array.

- The .NET Framework provides several built-in generic collections that may be categorized as indexed, keyed, or ordered. `ArrayLists` are a type of indexed collection. A `Hashtable` is a keyed type collection. Stacks and queues are ordered type collections.

- Enumerators are used to iterate through keyed and ordered collections.

- Hash tables store unique key values along with the item data.

- Stacks and queues are appropriate when the order in which items are received and processed is important. Stacks use LIFO, whereas queues use FIFO.

KEY TERMS

Define each of the following terms, as it relates to object-oriented programming:

Essential Terms

- `Add` (`ArrayList`) method
- array
- `Array.Copy` method
- `Array.Reverse` method
- `Array.Sort` method
- `ArrayList`
- bubble sort
- `Clear` (`ArrayList`) method
- collection
- dimension
- dimensionality
- dynamic array
- element
- `GetUpperBound` method
- `IndexOutOfRangeException`
- initialize (an array)
- initialize (array elements)
- `Length` property
- new
- rank
- `Reverse` (`ArrayList`) method
- sequential search
- single-dimensional array
- `Sort` (`ArrayList`) method
- static array
- subscript

Bonus Terms

- collection
- `Current` (enumerator) property
- `Dequeue` method
- `Enqueue` method
- enumerators
- FIFO
- hash table
- jagged array
- LIFO
- `MoveNext` (enumerator) property
- multidimensional arrays
- `Pop` method
- `Push` method
- queue
- `Reset` (enumerator) property
- `SortedList`
- stack

REVIEW QUESTIONS

Essential Questions

1. An array is a noncontiguous set of memory locations that share the same name. True or false?

2. An array subscript refers to an individual item value in an array. True or false?

3. An array index is used to identify which array element you want to use based on its location or offset within the array. True or false?

4. A single-dimensional array requires one subscript to identify a specific array element. True or false?

5. The `Length` property of an array identifies the maximum number of characters that an individual array element can store. True or false?

6. A sequential search can be applied to any type of array to locate a desired lookup value. True or false?

7. The easiest way to sort the numeric items in a **ListBox** is to set the **Sorted** property to **true**. True or false?

8. An acceptable way to sort items in an array in descending order is to use the **Reverse** method after using the **Sort** method. True or false?

9. To sort items in an **ArrayList** in descending order, use the **Reverse** method after using the **Sort** method. True or false?

10. To remove an item in an **ArrayList**, use the **Clear** method with the index number of the item to be deleted. True or false?

11. To iterate through all elements of an array without having to use an index counter, a _____ loop should be used.

12. To determine the largest subscript of the single-dimensional array **student**, use _____.

13. If the **hours** array has five elements (5, 23, 10, 15, 6), to reference the value 5, use _____.

14. To assign the fifth item in the **ArrayList** named **sampleAL** to the variable **example**, use the C# statement: _____.

15. To insert the value "X" to the end of the **ArrayList** symbol, use _____.

16. Write a definition for a single-dimensional array named **purchase** that will be used to hold the dollar amount of up to 100 purchased items.

17. If the array **answer** holds decimal values that could be as large as $1,000.00, write the code needed to display an individual **answer** item within a field that is 10 characters wide and is right-aligned.

18. What happens if you write a program loop that attempts to access an array element that doesn't exist?

19. Write the general logic for performing a bubble sort on two related arrays.

20. Write the code snippet that will add the list of names in the static array **names** to the **ArrayList students**.

Bonus Questions

1. True or false? To define a two-dimensional double array to hold rates, use
   double rates [,] = new double [,];

2. To determine the largest column subscript of the two-dimensional array names, use
   names.GetUpperBound(1). True or false?

3. An **ArrayList** is an indexed type of collection. True or false?

4. Stacks and queues are keyed type collections. True or false?

5. An Enumerator is used to access items in a collection in random order. True or false?

6. If a **ListBox** contains ten names, including Jane, and you have three parallel arrays (ID, phone, grade) that contain related information for each name, use _____ to access the related information in the three arrays after Jane's name is highlighted in the list.

7. To add an item to a **Hashtable**, both a(n) _____ and a(n) _____ are required.

8. To remove an item in a **Hashtable**, you must provide the _____.

9. How do you add and remove items in a queue?

10. How do you add and remove items in a stack?

PROGRAMMING EXERCISES

Essential Exercises

1. Write a C# program that computes and stores the first 20 prime numbers in a single-dimensional array. Use a loop to display the array index plus 1 and the value of the prime number at that index.

2. Write a C# program to get grades from the user to add to an array. Once the Stats button is clicked, the program should compute and display the average, high, and low scores using the values currently stored in the array.

3. Write a C# program that computes and stores the name and total points for up to 25 students in a class. When the OK button is clicked, the class statistics should be displayed, along with the student names and grades.

4. Add the following features to Exercise 3: the names and grades should be displayed, ordered alphabetically by name or in descending order by grade.

5. Write a C# program to manage your to do list. Use an **ArrayList** to store the tasks.

Bonus Exercises

1. Write a C# program to display a mileage table. Show the range of gallons at fill-up from 15 gallons to 30 gallons in increments of 3 gallons. Show the range of distance traveled from 150 miles to 450 miles in increments of 50 miles.

2. Write a C# program to display a sales tax table. Show the range of sales tax from 3% to 7.5% in increments of 0.5%. Show the range of purchases from 50 dollars to 500 dollars in increments of 50 dollars.

3. Write a C# program that uses a single-dimensional array to store fifteen student names and a two-dimensional array to store four test scores for the fifteen students. The program should display in a **ListBox** each student's name, four test scores, and total points on all four tests. At the end, it should display the average score earned for each test as well as the average total points for the class.

4. Write a C# program that uses a hash table to store student grades and uses the student name as a key value. The program should allow the user to view all grades by student names, look up a student's grade by his/her name, remove a student from the class, or start over (erase the collection).

5. Write a C# program to mimic a print queue. Provide a text box to identify the item being added to the queue. After an item has been printed, a Remove button should be used to remove the item from the print queue. In the case of a printer jam, a Clear button should remove all items from the print queue.

10

ENCAPSULATION

In the Essentials section you will learn:

♦ The goals of encapsulation

♦ The difference between **public** and **private** object members

♦ How an object's interface is implemented

♦ Object constructors

♦ How to add object behavior

♦ Object reference variables

♦ How to use **ArrayLists**

In the Bonus section you will learn:

♦ Memory management and garbage collection

♦ The program stack and managed heap

♦ The meaning of "out of scope"

♦ Class destructors

After you read this chapter, you should better understand the various methods you can use to access objects and how to use these methods correctly. You should also understand the benefits that encapsulation makes available to you as a programmer.

ESSENTIAL TOPICS

ENCAPSULATION REVIEW

In Chapter 1 we discussed some of the advantages that encapsulation makes available to you as a programmer. However, now that you have a more complete understanding of the language fundamentals of C#, we can revisit those programming advantages and learn how to better exploit them in our programs.

In Chapter 1, Figure 1-3 shows how the properties and methods of an object reside within the confines of the object itself. By placing the properties and methods inside the object, programmers can control how those properties and methods are accessed by the world outside the object—this is *encapsulation*. In other words, you are encapsulating an object's data (properties) and the code that manipulates that data (methods) within the object itself. By restricting the access to the object's data and its methods, you can minimize the risk that other elements of the program contaminate that data. This is the fundamental idea behind encapsulation: hide the data and methods that operate on that data. Encapsulation, therefore, helps to preserve the correct **state** of the object's data by limiting the outside world's access to that data.

Encapsulation makes the task of debugging a program easier because an object's data can be isolated within the object. As you have already experienced, the hard part of debugging is finding where the bug lives. Once found, correcting the bug is usually fairly easy. Encapsulation reduces the time it takes to isolate a program bug and, hence, reduces the time it takes to debug a program.

CREATING YOUR OWN CLASSES

The primary vehicle for encapsulation in C# is the class. You have read about classes from the very first chapter. In this section, however, you are going to create a project with multiple classes. Up to this point, all of the properties and methods have been defined within a single class—the main form. That design approach works well when the goal is to teach you about the fundamentals of C#. Now, however, you are ready to go beyond the bare essentials and realize the real strengths of C#. Indeed, it is your ability to write your own classes that gives C# its real power and flexibility.

Start by creating a new project named ContactsList in the usual manner. Now you need to add a class to the project by using the Add Class menu selection of the Project, as shown in Figure 10-1.

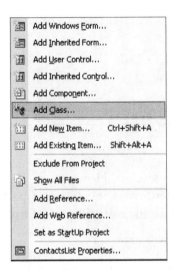

Figure 10-1 Adding a new class to a project

After you have selected the Add Class menu option, you are presented with a dialog box that asks you for the name of the class. Name the new class `clsContact`. The naming rules for classes are the same as those for variables. Our style preference, however, is to precede the class name with "cls" and then follow the same capitalization style convention for words within the class name. Figure 10-2 displays this dialog. Note that the Code File template (not the Class template) is selected in Figure 10-2. The ".cs" file extension is automatically supplied by Visual Studio and indicates a "C Sharp" source file.

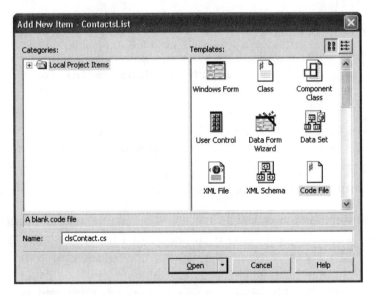

Figure 10-2 The Add New Item dialog box

After you click the Open button in Figure 10-2, type the code snippet shown in Figure 10-3 into `clsContact`.

```
using System;

public class clsContact
{

}
```

Figure 10-3   Code snippet for clsContact

You now have the clsContact.cs file constructed as a stand-alone class. However, if you look at the Visual Studio Solution Explorer, you can see that the **clsContact** class is a part of the ContactsList project. You have just created a class that is a separate file, yet still part of the project!

You are now ready to start adding code to the new **clsContact** class.

ACCESS SPECIFIERS FOR METHODS AND PROPERTIES

C#'s access specifiers give you control over which program elements have access to an object's properties and methods. As mentioned in Chapter 7, an access specifier determines the degree to which an object's properties and methods can be accessed outside the object itself. C# provides four access specifiers: **private**, **public**, **protected**, and **internal**. For the moment, we defer our discussion of the **protected** and **internal** access specifiers because they are used in contexts (e.g., inheritance and assemblies) that we are not yet ready to discuss.

The private Access Specifier

Suppose that you have defined a class that begins with the code shown in Figure 10-4.

```
public class clsContact                    // Start of class definition
{
        private string mFirstName;
        string mLastName;
        // More code…
}                                          // End of class definition
```

Figure 10-4   A class definition using the private access specifier

Figure 10-4 shows variable definitions for two variables names—**mFirstName** and **mLastName**. We prefer to use the convention of prefixing class data members with a lowercase letter "m". This style convention makes it easier to identify the variable as a data member of the class. Simply stated, a *data member* is a variable that is defined within a class statement block. (Usually, a data member is used to hold the state of a class property.) The data member named **mFirstName** is explicitly defined using the **private** access specifier. Because **mFirstName** is defined using the **private** access specifier, this data member is accessible only within the **clsContact** class. In other words, the current value associated with **mFirstName** is available only to the code that appears between the start and end of the **clsContact** class definition. Any program code outside the **clsContact** class definition is totally unaware of **mFirstName**. This also means that no other element of the program outside the **clsContact** class can directly access **mFirstName**.

What about access to the data member named **mLastName**? In this statement, we have not used an explicit access specifier, but simply defined the data member using its data type specifier. The omission of an explicit access specifier for a data definition within a class defaults to the **private** access specifier. This means that `mFirstName` and `mLastName` both have **private** access within the program. Once again, this means that no program element outside the `clsContact` class has direct access to either `mFirstName` or `mLastName`. Both data members are encapsulated and hidden within the `clsContact` class.

tip ▶ Even though C# defaults an access specifier to **private** if you omit it, you should always specify either **public** or **private**. Explicit code results in clearer code.

So what does all this mean in terms of using an object in a program? Consider the following program statements that might exist somewhere outside the `clsContact` class:

```
clsContact myFriend = new clsContact();
string aLastName;

myFriend.mFirstName = "Nicholas";          // Error!!
aLastName = myFriend.mLastName;            // Error!!
```

The first statement creates an instance object of the `clsContact` class named `myFriend`, whereas the second statement creates a **string** named `aLastName`. Because `mFirstName` and `mLastName` are **private** members of the `clsContact` class, the next two statements generate error messages. The error messages result because those two class members were defined using the **private** access specifier and, hence, are not directly accessible outside the `clsContact` class. From a perspective that is outside the `clsContact` class, the `myFriend` object does not permit direct access to either the `mFirstName` or `mLastName` class members because they are **private** to the object.

The public Access Specifier

The **public** access specifier does permit direct access to a class member. Let's modify the code snippet in Figure 10-4 to use the **public** access specifier. The changes are shown in Figure 10-5.

```
public class clsContact              // Start of class definition
{
    private string mFirstName;
    string mLastName;
    public string HomePhone;
    // More code...
}                                    // End of class definition
```

Figure 10-5 A class definition using the public access specifier

Note that we have used the **public** access specifier for a third class member named `HomePhone`. (You must explicitly use the **public** keyword because omitting it would cause the members to default to **private** access.) The impact of this change is that the `HomePhone` member is directly available to other parts of the program. To illustrate the impact of the change, consider the following statements:

```
clsContact myFriend = new clsContact();

myFriend.HomePhone = "1112345678";   // No error because it's public
```

Note that the statement that changes the `HomePhone` class data member does not generate a compiler error message. This is because the `HomePhone` class member is defined within the `clsContact` class using the `public` access specifier. The good news is that the compiler does not generate a compiler error message. The bad news is that the compiler does not generate an error message. In other words, the `public` storage class is a mixed blessing because it removes one level of protection against data contamination by permitting direct access to the members of the class through its object.

Figure 10-5 illustrates another style convention used by the authors. If a class data member uses the `public` access specifier, we drop the "m" prefix for that class member. This convention informs you that the class data member was defined using the `public` access specifier.

In some cases the extra protection is needed, but that protection may not be needed in all cases. How do you choose which access specifier to use? The answer to that question is the subject of the next section.

WHICH ACCESS SPECIFIER IS BEST?

Thinking about encapsulation using the `private` access specifier should cause a little head scratching on your part. If the `private` access specifier isolates the value of a member variable within the object, how is it possible to read or change the state of an object? After all, it is the member variables of a class and their values that determine the state of an object. If they are totally encapsulated using the `private` access specifier, how can you use (or alter) the state of the object in other parts of a program?

On the other hand, using the `public` access specifier means that any element of a C# program can change the state of the object by simply using the object's dot notation. Exposing the class members using the `public` access specifier negates some of the encapsulation protection that makes program debugging easier and safer in many ways. This appears to be a true dilemma: two choices, both bad!

Fortunately, the solution to the dilemma is fairly easy. All you have to do is define a public interface for the class.

Class User Interfaces

In the simplest of terms, a **class user interface** defines the way in which you wish to have the outside world use your class. In Chapter 1, you learned to view an object as though it were a shell. Inside the shell are the properties and methods that make the object do whatever task you have defined for it. The `private` and `public` keywords control how those properties and methods can be accessed by program elements that exist outside the class. By thoughtful use of the `public` and `private` keywords, in conjunction with the properties and methods contained within the class, you control how other program elements interface with objects of the class. In other words, you are responsible for the design and implementation of the class's user interface. (Most programmers simply use the words "class interface" to refer to a class's user interface, a convention we will adopt for the remainder of the text.)

To illustrate a class interface, let's continue to use the code shown in Figure 10-4. Let's further suppose that you wish to allow the programmer who uses your class to alter the value of `mFirstName`, but you still want to have some element of control over the variable. The new code appears in Figure 10-6.

```
1    using System;
2
3    public class clsContact
4    {
5        // List of the class data members
6        private string mFirstName;
7        private string mLastName;
8        public clsPhoneNumber HomePhone;
9        public clsPhoneNumber MobilePhone;
10       public DateTime BirthDate;
11
12       // ----------- Accessor methods for data members ----------------
13
14       // Purpose: to read or write the mFirstName data member
15       public string FirstName
16       {
17           get
18           {
19               return mFirstName;
20           }
21
22           set
23           {
24               string temp;
25
26               // Make everything lowercase
27               value = value.ToLower();
28               // Pull out the first letter
29               temp = value.Substring(0,1);
30               // Build by making first letter upper case and add the rest
31               value = temp.ToUpper() + value.Substring(1,value.Length - 1);
32               mFirstName = value;
33           }
34       }
35
36       // More code...
37   }// End class code
38
39
```

Figure 10-6 A class definition using get and set accessor methods

Notice the additions to the code. The new code contains a class property method named
FirstName. A class **property method** consists of a statement block that is designed to provide
public access to a **private** data member of a class. (Observe that, unlike a property data member, a property method does not use the lower case "m" character at the start of the property method name. Recall that our style convention is to drop the "m" prefix from **public** data items.) The **public** access specifier is used for the new method named FirstName. Because the **public** access specifier is used, the property method named FirstName is available to program elements outside of the class.

You can see two new keywords, **get** and **set**, within the FirstName property method code. These two new keywords are used to define two specific methods called *accessor methods*. The **get** accessor method is called whenever an object needs to read the value of a **private** data member within a class. The **set** accessor method is called whenever an object needs to change, or write, a new value for a **private** data member.

Consider for a moment what these two accessor methods mean. A program statement such as:

```
myFriend.FirstName = "Nicholas";
```

allows the user of the class to change the mFirstName data member to "Nicholas". This statement shows that the user of the object can change the state of the object even though property member mFirstName is defined with the **private** storage class! In other words, you have defined a **public** accessor method by which you can interact with a **private** member of the class. Make sure you understand the difference between the name of the accessor method (FirstName) and the class member name (mFirstName). That is, FirstName is an accessor method that allows the outside world to read or change the state of a private property (mFirstName) of the class.

By writing the appropriate **get** and **set** methods for each **private** data member in the class using the **public** access specifier for its associated property method, you provide access to those **private** data class members you wish to expose to the outside world. Note that this also means you control how the outside world uses your class. To access a **private** class member, the user is forced to go through your **public get** and **set** accessor methods. In a very real sense, you now have the benefits of encapsulation, but the user of your class still has the means to change the state of the object. This added level of protection can be important if you wish to do some processing, such as data validation, before you allow a private data member to be changed. (Additional details are supplied in the section titled "Why Not Just Use the public Keyword for All Class Members?")

How to Determine Whether get or set Is Called

How does the C# compiler know whether to call the **get** or **set** method for a given data member? As you have seen in this section, a **get** method is used to read, or retrieve, a data member's value. (Using the terms you learned in the Bonus section of Chapter 3, a **get** method is used to fetch the **rvalue** of a data member.) Therefore, a statement similar to:

```
aFirstName = myFriend.FirstName;        // This statement does a get
```

performs a **get** operation because it reads (gets) the value of mFirstName and assigns that value into aFirstName. The state of the myFriend object remains unchanged, but the value of aFirstName is assigned the contents of mFirstName. Remember that the assignment operator always takes the value of the expression on the right side of the equal sign and assigns it into the operand on the left side of the equal sign.

On the other hand, a **set** method is used to *change* (set) the value of a data member. The statement:

```
myFriend.FirstName = aFirstName;        // This statement does a set
```

retrieves the current value for aFirstName, copies the value of aFirstName into mFirstName using the **set** method of the FirstName property method. In other words, this statement performs a **set** operation to change the value of mFirstName inside the object. Of course, this also means that the state of the myFriend object is changed by the statement because one of the object's data members (mFirstName) was changed.

The C# compiler knows whether to use the **get** or **set** method in an assignment operation by observing whether the myFriend object appears on the left (a **set** operation) or right (a **get** operation) side of the assignment operator. Stated differently, the C# compiler examines the semantic *context* in which the object is used to determine which accessor method to use.

To further explain how **set** operations are performed, look at the **set** statement block presented in Figure 10-6. Can you find a definition of the **value** variable anywhere in the code? (Hint: No!) How is this possible? C# demands that you define a variable before you use it, yet the code in Figure 10-6 compiles without complaint. The reason is that C# automatically creates what we like to call a *ghost variable* named **value** for any **public** property method that has a **set** statement block. The data type of **value** is determined by the property method's type specifier. In line 15 of Figure 10-6, you can see that the type specifier for the **FirstName** property method is **string**. Because the property method's type specifier is **string**, that becomes the data type for **value**. Note that the name of the ghost variable is always the same: **value**.

The exact content of **value** is determined by the expression in which the property method is used. Earlier in this section you saw the statement:

```
myFriend.FirstName = aFirstName;      // This statement does a set
```

In this expression, **value** receives the contents of **aFirstName** when the **set** operation named **FirstName** is called.

WHY NOT USE THE PUBLIC KEYWORD FOR ALL CLASS MEMBERS?

You might still be asking yourself: "Why bother with the **get** and **set** methods for **mFirstName**? After all, if you make it a **public** data member, the user can simply change the value directly." Although that is true, adding the **get** and **set** methods allows you to retain some control over the content of the member data value. If you study the code in the **set** method in Figure 10-6, you can see that the code transforms whatever name the user enters so that it starts with a capital letter, whereas the remainder of the name is all lowercase letters. For example, if you typed in "jenn" for the first name, it would be assigned into **mFirstName** as "Jenn". One of the reasons, therefore, for using property methods is so you can perform any data checking, validation, or other processing that you might need before the value is assigned into the class data member.

Guidelines for Designing Accessor Methods

Your ability to properly design a class and its properties and methods will grow with experience. However, the following guidelines should help you design good property methods.

Accessor methods allow you to:

- Make a read-only property by coding only a **get** accessor method
- Make a write-only property by coding only a **set** accessor method
- Execute code whenever a property is accessed, such as to validate the contents of the value being set
- Change the way the data is stored internally in the class without affecting other parts of the project
- Make properties that are based on the values of other properties

Let's consider each of these in greater detail.

A read-only property is used when you want to be able to read a data member, but not allow it to be changed outside the class. An example might be the odometer on a car. Most state laws take a dim view of people resetting the odometer reading on a car. In those cases where you only wish to read a property's value, you would simply write code for the **get** accessor method and omit the **set** accessor method. This has the effect of making the property a read-only member of the class.

If you needed a write-only property, you would write code for the **set** accessor method and omit the code for the **get** accessor method. Perhaps you have some unique value that needs to be written to a piece of hardware, but you don't need to read its value during program execution.

If you need to execute code whenever a property is accessed, you add additional logic in the **get** and/or **set** accessor methods. For example, the **FirstName** property in Figure 10-6 is implemented by coding a **get** accessor method that simply returns the private value of **mFirstName**. However, the **set** accessor method changes the name so it starts with a capital letter and is followed by lowercase letters.

The fourth guideline suggests coding accessor methods when the data type of a property changes. For example, suppose the **BirthDate** property had been implemented by defining a public variable of type **DateTime**. Then later you decide that **string** is a better data type for **BirthDate**. However, you can't simply change the data type of the **BirthDate** because any code outside this class that uses this property would have to treat **BirthDate** as a **string** value rather than a **DateTime**. So, how can you properly make such a data type change?

Keep in mind that when you use **public** accessor methods for a **private** data member, you are free to change the data member's **private** data type without impacting the way previous versions of the code worked. In the case of the **BirthDate** example, you could do the following:

- Change **BirthDate** from a **DateTime** data type to a **string**
- Change its name to **mBirthDate**
- Change the access specifier to **private** instead of **public**
- Code a **get** accessor method that converts **mBirthDate** to a **DateTime** and returns it
- Code a **set** accessor method that is passed a **DateTime** in **value**, converts it to a **string**, and assigns it into **mBirthDate**.

The user of the class can be totally unaware of our change to **mBirthDate**, and the code works just as it did before the change. If you study the changes carefully, you will find that all the changes are hidden inside the object. That is, you have encapsulated the details of the change inside the class, so it appears as though nothing has changed to the outside world. The beauty of this is that all the code that uses this object functions exactly as it did before, even though you changed the way **mBirthDate** is stored internally within the object.

The final guideline simply states that if you wish to fabricate a new property from existing properties, it's best to use a **public** property method for the derived data member. For example, consider the code shown in Figure 10-7.

```
public string LastFirstName
{
    get
    {
        return mLastName + ", " + mFirstName;
    }
}
```

Figure 10-7 The clsContact class code snippet

Notice in the **LastFirstName** property method that only the **get** accessor method is provided. This makes **LastFirstName** a read-only method to the outside world. This also means that you have control over the code that determines the value for **LastFirstName**. In fact, you don't even need an **mLastFirstName** data member because the property method code is so simple, the code simply "rebuilds" the value each time the user wants it from the existing **mLastName** and **mFirstName** properties.

Figure 10-8 shows a sample run of the program code. The screen shot was taken after all the data had been entered. What is not obvious is that the phone numbers were entered as a dense list of numbers (e.g., 5558565) and reformatted by the program. The complete program code is presented later in the chapter.

Figure 10-8   Sample run of the Contacts List program

The list of design guidelines presented earlier in this section should help you decide whether to make a class data member a **public** or **private** member of the class. At first glance, it may appear that the class properties that use the **public** access specifier do not follow the spirit of encapsulation. However, because even **public** class members must be accessed through the object's dot operator syntax, **public** members are still afforded many of the encapsulation benefits. Always keep in mind, however, that any **public** property or method becomes part of the user interface for your class.

SETTING THE INITIAL STATE OF AN OBJECT VARIABLE

As you've learned in previous chapters, a statement such as:

```
clsContact myFriend = new clsContact();
```

defines an object instance variable of the **clsContact** class named **myFriend**. It is the code found within the **clsContact** class that determines the initial state of the object named **myFriend**. Once the memory address of **myFriend** has been determined by the operating system, all of its data members are initialized to appropriate values by default. For example, numeric data types are initialized to 0, and reference data types are set to **null** by default. The **null** literal value represents a null reference, meaning that the reference variable does not refer to any object.

Data Member Initialization

However, what if you want your object's initial state to be something other than that produced by the default values? The purpose of this section is to show you how you can alter the default initial state of an object variable. There are two ways to alter the initial state of an object: first, data member **initialization**, or second, using one or more constructors. We discuss each of these in turn.

As shown in Figure 10-6, our `clsContact` class has five data members:

```
6          private string mFirstName;
7          private string mLastName;
8          public clsPhoneNumber HomePhone;
9          public clsPhoneNumber MobilePhone;
10         public DateTime BirthDate;
```

Given the way the code is written in Figure 10-6, all of the data members (except `BirthDate`) are initialized at runtime to **null**.

Let's suppose, however, that for some reason, you wish to initialize each data member to non-default values. This is not as strange as it sounds. For example, as you developed the code for the program shown in Figure 10-6, you wanted predefined values for each field to be used so you don't have to repeatedly type the values used for testing purposes. Therefore, you should change the code to:

```
private string mFirstName = "Nicholas";
private string mLastName = "Hartman";
```

The impact of these changes is that the initial state of the object has been changed from what it was in Figure 10-6 to what now appears in Figure 10-9. That is, the default value of **null** for both **mFirstName** and **mLastName** data members at the instant the object is instantiated have been replaced with "Nicholas" and "Hartman", respectively. (You can verify that this is the case by placing a breakpoint on the statement line that defines **mFirstName** and observing each member's value in a watch window as you go through the program one line at a time.)

```
3     public class clsContact
4     {
5         // List of the class data members
6         private string mFirstName = "Nicholas";
7         private string mLastName = "Hartman";
8         public clsPhoneNumber homePhone;
9         public clsPhoneNumber mobilePhone;
10        public DateTime BirthDate;
11
```

Figure 10-9   Setting the initial state of a clsContact object using member initialization

You also need to change the `frmMain()` code to:

```
public frmMain()
{
    InitializeComponent();
    contact = new clsContact();

// Test code...remove later###
    txtFirstName.Text = contact.FirstName;
    txtLastName.Text = contact.LastName;
}
```

Now, when the program starts, the name text boxes are already filled in with the test name, and you don't have to retype it each time you run the program during development and testing. Also, the code shows how a data definition and initialization statement of a member causes the object to be created with a known state for the object using non-default values. Note the comment that the code is to be removed later.

tip ▶ If you use three consecutive sharp signs (###) in the comment, this helps you locate such sections of code for removal later. You can use the search facility (that is, the Ctrl-F keys) of the code editor to locate and remove these comments easily.

CLASS CONSTRUCTORS

Using a **class constructor** represents a second way to set the initial state of an object. A class constructor is a class method that is called automatically each time a new object of the class is instantiated. Every class has a default constructor, even though the code for the default constructor is not visible in the code for the class. The default class constructor is responsible for setting the initial value of each data member to 0 or **null**, whichever is appropriate for each data member. To illustrate, in the following statement, **clsContact()** is actually a call to the default constructor of the **clsContact** class.

```
clsContact myFriend = new clsContact();
```

Because this statement follows the general syntax used to create an instantiation of a class object, it follows that every class has a default constructor. Note that the name of the class constructor must be the same name as that of the class.

You can, however, write your own constructor, as shown in Figure 10-10.

```
1    using System;
2
3    public class clsContact
4    {
5        // List of the class data members
6        private string mFirstName = "Nicholas";
7        private string mLastName = "Hartman";
8        public clsPhoneNumber HomePhone;
9        public clsPhoneNumber MobilePhone;
10       public DateTime BirthDate;
11
12       // ----------- Class constructors -----------
13       public clsContact()
14       {
15           // Default values for debugging...remove later ###
16           mFirstName = "Nicholas";
17           mLastName = "Hartman";
18       }
19
20       // Class constructor #2
21       public clsContact(string first, string last)
22       {
23           mFirstName = first;
24           mLastName = last;
25       }
26
```

Figure 10-10 A constructor for the clsContact class

10

Again, notice in Figure 10-10 that the class constructor must have the same name as the class itself, `clsContact`. A second rule is that a constructor is not allowed to return a value. This second rule has two important implications. First, you cannot have a return data type specifier in the signature of the constructor. In other words, if you write:

```
public void clsContact()
{
```

for the signature of the constructor, the compiler issues the error message:

```
'clsContact': member names cannot be the same as their enclosing type
```

This error message from the compiler is a little misleading because you might think you have mistyped the name of a method or some similar mistake. Actually, the compiler is complaining about the **void** keyword in the constructor's signature. If you remove the **void** keyword from the signature, the error message disappears. If you think about it, you realize that attempting to return a value to an instance of an object doesn't make any sense. What would the return value be assigned into? After all, the job of the constructor is to create an instance of the object and initialize any non-default values you may wish to use to establish a (non-default) state. There simply is no need for a return value.

Another consequence of the second rule is that a constructor cannot return a value. Therefore, code similar to:

```
public clsContact()
{
    mFirstName = "Nicholas";
    mLastName = "Hartman";
    return 1;                          // ERROR!!!
}
```

generates an error message because a class constructor cannot return a value. Removing the **return** statement from the code fixes this problem.

Within the constructor, you may place any code you wish to have executed at the moment an object of the class is instantiated. In Figure 10-10, you are setting the initial state of the `clsContact` object to the same default values discussed in the previous section. (See Figure 10-9.)

Given that the code in Figures 10-9 and 10-10 produce identical results for the initial state of the object, which is the better choice? Because we believe that less code is better than more code, the code shown in Figure 10-9 is a better choice because there is no constructor code to write. The code in Figure 10-9 simply initializes the members to the appropriate default values as part of the data definitions. If that's the case, why ever use an explicit constructor?

WHY USE AN EXPLICIT CONSTRUCTOR?

There are two reasons to use an explicit constructor rather than relying on the default (implicit) constructor. The first reason is that you may wish to use an additional program statement, such as an **if** statement, to conditionally set the initial state of the object. For example, there may be a piece of data named `whichCountry` that assumes a certain value. Perhaps its value determines whether the U.S. or European style for formatting a phone number is used for the object. In such a case, the constructor might look like:

```
public clsContact()
{
    if (whichCountry == 2)
    {
        spacer = '.';          // European
    }
    else
    {
        spacer = '-';          // USA
    }
}
```

In this constructor code, you can set the initial state of the object based upon the value of an external data value (that is, the value of **whichCountry**). Doing this requires the use of a logic (**if-else**) statement and the value of **spacer**. You cannot use logic statements if you are relying on the default initialization of the data members shown in Figure 10-9. Therefore, you must use a constructor if you need to use program statements to determine what the initial values for the object are to be.

A second reason for using a constructor is because you can dynamically set the initial state of an object by passing parameters to the constructor. For example, suppose you find the statement to instantiate the object written as:

```
clsContact myFriend = new clsContact(txtFirstName.Text, txtLastName.Text);
```

Notice that the statement has added two parameters to the **clsContact()** constructor. To avoid having this statement cause a compiler error, you must provide a constructor that matches the parameters in the signature of the constructor. The required new constructor might be written:

```
public clsContact(string first, string last)
{
    mFirstName = first;
    mLastName = last;
}
```

Taken together, the statement that instantiates the object coupled with the new constructor sets the initial state of the object to use whatever names were written into text boxes **txtFirstName** and **txtLastName**.

Once again you're scratching your head asking: "Wait a minute! Don't we now have two constructors with the same name? How does the compiler handle this?" Good question. The compiler solves this problem by allowing overloaded constructors.

OVERLOADED CONSTRUCTORS

What is an overloaded constructor? As you will recall from Chapter 7, a constructor, or any other C# method, is said to be *overloaded* whenever there are two methods in the namespace sharing the same name. In our example, the overloaded method just happens to be the constructor named **clsContact()**. Figure 10-11 shows the new class code.

```
  1    using System;
  2
  3    public class clsContact
  4    {
  5        // List of the class data members
  6        private string mFirstName = "Nicholas";
  7        private string mLastName = "Hartman";
  8        public clsPhoneNumber HomePhone;
  9        public clsPhoneNumber MobilePhone;
 10        public DateTime BirthDate;
 11
 12        // ----------- Class constructors -----------
 13        public clsContact()
 14        {
 15            // Default values for debugging...remove later ###
 16
 17            mFirstName = "Nicholas";
 18            mLastName = "Hartman";
 19        }
 20
 21        // Class constructor #2
 22        public clsContact(string first, string last)
 23        {
 24            mFirstName = first;
 25            mLastName = last;
 26        }
 27
 28            // More class code...
115
116    }
```

Figure 10-11   Using an overloaded constructor for the clsContact class

The C# compiler compiles the code shown in Figure 10-11 without complaint. How is this possible when the two constructors have the same name? The compiler does not get confused because the signatures for the two constructor methods are different. As discussed in Chapter 7, the signature of a method extends from the start of the method name and continues to the opening curly brace of the method. In our example, the signatures for the two constructors are shown in Figure 10-12.

```
clsContact()
clsContact(string first, string last)
```

Figure 10-12   Constructor signatures for clsContact() constructor methods

The important thing to remember about any overloaded method is that, although the names are the same, the parameter lists between the parentheses must be different. In Figure 10-11, the signatures follow this rule because the second signature contains two parameters whereas the first signature contains none. Therefore, if you use the code shown in Figure 10-11, the statements:

```
clsContact myFriend = new clsContact();
clsContact yourList = new clsContact("Katherine", "Cioce");
```

instantiate two **clsContact** objects. However, the objects are created with different initial states because different constructors were used to create the two objects. Always keep in mind that if you do write a constructor of your own, you are, in effect, replacing the default constructor with your own version.

WHY METHOD OVERLOADING IS A GOOD THING

Method overloading is a very powerful feature of C# because it adds flexibility. You now have one method name that can do double duty. That's the good news. The bad news is that you have to remember how to call each of the overloaded methods. Actually, Microsoft anticipated this problem quite nicely, as shown in Figure 10-13.

Look at the third statement in Figure 10-13 that contains:

```
clsContact contact = new clsContact();
```

As soon as you type the opening parenthesis for **clsContact(**, the Intellisense feature of VS.NET opens a small rectangle that states that there is more than one method with the name **clsContact**. In other words, you now know that **clsContact()** is an overloaded method. By clicking on the up and down arrows of the Intellisense box shown in Figure 10-13, you can view the signatures for each overloaded version of the constructor method. The figure shows that the up arrow was clicked to see the second signature for **clsContact**. The "2 of 2" you see in the figure tells you there are two versions of the method and that currently you are viewing the second method. The remainder of the boxed message shows the second of the two signatures for **clsContact()**. Also note that Intellisense is smart enough to use the same parameter names you used when you defined the method. (This is another reason to create variable names that give some clue to their purpose.) The Intellisense feature makes it easy to review the signatures for any overloaded method, not just constructors.

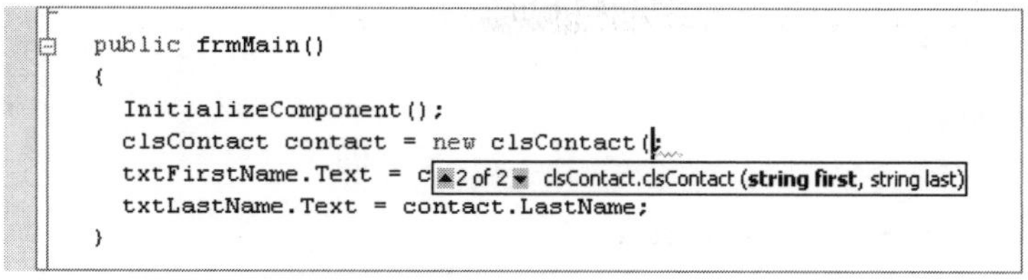

```
public frmMain()
{
    InitializeComponent();
    clsContact contact = new clsContact(|
    txtFirstName.Text = c [▲ 2 of 2 ▼  clsContact.clsContact (string first, string last)]
    txtLastName.Text = contact.LastName;
}
```

Figure 10-13   Using Intellisense to view method signatures

REMOVING OBJECTS FROM A PROGRAM

If you look closely at the code in Figure 10-13, you can see that we have defined a **clsContact** object named **contact**. The instantiation of the object named **contact** means that the common language runtime (CLR) has provided our program with enough memory to store one **clsContact** object named **contact**. When the program leaves the method in which the object is defined (that is, **frmMain()**), the object is no longer accessible in the program. When the closing brace of **frmMain()** is reached, the object named **contact** is no longer in scope.

However, simply because an object is out of scope does not mean that it has been removed from memory. Instead, the "dead" object may just hang around wasting memory until the CLR reclaims the memory that was allocated to it. (We discuss this memory reclamation process in the Bonus Topics section of this chapter.) If you add the statement:

```
contact = null;
```

just before the closing brace of the method in which the object is defined, you are marking the object for reclamation by the CLR. In other words, assigning the value **null** to an object tells the CLR that you are finished using the object and the CLR can reclaim the memory associated with the object. However, the statement does not force the CLR to perform the memory reclamation at that instant in the program. What actually happens is that the statement tells the CLR that the memory allocated for the object *can* be reclaimed, but the CLR actually reclaims the memory whenever it determines it is most efficient to do so. (Memory reclamation is fairly time-consuming.)

If you can't actually control when memory reclamation takes place, why bother setting objects to **null**? After all, objects are also marked for reclamation when they go out of scope. While setting objects to **null** does not force the CLR to instantly reclaim their memory, it is a form of documentation that tells the reader of the code that you are finished using the object. In very complex methods that involve a large amount of code with looping constructs, it may be that the CLR can reclaim the memory before the method has finished its task and the local data go out of scope. To be honest, because the CLR reclaims memory when it deems it appropriate to do so, most programmers do not explicitly set the object to **null** when they finish using the object. We are simply presenting the assignment here to demonstrate that such statements do document your intentions if nothing else.

Figure 10-14 shows the complete source code for the Contacts List program. Note that the program produces the output shown in Figure 10-8. The code for the form, **frmMain()**, is shown first, followed by **the clsContact** and **clsPhoneNumber** class code.

```
 1    using System;
 2    using System.Collections;
 3    using System.Windows.Forms;
 4
 5    public class frmMain: Form
 6    {

29        #region Windows Form Designer generated code

280
281       clsContact contact;
282       clsPhoneNumber phone;
283       ArrayList myFriends = new ArrayList();
284
285       public static void Main()
286       {
287           frmMain main = new frmMain();
288           Application.Run(main);
289       }
290
291       public frmMain()
292       {
293           InitializeComponent();
294           contact = new clsContact();
295           txtFirstName.Text = contact.FirstName;
296           txtLastName.Text = contact.LastName;
```

Figure 10-14   Complete test code for the Contact List program

```
297        }
298
299        // Adds a new contact to the list.
300        private void btnAdd_Click(object sender, System.EventArgs e)
301        {
302
303            // Validate the input values.
304
305            if (validateInput() == false)
306            {
307                return;
308            }
309
310            // Instantiate and populate the new Contact item.
311
312            contact = new clsContact();
313            getInputValues(contact);
314
315            // Reset the UI by displaying the new contact in the listbox and clearing
316            // the input controls. Note the listbox has DisplayMember = LastFirstName.
317
318            lstContacts.Items.Add(contact);
319            txtHomePhone.Text = contact.HomePhone.ToString();
320            txtMobilePhone.Text = contact.MobilePhone.ToString();
321            txtAge.Text = contact.Age.ToString();
322
323            contact = null;
324        }
325
326        // Clears out the input controls.
327        private void btnClear_Click(object sender, System.EventArgs e)
328        {
329            clearInputControls();
330        }
331
332        // Close the form to end the application.
333        private void btnClose_Click(object sender, System.EventArgs e)
334        {
335            Close();
336        }
337
338        // Removes the selected contact from the list.
339        private void btnDelete_Click(object sender, System.EventArgs e)
340        {
341            clsContact contact;
342
343            // Make sure an item is selected in the listbox.
344            if (lstContacts.SelectedItem == null)
345            {
346                return;
347            }
348
349            contact = (clsContact)lstContacts.SelectedItem;
350
351            // Ask the user for confirmation.
352
353            if (messageBoxYesNo("Are you sure you want to delete " +
                        contact.LastFirstName + "?") == DialogResult.No)
354            {
```

Figure 10-14 Complete test code for the Contact List program (continued)

```
355                    return;
356              }
357
358         // Remove the contact from the listbox and array list.
359
360         lstContacts.Items.Remove(lstContacts.SelectedItem);
361         myFriends.Remove(contact);
362         contact = null;
363
364     }
365
366     // Update the selected contact with the new input values.
367     private void btnUpdate_Click(object sender, System.EventArgs e)
368     {
369         clsContact contact;
370
371         // Make sure an item is selected in the listbox.
372
373         if (lstContacts.SelectedItem == null)
374         {
375             return;
376         }
377
378         // Validate the input values.
379
380         if (validateInput() == false)
381         {
382             return;
383         }
384
385         // Populate the existing contact item with the new values.
386
387         contact = (clsContact)lstContacts.SelectedItem;
388         getInputValues(contact);
389
390         // Reset by making sure the new FullName is displayed. Do this
391         // by removing and then re-adding the contact. Finally, clear the
392         // input controls.
393
394         lstContacts.Items.Remove(contact);
395         lstContacts.Items.Add(contact);
396         clearInputControls();
397         contact = null;
398
399     }
400
401     // Clears the input controls.
402     private void clearInputControls()
403     {
404         txtFirstName.Text = "";
405         txtLastName.Text = "";
406         txtHomePhone.Text = "";
407         txtMobilePhone.Text = "";
408         txtBirthDate.Text = "";
409         txtAge.Text = "";
410         txtSearch.Text = "";
411         lblSearch.Visible = false;
412         txtSearch.Visible = false;
```

Figure 10-14 Complete test code for the Contact List program (continued)

```
413              txtFirstName.Focus();
414         }
415
416     // Populates the passed contact object with the values of the input controls.
417     private void getInputValues(clsContact contact)
418     {
419         contact.FirstName = txtFirstName.Text;
420         contact.LastName = txtLastName.Text;
421         contact.HomePhone = new clsPhoneNumber(txtHomePhone.Text, 1);
422         contact.MobilePhone = new clsPhoneNumber(txtMobilePhone.Text);
423         contact.BirthDate = DateTime.Parse(txtBirthDate.Text);
424
425         // Add the new contact to the list.
426         myFriends.Add(contact);
427     }
428
429     // Displays the property values for the selected contact values.
430     private void lstContacts_DoubleClick(object sender, System.EventArgs e)
431     {
432         // Make sure an item is selected in the listbox.
433
434         if (lstContacts.SelectedItem == null)
435         {
436             return;
437         }
438         int index = (int) lstContacts.SelectedIndex;
439         // Get the reference to the selected contact.
440
441         ShowContact(index);
442     }
443
444     // Show the info for the contact at index
445     private void ShowContact(int index)
446     {
447         contact = (clsContact) myFriends[index];
448
449         // Display the contact's property values.
450
451         txtFirstName.Text = contact.FirstName;
452         txtLastName.Text = contact.LastName;
453         txtHomePhone.Text = contact.HomePhone.ToString();
454         txtMobilePhone.Text = contact.MobilePhone.ToString();
455         txtBirthDate.Text = contact.BirthDate.ToString("d");
456         txtAge.Text = contact.Age.ToString();
457     }
458
459     // Display a proper message box with only an OK button.
460     private void messageBoxOK(string msg)
461     {
462         MessageBox.Show(msg, Text, MessageBoxButtons.OK, MessageBoxIcon.Information);
463     }
464
465     // Display a proper Yes or No question message box.
466     private DialogResult messageBoxYesNo(string msg)
467     {
468         return MessageBox.Show(msg, Text, MessageBoxButtons.YesNo,
469                     MessageBoxIcon.Question);
        }
470
```

Figure 10-14 Complete test code for the Contact List program (continued)

```
471        // Validate the contents of the input values on the form. This method
               returns true if everything is OK
472        // and false if something is invalid.
473        private bool validateInput()
474        {
475            // Check to make sure a first and last name have been entered.
476
477            if (txtFirstName.Text == "")
478            {
479                messageBoxOK("First Name is required.");
480                txtFirstName.Focus();
481                return false;
482            }
483
484            if (txtLastName.Text == "")
485            {
486                messageBoxOK("Last Name is required.");
487                txtLastName.Focus();
488                return false;
489            }
490
491            // Validate Birth Date.
492
493            try
494            {
495                DateTime birthDate = DateTime.Parse(txtBirthDate.Text);
496            }
497            catch (Exception)
498            {
499                messageBoxOK("Birthdate is required and must be a valid date.");
500                txtBirthDate.Focus();
501                return false;
502            }
503
504            phone = new clsPhoneNumber(txtHomePhone.Text,1);
505            txtHomePhone.Text=phone.ToString();
506
507            // If we get here, then everything must be OK.
508            return true;
509        }
510
511        private void btnSearch_Click(object sender, System.EventArgs e)
512        {
513            lblSearch.Visible = true;
514            txtSearch.Visible = true;
515            txtSearch.Focus();
516        }
517
518
519        private void txtSearch_Leave(object sender, System.EventArgs e)
520        {
521            int index;
522            string buff;
523            string firstLetter;
524
525            clsContact tempContact = new clsContact();
526
527            index = 0;
528
```

Figure 10-14   Complete test code for the Contact List program (continued)

```
529                    // Copy the name entered in the text box to lowercase
530                    buff = txtSearch.Text;
531                    buff = buff.ToLower();
532
533                    // Get the first letter
534                    firstLetter = buff.Substring(0,1);
535                    // Make first letter uppercase and add the rest
536                    buff = firstLetter.ToUpper() + buff.Substring(1, buff.Length - 1);
537
538                    // Spin through list to see if name is present
539                    while (index < myFriends.Count)
540                    {
541                        tempContact = (clsContact) myFriends[index];
542
543                        if (tempContact.LastName == buff)
544                        {
545                            ShowContact(index);
546                            return;
547                        }
548                        index++;
549                    }
550                    messageBoxOK("Name not found in list");
551            }
552
553    }
554
```

```
1      using System;
2
3      public class clsContact
4      {
5          // List of the class data members
6          private string mFirstName = "Nicholas";
7          private string mLastName = "Hartman";
8          public clsPhoneNumber HomePhone;
9          public clsPhoneNumber MobilePhone;
10         public DateTime BirthDate;
11
12         // ----------- Class constructors -----------
13         public clsContact()
14         {
15             // Default values for debugging…remove later ###
16             mFirstName = "Nicholas";
17             mLastName = "Hartman";
18         }
19
20         // Class constructor #2
21         public clsContact(string first, string last)
22         {
23             mFirstName = first;
24             mLastName = last;
25         }
26
27
28         // ----------- Accessor methods for data members -----------
29
```

10

Figure 10-14   Complete test code for the Contact List program (continued)

```
30          // This accessor reads or writes mFirstName. If the name does not
31          // start with a capital letter, it is forced to a cap.
32          public string FirstName
33          {
34              get
35              {
36                  return mFirstName;
37              }
38
39              set
40              {
41                  string temp;
42
43                  // Make everything lowercase
44                  value = value.ToLower();
45                  // Pull out the first letter
46                  temp = value.Substring(0,1);
47                  // Build by making first letter uppercase and add the rest
48                  value = temp.ToUpper() + value.Substring(1,value.Length - 1);
49                  mFirstName = value;
50              }
51          }
52
53          // Read or write the mLastName data member
54          public string LastName
55          {
56              get
57              {
58                  return mLastName;
59              }
60
61              set
62              {
63                  string temp;
64
65                  // Make everything lowercase
66                  value = value.ToLower();
67                  // Pull out the first letter
68                  temp = value.Substring(0,1);
69                  // Build by making first letter uppercase and add the rest
70                  value = temp.ToUpper() + value.Substring(1,value.Length - 1);
71                  mLastName = value;
72              }
73          }
74
75          // Returns the last name concatenated with the first name.
76          public string LastFirstName
77          {
78              get
79              {
80                  return mLastName + ", " + mFirstName;
81              }
82          }
83
84          // ----------- End Accessor methods for data members -----------
85
86          // Returns age based on the birthdate and current date.
87          public byte Age
88          {
```

Figure 10-14   Complete test code for the Contact List program (continued)

```
 89             get
 90             {
 91                 // Get the birthdate value for the current year.
 92
 93                 DateTime thisYearBirthDate = new DateTime(DateTime.Now.Year,
 94                                         mBirthDate.Month, mBirthDate.Day);
 95                 // Calculate and return the age based on whether the birthdate has
                       occurred this year or not.
 96
 97                 if (thisYearBirthDate <= DateTime.Now)
 98                 {
 99                     return (byte)(DateTime.Now.Year - mBirthDate.Year);
100                 }
101                 else
102                 {
103                     return (byte)(DateTime.Now.Year - mBirthDate.Year - 1);
104                 }
105             }
106         }
107
108         // A destructor for an object
109         ~clsContact()
110         {
111             mFirstName = null;
112             mLastName = null;
113             HomePhone = null;
114             MobilePhone = null;
115         }
116
117     }
```

```
 1     using System;
 2
 3     public class clsPhoneNumber
 4     {
 5         // The private string we use to store the formatted phone number.
 6         private string mPhoneNumber = "";
 7
 8         // Default values for USA. USA = 1, Europe = 2
 9         private int mWhichCountry = 1;
10
11         // USA = '-', Europe = '.'
12         private char mSpacer = '-';
13
14         // The ToString method is overridden to return the formatted phone number.
15         public override string ToString()
16         {
17             return mPhoneNumber;
18         }
19
20         // This constructor takes a string value as the argument, and
21         // removes any character that isn't one of the numbers 0 - 9,
22         // then saves it formatted as (999) 999-9999.  An exception is
23         // thrown if the string contains more than 10 numeric characters.
24         public clsPhoneNumber(string value)
25         {
```

Figure 10-14 Complete test code for the Contact List program (continued)

10

```
26              // Skip the reformatting if all we have is an empty string.
27              string temp;
28
29              if (value == "")
30              {
31                  mPhoneNumber = "";
32                  return;
33              }
34              temp = checkString(value);
35              formatPhoneNumber(temp);
36          }
37
38          // The first parameter is the phone number. This constructor uses a
39          // second parameter to decide the country-specific formatting to use.
40          // Currently, 1 is the US and 2 is Europe.
41          public clsPhoneNumber(string value, int countryCode)
42          {
43              string temp;
44
45              mWhichCountry = countryCode;
46
47              // Skip the reformatting if all we have is an empty string.
48              if (value == "")
49              {
50                  mPhoneNumber = "";
51                  return;
52              }
53
54              // Change the character between digits based on locale preference
55              switch (mWhichCountry)
56              {
57                  case 1:// USA
58                      mSpacer = '-';
59                  break;
60
61                  case 2:// Europe
62                      mSpacer = '.';
63                  break;
64
65                  // Add any new country case codes here
66
67                  // Default assumes USA
68                  default:
69                      mSpacer = '-';
70                  break;
71              }
72              temp = checkString(value);
73              formatPhoneNumber(temp);
74          }
75
76          //Format the phone number based upon its length, which
77          //may or may not include an area code.
78          private void formatPhoneNumber(string digits)
79          {
80              switch (digits.Length)
81              {
82
83                  case 7://Default for no area code
```

Figure 10-14 Complete test code for the Contact List program (continued)

```
84                        mPhoneNumber = digits.Substring(0, 3) + mSpacer + digits.
                             Substring(3, 4);
85               break;
86
87               case 10:// Format with area code
88                   mPhoneNumber = "("
89                   + digits.Substring(0, 3)
90                   + ") "
91                   + digits.Substring(3, 3)
92                   + mSpacer
93                   + digits.Substring(6, 4);
94               break;
95
96               default:// Throw an exception if we don't find ten digits.
97                   throw new Exception("Improper number of numeric digits.");
98           }
99       }
100
101      // Checks whether the string contains digit characters only.
102      private string checkString(string value)
103      {
104          char digit;
105          string digits = "";
106
107          // Remove any character that isn't a digit character 0 - 9.
108          for (int index = 0; index < value.Length; index++)
109          {
110              digit = value[index];
111              if (digit >= '0' && digit <= '9')
112              {
113                  digits += digit;
114              }
115          }
116          return digits;
117      }
118
119  }
```

Figure 10-14 Complete test code for the Contact List program (continued)

The coding style demonstrated in Figure 10-14 is not etched in stone. It is simply a style that has served us well over the years. If you write code as part of a team, the team should get together and create a coding style that meets your needs. It can be whatever you wish it to be (within reason). However, once the team selects a coding style, all members of the team should stick with it. If there are multiple teams within the corporation, then coding style should be a corporate decision that all programmers can agree to use. Consistency of coding style does make it easier to debug and maintain the code.

HOW THE PROGRAM WORKS

The code presented in Figure 10-14 is fairly straightforward, and is similar to that which you have seen in previous chapters. The code waits for you to enter the appropriate information into the text boxes. When you click the Add button, the information contained in the text boxes is copied into a **clsContact** object via the call to **getInputValues()**. The name is then copied to the list box and the input text boxes are cleared.

Perhaps the only surprise is in the way you might edit the contents of the `contact` list. In the `lstContacts_DoubleClick()` event code, you see the statement:

```
clsContact contact = (clsContact) lstContacts.SelectedItem;
```

This statement takes the information associated with the highlighted name from the `lstContacts` list box that you just double-clicked, casts the information to a `clsContact` object, and then copies the data into the `clsContact` object name `contact`. The remainder of the `lstContacts_DoubleClick()` event code simply copies the `contact` information into the appropriate text boxes. The cast is necessary because a list box object (`lstContacts`) is not the same as a class (`clsContact`) object. (Recall that a cast is a mechanism that allows us to convert apples to oranges. Casts are discussed in Chapter 4.)

Storing the Contacts

Consider the following two program lines from Figure 10-14:

```
283          ArrayList myFriends = new ArrayList();

425             myFriends.Add(contact);
```

Line 283 defines an `ArrayList` named `myFriends`. Each time the user enters the information for a new contact and clicks the Add button, Line 425 adds the new friend to `myFriends`. This is one of the really great features of `ArrayList`—you can add objects to the array with a single, simple statement, and C# takes care of all of the details necessary to dynamically expand the list. Likewise, lines 539 through 549 show how simple it is to search the `myFriends ArrayList` for a specific friend. Finally, the line:

```
361             myFriends.Remove(contact);
```

shows how easy it is to remove an object from `myFriends`. If you had used a simple array type to store the `clsContact` data, you would have to write a considerable amount of code to remove a name from the middle of the list. With an `ArrayList`, a single line of code takes care of it.

Spend some time studying the code in Figure 10-14. We have purposely said nothing about the code in the `clsPhoneNumber` class. Figuring out what the `clsPhoneNumber` code does should help solidify your understanding of how to write code for a class.

One last point about Figure 10-14—line 15 of the clsPhoneNumber appears as:

```
15        public override string ToString()
```

C# provides a `ToString` method for every object. By default, the `ToString` method returns a string that is the name of the class to which the object belongs. For example, after executing the lines:

```
string buff;
clsContact contact = new clsContact();
buff = contact.ToString();
```

the variable `buff` would contain `clsContact`. By overriding the `ToString` method, you can return a string that can be just about anything you wish it to be. Line 15 of the `clsPhoneNumber` code simply changes the default behavior of `ToString` to return a formatted phone number instead of `clsPhoneNumber`.

BONUS TOPICS

MEMORY MANAGEMENT

Even though it's common for a home computer to have a good amount of memory, as a programmer, you should still be concerned with managing your memory resources. Microsoft's Visual Studio languages, including C#, provide for automatic memory management through the CLR. This means that problems such as memory leaks (i.e., forgetting to release a memory resource before the program ends) are virtually eliminated. Because most C# programs use the CLR, their execution is controlled by the CLR in a process called **managed execution**.

One component of the CLR is named the garbage collector. It is the **garbage collector**'s responsibility to respond to all memory requests made by your program during managed execution. Figure 10-15 can help you understand how the garbage collector performs its memory allocation task. (We are going to make some simplifying assumptions about the memory management process to make the explanation easier to follow.)

As you can see in Figure 10-15, the Windows operating system occupies the lowest section of memory. The next block of memory is used to store Visual Studio and the C# compiler. Following that section of memory is the program you are developing. Above the section of memory devoted to your program is the **managed heap**, which is where the garbage collector does most of its magic. You'll learn more about the managed heap in a few moments.

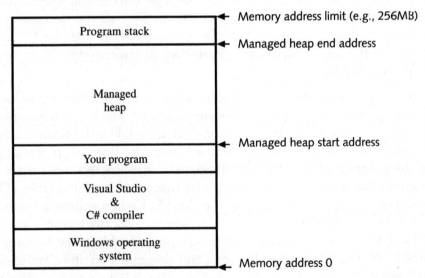

Hypothetical system's memory space

Figure 10-15   Typical memory map

THE PROGRAM STACK

At the very top of memory is the program stack. For the most part, the **program stack** is used to store local variables that are defined in program methods. Think of the program stack as starting at the very last byte of memory in your system. Each time you define a variable in a method, a chunk of memory large enough to hold that variable is allocated on the stack. For example, if your method defines an **int** variable, 4 bytes of memory are allocated for that variable and that memory address would be recorded in the symbol table's **lvalue** column. (See the Bonus Topics section in Chapter 3 for details about the symbol table and how it works.) If you define another variable in the same method, for example a **double**, it would also have its memory address (**lvalue**) recorded in the symbol table. However, the **double's lvalue** would be stored at a memory address that is 4 bytes lower in memory than the top of the stack because of the **int** that was stored earlier. In other words, as new data items are allocated on the stack, the **lvalue** for each new address is less than those defined earlier in the program. Therefore, *memory allocations done on the stack grow towards low memory.*

The C# compiler always keeps track of where the next available byte of **stack memory** is located. It does this with an internal variable called the stack pointer. The sole purpose of the **stack pointer** is to hold the memory address of where the next available byte of stack memory is located. It follows that, each time you define a new variable within a memory, the stack pointer is adjusted downwards by the amount of memory required to store the most recently defined variable on the stack.

A limited amount of memory is set aside for the program stack. Suppose the stack contains 64K of memory. If you try to define new variables that allocate more memory in a method than has been set aside for the stack, it is possible to get an out-of-memory error message from the compiler. For example, if you tried to define a new variable within a loop, given enough iterations of the loop, you would eventually run out of stack memory.

Out of Scope

Assuming that you don't get an out-of-memory error message during the execution of the method, when the compiler reaches the closing brace of the method, all the data items defined within the current method go "out of scope." Out of scope also means that the C# compiler resets its stack pointer back to the top of memory and removes all associated memory references to those variables from the symbol table.

If you think about the process, as your program executes and calls various program methods, you realize that there is a growing and shrinking process occurring in the stack and the symbol table as new methods come and go during program execution. (We have taken the term symbol table here very loosely, but it aligns well for purposes of discussion with the Bonus Topics section from Chapter 3.) Each time the program enters a new method, memory allocations are made on the stack, the stack pointer grows downward, and new entries are made in the symbol table. (The time it takes to perform these tasks is often referred to as the overhead when calling a method. This topic was discussed in Chapter 7.) When the program statements associated with a method are finished executing, all local variables are removed from the symbol table (they become out of scope), the stack pointer is reset to the top of memory, and program execution resumes at the point where the method was called.

Even though much takes place in managing the stack, the CPUs that support Windows have relatively efficient stack instructions. The end result is that, even though much happens when managing the stack, the CPU instructions perform the functions quite efficiently, so program execution zips along quite fast. The important thing to remember about stack memory management is that all local variables located on the stack are deallocated from the stack simply by resetting the stack pointer—a very fast operation. The same cannot be said for data allocated on the heap.

Managed Heap

In the discussion of the stack, there was a simplifying assumption that all variables defined in the method are allocated on the stack. Well, that is really not the case. No object references are allocated from stack memory. Instead, all object references are allocated from the managed **heap memory** space. (See Figure 10-15.) The mechanics is similar to memory allocation from the stack, but the memory allocations are controlled by the Windows Memory Manager (WMM), which is also in charge of garbage collection. Because garbage collection is also part of the CLR, memory allocations controlled by the garbage collector are referred to as **managed memory allocations**. (There are ways to allocate memory without going through the garbage collector called **unmanaged memory allocations**, but the process is usually slower and, hence, is discouraged.)

Managed memory allocations are performed through the CLR in concert with the WMM for resource management. Just like the stack pointer mentioned earlier, the WMM also manages a pointer that tracks the next unused block of heap memory available in the system. As you define object references in your program, the WMM allocates the amount of memory the new object requires and increases the managed heap's memory pointer. Because of the way the WMM works, heap memory allocations are almost as fast as stack memory allocations.

Alas, releasing heap memory allocations requires more than simply resetting the memory pointer as the stack does. One reason that releasing memory from the heap is slow is that some object references persist even though we have stopped executing a program method. In other words, an object reference may hang around even though the closing brace for the method has been reached and the reference has gone out of scope. The reason is that reclaiming those memory resources associated with the reference through the CLR is a relatively time-consuming process, so the CLR determines the "best" time to reclaim those resources rather than your code making the decision. This is one reason code that is controlled by the CLR is called managed code. That is, some decisions such as memory reclamation are managed by the CLR rather than by the code you write.

For example, the following code snippet taken from Figure 10-14 illustrates the problem:

```
291         public frmMain()
292         {
293             InitializeComponent();
294             contact = new clsContact();
295             txtFirstName.Text = contact.FirstName;
296             txtLastName.Text = contact.LastName;
297         }
298
```

When you finish the call to the `clsContact()` constructor (that is, the part of the statement that contains `new clsContact();`), you still need `contact` to be available (that is, in scope) in the program for the assignment statements that follow. Hence, `contact` is allocated on the heap. (Another reason the variable `contact` is allocated on the heap is that it is an object reference rather than a value variable.) As long as there are code references to `contact` at any point in the program, the program cannot discard the memory associated with the `contact`. Only after all references to `contact` have been processed can the garbage collector free the memory associated with `contact`. The process of freeing heap memory for reuse in the program is called **garbage collection**.

10

For reasons we need not study here (e.g., memory compaction), garbage collection is a time-consuming process. Therefore, the programmer does not directly control the actual timing of the garbage collection process in managed code. Instead, it is the algorithms that control the garbage collector that determine the optimal time for the garbage collection process to take place. The best you can do to free memory resources is to explicitly tell the garbage collector that you are finished using an object reference.

FREEING OBJECT REFERENCES

C# provides three ways to release an object reference. These include:

1. The object reference goes out of scope.

2. The object reference is set to **null**.

3. A destructor is used.

We discuss each of these in turn.

Object Reference Goes out of Scope

The first way to release an object reference is simply to let it go out of scope. As you already know, any data item goes out of scope when the closing brace that contains the definition of the object is reached. When an object reference goes out of scope, there can no longer be any valid references to the object. When that happens, the object reference is marked for garbage collection.

Assigning the Value null

A second way to release the memory associated with an object reference is to explicitly set the reference variable to **null**. You can see an example of this in line 323 of the **btnAdd_Click()** event in Figure 10-14 and the statement:

```
contact = null;
```

Note that this statement marks the object reference, **contact**, for garbage collection. The keyword **null** simply indicates that the contents of the **contact** object reference is now "garbage." It's up to the garbage collector to determine the best time for collecting the garbage.

Figure 10-16 illustrates a complication about freeing object references.

```
clsContact contact = new clsContact();
clsContact copyContact = contact;

// Code that does something to the object

contact = null;
```

Figure 10-16 Problem freeing memory using null

Given the code in Figure 10-16, what happened to object reference **copyContact**? Recall that **copyContact** actually refers to **contact**—that is, it refers to the exact same **lvalue** in the managed heap. Because **copyContact** still contains a valid (non-**null**) reference to an object, the garbage collector cannot reclaim **contact**'s memory. Therefore, if two reference variables refer to the same object, the memory associated with that object cannot be freed until *both* reference variables contain **null** or the reference variables go out of scope.

Using Destructors

A third way to remove an object reference is to write a destructor for the object's class. As you learned earlier in this chapter, the name for a class constructor is the same as the class name. A **class destructor** also has the same name as the class, but it is prefixed with a tilde character (~). Sample code for a destructor can be seen in Figure 10-17.

```
108        // A destructor for an object
109        ~clsContact()
110        {
111            mFirstName = null;
112            mLastName = null;
113            HomePhone = null;
114            MobilePhone = null;
115        }
116
117    }
```

Figure 10-17 Sample class destructor

Note that a destructor cannot have any arguments nor can it return a value. Because a destructor cannot have any arguments, it cannot be overloaded. (Think about it. If you cannot have any arguments, how could the signatures be different?) In fact, you cannot prefix a destructor name with an access specifier such as **public** or **private**.

A destructor implicitly calls the **Object.Finalize** method of the CLR, so the code presented in Figure 10-17 actually becomes the code shown in Figure 10-18.

```
~clsContact()
{
    try
    {
        mFirstName = null;
        mLastName = null;
        HomePhone = null;
        MobilePhone = null;
    }
    finally
    {
        base.Finalize();
    }
}
```

Figure 10-18 Actual destructor code

Why use a class destructor when you can remove an object reference by using a **null** assignment? The primary reason is because you may want to perform certain tasks on the object before it is destroyed. For example, if the class works with disk files, you could place code in the destructor that closes the relevant files before the object is destroyed. Another common example is to close a network or printer connection that might be associated with the object. In general, a destructor is a good place to write any code you want to execute to "tidy things up" before the object is marked for oblivion.

To be honest, most programmers are a little lazy about removing an object reference from memory. They simply let the object go out of scope, and quite often that's okay. This is especially true in managed code because garbage collection is ultimately determined by the CLR. In most cases, using the keyword **null** is more of a documentation effort than a statement that actually triggers garbage collection. If you would like more information about the complexities of the garbage collection process, see the Visual Studio Help discussions of the topic.

SUMMARY

Essential Topics

- Encapsulation is a critical element of object-oriented programming and promotes the concepts of hiding the data and the methods of an object.

- You can add a new class to a project as a separate file, making the new class a part of the program being developed. At the same time, because it is in a separate file, it can be reused in other projects by simply including the class file in the new project's namespace.

- The **public** and **private** access specifiers are the most common used in the class code. The **private** access specifier limits the visibility of the data member or method to the class in which it is defined. The **public** access specifier, however, allows the outside world to access that member or method through an instance object of the class using the dot notation. You use the **public** access specifier to define the class's user interface.

- A user interface refers to the way you've designed the class to be used by those who wish to use your class. It is the **public** data members and methods that form the user interface. The user interface is implemented with a combination of **get** and **set** methods for the properties.

- If needed, class constructors can be overloaded to establish different starting states for an object of the class. Class constructors must use the same name as the class.

- It is easy to manage objects using an **ArrayList**. The **ArrayList** data structure offers several advantages over simple arrays because of the ease with which it can be managed.

- Objects should be removed from a program when you are finished using them. The most common way is to simply allow the variable to go out of scope. A second way is to assign the variable the value **null**. Although such an assignment marks the variable for garbage collection, code that is managed by the CLR performs a garbage collection process only when the CLR determines it's best to do so. A third way to remove an object reference is to write a destructor for the object's class.

Bonus Topics

- Removing objects when you are finished with them helps the garbage collection process to use system memory as efficiently as possible.

- You also learned how the program stack is used during program execution in a C# program and how the stack relates to the concept of out-of-scope variables. You then learned about the difference between variables placed on the stack and those placed in the managed heap space.

- You also learned how to write class destructors and the purpose they serve.

KEY TERMS

Define each of the following terms, as it relates to object-oriented programming:

Essential Terms

- class interface
- class constructor
- **get** accessor method
- **null**
- **public**
- **private**
- initialization
- state
- **Set** accessor method
- managed execution

Bonus Terms

- class destructor
- garbage collection
- heap memory
- managed heap
- managed memory allocation
- memory management
- stack memory
- stack pointer
- unmanaged memory allocation

REVIEW QUESTIONS

Essential Questions

1. A major feature of encapsulation is data hiding. True or false?

2. The **private** access specifier is the default for the data members of a class. True or false?

3. The **set** accessor method is used when you wish to read the value of a data member. True or false?

4. As a general rule, if an accessor method appears on the right side of an assignment operator, the code is performing a **get** operation. True or false?

5. Reference variables are initialized to **null** by default. True or false?

6. C# does not supply default constructors for a class. True or false?

7. The principle of encapsulation means you should never define a class member with the **public** access specifier. True or false?

8. The return data type for overloaded methods must be the same. True or false?

9. Class methods are not allowed to return a data type value. True or false?

10. Class constructor methods are a special case and are allowed to return a data value. True or false?

11. A data cast allows you to convert one data type to another data type. True or false?

12. The _____ access specifier is used when you wish to hide a data member from the rest of the program.

13. A(n) _____ defines the way in which you wish to have the outside world use your class.

14. A read-only property is one in which there is only a(n) _____ accessor method for a data member.

15. A method defined within a class using the **private** access specifier is called a _____ method.

16. A common way to initialize an object to a known state at the time of its creation is to _____.

17. Briefly list the benefits of encapsulation.

18. What is an overloaded method?

19. Under what circumstances would you write a constructor for a class?

20. What is a method signature?

21. In a few sentences, describe what the **clsPhoneNumber** class does.

Bonus Questions

1. The Windows Memory Manager and the CLR's garbage collector work together to allocate memory resources used in a C# program. True or false?

2. In C#, global variables are stored in the program stack. True or false?

3. The stack pointer is used to track the next available memory location in the stack. True or false?

4. You can make a read-only property by not providing code for the **get** property method. True or False?

5. As a style convention, public data members in a class should be prefixed with a lowercase "m". True or False?

6. Assigning the value _____ to a reference variable is one way to tell the system that you are finished using this reference variable.

7. Draw a typical system's memory map and label the program stack, the heap, the operating system, and your application.

8. If a class needs to "clean up after itself," a good place for such code is in the class _____.

9. Why is it a bad idea to use graphical user interface (GUI) component names, such as **txtFirstName.Text**, when designing a class method?

10. C# programs that use the common language runtime (CLR) to control their execution use a process called _____.

PROGRAMMING EXERCISES

In the following exercises, you should write not only the class code, but also a small program to test the class.

1. Take a program exercise from any of the previous chapters and break it into a separate class and its test code. Use whatever class and method name seems appropriate.

2. Write the code for a class named **clsBinDec** that has a method named **convertDecToBin()**. The method accepts an integer value passed to it and returns a string with that integer number's binary representation. That is, if you pass in the integer value 10, the method returns a string: "0000 0000 0000 0000 0000 0000 0000 1010". Note that each nibble (4 bytes) is separated with a blank space.

3. Add a second method to the class named **clsBinDec** from Exercise 2 that is named **convertBinToDec()**. This method accepts a string containing the binary representation of an integer number and returns an **int** to the caller. For example, if you pass the string "0000 0000 0000 0000 0000 0000 0000 1010" to the method, it returns 10 as an integer value.

4. Programming Exercise 9 from Chapter 7 stated: Write a **static** leap year method that returns the value 1 if it is a leap year, and 0 if it is not a leap year. The algorithm is: If the year can be evenly divided by 4, but not by 100, it is a leap year. However, years that are evenly divisible by 400 are also leap years. Write a new class named **clsDateStuff** that incorporates a method named **leapYear()** that accepts an integer value as its argument.

5. Add two more methods to the **clsDateStuff** class named **getDays()**. The first method accepts a single integer value that is decoded as January = 1, February = 2, and so on. The overloaded version of the method accepts two arguments; the first is an integer denoting the month, and the second argument is an integer value that represents the year. The overloaded version is expected to return the proper number of days for leap years.

6. Write a class with a method that accepts two military times, such as 0830 and 1420, and returns the number of minutes between the two times. Call the class **clsMilitaryTime** and the method **militaryTimeDiff()**.

10

7. Write a class named **clsMoney** with a method named **getChange()** that accepts a **decimal** argument named **amount** plus four other integer arguments named **quarters**, **dimes**, **nickels**, and **pennies**. The method determines the proper number of coins necessary to return the exact change held in **amount**. For example, the call:

```
getChange(.75, quarters, dimes, nickels, pennies);
```

should return with **quarters** equal to 3 and the other arguments equal to 0.

CHAPTER

11

OBJECT PERSISTENCE USING DATA FILES

In the Essentials section you will learn:

- ◆ What object persistence is and why it is needed
- ◆ How the Windows File System is organized into drives, folders, and files
- ◆ How to use the `Directory` and `Path` classes in the `System.IO` namespace to manipulate the Windows File System
- ◆ The difference between text and binary data files
- ◆ How to persist object state information to sequential text files using the `StreamReader` and `StreamWriter` classes in the `System.IO` namespace
- ◆ How to persist object state information using tab-delimited text files using the `StreamReader` and `StreamWriter` classes in the `System.IO` namespace
- ◆ What object serialization is
- ◆ How to catch exceptions that might be thrown from file input and output operations

In the Bonus section you will learn:

- ◆ How to allow the user to specify a filename and location
- ◆ How to read information from fixed-width text files
- ◆ How to persist object state information using binary data files

In all the examples presented so far in this text, data have existed only in the computer's random access memory. When the programs end, the data are gone. Almost all applications benefit if some of the data can be saved between executions of the application. In other words, applications are more useful if the state of the objects that make up the application persists between the time the application is closed and the next time it is started. Modern information systems store this object state either in data files or in a relational database. Persisting objects to data files is the subject of this chapter. Persisting objects to a relational database is the subject of Chapter 13.

ESSENTIAL TOPICS

WHY IS OBJECT PERSISTENCE NEEDED?

In the applications discussed so far in this text, users enter information into the application using the application's user interface (UI), and then the program validates the data, processes the data, and displays the results of the processing to the user. When the user closes the application, any data that may have been entered are lost. The data are lost because the program merely saved the input values into variables, and as you've learned, variables are just names given to addresses in the computer's **random access memory (RAM)**. Computer RAM is sometimes called **volatile memory** because it loses its contents when the electricity is turned off. So, even if you didn't end the application before turning off the power to your computer, the contents of the computer's RAM would be lost.

In addition to volatile memory, computers have another way to store data, and its name is similar—non-volatile memory. **Non-volatile memory** is memory that doesn't lose its contents when the electricity is turned off. Non-volatile memory is also known as **external storage**. The most common device that computers use for non-volatile memory is a **hard drive**. (Hard drives are sometimes called disk drives or fixed disks.) A PC almost always has some type of fixed disk drive, but there are many other examples of external storage. Removable 3.5-inch disks (sometimes called floppy disks), Universal Serial Bus (USB) storage devices, magnetic tapes, compact discs (CDs), Compact Flash (CF) memory cards, and Secure Digital (SD) memory cards are all examples of non-volatile memory. Even portable music players and digital cameras connected to a computer through a USB port can serve as external storage.

> **External Storage**
>
> Because a fixed disk drive is one of the oldest and most common forms of non-volatile memory used by a computer, we use the term *disk* to refer to all forms of external storage. Note that the code you write to save data to a disk drive can also be used to save the data to other forms of external storage such as a USB storage device.

If non-volatile memory doesn't lose its contents, why do computers even bother using volatile memory? The reason is that volatile memory access is much faster than non-volatile memory access. To provide the best performance, computer software stores data in RAM while it is being manipulated. Then, after processing has finished, any information that needs to be recalled later is saved to disk.

In object-oriented terminology, **persistence** means storing an object in non-volatile memory. In other words, an object is made persistent by saving the information about its state to disk. In this chapter, you learn how to make objects persistent by saving their state information to sequential text files. (In Chapter 13, you will learn how to persist objects using a relational database management system.) Before you can learn to code for persistence, you must become familiar with the Windows File System.

THE WINDOWS FILE SYSTEM

The **Windows File System (WFS)** is the part of the Windows Operating System (OS) that handles the tasks of saving data to, and retrieving data from, external storage devices. Fortunately, it isn't vital for application developers to know exactly how the WFS does its job. It is also not essential to know where the WFS physically stores the data. What is important to know, however, is how data are logically organized on disk.

Much of the terminology used when discussing the WFS should be familiar to you, either because you have experience using a Windows PC or because many of the terms are carried over from a time when information was processed using paper. These terms include documents, files, and folders. At a general overview level, a PC stores data on external storage devices in a hierarchical fashion. A PC contains one or more disks. The space on a disk is organized into zero or many folders. Each folder contains zero or many subfolders or **files**.

Disks

A typical Windows PC contains one or more external storage devices. To uniquely identify each disk, Windows assigns each a one-character letter. For example, a PC's 3.5-inch disk drive normally is the "A drive," its fixed disk drive is the "C drive," and its CD drive is the "D drive."

Sometimes a physical storage device is divided into several logical drives called **partitions**. In this case, each partition is given a unique drive letter. With all the external storage options available, it is not uncommon for a PC to have five to ten drive letters assigned.

11

Folders

Folders are used to group related files. A folder can contain zero or more files, or zero or more subfolders. A subfolder can, in turn, contain zero or more files, or zero or more subfolders of its own. Because folders are arranged in a hierarchy, they are often shown in a graphical user interface (GUI) using a tree structure as shown in Figure 11-1. A tree structure is so named because visually it resembles an upside-down tree branching out to the right from a single root at the top.

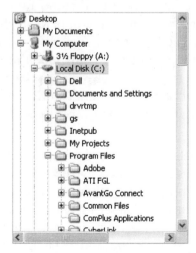

Figure 11-1   Windows folders shown in a hierarchy

Each folder is given a name so that it can be identified. Folder names must contain between 1 and 255 characters. Almost any character can be used as part of a filename, with the exception of the special characters ? * / \ : ; < >. Folder names are not case sensitive, but they are case-aware. This means that you can use a mixture of uppercase and lowercase letters when naming folders, but folder names must differ by more than just the case of the letters that make up the folder's name. For example, creating a folder named "My Documents" and another named "my documents" within the same subfolder is not allowed. Multiple folders can have the same name, but a subfolder's name must be unique within the folder in which it is contained.

In older versions of Windows (and in other operating systems) folders are called **directories**. (Microsoft started using the term "folders" instead of "directories" beginning with Windows 95 in order to make the term more analogous to the paper documents.) Don't be surprised if you find some of the .NET documentation and classes still using the term "directories." Just remember that directories and folders are the same thing.

Files

Files contain a sequence of bytes that represent information. For example, Microsoft Word stores information about each document you type in a file, a song can be stored in an MP3 file, and VS.NET stores the programs you are learning to write in files. Persisting objects to files is important not only because it eliminates the need for data to be reentered each time an application is run, but also because it allows information to be shared between people, or between applications. For example, one person can create a graphic using a drawing program, save it as a JPEG file, and e-mail it to someone else to view or edit.

Each file is given a name so that it can be identified. Files must be named using the same rules as folders. The filename must contain between 1 and 255 characters, the special characters ? * / \ : ; < > are not allowed, filenames are not case-sensitive, and filenames must be unique within the folder in which they are contained.

File Naming Conventions

In the first 13 years or so of the PC's existence, filenames were restricted to no more than eight uppercase characters, followed by a dot character, followed by three uppercase characters. This naming convention was known as the 8.3. (read "eight dot three") format. Many of the files that make up the Windows OS still use 8.3 naming format. Ask anyone who is old enough to remember and they'll tell you what a pain it was trying to give descriptive names to files when you only had 11 uppercase characters to work with! It wasn't until 1995 and Windows 95 when PC users were finally able to use long filenames and mixed-case letters.

Most files contain little or no information about how the data are organized within the file. How the information is stored in a file, called the **file format**, is determined by the software that is used to create the file. Sometimes the file formats are very simple, and other times they are very complex. (Don't panic, you'll be using simple file formats in this chapter.) Many times, file formats are standardized so that files can be used by many applications from different vendors. For example, the MP3 format is a standard file format used to store music, and HTML (Hypertext Markup Language) is a standard format for describing how a Web page should be displayed in a Web browser.

Files on a PC normally have a three (sometimes four) character suffix. This suffix, or **file extension**, is used to help identify the file's type. For example, Microsoft Word documents have a .doc extension, compressed files might have a .zip extension, and executable programs have an .exe extension.

Many computer users who are not familiar with the WFS confuse a file extension with the contents of the file. The file extension *does not dictate what is contained within the file*. Rather, files of the same type are given the same extension to make them easier to work with. For example, when you double-click a file, Windows attempts to see if an application is installed on your computer that knows how to process a file with that extension. If Windows finds such an application, it starts the application and tells the application to open the file. For example, if you double-click a file with an .sln extension, Windows starts VS.NET and tells it to open your C# application solution. However, just because a file has an .sln extension doesn't mean it is indeed a VS.NET file. After all, there is nothing to prevent some devious person from renaming a .doc file to .exe and giggling when you try to run the file. To experiment, find a file on your computer, rename it so that is has a .doc extension, double-click it, and see if Microsoft Word starts and tries to open it. Don't be surprised if you see an error message.

Many Windows computers, by default, hide information about the file system from you. For the average computer user, this may indeed be a good idea. However, we believe that as a software developer you benefit by seeing everything about the file system, including file extensions, paths, and hidden files. To configure Windows Explorer to show you as much information as possible, follow these steps:

1. Start the Windows Explorer by double-clicking the **My Computer** icon, or by clicking **Start → Run**, and type **explorer** in the Run dialog box.

2. From the Windows Explorer menu, choose **View → Details**.

3. From the Windows Explorer menu, choose **Tools → Folder Options**.

4. From the View tab (shown in Figure 11-2), select the **Apply to All Folders** button and select Yes to the confirmation dialog so that the Windows Explorer will show the details for all folders and files.

5. From the Advanced settings list on the View tab, set these options:

- **Display the contents of system folders** should be checked.

- **Display the full path in the address bar** should be checked.

- **Display the full path in the title bar** should be checked.

- **Hidden files and folders** should be set to **Show hidden files and folders.**

- **Hide extensions of known file types** should not be checked.

11

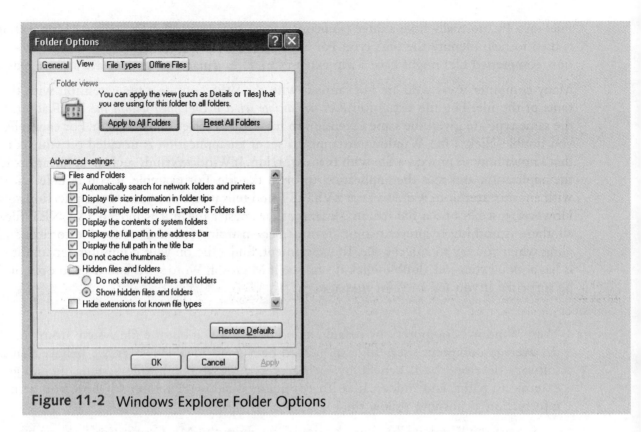

Figure 11-2 Windows Explorer Folder Options

To completely and uniquely identify a file's location, you need to know:

1. The drive letter of the disk

2. The folders and subfolders in which the file is contained

3. The filename

4. The file extension

The drive letter is followed by a colon and backward slash (:\ ), folders are separated by backward slashes ("backslashes"), and the filename and extension are separated by a dot. The drive letter and folder names are known collectively as the file's **path**. A few samples are shown in Figure 11-3.

```
C:\AUTOEXEC.BAT
C:\WINDOWS\NOTEPAD.EXE
C:\Program Files\WinZip\WINZIP32.EXE
C:\Program Files\Microsoft Office\Office\WINWORD.EXE
D:\My Projects\CarpetCost\CarpetCost.sln
D:\My Music\BoDeans\Resolution\01 - If It Makes You.mp3
```

Figure 11-3 Sample files shown with complete paths

THE .NET System.IO NAMESPACE

Recall that the .NET framework groups classes for similar functionality into namespaces. You might expect there to be a namespace that contains classes for interacting with the WFS. **System.IO** is that namespace. The classes within the **System.IO** namespace can be grouped into two distinct functions: 1) classes that manipulate the file system (for example, creating folders and deleting files), and 2) classes for saving and retrieving data to and from external storage devices.

The classes for manipulating the file system are covered in this section. Later sections show you how to use **System.IO** classes to persist state information to and from a file. A complete discussion of all **System.IO** classes is beyond the scope of this text. Instead, we present several of the classes and methods we think you'll find most useful. After reviewing the following sections, it is recommended that you use the VS.NET Help to discover more details.

System.IO.Directory

The **Directory** class exposes methods that can be used to create, delete, move, and list subfolders and files. (Recall the term *folder* is now more commonly used than the older term *directory*, but the older term is used in many technical references such as the **System.IO** namespace.) Because the methods are defined as **static**, they must be called using the class name and not using an instance variable name. Table 11-1 lists the essential methods of the **Directory** class.

Table 11-1   Essential System.IO.Directory methods

Method	Description
Directory.CreateDirectory	This method creates the folder specified in the argument. If the folder already exists, calling this method has no effect.
	This example creates a folder named "C:\My Projects".
| | ```
1    string newFolderName;
2    newFolderName = @"C:\My Projects";
3    Directory.CreateDirectory(newFolderName);
``` |
| Directory.Delete | This method deletes the folder specified in the argument. An exception is thrown if the folder cannot be deleted for some reason, for example, if a file within the folder is being used. Note that this method does not send the folder to the Recycle Bin, nor does it ask the user for a confirmation, so be sure to use this method with caution. |
| | This example deletes the folder "C:\My Projects". Note that an exception is thrown if the folder is not empty. |
| | ```
1    string folderName;
2    folderName = @"C:\My Projects";
3    Directory.Delete(folderName);
``` |
| | If you want to delete a folder and all its contents, including subfolders, pass **true** as a second argument: |
| | ```
1    string folderName;
2    folderName = @"C:\My Projects";
3    Directory.Delete(folderName, true);
``` |
| Directory.Exists | This method returns **true** or **false**, depending on whether the path passed as an argument exists or not. |
| | This example displays a message if the folder "C:\My Projects" does not exist. |
| | ```
1    string folderName;
2    folderName = @"C:\My Projects";
3
4    if (Directory.Exists(folderName) == false)
5    {
6        messageBoxOK(folderName + " does not exist.");
7    }
``` |

11

Table 11-1   Essential System.IO.Directory methods (continued)

Method	Description
Directory.GetDirectories	This method returns a collection of subfolders found in the folder passed as an argument.
	This example adds all the subfolders within folder `"C:\My Projects"` to a list box.

	<pre>1 string folderName;
	2 folderName = @"C:\My Projects";
	3 lstSubFolders.Items.Clear();
	4 foreach (string subFolder in Directory.GetDirectories(folderName))
	5 {
	6 lstSubFolders.Items.Add(subFolder);
	7 }</pre>

	The GetDirectories method accepts a second parameter. When it is passed a search pattern as the second argument, only those folders whose names match the pattern are returned. For example, to get only folders that begin with "My" use:
	`Directory.GetDirectories(folderName, "My*")`
Directory.GetFiles	This method returns a collection of files found in the folder passed as an argument.
	This example adds all the files within the folder `"C:\My Projects"` to a list box.

	<pre>1 string folderName;
	2 folderName = @"C:\My Projects";
	3 lstFiles.Items.Clear();
	4 foreach (string file in Directory.GetFiles(folderName))
	5 {
	6 lstSubFolders.Items.Add(file);
	7 }</pre>

	The GetFiles method accepts a second parameter. When passed a search pattern as the second argument, only those files whose names match the pattern are returned. For example, to get only files of type .MP3, use:
	`Directory.GetFiles(folderName, "*.mp3")`
Directory.Move	Calling this method moves a folder and its contents, including subfolders and files, to a new folder location.
	This example moves a folder named `"C:\My Projects"` and its contents to `"X:\Shared\My Projects"`:

	<pre>1 string oldFolderName;
	2 string newFolderName;
	3
	4 oldFolderName = @"C:\My Projects";
	5 newFolderName = @"X:\Shared\My Projects";
	6
	7 Directory.Move(oldFolderName, newFolderName);</pre>

	Note that the folder and its contents are moved, not copied. Therefore, this method can effectively be used to rename a folder by "moving" it with a different filename. For example:

	<pre>1 string oldFolderName;
	2 string newFolderName;
	3
	4 oldFolderName = @"X:\Shared\My Projects";
	5 newFolderName = @"X:\Shared\My New Projects";
	6
	7 Directory.Move(oldFolderName, newFolderName);</pre>

System.IO.File

The `File` class exposes methods that can be used to copy, delete, and move files. The `File` methods are defined as **static** just as they are in the `Directory` class. Therefore, they must be called using the class name and not using an instance variable name. Table 11-2 lists the essential `File` methods.

Table 11-2 Essential System.IO.File methods

Method	Description
`File.Copy`	This method can be called to make a copy of a file.
	The following example copies a file named `"C:\My Projects\Employees.dat"` to `"X:\Backups\Employees.bak"`:
| | ```
1    string fileName;
2    string copyName;
3
4    fileName = @"C:\My Projects\Employees.dat";
5    copyName = @"X:\Backups\Employees.bak";
6
7    File.Copy(fileName, copyName);
``` |
| | Note that if the destination name (copyName) already exists, an exception is thrown. To force the copy to overwrite the existing file, pass **true** as a third argument to the Copy method as shown here: |
| | ```
File.Copy(fileName, copyName, true);
``` |
	An exception is also thrown if the destination contains a path that doesn't exist.
`File.Delete`	This method deletes the file specified in the argument. Note that this method does not send the file to the Recycle Bin, nor ask the user for a confirmation, so be sure to use it with caution. An exception is thrown if the file cannot be deleted for some reason—for example, if the file is being used by another program.
	This example deletes the file `"C:\My Projects\Employees.dat"`.
| | ```
1    string fileName;
2    fileName = @"C:\My Projects\Employees.dat";
3    File.Delete(fileName);
``` |
| `File.Exists` | This method returns **true** or **false** depending on whether the path and filename passed as an argument exists or not. |
| | This example displays a message informing the user as to the existence of the file `"C:\My Projects\Employees.dat"`. |
| | ```
1    string fileName;
2    fileName = @"C:\My Projects\Employees.dat";
3
4    if (File.Exists(fileName) == true)
5    {
6        messageBoxOK(fileName + " does exist.");
7    }
8    else
9    {
10       messageBoxOK(fileName + " does not exist.");
11   }
``` |

11

Table 11-2   Essential System.IO.File methods (continued)

Method	Description
`File.Move`	Calling this method moves a file from one folder to another.
	This example moves a file named `"C:\My Projects\Employees.dat"` and its contents to `"X:\Shared\My Projects\Employees.dat"`:

	<pre>1 string fileName;
	2 string newFileName;
	3
	4 fileName = @"C:\My Projects\Employees.dat";
	5 newFileName = @"X:\Shared\My Projects\Employees.dat";
	6
	7 File.Move(fileName, newFileName);</pre>

	Note that this method can also be used to rename a file by "moving" it to the same folder but with a different filename. For example:

	<pre>1 string fileName;
	2 string newFileName;
	3
	4 fileName = @"C:\My Projects\Employees.dat";
	5 newFileName = @"C:\My Projects\NewEmployees.dat ";
	6
	7 File.Move(fileName, newFileName);</pre>

System.IO.Path

The methods in the **Path** class don't actually manipulate folders and files. Instead, the methods in the **Path** class can be used to manipulate the strings that define a folder's or file's path. Table 11-3 lists the essential **Path** methods.

Table 11-3   Essential System.IO.Path methods

Method	Description
`ChangeExtension`	This method can be called to change the file extension of the filename passed to it. It returns a string containing the new path and filename. This example:
	`Path.ChangeExtension(@"C:\Employees.dat", "bak")`
	returns a string containing:
	`"C:\Employees.bak"`
`Combine`	Call this method to concatenate a subfolder or filename to a path. It returns a string containing the new path. For example:
	`Path.Combine(@"C:\My Projects\", "Employees.dat")`
	returns a string containing:
	`"C:\My Projects\Employees.dat"`
	You might wonder why you should use `Path.Combine` rather than simply using the string concatenation operator (+) to combine a path with a filename. The reason is that `Path.Combine` does more than just concatenate the two strings. It checks the first argument to see if it ends in a backslash. If the argument doesn't end in a backslash, `Path.Combine` adds one before combining it with the second argument. In other words, these two examples of `Path.Combine`:
	`Path.Combine(@"C:\My Projects", "Employees.dat")` `Path.Combine(@"C:\My Projects\", "Employees.dat")`
	return the same value. But these two concatenations don't:
	`@"C:\My Projects\" + "Employees.dat"` `@"C:\My Projects" + "Employees.dat"`

Table 11-3 Essential System.IO.Path methods (continued)

Method	Description

`GetDirectoryName`	This method returns a string containing the path, without the filename, for the path passed as the argument. This example:
	
	`Path.GetDirectoryName(@"C:\My Projects\Employees.dat")`
	
	returns a string containing:
	
	`"C:\My Projects"`

`GetExtension`	You can pass this method a filename or a path that includes a filename and it returns a string containing the file's extension, including the dot. For example:
	
	`Path.GetExtension(@"C:\My Projects\Employees.dat")`
	
	returns a string containing:
	
	`".dat"`

`GetFileName`	This method returns a string containing the filename with the file extension of the path that is passed as an argument. For example:
	
	`Path.GetFileName(@"C:\My Projects\Employees.dat")`
	
	returns a string containing:
	
	`"Employees.dat"`

`GetFileNameWithoutExtension`	This method returns a string containing the filename *without* the file extension of the path that is passed as an argument. For example:
	
	`Path.GetFileName(@"C:\My Projects\Employees.dat")`
	
	returns a string containing:
	
	`"Employees"`

11

TYPES OF FILES

Although there are probably hundreds of file types in use on PCs, each is unique in the way the data are arranged in the file, we can reduce these differences to two basic file types: text files and binary files. You need to understand these two basic file types because the ways in which their data are stored and retrieved from disk are different.

Text and Binary Files

Data can be stored in a file as plain-text strings or as binary data. Some examples of file extensions you might be familiar with for binary files are .exe, .mp3, .jpg, and .doc. **Text files** usually have a file extension of .txt, but as you've learned, having a .txt extension doesn't guarantee that they contain plain text. Likewise, a file with an extension other than .txt might contain plain text. Both text and binary data files have advantages and disadvantages.

When stored as plain text, all information is stored as strings. Data that are not normally stored as text strings in RAM, such as numbers, dates, and Booleans, must be converted to strings before being saved to a text file. In the same way, when these non-string types are restored from a text file, they must be converted back to the appropriate data types. This type conversion is the same process that a program uses when accepting input from a text box and displaying the results to the user. This conversion to and from strings is not necessary when saving data to a binary data file because variable values are represented in the same way in the file as they are in RAM. Therefore, saving data to a binary data file executes more efficiently than saving data to a text file. Storing some values in binary format can also result in a smaller file size.

However, plain-text files do have several advantages over binary data files. First, text files are a good choice for data that must be shared among different applications, especially when those applications run on computers with different operating systems. For example, the way numbers are stored in binary format on a Windows computer may not be the same as the way numbers are stored in binary form on a computer running the Linux OS. Text files, therefore, are often used to communicate data between two dissimilar systems because text characters generally are stored in the same way on these different computing systems. HTML files are a good example of using plain text to communicate information between different computer systems. Similarly, text files can be used to export and import data between different applications. For example, you can export data from a Microsoft Excel spreadsheet as a plain-text file, and then import it into Microsoft Access.

One final advantage of plain-text files, and the most important for our purposes at this time, is that saving data to plain-text files makes testing and debugging your programs easier—especially for students beginning to learn to program. The reason testing and debugging are easier is that the contents of the text file can be viewed using a simple text editor application like Windows Notepad. Viewing and comprehending the contents of a binary file requires knowledge beyond the scope of this text. (Note, however, that the Bonus Section of this chapter does demonstrate how to save and restore object state using binary data files.) Figure 11-4 shows two text files and one binary data file opened in Windows Notepad. Can you tell which one is the binary file?

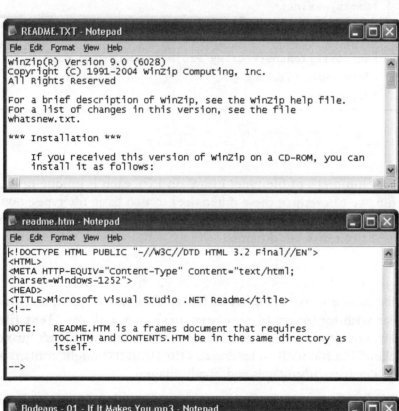

Figure 11-4   Text and binary files opened in Notepad

Sequential Data Files

Another classification of data files involves how your program accesses them. Files can be accessed either randomly or sequentially. With random access files, your program can process the data at any location in the file at any time. A common analogy is a DVD player that lets you skip from one part of a movie to the next without having to watch the parts in between. With sequential access files, the data in the file are accessed by beginning at the start of the file and reading the data one piece at a time in sequential order until all data have been processed. **Sequential files** are like VHS videotape players in which you have to fast forward or rewind, reading all the tape in between, as you move from one part of the video to another. Because sequential access is simpler to program and is quite useful for certain applications, we are limiting our discussion to sequential file access.

Before you study the C# source code to process sequential data files, you need to know how data are organized within this type of file. You also need to be familiar with the terminology used to describe this organization. Consider the sample employee information shown in Table 11-4.

Table 11-4   Sample employee information

Plant	Dept	EmplID	LastName	FirstName	DateHired	SalaryInd	Gender	PayRate
ATL	1200	010860008	Peace	Warren	12/28/1981	Yes	M	58,000.00
ATL	1200	112380012	Melon	Walter	01/28/1980	Yes	M	56,000.00
ATL	1200	112590013	Warmwater	Luke	12/28/1981	No	M	6.90
ATL	1200	112730014	Lesse	Moira	01/28/1980	Yes	F	152,800.00
PAC	1000	112900043	Feeding	Karen	07/20/1985	Yes	F	305,200.00
ATL	1100	113230004	Whelan	Rod	12/28/1981	Yes	M	98,200.00
ATL	1200	011480009	Mellow	Marcia	01/28/1980	No	F	22.45
ATL	1200	115320015	Vader	Ella	12/28/1981	Yes	F	34,270.00
ATL	1200	115510016	Kleerly	Seymour	12/28/1981	Yes	M	17,000.00
CTL	3000	011700024	Seville	Barbara	03/07/1984	No	F	13.70

11

A **record** is a set of information that describes a single entity. Each record contains the same type of information about each entity. A sequential data file can contain zero or more records. If the data in Table 11-4 were saved to a sequential data file, the file would contain 10 records. If a file happens to contain zero records, the file is said to be empty. While not a usual occurrence, empty files do make sense in some cases. For example, if a file contained the sales records for your organization for a given month and you had no sales during that month, then your sales records file for that month would be empty.

A record can contain one or more pieces of information about each entity. Each piece of information is called a **field**. Each record in Table 11-4 contains nine fields (Plant, Dept, EmplID, LastName, FirstName, DateHired, SalaryInd, Gender, and PayRate). If you recall the discussion in Chapter 10 about object properties, you should note that the fields in a record are like the properties of an object. The fact that some or all the fields have different values is what makes it possible to distinguish one record from another.

There are many common formats for saving information in sequential data files using plain text. Some examples include fixed-width, comma-separated values (CSV), and tab-delimited. Figure 11-5 shows how the information from Table 11-4 might look if it were saved in these formats and then opened using Notepad. Note there is no information in the files that indicates what the data are—they are just a series of characters. Remember, the content of a data file is determined by the application, or applications, that process it.

Fixed-width text file

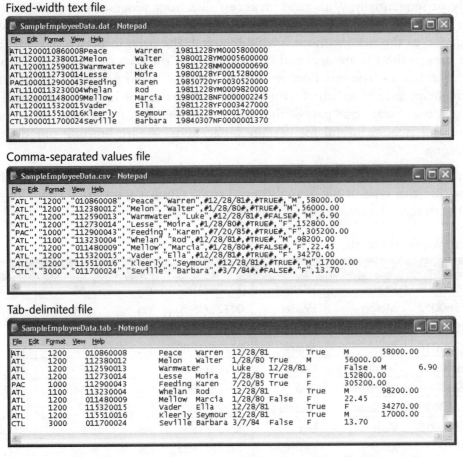

Comma-separated values file

Tab-delimited file

Figure 11-5 Employee information saved in fixed-width, CSV, and tab-delimited format

C# doesn't have an easy mechanism for processing CSV files, so the examples in the Essentials Section of this chapter use tab-delimited files for persisting object state. (You can read about fixed-width files in the Bonus Section of this chapter.)

Tab-delimited files are so named because a single tab character is placed between each field in the records. The tab characters allow programs to know where one field ends and another begins. When a tab-delimited file is opened using a text editor application (for example, Notepad), the tab characters aren't displayed on the screen. Instead, the text editors display the fields in predefined columns. If the information for one field overflows into the next field, as it does for the last name in record 3 of the bottom sample in Figure 11-5, the columns won't align perfectly. But don't be fooled. There is only 1 byte between the fields in the file—the tab character.

Similarly, each record ends with a special 2-byte sequence, so programs can determine the end of a record. This 2-byte sequence is called **carriage return and line feed (CRLF)**, and can be coded in C# using the string **"\r\n"**. (The **\r** and **\n** escape sequences were discussed in Chapter 3.) The CRLF name is a legacy term from the early days of computing when printers were modeled after manual typewriters (see the sidebar).

Just as text editor applications don't display tab characters, they generally don't display the CRLF characters either. Instead, text editors display the next record beginning on the next line whenever a CRLF is found.

Borrowing from Outdated Technology

Many terms used with modern computer technology existed long before computers did. The inventors of computer systems often used terminology from other domains to describe parts of these new systems. For example, folders and files were used with paper documents before they were used with a computer's file system. Carriage return and line feed are other examples.

Carriage return and line feed date back to the earliest manual typewriters. These typewriters had a carriage mechanism that held a piece of paper and moved the paper under the striking area of the typewriter keys. When the typed text reached the right margin of the typewriter, a bell would ring and the typewriter operator had to slide a big lever to return the carriage back to the left margin of the paper. At the same time, the paper would be advanced up by the height of one row of typed text—the line feed—so the operator could continue typing.

Because early computer printers were adapted from typewriter technology, the terms carriage return and line feed continue to be used today.

PERSISTENCE USING SEQUENTIAL TEXT FILES

11

The steps used to process a file are almost always the same no matter what programming language you use. The terminology for processing files is the same you use when describing how a person uses a paper file. First, the file is opened. Next, you read data from the file, or write data to it. Last, the file is closed when you are finished with it. Reading data from a file is another form of input and writing data to a file is another form of output. Therefore, you often see the term **File I/O** when file input and output processing is discussed.

When a computer program reads data from a file, the information is copied from disk to the variables in memory. When processing text files, the numbers, dates, and Booleans must be converted from textual string values to the appropriate C# data types, just as you convert input from a text box. Writing data to a file causes the contents of variables to be copied to disk. With text files, numbers, dates, and Booleans, the values must be converted to a string representation, just as when they are displayed on a UI form.

If you were guessing that the .NET class library contains classes that allow you to easily read and write tab-delimited text files, you'd be only half-right. To read and write sequential text files with C#, you use the .NET **StreamReader** and **StreamWriter** classes, but you have to write your own code to use streams with tab-delimited text files. Streams are a concept C# uses for input and output, but streams are not limited to files. For example, streams are used when sending data to another program over a network connection. Streams are more flexible than files, but with this extra flexibility comes more complexity.

To illustrate how to save an object's state to a sequential text file, let's make a form persist information about its state. When the application is closed, the form should save its screen position and then move itself back to that same position when the application is restarted. Saving program information before terminating is common with many Windows applications. (Guess how your favorite spreadsheet or word processing program remembers the names of the last several files you worked with.)

The first step is to start a new project. Alternatively, you can modify one of the projects you created in a previous chapter. The code in this section assumes a new project named **StatefulForm**. There is only one set of properties to set differently than you have for the forms in other programs—make sure you set **FormBorderStyle = Sizable** and **StartPosition = Manual**. A **FormBorderStyle** of **Sizable** lets the user resize the form as well as move it around on the screen. Setting **StartPosition = Manual** indicates that the form's startup position is set using code rather than automatically centering it on the screen as you've done before.

 tip ▶ Don't forget to add the **using** statement for the **System.IO** namespace to any class that contains file I/O processing:

```
1    using System;
2    using System.IO;
3    using System.Windows.Forms;
```

Next, you need to choose a filename to store the form's state information and the path where you want the file to exist. For a path, you could choose something simple like **"C:\"**, but coding a path in your program like this (so-called **hard coding**) isn't a good idea for real applications. Hard-coded paths aren't a good idea because a path that exists on your computer might not exist on someone else's computer. Hard-coded paths can result in exceptions if the program is ever run on a computer different from the one on which it was developed.

Instead of using hard-coded paths, you should set the path for the state file to the folder where the application is running. This path can easily be determined when the application runs by using **Application.StartupPath** to get the full path to the location from which the application's .exe file is run. The filename of the state file can be just about anything. For this example, use **FormState.dat**.

Using a .dat File Extension

When the file contains textual data that are to be read directly without further processing, such as an e-mail or letter, it is common to use the .txt file extension. However, when a textual file contains data that are stored in a text file, it is common to use a .dat file extension. Files with a .dat extension often contain data that have to be processed (that is, converted from a string data type to perhaps a numeric data type) before they can be used.

For testing purposes, you should first write the code to store the form's state information. After you are sure that this code works properly, you can then write the code that restores the form's state. When the user closes a form, the form's **Closing** event is executed. Therefore, you need to write the code to store the form's state in the **frmMain_Closing** method, as shown in Figure 11-6. Don't forget to use the Properties Window to connect this method with the **Closing** event, as shown in Chapter 2.

```
66   private void frmMain_Closing(object sender, System.ComponentModel.CancelEventArgs e)
67   {
68        // Save the form's position and size to the state file.
69
70        string pathFileName = Path.Combine(Application.StartupPath, "FormState.dat");
71
72        StreamWriter sw = new StreamWriter(pathFileName);
73
74        sw.WriteLine(Left.ToString());
75        sw.WriteLine(Top.ToString());
76        sw.WriteLine(Width.ToString());
77        sw.WriteLine(Height.ToString());
78
79        sw.Close();
80   }
```

Figure 11-6 Saving a form's position and size to a sequential text file

Let's review the code in Figure 11-6. The statement on line 70 creates a string that contains the full path and filename for the state file by combining the path of the application's executable file with the string literal **FormState.dat**. The statement on line 72 instantiates a **StreamWriter** object. Because the filename is passed to the **StreamWriter**'s constructor, the file is opened and the **StreamWriter** object is associated with the file. It is important to note that, if you open a file in this manner and the file already exists, the existing file is overwritten. If you don't intend to replace the existing file with a new one, you should add code to determine if the file exists before opening it.

The statements on lines 74 through 77 call the **StreamWriter**'s **WriteLine** method to save the form's **Left**, **Top**, **Width**, and **Height** properties to the file. The **WriteLine** method writes one record to the file. The **WriteLine** method also automatically adds CRLF to the end of each record as it is written to the file. Note how the form's position and size properties are converted to strings because we want to illustrate that the data are stored as plain text. Finally, the statement on line 79 closes the file.

11

How Buffering Works

You should know that when you call the **StreamWriter**'s **WriteLine** method, the data aren't immediately written to the disk file. Instead, the Windows operating system uses a process of buffering (sometimes called caching) when performing file I/O.

Buffering simply means that a chunk of volatile memory is used to hold data that need to be written to a file. When the amount of data in the buffer reaches a limit set by Windows, the contents of the buffer are physically written to the file. Because this buffer size is likely much larger than a single record, your code might call the **WriteLine** method many times before the data are actually written to disk. Whenever you close a file, any data remaining in the buffer are written to disk. Therefore, if you try to view the contents of an output file before the application has closed it, you might not see all the records that have been written to it. For that reason, it is important to always remember to close the file. If the file is never closed, data remaining in the buffer may never get physically written to the file.

Operating systems use buffering to speed execution because writing a small amount of data to disk is much less efficient than saving a small amount of data in memory.

After you've coded the **Closing** event method, run the application, move the form to a new position and resize it, and then close the form. (The first time you run this application, you should see the form start in the upper-left corner of the screen. The form appears there because we haven't yet added code to reposition the form at startup.) When you closed the application, the form's position and size should have been saved in the state file. To verify that the application worked, follow these steps:

1. Use the Windows Explorer to navigate to your application's startup folder (this should be the same path as that for the location where your source code is saved).

2. Navigate to the bin\debug folder.

3. Find the file named FormState.dat.

4. Open this file with Notepad and observe its contents.

The contents should be similar to Figure 11-7, except that the number values will be different. You should see four records, each with one field. These numbers should be integers that represent the position and the size of the form when it was closed. Note that we could have written just one record that contained all four values and separated the fields with tabs. For simplicity's sake, we used this four-record, single-field format. (Using tabs as field separators is covered in the next section.)

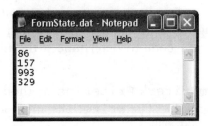

Figure 11-7   FormState.dat viewed using Notepad

To restore the form to its previous position and size, add code to the form's constructor method as shown in Figure 11-8. The program examples from earlier chapters included only line 5, so the main form for those applications always starts at the same place. Now when the application begins, the location and size of the form are changed based on the information that was stored in the **FormState.dat** file.

```
66    public frmMain()
67    {
68        // Initialize the UI.
69
70        InitializeComponent();
71
72        // Restore the form's position and size from the state file if it exists.
73
74        string inputValue;
75        string pathFileName = Path.Combine(Application.StartupPath, "FormState.dat");
76
77        if (File.Exists(pathFileName) == true)
```

Figure 11-8   Restoring a form's position and size from a text file

```
78        {
79                StreamReader sr = new StreamReader(pathFileName);
80
81                inputValue = sr.ReadLine();
82                Left = int.Parse(inputValue);
83
84                inputValue = sr.ReadLine();
85                Top = int.Parse(inputValue);
86
87                inputValue = sr.ReadLine();
88                Width = int.Parse(inputValue);
89
90                inputValue = sr.ReadLine();
91                Height = int.Parse(inputValue);
92
93                sr.Close();
94        }
95     }
```

Figure 11-8 Restoring a form's position and size from a text file (continued)

The purpose of the code in Figure 11-8 is as follows: Line 43 defines a string variable that is used to hold the value of each input record as it is read in from the state file. The statement on line 43 creates a string that contains the full path and filename just as was done when saving the state information.

Line 46 uses the **File.Exists** method to determine if the state file exists or not. If it does exist, the statements on lines 48 through 62 are executed. Normally the state file should exist, but it might not for some reason (for example, when the application is run for the first time). If you try to open a file for input that doesn't exist, an exception is thrown, so it's best to make sure that it exists before you try to open it. More coverage on how to use exception handling with files is presented in a later section in this chapter.

The statements on lines 50 through 60 are similar. An input record is read by calling the **StreamReader**'s **ReadLine** method. The **ReadLine** method gets one record from the input state file by reading all the data up to the CRLF (just one field in this example) and returns its contents as a string. In the code in Figure 11-8, that string value is then stored in variable **inputValue**. Note that the string returned from the **ReadLine** method does not include the CRLF end-of-record marker. After an input record is read, the **int.Parse** method is used to convert the input record values to integers. These integer values are then assigned to the form's **Left**, **Top**, **Width**, and **Height** properties. Finally, the statement on line 62 closes the file.

For the form's state to be saved and restored correctly, it is important to note that the order of the records written to the file must match the order of the records read from the file. In other words, the records are written so the first record contains the **Left** value, the second record contains the **Top** value, the third record contains the **Width** value, and the fourth record contains the **Height** value. Therefore, when restoring the state, the values must be read from the file in this same order. If you read these values in the wrong order, then the form's initial state will not be what you expect.

The previous example should give you an idea of how to process sequential text files using the `System.IO` namespace and streams for input and output. The code as shown in Figure 11-6 and 11-8 should work in most cases, but it needs enhancements to make it robust enough for real applications. Some suggested modifications include:

- When saving the form's position and size, first check to make sure that the form isn't minimized (a minimized form has `Left` and `Top` values of –32,000).

- Save and restore the form's `WindowState` property value so that the form can be restored to a maximized state if it was maximized when the form was closed.

- If the state file doesn't exist, default the position of the form to be the center of the screen.

- When restoring the form's position and size, make sure that it is not moved off the edge of the screen and therefore not visible to the user. This can happen if the user changes the screen's resolution from large (1920 × 1200) to small (800 × 600).

- Always add appropriate exception handlers when processing files.

These enhancements are left as an exercise for you. The next section shows a more complete example of persisting objects to a sequential data file.

A PROGRAM EXAMPLE

In Chapter 10, you created a class that encapsulated the properties and methods of a single contact object. A simple UI allowed the user to add, update, and delete these contact objects in a list. If ever a program were in need of persisting state information between executions, the contact program is. After all, why would anyone bother to type in all that contact information if it would be lost as soon as the application closes?

Serialization and Persistence

When storing an object's state, you often run into the term serialization. As with much object-oriented terminology, serializing is a big word with a simple meaning. **Serialization** is defined as converting an object's state information to a simple stream, or string, of data. This stream of data can be used to send the object to another computer over a network connection, or as you learn in this section, to make the object persistent. You should be aware that a complete discussion of serialization is beyond the scope of this text. The examples presented here are purposefully kept simple.

Tab-delimited sequential text files are a good choice for the Contacts List program. Tab-delimited text files can be easily imported into a database application such as Microsoft Access, and because their contents are plain text, you can easily verify a file's contents by opening the file in Notepad.

Before you begin enhancing the Contacts List program first presented in Chapter 10, you have several decisions to make:

1. What should the name of the file be, and what folder should it be saved in?

2. When should the contact objects be saved to the file?

3. When should the contact objects be restored from the file?

4. Which object should be responsible for persisting the contact objects?

For now, we suggest the file be named something descriptive, for example `Contacts.dat`, and be stored in the same folder as the application's .exe file (as was done with the `FormState.dat` file). When to save and restore the contact objects is also pretty obvious. When the application first starts, it makes sense to restore all contacts from the file and display them in the list box. The user can then add, update, and delete the contacts as needed. Finally, when the application closes, the list of contact objects should be saved back to the file, overwriting the old contents with the new list of contacts.

Now you have a plan for *where*, and *when*, but how about *which* objects should be responsible for persisting the contact objects? It turns out that at least two classes have to share this responsibility. The file needs to contain the state information for each contact object. Because the only object that has access to all of a contact object's state information is `clsContact`, it does part of the work. However, a single contact object only knows about itself. The only class that knows about all the contact objects in the list is `frmMain`. So, both `frmMain` and `clsContact` need enhancements in order to persist the entire list of contact objects to a file.

Saving the Contacts

To save the contact list to a file, you need to make these enhancements:

1. In `clsContact`, a public `Serialize` method needs to be added. When called, this method returns a single string that contains the current contact object's state information with each piece of state information (that is, its fields) separated by tab characters.

2. When the application is closing (the `frmMain_Closing` event), `frmMain` calls a `saveContacts` helper method. (You could add the logic directly in the `frmMain_Closing` method, but as you learned in Chapter 7, a well-behaved method has a single purpose so a private helper method should be created.) The `saveContacts` method opens a file using a `StreamWriter` object. Then, for each contact in the list, it calls the contact's `Serialize` method, and writes the returned string containing the contact's state information to a record in the file using the `StreamWriter`'s `WriteLine` method. After all contacts have been written, the file is closed.

3. The `saveContacts` method needs a path and a filename to use when opening the file. Because this same filename is needed later when the contacts are restored from the same file, the variable that contains the filename should be defined as a class member and initialized in the form's constructor. See Figure 11-9. Note that the path for the file defaults to the same path as that of the location from which the application's .exe is run using the `Application.StartupPath` property.

```
1    using System;
2    using System.IO;
3    using System.Windows.Forms;
4
5    public class frmMain: Form
6    {
7        private string mContactsFileName;

242  public static void Main()
243  {
```

Figure 11-9 Initializing the filename in the constructor

```
244          frmMain main = new frmMain();
245          Application.Run(main);
246    }
247
248    public frmMain()
249    {
250       InitializeComponent();
251
252       mContactsFileName = Path.Combine(Application.StartupPath, "Contacts.dat");
253    }
```

Figure 11-9 Initializing the filename in the constructor (continued)

Figure 11-10 shows the **clsContact.Serialize** method. This method is pretty straightforward. Each piece of state information is concatenated into one long string, and then returned to the calling method so that it can be written as a record. The **"\t"** escape sequence is used to place a tab character between each field. Note that the private member variables, which hold the state information for the contact, are used for the first and last name.

```
123    public string Serialize()
124    {
125        return mFirstName              + "\t"
126            + mLastName                + "\t"
127            + HomePhone.ToString()     + "\t"
128            + MobilePhone.ToString()   + "\t"
129            + BirthDate.ToString();
130    }
```

Figure 11-10 The clsContact.Serialize method

It's a good idea to write a helper method to save the contact information. The helper method can be called when you close the form as well as within any other method in which the contacts should be saved (such as the click event method for a save contacts button). Figure 11-11 shows the changes to the **frmMain_Closing** event method and the **saveContacts** method. The **frmMain_Closing** event simply calls the **saveContacts** helper method.

```
354    private void frmMain_Closing(object sender, System.ComponentModel.CancelEventArgs e)
355    {
356        saveContacts();
357    }


443    private void saveContacts()
444    {
445        StreamWriter sw = null;
446        sw = new StreamWriter(mContactsFileName);
447        foreach (clsContact contact in lstContacts.Items)
448        {
449            sw.WriteLine(contact.Serialize());
450        }
451        sw.Close();
452    }
```

Figure 11-11 The frmMain_Closing event calling the saveContacts method

To make testing easier, it is recommended that you complete the previously mentioned enhancements to `clsContact` and `frmMain` before attempting to add the code that restores the contacts. After all, you can't test the loading of the contacts back into memory if they've never been saved to a file. To test the code, set a breakpoint in the `frmMain_Closing` method. Run the program, enter a few contacts, and close the application. Step through the code to make sure that the contact data are serialized and are written to the file. After your program finishes closing, use Notepad to open the `Contacts.dat` file and visually inspect the contents to make sure that the information was saved correctly.

Restoring the Contacts

When you are satisfied that the list of contacts is being saved, you can now make enhancements to restore the contacts from the file:

- In `clsContact`, add a **public** `Deserialize` method. This method works in just the opposite manner to the `Serialize` method. Instead of converting the object's state information to a tab-delimited string, the `Deserialize` method should be passed a tab-delimited string that was once created by the `Serialize` method. `Deserialize` then splits the string up and stores values back into the state, or property, variables of the object.

- As you might expect, the process of restoring the contacts from the file works in just the opposite manner to saving them. When the application is starting, the `frmMain` constructor method calls the helper method `loadContacts`. The `loadContacts` method opens a file using a `StreamReader` object. The first record is read, which contains a tab-delimited (serialized) string. A new contact object is instantiated and this new object's `Deserialize` method is called and passed the tab-delimited string to restore its state. The contact object's data are then displayed in the list box on the form. This process is repeated for the second record, the third record, and so on until all records have been processed.

Figure 11-12 shows the `clsContact.Deserialize` method. This method works in reverse of the `Serialize` method. Instead of concatenating all the state information into a big string, it restores the state information of the object by splitting up a big string into separate smaller strings. Each string value is then used to assign a property value back into each of the object's state variables. This processing of splitting a string into many values is often called **parsing**. Because each field value in the string is separated by a tab character, you can use the **string** class's `Split` method to separate the string into its appropriate values. The `Split` method returns an array of strings. Each element from the array can then be used to assign a value back into a state variable. Because all information is in the form of a string, some values have to be converted back into the correct data types (for example, phone numbers and birthdate).

11

```
133     public void Deserialize(string serializedContact)
134     {
135         string[] values = serializedContact.Split('\t');
136
137         mFirstName = values[0];
138         mLastName = values[1];
139         HomePhone = new clsPhoneNumber(values[2]);
140         MobilePhone = new clsPhoneNumber(values[3]);
141         BirthDate = DateTime.Parse(values[4]);
142     }
```

Figure 11-12   The clsContact.Deserialize method

Figure 11-13 shows the changes to the frmMain constructor and the loadContacts method. Line 255 in the constructor is added to call the restoreContacts method when the application starts. The restoreContacts method requires some explanation.

```
248     public frmMain()
249     {
250       InitializeComponent();
251
252       mContactsFileName = Path.Combine(Application.StartupPath, "Contacts.dat");
253       restoreContacts();
254     }


418     private void restoreContacts()
419     {
420         StreamReader sr = null;
421         string inputLine;
422         clsContact contact;
423
424         lstContacts.Items.Clear();
425
426         if (File.Exists(mContactsFileName) == true)
427         {
428             sr = new StreamReader(mContactsFileName);
429
430             inputLine = sr.ReadLine();
431             while (inputLine != null)
432             {
433                 contact = new clsContact();
434                 contact.Deserialize(inputLine);
435                 lstContacts.Items.Add(contact);
436                 inputLine = sr.ReadLine();
437             }
438             sr.Close();
439         }
440     }
```

Figure 11-13   Changes to the frmMain constructor and the restoreContacts method

Line 455 defines a StreamReader object the method uses to read in the contact state information. Line 456 defines a String variable to hold the contents of each record as it is read in from the file, and line 457 defines a variable used when instantiating a new contact object each time a record is read. Line 459 clears the contents list box to make sure that it is empty before the contacts are added to it.

Line 461 checks to make sure the file exists. If the `Contacts.dat` file doesn't exist, it doesn't necessarily mean that anything is wrong. It might just mean that the user hasn't entered any contacts yet, in which case the user is presented with an empty list. Line 463 instantiates the `StreamReader` object and passes the filename to its constructor to open the file.

Line 465 attempts to read the first input record. Note we said *attempts* to read it because, if the file exists but has no records (it is empty), the `ReadLine` method returns a `null` value. When processing a file sequentially using a `StreamReader` object, your program knows it has read all the records when `ReadLine` returns the value `null`. When all records have been read, the condition is known as end of file, or simply EOF.

The `while` loop, formed by lines 466 through 472, processes each record in the same manner. A new contact object is instantiated, and the input record is passed to its `Deserialize` method to restore its state. Next, the contact is added to the list box. Finally, line 471 attempts to read the next input record. The `while` loop is repeated until all records have been processed and `inputLine` equals `null`, at which time line 473 is executed to close the file.

That's all there is to persisting a list of objects to a file! Add `Serialize` and `Deserialize` methods to the object's class. Use a `StreamWriter` object to write the serialized object's state to a sequential data file, and use a `StreamReader` object to read and restore the serialized objects from a sequential file. That's almost all there is to it. You still need to add code to catch exceptions.

Catching Exceptions

When run, the application presented in the previous section should work fine as long as nothing is wrong with the `Contacts.dat` file. However, many things can go wrong when a program is processing files. The `restoreContacts` method does check to see if the file exists before attempting to process it, but just because it exists, doesn't mean that it can be processed without problems. For example, opening a file can fail if the file is in use by another program, or if the user doesn't have permissions to read the file. Even if the file can be opened, the content of the file could be corrupt and cause the `clsContact.Deserialize` method to fail.

You learned in Chapter 6 that when such errors occur at run time, an exception is thrown. If your code doesn't catch the exception, your program terminates abnormally. To make sure that the Contacts List application won't terminate because of a file exception, general exception handlers should be added to the `saveContacts` and `restoreContacts` methods. In fact, a good rule of thumb is that any code that processes files should always be wrapped in a `try` block.

The `saveContacts` and `restoreContacts` methods with general exception handlers are shown in Figures 11-14 and 11-15. Note that proper exception handling adds a considerable number of statements.

11

```
457    private void saveContacts()
458    {
459        StreamWriter sw = null;
460        try
461        {
462            sw = new StreamWriter(mContactsFileName);
463            foreach (clsContact contact in lstContacts.Items)
464            {
465                sw.WriteLine(contact.Serialize());
466            }
467        }
468        catch (Exception ex)
469        {
470            messageBoxOK("Error saving contacts to file "
471                + mContactsFileName + ". " + ex.Message);
472        }
473        finally
474        {
475            if (sw != null)
476            {
477                sw.Close();
478            }
479        }
480    }
```

Figure 11-14 The saveContacts method with exception handling

```
418    private void restoreContacts()
419    {
420        StreamReader sr = null;
421        string inputLine;
422        clsContact contact;
423
424        lstContacts.Items.Clear();
425
426        try
427        {
428            if (File.Exists(mContactsFileName) == true)
429            {
430                sr = new StreamReader(mContactsFileName);
431
432                inputLine = sr.ReadLine();
433                while (inputLine != null)
434                {
435                    contact = new clsContact();
436                    contact.Deserialize(inputLine);
437                    lstContacts.Items.Add(contact);
438                    inputLine = sr.ReadLine();
439                }
440            }
441        }
442        catch(Exception ex)
```

Figure 11-15 The restoreContacts method with exception handling

```
443        {
444            messageBoxOK("Error restoring contacts from file "
445              + mContactsFileName + ". " + ex.Message);
446        }
447        finally
448        {
449            if (sr != null)
450            {
451                sr.Close();
452            }
453        }
454    }
```

Figure 11-15 The restoreContacts method with exception handling (continued)

In both Figures 11-14 and 11-15, pay particular attention to the **finally** block. Recall that the **finally** block is always executed whether an exception occurs or not. Until now, you didn't really have a good reason to use the **finally** block, but the **finally** block is the perfect place to close files. However, you can't simply close the file. Instead, you must first make sure that the file was actually opened. If you attempt to close a file that is never opened, another type of exception is thrown. The approach used in Figures 11-14 and 11-15, is to compare the **StreamWriter** or **StreamReader** variable to **null**. If the variables don't have a value **null**, then the files were opened and so need to be closed. If the files weren't opened, then the variables have a value of **null** and therefore don't need to be closed.

Now you know the minimum work involved in creating a robust application that persists an object to a sequential tab-delimited file. The next section describes how your program can allow the user to specify the name and paths of files, as well as how your application can persist object state to different types of files.

BONUS TOPICS

FILE OPEN AND FILE SAVE DIALOGS

In the examples presented earlier in this chapter, objects have been persisted to a file that is always in the same folder as the application's .exe. For some types of data, this default behavior works well. For example, you want your application to automatically restore the form state information (position and size) without user intervention as you did earlier in the chapter. However, applications can often be made more useful if they allow the user to specify a filename and path when the file is opened.

The task of asking a user to specify a filename and path occurs so frequently that the .NET Framework includes two classes to make this task easier—**OpenFileDialog** and **SaveFileDialog**. These two don't actually open or save anything. Instead, they just allow the user to easily specify a filename and path. You use **OpenFileDialog** when you want to ask the user to specify a filename and path for a file that should already exist. You use **SaveFileDialog** when you want to ask the user to specify a filename and path for a new file (one that doesn't already exist). Figure 11-16 shows the GUI for both dialogs.

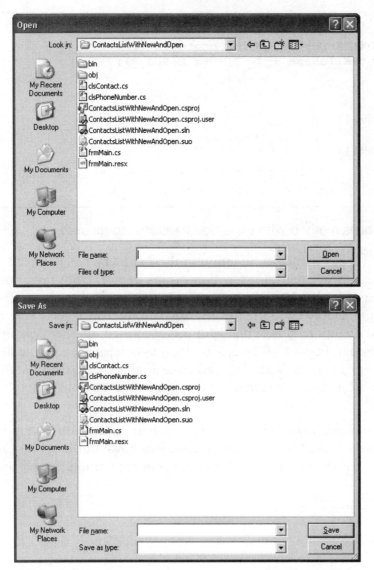

Figure 11-16   The OpenFileDialog and SaveFileDialog classes in action

The Contacts List program is one such application that could benefit from allowing the user to specify the filename and path. Users could then have multiple contacts files. For example, one contacts file for business contacts and another for personal contacts. Adding this functionality turns out to be pretty easy.

The Contacts List UI must be changed to give users a way to tell the program when to open a contacts file. The users also need a way to tell the program to create a new contacts file. Figure 11-17 shows a modified UI for the Contacts List application that contains New and Open buttons. For ease of use, the application should automatically save any existing contacts whenever the application closes, just before a file is opened, and just before creating a new file.

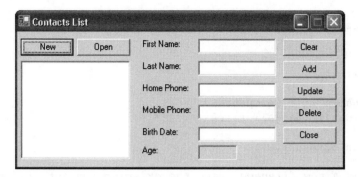

Figure 11-17 The Contacts List UI with New and Open buttons

The changes to the source code are also fairly minor. The previous version of the Contacts List application uses a default filename and path when the application starts and automatically loads the contacts from this file. If you allow the user to specify the filename, you shouldn't automatically load a file. So the **frmMain** constructor needs to be changed to initialize the filename to **null**, and the call to the **restoreContacts** method needs to be removed. The previous version of the Contacts List application also automatically saved the contacts when the application closed. In the new version, it might be the case that the user opens the application and immediately closes it without ever opening a file. So, the **frmMain_Closing** method needs to be modified to first check to see if a filename has ever been specified before calling the **saveContacts** method. The changes to the constructor and **frmMain_Closing** are shown in Figure 11-18.

11

```
270    public frmMain()
271    {
272       InitializeComponent();
273
274       mContactsFileName = null;
275    }


424    private void frmMain_Closing(object sender, System.ComponentModel.CancelEventArgs e)
425    {
426       if (mContactsFileName != null)
427       {
428           saveContacts();
429       }
430    }
```

Figure 11-18 Changes to the frmMain constructor and frmMain_Closing event method

The only other changes necessary are to add event methods for the New and Open buttons that have been added to the user interface. These two methods are shown in Figure 11-19 and Figure 11-20.

```
368    private void btnOpen_Click(object sender, System.EventArgs e)
369    {
370       OpenFileDialog ofd;
371       ofd = new OpenFileDialog();
372
373       ofd.Title = "Select a Contacts file to open";
374       ofd.Filter = "Contacts (*.dat)|*.dat|All files (*.*)|*.*";
375
376       if (ofd.ShowDialog() == DialogResult.OK)
377       {
378          // If the user specified a new filename, save the existing contacts (if a
379          // filename is present), and restore the contacts from the new file.
380
381          if (mContactsFileName != null)
382          {
383             saveContacts();
384          }
385          mContactsFileName = ofd.FileName;
386          restoreContacts();
387       }
388    }
```

Figure 11-19 The btnOpen_Click event method

Lines 370 and 371 in the **btnOpen_Click** method define and then instantiate an **OpenFileDialog** object. Line 373 sets the dialog's **Title** property. The **Title** property serves the same purpose as the **Text** property of a normal form and is used to indicate what text shows as the form's caption. The default value for the **Title** property is **"Open"**, so line 373 changes it to be more descriptive for the Contacts List program.

Line 374 requires some explanation. The **Filter** property is used to populate the contents of the drop-down list that lets the user choose from a list of different file types. Because the drop-down list could contain many values, the designers of the **Filter** property chose to let you specify many values by setting this one property one time. The way you specify these many values is to concatenate them into a big string in which each value is separated by the vertical line character (|). However, it is even more complicated than that. The values are actually value pairs. The first part of the pair is the description the user sees in the list. The second value is the pattern the dialog uses to display matching files.

Line 374 in Figure 11-19 adds two file types to the drop-down list. The first item has a description of **Contacts (*.dat)** and the dialog uses a pattern of ***.dat** to display existing files when the user chooses the first item from the list. The second item has a description of **All files (*.*)**, and the dialog uses a pattern of ***.*** to display existing files when the user chooses the second choice from the list. Note that the first element (for example, **Contacts (*.dat)**) is what the user sees in the drop-down list box, whereas the second related element (***.dat**) is what the computer uses to search the disk for that type of file.

Line 376 calls the **ShowDialog** method, which shows the dialog to the user. Note that this form is shown as a modal dialog just as the **MessageBox** is shown. **Modal** means that statement 381 won't be executed until after the dialog is dismissed by the user. Line 376 compares the **ShowDialog** return value to **DialogResult.OK** and, if they are equal, the statements on lines 381 through 386 are executed to save the existing file and load the contents of the new file.

```
343   private void btnNew_Click(object sender, System.EventArgs e)
344   {
345       SaveFileDialog sfd;
346       sfd = new SaveFileDialog();
347
348       sfd.Title = "Enter a name and location for the new Contacts file";
349       sfd.Filter = "Contacts (*.dat)|*.dat|All files (*.*)|*.*";
350
351       if (sfd.ShowDialog() == DialogResult.OK)
352       {
353           // If the user specified a new filename, save the existing contacts (if a
354           // filename is present), store the new filename, and clear the user interface.
355
356           if (mContactsFileName != null)
357           {
358               saveContacts();
359           }
360           mContactsFileName = sfd.FileName;
361           lstContacts.Items.Clear();
362           clearInputControls();
363       }
364   }
```

Figure 11-20   The btnNew_Click event method

When you understand the logic in the **btnOpen_Click** event method, you should have no problem understanding the logic in the **btnNew_Click** method because they work in a very similar manner. However, a couple of points do need to be made. The code uses the **SaveFileDialog** class even though the data aren't immediately saved to the new file. Recall you use **SaveFileDialog** when you want to ask the user to specify a filename and path for a new file (one that doesn't already exist), which is the case here. Also note lines 361 and 362. Because the user is indicating a need to create a new contacts file, lines 361 and 362 clear the contents of the UI.

FIXED-WIDTH TEXT FILES

Earlier in the chapter you learned that there are many common formats for saving information in sequential data files. One of these formats is fixed-width text files. Fixed-width text files are not the most common format used by PC applications, but fixed-width text files are frequently found with applications that run on other computing platforms. For example, programs that are written using the Cobol programming language and are run on mainframe computers most often store information in fixed-width files. Writing applications that interface with data from other systems is a common programming task, so learning how to process fixed-width text files is worth a closer look.

The format of fixed-width text files is similar to tab-delimited text files in that the file contains zero or many records, each record contains information about a single entity, and each record normally is terminated by a CRLF. What is different is the way the fields in each record are organized. With tab-delimited files, each field is of variable length depending on the field's contents, and fields are delimited by a tab character. After all, people with short names use less disk storage in a tab-delimited text file than people with long names. In **fixed-width text files**, the contents of each field in each record is always the same number of characters, and there is nothing in the file that delimits where a field begins and ends. The only way to process such files is to have documentation that describes the

record layout of the file. In other words, you need to know the columns of where each field begins and ends.

The good news about fixed-width sequential text files is that you process them very much the same as you process tab-delimited files. You first open the file. Next you use the **ReadLine** method of the **StreamReader** class or the **WriteLine** method of the **StreamWriter** class for reading or writing records. Finally, the file is closed when you are finished using it. The bad news about fixed-width files is that parsing the input records and formatting the output records require more tedious coding than with tab-delimited records. However, after you learn the techniques, it's not that complicated.

To illustrate, add a feature to the Contacts List application that allows the user to import contact information from a fixed-width text file. The contents of the import file are shown in Figure 11-21 using Windows Notepad.

Figure 11-21   The contents of a fixed-width text file for importing contact information

When you look at the contents of the file in Figure 11-21, you might be able to guess what some of the data are, but you can't be sure unless you have some documentation. The record layout for the sample import file is shown in Table 11-5.

Table 11-5   The record layout for the import file

Field name	Starts in column	Length	Ends in column
Last Name	1	10	10
First Name	11	10	20
Birthdate Month	21	2	22
Birthdate Day	23	2	24
Birthdate Year	25	4	28
Home Phone	29	10	38
Mobile Phone	39	10	48
Not used	49	2	50

The first change to the Contacts List program is to add an Import button to the UI. When this button is clicked, the program presents the user with the **OpenFileDialog** to allow the user to choose an import file (see Figure 11-22). If the user specifies a file, a private helper method is called to process the records.

```
355    private void btnImport_Click(object sender, System.EventArgs e)
356    {
357        OpenFileDialog ofd;
358        ofd = new OpenFileDialog();
359
360        ofd.Title = "Select a Contacts file to import";
361        ofd.Filter = "Import files (*.txt)|*.txt|All files (*.*)|*.*";
362
363        // If the user specified an import file, call the helper method to
364        // process it.
365
366        if (ofd.ShowDialog() == DialogResult.OK)
367        {
368            importFixedWidthContacts(ofd.FileName);
369        }
370    }
```

Figure 11-22 The btnImport_Click event method

Reading Fixed-Width Records

The technique for parsing fixed-width records is to read each record into one long string variable, then use the string's **Substring** method to get from the input record the characters that represent each field. For values that are stored as strings in your program, you must use the string's **TrimEnd** method to remove any trailing spaces that exist in the string returned from the **Substring** method. For a value that is stored as a number in your program, you can use the **Parse** method to convert the string to the correct numeric data type.

The fixed-width text file shown in Figure 11-21 can be imported to the Contacts List program using the method shown in Figure 11-23. The code within this method is described in the following paragraphs.

```
511    private void importFixedWidthContacts(string importFileName)
512    {
513        StreamReader sr = null;
514        clsContact contact;
515
516        string inputLine;
517        string year;
518        string month;
519        string day;
520
521        try
522        {
523            // Open the import file.
524
525            sr = new StreamReader(importFileName);
526
527            inputLine = sr.ReadLine();
528            while (inputLine != null)
```

Figure 11-23 Importing contacts from a fixed-width file

```
529                   {
530                       // Instantiate a new contact object and set its properties.
531
532                       contact = new clsContact();
533
534                       contact.LastName = inputLine.Substring(0, 10);
535                       contact.LastName = contact.LastName.TrimEnd();
536
537                       contact.FirstName = inputLine.Substring(10, 10);
538                       contact.FirstName = contact.FirstName.TrimEnd();
539
540                       month = inputLine.Substring(20, 2);
541                       day = inputLine.Substring(22, 2);
542                       year = inputLine.Substring(24, 4);
543                       contact.BirthDate =
544                           new DateTime(int.Parse(year), int.Parse(month), int.Parse(day));
545
546                       contact.HomePhone = new clsPhoneNumber(inputLine.Substring(28, 10));
547                       contact.MobilePhone = new clsPhoneNumber(inputLine.Substring(38, 10));
548
549                       // Add the new contact to the list and try to get the next input record.
550
551                       lstContacts.Items.Add(contact);
552                       inputLine = sr.ReadLine();
553                   }
554               sr.Close();
555           }
556           catch(Exception ex)
557           {
558               messageBoxOK("Error importing contacts from file "
559                   + importFileName + ". " + ex.Message);
560           }
561           finally
562           {
563               if (sr != null)
564               {
565                   sr.Close();
566               }
567           }
568       }
```

Figure 11-23 Importing contacts from a fixed-width file (continued)

The `importFixedWidthContacts` method is very similar to the `restoreContacts` method shown in Figure 11-15. The only difference is how the input records are parsed. In `restoreContacts`, each record is passed to the contact object's `Deserialize` method for parsing. You could add a method to the `clsContact` class that would handle the fixed-width record, but because `clsContact` wasn't responsible for creating the records in the import file, we didn't choose to make it responsible for parsing them. Instead, lines 534 through 547 handle the task of parsing the fixed-width records.

Line 534 uses the `inputLine` object's `Substring` method to get the first 10 characters from the input record (recall the first argument to the `Substring` method is zero-based) and assigns them to the `LastName` property of the contact object. Line 535 then uses the string object's `TrimEnd` method to remove any trailing spaces. The same process is used on lines 537 and 538 for the `FirstName` property.

Lines 540 through 544 are used to get the birthdate value out of the input record. First, lines 540 through 542 use the **Substring** method to get the month, day, and year values from the input record. Lines 543 and 544 instantiate a new **DateTime** object and pass the year, month, and day values to the **DateTime** constructor. Note that, because the year, month, and day values are stored as strings, **int.Parse** is first used to convert them to integers before they get passed to the constructor. Similarly, lines 546 and 547 use the **Substring** method to get the 10 characters that make up the home and mobile phone numbers and pass these 10 characters to the **clsPhoneNumber** constructor.

Finally, line 551 adds the new contact to the list box and line 552 gets the next record, just as was done with the tab-delimited record. Of course, the **importFixedWidthContacts** method wraps all file processing logic in a **try/catch** block just in case an exception is thrown while processing the import file.

Writing Fixed-Width Records

The technique for writing fixed-width records is to concatenate the values of the variables that make up the output record into one big string and then write it to the file using the **WriteLine** method of the **StreamWriter** class. For values stored as strings in your program, you have to first make a copy of the variable that is fixed-length. If the number of characters in the original string is less than the number of characters you need in the output record, you can use the string's **PadRight** method to add spaces to the end of a string. If the number of characters in the original string is greater than the number of characters you need in the output record, you can use the string's **Substring** method to copy only the number of characters needed from the beginning of the original string. The following code snippet shows how to make a copy of the variable named **address** always contain exactly 20 characters:

```
string fixedAddress;
if (address.Length < 20)
{
    fixedAddress = address.PadRight(20);
}
else
{
    fixedAddress = address.Substring(0, 20);
}
```

Note you could combine the calls to the **PadRight** and **Substring** methods into a single statement like this:

```
fixedAddress = address.PadRight(20).Substring(0, 20);
```

This shorter version works because **PadRight** doesn't change the value of the string if it already contains 20 characters. We leave adding a feature to the Contacts List program that creates a fixed-width export file for you to do as an exercise.

PERSISTENCE USING BINARY DATA FILES

Earlier in the chapter you learned saving object state to text files is especially useful for beginning programmers because viewing the contents of these kinds of files is so easy—just open them with a text editor such as Notepad. However, you also learned that text files can be less efficient than binary data files because, with text files, any data that are not stored as text within your program must be converted to a string before they can be written to the file. And when reading text files, the data in the input records must be converted from a string back into numeric values. This extra conversion back and forth isn't necessary with binary files. With binary files, the values are stored on disk using exactly the same bit pattern as that used for the values stored in computer memory. No conversion is necessary, which increases processing speed.

Processing binary files is in some ways the same as processing text files. Before the file can be processed, it has to be opened. And when it is finished processing, the file is closed. Data are also read from or written to the file. However, binary data files don't typically contain records that end with CRLF. The concept of a record is still there, and the information about a single entity is grouped together, but there is no CRLF at the end of each record. Instead, data values are saved by writing them to the binary file field by field. To restore the values, they are read back in the same sequence in which they were written.

You've learned that C# uses the concept of streams for file input and output. For processing sequential text files, **StreamReader** and **StreamWriter** can be used. To process binary files, you have to use both a **FileStream** object and either a **BinaryReader** or **BinaryWriter** object. The **FileStream** object is used to open the file. **BinaryReader** has methods that allow you to read various data types as binary values from the file, and **BinaryWriter** has methods that write various data types as binary values to the file.

To illustrate binary files, we again change the Contacts List program. This time we change the Contacts List program to serialize object state to a binary file rather than using tab-delimited records. After you test the program, you can examine the contents of a binary file using VS.NET. Because you aren't changing the UI for the Contacts List application, the only methods we need to change are the **saveContacts** and **restoreContacts** methods, as well as the **Serialize** and **Deserialize** methods in **clsContact**. Figure 11-24 shows the **saveContacts** method modified to persist the contacts to a binary file.

```
460    private void saveContacts()
461    {
462        FileStream fs = null;
463        BinaryWriter bw = null;
464
465        try
466        {
467            fs = new FileStream(mContactsFileName, FileMode.Create);
468            bw = new BinaryWriter(fs);
469
470            foreach (clsContact contact in lstContacts.Items)
471            {
472                contact.Serialize(bw);
473            }
474        }
475        catch (Exception ex)
476        {
477            messageBoxOK("Error saving contacts to file "
478                + mContactsFileName + ". " + ex.Message);
479        }
```

Figure 11-24   The saveContacts method modified to use a binary data file

```
480        finally
481        {
482            if (bw != null)
483            {
484                bw.Close();
485            }
486
487            if (fs != null)
488            {
489                fs.Close();
490            }
491        }
492    }
```

Figure 11-24 The saveContacts method modified to use a binary data file (continued)

For the most part, the new **saveContacts** method is the same as the previous versions. The difference is the stream objects that are used. Lines 462 and 463 define the **FileStream** and **BinaryWriter** objects that are used when writing the property values to the file. Line 467 instantiates the **FileStream** object and passes the filename to be opened along with a second argument, **FileMode.Create**, that tells the **FileStream** object to create the file. (Note that if the file already exists, the existing file is deleted.) Line 468 instantiates the **BinaryWriter** object and passes the **FileStream** object to the constructor. This causes the **BinaryWriter** object to be associated with the file opened by the **FileStream** object.

Lines 470 through 473 loop through the list of **clsContact** objects and calls the contact's **Serialize** method. Unlike the tab-delimited version, the **Serialize** method is modified so that it writes its state values directly to the file rather than returning a string containing the object's state.

Lines 482 through 490 call the **Close** method for both the **BinaryWriter** and the **FileStream** objects. Note that both objects have to be closed and are compared to **null** to determine if they have been opened before attempting to close them.

The changes to the **restoreContacts** method are similar to the changes made to the **saveContacts** method, except **restoreContacts** defines and instantiates a **BinaryReader** object. Figure 11-25 lists the modified **restoreContacts** method. The only other thing that might need some explanation is the **while** loop on line 432. The **PeekChar** method of the **BinaryReader** object looks ahead one byte in the file stream. If there is no next character in the file (all bytes have been read from the file), **PeekChar** returns a value of −1 to indicate the end of file (EOF) has been reached.

```
417    private void restoreContacts()
418    {
419        FileStream fs = null;
420        BinaryReader br = null;
421        clsContact contact;
422
423        lstContacts.Items.Clear();
424
425        try
```

Figure 11-25 The restoreContacts method, modified to use a binary data file

```
426          {
427              if (File.Exists(mContactsFileName) == true)
428              {
429                  fs = new FileStream(mContactsFileName, FileMode.Open);
430                  br = new BinaryReader(fs);
431
432                  while (br.PeekChar() != -1)
433                  {
434                      contact = new clsContact();
435                      contact.Deserialize(br);
436                      lstContacts.Items.Add(contact);
437                  }
438              }
439          }
440          catch (Exception ex)
441          {
442              messageBoxOK("Error restoring contacts from file "
443                  + mContactsFileName + ". " + ex.Message);
444          }
445          finally
446          {
447              if (br != null)
448              {
449                  br.Close();
450              }
451
452              if (fs != null)
453              {
454                  fs.Close();
455              }
456          }
457     }
```

Figure 11-25 The restoreContacts method, modified to use a binary data file (continued)

The other changes necessary to make the Contacts List application use binary data files require changing the **Serialize** and **Deserialize** methods in **clsContact** to use **BinaryWriter** and **BinaryReader** objects. The new **Serialize** and **Deserialize** methods are shown in Figure 11-26.

```
419     public void Serialize(BinaryWriter writer)
420     {
421         writer.Write(mFirstName);
422         writer.Write(mLastName);
423         writer.Write(HomePhone.ToString());
424         writer.Write(MobilePhone.ToString());
425         writer.Write(BirthDate.Year);
426         writer.Write(BirthDate.Month);
427         writer.Write(BirthDate.Day);
428     }
```

Figure 11-26 clsContact Serialize and Deserialize methods using a binary data file

```
432     public void Deserialize(BinaryReader reader)
433     {
434         string tempPhone;
435         int year;
436         int month;
437         int day;
438
439         mFirstName = reader.ReadString();
440         mLastName = reader.ReadString();
441
442         tempPhone = reader.ReadString();
443         HomePhone = new clsPhoneNumber(tempPhone);
444
445         tempPhone = reader.ReadString();
446         MobilePhone = new clsPhoneNumber(tempPhone);
447
448         year = reader.ReadInt32();
449         month = reader.ReadInt32();
450         day = reader.ReadInt32();
451         BirthDate = new DateTime(year, month, day);
452     }
```

Figure 11-26 clsContact Serialize and Deserialize methods using a binary data file (continued)

11

Let's examine the changes to the **Serialize** method first. The **BinaryWriter** class has a public method named **Write** that is overloaded so that you can pass it any of the simple data types, for example numbers, Booleans, and strings. When called, the **Write** method simply copies the values of the variables from RAM to the disk file associated with the **BinaryWriter** class. Unfortunately, the **BinaryWriter** class doesn't have methods to write the values of more complex data types such as **DateTime** or any class you define like **clsPhoneNumber**. This means you are responsible for figuring out a way to store the values of these data types. For the **BirthDate** property, we save the date's **Year**, **Month**, and **Day** property values as integers to the file (we aren't using the time portion of **BirthDate**, so it isn't saved). We convert phone numbers to strings before saving them to the file.

The changes to **Deserialize** are a little more complicated. Recall that a method can only be overloaded by having a unique parameter list. This means that the **BinaryReader** object can't have a single method that knows how much data to read based on the variable that holds the return value. Instead, it has methods named to read each of the simple data types (**ReadBoolean**, **ReadByte**, **ReadDecimal**, **ReadDouble**, **ReadString**, and so on). Note that, to read a type **int**, you call the **ReadInt32** method because an **int** data type is stored using 32 bits. **Deserialize** must read back the field values in the same order they were written using the **Serialize** method, and the same data types must be used.

Viewing the Contents of a Binary Data File

You learned earlier that you can use the Windows Notepad application to view the contents of a text file. You can open binary data files with Notepad, but you won't be able to view much. Notepad expects each sequence of 8 bits to represent a text character and so tries to interpret every file it opens that way (see Figure 11-4). However, if you store numeric values in a binary data file without converting them to text, you have to use an application that knows how to display data in binary format. You've been using VS.NET to write and test your programs, but VS.NET can also be used to view binary data files.

To see for yourself, use the binary data file version of the Contacts List program to add a single contact and save it to a file. Next open this file using VS.NET by choosing File → Open → File from the VS.NET menu bar and select the binary data file containing this one contact. VS.NET displays the contents of the file using a format like that shown in Figure 11-27.

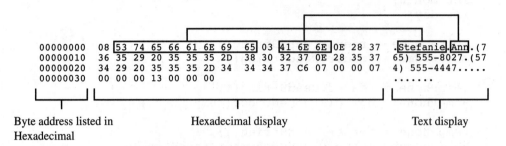

Figure 11-27   Hexadecimal display of a binary data file

VS.NET displays the contents of binary data files in the so-called hexadecimal format. Whereas a text editor application such as Windows Notepad displays every 8 bits as a character, **hexadecimal** format displays every 4 bits as a character. Because 4 bits have 16 unique combinations, hexadecimal is sometimes known as a base 16 numbering system. In hexadecimal format, the value zero is displayed as character **"0"**, the value one is displayed as character **"1"**, and so on. But the value of 10 is displayed as **"A"**, the value 11 is displayed as **"B"**, and the value 15 displayed as **"F"**.

From 11-27, you can see that the first byte contains hexadecimal **"08"** which is the length of the first name string. The second byte contains hexadecimal **"53"**, which represents the letter **"S"**. The third byte contains hexadecimal **"74"**, which represents the letter **"t"**, and so on. Perhaps the most important thing to notice is that the values of the year, month, and day portion are stored as integers and not text characters. Can you find them in Figure 11-27? The birthdate for this contact is July, 19, 1990.

> **tip ▶** If you use VS.NET to open a text file, by default it displays the file's contents as text, and not as hexadecimal. You can trick VS.NET into displaying the contents of a text file in hexadecimal format by renaming the file's extension to .bin before you open it in VS.NET.

Summary

Essential Topics

- Computer RAM is sometimes called volatile memory because it loses its content when the electricity is turned off. Non-volatile memory is memory that doesn't lose its content when the electricity is turned off. Non-volatile memory is also known as external storage. The most common device computers use for non-volatile memory is a computer's hard drive.

- Persistence means storing an object in non-volatile memory. In other words, an object is made persistent by saving its state information to disk.

- The Windows File System (WFS) is the part of the Windows Operating System (OS) that handles the task of saving data to, and retrieving data from, external storage devices. The WFS organizes external storage devices by giving each a drive letter. A disk can contain zero or more folders (directories). Each folder can contain zero or more files, and zero or more subfolders.

Folders and files have the same naming rules. A file's path includes a drive letter and a list of folders and subfolders.

▫ The .NET **System.IO** namespace contains classes with methods that can be used to manipulate the WFS. The most essential of these classes include **System.IO.Directory**, **System.IO.File**, and **System.IO.Path**.

▫ Data can be stored in a file in either text or binary format. Binary files can process data faster and can save disk space. Text files are useful when the files could be used by applications on different computing systems. Because text files can be easily read using a simple text editor such as Windows Notepad, text files also make testing and debugging a program easier.

▫ Files can either be accessed randomly or sequentially. With a random access file, your program can process the data at any location in the file at any time. With a sequential access file, the data in the file are accessed by beginning at the start of the file and reading the data a piece at a time in sequence until all data have been processed. A sequential data file can contain zero or more records. A record can contain one or more pieces of information about each entity. Each piece of information is called a field.

▫ The terminology and processing steps you use to describe computer file processing are the same as those you use to describe how a person uses a paper file. First, the file must be opened. After it is opened, a program can read and write data to the file. When finished, it is essential that the program explicitly close the file.

▫ In C#, you use the **StreamReader** and **StreamWriter** classes to process sequential files. **StreamReader** has a **ReadLine** method you can use to read a record from a sequential input text file. **StreamWriter** has a **WriteLine** method you can use to write a record to a sequential output text file.

▫ Serialization is defined as converting an object's state information to a simple stream, or string, of data. This stream of data can be used to send the object to another computer over a network connection, or to make the object persistent.

▫ Because exceptions are common when processing files, you should always enclose file I/O logic within a **try** block to catch any exceptions that might occur. The **finally** block is the best place to close a data file. This ensures the file is closed even if an exception occurs while processing the file.

Bonus Topics

▫ The .NET framework includes the **OpenFileDialog** and **SaveFileDialog** classes you can use to allow users to specify a file path and filename. Use **OpenFileDialog** for files that should already exist, and **SaveFileDialog** for new files. Both classes have similar properties that let you customize the title shown on the dialogs and the filter used to indicate which files should be shown. To use these classes, instantiate an instance of either and call its **ShowDialog** method. The filename specified by the user can then be retrieved using the dialog object's **FileName** property.

▫ Fixed-width files are commonly used by applications that run on non-PC platforms. A common task of programming is writing programs that interface with other applications. Fixed-with text files are organized as records within a file, but to know how to parse them, you need to know where each field begins and ends within each record.

▫ Fixed-width text files can be processed in C# by using the same **StreamReader** and **StreamWriter** classes used for processing tab-delimited records. You use the **ReadLine** method of the **StreamReader** class or the **WriteLine** method of the **StreamWriter** class for reading and writing records. Fields can be parsed out of a fixed-width input record using the **Substring** and **TrimEnd** methods of the **string** class. Fixed-width output records can be created using the **Substring** and **PadRight** methods of the **string** class.

❑ Binary data files can execute more efficiently and use less disk space than text files because data are represented in the file in the same format as in computer RAM. However, the contents of binary files are more difficult to view because a simple text editor application cannot be used to view their contents. Instead, an application that can display binary data in hexadecimal must be used, and you need to be able to read data represented in hexadecimal format.

❑ The .NET framework classes you can use for binary file input and output are **FileStream**, **BinaryReader**, and **BinaryWriter**. **FileStream** is used to open a binary data file. **BinaryReader** contains methods for reading a field value from a binary file. **BinaryWriter** contains an overloaded **Write** method that allows you to write the contents of simple data types to a file.

KEY TERMS

Define each of the following terms, as it relates to object persistence:

Essential Terms

- ❑ buffering
- ❑ carriage return and line feed (CRLF)
- ❑ directory
- ❑ external storage
- ❑ field
- ❑ file
- ❑ file extension
- ❑ file format
- ❑ file I/O
- ❑ folder
- ❑ hard coding
- ❑ hard drive
- ❑ non-volatile memory
- ❑ parsing
- ❑ partition
- ❑ path
- ❑ persistence
- ❑ random access memory (RAM)
- ❑ record
- ❑ sequential file

- ❑ serialization
- ❑ **StreamReader**
- ❑ **StreamWriter**
- ❑ **System.IO**
- ❑ text file
- ❑ volatile memory
- ❑ Windows File System (WFS)

Bonus Terms

- ❑ **BinaryReader**
- ❑ **BinaryWriter**
- ❑ **FileStream**
- ❑ **Filter**
- ❑ fixed-width text files
- ❑ hexadecimal
- ❑ modal
- ❑ **OpenFileDialog**
- ❑ record layout
- ❑ **SaveFileDialog**

REVIEW QUESTIONS

Essential Questions

1. Non-volatile memory loses its contents when the electricity is turned off. True or false?

2. To uniquely identify each external storage device, the Windows File System assigns each one a letter. True or false?

3. File and folder names must contain between 1 and 128 characters and can't contain the special characters ? * / \ : ; < >. True or false?

4. Most files contain little or no information about how the data are organized within the file. True or false?

5. The file extension dictates what is contained within the file. True or false?

6. Binary files are generally easier for beginner programmers to use. True or false?

7. When saving data to a binary file, numbers, Booleans, and dates must first be converted to a string. True or false?

8. The `Application.StartupPath` property can be used to determine the path of where an .exe file is run from. True or false?

9. `Serialization` is defined as converting an object's state information to a simple stream, or string, of data. True or false?

10. When a `StreamReader` has reached the end of file condition, it sets its EOF property = `true`. True or false?

11. Non-volatile memory is also known as _____.

12. _____ means to store an object in non-volatile memory.

13. The .NET _____ namespace has classes that manipulate the Windows File System, and classes for saving and retrieving data to and from external storage devices.

14. The end of a record in sequential files is marked by _____.

15. The _____ class has methods that can be used to manipulate the strings that define a folder's or file's path.

16. Explain why computers use a combination of volatile and non-volatile memory rather than just one or the other.

17. List at least two reasons you might choose to store data in a text file rather than a binary file.

18. What class and method is used to read a record from a sequential text file?

19. What class and method is used to write a record to a sequential text file?

20. Explain where you should write the code to close a file. What happens when file I/O causes an exception?

Bonus Questions

1. The `OpenFileDialog` class is used to instantiate an object of type `StreamReader`. True or false?

2. The `Filter` property is used by both `OpenFileDialog` and `SaveFileDialog` to limit which files are displayed on the form. True or false?

3. Fixed-width files have no field delimiter character between field values in each record. True or false?

4. When reading a binary file in a **while** loop, your program knows that all data in the file have been read when the binary reader object's **PeekChar** method returns –1. True or false?

5. Binary data can be viewed using Windows Notepad by selecting Hexadecimal from Notepad's View menu. True or false?

6. To show either an **OpenFileDialog** or **SaveFileDialog** object, you call the object's _____ method.

7. The _____ class is used to read data from a binary file, and the _____ class is used to write data to a binary file.

8. Which methods of which class are used for reading and writing records in fixed-width files?

9. Explain the process of parsing a fixed-width record into its various field values.

10. Write a single C# statement that causes the contents of a string variable named **emailAddress** to always contain exactly 30 characters.

PROGRAMMING EXERCISES

Essential Exercises

1. Modify the example presented in the chapter that saves a form's state to include these enhancements:

   ◻ When saving the form's position and size, first check to make sure that the form isn't minimized.

   ◻ Save and restore the form's **WindowState** property value so that the form can be restored to a maximized state if it was maximized when the form was closed.

   ◻ If the state file doesn't exist, default the position of the form to be the center of the screen.

   ◻ When restoring the form's position and size, make sure that it will not be moved off the edge of the screen and therefore not be visible to the user. This can happen if the user changes the screen's resolution from large (1920 × 1200) to small (800 × 600).

   ◻ Appropriate exception handlers should always be added when processing files.

2. Move the code from Exercise 1 to a new class named **clsFormState** so that the code for saving and restoring a form's state can be more easily reused. Define a constructor in **clsFormState** that takes a **Form** object as the only argument and save this **Form** reference as state information in **clsFormState**. Define a **Save** and **Restore** method in **clsFormState** that should be called whenever the form is closing and loading, respectively.

3. Develop an application that uses the **System.IO.Directory** class to allow the user to navigate through the Windows File System and move, rename, and delete folders.

4. Enhance the application in Exercise 3 to allow the user to move, rename, and delete files.

5. Modify the **clsContact.Deserialize** method in the Contacts List application presented in this chapter to perform data validation on the string it is passed. Make sure that when the string is split, it has the correct number of elements, and make sure each element is of the correct data type before assigning to the state variables. If any errors are found, throw an exception with an appropriate descriptive message.

6. Write a program to manage persistence of a student class, which contains a student's name, ID, section, classification, and grade. The student file should be a sequential tab-delimited text file. The user interface should allow the user to open a file and display the contents in a list box.

Bonus Exercises

1. Modify the Contacts List program so that it always saves data in fixed-width text files rather than tab-delimited files.

2. Develop an application that uses a recursive method call to search a folder and all its subfolders to find files with names that match a pattern (for example, `*.jpg`). Use `Directory.GetFiles` to find matching files in the current folder. Use `Directory.GetDirectories` to get a list of subfolders for the current folder. Your user interface should allow the user to specify the starting folder to search. Display all matching files in a list box. Because the search logic might run for several minutes, your user interface should include a button that allows the user to cancel the search. To allow the user interface to be refreshed and to allow the user to click the Stop button, call the `Application.DoEvents` method from inside the recursive iteration.

3. Write a program that can display the contents of a binary file in hexadecimal format similar to that shown in Figure 11-27. Allow the user to select a file using the `OpenFileDialog` class. To display the output to the user, use a text box with its `Multiline` property set to *True*, `ScrollBars` set to *Both*, and `WordWrap` set to *False*. To read the contents of the file, use the `BinaryReader`'s `ReadByte` method to read a single byte at a time. You can convert a **byte** value to a string formatted in hexadecimal format using `byteVariable.ToString("X2")`.

11

12

USER INTERFACE OBJECTS

In the Essentials section you will learn:

- Properties, events, and methods common to most user interface controls derived from the `System.Windows.Forms` class
- Additional properties, events, and methods for forms, labels, text boxes, and buttons
- How one form can show another form
- How one form can show another form as a modal dialog
- Which properties to set for common form styles
- When and how to use user interface controls including the `CheckBox`, `ComboBox`, `DateTimePicker`, `GroupBox`, `ListView`, `MainMenu`, `ContextMenu`, `NumericUpDown`, `RadioButton`, `Timer`, `ToolBar`, and `StatusBar` controls

In the Bonus section you will learn:

- Proper user interface design guidelines
- How to achieve special effects using forms
- How to generate printed paper reports

The examples presented so far in this text have used just a few user interface objects. These objects are forms, labels, buttons, text boxes, and sometimes list boxes. We limited the use of controls to just these few because the intent of this book is to teach object-oriented programming using C# and not necessarily to show you how to use all the classes in the .NET Framework. However, one of the most rewarding parts of software development is creating applications that other people want to use. These days, users expect applications to have a good user interface. An application doesn't necessarily need to allow the interface to be completely customizable, but the user interface should not appear amateurish. The purpose of this chapter is to show you how to give your applications a professional appearance using many of the user interface objects available to .NET developers.

ESSENTIAL TOPICS

You've already learned how to use the Form Designer, Toolbox, and Properties window to build simple GUIs using forms, labels, text boxes, and buttons. While doing so, you surely noticed that the Toolbox contains over 40 user interface objects. Most of these objects have over 100 different properties, events, and methods! That's quite a lot of information to try to absorb. You can find a complete reference for each control in the VS.NET Help system. Just select a control in the Toolbox and press F1. The trouble is, this reference lists everything about each control and doesn't make a distinction between what you can use, and what you are likely to use. Luckily, most applications use only a subset of these controls and just a small fraction of their properties, events, and methods. These essential controls are what you'll find in the following sections of this chapter.

Most of the time, you use the Form Designer and the Properties Window to configure the user interface objects to behave the way you want. However, almost all property values can be set from code. Recall that you used the Form Designer and Properties window to generate code to instantiate the objects and set their property values. The resulting code is placed in the "Windows generated code" region of the form's class.

The next section discusses properties, events, and methods common to most controls. Later sections in the chapter cover the details of the essential controls. The Program Example section creates a professional-looking user interface for the Contacts List program developed in Chapters 10 and 11. While reading this chapter, we encourage you to have VS.NET open and use the Form Designer and Properties Window to experiment with the controls as you read about them. The sample project files that accompany this text also contain many projects that demonstrate the appearance and behavior of these essential user interface objects.

COMMON PROPERTIES, EVENTS, AND METHODS

You learned in Chapter 2 that user interface controls are contained in the `System.Windows.Forms` namespace. What hasn't been mentioned yet is that most controls are derived from the same base class named `System.Windows.Forms.Control`. Any control that is derived from `System.Windows.Forms.Control` inherits the properties, events, and methods defined in that class. Rather than repeat this common interface for each control, the common properties, events, and methods you are likely to use are listed next.

Anchor Property

The `Anchor` property is useful for a control that is placed on a **form** that can be resized by the user. If the form can't be resized, `Anchor` doesn't have much purpose. The `Anchor` property allows a control to always remain positioned at the left, top, right, or bottom of a form as the form is resized. You can set `Anchor` to be any combination of `Left`, `Top`, `Right`, and `Bottom`. For example, you might set the `Anchor` property of a button to be `Bottom`, `Right` if you want the button to always appear at the lower right of the form.

`Anchor` also can cause a control to change its size whenever the form resizes by setting it to include either `Left` and `Right`, or `Top` and `Bottom`. When the form is resized, the control is automatically resized in proportion to the size of the control in the Form Designer and the current size of the form as it is being resized by the user. Probably the best use for `anchor` is to cause another control, such as a `Listbox` or `ListView`, to fill the interior of the form as it is resized. In this case, you would set the `Anchor` property to `Top`, `Left`, `Right`, and `Bottom`.

BackColor and ForeColor Properties

The `BackColor` and `ForeColor` properties allow you to get or set the background or foreground colors of an object. Specific colors can be specified using the Properties window or from code using values from the `Color` class, for example `Color.Red`, `Color.Blue`, and `Color.BlanchedAlmond`. However, even though you can set these colors to something other than the defaults, you normally shouldn't. The reason is because Windows allows the user to configure the color scheme he or she wants for user interface elements. You personally might like the way your user interface looks when everything is colored pink, but the user of your application might prefer the Windows Spruce or some other color scheme.

Enabled Property

The `Enabled` property determines if a control can respond to events and if the user can interact with a control. If set to **true**, the control is enabled and can respond to events. If set to **false**, the control is disabled and often appears grayed out to let the user know that he or she can't interact with the control at that time. For example, an enabled **TextBox** control allows text to be entered, and one that is disabled does not. You might use `Enabled` to enable or disable menu items or buttons based on the state of the application.

Font Property

The **Font** property is used to change the way that text is displayed on controls that display text. The `Font` property is an object itself with its own set of properties. A `Font` object has properties for **Bold**, **Italic**, **Name**, **Size**, **Strikeout**, and **Underline**, among others. You can use the Properties Window to change the initial **Font** a control uses. You can also set the **Font** property during program execution, but it is not quite as easy as you might guess. Most of the **Font** properties are read-only so you can't directly set them. To change the **Font** property of an object, you must first instantiate a new **Font** object and pass details about the new font to the constructor, and then set the **Font** property of the object to this new **Font** object. For example, you could make a button use a bold font by using code similar to:

```
Font newFont = new Font(btnOK.Font, FontStyle.Bold);
btnOK.Font = newFont;
```

Note that the **Font** constructor is overloaded, enabling you to construct **Font** objects many different ways. The previous example uses a constructor that accepts an existing **Font** object to use as a base for the new font, and passes a second argument to change the font style to be bold. Also note that the **Font** object is contained in the **System.Drawing** namespace, so the previous example assumes a **using** directive for this namespace is defined.

However, you should leave the **Font** property set to the default value for the same reason you should leave the `BackColor` and `ForeColor` properties set to their defaults—Windows allows the user to choose the appearance (including fonts) for user interface elements. The user—not the developer—should decide the fonts and colors used in a user interface. If you use specific colors and fonts in your user interface, they will override the appearance settings in the Windows Control Panel. Additionally, if you develop the application using a font that exists on your computer and that font doesn't exist on the computer running the program, the user interface may not be displayed correctly. Fonts are not compiled into the application's .exe file.

12

Image Property

Many controls can display a graphic on themselves. The **Image** property is used to indicate which graphic file to display. The **Image** property can be set using the Properties window, or during program execution by loading the image from a file using code similar to:

```
btnOK.Image = Image.FromFile(@"C:\button.jpg");
```

Images can be loaded from many popular image file formats including .bmp, .gif, .jpg, .ico, .png, and .wmf.

Left, Top, Width, and Height Properties

These properties are used to determine the position and size of a control on its container (a container is usually a form). **Left** refers to the object's horizontal position and **Top** refers to the object's vertical position relative to the top-left corner of the container. **Width** refers to the horizontal size, and **Height** refers to the vertical size of the object. Values are specified using the number of pixels. These values are normally set when you position controls on the form using the Form Designer. However, you might also set them during program execution if controls need to be repositioned or resized when the form is resized (see also the **Anchor** property).

Locked Property

The **Locked** property can only be set using the Properties window and cannot be set at program execution. The **Locked** property is available only as an aid in form layout. If you set a control's **Locked** property to **true**, the control's position cannot be changed. A useful user interface design technique is to lock the controls on a form after you are satisfied with their arrangement. This prevents the controls from accidentally being moved or resized.

 tip ▶ You can easily lock (or unlock) all controls on a form by right-clicking the form in the Form Designer and choosing Lock Controls from the pop-up menu. The Form Designer shows locked controls with a border that is only slightly different from unlocked controls. If you find you can't move or resize a control, make sure that it isn't locked.

Name Property

The **Name** property is the value you give to a control so that you can refer to it in code. Because you almost always set the **Name** property of a control, it appears in the Properties window as (**Name**) so that it is sorted to the top of the list when the Properties window is sorted alphabetically. The coding guidelines used in this text suggest a three-character prefix be used for the name of controls that indicates the control's type. For example, text boxes are prefixed with **txt**. See the sections that follow for the recommended prefix for each control type.

TabIndex and TabStop Properties

The **TabIndex** and **TabStop** properties are used to control the order in which the user can move the focus from one control to another by pressing Tab or Shift+Tab on the keyboard. When your program is executing and the user presses Tab, the control with the next highest **TabIndex** value that can receive the focus is found, and the focus is set to that control. Pressing Shift+Tab does the same thing except the control with the next lowest **TabIndex** value is found. That is, Shift+Tab moves the focus back to the previous control. If a control cannot receive the focus, the focus is moved to the control with the next highest (or lowest for Shift+Tab) **TabIndex** value.

Some controls, such as **Label**s, can never receive the focus. If you don't want the cursor to stop on a control that can normally receive the focus, you can set its **TabStop** property to **false**. Controls that are used for output purposes only, such as a text box with its **ReadOnly** property set to **true**, should have **TabStop** set to **false**.

TabIndex is automatically assigned when you add a control to a form using the Form Designer. The first control added to the form has a **TabIndex** value of 0, the second has a **TabIndex** value of 1, and so on. As you make changes to the UI by adding or removing controls, these index values may not be in the order you want.

The logical tab order on a form should start in the upper left of a form and move down and to the right. To set the **TabIndex** properties correctly, wait until after you have added all controls to a form and arranged them in suitable positions. Next, open the Properties window and click the control in the upper left of the form, click **TabIndex** in the Properties window, and type 0. Then click the second control on the form, click **TabIndex** in the Properties window, and type 1. Repeat this process, each time incrementing the **TabIndex** value, until you have set the **TabIndex** property for all controls on the form. You should set the **TabIndex** property even for controls that can't receive the focus, like labels, especially if that control has an access key defined (see the **Text** property in the next section).

 You can also set the **TabIndex** property for the controls on a form by using the Form Designer. With the form opened in the Form Designer, select Tab Order from the VS.NET View menu. You can now set the **TabIndex** properties by clicking the controls in the same sequence you want for the tab order. When finished, again select Tab Order from the VS.NET View menu to return to the normal layout mode.

Text and TextAlign Properties

The **Text** property simply indicates what text is displayed on the control. Different controls display the text in different locations. For example, a form displays the **Text** property in its title bar, and the user can change the value of a text box's **Text** property by typing characters in the text box.

The **TextAlign** property is used to control where on the control the text is displayed. For example, you can use it to make the text display left-justified, right-justified, or centered. If a text box is used to output numeric values only, it may be acceptable to display the text as right-justified. If a text box is used for input, left-justified is best because users find typing text into a right-justified text box awkward. The text within a **Label** control is also sometimes displayed right-justified or centered to make a more visually appealing user interface. If a button shows an image and text, you might make the text display bottom center. Otherwise, you should generally leave it at its default value.

For many controls, if you include an ampersand (&) embedded within the text for the **Text** property, the ampersand isn't displayed, but the character just after the ampersand is displayed with an underline (unless you also set the **UseMnemonic** property to **false**). Therefore, if the Text property is defined:

&Close

on a button, the displayed text on the button becomes:

Close

The character following the ampersand defines an **access key**, or mnemonic key for that control. Users can set the focus to a control, or select the control, by pressing Alt and the underlined letter (that is, the access key) on the keyboard. For example, you can select the OK button on most dialogs by pressing Alt+O, and you can select the File menu in many applications by pressing Alt+F. User interface design guidelines suggest that you define access keys whenever possible, for example on buttons, check boxes, group boxes, labels, menus, and radio buttons. (These guidelines permit the user to run your program using either a mouse or the keyboard or a combination of both.) If a control that *cannot* receive the focus has an access key defined, and the user presses that access key on the keyboard, the focus is moved to the control with the next highest `TabIndex` value.

Note that some versions of Windows have an option that hides the underlined characters for access keys until the Alt key is pressed. See the Windows Control Panel → Display → Appearance → Effects for more information.

Visible Property

The `Visible` property indicates whether a control can be seen when the program executes. Setting this property using the Form Designer won't hide the control until the program is run (if it did hide it, you might forget you added it to the form). Setting the `Visible` property to **true** is the same as calling the control's `Show` method, whereas setting the `Visible` property to **false** is the same as calling the control's `Hide` method. User interface design guidelines suggest that people find controls that disappear and reappear to be a distraction. Unless you have a good reason not to do so, you should consider enabling and disabling the controls using the `Enabled` property instead of hiding and showing them. One exception to this is if your application allows the user to configure which elements of the user interface he or she wants to see. For example, you might have an option that allows the user to show and hide toolbars and status bars.

Click and DoubleClick Events

The `Click` event is likely the most common method for which you write event methods. The `Click` event occurs whenever the user clicks the object with the mouse. `DoubleClick` works similarly, except that it occurs when the user double-clicks a control. Click events can also occur from keyboard actions. For example, a button can receive a `click` event when it has the focus and the user presses the space bar or presses the button's access key. This behavior is useful because it allows the user to use the keyboard for most tasks rather than having to reach for the mouse. The `Click` and `DoubleClick` events do not receive any information about the state of the mouse (for example, which button was used to click the object) at the time of the click or double-click. If you need information about the mouse, use the `MouseDown` and `MouseUp` events instead.

Enter and Leave Events

The `Enter` event occurs when an object first gets the focus, and the `Leave` event occurs when the focus leaves the control. Users normally change the focus by pressing the Tab key, pressing access keys, or clicking controls with the mouse. However, the `Enter` and `Leave` events can also occur when the focus is changed by code calling an object's `Focus` method.

One use for coding an `Enter` method is to automatically select the contents of a text box when the text box receives the focus. This can make data entry easier for the users because they can enter new values into the text box without first having to delete the previous contents. For example, the following method is used to select the contents of a text box named `txtPassword` whenever it receives the focus:

```
private void txtPassword_Enter(object sender, System.EventArgs e)
{
    txtPassword.Select(0, txtPassword.TextLength);
}
```

Thinking that the program should notify the user as soon as possible that something has been entered incorrectly, programmers sometimes try to put data validation logic in the **Leave** method of an event. As mentioned in Chapter 5, we don't recommend this approach. However, it is sometimes a good idea to reformat the contents of a text box in its **Leave** event. For example, suppose that you have a text box that allows the user to input a date value. You might choose to code a **Leave** event method in a manner similar to:

```
1    private void txtDateHired_Leave(object sender, System.EventArgs e)
2    {
3        DateTime date;
4        try
5        {
6            date = DateTime.Parse(txtDateHired.Text);
7            txtDateHired.Text = date.ToShortDateString();
8        }
9        catch
10       {
11           // Ignore the exception.
12       }
13   }
```

This reformatting acts as a confirmation to the users that they've entered an acceptable value because they see it change as they Tab away from the text box. Note that a **try-catch** block must be used to catch the exception that might be thrown by the **Parse** method if the text box doesn't contain a valid date value. The data validation code in another part of the program is responsible for informing the user about the error.

Note that form objects don't support the **Enter** and **Leave** events. Instead, forms use the **Activated** and **Deactivated** events.

Use Enter and Leave rather than GotFocus and LostFocus

The **Enter** and **Leave** events were first introduced in .NET. Previous to .NET, controls had **GotFocus** and **LostFocus** that were used for the same purpose. Curiously, the **GotFocus** and **LostFocus** events are still supported by most user interface controls in .NET. However, the Properties window doesn't list them in the Events list. Because the future of **GotFocus** and **LostFocus** is questionable, we recommend you instead use the **Enter** and **Leave** methods.

KeyDown, KeyPress, and KeyUp Events

These key events occur as a result of the user pressing keys on a keyboard when a control has the focus. When a key is pressed, the **KeyDown** event occurs first, followed by the **KeyPress** event, and finally the **KeyUp** event. The difference between the **KeyPress** and **KeyDown** events is that the **KeyPress** event is triggered only by character keys. To do something special when a character is typed, use **KeyPress**. To handle navigation keys, such as the arrow keys, use either the **KeyDown** or **KeyUp** event.

The event method for **KeyPress** is passed an argument of type **KeyPressArgs**, and the event method for **KeyDown** and **KeyUp** are passed an argument of type **KeyEventArgs**. These objects have properties that give you information about the state of the keyboard at the time the key was pressed. For example, the **Control** property of **KeyEventArgs** can be used to determine if the Control key was pressed when the event occurred.

12

The **KeyPress** event is sometimes used to limit which characters can be typed into a text box. For example, suppose that your application requires the user to enter an IP address for a computer in the format *999.999.999.999*, where *9* is any numeric character. For such a text box, the only valid characters are the numeric characters 0 through 9 and the dot character. You could limit the input to only these characters using a **KeyPress** event method such as the following:

```
1   private void txtIPAddress_KeyPress(object sender, System.Windows.Forms.KeyPressEventArgs e)
2   {
3       if ((e.KeyChar < '0' || e.KeyChar > '9') && e.KeyChar != '.')
4       {
5           e.Handled = true;
6       }
7   }
```

In the previous example, the **Handled** property of the **KeyPressEventArgs** object is set to **true** for any character other than the number characters and the dot character. Setting the **Handled** property to **true** causes the keystroke to be ignored. However, you should note *this technique doesn't prevent the text box from having other characters in it*, so further validation is necessary. A user can still put non-numeric characters into the text box by pasting them from the clipboard. Pasting text into a text box doesn't cause the **KeyPress** event to be executed.

Focus Method

You've been using the **Focus** method since Chapter 2 in your data validation logic to move the focus to a text box that contains an invalid value. We include the **Focus** method here for completeness. Because forms do not have a **Focus** event, use the form's **Activate** method instead.

Hide and Show Methods

The **Hide** and **Show** methods can be used to make a control invisible or visible. Calling the **Hide** method is the same as setting the object's **Visible** property to **false**. Calling the **Show** method is the same as setting the object's **Visible** property to **true**. See the **Visible** property for more information. Note that hiding a form isn't the same as closing it.

Refresh Method

Normally Windows applications automatically redraw their controls on the screen during otherwise idle times. This refresh behavior is by design and is done to make applications execute more efficiently. However, sometimes you want your application's user interface to be updated immediately rather than letting Windows perform the refresh when it wants to, for example, when your program has a loop that processes for a very long time and during this loop you want to provide the user with some feedback that indicates the program is still executing.

Suppose that your program has to process a sequential text file containing millions of records. You might include code within the loop to update a status bar with the number of records processed, as shown in Figure 12-1.

```
1          StreamReader sr = null;
2          string inputRecord;
3          int recordCounter = 0;
4
5          sr = new StreamReader(mFileName);
6
7          inputRecord = sr.ReadLine();
8          while (inputRecord != null)
9          {
10
11             // Do something here to process the input record.
12
13             recordCounter++;
14             stbProgress.Panels[0].Text = "Processing record " + recordCounter.ToString();
15             stbProgress.Refresh();
16
17             inputRecord = sr.ReadLine();
18         }
19         stbProgress.Panels[0].Text = "Finished.";
20         sr.Close();
```

Figure 12-1 Forcing a control to redraw itself by calling its Refresh method

Without the call to the **Refresh** method on line 15, the status bar wouldn't be updated until the loop finishes, and the user might think the program is "locked up." Note that, for brevity's sake, the example in Figure 12-1 doesn't include code to actually process the input record, nor does it include code to catch exceptions.

12

FORM OBJECTS

Forms are the foundation for building GUIs for Windows applications. Forms are used to create the main user interface for an application, floating Toolbox windows, and dialogs. (When a form is shown as a **modal dialog**, the form is always displayed on top of other forms in the application. As long as the modal form is displayed, the other forms in the application cannot receive the focus until the user closes the modal form.) This section lists the essential properties, events, and methods for **Form** objects. Figure 12-2 labels typical components of a form with the terms used in this chapter. Table 12-1 lists the essential **Form** properties, events, and methods.

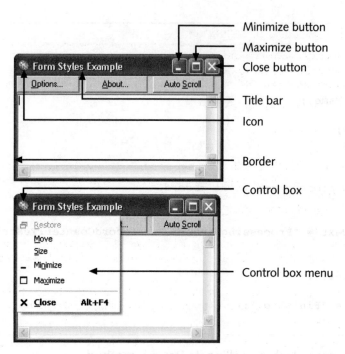

Minimize button

Maximize button

Close button

Title bar

Icon

Border

Control box

Control box menu

Figure 12-2   Components of a form

As mentioned earlier, we encourage you to have VS.NET open and use the Form Designer and Properties window to experiment with the controls as you read about them. You can also review the example project files that accompany this text as they also demonstrate the appearance and behavior of these essential user interface objects.

Table 12-1   Essential Form properties, event, and methods

`AcceptButton` and `CancelButton` properties	The `AcceptButton` property allows you to indicate which button on the form should be clicked when the user presses the Enter key on the keyboard. The `CancelButton` property allows you to indicate which button on the form should be clicked when the user presses the Escape key on the keyboard. A normal dialog-style form would have the `AcceptButton` property set to the OK button and the `CancelButton` property set to the Cancel button. If a dialog has only an OK button, for example an About dialog, it is acceptable to have `AcceptButton` and `CancelButton` set to the same button.
`AutoScroll` property	Setting the `AutoScroll` property of a `Form` object to **true** causes the form to automatically display scroll bars if any controls are located on the form outside the form's visible area. The default value is **false**. If a form contains numerous controls, you might consider using this property so that the user can get to all controls even if the form is sized to be small. However, users may not notice the scroll bars on the form and so may ignore any controls they can't see. For forms with numerous controls, a better user interface design is to use tabs. See the `TabControl` for more information.
`ControlBox` property	Setting the `ControlBox` property to **true** or **false** determines if the form displays the control box in the upper-left corner of a form or not. The default value is **true**, because most forms should display the control box. The control box menu can be accessed from the keyboard by pressing Ctrl+Space. Examples of forms that might not display a control box are so-called "splash screens" that are displayed when your application first starts, and floating-toolbar-style forms.

Table 12-1   Essential Form properties, event, and methods (continued)

Controls property	A form's `Controls` property is actually a collection of objects of type `System.Windows.Forms.Control`. You could use this property to loop through all the controls on a form and perform an action. The following example disables all controls on a form: ```foreach (Control control in Controls)\n{\n control.Enabled = false;\n}```
DrawGrid, GridSize, and SnapToGrid properties	These three properties have no effect during program execution. Rather, these properties are set in the Properties window to help you lay out the controls on a form when you are designing an application's user interface. When used together, these properties help you ensure that groups of controls are aligned at the proper location. Setting `DrawGrid` to **true** displays a series of alignment dots according to the values set in the `GridSize` property. These alignment dots are not displayed during program execution. When `SnapToGrid` is set to **true**, an object's position and size is automatically adjusted so that it has the value of the nearest alignment dot.
FormBorderStyle property	The `FormBorderStyle` property is used to indicate the appearance and behavior of a form object's border. Most commonly it is used to determine if a form can be resized or not. See the "Properties for Common Form Styles" section later in this chapter for more information.
Icon property	The `Icon` property can be set to an icon file (file extension .ico) to cause the icon to be displayed in the form's control box and to be shown on the Windows taskbar when the form is minimized. When set using the Properties window, the icon file is included in the assembly (.exe) so you don't have to distribute any icon files with the application. Modal dialog-style forms should not have the icon property set. See the "Properties for Common Form Styles" section later in this chapter for more information.
KeyPreview property	When you set the `KeyPreview` property to **true**, all keyboard events are sent to the form's `KeyPress`, `KeyDown`, and `KeyUp` event methods before they are sent to the control that would normally receive them. The `KeyPreview` property allows you to write a single keyboard event method that is executed no matter which control has the focus. For example, you could set `KeyPreview` to **true** and write a `KeyDown` event method for the form that closes the application whenever the F3 button is pressed: ```1 private void frmMain_KeyDown(object sender, KeyEventArgs e)\n2 {\n3 if (e.KeyCode == Keys.F3)\n4 {\n5 Close();\n6 e.Handled = true;\n7 }\n8 }``` Note that the statement on line 6 sets the `KeyEventArgs` object's `Handled` property to **true** which prevents the F3 keystroke from being passed to whichever control has the focus.
MaximizeBox and MinimizeBox properties	Setting these properties to **true** or **false** determines if the form displays maximize and minimize boxes. See the "Properties for Common Form Styles" section later in this chapter for more information.
MaximumSize and MinimumSize properties	For forms that have their `FormBorderStyle` property set to one of the values that allow resizing, `MaximumSize` and `MinimumSize` can be used to place limits on how much the user can resize the form. Leaving these properties to their default values of 0, 0 indicates that no maximum or minimum size is specified for the form.
ShowInTaskbar property	Setting the `ShowInTaskbar` property to **true** or **false** determines if the form displays in the Windows taskbar when the form is minimized. See the "Properties for Common Form Styles" section later in this chapter for more information.

12

Table 12-1   Essential Form properties, event, and methods (continued)

`StartPosition` property	This property determines where a form is placed on the computer screen when it is first displayed. Two common values are `CenterScreen` and `CenterParent`. By default, a form is placed at the upper-left portion of the display (called the `WindowsDefaultLocation` in the `StartPosition` drop-down list).
	When `StartPosition` is set to `CenterScreen`, the form is centered horizontally and vertically on the screen. `CenterScreen` is a good value to use for the main form of an application. When `StartPosition` is set to `CenterParent`, the form displays centered over the form that displayed it. `CenterParent` is the value to use for modal-dialog-style forms.
	Another value sometimes used for `StartPosition` is `Manual`. When `StartPosition` is set to `Manual`, you include code in the form's constructor to position and size the form. For example, a `StartPosition` of `Manual` was used in Chapter 11 when code was added to restore a form to its previous position by using an application state file.
	See the "Properties for Common Form Styles" section later in this chapter for more information.
`TopMost` property	Setting the `TopMost` property to **true** for a form causes the form to always be at the front of the display. In other words, all other windows are displayed behind this form. This property normally should be left to its default value of **false** but some types of forms, such as a floating toolbar, non-modal dialog, or a splash screen, work better with `TopMost` set to **true**.
`TransparencyKey` property	See the "Special Effects with Forms" section in the bonus topics of this chapter.
`Closing` event	You know that when an object is instantiated, its constructor method is executed. You put initialization code in this constructor. When a form object is being closed, either by the user or by code calling the form's `Close` method, the form's `Closing` event occurs. You can add code to this event method to do any type of "clean up" operations such as saving application state, closing data files, and releasing network connections.
`Close` method	You should be familiar with the `Close` method by now. Calling a form's `Close` method causes the form to be unloaded from memory. Calling a form's `Close` method triggers its `Closing` event.

The Form Show and ShowDialog Methods

All examples presented in this text have been applications that use a single form. Most real applications require more than one form. The common technique for having more than one form in an application is to have a main form (what you've been naming **frmMain**) that is instantiated and shown when the application starts. This main form can then instantiate other form objects and show them layered "on top" of the main form. Instantiating a form object only causes it to be created in memory. To display the form on the computer screen, you must call either its **Show** or **ShowDialog** method. Both methods cause the form to be shown, but the shown forms behave differently.

After the **Show** method is called, execution immediately continues with the statement that follows the call to the **Show** method. The user is then free to switch between the two forms. Closing the main form ends the application.

Calling **ShowDialog** causes the form to be displayed modally. When a form is shown modally using the **ShowDialog** method, the statement following the **ShowDialog** method isn't executed until the modal form is closed. The **ShowDialog** method also returns a value of type **DialogResult** that can be checked to determine how the users closed the form (that is, did they click a Yes, No, or Cancel button?).

The example that follows displays a modal form and checks to see if the user closed the form by clicking the OK button. If the OK button was clicked, a private helper method is called to save the options. Note that the decision statement on line 8 is not executed until the *options* form has been closed.

```
1    private void mnuOptions_Click(object sender, System.EventArgs e)
2    {
3        frmOptions options;
4        DialogResult result;
5
6        options = new frmOptions();        // instantiate options form
7        result = options.ShowDialog();     // show options form and save result
8        if (result == DialogResult.OK)     // call saveOptions if OK clicked on options form
9        {
10           saveOptions();
11       }
12   }
```

See the sample program discussed later in this chapter for more examples of using multiple forms in an application.

Properties for Common Form Styles

Most forms you create are one of three styles:

1. A main form that doesn't allow resizing

2. A main form that does allow resizing

3. A modal dialog form

The forms you've created for the examples so far in this text have been of the first style. Examples later in this chapter explain a use for the other two styles. When a main form allows resizing, at least one control in the form should also resize. Modal dialogs normally don't allow resizing and require the user to dismiss them before continuing to use other parts of the application. Modal dialogs typically have both an OK and Cancel button.

To make a form behave properly for the three styles mentioned earlier, set the form values as shown in Table 12-2.

Table 12-2   Property values for common Form styles

Form style	Property	Value
A main form that doesn't allow resizing	ControlBox	True
	FormBorderStyle	FixedSingle
	Icon	An appropriate icon file
	MaximizeBox	False
	MinimizeBox	True
	ShowInTaskbar	True
	StartPosition	CenterScreen or Manual
A main form that does allow resizing	ControlBox	True
	FormBorderStyle	Sizable
	Icon	An appropriate icon file
	MaximizeBox	True
	MinimizeBox	True
	ShowInTaskBar	True
	StartPosition	CenterScreen or Manual

Table 12-2   Property values for common Form styles (continued)

Form style	Property	Value
A modal dialog form	AcceptButton	btnOK
	CancelButton	btnCancel
	ControlBox	False
	FormBorderStyle	FixedDialog
	Icon	Not applicable
	MaximizeBox	False
	MinimizeBox	False
	ShowInTaskbar	False
	StartPosition	CenterParent

LABEL OBJECTS

Label controls are typically used to display static text next to another control, most commonly a text box. Many other controls that can be used for data input, such as check boxes and radio buttons, have their own **Text** property, and so using a **Label** control to identify them isn't necessary. Table 12-3 lists essential properties for the **Label** control.

Table 12-3   Essential Label properties

Name property	The suggested three-character prefix for Label controls is lbl.
	When a label is used solely for decorative purposes (i.e., when you never have to access it from your code), it is common practice to keep the label's Name property at whatever value the Form Designer generated for it. Sometimes labels are used to display output values. When used for output, the label should be given a descriptive value for its Name property so that it can be accessed from code.
AutoSize property	Setting the AutoSize property of a label to **true** causes the label to be resized so that the contents of the Text property are always displayed. If AutoSize is set to **false**, the label can be stretched vertically to cause the text to wrap over several lines. The default value is **false**. It is recommended that this property be set to **true**.
Image property	The graphical image to display as part of the label.
Text property	The text to display on the label.

TEXTBOX OBJECTS

Text boxes are used to allow the user to enter input values using the keyboard. A text box can also be used for displaying output values. Text boxes can be made to accept or display just a few characters, or to allow complete documents to be edited. See Figure 12-3 for text box examples. You cannot set the height of a single-line text box. The height of a single-line text box is determined by the size of the font being used in the text box. Table 12-4 lists essential properties for the **TextBox** control.

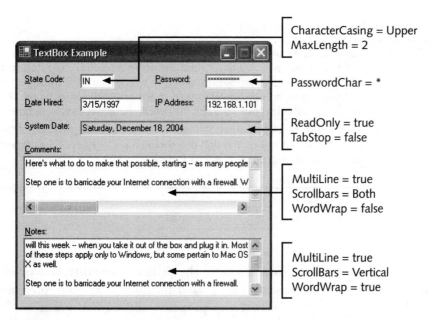

Figure 12-3 TextBox examples

Table 12-4 Essential TextBox properties

Name property	The suggested three-character prefix for `TextBox` controls is `txt`.
AcceptsReturn property	If `AcceptsReturn` is set to **true** and the user presses the Enter key on the keyboard for a text box that has its `MultiLine` property set to **true**, a new line is created in the text box. Otherwise, pressing the Enter key has the same effect as clicking the button set for the form's `AcceptButton` property.
CharacterCasing property	The `CharacterCasing` property can be set to Upper or Lower to force all keystrokes to be converted to uppercase or lowercase characters. For example, it might be useful to set `CharacterCasing` to Upper for a text box that accepts a two-character state abbreviation code.
Lines property	This property gets or sets an array of strings where each element in the array represents one line in the text box. The `Lines` property of `TextBox` is useful only when the `MultiLine` property is set to **true**.
MaxLength property	The `MaxLength` property can be used to limit the number of characters that can be typed into a text box. The default value allows 32,767 characters to be entered or displayed in the text box. Setting `MaxLength` is important when the text box is used for a string value stored in a file or database table that has a maximum number of characters defined.
MultiLine, ScrollBars, and WordWrap properties	These three properties all work with each other to create a style of text box that accepts or displays multiple lines of text. The default value for `MultiLine` is **false** which means the text box processes only one line of text. Setting `MultiLine` to **true** allows many lines of text to be entered or displayed. If `MultiLine` is **true**, the vertical size of the text box should be sized greater than one line so the user knows multiple lines can be used.
	The `ScrollBars` property should also be changed from the default to allow the user to scroll the text contained in the text box. If you want the text to be automatically wrapped as the user types it, set `WordWrap` to **true** and `ScrollBars` to `Vertical`. If you want the user to control when to advance to the next line by pressing the Enter key, set `WordWrap` to **false** and `ScrollBars` to `Both` (both horizontal and vertical).

Table 12-4   Essential TextBox properties (continued)

PasswordChar property	The PasswordChar property is used when you are using a text box to accept a password from a user and you don't want the actual password characters to be displayed as the user types them. Set this property to any character, usually an asterisk (*), and that character is displayed instead of the actual character typed. Note the Text property of the text box contains the actual characters that were typed.
ReadOnly property	Set ReadOnly to **true** to prevent the user from typing in the text box. When used only to display output values, the text box should have its ReadOnly property set to **true** and its TabStop property set to **false**.
Text property	The characters displayed in the text box.

BUTTON OBJECTS

Almost all Windows applications use buttons and menus as the primary user interface objects users click to request that some action be performed. You've used buttons in all examples beginning with Chapter 2, so you already know they have a **Text** property and **Click** event.

Buttons also support the previously mentioned **Image** property, so they can display a graphic. Buttons also have an **ImageAlign** property that determines where on the button the image is shown (see Figure 12-4). However, user interface design guidelines suggest that, most of the time, buttons shouldn't display a graphic. Instead, buttons on a form should all be a uniform size and we recommend you leave them at their default size of 75 × 23 pixels. One exception to this guideline is when you use buttons to make a toolbar at the top of a form and for some reason don't want to use the **ToolBar** control.

Table 12-5 lists essential properties and events for the **Button** control.

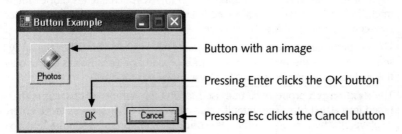

Button with an image

Pressing Enter clicks the OK button

Pressing Esc clicks the Cancel button

Figure 12-4   Button examples

Table 12-5   Essential Button properties and events

Name property	The suggested three-character prefix for Button controls is btn.
Image and ImageAlign property	These properties are used to indicate the image file to display and where on the button the image is displayed.
Text and TextAlign properties	These properties are used to indicate the text, and the location of the text, on the button.
Click event	The Click event occurs when the user clicks the button with the mouse or keyboard.

CheckBox Objects

CheckBox objects are typically used to represent Boolean values denoted by displaying the box as checked or unchecked. See Figure 12-5. **CheckBox** objects have their own **Text** property, so there is no need to use a **Label** control to identify them on a form. Table 12-6 lists essential properties and events for the **CheckBox** control.

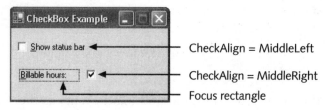

Figure 12-5   CheckBox examples

Table 12-6   Essential CheckBox properties and events

Name property	The suggested three-character prefix for CheckBox controls is chk.
CheckAlign property	The CheckAlign property can be used to position the check box to the left or right of the text. Normally the default value of MiddleLeft should be used. However, you might sometimes change this value to MiddleRight to make the check box align vertically with other controls on the form.
Checked property	The Checked property is used when representing a Boolean value. If Checked has a value of **true**, the check mark is shown. If Checked has a value of **false**, the check mark is not shown.
Text property	The text that displays next to the check box.
CheckedChanged event	The CheckedChanged event occurs whenever the Checked property is changed either by the user or from code. You might add code to this event to enable or disable other controls on the form, depending on the value of the Checked property.

ComboBox Objects

The **ComboBox** control combines the features of a text box and list box into a single control. A **ComboBox** consists of text box, a drop-down button, and a scrollable list. See Figure 12-6. The **ComboBox** control is typically used when the user must select a value from a predefined list or enter a value not in the list. You can set properties so that the user must just select a value from the list, or it can also be configured so that the user can type text into the text box portion or select a value from the list. When configured so that the user can select only an item from the list, it behaves much the same as a **ListBox** control. However, it requires much less space on the form.

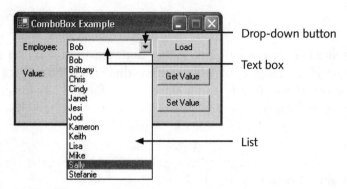

Figure 12-6 ComboBox example

The **ComboBox** control has many of the same properties, methods, and events as the **ListBox** control. Because you already know how to use the **ListBox** control, the **ComboBox** control should be easy for you to use. Table 12-7 lists essential properties for the **ComboBox** control.

Table 12-7 Essential ComboBox properties

`Name` property	The suggested three-character prefix for `ComboBox` controls is `cbo`.
`DropDownStyle` property	This property controls whether the user can type text directly into the text box portion of the control, or if the user must select a value from the list. Set to `DropDown` if you want the user to be able to type text or select from the list. Set to `DropDownList` if the user must select a value from the list.

`Items` property	The `Items` property is a collection of the selectable objects shown in the list portion of the control. The `Items` property can be set using the properties window, but items are typically added to the list by calling the `Items.Clear` and `Items.Add` methods. For example:
	
	`cboEmployee.Items.Clear();`
	
	`cboEmployee.Items.Add("Sally");`
	`cboEmployee.Items.Add("Kameron");`
	`cboEmployee.Items.Add("Stefanie");`
	`cboEmployee.Items.Add("Keith");`
	`cboEmployee.Items.Add("Janet");`
	`cboEmployee.Items.Add("Bob");`
	`cboEmployee.Items.Add("Cindy");`
	
	Note that, in a real program, the items might be added using values from a file or database table.

`MaxDropDownItems` property	The `MaxDropDownItems` property controls how many items are displayed in the drop-down list. The default value is just 8, so consider changing it to a higher value to make it easier for the user to select a value. A value of 12 or 15 is a good choice. If the list contains less than 20 total items, you should consider setting `MaxDropDownItems` to the number of total items in the list so that the user won't have to scroll the list when choosing a value.

`Sorted` property	Indicates if the values in the list are automatically sorted into ascending alphabetical order or not. Note that if you later add the statements:
	
	cboEmployee.Items.Add("AJ");
	cboEmployee.Items.Add("Jennifer");
	cboEmployee.Items.Add("Katherine");
	cboEmployee.Items.Add("Tony");
	
	after the initial values are set, these names are inserted into the list shown in Figure 12-6 at the appropriate alphabetic locations, regardless of the order of the statements.

`Text` property	The text value shown in the text box portion of the control.

DateTimePicker Objects

As its name suggests, the **DateTimePicker** control is used to represent a **DateTime** value. Whereas a **DateTime** value includes both a date and a time portion, the **DateTimePicker** can be used to represent a date value or a time value, but not both at the same time. Users choose a date value by typing in the month, day, and year parts of a date, or by selecting the date from a drop-down calendar. Times can be indicated by typing in hour, minute, and second values, or by using up and down (often called *spin*) buttons. Figure 12-7 shows the three formats the **DateTimePicker** object can assume based on how its properties are set (date, time or drop-down calendar). Table 12-8 lists essential **DateTimePicker** properties.

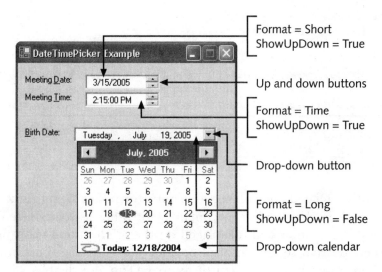

Figure 12-7   DateTimePicker examples

Table 12-8   Essential DateTimePicker properties

Name property	The suggested three-character prefix for DateTimePicker controls is dtp.
Format property	The Format property determines the look and behavior of the DateTimePicker object. For dates, you set Format to either Long or Short. The exact contents of Long and Short are determined the by Regional Settings in the Windows control panel. Generally, the Long format spells out the name of the day and month, and Short represents the month as a number.
	Set a DateTimePicker object's Format property to Time when representing the time portion of a DateTime type. You can also set Format to Custom and set the CustomFormat property if you want more control over how the date and time elements are displayed.
MaxDate and MinDate properties	The MaxDate and MinDate properties can be set to limit the date range the object displays. When set, users cannot enter or select a date greater than the MaxDate value, or a date less than the MinDate value.
ShowUpDown property	The ShowUpDown property determines if the DateTimePicker object is drawn with the up and down buttons (sometimes called spin buttons). Setting this property to **true** for dates causes the up and down buttons to display instead of the drop-down button. Users can then use the up and down buttons to change the values of the month, day, and year portions of the date. This option should be set to **true** when the DateTimePicker object is used to represent a time-only value because the drop-down button still displays a month calendar.

Table 12-8   Essential DateTimePicker properties (continued)

Value property	The `Value` property is used to get or set the date or time the control is representing. The `Value` type of the `DateTimePicker` is actually a `DateTime` value, so it contains both a date and time portion even if it doesn't visually represent both. If the value you need to represent includes both a date and time, you use two `DateTimePicker` controls with one representing the date and the other representing the time. You should then get and set the `DateTimePicker` `Value` property using code similar to:

```
private DateTime mMeetingDateTime = DateTime.Now;
...

    // Set the DateTimePicker objects to display the values of the variables.

    dtpMeetingDate.Value = mMeetingDateTime;
    dtpMeetingTime.Value = mMeetingDateTime;
...

    // Get the DateTimePicker values and store in a single variable.

    mMeetingDateTime = dtpMeetingDate.Value.Date + dtpMeetingTime.Value.TimeOfDay;
```

GROUPBOX OBJECTS

A **GroupBox** is used to group other related controls together on a form. The **GroupBox** control is different than most other controls in that it acts as a container for other user interface objects. Objects that act as containers can have other controls placed on them. The **Location** property of these other controls are then relative to the **GroupBox** and not the form containing the **GroupBox**. Setting the **Enabled** property of the **GroupBox** to **false** also disables all controls contained within the **GroupBox**.

The suggested three-character prefix for **GroupBox** controls is **grp**. The only other essential properties are the previously mentioned **Enabled** and **Text** properties. See the "RadioButton Objects" section for more information.

LISTVIEW OBJECTS

You learned in Chapter 8 how to use a **ListBox** control to display a list of text. **ListBox** controls work fine when you have only one value to display, but what do you use when you want to display more than one column for each row? Previous techniques have showed you how to format the text in the list box so that it appears as if there is more than one column, but this technique can make your application appear amateurish. For situations in which you want to display multiple columns of data, you should use the **ListView** control rather than a **ListBox** control. (For example, the Windows Explorer uses the **ListView** control when displaying detailed information about files.) Figure 12-8 shows an example of a **ListView** control.

ListView controls have many advantages over **ListBox** controls, including the following:

- **ListViews** have real columns.
- **ListViews** can have column headings.
- Data in the columns can be left- or right-justified.
- The columns in a **ListView** can be resized by the user.

- The columns in a `ListView` can be reordered by the user.

- `ListViews` automatically show horizontal and vertical scroll bars when needed.

- Clicking a column heading can cause the contents of the list to be sorted, provided that you add the necessary code.

The only reason you might not want to use `ListView` controls is that they are a little more complex to work with than a simple `ListBox` control. If you need to display a list of data that contains a single column, you should use a `ListBox` control. Otherwise, consider using a `ListView` control.

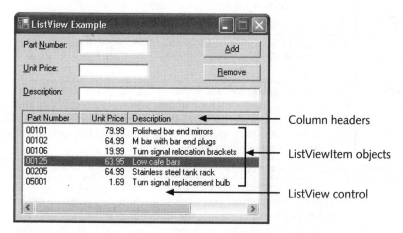

Figure 12-8 ListView example

The `ListView` control is one of those objects that contains other objects. Specifically, `ColumnHeader` objects define the columns to display in the list, and `ListViewItem` objects are used to represent each row in the list. The essential properties used for the `ListView` control and its parts are shown in Table 12-9. The next section describes how to use the `ListView` from code.

Table 12-9 Essential ListView properties

`ListView.Name` property	The suggested three-character prefix for `ListView` controls is `lvw`.
`ListView.AllowColumnReorder` property	Set this value to **true** if you want the user to be allowed to reposition the columns in the list by dragging them with the mouse.
`ListView.Columns` property	This property refers to the collection of `ColumnHeader` objects that define the columns in the list. These values are normally set using the Properties window.
`ListView.FullRowSelect` property	Set this value to **true** if you want the user to be able select a row in the list by clicking anywhere in the list. If it is set to **false**, the user can only select the row by clicking the text in the first column.
`ListView.MultiSelect` property	Set this to **true** if you want the user to be able to select more than one item in the list.
`ListView.Sorting` property	Like the `ListBox` control, the `ListView` control can automatically sort its contents. You can set this property to either `Ascending` or `Descending`, if you want the list to be automatically sorted by the value of the first column. Set this to `None` if the contents of the list are unordered or if your code sorts the data before adding it to the list. Note that this automatic sorting sorts values as if they are strings and so won't produce good results for non-string data types.
`ListView.View` property	The `ListView` can actually display data in many different ways. The most useful, and the only one you'll likely use, sets the `View` property to `Details`.

Table 12-9   Essential ListView properties (continued)

`ListView.Items` property	This property refers to the collection of `ListViewItem` objects that represent the rows shown in the list. These values are normally added from your program after it has read data from a file or database.
`ListView.SelectedItems` property	This property refers to the collection of `ListViewItems` that are currently selected in the list. If the `MultiSelect` property is **false**, this collection contains at most one item.
`ListView.ListViewItemSorter` property	In the `ColumnClick` event, set this property to a class that knows how to sort the rows displayed in the `ListView`. See the "Sorting the Contents of a ListView" section for more information.
`ColumnHeader.Text` property	This property is simply the text that appears in the column header.
`ColumnHeader.TextAlign` property	This property determines if the data in the column should be left- or right-aligned. Generally, only columns containing numeric values should be right-aligned.
`ColumnHeader.Width` property	This property determines the width of the column in pixels. It is common to use a trial-and-error method of determining the best width for a column. The users can always resize the columns if they need to be bigger or smaller, but the initial widths of the columns shouldn't require the user to resize them in order to see the information.
`ListViewItem.SubItems` property	The `SubItems` property refers to the value of each column in a single row.

`ListViewItem.Tag` property	The `Tag` property is not used by the `ListView` or `ListViewItem` itself. Instead it is available for you to store a reference to another object. For example, if you are displaying the contents of an `ArrayList` in a `ListView`, you could set each item's `Tag` property to the reference of the object in the `ArrayList` it represents. For example:
	
	`foreach (clsTimeLogEntry entry in mArrayList)`
	`{`
	`    if (entry.Billable == true)`
	`    {`
	`        ListViewItem item =`
	`            new ListViewItem(entry.EmployeeID);`
	`        item.SubItems.Add(`
	`            entry.DateWorked.ToShortDateString());`
	`        item.SubItems.Add(`
	`            entry.HoursWorked.ToString("0.00"));`
	
	`        item.Tag = entry;`
	
	`        lvwMain.Items.Add(item);`
	`    }`
	`}`
	
	You can then use the Tag property of the `ListViewItem` to get a reference back to the object displayed in the `ListViewItem`. For example:
	
	`clsTimeLogEntry entry =`
	`    (clsTimeLogEntry)lvwMain.SelectedItems[0].Tag;`
	
	This technique is especially useful when the items in the `ListView` are sorted in an order that doesn't match the order in the `ArrayList`.

Adding Columns to a ListView

Columns are normally added using the Properties window and by clicking the ▦ button next to the Columns property to show the ColumnHeader Collection Editor window (see Figure 12-9). Be sure that you set the **View** property to **Details** before showing this form so that you can see the columns appear on the **ListView** as you add them. To add a column header, click the **Add** button and then set the properties for that column header in the right-hand pane. Notable properties you'll want to set are **Text, TextAlign,** and **Width.** Other buttons on the ColumnHeader Collection Editor window allow you to remove columns and rearrange their order.

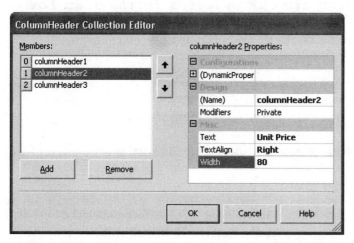

Figure 12-9 ColumnHeader Collection Editor window

Adding Rows to a ListView

There are many techniques for adding rows to a **ListView,** but we feel the technique presented here is the easiest. First instantiate a **ListViewItem** object and pass its constructor a string for the contents of the first column. Next, call the **ListViewItem** object's **SubItems.Add** method and pass it a string for the contents of the second column. Continue calling the **SubItems.Add** method until all columns have been populated. Finally, add the **ListViewItem** object to the **ListView** object by calling the **ListView** object's **Items.Add** method. Note that the contents of a column are always a string. These steps are illustrated in the following code snippet:

```
1        ListViewItem item;
2
3        item = new ListViewItem(partNumber);
4
5        item.SubItems.Add(unitPrice.ToString("C"));
6        item.SubItems.Add(description);
7
8        lvwParts.Items.Add(item);
```

Determining Which Rows Are Selected

To determine if any rows are selected in a **ListView,** you check the value of the **ListView** object's **SelectedItems.Count** property. If it has a value of zero, then no rows have been selected.

If the **Items.Count** property has a value greater than zero, then at least one row has been selected. You can get a reference to the **ListViewItem** objects selected by using the **ListView** object's **SelectedItems** collection.

Removing a Row from a ListView

Removing a row from the **ListView** object works similarly to other collection types—just call the **ListView** object's **Items.Remove** method and pass it a reference to the **ListViewItem** property you want to remove. The following example makes sure at least one item is selected in the `ListView` and then removes the first item selected:

```
1     // Make sure an item is selected in the list box.
2
3     if (lvwParts.SelectedItems.Count == 0)
4     {
5         return;
6     }
7
8     // Remove the item from the list box.
9
10    lvwParts.Items.Remove(lvwParts.SelectedItems[0]);
```

Sorting the Contents of a ListView

A nice feature to add to a `ListView` control is to cause its rows to be sorted based on the value of a certain column whenever that column's header is clicked. To add this behavior, you must first define a class that knows how to compare two rows in your `ListView`. Then, in the `ListView`'s `ColumnClick` event method, set the `ListView`'s `ListViewItemSorter` property to an instance of this class. For example:

```
private void lvwParts_ColumnClick(object sender, System.Windows.Forms.ColumnClickEventArgs e)
{
    lvwParts.ListViewItemSorter = new clsListViewComparer(e.Column);
}
```

The `ListView` control then makes repeated calls to the `Compare` method defined in the comparer class, passing it two `ListViewItem` objects to compare so the rows can be put in the correct order. After all rows have been compared, the rows are redisplayed in the new sequence.

Figure 12-10 defines a class that knows how to compare the rows of the `ListView` object shown in Figure 12-8. Note that the constructor for the class must be passed the column that is being compared. This column value is stored in a private member variable so that when the `Compare` method is called, it knows which data type to use to compare the two values. The `Compare` method indicates which of the values it is passed is greater by returning one of three values: a -1 if the first value is less than the second, a 1 if the first value is greater than the second, or a zero if both values are equal. If you want the rows sorted in descending order, return -1 if the first value is greater than the second, and 1 if the first value is less than the second. Note that the column containing price must be converted to a **decimal** value before the values can be compared.

```
1    using System;
2    using System.Collections;
3    using System.Windows.Forms;
4
5    public class clsListViewComparer: IComparer
6    {
7        private int mColumnToCompare;
8
9        public clsListViewComparer(int column)
10       {
11           mColumnToCompare = column;
12       }
```

Figure 12-10   A class that compares two rows of a ListView control

```
13
14          // Compares two values, depending on the column being sorted.
15          // Column 0 = Part Number (string)
16          // Column 1 = Price        (decimal)
17          // Column 2 = Description (string)
18          public int Compare(object object1, object object2)
19          {
20              ListViewItem item1;
21              ListViewItem item2;
22              string text1;
23              string text2;
24              decimal decimal1;
25              decimal decimal2;
26
27              // The Compare method is always passed plain old object references
28              // so cast them as ListViewItem objects.
29
30              item1 = (ListViewItem)object1;
31              item2 = (ListViewItem)object2;
32
33              // Get the text values for the column being sorted.
34
35              text1 = item1.SubItems[mColumnToCompare].Text;
36              text2 = item2.SubItems[mColumnToCompare].Text;
37
38              if (mColumnToCompare == 1)
39              {
40                  // To compare prices, first convert the strings to decimals so
41                  // their numeric values can be compared.
42
43                  decimal1 = decimal.Parse(text1);
44                  decimal2 = decimal.Parse(text2);
45
46                  if (decimal1 < decimal2)
47                  {
48                      return -1;
49                  }
50                  if (decimal1 > decimal2)
51                  {
52                      return 1;
53                  }
54                  else
55                  {
56                      return 0;
57                  }
58              }
59              else
60              {
61                  // All other columns are compared as strings so we can use the
62                  // String.Compare method to do a case-insensitive compare.
63
64                  return String.Compare(
65                      item1.SubItems[mColumnToCompare].Text,
66                      item2.SubItems[mColumnToCompare].Text, true);
67              }
68          }
69      }
```

Figure 12-10 A class that compares two rows of a ListView control (continued)

MENU OBJECTS

As previously mentioned, almost all Windows applications use menus and buttons as the primary user interface objects users click to request that some action be performed. You already know how to add event methods to buttons.

.NET has two styles of menus—main menus that are displayed from a form's menu bar, and context menus that can pop up just about anywhere when the user right-clicks on something. In reality, main menus and context menus are two separate controls, but because they share many of the same properties and events, and because they are added to a form in the same way, we cover both styles in this section. Figure 12-11 shows each menu type along with the menu terminology used for each menu type.

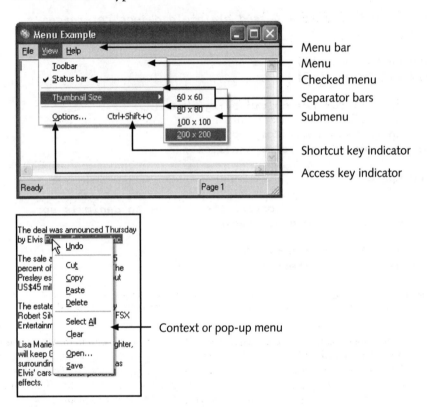

Figure 12-11   Menu examples and terminology

Adding Menus to Forms

Adding event methods to menus is easy, but adding menus to a form is a little more complex. To begin, drag a **MainMenu** control from the Toolbox to the form. When you add a menu to a form, a small icon that represents the menu is displayed at the bottom of the Form Designer window in what is called the **Control tray**. You add menu items, separator bars, and submenus by typing the caption for the menus in places provided as shown in Figure 12-12. Menu items can also be reordered by dragging them with the mouse.

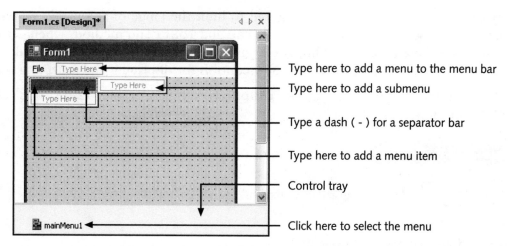

Figure 12-12   Adding menus using the Form Designer

Context menus are added in the same way, except that you drag a **ContextMenu** control from the Toolbox to the form. To cause a **ContextMenu** object to be displayed at execution time, you set the **ContextMenu** property of some other control to the context menu added to the form. The context menu then pops up whenever the user right-clicks that control.

After you add the menus the way you like them, you set properties and add event methods using the Properties window just as with other objects. Note that each menu item is an individual object and so each has its own property values and event method. Table 12-10 lists essential menu properties and events.

Table 12-10   Essential menu properties and events

`Name` property	The suggested three-character prefix for menu controls is mnu.
`Checked` property	This property is used to indicate if a check mark should be drawn next to the menu item. A value of **true** draws the check mark and a value of **false** doesn't draw the check mark.
`Shortcut` property	This property can be used to assign a shortcut key to the menu item. When the user presses the shortcut key, the menu object's `Click` event is triggered. Shortcut keys are function keys, or a letter on the keyboard along with some combination of Ctrl, Shift, and Alt. You can implement shortcut keys to give the user an additional option for selecting menu commands rather than using the mouse or access keys.
`Text` property	This property is used to set the text value that appears on the menu item. Menu items normally include an access key, so be sure to include an ampersand in front of the appropriate character in the `Text` property.
`Click` event	The `Click` event occurs when the user clicks the menu with the mouse or keyboard.

NumericUpDown Objects

The **NumericUpDown** control is used to visually represent numbers and to give the user a way to input a numeric value without using the keyboard. In addition to typing an input value, the **NumericUpDown** control has tiny up and down buttons (sometimes called spin buttons) that the user can click to change the displayed value.

The `NumericUpDown` control can be configured to limit the range of acceptable values, and it has a `Value` property so you don't have to use `Parse` and `ToString` methods when getting and setting its value. For these reasons, and because it gives the user additional options for data input, you should consider using it instead of `TextBox` controls for displaying and accepting numbers.

Figure 12-13 shows examples of `NumericUpDown` objects. Table 12-11 lists essential `NumericUpDown` properties.

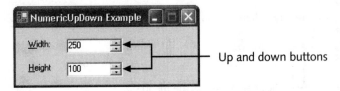

Figure 12-13   NumericUpDown examples

Table 12-11   Essential NumericUpDown properties

Name property	The suggested three-character prefix for `NumericUpDown` controls is num.
`DecimalPlaces` property	The `DecimalPlaces` property simply indicates how many decimal places the control should display. Set to 0 for integer values and 2 for monetary values.
`Increment` property	The `Increment` property indicates what value should be added or subtracted from the current value when the user clicks the up or down buttons on the control.
`InterceptArrowKeys` property	When set to **true**, the `InterceptArrowsKey` property allows the user to select values by using the up and down arrow keys on the keyboard. We recommend that you keep the default value of **true** for this property.
`Minimum` and `Maximum` properties	These two properties limit the range of values that can be displayed and selected with the `NumericUpDown` control. If the value displayed has already reached the maximum value, clicking the up button has no effect. If the value displayed has already reached the minimum value, clicking the down button has no effect. Note these two values are required and default to 0 and 100, respectively, so you almost always have to change them after adding one of these controls to a form.
`ThousandsSeparator` property	This property is used to indicate if a thousands separator character (normally a comma) should be displayed or not. Set this property to **true** to display the thousands separator character and to **false** if you don't want it displayed.
`Value` property	The `Value` property is used to set or get the numeric value of the text displayed. Unlike a `TextBox`, you don't have to use `Parse` and `ToString` methods when getting and setting a `NumericUpDown` control's numeric value. Note the `Value` property is of type **decimal** so you might need to use casting to convert the `Value` property to other numeric data types. For example: `Height = (int)numHeight.Value;`

RADIOBUTTON OBJECTS

`RadioButton` objects are used to allow the user to choose a single value from a set of choices. Normally this value is selected from at least three choices, but you might also use two `RadioButtons` to represent a single **Boolean** value instead of a `CheckBox` control. If the range of choices is more than about five, you should choose another user interface item, such as a `ComboBox`, to represent the value.

When one `RadioButton` object has its `Checked` property set to **true**, either by code or when the user selects it, all other `RadioButtons` in the same container control automatically have their `Checked` property set to **false**. Because this mutually exclusive behavior is indicated by the container control, you often place **RadioButton** controls within a **GroupBox** control (see Figure 12-14). Table 12-12 lists essential **RadioButton** properties and events.

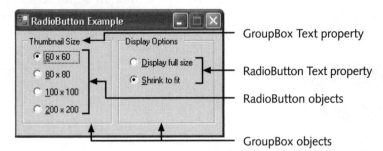

GroupBox Text property

RadioButton Text property

RadioButton objects

GroupBox objects

Figure 12-14 RadioButton and GroupBox examples

Table 12-12 Essential RadioButton properties and events

Name property	The suggested three-character prefix for RadioButton controls is rad.
Checked property	The Checked property is used to indicate if this object is selected or not. If Checked has a value of **true**, the RadioButton appears selected. If Checked has a value of **false**, the RadioButton does not appear selected. Only one RadioButton in the same container control can have a Checked value of **true**.
Text property	The text that displays next to the button.
CheckedChanged event	The CheckChanged event occurs whenever the Checked property is changed either by the user or from code.

12

TIMER OBJECTS

You can use the **Timer** control to cause an event method to be executed at a regular interval. For example, you might use a **Timer** control to display the current system time, or to implement a feature that automatically saves data to a file every 10 minutes. **Timer** objects have no visual representation to the user and so don't appear when your application is running. Table 12-13 lists the essential **Timer** properties and events.

Table 12-13 Essential Timer properties and events

Name property	The suggested three-character prefix for Timer controls is tmr.
Enabled property	The Enabled property indicates if the timer is executing or not. When Enabled is set to **false**, the Tick event is not triggered.
Interval property	The Interval property is used to indicate how frequently the Tick event should be triggered. The Interval property is defined in milliseconds. For example, a value of 1,000 triggers the Tick event every second, a value of 60,000 triggers the Tick event once every minute, and a value of 3,600,000 triggers the Tick event once every hour.
Start and Stop methods	You can call the Start and Stop methods to indicate if the timer is executing or not. These methods have the same effect as setting the timer's Enabled property to **true** or **false**.
Tick event	The Tick event is triggered when the timer's Interval has been reached. Care must be used that the code placed within a Tick event executes faster than the Interval value. The following example updates a text box with the current system time. ```private void tmrClock_Tick(object sender, System.EventArgs e)\n{\n txtSystemTime.Text = DateTime.Now.ToLongTimeString();\n}```

TOOLBAR OBJECTS

Toolbars are placed on a form to give users a quick way to request that an action take place (see Figure 12-15). Toolbar buttons usually correspond to menu commands, but the toolbar requires fewer mouse clicks. Users typically have the option of showing or hiding the toolbar.

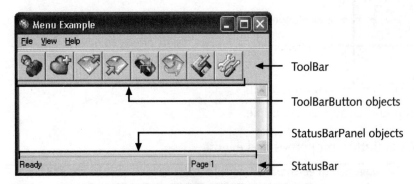

Figure 12-15   ToolBar and StatusBar controls

One technique for creating a toolbar on a form is to simply arrange a set of buttons containing images along the top of the form. A more formal style is to use the **ToolBar** control. Table 12-14 lists the essential **ToolBar** control properties and events.

Table 12-14   Essential ToolBar properties and events

`Name` property	The suggested three-character prefix for `ToolBar` controls is `tlb`.
`Appearance` property	The `Appearance` property can be set to either `Normal` or `Flat` depending how you want the buttons on the toolbar to appear.
`Buttons` property	This is the collection of buttons that are present on the toolbar. See the "Adding Buttons to a Toolbar" section for more information.
`ButtonSize` property	The `ButtonSize` property determines the width and height of the buttons shown on the toolbar. A pixel size of 40 × 40 is good if the button icons are the larger 32 × 32 size.
`Dock` property	This property determines where on the form the toolbar appears. Toolbars normally are docked to the top of the form, but this property also allows you to dock them on the left, right, or bottom of the form.
`ShowToolTips` property	The `ShowToolTips` property determines if the ToolTip text for a button is displayed in a small pop-up window when the user hovers the mouse over a button. For most purposes, this value should be set to **true**. The ToolTip text for a toolbar button is defined by setting the `ToolBarButton's ToolTipText` property. See the discussion for Figure 12-30 for more information.
`ImageList` property	The `ImageList` property is set to the `ImageList` control that contains the collection of images you want to use when assigning a graphical image to the toolbar buttons. See the "Adding Buttons to a Toolbar" section for more information.

Table 12-14   Essential ToolBar properties and events (continued)

ButtonClick event	This event occurs whenever the user clicks any of the buttons on the toolbar. To determine which button was clicked, the event method is passed an argument of type `ToolBarButtonClickEventArgs` that contains a reference to the button that was clicked. You can then compare this reference to the names you've given to the buttons, for example:

```
private void tlbMain_ButtonClick(object sender, ToolBarButtonClickEventArgs e)
{
    if (e.Button == tbbAdd)
    {
        addEntry();
    }
    else if (e.Button == tbbUpdate)
    {
        updateEntry();
    }
    ...
}
```

Adding Buttons to a Toolbar

The **ToolBar** control is an object that contains a collection of **ToolBarButton** objects, which you also have to know how to use when adding a toolbar to a form. Buttons are normally added to a toolbar using the Properties window and by clicking the ▣ button next to the **Buttons** property to show the ToolBarButton Collection Editor window (see Figure 12-16). To add a button, click the Add button and set the properties for that button in the right-hand pane.

The suggested three-character prefix for **ToolBarButton** controls is **tbb**. Other **ToolBarButton** properties you'll want to set include **Text** or **ToolTipText**. The **Text** property is displayed on the button, and the **ToolTipText** is displayed if the user hovers the mouse over the button. You should set either the **Text** or **ToolTipText** property, depending on the style of toolbar button you want.

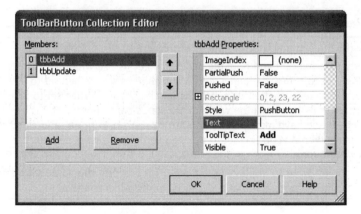

Figure 12-16   ToolBarButton Collection Editor window

Unfortunately, adding an image to a toolbar button isn't as straightforward as adding an image to a regular button. To add an image to a toolbar button, you don't set the toolbar button's **Image** property. Instead, you set its **ImageIndex** property, but first you must first add an **ImageList** control to the form.

The **ImageList** control serves as a holder for a collection of images that other controls can use. You add images to its Images collection by clicking the ▣ button next to the **Images** property to show the Image Collection Editor window and adding image files. Images can be loaded from many file formats including .bmp, .gif, .jpg, .ico, .png, and .wmf.

After an `ImageList` has been added to the form, and its `Images` property is set to a collection of images loaded from graphics files, you set the `ToolBar` control's `ImageList` property to this `ImageList` object. Then set the `ImageIndex` for each `ToolBarButton` on the toolbar. The `ImageIndex` property indicates which image in the `ImageList's` `Image` collection to use.

STATUSBAR OBJECTS

`StatusBar` objects are placed at the bottom of a form to give the user some additional information about the state of the application (see Figure 12-15). Status bars are normally output only, meaning that users don't interact with them. Users typically have the option of showing or hiding status bars. A status bar is divided into one or more **status bar panels**, depending on what information you wish to be displayed.

Table 12-15 lists the essential `StatusBar` properties, and Table 12-16 lists the essential `StatusBarPanel` properties.

Table 12-15   Essential StatusBar properties and events

Name property	The suggested three-character prefix for `StatusBar` controls is stb.
Dock property	This property determines where on the form the status bar appears. Status bars are almost always docked at the bottom of the form.
Panels property	Panels are added to a toolbar using the Properties window and by clicking the ⬚ button next to the `Panels` property to show the StatusBarPanel Collection Editor window. To add a panel, click the Add button and set the properties for that button in the right pane. Essential `StatusBarPanel` properties are described in Table 12-16.
ShowPanels property	Set the `ShowPanels` property to **true** so the panels contained in the `Panels` property collection are displayed.

Table 12-16   Essential StatusBarPanel properties and events

Name property	The suggested three-character prefix for `StatusBarPanel` controls is sbp.
AutoSize property	This property determines if and how the panel changes its size when the form is resized. When set to `None`, the panel does not change its size. When set to `Contents`, the panel sizes itself to match the text it contains. When set to `Spring`, the panel changes its size to fill the width of the status bar. A normal status bar on a resizable form would have most panels with `AutoSize` set to `None`, and either the first or last panel with `AutoSize` set to `Spring` so that at least one status bar panel is resized with the form.
Text property	This is the text you want to display in the panel. This property should be set from code whenever the state information that is displayed in the panel changes.

A PROGRAM EXAMPLE

Now that you have some idea about when and how to use the essential user interface controls, it's time to take another look at the Contacts List application first introduced in Chapter 10 and enhanced in Chapter 11. The user interface for the Contacts List application can be greatly enhanced by using many of the controls you just learned about. Walking you through the steps to make all the changes would be too lengthy. Instead, the list of enhancements is listed in the next few sections and noteworthy code segments are presented and discussed. You are strongly encouraged to try to make these enhancements yourself, but if you get stuck, you can review the project solution files that accompany this text.

Figure 12-17 shows an example of the new and improved user interface for the Contacts List application.

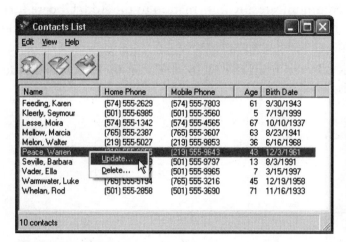

Figure 12-17   New and improved Contacts List application

Summary of Changes

Many changes have been made to the Contacts List application including the following:

- Three forms are now used instead of one. The main form lists all contacts added. A second form is used as a modal dialog for adding new contacts and updating existing contacts. A third form shows version and copyright information.

- The main form can now be resized by the user, and can be minimized or maximized.

- The main form contains a toolbar and status bar, which can be hidden by the user using the View menu. A panel on the status bar displays the total number of contacts in the list.

- The main form now contains menus and toolbar buttons, so users can indicate that they are ready to add, update, or delete a contact.

- All contacts are displayed on the main form using a `ListView` control. Clicking the `ListView` column headers sorts the contents of the list in ascending order by the column clicked.

- Double-clicking a contact in the `ListView` shows the Update Contact dialog for that contact.

- Right-clicking a contact in the `ListView` control shows a context menu from which the user can choose to update or delete the selected contact.

- The Add/Update dialog uses the `DateTimePicker` control for the Birthdate value.

- A menu command on the main form shows an "About" dialog with version and copyright information.

Interform Communication

When you develop an application that uses more than one form, you almost always need to communicate information between the forms. Communicating between forms has not been discussed in this text yet, but the way it is done should not surprise you if you remember that a form is just another kind of object. Objects communicate with each other using their public properties and methods. In the Contacts List example, the main form instantiates and shows the Add/Update form. In order for the main form to communicate any information to the Add/Update form, code has to be added to the Add/Update form to accept this information either as method arguments or properties. Here's a more detailed example and explanation.

When the About menu command is selected from the Help menu on the main form, the About dialog, shown in Figure 12-18, is displayed.

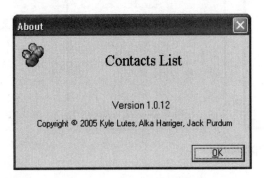

Figure 12-18   New and improved Contacts List application

You can see from Figure 12-18 that the About dialog displays information about the Contacts List application. It would have been easy to set these properties when designing the About form, but because one goal of OOP is to make reusable classes, the About form contains no code specifically related to the Contacts List application. Instead, the main form passes the application-specific information to the About form when it instantiates it, as shown here:

```
365    private void mnuHelpAbout_Click(object sender, System.EventArgs e)
366    {
367        frmAbout about;
368        about = new frmAbout(this, mVersion, mCopyright);
369        about.ShowDialog();
370    }
```

Note how line 368 passes as the first argument the keyword **this**, which contains a reference to the current object (that is, the `frmMain` object). The About form needs a reference to the main form so that it can get the main form's `Icon` and `Text` properties to display on the About dialog. Passing a reference from one object to a second so that the second can access the first object's properties and methods is sometimes called a **callback reference**. Note also that the return value from the call to the About form's `ShowDialog` method on line 369 is ignored because no information is being communicated back to the main form.

In order for the About form to accept the details about the application, the constructor for the About form takes three arguments, as shown here:

```
096   public frmAbout(Form parent, string version, string copyright)
097   {
098       InitializeComponent();
099
100       picIcon.Image = parent.Icon.ToBitmap();
101       lblAppTitle.Text = parent.Text;
102       lblVersion.Text = version;
103       lblCopyright.Text = copyright;
104   }
```

The arguments passed to the **frmAbout** constructor are then used to display the relevant information about the application on the About form.

Similar communication must take place between the main form and the Add/Update form. Because the Add/Update form serves two purposes, the main form must tell it whether it is adding or updating a contact whenever it is displayed. Additionally, the main form passes the Add/Update form a reference to the contact object it is adding or updating. Because the user has several ways to request add or update, the main form uses private helper methods to start the add or update process. These helper methods are called from the various menu and toolbar button event methods. The two private helper methods are shown in Figure 12-19. Figure 12-20 shows the corresponding relevant methods from **frmAddUpdate**.

12

```
424   // Adds a new contact to the list.
425   private void addContact()
426   {
427       clsContact contact = new clsContact();
428       frmAddUpdate addUpdate;
429
430       addUpdate = new frmAddUpdate(this, "Add", contact);
431       if (addUpdate.ShowDialog() == DialogResult.OK)
432       {
433           addContactToListView(contact);
434           updateStatusBar();
435       }
436   }

482   // Updates the selected contact to the list.
483   private void updateContact()
484   {
485       clsContact contact;
486
487       // Make sure an item is selected in the list box.
488
489       if (lvwContacts.SelectedItems.Count == 0)
490       {
491           return;
492       }
493
494       contact = (clsContact)lvwContacts.SelectedItems[0].Tag;
495
496       frmAddUpdate addUpdate = new frmAddUpdate(this, "Update", contact);
497       if (addUpdate.ShowDialog() == DialogResult.OK)
```

Figure 12-19 frmMain communicating with frmAddUpdate

```
498          {
499              lvwContacts.Items.Remove(lvwContacts.SelectedItems[0]);
500              addContactToListView(contact);
501              updateStatusBar();
502          }
503     }
```

Figure 12-19 frmMain communicating with frmAddUpdate (continued)

You should also see, on lines 430 and 496 in Figure 12-19, that the **frmAddUpdate** constructor is also passed **this** as the first argument so the Add/Update form can use it as a callback reference. The Add/Update form needs this reference to the main form so that it can call the main form's **MessageBoxOK** method when validating the input values. For example:

```
251          if (txtFirstName.Text == "")
252          {
253              mMainForm.MessageBoxOK("First Name is required.");
254              txtFirstName.Focus();
255              return false;
256          }
```

In previous chapters, the **MessageBoxOK** method was defined **private**, which worked fine because it was called from only within the main form's class. Now that **MessageBoxOK** needs to be called from more than one class, the method has been defined as **public** in **frmMain**.

After the Add/Update form gets a reference to a contact, it displays the contact's property values on the form when in Update mode. When in Add mode, the controls on the Add/Update form are left blank. When the user clicks OK for either an add or update, the contents of the form are validated, and the values from the form are assigned to the contact object. The Add/Update form communicates whether the user clicked the OK or Cancel button by setting its **DialogResult** property that is returned from the **ShowDialog** method. (Note that setting the **DialogResult** property also causes the form to be closed.) The main form then checks the return value of the **ShowDialog** method to determine if the contact should be added or updated in its **ListView**.

```
199     public frmAddUpdate(frmMain mainForm, string addUpdateMode, clsContact contact)
200     {
201         InitializeComponent();
202
203         mMainForm = mainForm;
204         mAddUpdateMode = addUpdateMode;
205         mContact = contact;
206
207         Text = mAddUpdateMode + " Contact";
208
209         // Display the contact's property values during updates.
210
211         if (mAddUpdateMode == "Update")
212         {
213             txtFirstName.Text = contact.FirstName;
214             txtLastName.Text = contact.LastName;
215             txtHomePhone.Text = contact.HomePhone.ToString();
216             txtMobilePhone.Text = contact.MobilePhone.ToString();
217             dtpBirthDate.Value = contact.BirthDate;
218             txtAge.Text = contact.Age.ToString();
```

Figure 12-20 frmAddUpdate communicating with frmMain

```
219        }
220    }
221
222    // When the cancel button is clicked, set the DialogResult to close the form.
223    private void btnCancel_Click(object sender, System.EventArgs e)
224    {
225        DialogResult = DialogResult.Cancel;
226    }
227
228    // Validate the input values and save them to the contact object.
229    private void btnOK_Click(object sender, System.EventArgs e)
230    {
231        if (validateInput() == false)
232        {
233            return;
234        }
235
236        mContact.FirstName = txtFirstName.Text;
237        mContact.LastName = txtLastName.Text;
238        mContact.HomePhone = new clsPhoneNumber(txtHomePhone.Text, 1);
239        mContact.MobilePhone = new clsPhoneNumber(txtMobilePhone.Text);
240        mContact.BirthDate = dtpBirthDate.Value.Date;
241
242        DialogResult = DialogResult.OK;
243    }
```

Figure 12-20   frmAddUpdate communicating with frmMain (continued)

12

BONUS TOPICS

USER INTERFACE DESIGN GUIDELINES

The beginning of this chapter stated that one of the most rewarding parts of software development is creating applications for other people to use, and that users expect applications to have an attractive and practical user interface. The Essential Topics section in this chapter has focused on various user interface objects you can use and how to use them. The purpose of this section is to list several guidelines you should follow when designing user interfaces for your applications.

Although entire books are devoted to proper user interface design, this section lists several fundamental principles that can make your programs appear more professional and be easier to use.

tip ▶   The best user interface is the one that users don't notice because it can be used intuitively.

Figure 12-21 shows a dialog-style form designed by a student who didn't follow these guidelines, and Figure 12-22 shows the form after receiving a makeover using the following guidelines:

- One benefit of a graphical user interface (GUI) is that different applications share a common "look and feel." Try to make your application's UI look similar to other popular Windows applications. Users find programs with a familiar UI easier to use. Also, Microsoft has spent more money researching its UI style than any of us will ever make in a lifetime. There is no good reason not to ride the coattails of its research.

- Simpler is usually better. Only add controls to forms to increase usability and not to add decorations. Avoid changing default color and font properties. Use sound, color, and animation sparingly, if at all.

- All forms should be usable on a computer with a screen resolution of 800 × 600 pixels with the Windows Taskbar showing.

- All forms should have appropriate values set for the `ControlBox`, `FormBorderStyle`, `Icon`, `MaximizeBox`, `MinimizeBox`, `ShowInTaskBar`, and `StartPosition` properties. See Table 12-3 for more information.

- An application's UI should be completely available using the keyboard only and should not require the use of a mouse. Set appropriate tab orders, and define Access Keys and Shortcut Keys when available.

- When appropriate, vertically and/or horizontally align controls to establish a visual grid by making controls the same size. Keep in mind that most people read from left to right, top to bottom, and the tab order of the controls should reflect that fact.

- All the text on forms and error messages should be written using good grammar and should not contain spelling errors. Avoid error messages that are overly polite (no need to include "please"), cute, or humorous.

- Message boxes should normally follow the two main styles presented in Chapter 5. The title of the message box should be the title of the application, they should include an information or question mark icon, and they should have appropriate buttons.

- Use "…" after the text on menu commands and buttons that require the user to complete at least one more step (such as responding to a confirmation dialog) before the action is complete.

- Labels that are used to identify text boxes and other controls should use consistent capitalization and should be followed with a colon.

- If your program performs a lengthy process (over three seconds) change the cursor to an hourglass while the long running process executes and change it back when the process finishes. For example:

```
Cursor.Current = Cursors.WaitCursor;
try
{
    // Do lengthy processing here.
}
finally
{
    Cursor.Current = Cursors.Default;
}
```

- Set your application Assembly Name to the name to be used for the .exe file, and set the Application Icon to the same icon used for the application's main form (Project → Properties → Common Properties → General). This icon appears next to the application's .exe file when viewed in the Windows Explorer.

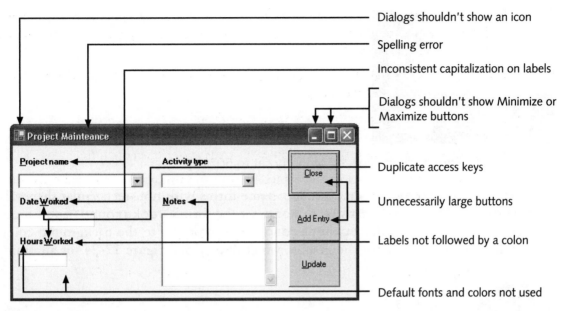

Dialogs shouldn't show an icon

Spelling error

Inconsistent capitalization on labels

Dialogs shouldn't show Minimize or Maximize buttons

Duplicate access keys

Unnecessarily large buttons

Labels not followed by a colon

Default fonts and colors not used

Figure 12-21   User interface design guidelines not followed

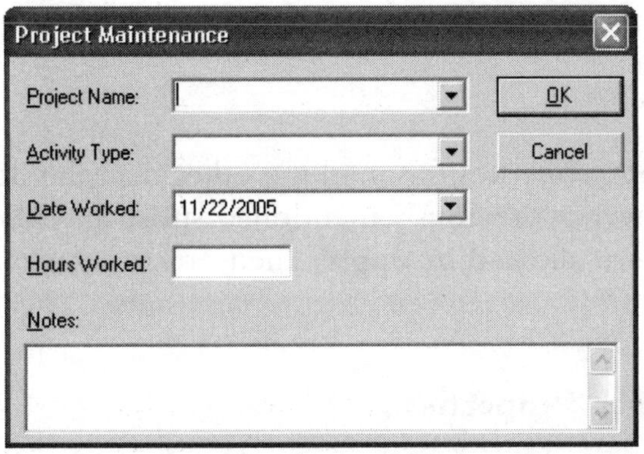

Figure 12-22   User interface design guidelines followed

SPECIAL EFFECTS WITH FORMS

Normally you should avoid making forms appear unusual for the reasons mentioned in the previous section. However, sometimes it is appropriate or at least acceptable to abandon normalcy. Historically, programmers add pizzazz to an application's user interface in the "splash screen" that appears when an application first starts, or when the About dialog is displayed that shows version and copyright information.

The form's `Opacity` and `TransparencyKey` properties can be used to create forms with appealing visual effects. Setting the `Opacity` property to anything less than 100% causes the form to appear to be see-through, as shown in Figure 12-23.

Figure 12-23   Form with its Opacity property set to 50%

The **TransparencyKey** property lets you create forms with non-rectangular shapes. If you set a form's object's **FormBorderStyle** to **None**, set the form's **BackgroundImage** property to a graphic file, and set the form's **TransparenceyKey** property to the background color used in the graphic, the background of the graphic won't display. See Figure 12-24 for an example.

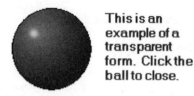

Figure 12-24   A transparent form

Using the **Opacity** and **TransparencyKey** properties for anything other than the default values isn't recommended for most forms. However, as previously mentioned, splash and About forms are examples of forms where programmers are allowed to display their artistic creativity. Game applications are another example.

> **Using the Opacity and TransparencyKey Properties**
>
> The visual effects created with the **Opacity** and **TransparencyKey** properties only work with Windows 2000 and Windows XP, and presumably any later versions of Windows.
>
> At the time this text was written, a bug existed with the **TransparencyKey** property causing it to work improperly on computers that had their display set to a color depth greater than 24-bit. If the **TransparencyKey** property doesn't work for you, try setting your color-quality to 16-bit (Control Panel → Display → Settings → Color quality).

PRINTING REPORTS

Up to now, the only way for people to view the information your application manages has been by viewing it on the computer screen. However, if you develop an application that lets users view and enter information, chances are that at some point they will want to print it on paper. Sending information to a printer is the subject of this section.

Objects Used for Printing Reports

The .NET Framework contains many classes that are used to print paper reports. Each of these classes has numerous properties, events, and methods. As usual, you can get good results using just a small number of them. Producing a report requires you to use at least six classes that interoperate with each other. Rather than include an exhaustive list of everything you can do when creating reports, we give a brief overview of these six classes in Table 12-17. (For a complete description, consult the VS.NET Help.) We then illustrate how to use these six classes by adding a report to the Contacts List application that was enhanced earlier in this chapter to use a better user interface.

When you write code to produce a report, your code uses methods of graphical objects to "draw" the information on the report. These same graphical objects are used when drawing shapes and text on the screen. Except where indicated, the .NET Framework includes these classes in the `System.Drawing` namespace. In the rest of this section, the terms draw and print are used interchangeably.

Table 12-17   Classes used when printing reports

Class	Overview

Font	The Font class is used to define the font object that is used when text is drawn on a report. The Font class lets you define attributes (font style, size, bold, italic, and the like) that determine how the text appears. This example:
	
	`Font font = new Font(FontFamily.GenericSerif, 16, FontStyle.Italic);`
	
	creates an italicized serif font, size 16. The constructor used doesn't request a font using an exact font name. Instead, the fonts are requested using a generic font family style. If you instantiate a font using an exact font name and that font doesn't exist on the user's computer, your report may not print correctly.
	
	The Font class constructor is overloaded with 13 different parameter lists! Here are a few more examples of instantiating font objects:
	
	`Font font1 = new Font(FontFamily.GenericSansSerif, 10);`
	`Font font2 = new Font("Arial", 12, FontStyle.Bold);`
	`Font font3 = new Font(font1, FontStyle.Italic);`

Pen	The **Pen** class is used to draw lines of a specified color and width. When instantiating Pen objects, you pass a color and width to the constructor: `Pen pen = new Pen(Color.Black, .015F);` In this example, a black pen is created with a width of .015 inches. The "F" after .015 reminds the reader that the second argument (pen width) is a **float** data type.
SolidBrush	The **SolidBrush** class is used to specify the color that is used to fill the interior of a shape being drawn. Shapes include rectangles, ellipses, polygons, text characters, or any other bounded shape. When instantiating Brush objects, you pass the color to the constructor: `SolidBrush brush1 = new SolidBrush(Color.Black);`
Graphics	The **Graphics** class contains methods that draw shapes on a drawing surface. For example, the Graphics class contains DrawString and DrawLine methods that are frequently used when printing a report. Note that a Graphics object is not the drawing surface itself. Rather, it just exposes the methods that are used to draw on its associated drawing surface.
PrintDocument	The **PrintDocument** class is used to instantiate a drawing object that is destined for a printer. The PrintDocument class is the drawing surface you draw on with the methods from the Graphics class. This class is contained in the System.Drawing.Printing namespace.

12

Table 12-17   Classes used when printing reports (continued)

Class	Overview
`PrintPreviewDialog`	Most of the time when your program produces a report, you want the user to have a chance to preview it before it is sent to the printer. You'll appreciate this feature too while testing your reporting logic. It saves a lot of paper.
	The `PrintPreviewDialog` provides this feature with just a few lines of code on your part. To add print preview to your application, you just instantiate a `PrintPreviewDialog`, associate it with a `PrintDocument`, and call its `ShowDialog` method.
	This class is contained in the `System.Windows.Forms` namespace.

A Report Example

Before you begin writing code to produce a report, you must first design the report. You've been using the VS.NET Form Designer to design form-based user interfaces as you develop each application. However, there is no such tool for designing reports. Instead, you might use a word processor or just sketch it out with paper and pencil.

The report we are adding to the Contacts List application uses a tabular style. This style typically consists of **page headers** (sometimes called headings) that might list the name of the report and **column headers** that identify the contents of each column. After the headers, one or more detail lines are printed. **Detail lines** contain whatever information you want to show for each of the data items being printed. At the bottom of each page is a footer. **Page footers** might contain the date the report was printed and page numbers. The Contacts List Report that is added to the Contacts List application mimics the content of the `ListView` control on the main form. The design is shown in Figure 12-25.

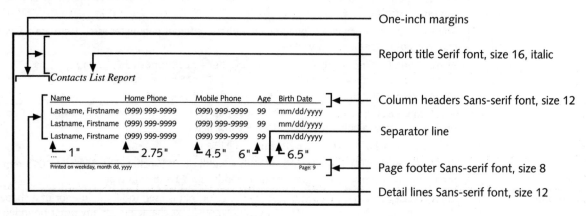

Figure 12-25   Contacts List Report design

After you have designed a report, the next step is to come up with a plan on how to add the code that prints the report. The user needs a way to request the report be printed. Typically this is done using menu commands and sometimes toolbar buttons, so that is what has been done to the Contacts List application, as shown in Figure 12-26.

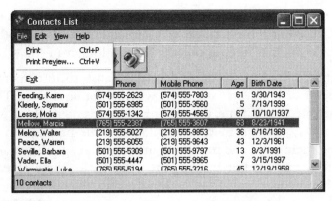

Figure 12-26   Contacts List UI with Print Preview menu items and toolbar buttons

Because the user requests that a report be printed using controls on the main form, you might consider adding all the code that prints the report to the **frmMain** class. However, in Chapter 10 you learned about the benefits of encapsulation. Creating a new class to contain the logic necessary to create the report is an excellent example of effective use of encapsulation. The example code in this section names this new class **clsContactsListReport**.

The public interface for the **clsContactsListReport** needs only two methods—**PrintReport** and **PrintReportWithPreview**. The only external information the class needs is a collection of **clsContact** objects to print. The main form has this collection in its **ListView** control. After you complete the coding for the report class, the main form can instantiate it, passing the **ListView** to the print class's constructor. After the constructor has been called, call its **PrintReport** or **PrintReportWithPreview** method, as shown in Figure 12-27. Designing the interface to the new class is the easy part. Writing the code contained within the class requires more explanation.

```
434        private void mnuPrint_Click(object sender, System.EventArgs e)
435        {
435            clsContactsListReport report = new clsContactsListReport(lvwContacts);
437            report.PrintReport();
438        }
439
440        private void mnuPrintPreview_Click(object sender, System.EventArgs e)
441        {
442            clsContactsListReport report = new clsContactsListReport(lvwContacts);
443            report.PrintReportWithPreview();
444        }
```

Figure 12-27   Using clsContactsListReport in menu event methods

Before showing the code that prints the report, some discussion is necessary of how C# code can create a report. The **PrintDocument** class is the primary class used when printing reports. Your code uses this class by instantiating an object of type **PrintDocument**, and then calling its **Print** method. **Print** takes no arguments and just starts the printing process. The **PrintDocument** object then fires three events for which you can add event methods to contain the code to produce the report.

The first event, **BeginPrint**, occurs one time just after you call the **Print** method. You add code to this method to perform initialization functions, for example to initialize page counter variables. The second event, **PrintPage**, is fired once for every page in the report. **PrintDocument** fires this event over and over until your code tells it there are no more pages to print. After all the pages have been printed, the `EndPrint` event is fired. You might add code to this method to perform any termination or "cleanup" tasks such as freeing objects you no longer need.

Because the `PrintPage` event might be fired many times, it makes sense to instantiate in the `clsContactsListReport` constructor any objects you need when printing a page. This way, these objects won't have to be instantiated each time the `PrintPage` event method is called. Instantiating these objects in the `PrintPage` event method would cause the program to execute slightly less efficiently than instantiating them once and reusing them for each page. When an object is going to be instantiated in one method and used in another, the variables for these objects must be defined using class scope. Because they are used only from within the class, they should be defined as **private**. Figure 12-28 shows how we define the first part of `clsContactsListReport`. Explanations are included in the following paragraphs.

```
1   using System;
2   using System.Drawing;
3   using System.Drawing.Printing;
4   using System.Windows.Forms;
5
6   public class clsContactsListReport
7   {
8       private int mPageNumber;
9       private int mNumberContactsPrinted;
10      private ListView mContactsListView;
11
12      private PrintDocument mPrintDocument;
13      private Font mReportHeaderFont;
14      private Font mReportDetailFont;
15      private Font mReportFooterFont;
16      private Pen mReportPen;
17      private SolidBrush mReportBrush;
18
19      // Instantiate all the objects needed for printing the report.
20      public clsContactsListReport(ListView listView)
21      {
22          mContactsListView = listView;
23
24          mReportHeaderFont = new Font(FontFamily.GenericSerif, 16, FontStyle.Italic);
25          mReportDetailFont = new Font(FontFamily.GenericSansSerif, 12);
26          mReportFooterFont = new Font(FontFamily.GenericSansSerif, 8);
27          mReportPen = new Pen(Color.Black, .015F);
28          mReportBrush = new SolidBrush(Color.Black);
29
30          mPrintDocument = new PrintDocument();
31          mPrintDocument.BeginPrint += new PrintEventHandler(beginPrint);
32          mPrintDocument.PrintPage  += new PrintPageEventHandler(printPage);
33      }
```

Figure 12-28 The beginnings of clsContactsListReport

Lines 1 through 4 include the **using** directives for the objects that are used when printing the report. The `System.Drawing` and `System.Drawing.Printing` namespaces contain the objects for drawing text and lines on the report. The `System.Windows.Forms` namespace contains the `PrintPreviewDialog` and the `ListView` classes. See Table 12-17 for more information.

Lines 8 through 17 define the objects that are needed when printing the report. Note that because the report design includes three separate styles of fonts—one each for the report title, column headers and detail lines, and footers—a font object for each style is defined in lines 13, 14, and 15. These font objects are instantiated in the class constructor in lines 24 through 26.

Line 27 instantiates the **Pen** object that is used to draw the separator lines on the report. Line 28 instantiates the **SolidBrush** object, which is used to fill the text characters drawn for all sections of the report.

Line 30 instantiates the **PrintDocument** object that has the text and separator lines drawn upon it. Lines 31 and 32 define which event methods should be called for the **BeginPrint** and **PrintPage** events. You probably haven't seen statements like these, but your programs have contained them ever since the first program in Chapter 2. Normally, the Form Designer generates them when you use the Properties window to connect events to event methods. This sample report doesn't use the Form Designer to define the **PrintDocument** object, so you have to write the code that defines which methods should be called for the events.

The next part of the class implements the **public** PrintReport and PrintReportWithPreview methods. These methods are shown in Figure 12-29. For the PrintReport method, the only thing to do is call the **PrintDocument** object's **Print** method. Recall that calling the **Print** method starts the process by triggering the **PrintDocument**'s **BeginPrint**, **PrintPage**, and **EndPrint** events. Because lines 31 and 32 in Figure 12-28 assign event handler methods to these events, the **beginPrint** and **printPage** methods are called. Note the sample report doesn't use a method for the **EndPrint** event because no clean up tasks are necessary.

```
35          // Send the report to the default printer.
36          public void PrintReport()
37          {
38              mPrintDocument.Print();
39          }
40
41          // Show the report in a print preview dialog.
42          public void PrintReportWithPreview()
43          {
44              PrintPreviewDialog printPreviewDialog = new PrintPreviewDialog();
45              printPreviewDialog.Document = mPrintDocument;
46              printPreviewDialog.ShowDialog();
47          }
```

Figure 12-29 The PrintReport and PrintReportWithPreview public methods

The implementation for the **PrintReportWithPreview** method is also easy. Line 44 instantiates a **PrintPreviewDialog** object. Line 45 is the key to understanding how the **PrintPreviewDialog** works. The **PrintPreviewDialog** class exposes a **Document** property that must be set to a valid **PrintDocument** object. When you call the **PrintPreviewDialog** object's **ShowDialog** method (or the **Show** method if you don't want the **PrintPreview** form to show modally), the **PrintPreviewDialog** object turns right around and calls the **PrintDocument** object's **Print** method, which causes the **PrintDocument** object's **BeginPrint**, **PrintPage**, and **EndPrint** events to be triggered. The difference is that the **PrintPreviewDialog** instructs the **PrintDocument** object to draw itself on the print preview form, rather then sending the report to the default printer.

12

All that's left to do to complete the `clsContactsListReport` is to add the code that handles printing the information on the report. In other words, you need to code the `beginPrint` and `printPage` event methods. The `beginPrint` event method is shown in 12-30 and simply initializes a couple of variables. The `mPageNumber` variable is used to print a page number on each page of the report, and `mNumberContactsPrinted` is used to keep track of how many contacts have been printed so the code will know when to stop printing pages.

The real work is done with the `printPage` method. However, before you write that code, you need to understand the way that text and graphics are drawn on the report. The `printPage` method is passed an argument that is a reference to a `PrintPageEventArgs` object. The `PrintPageEventArgs` class has various properties that are used to communicate between your method and the `PrintDocument` object. Most importantly, `PrintPageEventArgs` has a property that gives you a reference to the `Graphics` object whose methods you use to draw text and graphics on the report. `PrintPageEventArgs` has a `HasMorePages` property that you set to **false** when your code determines it has finished printing all pages.

Additionally, `PrintPageEventArgs` has a `PageSettings` property, which is a reference to a `PageSettings` object that contains properties that hold further information about the report. For example, you can set the `PageSettings.Landscape` property to **true** or **false**, depending on whether you want the report printed in landscape or portrait mode.

As mentioned earlier, you print text (and draw other graphics) on a report by using methods from the `Graphics` class. To know where on the page the text should be printed, the methods are passed the location of where the text is to be drawn. A coordinate system containing horizontal and vertical positions is used to specify this location. The coordinate system is typically described using x and y values, where x is the horizontal position and y is the vertical position. The upper-left position on the page is location 0, 0. As the x value becomes bigger, the horizontal position moves to the right. As the y value becomes bigger, the vertical position moves toward the bottom of the page. Fortunately, the `Graphics` class has a `PageUnit` property that you can set to one of a number of values, so you can indicate locations using your favorite unit of measure. For example, `PageUnit` can be set to `GraphicsUnit.Inch`, `GraphicsUnit.Millimeter`, or `GraphicsUnit.Point`.

Now that you know about the `PrintPageEventArgs` object, the `Graphics` object, and the coordinate system for drawing, you should review the code for the `printPage` event method shown in Figure 12-30. Notice that the `printPage` event method enlists the help of two helper methods—`printPageHeadersAndFooters` and `printDetailLine`—to do the actual drawing of the text. These two helper methods are shown in Figure 12-31 and Figure 12-32.

```
49    // Initialize anything necessary before the report is printed. Note
50    // these can't be initialized in the constructor because the constructor is
51    // called only once for print preview, but beginPrint is called when the
52    // report is shown on the preview dialog, and again if the user chooses
53    // to send the report to the printer from the preview dialog.
54    private void beginPrint(object sender, PrintEventArgs e)
55    {
56        mPageNumber = 0;
57        mNumberContactsPrinted = 0;
58    }
```

Figure 12-30 The printPage event method

```
59
60          // Prints a single page on the report.
61          private void printPage(object sender, PrintPageEventArgs e)
62          {
63              float vertPagePosition;
64              clsContact contact;
65
66              // Use inches for all measurements.
67
68              e.Graphics.PageUnit = GraphicsUnit.Inch;
69
70              // Print the headers and footers.
71
72              printPageHeadersAndFooters(e);
73
74              // Print the detail lines until we reach the end of the page or
75              // until we run out of contacts to print.
76
77              vertPagePosition = 1.75F;
78              while (mNumberContactsPrinted < mContactsListView.Items.Count
79                  && vertPagePosition < 9.75)
80              {
81                  contact = (clsContact)mContactsListView.Items[mNumberContactsPrinted].Tag;
82
83                  printDetailLine(contact, e, vertPagePosition);
84
85                  mNumberContactsPrinted++;
86                  vertPagePosition += .25F;
87              }
88
89              // See if there are more pages to print.
90
91              if (mNumberContactsPrinted < mContactsListView.Items.Count)
92              {
93                  e.HasMorePages = true;
94              }
95              else
96              {
97                  e.HasMorePages = false;
98              }
99          }
```

Figure 12-30 The printPage event method (continued)

The variable **vertPagePosition** defined on line 63 is used to track where on the page each detail line should be printed. As each detail line is printed, **vertPagePosition** is incremented by .25 (¼ inch).

The loop in lines 78 through 87 is used to iterate through the collection of **clsContact** objects contained in the **ListView**'s collection. Note the loop terminates when all contacts have been printed, or the **vertPagePosition** indicates the end of the page has been reached. (In other words, when the contacts have been printed past 9.75 inches at the bottom of the page.) Finally, lines 91 through 98 set **PrintPageEventArgs HasMorePages** to either **true** or **false**, depending on whether all the contacts have been printed or not. If it is set to **true**, the **PrintDocument** object fires another **PrintPage** event, which causes the **printPage** method to be called.

```
101        // Prints the report title, column headers, and page footer.
102        private void printPageHeadersAndFooters(PrintPageEventArgs e)
103        {
104            // Print page header.
105
106            e.Graphics.DrawString("Contacts List Report",
107                mReportHeaderFont, mReportBrush, 1.0F, 1.0F);
108
109            e.Graphics.DrawString("Name",
110                mReportDetailFont, mReportBrush, 1.0F, 1.5F);
111
112            e.Graphics.DrawString("Home Phone",
113                mReportDetailFont, mReportBrush, 2.75F, 1.5F);
114
115            e.Graphics.DrawString("Mobile Phone",
116                mReportDetailFont, mReportBrush, 4.5F, 1.5F);
117
118            e.Graphics.DrawString("Age",
119                mReportDetailFont, mReportBrush, 6.0F, 1.5F);
120
121            e.Graphics.DrawString("Birth Date",
122                mReportDetailFont, mReportBrush, 6.5F, 1.5F);
123
124            e.Graphics.DrawLine(mReportPen, 1.0F, 1.71F, 7.5F, 1.71F);
125
126            // Print the page footer.
127
128            e.Graphics.DrawLine(mReportPen, 1.0F, 9.9F, 7.5F, 9.9F);
129
130            e.Graphics.DrawString("Printed on " + DateTime.Now.ToLongDateString(),
131                mReportFooterFont, mReportBrush, 1F, 10F);
132
133            mPageNumber++;
134            e.Graphics.DrawString("Page: " + mPageNumber.ToString(),
135                mReportFooterFont, mReportBrush, 7F, 10F);
136        }
```

Figure 12-31   The printPageHeadersAndFooters helper method

When reviewing the code in Figures 12-31 and 12-32, it might be helpful for you to refer back to the report design in Figure 12-26. The logic contained in both **printPageHeadersAndFooters** and **printDetailLine** is very similar. The only real difference is what information is printed. The **printPageHeadersAndFooters** method calls the **Graphics** object's **DrawString** method to draw the string literals for the report title, column headers, and page footers. It also calls the **Graphics** object's **DrawLine** method to draw the separator lines. Note that the **DrawString** method is passed five arguments: (1) the text to draw, (2) the font object to use when drawing the text, (3) the brush object to use that fills the characters with a color, (4) the x-coordinate of the location at which to print the text, and (5) the y-coordinate of the location at which to print the text. All measurements are given in inches as **float** values so that fractional values can be used. The F suffix on the numbers tells the C# compiler to treat the number literals as **floats**.

```
138        // Prints a detail line for the contact passed.
139        private void printDetailLine(clsContact contact,
140            PrintPageEventArgs e, float vertPagePosition)
141        {
142            e.Graphics.DrawString(contact.LastFirstName,
143                mReportDetailFont, mReportBrush, 1.0F, vertPagePosition);
144
145            e.Graphics.DrawString(contact.HomePhone.ToString(),
146                mReportDetailFont, mReportBrush, 2.75F, vertPagePosition);
147
148            e.Graphics.DrawString(contact.MobilePhone.ToString(),
149                mReportDetailFont, mReportBrush, 4.5F, vertPagePosition);
150
151            e.Graphics.DrawString(contact.Age.ToString(),
152                mReportDetailFont, mReportBrush, 6.0F, vertPagePosition);
153
154            e.Graphics.DrawString(contact.BirthDate.ToShortDateString(),
155                mReportDetailFont, mReportBrush, 6.5F, vertPagePosition);
156        }
```

Figure 12-32 The printDetailLine helper method

This section has shown you how to produce a report with a print preview feature. Adding a report to your application requires you to use a number of objects, but after you understand how they all work together, reporting logic is rather straightforward, even though writing the code to print each value can be tedious. The sample report should give you a good starting point for other reports your applications may need to produce. Be aware that this section is only an introduction to creating reports using C# and .NET. Other .NET classes exist that you can use to make your reports even more flexible. For example, you might consider allowing the user to choose which printer to send the report to, which fonts to use, page margins, and whether the report should be printed in color or grayscale.

12

SUMMARY

Essential Topics

- ▫ Most user interface controls are derived from the same base class named **System.Windows.Forms.Control**. Any control that is derived from this class inherits the properties, events and methods defined in the **System.Windows.Forms.Control** class.

- ▫ The **TabIndex** and **TabStop** properties are used to control how the user can move focus from one control to another by pressing Tab and Shift+Tab on the keyboard. The logical tab order on a form should start in the upper left of a form and move down and to the right. To get the **TabIndex** properties set correctly, wait until after you have added all controls to a form and arranged them in suitable positions. Then set the **TabIndex** using the Properties window.

- ▫ If you include an ampersand (&) for the **Text** property of many controls, the ampersand won't display and the character just after the ampersand is displayed underlined. This lets you define an access key for that control. Users can set the focus to a control, or select the control, by pressing Alt and the underlined letter on the keyboard.

- ▫ The **Click** event is likely the most common method for which you write event methods. The **Click** event occurs whenever the user clicks the object with the mouse. **Click** events can also occur from some keyboard actions.

- Forms are the foundation for building GUIs for Windows applications. Forms are used to create the main user interface for an application, floating Toolbox windows, and modal dialogs. To make a form display on the computer screen, the form must be instantiated and its `Show` or `ShowDialog` method must be called. The `ShowDialog` method returns a value of type `DialogResult` that can be checked to determine how the user closed the form.

- Most forms you create are one of three styles: (1) a main form that doesn't allow resizing, (2) a main form that does allow resizing, or (3) a modal dialog form. To make a form behave in one of these three styles, its `ControlBox`, `FormBorderStyle`, `Icon`, `MaximizeBox`, `MinimizeBox`, `ShowInTaskBar`, and `StartPosition` properties must be set correctly.

- `Label` controls are typically used to display static text next to another control.

- `TextBox` controls are used to allow the user to enter input values using the keyboard.

- Buttons and menus are two of the primary user interface objects that users click to request that an action be performed. .NET has two styles of menus—main menus that are displayed from a forms menu bar, and context menus that can pop up just about anywhere.

- `CheckBox` controls are typically used to represent Boolean values by displaying boxes as checked or unchecked.

- The `ComboBox` control combines the features of a `TextBox` and a `ListBox` control into a single control.

- The `DateTimePicker` control is used to represent a `DateTime` value. The `DateTimePicker` can be used to represent a date value or a time value, but not both at the same time.

- A `GroupBox` is used to group other related controls on a form. When used in conjunction with certain other controls, such as radio button controls, a `GroupBox` causes those controls to behave in a mutually exclusive fashion.

- `ListView` controls have many advantages over `ListBoxes`. If you need to display a list of data that contains a single column, you should use a `ListBox`. Otherwise, consider using a `ListView` control.

- `RadioButton` objects are used to allow the user to choose a single value from a set of choices.

- The `Timer` control can be used to cause an event method to be executed at a regular interval.

- Toolbars are placed on a form to give users a quicker way to request that an action take place than selecting a menu command.

- Status bars are placed at the bottom of a form to give the user some additional information about the state of the application.

- Objects communicate with each other using their public properties and methods. Because a form is just a type of object, public methods and properties can be added to a form class to enable the forms to pass information back and forth.

Bonus Topics

- By following several user interface design guidelines, you can make your programs appear more professional and be easier to use. The best user interface is the one users don't notice because it aids them in performing their work and doesn't get in their way.

- The **Form Opacity** and **TransparencyKey** properties can be used to create forms with interesting visual effects. Normally these properties shouldn't be used for any forms that the user frequently uses. However, some acceptable uses include splash and About forms.

- An application that lets users view and enter information most likely needs a way to print the information to a paper report. Producing a report requires you to use at least six classes, which all interoperate. Classes used for creating reports that are contained in the **System.Drawing** namespaces include the **Font**, **Pen**, **SolidBrush**, and **Graphics** classes. Additional classes used when printing reports include the **PrintDocument** class from the **System.Drawing.Printing** namespace and the **PrintPreviewDialog** class from the **System.Windows.Forms** namespace.

- The bulk of the code you write to produce a report is contained within the PrintDocument's PrintPage event method. Drawing methods are passed x- and y-coordinates that specify the location where text and graphics should be drawn, where x is the horizontal position and y is the vertical position.

KEY TERMS

Define each of the following terms, as it relates to user interface objects:

Essential Terms

- access key
- button
- callback reference
- CheckBox
- ComboBox
- ContextMenu
- control tray
- DateTimePicker
- form
- GroupBox
- Label
- ListView
- MainMenu
- modal dialog
- NumericUpDown
- RadioButton
- status bar panel
- StatusBar
- TextBox
- Timer
- ToolBar

Bonus Terms

- column headers
- detail lines
- Font class
- Graphics class
- Opacity
- page footers
- page headers
- Pen class
- PrintDocument
- PrintPreviewDialog
- SolidBrush

12

REVIEW QUESTIONS

Essential Questions

1. Nowadays, users expect applications to have a professional looking user interface. True or false?

2. The `BackColor` and `ForeColor` properties exist to give the application developer a way to express his or her creativity. True or false?

3. The `Locked` property can be set to prohibit the user from typing text into a text box. True or false?

4. `Click` events are triggered when the user clicks a control with the mouse, but they can also occur through a keyboard action. True or false?

5. It's a good idea to perform data validation in a control's `Leave` event so that you can inform the user as soon as possible if the input value is bad. True or false?

6. Your code can identify how the user dismissed a modal dialog form by checking its `DialogResult` property. True or false?

7. The buttons on a form the user is most likely to click should be drawn with a bigger size. True or false?

8. `RadioButton` controls are typically used to represent Boolean values. True or false?

9. .NET has two styles of menus—main menus that display from a forms menu bar, and context menus that can pop up just about anywhere. True or false?

10. When one `RadioButton` has its `Checked` property set to **true**, all other `RadioButtons` in the same container control automatically have their `Checked` property set to **false**. True or false?

11. The `ComboBox` control combines the features of a _____ and _____ into a single control.

12. Most user interface controls are derived from the base class named _____.

13. The _____ and not the _____ should decide the fonts and colors used in a user interface.

14. You define an access key for a control by including a _____ in a control's _____ property.

15. Almost all forms you define in an application are one of _____ styles.

16. Describe how an application determines which control to move the cursor to when the user presses the Tab key on the keyboard.

17. Which property values must you set if you want the user to use a text box to enter many lines of text?

18. Which property values should you set if you want to use the `DateTimePicker` control to allow the user to enter a time of day?

19. List at least five advantages that a `ListView` control has over a `ListBox` control.

20. Describe the process of adding images to a toolbar button using the `ToolBar` control.

Bonus Questions

1. To make users notice your application, you should try to make its user interface unique. True or false?

2. An application's UI should be completely available using the keyboard only and should not require the use of a mouse. True or false?

3. The **PrintPreviewDialog** class allows you to add print preview features to your application with just a few lines of code. True or false?

4. A report printed from your application is a good example of appropriate use of encapsulation to contain the code to create the report in a class. True or false?

5. The **SolidBrush** class is used to draw solid lines on a report. True or false?

6. The **Form** _____ and _____ properties can be used to create forms with interesting visual effects.

7. A report design typically contains _____, _____, and _____ sections.

8. The **Graphics** class _____ property can be set to allow you to specify x- and y-coordinates using inches or millimeters.

9. List the six classes that are typically used when adding report printing to an application. In which namespaces are these classes contained?

10. Explain how the **PrintDocument** object knows when to stop triggering the **PrintPage** event.

12

PROGRAMMING EXERCISES

Essential Exercises

1. Enhance the solution to the Contacts List application to include a Contact Type property for each contact. Contact Type choices should be Personal, Business, or Family. This enhancement requires changes to **clsContact** to add the new property, and to serialize and deserialize the Contact Type value. Changes will also be necessary to **frmAddUpdate** to allow the user to view and update this new property using radio buttons contained in a group box.

2. Enhance the solution to the Contacts List application to use a **Timer** control that automatically saves the contacts list to the sequential data file every *n* minutes, where *n* is a value between 1 and 60 and is specified by the user. Add a new "Options" form so that the user can specify the auto save minutes increment using a **NumericUpDown** control. Update the status bar with an informative message while the contacts list is being saved.

3. Enhance the solution to the Contacts List application to improve the way items are sorted in the **ListView**. The current solution always sorts the rows in the list in ascending order. Your enhanced solution should toggle the sorting between ascending and descending order.

4. Develop an application that uses the **System.IO.Directory** and **System.IO.File** classes to display a list of all files for a given folder in a **ListView** control in a manner similar to the way in which the Windows Explorer shows details about files. Your list should include filename, file size, and date modified. Your user interface should include a context menu that pops up whenever a file is right-clicked in the list view. The context menus should include menu commands that allow the user to delete and rename the file. Be sure to ask the user for confirmation before deleting a file.

5. Write a program that allows you to maintain a list of courses you have completed while at college. Your new application should have the same basic functionality as the Contacts List application. Each course object should have properties for the course code (for example, IS101), the course title, instructor's name, term completed (for example, Fall 2005), and letter grade earned. Display the number of courses completed, and grade point average (GPA) on the main form's status bar.

Bonus Exercises

1. Develop a reusable form that can be used as a splash window that displays when an application first starts. The application title, as well as the number of seconds the window is displayed, should be passed to the form's constructor. The splash form should always display on top of other forms. Use a timer in the splash form to make the splash form close itself after the specified time has passed. Use the form's **Opacity** and/or **TransparencyKey** properties to make the splash form more interesting.

2. Add some animation to the About form of the Contacts List application by including a **Timer** control that moves the icon around the form whenever the form is displayed.

3. Enhance the version of the Contacts List application that prints the report to give the user more control over how the report is printed. New options should include the option to specify the fonts to use for the various sections of the report, and whether to print the report in portrait or landscape mode. You can populate the contents of a **ComboBox** control by looping through the **InstalledFontCollection** object like this:

```
foreach (FontFamily font in InstalledFontCollection)
{
        cboFonts.Items.Add(font.Name);
}
```

DATABASE CONNECTIVITY WITH
ADO.NET

In the Essentials section you will learn:

♦ What a relational database is

♦ What database management systems are and why they are used

♦ Fundamental relational database terminology

♦ The Structured Query Language (SQL) syntax for creating, retrieving, updating, and deleting data in a database

♦ How to use the `OleDbConnection`, `OleDbCommand`, and `OleDbDataReader` classes in ADO.NET

In the Bonus section you will learn:

♦ How to use bound controls to display a database table

♦ The difference between bound and unbound controls

♦ How to create a Microsoft Access database from a C# program

♦ How to write aggregate queries

You already have the skills to develop a variety of Windows desktop applications that use objects, methods, loops, decisions, arrays, and collections. In Chapter 11, you learned how to persist object state to non-volatile storage using sequential files. However, the nature of sequential files makes them unsuitable for many business applications. Storing information using a database management system is a better alternative in many situations. This chapter introduces you to database terminology and shows you how to use ADO.NET in your C# programs to maintain data in a simple Microsoft Access database.

ESSENTIAL TOPICS

DATABASE MANAGEMENT SYSTEMS

You already know that many programs need to persist object state information. Simple sequential data files were the predominant technique used for storing data in the early days of automated computer systems. However, even though sequential files still work well for some applications, the norm for modern business applications is to store data in a database.

A **database** is a collection of information organized in such a way that it can be accessed, managed, and updated quickly and easily. A **database management system (DBMS)** is a collection of programs that manage the data in the database. The DBMS software handles the mechanics of creating, storing, retrieving, and updating the data in the database file. DBMSs are sometimes referred to as **database engines**. A DBMS offers many advantages over simple sequential files. A DBMS allows data to be accessed randomly rather than sequentially, resulting in much-improved performance, and it improves data integrity by providing replication and backup services. A DBMS includes security features that can be used to limit "who does what" to the data, which allows you to build more secure applications.

There are many popular DBMSs used in organizations today. These DBMSs range from small systems designed to run on personal computers for a single user, to server-based DBMSs for large-scale enterprise applications that allow thousands of concurrent users to share information. The three leading vendors of enterprise DBMSs are Oracle, IBM, and Microsoft. When people say they are using a particular type of database, they are usually referring to the vendor or name of the DBMS. For example, if a recruiter tells you his company uses Oracle, he means that the company's business applications store data in a database using the Oracle DBMS. IBM's DBMS product is named DB2, and Microsoft's enterprise DBMS product is named SQL Server. These enterprise DBMSs are not cheap, and the licenses to use them can cost anywhere from a few thousand dollars to over a million dollars. Many organizations also use MySQL, which is a free, open-source alternative to the big vendors' database products.

You probably won't have access to an enterprise DBMS while reading this book, so the examples in this chapter are limited to using a personal DBMS. More specifically, the Microsoft Jet DBMS is used for the examples in this chapter. The Microsoft Jet DBMS is the same database engine used by Microsoft Access. Access databases typically have a file extension of .mdb. Because Jet is used by Access, Jet databases are commonly referred to as Microsoft Access databases.

You don't need to have Microsoft Access installed on your PC in order to use the Jet database engine from C# because it, and other data access components, are included with VS.NET. However, having Microsoft Access available does make debugging your programs easier because you can use it to verify the contents of the databases your programs manipulate. You should know that, even though the examples in this chapter use a personal DBMS, they are also written to work equally well with an enterprise DBMS.

RELATIONAL DATABASES

A problem with storing information in simple sequential data files is that information is often duplicated in many files. For example, suppose that you have a checking account, a savings account, a car loan, and a student loan at the same bank. If the bank stored your personal information for each of your accounts in separate files, your name and address would be duplicated four times!

Although the wasted disk space is not a major concern due to the relatively low cost of data storage media, the duplicate entries create an opportunity for errors by violating the integrity of your information in the bank's files. If you move and send the bank your new address, there is a chance that your address may not be changed in all four places. If this were to happen, the bank would have erroneous information about you in their files, and determining which address is correct would pose a problem for the bank's employees.

The goal of a relational database is to solve this redundant data problem by defining relationships between different types of data stored in the database. A **relational database management system (RDBMS)** is a collection of programs that enable you to control or manage data in a relational database. RDBMSs are used by virtually all business applications. Their prevalence is so common that most people use the broader name of DBMS instead of the more specific name of RDBMS. In fact, the five DBMSs mentioned earlier by name (Oracle, DB2, SQL Server, MySQL, and Microsoft Jet) are all relational database management systems. Therefore, this chapter also uses the more common term DBMS even though all examples use relational databases.

Relational Database Terminology

To understand how data is organized in a relational database, you also need to be familiar with the terminology used to describe this data organization. As you read about these terms, you may notice that they are similar to the terminology used for files as presented in Chapter 11. Therefore, let's begin with a quick review of sequential data files.

In Chapter 11, you learned how to persist an object's state to a sequential data file. Let's review how sequential files work. If your application handles multiple objects all of the same class, the state information for all objects is stored collectively in a single sequential file. Sequential files are organized into zero or more records, in which each record represents a single object's state information. Each record consists of multiple fields, in which each field represents a single piece of information about a single object.

A **relational database** is a database that organizes its data into a set of one or more related tables. A relational database **table** consists of zero or more rows and one or more columns of data. Each **row** in a database table is analogous to a single record in a sequential file, and each **column** in a database table is analogous to a field in a sequential file record (see Table 13-1). The terms **row** and **record**, and **column** and **field** are often used interchangeably. When used to make objects persistent, each row in a table often contains the state of a single object.

Table 13-1   Relational database terminology

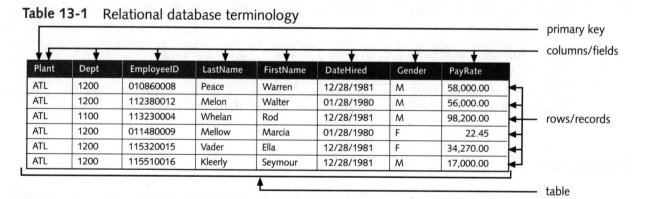

A well-designed relational database table should define one or more columns as the primary key. The **primary key** of a table must contain a value that uniquely identifies each row in the table and is therefore sometimes referred to as a **unique identifier**. Often the name of the column that serves as the primary key in a table includes "ID" in its name. Some examples of fields used as primary keys include Student ID, Employee ID, and Account ID. In addition to being unique, identifiers should be chosen using values that are unlikely to ever change. Therefore, names, telephone numbers, and e-mail addresses are not good choices for primary keys.

The data in a relational database table looks much like the data that is stored in sequential data files as described in Chapter 11. In fact, if you prefer to maintain your application data in a database rather than in sequential data files, you can create a table with columns that match the fields in the records of the sequential file. You can see this for yourself when you review the revised Contact List program example presented later in this chapter.

INTRODUCTION TO SQL

Structured Query Language (SQL) is the industry standard language for working with relational databases. In conversation, the word "SQL" is pronounced as "sequel" or by saying each letter as "es-queue-el." SQL is used to define the statements you use to manipulate the data in the database. Common examples of SQL statements are those used to create new rows, retrieve (read or query) data, update existing data, and delete existing rows.

 tip ▶ The four common database actions are collectively referred to as **CRUD**. CRUD is an acronym for create, retrieve or read, update, and delete.

Regardless of which programming language or DBMS you use, the approach for developing a database-driven program is nearly the same. That is, when you write a program that interacts with a DBMS, your program builds SQL statements in string variables and then passes them to the DBMS to be executed. For this reason, knowing some basic SQL syntax is necessary when developing applications that store, retrieve, and manipulate information in a database.

Because SQL is a standard that is supported by most database engines, your applications will work with DBMSs from different vendors with little or no changes. However, as is the case with most standards, each vendor's implementation of SQL may be slightly different even though conceptually the same. Because the examples in this chapter use the Jet DBMS, the SQL examples are presented using syntax that works with the Jet database and is still as close to the standard SQL syntax as possible.

The discussion that follows uses an Access database file named EmployeeDatabase.mdb and a table named Employees (see Figure 13-1) to illustrate essential SQL statements. If you have Microsoft Access installed on your PC and wish to try these SQL statements out for yourself, the EmployeeDatabase.mdb file can be found in the supplemental files that accompany this book.

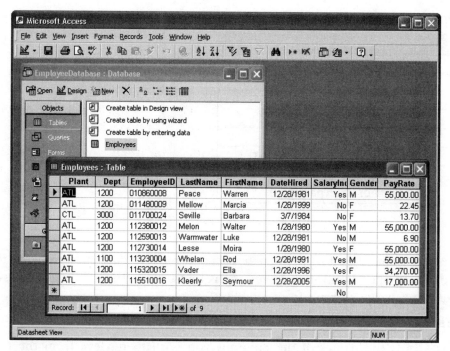

Figure 13-1 Employees table in the EmployeeDatabase.mdb Access database

Figure 13-2 shows the Employees table opened in design view using Microsoft Access. To use Microsoft Access to view the design of a table, open the database file, right-click the table, and choose Design View from the pop-up menu.

13

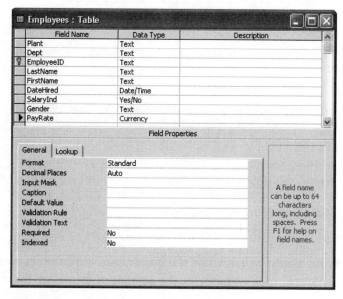

Figure 13-2 Design of the Employees table

In this view, you should notice that several data types for the fields have been used. (See the second column in Figure 13-2.) The data types used by Access are similar to the C# value data types, even though they aren't defined using exactly the same keywords. Table 13-2 provides a cross-reference list of C# data types to Access data types. You need this cross-reference when you define C# variables to hold the data values found in an Access table.

Table 13-2 C# and Access data types cross-references

C# data types	Microsoft Access data types
bool	Yes/No
DateTime	Date/Time
decimal	Currency
double	Number (field size Double)
int	AutoNumber
int	Number (field size Long Integer)
string	Memo
string	Text (limit of 255 characters)

Retrieving Data

The SQL **SELECT** statement is used to perform a query to retrieve data. It is probably the most common type of database operation found in programs that use a DBMS. The general syntax of a **SELECT** statement to retrieve all rows from a table is:

        SELECT *listOfFields* FROM *tableName*

Where **listOfFields** is the names of the columns you wish to retrieve from the table, and **tableName** is the name of the database table that contains the records you want to query. When more than one column name is used in **listOfFields**, the column names must be separated by commas. For example:

        SELECT EmployeeID FROM Employees

        SELECT EmployeeID, LastName, FirstName FROM Employees

Alternately, you can use an asterisk (*) for **listOfFields** to retrieve the values for all columns in the table:

        SELECT * FROM Employees

 tip ▶ Always code SQL keywords in uppercase when formatting SQL statements within a program to increase readability.

The WHERE Clause

If you are interested in retrieving only those records that meet a certain criteria, you can append the optional **WHERE** clause to the **SELECT** statement as follows:

        SELECT *listOfFields* FROM *tableName* WHERE *criteriaExpression*

The **criteriaExpression** in a **WHERE** clause behaves like the conditional expressions used in C# decision statements. These expressions include one or more of the operators shown in Table 13-3.

Table 13-3 Operators used in an SQL WHERE clause

Purpose	SQL operator
Less Than	<
Greater Than	>
Less Than or Equal To	<=
Greater Than or Equal To	>=
Equal To (Equality)	=
Not Equal To (Inequality)	<>
Similar to	LIKE
Between	BETWEEN...AND
Conditional Logical And	AND
Conditional Logical Or	OR
Logical Not	NOT

Shown here are a few examples of queries using the **WHERE** clause:

```
SELECT * FROM Employees WHERE PayRate < 10.00
```

```
SELECT * FROM Employees WHERE SalaryInd = True AND PayRate > 80000.00
```

As with C# decision statements, parentheses can be used to control operator precedence:

```
SELECT * FROM Employees
WHERE (SalaryInd = True AND PayRate > 80000.00)
OR (SalaryInd = False AND PayRate > 20.00)
```

C# uses the double quotation mark character (") as a delimiter to define string literal constants. However, most database engines expect the single quotation mark, or apostrophe character (') as the string literal delimiter to be used in SQL statements. So, to specify a string literal in an SQL statement, you enclose it in single quotation marks, as shown here:

```
SELECT * FROM Employees WHERE Dept = '1200'
```

```
SELECT * FROM Employees WHERE PayRate < 10.00 AND Gender = 'M'
```

If you want to retrieve only a specific row, use the table's primary key in the **WHERE** clause:

```
SELECT * FROM Employees WHERE EmployeeID = '1005510016'
```

Note that when comparing text values, the Jet DBMS performs a case-insensitive compare. Other DBMSs may do case-sensitive compares

Date literal constants are also enclosed in single quotation where the date is formatted as **'yyyy-mm-dd'**, where **yyyy** is the four-digit year, **mm** is the two-digit month number, and **dd** is the two-digit day. For example:

```
SELECT * FROM Employees WHERE DateHired < '2000-01-01'
```

When comparing text values, you can also use the percent (%) character with the **LIKE** operator to perform wildcard searches. For example, to retrieve all column values for all employees who work in department 1200 and whose first name starts with "W", use the following SQL statement:

```
SELECT * FROM Employees WHERE Dept = '1200' AND FirstName LIKE 'W%'
```

Note that when executing a query from within Microsoft Access, you have to use an asterisk (*) rather than a percent (%) for the wildcard character used with the **LIKE** operator.

13

Alternative SQL Syntax

The SQL syntax used in the chapter is known to work with the Jet database engine. If you read other references on Microsoft Access and Jet SQL statements, you might see other syntax being used. This is possible because Microsoft Access and the Jet DBMS allow non-textual values to be formatted in a variety of ways. For example, dates can be formatted as `#mm/dd/yy#` in addition to `'yyyy-mm-dd'`, and Boolean values can be represented as `Yes` and `No`, instead of `True` and `False`.

We chose not to use these alternative representations because they are unique to Microsoft Access and are not standard SQL syntax, as is used in this chapter.

You might also see references to the Microsoft Access SQL use of column names containing spaces surrounded by square braces, like this:

```
SELECT [Employee Number] FROM Employees
```

Many enterprise DBMSs don't allow column names to contain spaces, so the examples in this chapter don't either.

The `BETWEEN...AND` operators are used to retrieve all values inclusively within a given range. For example, to retrieve all employees who were hired in the 1990s, use either of the following SQL statements:

```
SELECT * FROM Employees WHERE DateHired BETWEEN '1990-01-01' AND
'1999-12-31'

SELECT * FROM Employees WHERE DateHired >= '1990-01-01' AND DateHired <=
'1999-12-31'
```

The ORDER BY Clause

The rows returned from a query aren't guaranteed to be in any particular order. In previous chapters, you learned how various sorting techniques could be used to arrange the data in a more user-friendly sequence. Querying from a database using SQL makes sorting significantly easier!

To change the order of the records that are retrieved, you simply append the optional **ORDER BY clause** to the SQL statement:

```
SELECT listOfFields FROM tableName WHERE criteriaExpression ORDER BY sortColumns
```

where `sortColumns` consists of a comma-separated list of the sort fields and sort order. The sort order may be `ASC` (for ascending) or `DESC` (for descending). ASC is the default sort order, so you need to specify `DESC` only if you want the sort to be descending. If multiple sort fields are listed, then the order in which the fields appear in the list determines the primary sort field, the secondary sort field, and so on. For example, to retrieve all male employees sorted in descending order by last name use:

```
SELECT * FROM Employees WHERE Gender = 'M' ORDER BY LastName DESC
```

The `ORDER BY` clause can be used with or without the `WHERE` clause. For example, to retrieve all employees in ascending order by plant, and within each plant by department, and within each department by EmployeeID, use:

```
SELECT * FROM Employees ORDER BY Plant, Dept, EmployeeID
```

All the previous examples only retrieved the data from the database. However, you also need the ability to make changes to the data in the database. The next three sections show you the SQL statements that are used to add rows to a table, remove rows from a table, and update column values.

Inserting Rows

The SQL INSERT statement is used to add a single row to a database table. The general syntax of the INSERT statement is as follows:

```
INSERT INTO tableName (listOfFields) VALUES (listOfValues)
```

As before, the tableName is the name of the table in which this row is inserted. The listOfFields is a comma-separated list of the column names in that table for which you are providing values. The listOfValues is a comma-separated list of the actual values being assigned to each of the listed fields. The order of the column names in listOfFields does not have to match the order of the columns as defined in the table, but the order of the column values must match the column names specified in listOfFields.

Remember that if any of the fields are **string** or **date** types, you need to make sure that you use delimiters around the values assigned to these fields. To illustrate, a new row can be inserted into the Employees table by using the following SQL INSERT statement:

```
INSERT INTO Employees (
EmployeeID, LastName, FirstName, DateHired, SalaryInd, Gender, PayRate,
Plant, Dept)
VALUES
('115534123', 'Encharge', 'Ben', '1979-05-15', True, 'M', 500000.00,
'PAC', '1100')
```

13

Updating Rows

The SQL UPDATE statement is used to modify one or more column values for one or more rows in a table. The general syntax of the UPDATE statement is:

```
UPDATE tableName SET (listOfFieldAssignments) WHERE criteriaExpression
```

The tableName is the name of the table in which the values will be changed. The listOfFieldAssignments is a comma-separated list of column names and new values. For example, suppose an employee transferred to a new department because of a promotion and is now paid a salary instead of an hourly wage. The following SQL UPDATE statement uses the primary key in the WHERE clause to update that employee's record in the database:

```
UPDATE Employees SET Dept = '1200', SalaryInd = True, PayRate = 48000.00
WHERE EmployeeID = '011480009'
```

Most of the time SQL UPDATE statements include a WHERE clause. However, you can omit the WHERE clause if you need to update all rows in a table. For example, the following statement gives all employees a 5% raise:

```
UPDATE Employees SET PayRate = PayRate * 1.05
```

Deleting Rows

The SQL DELETE statement is used to remove one or more rows from a table. The general syntax of the DELETE statement is:

```
DELETE FROM tableName WHERE criteriaExpression
```

where **tableName** and **criteriaExpression** are the same as mentioned previously. To delete a specific record, use the primary key in the **WHERE** clause as shown here:

```
DELETE FROM Employees WHERE EmployeeID = '011480009'
```

If the primary key isn't used in the **WHERE** clause, multiple rows can be deleted using a single SQL **DELETE** statement. This next example deletes all Employees in Plant PAC:

```
DELETE FROM Employees WHERE Plant = 'PAC'
```

If you want to remove all rows from a table, you can omit the **WHERE** clause completely:

```
DELETE FROM Employees
```

However, needing to remove all rows from a table is unusual. Most of the time, your SQL **DELETE** statements use the primary key in the **WHERE** clause to delete a single row.

FORMATTING SQL STATEMENTS IN CODE

The SQL examples presented in the previous section of this chapter all contained constant values. If you need to give one of these SQL statements to a database engine to execute, you must first put it into a string variable. For example, passing the **sql** variable in the following statement to a DBMS deletes all employees who work in Plant PAC:

```
string sql;
sql = "DELETE FROM Employees WHERE Plant = 'PAC'"
```

It is unusual for a complete SQL statement such as this to be hard-coded directly into a program. A more likely scenario is that the SQL statements are dynamically constructed by concatenating string constants and the values of variables. For example, suppose that a variable named **closedPlant** contained the name for a plant that was closing. An SQL **DELETE** statement might be constructed in your C# code using a concatenation statement like:

```
string closedPlant;
...
string sql;
sql = "DELETE FROM Employees WHERE Plant = '" + closedPlant + "'";
```

Because **Plant** is stored in the database as a text field, the value in the **closedPlant** variable must be surrounded by single quotes in the SQL statement. Therefore, the code that pieces together the SQL string must include the single quotes as part of the C# string that is concatenated using the value in the variable.

Recall that dates in SQL strings are also enclosed in single quotes, and the date is formatted as **'yyyy-mm-dd'**, where **yyyy** is the four-digit year, **mm** is the two-digit month number, and **dd** is the two-digit day. You can format an SQL statement that uses a value from a **DateTime** variable like this:

```
DateTime queryDate;
...
string sql;
sql = "SELECT * FROM Employees WHERE DateHired < '" +
queryDate.Format("yyyy-MM-dd") + "'";
```

When number values are used in SQL statements that associate fields defined in the database with numeric data types, those values must not be enclosed in single quotation marks in the SQL statement. Also remember that, when your code dynamically constructs an SQL statement containing the value of a numeric variable, the variable must be converted to a string before it can be concatenated onto the SQL statement string. The same is true for Boolean data types. The Jet DBMS expects Boolean values to be indicated in SQL statements by using the strings `True` and `False`, which happen to be the string value returned from the Boolean `ToString` method. Formatting SQL statements using numbers and Booleans is illustrated in the following example:

```
decimal maxPayRate;
bool paidSalary;
...
string sql;
sql = "SELECT * FROM Employees WHERE"
    + " SalaryInd = " + paidSalary.ToString()
    + " AND PayRate > " + maxPayRate.ToString();
```

One more point needs to be made about formatting SQL statements containing text values. You know that most DBMSs expect SQL statements to use the single quotation mark or apostrophe character as the text delimiter character. But what happens when that same character is contained within a text value that is stored in the database? For example, suppose a variable containing an employee's last name entered by the user was being used to construct the SQL **SELECT** statement as shown here:

```
string lastName;
...
string sql;
sql = "SELECT * FROM Employees WHERE LastName = '" + lastName + "'";
```

Now suppose that the `lastName` variable contains the value `O'Conner`, which contains an embedded apostrophe. After the SQL statement is concatenated, it contains the value:

```
SELECT * FROM Employees WHERE LastName = 'O'Conner'
```

When the database engine tries to interpret the SQL statement, an exception is thrown because the unmatched quotation marks in the statement cause an SQL syntax error.

An even more serious error can be caused if a devious user enters SQL commands into your user interface for values he or she knows the application uses when formatting SQL statements. Using the last name query example, suppose that the user fills in the last name text box on a form with:

```
Bob'; DELETE FROM Employees WHERE Gender <> 'X
```

If this input is then concatenated directly to the SQL **SELECT** statement using C# code like this:

```
string sql;
sql = "SELECT * FROM Employees WHERE LastName = '" + txtLastName.Text + "'";
```

the result is a variable containing the SQL statements:

```
SELECT * FROM Employees WHERE LastName = 'Bob'; DELETE FROM Employees WHERE
Gender <> 'X'
```

If your program then passes this value to a DBMS to be executed, the DBMS might just perform the query and delete all the employee records!

The solution to this so-called **embedded quotes problem** is to pass two single quotation marks whenever one single quotation mark is found in the text value. For example, to query for all employees whose last names are `O'Conner`, use an SQL **SELECT** statement containing a value of:

```
SELECT * FROM Employees WHERE LastName = 'O''Conner'
```

When the DBMS finds two sequential single quotation marks, it knows to treat them as one embedded apostrophe. So, the proper way to format an SQL statement containing the value of a string variable is to first replace each apostrophe in the string with two apostrophes. This can be easily accomplished using the **string** object's **Replace** method. For example:

```
string lastName;
...
string sql;
sql = "SELECT * FROM Employees WHERE LastName = '" + lastName.Replace("'",
"''") + "'";
```

Now if the devious user enters the same text in the text box, attempting to delete all the employee records, the value that is assigned to the **sql** variable is:

```
SELECT * FROM Employees WHERE LastName = 'Bob''; DELETE FROM Employees WHERE
Gender <> ''X'
```

The result of passing this string to the DBMS is that no record is returned because no record in the table has a **LastName** value of:

```
Bob'; DELETE FROM Employees WHERE Gender <> 'X
```

Getting all the quotation marks in the correct places and converting variables to the correct format quickly causes your C# source code to become confusing. This is especially true for lengthy SQL **INSERT** and **UPDATE** statements. Therefore, we recommend using helper methods that convert the various data types into the proper string format for use in SQL statements. Figure 13-3 shows the set of methods used in the Essential ADO.NET test application.

```
272    // Private helper methods overloaded to format frequently used data types
273    // to the proper SQL format.
274
275    private string toSql(bool boolValue)
276    {
277        return boolValue.ToString();
278    }
279
280    private string toSql(DateTime dateTimeValue)
281    {
282        return "'" + dateTimeValue.ToString("yyyy-MM-dd") + "'";
283    }
284
285    private string toSql(decimal decimalValue)
286    {
287        return decimalValue.ToString();
288    }
289
290    private string toSql(double doubleValue)
291    {
292        return doubleValue.ToString();
293    }
294
295    private string toSql(int intValue)
296    {
297        return intValue.ToString();
298    }
299
300    private string toSql(string stringValue)
301    {
302        return "'" + stringValue.Replace("'", "''") + "'";
303    }
```

Figure 13-3   Helper methods used to convert data types to proper SQL format

Note that these methods take advantage of method overloading so that the same method name is used no matter what data type the variable is. These helper methods make concatenating variable values to SQL statements a snap. Just be sure to pass the variables to the toSQL methods first, as shown in Figure 13-4. If you always remember to use the toSQL methods, your values will always be formatted correctly and you won't have to worry about problems caused by embedded quotation marks in text values.

```
string employeeID;
string dept;
bool salaryInd;
decimal payRate;
...
string sql;

sql = "UPDATE Employees SET "
    + " Dept = "         + toSQL(dept)       + ", "
    + " SalaryInd = " + toSQL(salaryInd) + ", "
    + " PayRate = "    + toSQL(payRate)
    + " WHERE EmployeeID = " + toSQL(employeeID);
```

Figure 13-4 Using the toSQL methods to construct an SQL UPDATE statement

Using methods like those shown in Figure 13-3 has the added bonus that, if your application changes in the future to use a different DBMS and that DBMS expects values to be formatted differently, you only need to change these helper methods and not each and every SQL statement contained within your application. (For example, SQL Server expects Boolean values to be represented by 1 and 0 instead of True and False).

13

DATABASE CONNECTIVITY USING ADO.NET

In order for your program to pass SQL statements to a DBMS for execution, it needs to first establish a connection to the database. The easiest way to do this in C# is to use **ADO.NET**. ADO.NET provides a set of classes that allows you to interact with various DBMSs. Although the examples in this chapter use ADO.NET to connect to a Microsoft Access database, ADO.NET allows you to connect to other DBMSs such as DB2, SQL Server, and Oracle. You can even use ADO.NET to connect to non-RDBMS data sources such as text files, Excel spreadsheets, or even XML files.

Several layers of objects and other software components are necessary for your application to be able to read and write data in a Jet database. Your application doesn't communicate directly with a DBMS; instead it communicates with the ADO.NET data provider classes. ADO.NET provides several sets of these data provider classes that know how to communicate with various DBMSs. Unfortunately, ADO.NET doesn't include data providers that know how to communicate directly with the Jet DBMS. However, ADO.NET does include data providers that know how to communicate with OLE DB. So what is OLE DB?

OLE DB is Microsoft technology that existed before Microsoft .NET. Rather than require applications to communicate directly with vendor DBMSs, Microsoft created **OLE DB** to act as a sort of "middle man" between application programs and vendor DBMSs. The idea was that instead of requiring application programmers to learn how to communicate with the various vendor DBMSs, programmers instead only needed to learn how to communicate with OLE DB. The vendors who sell DBMSs were then encouraged to write OLE DB driver software that would communicate between OLE DB and their DBMSs. This made the application developer's job easier because he or she could write code the same way no matter which DBMS was being used.

Database Connectivity Acronyms

Before Microsoft gave us ADO.NET, database connectivity was done using ADO. The acronym ADO stood for ActiveX Data Objects, or sometimes just Active Data Objects. If you've worked with computers for any amount of time, you have surely noticed that computer terminology is full of three-letter acronyms (TLAs). After a while, the original meaning becomes unimportant, and only the acronym is used. These days ADO.NET doesn't seem to stand for anything anymore, and people just refer to it as ADO.NET.

Microsoft is especially good at coming up with acronyms for its technologies. Microsoft has several other database technologies it promoted before ADO.NET that you might read about someday, including Data Access Objects (DAO), Remote Data Objects (RDO), Open Database Connectivity (ODBC), and, as mentioned before, Object Linking and Embedding Database (OLE DB).

Even though your C# program can't communicate directly with the Jet DBMS, it can use the ADO.NET OLE DB provider classes to communicate with OLE DB. Furthermore, because an OLE DB driver is available for Jet, the OLE DB provider classes can in turn communicate with the Jet OLE DB Driver, which communicates with the Jet DBMS to read and write data in the database. These layers are shown in Figure 13-5.

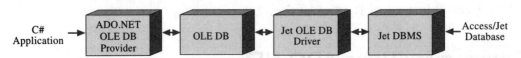

Figure 13-5   Connecting to the Jet DBMS using ADO.NET and OLE DB

You might wonder why all these layers of software are necessary. Layers of abstraction like these are often used in object-oriented programming to create more flexible software architectures. For example, your application can connect to the Jet DBMS using the ADO.NET OLE DB data provider classes. At a later time, you might decide to use IBM's DB2 DBMS. The only change you should have to make in your application is to tell ADO.NET to connect to DB2 instead of Jet. Hopefully, no other lines of code would need to be changed. Such a gain is but one of the benefits that encapsulation and OOP in general bring to the table.

The ADO.NET OLE DB Data Provider Classes

The database connectivity approach we recommend in this chapter uses three ADO.NET classes: (1) the OleDbConnection class, (2) the OleDbCommand class, and (3) the OleDbDataReader class. These three classes are defined in the **System.Data.OleDb** namespace, so be sure to include an appropriate **using** directive at the top of any classes that use them.

The OleDbConnection class provides connectivity to the DBMS. After you instantiate a connection object, you use that object to identify the OLE DB driver to use as well as the path and filename of the database file. The OleDbConnection object is then used to associate OleDbCommand and OleDbDataReader objects to the DBMS and database.

The `OleDbCommand` object allows you to execute SQL statements. Your program formats SQL statements and stores them in string variables and then passes them to an instance of the `OleDbCommand` class to be executed.

An `OleDbDataReader` object contains the rows from the database that are the result of a query statement that has been executed by an `OleDbCommand` object. Methods and properties in the `OleDbDataReader` class let you loop through all the rows that are returned from the query, as well as get the data value for each column in each row.

Using ADO.NET with C#

To illustrate using ADO.NET in C#, we present a sample application that illustrates the four basic CRUD (create, retrieve/read, update, and delete) operations. Rather than creating a realistic application that would contain a good deal of non-database logic, the functions of this sample program are limited to illustrating how to use SQL statements with the three previously mentioned ADO.NET classes. Additionally, the columns in the sample database are chosen to illustrate how to manipulate the seven most common data types we feel you will use when storing an object's state in a database. After you understand these basics, you will be ready to adapt them to be used in a real application.

The UI for our Essential ADO.NET test application is shown in Figure 13-6. As you can see, this minimalist UI is designed with only enough functionality to test basic CRUD functionality using ADO.NET with a Jet database named Sample.mdb.

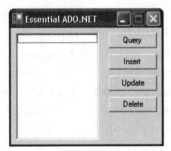

Figure 13-6 User Interface for the Essential ADO.NET test application

The data definition for the table this test application uses is also very minimalist. You can see from Figure 13-7 that the test table named `SampleTable` contains one column each for the seven most common data types you will use.

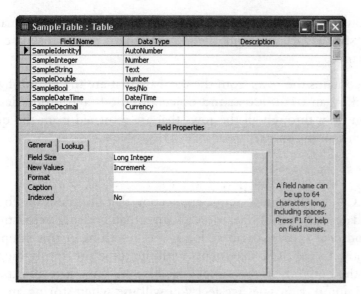

Figure 13-7   Design of SampleTable

The Essential ADO.NET application is created like most of the other simple applications presented in this text. That is, the application contains a single main form with buttons and a list box. The best way to test this application is to set breakpoints in each of the methods so you can watch each statement execute line by line. If you have Microsoft Access available, you can also open the Sample.mdb database file after each method is executed and observe the results. If you don't have Microsoft Access available, the Bonus Topics section includes a discussion of how to use bound controls to view the contents of a database table, which you might find useful.

The first part of the class that defines the main form, excluding the Form Designer–generated code, is shown in Figure 13-8. Line 2 contains the **using** directive for the **System.Data.OleDb** namespace. Line 8 defines and instantiates a private **OleDbConnection** object that the rest of the code uses to establish a connection to the Jet database engine. Lines 12 through 18 define C# variables of the seven different data types used in the test application.

```
1    using System;
2    using System.Data.OleDb;
3    using System.IO;
4    using System.Windows.Forms;
5
6    public class frmMain: Form
7    {
8        private OleDbConnection mDB = new OleDbConnection();
9
10       // Variables of frequently used data types to test inserting and updating.
11
12       private int      mIdentity;
13       private int      mInteger;
14       private string   mString;
15       private double   mDouble;
16       private bool     mBool;
17       private DateTime mDateTime;
18       private decimal  mDecimal;
```

Figure 13-8   The Essential ADO.NET test application frmMain class

```
 97        public static void Main()
 98        {
 99            frmMain main = new frmMain();
100            Application.Run(main);
101        }
```

Figure 13-8   The Essential ADO.NET test application frmMain class (continued)

Opening and Closing Database Connections

Just as with sequential data files, before you can read or write data to a database, you have to open a connection to it. When your program is finished reading and writing to it, your program should close the database connection. As mentioned earlier, database connections are opened and closed using an `OleDbConnection` object. The test application opens the connection when the application first begins execution and closes the connection when the application ends. You can see how this is done by observing the **frmMain** constructor and **Closing** event methods shown in Figure 13-9.

```
103    public frmMain()
104    {
105        InitializeComponent();
106
107        // Open the sample database.
108
109        try
110        {
111            // Set the connection string to open the sample database in the same
112            // folder as the EXE.
113
114            mDB.ConnectionString = "Provider=Microsoft.Jet.OLEDB.4.0;Data source="
115                + Path.Combine(Application.StartupPath, "Sample.mdb");
116            mDB.Open();
117        }
118        catch (Exception ex)
119        {
120            MessageBox.Show(ex.Message);
121        }
122    }

266    // Close the database connection when the form closes.
267    private void frmMain_Closing(object sender, System.ComponentModel.CancelEventArgs e)
268    {
269        mDB.Close();
270    }
```

Figure 13-9   frmMain's constructor and Closing event method

To open a database connection, you simply call the `OleDbConnection` object's `Open` method. (See line 116 in Figure 13-9. Also note how you should wrap calls to database methods in a **try-catch** block). Equally as easy, you close the database connection by calling the `OleDbConnection` object's `Close` method (see line 269 in Figure 13-9). Note that you don't have to wrap the call to the `Close` method in a **try-catch** block because it doesn't throw exceptions.

Before you can open a database connection, you must set the `OleDbConnection` object's `ConnectionString` property. (See lines 114 and 115 in Figure 13-9.)

The `ConnectionString` property tells OLE DB which OLE DB driver to connect to and can include other information that is passed along to the DBMS. The **connection string** to use when connecting to the Jet DBMS and a Microsoft Access database is:

```
Provider=Microsoft.Jet.OLEDB.4.0;Data source=filename
```

For example:

```
Provider=Microsoft.Jet.OLEDB.4.0;Data source=C:\My Projects\
EssentialADO.NET\bin\Debug\Sample.mdb
```

The *filename* in this string is the full path and filename of the database file to be opened. You can see from lines 114 and 115 in Figure 13-9 that the test application assumes that the Sample.mdb database file is located in the same folder as the application's .exe. You should note that the values you provide for database connection strings *must match exactly* the preceding sample shown, including uppercase and lowercase characters and spacing between words.

Database Connection Strings

The `OleDbConnection.ConnectionString` property differs, depending on which DBMS you are connecting to. The only difference between an application that uses the Jet DBMS and IBM's DB2 DBMS may be just the OLE DB connection string used.

The easiest way to find the correct connection string for the DBMS you are using is to do a Web search to find examples. There are so many variations of database connection strings that some Web sites are devoted only to this topic (for example, www.connectionstrings.com).

Inserting Rows

The code in Figure 13-10 shows an example of how to insert a record by passing an SQL `INSERT` statement to the Jet DBMS.

Lines 152 through 157 assign sample values to the various variables that will be used to form the SQL `INSERT` statement. All variable values are passed to the `toSQL` helper methods to convert them to strings of the correct format. Lines 162 through 180 format the SQL `INSERT` statement by concatenating string literals with the string values of the variables. Note that, to keep the sample application as simple as possible, the user interface doesn't allow the values to be entered and validated. If you'd like to experiment with different values, change the code, rebuild the application, and run it again.

Lines 184 and 185 show how you pass an SQL statement to the DBMS for processing. Line 184 instantiates a `OleDbCommand` object and passes the SQL statement and database connection object to its constructor. Line 185 calls the `OleDbCommand` object's `ExecuteNonQuery` method to execute the SQL `INSERT` statement.

 tip ▶ When debugging dynamically created SQL statements, assign the SQL statement to a variable so that you can inspect its contents to be sure that it is formatted correctly before it is passed to the DBMS to be executed.

```
146    // This method illustrates how to insert a row into a table.
147    private void btnInsert_Click(object sender, System.EventArgs e)
148    {
149        string sql;
150        OleDbCommand cmd;
151
152        mInteger = 12345;
153        mString = "Bob";
154        mDouble = 123.456F;
155        mBool  = false;
156        mDateTime = DateTime.Now;
157        mDecimal = 199.99M;
158
159        // Note the identity column isn't specified in the insert statement
160        // because it is calculated by the DBMS whenever a record is inserted.
161
162        sql = "INSERT INTO SampleTable ("
163
164            + "SampleInteger, "
165            + "SampleString, "
166            + "SampleDouble, "
167            + "SampleBool, "
168            + "SampleDateTime, "
169            + "SampleDecimal"
170
171            + ") VALUES ("
172
173            + toSql(mInteger)  + ", "
174            + toSql(mString)   + ", "
175            + toSql(mDouble)   + ", "
176            + toSql(mBool)     + ", "
177            + toSql(mDateTime) + ", "
178            + toSql(mDecimal)
179
180            + ")";
181
182        try
183        {
184            cmd = new OleDbCommand(sql, mDB);
185            cmd.ExecuteNonQuery();
186        }
187        catch (Exception ex)
188        {
189            MessageBox.Show(ex.Message);
190        }
191    }
```

Figure 13-10 Inserting a row into a Jet database using ADO.NET

A properly defined relational database table always contains a primary key that uniquely identifies each row in the table. Many times, the set of data that makes up the row contains no logical choice for a primary key. For example, suppose that you create a database to keep track of your collection of music CDs. In such a case, determining what to use as a primary key could pose a problem. Because this problem of not having an obvious choice for a primary key occurs frequently, the makers of database engines include a special data type that can be used to always guarantee a unique value. This column type is often called an Identity or Counter column.

Notice in Figure 13-7 that **SampleTable** is defined with a column named **SampleIdentity**, which is defined in the database table with type **AutoNumber**. Microsoft Access and the Jet DBMS provide the ability to generate a unique value for use as a primary key using the **AutoNumber** data type. Each time a row is inserted into a table with an **AutoNumber** field, the DBMS generates a unique value for that row. Therefore, the value for an **AutoNumber** column isn't included in the SQL **INSERT** statements. Different DBMSs use different schemes for generating unique identity values. An **AutoNumber** column in a Jet database is simply a sequential integer number.

When inserting a row into a database, the DBMS notifies your program if a problem was encountered by throwing an exception. The DBMS throws exceptions in situations like this:

- The SQL statement contains a syntax error (for example, unmatched quotation marks).
- A column value contains an invalid value (for example, a string value is indicated for a numeric column).
- A column value is required, and you don't include it in the **INSERT** statement.
- You provide a value for a primary key and a row already exists in the database with the same primary key value.

To avoid exceptions being thrown by the DBMS, you should review the design of the table to determine the data types of each column, determine the columns that require a value, identify which columns define the primary key, and identify any other rules that might exist for the table. Also, because of the many reasons the DBMS throws exceptions, it is imperative to put calls to database object methods inside of a **try-catch** block as shown in lines 182 through 190 in Figure 13-10.

Performing Queries

Now that you can insert rows into the database, you should next test to see if your program can get them back out. This is done by passing an SQL **SELECT** statement to the database engine by using an **OleDbCommand** object, which returns a reference to an **OleDbDataReader** object that encapsulates the rows resulting from the query. This process is illustrated in Figure 13-11. The sample application displays the results of the query by adding the values for the **SampleIdentity** columns to a list box on the form. Again, the best way to develop a good understanding of the concepts presented so far and to test this code is to set breakpoints and step through the code line by line.

```
193    // This method illustrates performing a query and looping through
194    // the results.
195    private void btnQuery_Click(object sender, System.EventArgs e)
196    {
197        string sql;
198        OleDbCommand cmd;
199        OleDbDataReader rdr;
200
201        lstMain.Items.Clear();
202
203        try
204        {
205            sql = "SELECT * FROM SampleTable ORDER BY SampleIdentity";
206            cmd = new OleDbCommand(sql, mDB);
```

Figure 13-11   Querying a table using ADO.NET and looping through the results

```
207              rdr = cmd.ExecuteReader();
208
209              while (rdr.Read() == true)
210              {
211                  mIdentity = (int)      rdr["SampleIdentity"];
212                  mInteger  = (int)      rdr["SampleInteger"];
213                  mString   = (string)   rdr["SampleString"];
214                  mDouble   = (double)   rdr["SampleDouble"];
215                  mBool     = (bool)     rdr["SampleBool"];
216                  mDateTime = (DateTime) rdr["SampleDateTime"];
217                  mDecimal  = (decimal)  rdr["SampleDecimal"];
218
219                  lstMain.Items.Add(mIdentity);
220              }
221              rdr.Close();
222          }
223          catch (Exception ex)
224          {
225              MessageBox.Show(ex.Message);
226          }
227      }
```

Figure 13-11 Querying a table using ADO.NET and looping through the results (continued)

Line 205 in Figure 13-11 creates a variable that holds an SQL SELECT statement. Line 206 instantiates an OleDbCommand object and passes it the SQL statement and the database connection object just as was done in Figure 13-10. However, because the SQL statement contains a query, the OleDbCommand object's ExecuteReader method is called instead of the ExecuteNonQuery method as was done when inserting a row. The ExecuteReader method returns a reference to an OleDbDataReader object, as shown on line 207.

Because a query can return more than one row, you need a way to loop through all the rows returned from the query. Looping through rows in an OleDbDataReader object is similar to reading records from a sequential file in that you use a **while** loop to process each row until all rows have been processed. The OleDbDataReader class contains a Read method that has the dual purpose of sequentially moving through the rows returned from the query and indicating when all rows have been processed. See line 209 in Figure 13-11. The Read method returns **true** as long as there are more rows to be processed and returns **false** when the end of the rows has been reached.

It is also important to understand how to get column values for the rows that result from a query. The syntax for getting a column value from an OleDbDataReader object is:

> *variable* = (*objectType*) *readerVariable*["*columnName*"];

where *variable* is the name of the variable to which the value is assigned, *objectType* is the data type of *variable*, *readerVariable* is the variable containing a reference to the OleDbDataReader object, and *columnName* is the name of the column as defined in the table. Note that *objectType* must match the data type of *variable* and the data type of the column as defined in the database. (See Table 13-2 for a cross-reference between C# and Access data types). Note how the extra spacing used on lines 211 through 217 in Figure 13-11 makes the code easier to read.

Finally, after all rows from the query have been processed, the OleDbDataReader object should be closed as shown on line 221 in Figure 13-11.

13

Updating and Deleting Rows

During the discussion on how to pass an SQL INSERT statement when using an OleDbCommand object, you should have noticed that there was nothing about the ExecuteNonQuery method that had anything to do with inserting rows. Instead, the SQL statement contained all the details about the action to be performed. We mention this here because if you understand how to pass SQL INSERT statements to the DBMS using an OleDbCommand object, then you also know how to pass SQL UPDATE and SQL DELETE statements because they are passed to the DBMS in exactly the same way as SQL INSERT statements. The only difference is the SQL statement itself. Figure 13-12 and Figure 13-13 show the methods from the sample application to illustrate updating and deleting a row in the sample database.

```
229     // This method illustrates how to update a record in a table.
230     private void btnUpdate_Click(object sender, System.EventArgs e)
231     {
232         string sql;
233         OleDbCommand cmd;
234
235         try
236         {
237             mIdentity = (int)lstMain.SelectedItem;
238
239             mInteger = 45678;
240             mString = "Cindy";
241             mDouble = 456.789F;
242             mBool  = true;
243             mDateTime = DateTime.Parse("12-03-2005");
244             mDecimal = 588.88M;
245
246             sql = "UPDATE SampleTable SET "
247
248                 + "SampleInteger = "  + toSql(mInteger)  + ", "
249                 + "SampleString = "   + toSql(mString)   + ", "
250                 + "SampleDouble = "   + toSql(mDouble)   + ", "
251                 + "SampleBool = "     + toSql(mBool)     + ", "
252                 + "SampleDateTime = " + toSql(mDateTime) + ", "
253                 + "SampleDecimal = "  + toSql(mDecimal)
254
255                 + " WHERE SampleIdentity = " + toSql(mIdentity);
256
257             cmd = new OleDbCommand(sql, mDB);
258             cmd.ExecuteNonQuery();
259         }
260         catch (Exception ex)
261         {
262             MessageBox.Show(ex.Message);
263         }
264     }
```

Figure 13-12   Updating a record in a Jet database using ADO.NET

Note again in Figure 13-12 how sample values are assigned to values on statements 239 through 244 to simplify the example code. Also note how line 237 in Figure 13-12 and line 132 in Figure 13-13 get the identity value that is currently selected in the list box. (This code assumes that an item is selected in the list box so be careful when testing.) Recall the identity value is defined as the primary key for the table and so is used in the **WHERE** clause of both the SQL **UPDATE** and SQL **DELETE** statements to make sure only one row is affected.

```
124     // This method illustrates how to delete a row from a table.
125     private void btnDelete_Click(object sender, System.EventArgs e)
126     {
127         string sql;
128         OleDbCommand cmd;
129
130         try
131         {
132             mIdentity = (int)lstMain.SelectedItem;
133
134             sql = "DELETE FROM SampleTable WHERE SampleIdentity = "
135                 + toSql(mIdentity);
136
137             cmd = new OleDbCommand(sql, mDB);
138             cmd.ExecuteNonQuery();
139         }
140         catch (Exception ex)
141         {
142             MessageBox.Show(ex.Message);
143         }
144     }
```

Figure 13-13   Deleting a record from a Jet database using ADO.NET

The Impedance Mismatch between OOP and Relational Databases

Before we present an example of using ADO.NET in a program example, you need to understand a significant problem you might encounter when using an object-oriented programming language such as C# with a relational database management system—the so-called impedance mismatch problem.

Most new business applications are developed with a modern object-oriented programming language such as C#, Java, or VB.NET. Most business applications persist their data to a relational database. However, mixing OOP with an RDBMS often results in a less than optimal solution. The reason for this is that the goals of OOP and relational databases are very different.

You've learned that one goal of OOP is to model real-world objects, and a goal of a relational database is to reduce redundancy. However, real-world objects almost always contain redundant data. Another goal of OOP is to facilitate code reuse through mechanisms such as encapsulation, inheritance, and polymorphism. Yet RDBMSs have no support for inheritance and polymorphism. Still another difference is something as basic as data types.

Both OOP languages and relational databases can represent data using simple data types such as integers, floating-point numbers, Booleans, date/times, and text characters. However, the way these values are stored in a relational database is often not the same way as how they are stored in an OOP language. For example, a relational database supports the notion of a field containing a null value when the value for a given data item is unknown. A customer's birthdate might contain a null value when stored in a database if the customer wants to keep his birthdate confidential. However, when dates are stored in a C# program, they always have a value, because the .NET **DateTime** data type is a value type not a reference type, and so it can never have a value of **null**.

These differences (and a few others) between OOP and relational database theory are collectively known as the **impedance mismatch** problem. You might ask yourself, "If OOP and relational databases aren't a good fit, then why are they the de facto standard for business application development?" The answer is because there simply isn't a better choice. Object-oriented database management systems do exist, but have never caught on as a good solution for business applications because of their poor processing performance.

Even given the impedance mismatch problem, it is possible to demonstrate persisting an object's state to a relational database, especially for relatively simple objects. If the business objects used in an application don't contain relationships and inheritance isn't used in the class definition, each unique object type can be represented using a single table in the database, where each piece of state information is mapped to a column in the table. Mapping a simple object structure such as this to a single database table is the subject of the next section.

A Program Example

Because modern OOP languages don't contain a mechanism to automatically save object state to a robust data management system, code must be included in each class to map that object's state information to one or more RDBMS tables. To illustrate how this can be done, we modify the Contacts List application one more time.

This time the Contacts List application from Chapter 12 is modified to use the Jet DBMS to save a contact object's state information to a Microsoft Access database file. Because no new features are being added to the program other than how the contact data is persisted, the remaining discussion focuses only on the changes necessary to use a database rather than sequential data files. You've also already learned how to use SQL with ADO.NET, so you need only learn where the code should go.

A summary of the changes includes the following:

- A Microsoft Access database file named Contacts.mdb is provided. The database contains a table named **Contacts** that stores the state for the **clsContact** objects.

- The main form defines and instantiates an **OleDbConnection** object to reference the database file (line 12 in Figure 13-14).

- When the application begins execution, a database connection is opened rather than opening the sequential file (lines 319 through 322 in Figure 13-14), and a new **refreshContacts** method is called to query the **Contacts** table and display each contact in the main form's list view (Figure 13-15).

- When the application ends, the database connection is closed (lines 344 through 347 in Figure 13-14).

- The **Serialize** and **Deserialize** methods in **clsContact** have been removed because the state information is no longer being saved to a tab-delimited text file.

- Four new methods have been added to **clsContact** that perform the four basic CRUD operations (see Figure 13-16).

- Whenever a contact is inserted, updated, or deleted, the main form tells the contact object to immediately update the database rather than waiting until the application ends to save the changes, as was done with the sequential file version (see Figure 13-17).

```
 12   private OleDbConnection mDB = new OleDbConnection();

311   public frmMain()
312   {
313      InitializeComponent();
314
315      // Open the database connection.
316
317      try
318      {
319          string contactsFileName = Path.Combine(Application.StartupPath, "Contacts.mdb");
320          mDB.ConnectionString = "Provider=Microsoft.Jet.OLEDB.4.0;Data source="
321           + contactsFileName;
322          mDB.Open();
323
324          refreshContacts();
325      }
326      catch(Exception ex)
327      {
328          MessageBoxOK(ex.Message);
329      }
330   }

344   private void frmMain_Closing(object sender, System.ComponentModel.CancelEventArgs e)
345   {
346       mDB.Close();
347   }
```

Figure 13-14 Opening and closing the connection to the Contacts database

```
578      // This method refreshes the list of contact objects by retrieving them
579      // from the Contacts database table.
580      private void refreshContacts()
581      {
582          string sql;
583          clsContact contact;
584          OleDbCommand cmd;
585          OleDbDataReader rdr = null;
586
587          lvwContacts.Items.Clear();
588
589          try
590          {
591              sql = "SELECT * FROM Contacts ORDER By ContactID";
592              cmd = new OleDbCommand(sql, mDB);
593              rdr = cmd.ExecuteReader();
594
595              while (rdr.Read() == true)
596              {
597                  contact = new clsContact();
598                  contact.RestoreStateFromQuery(rdr);
599                  addContactToListView(contact);
600              }
601              updateStatusBar();
```

Figure 13-15 Querying the Contacts database to restore the contact objects

```
602          }
603       finally
604       {
605          if (rdr != null)
606          {
607             rdr.Close();
608          }
609       }
610    }
```

Figure 13-15 Querying the Contacts database to restore the contact objects (continued)

```
124    // Purpose: Inserts this object into the Contacts database table.
125    public void Insert(OleDbConnection db)
126    {
127       string sql;
128       OleDbCommand cmd;
129
130       sql = "INSERT INTO Contacts ("
131
132          + "FirstName, "
133          + "LastName, "
134          + "HomePhone, "
135          + "MobilePhone, "
136          + "BirthDate"
137
138          + ") VALUES ("
139
140          + clsSql.ToSql(mFirstName)             + ", "
141          + clsSql.ToSql(mLastName)              + ", "
142          + clsSql.ToSql(HomePhone.ToString())   + ", "
143          + clsSql.ToSql(MobilePhone.ToString()) + ", "
144          + clsSql.ToSql(BirthDate)
145
146          + ")";
147
148       cmd = new OleDbCommand(sql, db);
149       cmd.ExecuteNonQuery();
150
151       // Re-query to get the ContactID of the record just inserted.
152
153       sql = "SELECT MAX(ContactID) AS MaxID FROM Contacts";
154       cmd = new OleDbCommand(sql, db);
155       mContactID = (int)cmd.ExecuteScalar();
156    }
157
158    // Purpose: Updates this object in the Contacts database table.
159    public void Update(OleDbConnection db)
160    {
161       string sql;
162       OleDbCommand cmd;
163
164       sql = "UPDATE Contacts SET "
165
```

Figure 13-16 CRUD methods in clsContact

```
166                  + "FirstName = "    + clsSql.ToSql(mFirstName)               + ", "
167                  + "LastName = "     + clsSql.ToSql(mLastName)                + ", "
168                  + "HomePhone = "    + clsSql.ToSql(HomePhone.ToString())     + ", "
169                  + "MobilePhone = " + clsSql.ToSql(MobilePhone.ToString()) + ", "
170                  + "BirthDate = "    + clsSql.ToSql(BirthDate)
171
172                  + " WHERE ContactID = " + clsSql.ToSql(mContactID);
173
174         cmd = new OleDbCommand(sql, db);
175         cmd.ExecuteNonQuery();
176     }
177
178     // Purpose: Deletes this object from the Contacts database table.
179     public void Delete(OleDbConnection db)
180     {
181         string sql;
182         OleDbCommand cmd;
183
184         sql = "DELETE FROM Contacts WHERE ContactID = "
185             + clsSql.ToSql(mContactID);
186
187         cmd = new OleDbCommand(sql, db);
188         cmd.ExecuteNonQuery();
189     }
190
191     // Restores the state of this object from the results of a query.
192     public void RestoreStateFromQuery(OleDbDataReader rdr)
193     {
194         string homePhone;
195         string mobilePhone;
196
197         mContactID  = (int)      rdr["ContactID"];
198         mFirstName  = (string)   rdr["FirstName"];
199         mLastName   = (string)   rdr["LastName"];
200         homePhone   = (string)   rdr["HomePhone"];
201         mobilePhone = (string)   rdr["MobilePhone"];
202         BirthDate   = (DateTime) rdr["BirthDate"];
203
204         HomePhone   = new clsPhoneNumber(homePhone);
205         MobilePhone = new clsPhoneNumber(mobilePhone);
206     }
```

Figure 13-16   CRUD methods in clsContact (continued)

```
438     // Adds a new contact to the database and the listview.
439     private void addContact()
440     {
441         clsContact contact = new clsContact();
442         frmAddUpdate addUpdate;
443
444         try
445         {
446             addUpdate = new frmAddUpdate(this, "Add", contact);
447             if (addUpdate.ShowDialog() == DialogResult.OK)
```

Figure 13-17   UI objects calling the contact object's Insert, Update, and Delete methods

```
448               {
449                   contact.Insert(mDB);
450                   addContactToListView(contact);
451                   updateStatusBar();
452               }
453           }
454       catch(Exception ex)
455       {
456           MessageBoxOK(ex.Message);
457       }
458   }
459

477   // Removes the selected contact from the database and listview.
478   private void deleteContact()
479   {
480       clsContact contact;
481
...
498       // Remove the contact from the database and listview.
499
500       try
501       {
502           contact.Delete(mDB);
503           lvwContacts.Items.Remove(lvwContacts.SelectedItems[0]);
504           updateStatusBar();
505       }
506       catch(Exception ex)
507       {
508           MessageBoxOK(ex.Message);
509       }
510
511   }
512
513   // Updates the selected contact in the database and the listview.
514   private void updateContact()
515   {
516       clsContact contact;
517
518       // Make sure an item is selected in the listview.
519
520       if (lvwContacts.SelectedItems.Count == 0)
521       {
522           return;
523       }
524
525       try
526       {
527           contact = (clsContact)lvwContacts.SelectedItems[0].Tag;
528
529           frmAddUpdate addUpdate = new frmAddUpdate(this, "Update", contact);
530           if (addUpdate.ShowDialog() == DialogResult.OK)
531           {
532               contact.Update(mDB);
533               lvwContacts.Items.Remove(lvwContacts.SelectedItems[0]);
534               addContactToListView(contact);
535               updateStatusBar();
```

Figure 13-17   UI objects calling the contact object's Insert, Update, and Delete methods (continued)

```
536             }
537         }
538         catch(Exception ex)
539         {
540             MessageBoxOK(ex.Message);
541         }
542     }
```

Figure 13-17 UI objects calling the contact object's Insert, Update, and Delete methods (continued)

BONUS TOPICS

BOUND CONTROLS

The database connectivity technique you've learned in the Essential Topics section uses SQL statements and just three ADO.NET classes for creating, retrieving, updating, and deleting data in a database table. The reason we have presented this approach is that it is a technique that works with most OOP languages and DBMSs. We also believe that having some knowledge of SQL syntax is important for anyone learning to develop information systems that use RDBMSs. Writing code to format the SQL statements can be a bit tedious, but in the long run it produces more robust and professional applications.

.NET includes another database connectivity technique that doesn't require knowledge of SQL and initially requires much less C# code. This approach uses bound controls. **Bound controls** allow you to connect UI objects directly to tables and columns in a database. Instead of writing C# code to move data back and forth between the UI controls and the database, properties are set on the controls that allow the data to be moved back and forth automatically.

Although bound controls might be acceptable in trivial applications for people who don't want, or don't know how, to write C# and SQL statements, real applications require C# code to add features such as:

- Deleting records
- Validating data
- Allowing the user to specify the database file to be opened
- Searching for specific records
- Calculating values based on other column values
- Allowing your application to dynamically create a database file

You may be able to accomplish all the above features while using bound controls, but your logic will quickly become fragmented and difficult to manage because the logic required to do so will be scattered among many event methods. Bound controls also violate the encapsulation spirit of object-oriented programming because your user interface is then connected directly to columns in the database instead of using classes to encapsulate the data.

13

Using Bound Controls to Display the Contents of a Database Table

To give you an idea of what is possible with bound controls, this section shows you how to create a program that can be used to view the contents of database tables without writing much code. Even though we don't recommend using bound controls for real applications, this technique might help you debug a different application that manipulates the data in a database. For example, if you don't have Microsoft Access on your computer, you might use this technique to display the entire contents of the sample database tables presented earlier in this chapter.

To try using bound controls for yourself, start a new project and complete the following steps. These steps use the Products.mdb Access database file supplied with supplemental files that accompanies this text, but you can try it using any Access database you have handy.

As you follow the steps, keep in mind that these VS.NET tools are really instantiating essential objects that allow you to interact with the database. First, a connection object identifies the type of database, the database filename, username, password, and other parameters that are needed to connect to the database. Second, a data adapter is used, which has a reference to the connection object and a specific database table. Third, a dataset object is an in-memory representation of the data you want to view. Finally, a new control, the `DataGrid`, is added to the form and bound to the dataset. The data adapter is used to fill the data set object with the data from the indicated data source, so you can view the data on the form. Although you can establish the binding at design time by assigning the `DataSource` property of the `DataGrid` control, this sample program binds the `DataGrid` to a dataset and fills the dataset using only two lines of code.

1. From the View menu, select **Server Explorer**.

2. In the Server Explorer window, right-click on **Data Connections** and select **Add Connection** from the pop-up menu.

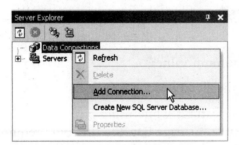

3. On the Provider tab in the Data Link Properties dialog, select **Microsoft Jet 4.0 OLE DB Provider**.

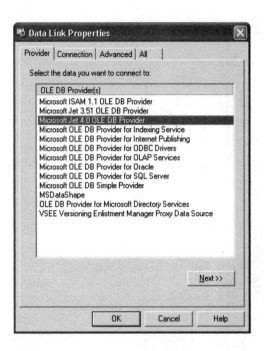

4. Click **Next** >> or switch to the Connection tab.

5. Click the ⬛ button and locate the desired database file from the Select Access Database dialog. Click **Open** when finished.

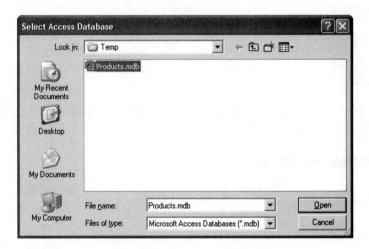

6. The filename should now appear in the Data Link Properties dialog under the Connection tab. Click the **Test Connection** button.

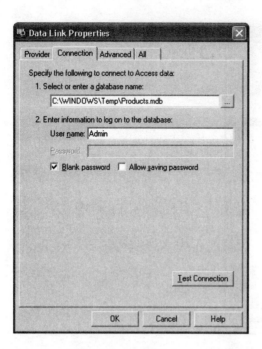

7. Assuming that the connection works, you should see the message box. Click the **OK** button to dismiss the confirmation dialog, and click the **OK** button on the Data Link Properties dialog.

8. In the Server Explorer window, expand the view until you can see the database tables in the file to which you connected.

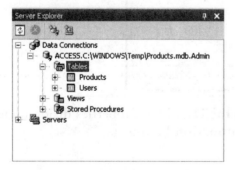

9. Drag the users table to the form.

10. You are asked whether or not you want to include the password to access the database file in the source code. Select **Don't include password**.

11. At this point, you see oleDbConnection1 and oleDbDataAdapter1 in the component tray.

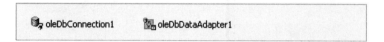

12. Select **oleDbConnection1** and rename it **oleConn** in the Properties window.

13. Select **oleDbDataAdapter1** and rename it **oleDAUsers** in the Properties window.

14. Click the **Generate Dataset** link (located below the list of properties).

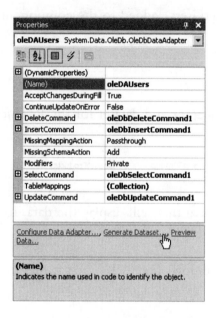

15. In the Generate Dataset dialog, name this dataset **dsetUsers** and make sure that **Add this dataset to the designer** is checked.

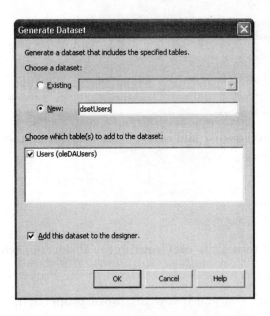

16. When you click **OK**, you should see dsetUsers1 added to the component tray.

17. Repeat these steps to add another data adapter and dataset for the Products table.

18. Now you need to add a control to the form that will display the data. To show the entire table, use the `DataGrid` control.

19. Drag the [DataGrid] icon from the Windows Forms Toolbox to the form.

20. Change the name to **dgridTable**.

21. Add three buttons on the form.

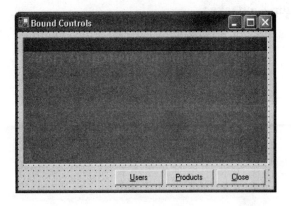

22. Add code to the Users and Products click **event methods**:

```
private void btnUsers_Click(object sender, System.EventArgs e)
{
    dsetUsers1.Clear();
    dgridTable.DataSource = dsetUsers1.Users;
    oleDAUsers.Fill(dsetUsers1);
}

private void btnProducts_Click(object sender, System.EventArgs e)
{
    dsetProducts1.Clear();
    dgridTable.DataSource = dsetProducts1.Products;
    oleDAProducts.Fill(dsetProducts1);
}
```

23. Run the program to verify that the **DataGrid** is initially empty. Clicking the Users button populates it using the users table, and clicking on the Products button populates it using the Products table.

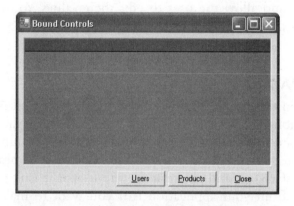

13

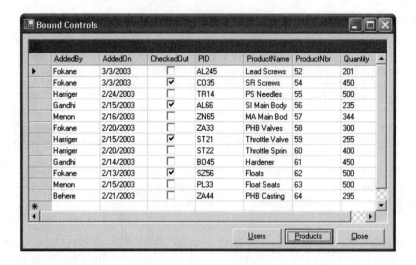

Bound controls are not limited to just displaying the contents of a table. For example, you can display individual columns of a row and allow the user to edit their values. You might also add navigation buttons to move through the database table row by row.

DYNAMICALLY CREATING A JET DATABASE

All the examples presented thus far in this chapter have assumed that a Microsoft Access database file exists before a connection is established. What if you don't want to require the file to already exist? Applications often need to create a database file programmatically. For example, if you don't want to distribute the MDB file with your program, you can add code to your program to see if the database file exists each time it starts up, and create it for the user if it isn't found. Another reason for creating the database file from your application is if you want to make the program more flexible by allowing the user to specify the path and filename of the database file.

Because ADO.NET is a general-purpose technology for database connectivity, it doesn't have the means to create a Microsoft Access database file programmatically. However, you can use ADOX for this purpose. So what's ADOX?

ADOX is a technology Microsoft released before ADO.NET, back when people were using ADO for database connectivity. You see, ADO also had no mechanism for dynamically creating Microsoft Access databases from code, but people wanted this ability. As a result, Microsoft released ADOX, or as it is more formally known, Microsoft ADO Ext. 2.7 for DDL and Security.

To illustrate using ADOX from your application, we present another sample application. The Bonus ADO.NET application is similar to the Essential ADO.NET application in that it isn't a real application and instead contains just enough code to show how to use ADOX to create a Microsoft Access database file, and then use ADO.NET to add a table and define columns for it. The Bonus ADO.NET application can be used to create the database file used by the Essential ADO.NET application.

To use ADOX in your application, you have to reference it from your project. Do so by selecting Project → Add Reference from the VS.NET menu. On the Add Reference dialog, select the COM tab and click the Browse button. From the Select Component dialog, browse until you find the `msadox.dll` file (usually found in the in the `c:\program files\common files\system\ado` folder). This file contains the ADOX classes that enable your program to create a database file.

Next add a `using` directive for the ADOX class library in the class file that will be creating the database file as shown on line 1 in Figure 13-35. Figure 13-35 shows the first part of the class that defines the main form for the Bonus ADO.NET sample application, excluding the code generated by the Form Designer of course. Note that line 3 contains the using directive for the `System.Data.OleDb` namespace because we need those classes to add the table and define its columns.

```
1    using ADOX;
2    using System;
3    using System.Data.OleDb;
4    using System.IO;
5    using System.Windows.Forms;
6
7    public class frmMain: Form
8    {
9        private OleDbConnection mDB = new OleDbConnection();
10

99       public static void Main()
100      {
101          frmMain main = new frmMain();
102          Application.Run(main);
103      }
104
105      public frmMain()
106      {
107          InitializeComponent();
108
109          // Set the connection string to open the sample database in the same
110          // folder as the EXE.
111
112          mDB.ConnectionString = "Provider=Microsoft.Jet.OLEDB.4.0;Data source="
113              + Path.Combine(Application.StartupPath, "Sample.mdb");
114      }
```

Figure 13-35 Using ADOX with ADO.NET

Creating the database file is really quite simple after you know which class and which method to use. Figure 13-36 illustrates how to instantiate an ADOX `Catalog` object (line 178) and then call its `Create` method (line 182). Note that the argument you pass to the `Create` method conveniently happens to be the exact same connection string you use with the `OleDbConnection` object (line 112 in Figure 13-35). To create the new database file, Jet requires the path for the file to exist. If you try to create a database file in a folder that does not exist, an exception is thrown. You should always call the `Create` method from within a `try-catch` block to catch this and any other exception that might be thrown.

```
173        // This method illustrates creating a brand new MDB database file.
174        // Note the project must reference Microsoft ADO Ext 2.7 (msadox.dll)
175        // and include a using "ADOX" directive.
176        private void btnCreate_Click(object sender, System.EventArgs e)
177        {
178            Catalog catalog = new CatalogClass();
179
180            try
181            {
182                catalog.Create(mDB.ConnectionString);
183            }
184            catch (Exception ex)
185            {
186                MessageBox.Show(ex.Message);
187            }
188        }
```

Figure 13-36 Programmatically creating a Microsoft Access database file

If you run the Bonus ADO.NET application and click the Create button, a database file named Sample.MDB should be created in the same folder as the application's .exe. You should then be able to open this file using Microsoft Access. If you do open it, you will see that the database file contains no tables. To add a table to a database, you use ADO.NET to pass DDL statements to Jet.

Data Definition Language (DDL)

After a new database file has been created, the next step is to use the SQL **Data Definition Language (DDL)** commands to add table and column definitions. To add a table to the database, use the **CREATE TABLE** statement syntax shown here:

```
CREATE TABLE tableName (column type, column type, ...)
```

where **tableName** is the name of the table to create, **column** is the name of the column to create, and **type** is a valid SQL data type for the column. You can also remove a table and all of its contents from a database using:

```
DROP TABLE tableName
```

Unfortunately, SQL data types use neither the same keywords as C# or Microsoft Access, so an expanded version of Table 13-2 provides a cross-reference between the C#, Access, and SQL data types in Table 13-4.

Table 13-4   C#, Access, and SQL data types cross-references

C#	Microsoft Access	SQL/DDL
bool	Yes/No	BIT
decimal	Currency	CURRENCY
DateTime	Date/Time	DATETIME
double	Number (field size Double)	DOUBLE
int	Autonumber	COUNTER
int	Number (field size Long Integer)	LONG
string	Text (limit of 255 characters)	TEXT(numberOfCharacters)
string	Memo	LONGTEXT

When sending DDL statements to the Jet DBMS, be sure you don't also have the MDB database file open in Microsoft Access. The reason is that in order for DDL statements to work, Jet needs to open the database file **exclusively** (meaning that no other applications can be using the file). If some other program is using the database file when you attempt to execute a DDL statement, an exception will be thrown.

Adding Tables and Columns to a Table

The code from the Bonus ADO.NET application that adds the table and columns to the database is shown in Figure 13-37. Lines 148 through 155 format the DDL statement that contains the table name, column names, and data types. Lines 159 through 161 pass the DDL statement to the DBMS to be executed. Note that `OleDbConnection` and `OleDbCommand` objects are used in the same manner as when an SQL `INSERT`, `UPDATE`, or `DELETE` statement was executed.

```
142        // This method illustrates adding a table to a database.
143        private void btnAddTable_Click(object sender, System.EventArgs e)
144        {
145            string sql;
146            OleDbCommand cmd;
147
148            sql = "CREATE TABLE SampleTable (" +
149                "SampleIdentity   COUNTER, "    +
150                "SampleInteger    LONG, "       +
151                "SampleString     TEXT(25), "   +
152                "SampleDouble     DOUBLE, "     +
153                "SampleBool       BIT, "        +
154                "SampleDateTime   DATETIME, "   +
155                "SampleDecimal    CURRENCY)";
156
157            try
158            {
159                mDB.Open();
160                cmd = new OleDbCommand(sql, mDB);
161                cmd.ExecuteNonQuery();
162            }
163            catch (Exception ex)
164            {
165                MessageBox.Show(ex.Message);
166            }
167            finally
168            {
169                mDB.Close();
170            }
171        }
```

Figure 13-37   Adding a table and columns using DDL and ADO.NET

Hopefully the sample code shown in Table 13-4 and Figure 13-37 shows you that including code in your application to programmatically create an Access database file isn't too complicated. To know how to use the Catalog class in ADOX, you need to understand just a little bit of DDL syntax, and you need to know which data types to use.

13

AGGREGATE QUERIES

In addition to retrieving rows and column values from the tables in a database, SQL provides a way for you to perform queries that return summary information about the data in a table. You could of course calculate summary information by performing a query and looping through the results, doing the calculations in C# code. However, SQL gives you a better option in the form of aggregate functions. **Aggregate functions** are calculations the DBMS knows how to execute. Table 13-5 lists some of the aggregate functions you might find useful.

Table 13-5   SQL aggregate functions

Aggregate function	Description
AVG	Average of the values in the selected numeric column
COUNT	Number of records with values in the specified column
MIN	Lowest value in the selected column
MAX	Highest value in the selected column
SUM	Sum of all values in the selected numeric column

The syntax for using aggregate functions in an SQL SELECT statement follows:

```
SELECT aggregateFunction(column) FROM tableName WHERE criteriaExpression
```

The *aggregateFunction* in this statement is one of the functions listed in Table 13-5, *column* is an applicable column name in the table, *tableName* is the name of the database table that contains the records you want to query, and *criteriaExpression* contains an expression that determines which rows to process. The *criteriaExpression* is the same as what was previously presented in the discussion about a regular SQL SELECT statement using the operators shown in Table 13-3. In addition, just like with a regular SQL SELECT statement, the WHERE clause is optional. When the WHERE clause is omitted, the aggregate function is performed on all rows in the table.

Here are some example SQL SELECT statements using aggregate functions:

- SELECT AVG(PayRate) FROM Employees WHERE SalaryInd = False AND Plant = 'ATL'

- SELECT COUNT(*) FROM Employees

- SELECT MIN(PayRate) FROM Employees WHERE PayRate < 10.00 AND Gender = 'M'

- SELECT MAX(DateHired) FROM Employees

- SELECT SUM(PayRate) FROM Employees WHERE SalaryInd = True

Using ADO.NET to pass an SQL aggregate query to the DBMS to be processed is much the same as performing a regular query. There is one key difference, however. Because a regular query might return more than one row, you call the ExecuteReader method of an OleDbCommand object, which returns a reference to an OleDbDataReader object. The OleDbCommand class has a different method you should use when the query returns a single value like that from an aggregate query. This method is named ExecuteScalar and returns a reference to a single object, which you can assign to a variable, as shown in Figure 13-38. Note that you need to use casting to convert the return value to the proper data type. When you use the ExecuteScalar method, there is no need to loop through the resulting rows because just one single value is returned.

```
1          string sql;
2          OleDbCommand cmd;
3
4          int nbrEmployees;
5          decimal avgHourlyPay;
6          DateTime mostRecentDateHired;
7
8          sql = "SELECT COUNT(*) FROM Employees";
9          cmd = new OleDbCommand(sql, mDB);
10         nbrEmployees = (int)cmd.ExecuteScalar();
11
12         sql = "SELECT AVG(PayRate) FROM Employees";
13         cmd = new OleDbCommand(sql, mDB);
14         avgHourlyPay = (decimal)cmd.ExecuteScalar();
15
16         sql = "SELECT MAX(DateHired) FROM Employees";
17         cmd = new OleDbCommand(sql, mDB);
18         mostRecentDateHired = (DateTime)cmd.ExecuteScalar();
```

Figure 13-38   Using SQL aggregate functions with ADO.NET

Using SQL aggregate functions to perform some of these computations rather than writing code to iterate through all rows and to compute the value manually not only takes less code on your part, it also increases performance because the DBMS does the work for you. Therefore, we recommend you use SQL aggregate functions to calculate summary information whenever you can.

13

SUMMARY

Essential Topics

◻ A database is a collection of information organized such that it can be accessed, managed, and updated quickly and easily. A database management system (DBMS) is a collection of programs that manage the data in the database. The DBMS software handles the mechanics of creating, storing, retrieving, and updating the data in the database file. Virtually all business applications store data using relational database management systems.

◻ A relational database is a database that organizes its data into a set of one or more related tables. A relational database table consists of zero or more rows and one or more columns of data. Each row in a database table is analogous to a single record in a sequential file, and each column in a database table is analogous to a field in a sequential file record. When used to make objects persistent, each row in a table often contains the state of a single object.

◻ Structured Query Language (SQL) is the industry standard language for working with relational databases. The SQL **SELECT** statement is used to retrieve data from a table, the SQL **INSERT** statement is used to insert data rows into a table, the SQL **UPDATE** statement is used to modify column values in a table, and the SQL **DELETE** statement is used to remove rows from a table. These four operations are collectively referred to as CRUD (create, retrieve, update, and delete).

◻ ADO.NET provides a set of classes that allow you to interact with various DBMSs. The **OleDbConnection** class provides connectivity to the DBMS. The **OleDbCommand** object allows you to execute SQL statements. An **OleDbDataReader** object contains the rows from the database that are the result of a query statement that has been executed by an **OleDbCommand** object. These three classes are contained within the **System.Data.OleDb** namespace.

◻ The impedance mismatch problem between OOP and relational databases is caused by their differing goals. One goal of OOP is to model real-world objects, and a goal of a relational database is to reduce redundancy. However, real-world objects almost always contain redundant data. Another goal of OOP is to facilitate code reuse through mechanisms such as encapsulation, inheritance, and polymorphism. Yet RDBMSs have no support for inheritance and polymorphism. Still another difference is that programming languages use different data types than relational databases do.

Bonus Topics

◻ Bound controls allow you to connect UI objects directly to tables and columns in a database. Instead of writing C# code to move data back and forth between the UI controls and the database, properties are set on the controls that allow the data to be moved back and forth automatically. Bound controls might work well enough in trivial applications, but real applications require C# code to add needed features. Using basic SQL statements from within your code will undoubtedly produce more robust and professional applications.

◻ Because ADO.NET is a general-purpose technology for database connectivity, it doesn't have the means to create a Microsoft Access database file programmatically. ADOX is a technology Microsoft released prior to ADO.NET that extends ADO and ADO.NET and can be used to dynamically create a database file. To use ADOX in your application, you must first reference the `msadox.dll` file from your project. After a database file is created using ADOX, you can use DDL statements to add tables and define columns.

◻ SQL aggregate functions are functions the DBMS knows how to execute that return summary information about the data in a table. Aggregate queries can be executed by calling an `OleDbCommand` object's `ExecuteScalar` method.

KEY TERMS

Define each of the following terms, as it relates to database connectivity:

Essential Terms
◻ ADO.NET
◻ column
◻ connection string
◻ CRUD
◻ database
◻ database engine
◻ database management system (DBMS)
◻ embedded quotes problem
◻ field
◻ impedance mismatch
◻ OLE DB
◻ OleDbCommand
◻ OleDbConnection
◻ OleDbDataReader
◻ ORDER BY clause
◻ primary key

◻ record
◻ relational database
◻ relational database management system (RDBMS)
◻ row
◻ Structured Query Language (SQL)
◻ table
◻ unique identifier

Bonus Terms
◻ ADOX
◻ aggregate functions
◻ bound controls
◻ Data Definition Language (DDL)
◻ exclusively (open a database)

REVIEW QUESTIONS

Essential Questions

1. A database is a collection of text files that describe related data and are stored in the same folder. True or false?

2. A DBMS is a collection of programs that manage the data in a database. True or false?

3. An RDBMS is equivalent to a DBMS. True or false?

4. The three leading vendors of enterprise RDBMSs are HP, Novell, and Oracle. True or false?

5. SQL is Microsoft's proprietary syntax for defining database queries. True or false?

6. The fields in a database table are identified as the column names. True or false?

7. Having multiple layers of abstraction when connecting to a database allows object-oriented programs to have more flexible architectures. True or false?

8. When using SQL in database-driven applications, if the DBMS changes, typically the only code that needs to change is the connection string that defines the type and location of the database. True or false?

9. The differences between OOP and relational databases is referred to as the impedance mismatch problem. True or false?

10. The `OleDbConnection`, `OleDbCommand`, and `OleDbDataReader` classes are the only ADO.NET classes you need to persist object state to a database. True or false?

11. A row in a database table is also known as a _____.

12. The four common database actions are collectively referred to as _____.

13. The _____ SQL statement is used to insert records into a database table.

14. _____ provides a set of classes that allow you to interact with DBMSs.

15. Explain the relevance of CRUD.

16. Write the SQL statement to retrieve all records from a table named Friends for which the friend's name starts with "Jo".

17. Write the SQL statement to add a record to a table named Products to assign the following values to the fields listed:

    ProdID: T243   Description: brass fasteners   UnitCost: 0.05   Quantity: 50000

18. Explain the result of passing the following SQL statement to the DBMS:

    ```
    DELETE FROM Friends
    ```

19. When using a Microsoft Access database, ADO.NET doesn't include data providers for the Jet DBMS. What alternative does a C# programmer have for writing applications that need to connect to an Access database?

20. Which ADO.NET class can be used to instantiate an object that contains rows that are the result of a query statement?

13

Bonus Questions

1. Using bound controls is a recommended approach when you need to get a database application written quickly. True or false?

2. Bound controls are specialized controls that you have to add to the Toolbox using the Insert menu's Add menu. True or false?

3. Bound controls are limited to displaying the contents of a database table, so they should be used only when you don't have Microsoft Access available on your PC. True or false?

4. ADO.NET has no provisions for creating a new Microsoft Access database file with C#. True or false?

5. You should always include a **try-catch** block around code that accesses database data to prevent your program from crashing due to errors in the SQL statements sent to the DBMS. True or false?

6. The _____ control can be used to display the contents of a table by setting its **DataSource** property.

7. The _____ method of the ADOX _____ object can be called to create a database file.

8. List three reasons you might use to convince someone that he or she shouldn't use bound controls.

9. To use ADOX in your applications, you must first add a reference to which file?

10. Write the DDL statement to create Table 13-1.

PROGRAMMING EXERCISES

Essential Exercises

1. Write a C# program that navigates the Employees table in the EmployeeDatabase.MDB file one row at a time.

2. Write a C# program that allows a user to look up select records in the Employees table in the EmployeeDatabase.MDB file by providing the plant location or asking to view information for all employees at all plants. Show the matching records using a **ListView** control.

3. Write a C# program that allows a user to look up select records in the Employees table in the EmployeeDatabase.MDB file by providing the complete or partial employee name. (In the case of multiple employees who match the lookup criteria, show the details for all matching employees.) Show the matching records using a **ListView** control.

4. Write a C# program that allows a user to look up select records in the Employees table in the EmployeeDatabase.MDB file by providing the minimum/maximum salary. Show the matching records using a **ListView** control.

5. Write a C# program that allows a user to add or delete records in the Employees table in the EmployeeDatabase.MDB file. The add form should contain input controls for all editable fields. The delete form should show a list of all employees and ask the user to indicate which employee should be removed.

6. Write a C# program that allows a user to specify a record to be updated in the Employees table in the EmployeeDatabase.MDB file. The form should display the current information and allow the user to change all fields except the primary key. After the OK button is clicked, the new values should be written to the database.

Bonus Exercises

1. Write a program that uses a bound **DataGrid** control to display the contents of the Employees table in the EmployeeDatabase.MDB file.

2. Modify the Contacts List application to check for the Contacts.MDB file when it begins execution. If not found, use ADOX to dynamically create the database file.

3. Write a C# program to create a ToDo database to track all the tasks you have to complete. Each record should have the task name, priority level (optional, low, medium, high, urgent), deadline, and completed indicator. Be sure to include an ID as an AutoNumber field.

14

INHERITANCE AND POLYMORPHISM

In the Essentials section you will learn:

♦ What inheritance is
♦ What subclasses are
♦ What the `protected` access specifier is and when to use it
♦ What method overriding is
♦ What virtual classes are
♦ What polymorphism is
♦ How to use polymorphism with messages
♦ What interfaces are

In the Bonus section you will also learn:

♦ How to use polymorphism to enhance existing objects
♦ How to use serialization to preserve the state of an object

We have stated numerous times in this text that, as a general rule, less code is preferable to more code. In this chapter we examine how inheritance promotes smaller program code size and code reuse. You will also learn how polymorphism can be used to simplify your code.

ESSENTIAL TOPICS

In this chapter we explore the final two legs of the OOP trilogy: inheritance (defined later in this chapter) and polymorphism (defined in Chapter 1). (You learned about encapsulation in Chapter 10.) As you will see, these two concepts work together to make complex applications simpler to write and easier to test, debug, and maintain.

WHAT IS INHERITANCE?

The concept of inheritance is based upon the idea that, although each object has a list of properties and methods that make it unique, there are often things that objects have in common. For example, suppose that you want to construct one object to describe a commercial office building and another object to describe an individual's home. Perhaps these objects will be used in a program you are developing for a client who invests in real estate. You begin by creating a list of properties and methods for each of the two objects. A hypothetical list of properties is shown in Figure 14-1.

Commercial office building	Private home
Street address	Street address
City and state	City and state
Number of rental units	Bedrooms
Number of parking spaces	Baths
Purchase price	Purchase price
Property taxes/year	Property taxes/year
Rent/square foot/year	Building style
Zoning code	Insurance cost
Insurance cost	
Restrooms/square foot	

Figure 14-1   Hypothetical properties list for real estate investments

No doubt you can think of other properties that might pertain to each object, but those listed in Figure 14-1 serve as a good starting point. Having created the list shown in Figure 14-1, you notice that the two types of real estate investments share several properties. Both property types have insurance costs and property taxes that must be paid. Each has a street address and a purchase price. You also know that you need to write property methods for each of these attributes. However, given that the properties are the same, it is quite likely that the code for the property methods will also be the same.

Then you have an epiphany.

Why not reorganize things a bit in an effort to simplify the objects? The result of such reorganization appears in Figure 14-2.

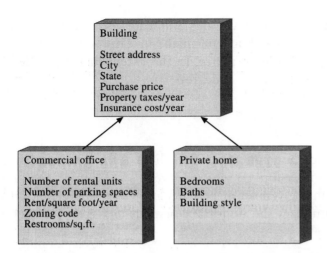

Figure 14-2 Reorganized properties list for real estate investments

In Figure 14-2, we have created a new class called `Building` that holds the list of properties that `Commercial office` and `Private home` classes have in common. At the same time, however, we have left those properties that are unique to the `Commercial office` and `Private home` classes encapsulated within their respective classes. In other words, the `Commercial office` class and the `Private home` class inherit those properties they have in common from the `Building` class object, but maintain those properties that are unique to each class.

In Figure 14-2, the `Building` class is called the base class, whereas the `Commercial office` and `Private home` classes are called subclasses. A **base class** may be thought of a class that holds those properties and methods that the subclasses have in common. Stated differently, a base class is a common denominator of properties and methods that the subclasses may share. A **subclass** is a group of one or more classes that have a relationship with a base class and share properties and methods with that base class.

Inheritance and "is a" Relationships

Note the nature of the relationship that is formed between the subclasses and base class. The synergy of the relationship is referred to as an **"is a" relationship**. That is, a commercial property *is a* building. Likewise, a private home *is a* building. Note, however, that the relationship is not reversible. You cannot say a building *is a* private home, because the building could also be a commercial property. Because the *is a* relationship is not reversible, the arrows shown in Figure 14-2 point only from the subclass to the base class.

You are now in a position to understand what inheritance is. **Inheritance** refers to the means by which subclasses of a base class may inherit the properties and methods those subclasses have in common with a base class. (Not all programmers use the same terms to describe inheritance. You will also hear the term parent class and child class used to refer to base class and subclass, respectively.)

Benefits of Inheritance

What do you gain by reorganizing Figure 14-1 into the structure shown in Figure 14-2? Note that the properties and methods seen in the `Building` class of Figure 14-2 no longer appear in the subclasses. This reorganization means that you have to write the code for the properties shown in the `Building` class in Figure 14-2 only once. You do not have to duplicate the code in the `Building` class in each subclass, as you would if you had used the organization shown in Figure 14-1.

14

One major benefit of inheritance is that you avoid writing duplicate code. Avoiding duplicate code means that there is less code to write, test, debug, and maintain. That is, the subclasses contain less code than they would if you didn't use inheritance. To the extent that less code is easier to understand, inheritance simplifies the application's code, too.

USING INHERITANCE

Suppose that a client wants you to develop an application. The client is the general manager for a local golf club that has four types of membership: (1) senior, (2) regular, (3) junior, and (4) social. Each membership type is associated with a given set of benefits and costs. The general manager provides you with Table 14-1 that summarizes the important benefits and costs for each membership type.

Table 14-1   Membership benefits and costs

Item	Senior*	Regular	Junior	Social
Dues per month	100	150	50	75
Food minimum per month	50	50	30	80
Golf rounds per year	Unlimited	Unlimited	Unlimited	3
Voting rights	Full	Full	Limited	None
Golf course assessments	Yes	Yes	Yes	No
Clubhouse assessments	Yes	Yes	Yes	Yes
Fee payment	Monthly	Monthly	Monthly	Quarterly

After discussions with the general manager, you learn that Social members join the club primarily to take advantage of the club's dining privileges as well as its tennis and pool facilities. The other three membership types are mainly people who enjoy playing golf. Age is the primary distinction between the Senior, Regular, and Junior members. The asterisk for Senior members means that not only must they be over age 65, but they must also have been members for at least 25 years. If a member does not meet both the age and membership criteria, that member is billed as a regular member.

After several more meetings with the general manager, plus two meetings with the club's accountant, you feel you are ready to design the application. How do you proceed?

USING INHERITANCE—PROGRAM ANALYSIS AND DESIGN

We can't possibly do justice to program analysis and design in one chapter. Indeed, some students take three semester-long courses on this topic alone. However, simply stated, **program analysis** is concerned with a full and complete definition of the problem(s) the program is designed to solve. Program analysis involves interviews with all those people, called **stakeholders**, who are affected by or have an interest in the program. The stakeholders can be customers, staff employees who use the program, management who might read reports generated by the program, plus a host of other people who might have an interest in the program. It's important to note that analysis is platform independent. That is, at the analysis stage, there is no regard to the language that will be used to write the program or the operating system that will host the program. Program analysis concentrates on the nature and definition of the problem and how the proposed program solves that problem.

Program design, on the other hand, does address the implementation of the program. At this stage in the program's development, you do consider the programming language, as well as the operating system that hosts the program. There are numerous methodologies that you could use in the design of a program, but one of the more popular is the application of the **Unified Modeling Language (UML)**. Although space prohibits a full discussion of UML here, suffice it to say that it is an approach to program analysis and design that works well with object-oriented programming techniques.

With respect to the membership program, we assume that you have talked with the interested stakeholders and you have a good understanding of what the program must do. Figure 14-3 shows how you think the major classes for the program should be organized.

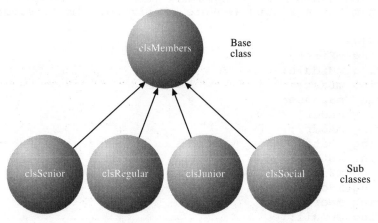

Figure 14-3   Class hierarchy

A class named `clsMembers` serves as the base class for the program. The purpose of `clsMembers` is to serve as a container for all those properties and methods that are used by each member type. For example, each of the four member types must have its name, address, phone number, and similar demographic information recorded. It is the value of each piece of data associated with each member that determines the state of each member (that is, an object that describes a member). Because we must manipulate such information for each member type, it makes no sense to duplicate the code that must administer the demographic state information in the class for each membership type when they can share that code through inheritance.

The purpose of each subclass, then, is to define those properties and methods that are unique to each membership type. Any property or method that distinguishes one member type from another should be placed in the appropriate subclass. (You can see these distinctions in Table 14-1.) Any property or method that is shared by all members should be placed in the base class.

Note the nature of the relationships suggested in Figure 14-3. A Senior member has an *is a* relationship to Member, just as a Junior *is a* Member. However, the relationship is not reversible. For example, a Member does not necessarily have an *is a* relationship to a Regular member. After all, a Member could be any one of the four possible member types. Because the relationships between subclasses and the base class are not reversible, the arrows depicted in Figure 14-3 point only from the subclasses to the base class to indicate the *is a* relationship.

Figure 14-4 shows the properties that you feel should be encapsulated within the `clsMembers` class shown in Figure 14-3.

```
1    using System;
2    using System.IO;
3    using System.Runtime.Serialization;
4    using System.Runtime.Serialization.Formatters.Binary;
5

16   [Serializable]
17   public class clsMember
18   {
19       // Constants
20       protected const int MONTHLY = 1;
21       protected const int QUARTERLY = 3;
22
23       protected enum VotingRights {NoVote, FullVote, LimitedVote}
24
25       // string types:
26       private string mFirst;
27       private string mMiddle;
28       private string mLast;
29       private string mSpouse;
30       private string mAddr1;
31       private string mAddr2;
32       private string mCity;
33       private string mState;
34       private string mZip;
35       private string mHomePhone;
36       private string mWorkPhone;
37       private string mEmail;
38       // int types:
39       private int mType;
40       // DateTime types:
41       private DateTime mJoined;
42       private DateTime mBirthdate;
43       // Protected members
44       protected string mSummary;
45       protected decimal mDues;
46       protected int mBillingCycle;
47       protected VotingRights mVotes;
48       protected int mGolfRounds;
49
50
```

Figure 14-4 Properties for the clsMembers base class

Most of the properties shown in Figure 14-4 have the **private** access specifier. Because we decided to declare them with the **private** access specifier, we also wrote code to provide **get** and **set** methods for those private properties. As we discussed in Chapter 7, these **get** and **set** methods provide a public interface for the class. A typical `get-set` method could be written like that shown in Figure 14-5.

```
64        public string FirstName
65        {
66            get
67            {
68                return mFirst;
69            }
70            set
71            {
72                mFirst = value;
73            }
74        }
```

Figure 14-5 A typical property method

As was explained in Chapter 7, the code shown in Figure 14-5 simply allows us to assign a new value into the `mFirst` property (a `set`) or to read its value (a `get`). Because we have coded the method using the **public** access specifier, this method becomes part of the public user interface for the `clsMember` class. Methods written using the **public** access specifier allow us to read or change the state of the `clsMember` object.

Why Create a Public User Interface?

We could have declared all the data members shown in Figure 14-4 using the **public** access specifier. This means that you have direct access to the data members by simply using the object's dot operator. Such a change does away with the need to write **get** and **set** methods to create a public user interface for each member of the class. However, the **public** access specifier takes away an element of control that you may wish to keep. For example, you might want to check the length of the member's first name before you accept a new value. Therefore, you might alter the code in Figure 14-5 to that shown in Figure 14-6.

```
64        public string FirstName
65        {
66            get
67            {
68                return mFirst;
69            }
70            set
71            {
72                // If it's too long...
73                if (value.Length > 10)
74                    value = value.Substring(0,10);
75
76                mFirst = value;
77            }
78        }
79
```

Figure 14-6 A modified property method

14

The modified code shown in Figure 14-6 truncates the string to ten characters if it is longer than ten characters. If we had used the **public** access specifier for **mFirst**, the user has direct access to **mFirst**, and there is no way to check its length before the new value is assigned into **mFirst**. By providing **public** property methods using **gets** and **sets** to implement a public user interface, you can write code to give you more control over the values that may change the property values. On the other hand, if there is no processing needed on the property (that is, no checking or validation is needed), make its access specifier **public**.

THE **protected** ACCESS SPECIFIER

If you look closely at Figure 14-4, you can see that some of the class members use a new access specifier called **protected**:

```
42          // Protected members
43          protected string mSummary;
44          protected decimal mDues;
45          protected WhenToBill mBillingCycle;
46          protected VotingRights mVotes;
47          protected int mGolfRounds;
```

During the analysis and design work, you probably noticed that there are certain properties for each member type that distinguished it from the other member types. Table 14-1 details these differences. Reviewing Table 14-1, you can see that member dues, their billing cycle, their golf rights, and their voting privileges vary according to membership type. The values of these data members distinguish one type of member from another. Because these data members do distinguish membership type, we do not want to make them part of the **clsMembers** public interface. We want each of these unique data members to be controlled in each subclass rather than in the base class. How can we do this?

If we use the **public** access specifier for these properties, anyone can access the property at any point in the program by simply using the object's dot operator. This would not give you the control you want for these unique data members with respect to each of the membership types. If you use the **private** access specifier for these data members and do not write **get-set** property methods for each of them, there is no public user interface for the data member. Without the **public user interface**, private data members are not visible outside the **clsMembers** class. This also means that these data members are not accessible to any of the subclasses (for example, **clsSenior**) where you want to control them.

As you might guess, the **protected** access specifier provides a solution to our problem. The **protected** access specifier provides access to the data member in the class where it is declared as well as any subclass derived from the class where the data member is declared. What this means, for example, is that **clsSenior** has access to data member **mDues** (which is declared in **clsMembers**) even though there is no public interface for it defined in **clsMembers**. This allows you to declare **mDues** in one place (for example, **clsMembers**), but control it in each subclass as you see fit.

Notice that we have also used the **protected** access specifier for the following declarations:

```
11          protected enum WhenToBill {Monthly = 1, Quarterly};
12
13          protected enum VotingRights {NoVote, FullVote, LimitedVote}
```

The first two statements (lines 11 and 13) simply declare named constants.

```
if (myObject.mBillingCycle == WhenToBill.Monthly)
        SendMonthlyBill(myObject);
```

Using the named constants makes understanding the code easier than if we had used a "magic number" in the code, as in:

```
if (myObject.mBillingCycle == 1)
        SendMonthlyBill(myObject);
```

Likewise, we can use the **enum** type to clarify the intent of the code:

```
if (myObject.mVotes == VotingRights.FullVote)
        SendBallot(myObject);
```

by avoiding numbers whose meaning isn't intuitively obvious.

In general, the **protected** access specifier provides us with the encapsulation benefits of the **private** access specifier, but allows the protected properties and methods to be accessed in any derived subclass.

Figure 14-7 presents the program code for the **clsMember** class as it currently stands. (We add more code to it later in this chapter.)

Discussion of Binary Files

The code in Figure 14-7 uses binary data files, which were discussed in the Bonus section of Chapter 11. Throughout this book, we have avoided referencing topics discussed in the Bonus section in the Essentials section. Alas, the exception proves the rule. Our opinion is that serialization is such an important topic that we must discuss it in the Essentials section even though an element of it (that is, binary files) is discussed in the Bonus section of an earlier chapter. It would be worthwhile for you to read the Bonus section on binary files in Chapter 11.

14

```
1    using System;
2    using System.IO;
3    using System.Runtime.Serialization;
4    using System.Runtime.Serialization.Formatters.Binary;
5
6
7    [Serializable]
8    public class clsMember
9    {
10       // Constants
11       protected enum WhenToBill {Monthly = 1, Quarterly};
12
13       protected enum VotingRights {NoVote, FullVote, LimitedVote}
14
15       // string types:
16       private string mFirst;
17       private string mMiddle;
```

Figure 14-7 The clsMember code

```
18        private string mLast;
19        private string mSpouse;
20        private string mAddr1;
21        private string mAddr2;
22        private string mCity;
23        private string mState;
24        private string mZip;
25        private string mHomePhone;
26        private string mWorkPhone;
27        private string mEmail;
28        // int types:
29        private int mType;
30        // DateTime types:
31        private DateTime mJoined;
32        private DateTime mBirthdate;
33        // Protected members
34        protected string mSummary;
35        protected decimal mDues;
36        protected WhenToBill mBillingCycle;
37        protected VotingRights mVotes;
38        protected int mGolfRounds;
39
40
41        // ------------ Constructor ------------
42        public clsMember()
43        {
44            // Set to default to these
45            mCity = "Indianapolis";
46            mState = "IN";
47            mZip = "46214";
48            mSummary = "";
49        }
50
51        // ------------ Property Methods ------------
52        #region "Property Methods"
53
54        public string FirstName
55        {
56            get
57            {
58                return mFirst;
59            }
60            set
61            {
62                // If it's too long, truncate it
63                if (value.Length > 10)
64                {
65                    value = value.Substring(0,10);
66                }
67                mFirst = value;
68            }
69        }
70
71        public string MiddleName
72        {
73            get
74            {
75                return mMiddle;
76            }
77            set
78            {
79                mMiddle = value;
```

Figure 14-7 The clsMember code (continued)

```
80                    }
81              }
82
83
84         public string LastName
85         {
86              get
87              {
88                    return mLast;
89              }
90              set
91              {
92                    mLast = value;
93              }
94         }
95         public string Spouse
96         {
97              get
98              {
99                    return mSpouse;
100             }
101             set
102             {
103                   mSpouse = value;
104             }
105        }
106
107
108        public string Addr1
109        {
110             get
111             {
112                   return mAddr1;
113             }
114             set
115             {
116                   mAddr1 = value;
117             }
118        }
119        public string Addr2
120        {
121             get
122             {
123                   return mAddr2;
124             }
125             set
126             {
127                   mAddr2 = value;
128             }
129        }
130
131        public string City
132        {
133             get
134             {
135                   return mCity;
136             }
137             set
138             {
139                   mCity = value;
140             }
141        }
142
```

Figure 14-7 The clsMember code (continued)

```
143        public string State
144        {
145            get
146            {
147                return mState;
148            }
149            set
150            {
151                mState = value;
152            }
153        }
154
155        public string Zip
156        {
157            get
158            {
159                return mZip;
160            }
161            set
162            {
163                mZip = value;
164            }
165        }
166
167        public string WorkPhone
168        {
169            get
170            {
171                return mWorkPhone;
172            }
173            set
174            {
175                mWorkPhone = value;
176            }
177        }
178
179        public string HomePhone
180        {
181            get
182            {
183                return mHomePhone;
184            }
185            set
186            {
187                mHomePhone = value;
188            }
189        }
190
191        public string Email
192        {
193            get
194            {
195                return mEmail;
196            }
197            set
198            {
199                mEmail = value;
200            }
201        }
202
203        public int MemberType
```

Figure 14-7   The clsMember code (continued)

```
204              {
205                  get
206                  {
207                      return mType;
208                  }
209                  set
210                  {
211                      mType = value;
212                  }
213              }
214
215              public DateTime Birthdate
216              {
217                  get
218                  {
219                      return mBirthdate;
220                  }
221                  set
222                  {
223                      mBirthdate = value;
224                  }
225              }
226
227              public DateTime Joined
228              {
229                  get
230                  {
231                      return mJoined;
232                  }
233                  set
234                  {
235                      mJoined = value;
236                  }
237              }
238              #endregion
239
240              // ------------ General Methods ------------
241
242              //Purpose: This method forms a string containing most of the demographic
243              // data for the member. We attempt to format it into columns for
244              // display, but proportional fonts don't work perfectly.
245              //
246              //Parameter list:
247              //    n/a
248              //
249              //Return value
250              //    string    the mSummary class member
251              //
252              //CAUTION: We attempt to format the data into columns for display,
253              // but proportional fonts don't work perfectly.
254              protected string MemberSummary()
255                  {
256                  string name;
257
258                  name = mFirst + " " + mMiddle + " " + mLast;
259                  mSummary = String.Format(" {0,-15} {1,-20} {2,10} {3,-3} {4,-11}",
260                      name, mAddr1, mCity, mState, mZip);
261
262                  return mSummary;
263              }
264
```

Figure 14-7   The clsMember code (continued)

```
265        //Purpose: This method is used to illustrate how we can override this
266        // method in a subclass.
267        //
268        //Parameter list:
269        //    n/a
270        //
271        //Return value
272        //     string    A message to indicate the action taken
273        //
274        public string SendBill()
275        {
276            return "The bill was sent.";
277        }
278
279        //Purpose: This method is used to serialize the data in an object using a
280        // binary format.
281        //
282        //Parameter list:
283        //    myFile    a clsMember object
284        //
285        //Return value
286        //     string    A message to indicate the action taken
287        //
288        public void SerializeMember(clsMember myFile)
289        {
290            IFormatter formatter = new BinaryFormatter();
291            Stream stream = new FileStream("MyFile.bin", FileMode.Create, FileAccess.Write,
                                              FileShare.None);
292            formatter.Serialize(stream, myFile);
293            stream.Close();
294        }
295
296        //Purpose: This method is used to deserialize the data in an object using a
297        // binary format.
298        //
299        //Parameter list:
300        //    myFile    a clsMember object
301        //
302        //Return value
303        //     string    A message to indicate the action taken
304        //
305        public void DeserializeMember(clsMember myFile)
306        {
307            IFormatter formatter = new BinaryFormatter();
308            Stream stream = new FileStream("MyFile.bin", FileMode.Open, FileAccess.Read,
                                              FileShare.Read);
309            myFile = (clsMember) formatter.Deserialize(stream);
310            stream.Close();
311        }
312        // ------------ Helper Methods ------------
313    }
```

Figure 14-7   The clsMember code (continued)

All the code in Figure 14–7 should look familiar to you. Note the statements for the class constructor shown in Figure 14–7 between lines 41 and 50. In most applications, you would not want to have the class properties initialized as shown in those statements. The reason is that those lines make an assumption about the state of each object that might be defined for each instance of the class. However, it makes sense to do so here because most of the members are "local" to the city where the golf course is. This saves the user from typing this information in each time a new object of **clsMember** is instantiated. The users can, of course, delete the default data provided by the constructor if they wish.

> **Methods for Presenting Data in Columns**
>
> In the following section, you learn how to use composite formatting as a means to align columnar data in a `ListBox` control. In Chapter 12, you learned how to use the `ListView` control to present columnar data. The discussion of composite formatting is presented here simply to give you another tool that might come in handy at some other time. You could use the `ListView` control if you wish.

Composite Formatting of String Data

Another strange statement appears in the `MemberSummary()` general method:

```
259   mSummary = String.Format(" {0,-15} {1,-20} {2,10} {3,-3}
                {4,-11}",
260             name, mAddr1, mCity, mState, mZip);
```

The statement uses what is called **composite formatting**, a feature that is embodied within the `Format()` method of the `String` class. The first argument is the **format string** which, in our example, contains five format item elements within the quoted format string. The syntax for a **format item** is:

{index[,alignment][:formatString]}

Each format item within the format string begins with an opening curly brace followed by an index number (`index`). Notice that there are five format items in our example and five arguments following the format string. As you might expect, the first format item:

{0,-15}

aligns with the first argument (that is, `name`) in the argument list. The next format item, `{1, -20}`, aligns with `mAddr1`, and so on.

The minus sign in the format item (for example, `{0,-15}`) defines the **alignment** we wish to use for the argument. The minus sign means we wish to left-justify the text within the field of 15 spaces. If you omit the minus sign, the text is right justified. The 15 means we wish to reserve a field of 15 characters in which to display the first argument (for example, `name`). If the variable's length exceeds its field allocation space, the entire string is still displayed.

In the format item syntax, the `formatString` provides you with many different options. Table 14-2 shows a few of them. In the Result column, we have used vertical bars (|) to denote the defined field widths. Note that, if you do not specify a field width, the field width becomes whatever character space it takes to display the data.

Table 14-2   Examples of composite formatting

Format item	Data	Result
{0}	"Jennifer"	|Jennifer|
{0,10}	"AJ"	| AJ|
{0,20}	"Katherine"	| Katherine|
{0,-20}	"Tony"	|Tony |
{0,20:C}	123	| $123|
{0,-20:C}	123	|$123.00 |
{0,dddd MMMM}	5/24/2005	|Tuesday May|
{0,10:hh}	9:15am	| 09|
{0:mm}	9:15am	|15|

You can use other format options. For additional information, see the Composite Formatting entry in the Visual Studio help.

> **Using Fixed Fonts for Data String Alignment**
>
> The information displayed in the **ListBox** control shown in Figure 14-8 uses the Courier New font. The Courier New font is a **fixed font**, which means each character uses the same display space. However, most of the fonts used in Windows are **proportional fonts**. With proportional fonts, the width of each character varies. For example, the letter "i" has a smaller width on the screen than does the letter "w." Because the character widths vary, displayed string data may not line up perfectly if you use proportional fonts. We used the Courier New font for the information shown in the list box in Figure 14-8 in an attempt to give the data a columnar appearance. As mentioned earlier, if alignment is a persistent problem, you may wish to use a **ListView** control.

Figure 14-8 shows a sample run of the program.

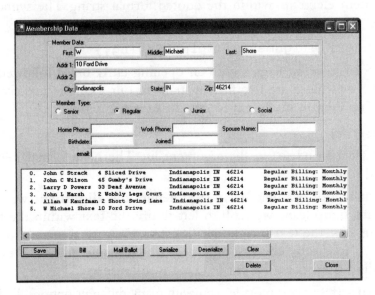

Figure 14-8   Sample program run

Note entry number 4 in Figure 14-8. The data for entry 4 has a name with 16 characters but uses a formatting width for the **name** field of 15 characters. As you can see in Figure 14-8, if your data overflows the width of a field, the data is *not* truncated. As a result of the field overflow, the alignment of the data in the list box is not perfect in Figure 14-8.

The frmMain Code

The sample output shown in Figure 14-8 was created by filling in the appropriate text boxes after the program started and then clicking the Save button. Figure 14-9 shows the code associated with **frmMain**. The first thing to notice in Figure 14-9 is how we have used the **region** keyword to reduce the number of lines that are visible in the listing. For example, line 570 has the statement:

```
570        #region "Button Code"
```

If you click on that line's expansion symbol, the region expands to reveal all the source code for the buttons used in the program. In Figure 14-9, we show how to use the region directive for the code associated with the form's radio buttons (expanded to lines 688 to 709). Using regions like this saves you time when scrolling through a long code listing by hiding code that has already been tested and debugged.

```
1    using System;
2    using System.Windows.Forms;
3    using System.IO;
4    using System.Runtime.Serialization;
5    using System.Runtime.Serialization.Formatters.Binary;
6
7    public class frmMain : System.Windows.Forms.Form
8    {

534
535      // Define a working instance of classes
536      clsMember myMember = new clsMember();
537      clsSenior mySenior = new clsSenior();
538      clsRegular myRegular = new clsRegular();
539      clsJunior myJunior  = new clsJunior();
540      clsSocial mySocial  = new clsSocial();
541
542      // Holds the member type
543      int which;
544      // How many have been entered
545      int classCounterIndex;
546
547      static void Main()
548      {
549          Application.Run(new frmMain());
550      }
551
552      public frmMain()
553      {
554          InitializeComponent();
555
556          // Default to regular member
557          txtMiddle.Text = myRegular.MiddleName;
558          txtFirst.Text = myRegular.FirstName;
559          txtLast.Text = myRegular.LastName;
560          txtAddr1.Text = myRegular.Addr1;
561          txtAddr2.Text = myRegular.Addr2;
562
563          txtCity.Text = myRegular.City;
564          txtZip.Text = myRegular.Zip;
565          txtState.Text = myRegular.State;
566          rbRegular.Checked = true;
567          which = 1;
568      }
569
570      #region "Button Code"
571      private void btnSave_Click(object sender, System.EventArgs e)
```

Figure 14-9   The frmMain source code

```
572         {
573             saveMemberData();
574
575             // Use these as defaults for next one
576
577
578             txtCity.Text = myRegular.City ;
579             txtZip.Text = myRegular.Zip;
580             txtState.Text = myRegular.State;
581             rbRegular.Checked = true;
582
583         }
584
585     private void btnClear_Click(object sender, System.EventArgs e)
586     {
587         ClearTextboxes();
588     }
589
590     private void btnBill_Click(object sender, System.EventArgs e)
591     {
592         lstOutput.Items.Add(" Senior: " + mySenior.SendBill());
593         lstOutput.Items.Add("Regular: " + myRegular.SendBill());
594         lstOutput.Items.Add(" Junior: " + myJunior.SendBill());
595         lstOutput.Items.Add(" Social: " + mySocial.SendBill());
596     }
597
598     private void btnMailBallot_Click(object sender, System.EventArgs e)
599     {
600         lstOutput.Items.Add(" Senior: " + mySenior.SendBallot());
601         lstOutput.Items.Add("Regular: " + myRegular.SendBallot());
602         lstOutput.Items.Add(" Junior: " + myJunior.SendBallot());
603         lstOutput.Items.Add(" Social: No ballot sent");
604     }
605
606     private void btnDelete_Click(object sender, System.EventArgs e)
607     {
608         btnClear_Click(sender,e);
609     }
610
611     private void btnExit_Click(object sender, System.EventArgs e)
612     {
613         Close();
614     }
615
616     #endregion
617
618     //Purpose: This method clears the text box data
619     //
620     //Parameter list:
621     //  n/a
622     //
623     //Return value
624     //  void
625     //
626     private void ClearTextboxes()
```

Figure 14-9 The frmMain source code (continued)

```
627              {
628                  txtMiddle.Text = "";
629                  txtFirst.Text = "";
630                  txtLast.Text = "";
631                  txtAddr1.Text = "";
632                  txtAddr2.Text = "";
633
634                  txtHomePhone.Text = "";
635                  txtWorkPhone.Text = "";
636                  txtSpouse.Text = "";
637                  txtBirthdate.Text = "";
638                  txtJoined.Text = "";
639                  txtEmail.Text = "";
640
641                  rbRegular.Checked = true;
642              }
643
644          private void txtState_Leave(object sender, System.EventArgs e)
645          {
646                  // Make the two-letter abbreviation upper case
647                  txtState.Text = txtState.Text.ToUpper();
648          }
649
650          //Purpose: This method determines what the member type is and builds
651          // an output string for the text box. (A real Save method would
652          // probably write the data to a database.)
653          //
654          //Parameter list:
655          //  n/a
656          //
657          //Return value
658          //  void
659          //
660          private void saveMemberData()
661          {
662              string indexString;
663              string final = "";
664
665              switch (which)
666              {
667                  case 0:// Senior
668                      TextToClass(mySenior);
669                      final = mySenior.Summary;
670                  break;
671                  case 1:// Regular
672                      TextToClass(myRegular);
673                      final = myRegular.Summary;
674                  break;
675                  case 2:// Junior
676                      TextToClass(myJunior);
677                      final = myJunior.Summary;
678                  break;
679                  case 3:// Social
680                      TextToClass(mySocial);
681                      final = mySocial.Summary;
682                  break;
683              }
```

Figure 14-9   The frmMain source code (continued)

```
684              indexString = String.Format("{0, 5}", classCounterIndex.ToString() + ". ");
685              lstOutput.Items.Add(indexString + final);
686              classCounterIndex++;
687          }
688      #region "Set the radio buttons"
689
690      private void rbSenior_CheckedChanged(object sender, System.EventArgs e)
691      {
692          which = 0;
693      }
694
695      private void rbRegular_CheckedChanged(object sender, System.EventArgs e)
696      {
697          which = 1;
698      }
699
700      private void rbJunior_CheckedChanged(object sender, System.EventArgs e)
701      {
702          which = 2;
703      }
704
705      private void rbSocial_CheckedChanged(object sender, System.EventArgs e)
706      {
707          which = 3;
708      }
709      #endregion
710
```

Figure 14-9   The frmMain source code (continued)

Figure 14-10 shows how the **clsSocial** subclass relates to the **clsMember** base class. Notice that in the constructor code for **clsSocial** (lines 6 through 11) we initialize several of the **protected** data members that are declared in **clsMembers**. Recall that the values for these data members for **clsSocial** are different than the other member types. Therefore, it makes sense to control these data members values in the **clsSocial** code.

In line 3 of Figure 14-10, the statement:

```
3 public class clsSocial : clsMember
```

says that we are declaring a new class named **clsSocial**, but that it is derived from the base class named **clsMember**. In other words, this line establishes the *is a* relationship to the base class. Notice that a colon separates the subclass (**clsSocial**) from the base class (**clsMember**). This relationship means that everything declared in the base class (**clsMember**) using the **public** or **protected** access specifier is available for use in the subclass (**clsSocial**). (Other languages, like C++, permit a subclass to inherit from two or more base classes in a process called "multiple inheritance." Multiple inheritance provides a quick means by which you cannot only shoot yourself in the foot, but also blow off your entire leg in the process. As a result of its inherent dangers, C# does not permit multiple inheritance.)

```
 1   using System;
 2
 3   public class clsSocial : clsMember
 4   {
 5       // Constructor for default values
 6       public clsSocial()
 7       {
 8           mDues = 75m;
 9           mBillingCycle = QUARTERLY;
10           mVotes = (int) VotingRights.NoVote;
11       }
12
13       // ------------ Special Property Methods ------------
14
15       public string Summary
16       {
17           get
18           {
19               string temp;
20
21               MemberSummary();
22               temp = " Social Billing: " + mBillingCycle.ToString();
23               temp += " Voting: " + mVotes.ToString();
24               temp += " dues: " + mDues.ToString();
25
26               return mSummary + temp;
27           }
28           set
29           {
30               mSummary= value;
31           }
32       }
33
34       //Purpose: This method simulates sending a bill to a social member, which
35       // should only be sent quarterly.
36       //
37       //Parameter list:
38       //  n/a
39       //
40       //Return value
41       //  stringA  message to indicate the action taken
42       //
43       //CAUTION: n/a
44       //
45       new public string SendBill()
46       {
47           int myMonth;
48           myMonth = DateTime.Now.Month;
49
50           if (myMonth % 3 != 0)
51           {
52               return "No bill this month.";
53           }
54           else
55           {
56               return "Quarterly bill sent";
57           }
58       }
```

Figure 14-10 Code for the clsSocial membership class

```
59
60        //Purpose: This method simulates sending a ballot to a social member, which
61        // should never be sent.
62        //
63        //Parameter list:
64        //   n/a
65        //
66        //Return value
67        //   stringA   message to indicate the action taken
68        //
69        //CAUTION: n/a
70        //
71
72        public string SendBallot()
73        {
74            return " No ballot sent.";
75        }
76
77    }
```

Figure 14-10   Code for the clsSocial membership class (continued)

Notice that the **get** method for Summary (lines 15 through 32) first calls **MemberSummary** from the base class. (You can find the **MemberSummary** code in Figure 14-7, lines 254 through 263.) The **MemberSummary** code simply builds a string that contains the general information about a member. Upon return, lines 22 through 26 in Figure 14-10 build the remainder of the member string, concatenating the information that is specific to a Social member to the general information held in **mSummary**. After the summary string for the member is built (see lines 669, 673, 677, and 681 in Figure 14-9), the string is added to the list box for display (line 685 in Figure 14-9). The result of these actions is one line of output, as can be seen in Figure 14-8.

So, what advantages does inheritance bring to the party? First, each of the subclasses can share the **MemberSummary** code in the base class. This means that we don't have to write, debug, and maintain four separate versions of the **MemberSummary** code for each member type. The second advantage is that, if we do need to do something unique for each subclass, we can place that specialized code in the subclass where it belongs. We added special code for the **clsSocial** class, for example, to build a slightly different version of the member string in the **Summary** property accessor method. (If you could scroll the content of the list box shown in Figure 14-8, you would see that the output is slightly different for each membership type.) The third advantage is that, because **mSummary** is a protected member of the base class, you can write **get** and **set** property methods in each of the subclasses if you wish. This means that you can have a public interface for **mSummary**, but each class can control its state as needed by that specific membership type. (We return to this advantage later in this chapter.)

Method Overriding

If you look at the data in Table 14-1, you can see that billing each member type is the same for everyone except the Social members. Instead of a monthly billing, Social members are billed only on a quarterly basis. In Figure 14-7, lines 274 through 286 simulate sending a bill by simply displaying a message on the screen. In an actual program that supported billing, there would likely be a considerable amount of code in the **SendBill** method to perform the database updates that would be necessary plus printing the bill itself. Clearly, we need a way to prevent sending monthly bills to the Social members. How would you do this?

You could do it in a manner similar to what we did when we displayed the general information about each member. That is, you could place the specific billing code in each subclass. That approach, however, means you would be duplicating a lot of code in each subclass.

A better solution to our problem is shown in Figure 14-10, lines 45 through 58. The statement in line 45:

```
45 new public string SendBill()
```

shows how you use the **new** keyword to preface a method named SendBill in clsSocial. However, also notice that line 283 in **clsMember** (see Figure 14-7) also declares a method named SendBill. The only difference between the two versions is the keyword **new** in clsSocial. The keyword **new** indicates that you wish to override the definition of SendBill found in clsMember with the declaration of SendBill found in clsSocial.

What overriding means is that, each time you have an object of clsSocial and you use the statement:

```
str = mySocial.SendBill();
```

the code for SendBill found in clsSocial is to be used instead of the SendBill code found in the base class. In other words, the **new** keyword in line 45 means that the declaration of SendBill found in clsSocial overrides, or replaces, the code for SendBill found in the base class (clsMember).

Polymorphism and Overriding

Note the polymorphic behavior being used here. We can issue a SendBill message call to each type of object, but each object is free to respond to the message as it sees fit. In the example shown here, a bill is only sent to a Social member if the date turns out to be a quarterly month. (The statement if (myMonth % 3 == 0) is only true every three months.) For any member type other than social, the SendBill method declared in the base class is used because none of the other subclasses override the SendBill method.

As a memory-jogger, we want to remind you that each time you see the keyword **new** at the start of a statement that looks like a method declaration, you can mentally substitute the word "overrides" in place of **new**. This should help you to remember that this version of the method is overriding a declaration in the base class. Note that, for overriding to work correctly, you must provide a version of the method in the base class for the method you are overriding in the subclass. Also, the signatures for the two versions of the method must be the same. Finally, and perhaps this is already obvious to you, there must be an inherited relationship between the base class method and the subclass that is using the overridden method.

14

USING INTERFACES

There may be times when you must have a method that applies to all subclasses, but each subclass must implement the method in a different manner. For example, Table 14-1 shows that Senior and Regular members have full voting rights, Junior members have limited voting rights, and Social members have no voting rights. This means that you must write code that allows each member to vote, with the exception of the Social members. Another complication, however, is that the ballot sent to Junior members is different from the ballot sent to Senior and Regular members. In a nutshell, you need to send: (1) a normal ballot to Senior and Regular members, (2) a limited ballot to Junior members, and (3) no ballot to Social members. **Interfaces** are especially useful when you need to provide a specific functionality in a subclass, but the way that functionality is implemented varies among subclasses.

The general syntax for an interface is:

```
[accessSpecifier] interface interfaceName
{
  //interface statement block
}
```

The valid access specifiers include **public** and **internal**. Unlike the **public** access specifier, which has unrestricted access, the **internal** access specifier limits the access to an item to the current assembly. (Unless you are using multiple assemblies, use the **public** access specifier.) If you do not supply an access specifier, the access specifier defaults to **public**.

For example, you can create a **Vote** interface with the following statements:

```
public interface Vote
{
  string SendBallot();
}
```

In this example, you are declaring that you wish to create a public interface named **Vote**. If you wish to implement this interface in your class, you *must* write code for a method named **SendBallot**. An interface, therefore, is a promise between you as the programmer and your code. It is important to note that the interface does not include the code, only a declaration of those elements that comprise the interface.

Implementing an Interface

Normally, interface declarations appear near the top of a class declaration. Therefore, the code shown in Figure 14-7 would change to that shown in Figure 14-11 if we added an interface declaration.

```
 6    public interface Vote
 7    {
 8         public string SendBallot();
 9    }
10
11    [Serializable]
12    public class clsMember
13    {
```

Figure 14-11   Adding an interface declaration to clsMember

Note that the interface declaration statements are *not* inside the **clsMember** class code, but are found outside the class code, as shown in Figure 14-11. Keep in mind that, given the interface declared in Figure 14-11, any class that chooses to implement the **Vote** interface must supply code for a method named **SendBallot** and a property named **voteCounter** with related **get** and **set** property methods. This also means that you either implement every aspect of the interface or you implement none of it—there is no middle ground.

Technically speaking, the declaration of the **Vote** interface could be placed with the **frmMain** code or in a separate file instead of with the **clsMember** code. Given that a properly declared interface has namespace scope, the interface declaration could be coded in either place. Our preference, however, is to place the interface declaration in the base class file for the subclasses that may expect to use the interface. If the interface is not used in an inherited relationship, we would place the interface declaration in the **frmMain** file or in a separate file.

Figure 14-12 presents the code for the **clsJunior** class. Look at line 3 in Figure 14-12. This line is verbalized as: "**clsJunior** is a subclass of **clsMember** and implements the **Vote** interface." Note the comma between the base class name and the interface name. If a class named, say, **clsTest** were not a subclass of some base class, you would write the class signature to implement the **Vote** interface as:

```
public class clsTest: Vote
```

If the interface is not part of a base class, you simply supply the interface name after the colon. In such cases, it is common to find the interface declaration (for example, lines 6 through 14 in Figure 14-11) contained at the top of the **frmMain** class file. In either case, however, you are making a promise that **clsJunior** does implement the **Vote** interface. If you wish to implement more than one interface, simply list each interface separated by a comma.

```
1    using System;
2
3    public class clsJunior: clsMember , Vote
4    {
5        // New property required by Vote interface
6        private int mJrVotes;
7
8        // Constructor for default values
9        public clsJunior()
10       {
11           mDues = 50m;
12           mBillingCycle = WhenToBill.Monthly;
13           mVotes = VotingRights.LimitedVote;
14       }
15       // ------------ Special Property Methods ------------
16
17       // New method required for interface property
18       public int voteCounter
19       {
20           get
21           {
22               return mJrVotes;
23           }
24           set
25           {
26               mJrVotes += value;
27           }
28       }
29
30       public string Summary
31       {
32           get
33           {
34               string temp;
35
36               MemberSummary();
37               temp = " Junior Billing: " + mBillingCycle.ToString();
38               temp += " Voting: " + mVotes.ToString();
39               temp += " dues: " + mDues.ToString();
```

Figure 14-12 Using the Vote interface in clsJunior

14

```
40
41              return mSummary + temp;
42          }
43      set
44      {
45          mSummary= value;
46      }
47  }
48
49
50  //Purpose: This method simulates sending a limited ballot to a junior member.
51  // This method is required by the Vote interface.
52  //
53  //Parameter list:
54  //n/a
55  //
56  //Return value
57  //stringA message to indicate the action taken
58  //
59  public string SendBallot()
60  {
61      return "A limited ballot was sent. Junior votes = " + mJrVotes.ToString();
62  }
63  }
```

Figure 14-12 Using the Vote interface in clsJunior (continued)

The actual code that implements the **SendBallot** method as required by the **Vote** interface appears in lines 59 through 62 of Figure 14-12. In this case, the code simply returns a string that is displayed in the list box, as shown in Figure 14-13.

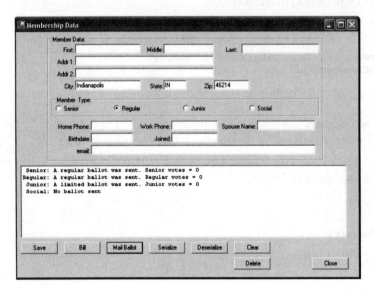

Figure 14-13 Clicking the Mail Ballot button

Figure 14-13 shows a sample run after the Mail Ballot button is clicked on the form. The code that produced the output shown in the list box is presented in Figure 14-14.

```
598          private void btnMailBallot_Click(object sender, System.EventArgs e)
599          {
600               lstOutput.Items.Add(" Senior: " + mySenior.SendBallot());
601               lstOutput.Items.Add("Regular: " + myRegular.SendBallot());
602               lstOutput.Items.Add(" Junior: " + myJunior.SendBallot());
603               lstOutput.Items.Add(" Social: No ballot sent");
604          }
```

Figure 14-14   The Click Event code for the Mail Ballot button

As you might guess from the code shown in Figure 14-14, **clsSenior**, **clsRegular**, and **clsJunior** all implement the **Vote** interface. However, because Social members cannot vote, there is no reason to implement the **Vote** interface for that class. Therefore, the code simply displays a message saying that no message is sent to Social members and the **SendBallot** method is not part of **clsSocial**.

Given what you've read, what does an interface add to our programming box of tools?

- The greatest advantage is that interfaces allow different classes to respond to the same message in whatever way the class deems fit. This is one way that classes can exhibit polymorphic behavior.

- Another major advantage is that interfaces force a discipline on your code by requiring you to provide certain functionality as a result of the interface declaration. This functionality promotes a consistent user interface for your classes.

- Also, by adding new interfaces to your classes as the need arises, you can enhance the functionality of the class without "breaking" earlier versions of the class code.

- Finally, it is important to note that interfaces permit polymorphic behavior in the absence of inheritance. That is, interfaces allow you to add identical user interfaces to classes even though the actual implementation may be different within each class that implements the interface.

14

Interfaces with Properties and Methods

The interface example shown in Figure 14-11 only requires that a **SendBallot** method be implemented in the interface. However, the need may arise where a new property is also required as part of the interface. For example, perhaps the **Vote** interface now requires a counter for the votes that are cast. We might expand the **Vote** interface to that shown in Figure 14-15.

```
1       using System;
2       using System.IO;
3       using System.Runtime.Serialization;
4       using System.Runtime.Serialization.Formatters.Binary;
5
6       public interface Vote
7       {
8           public string SendBallot();
9           public int VoteCounter
10          {
11              get;
12              set;
13          }
14      }
15
```

Figure 14-15 A property and method interface declaration

The new interface now includes a property named **VoteCounter**. The interface specifies that who-
ever uses this new **Vote** interface must provide **get** and **set** property methods for **voteCounter**.
To comply with the new **Vote** interface declaration, the code shown in Figure 14-12 would have
to be changed. Figure 14-16 shows an example of how the new interface might be coded. (These
are the missing lines from Figure 14-12.)

```
15          public int voteCounter
16          {
17              get
18              {
19                  return mRgVotes;
20              }
21              set
22              {
23                  mRgVotes += value;
24              }
25          }
26

45          //Purpose: This method is used to illustrate how we can override the
46          // ballot method.
47          //
48          //Parameter list:
49          //n/a
50          //
51          //Return value
52          //stringA message to indicate the action taken
53          //
54          //CAUTION: n/a
55          //
56          public string SendBallot()
57          {
58              return "A regular ballot was sent. Regular votes = " + mRgVotes.ToString();
59          }
60
61      }
```

Figure 14-16 Code to implement interface property and method

Note that line 6 in Figure 14-12 added a new property member to **clsJunior**. Lines 18 through
28 implement the **get** and **set** property methods as required by the interface declaration. We also

made a minor modification to line 63 in Figure 14-12 to show a simple use of the new property within the class. Because each member type has certain voting rights except the Social members, each of the other member types would likely implement the **Vote** interface as part of their class code. Interfaces are often written using just methods and properties, but they may also have events, too. Likewise, there are certain limitations on interfaces, too (that is, no constructors). If you need more specific information, consult the online Help facilities of Visual Studio.

BONUS TOPICS

SERIALIZING OBJECTS

It is very common to have objects that represent items for which you would like to maintain a permanent record. Examples might include purchase orders, invoices, payroll data, customer lists, and so on. As you learned in Chapter 11, serializing is a process by which an object is stored to a disk data file. Because serialization writes the properties for the object to a disk file, serialization provides a means by which you can permanently store the state of an object. Recall that deserialization is the process in reverse: reading the data previously stored by serialization back into the object.

Writing the Object's State

Figure 14-17 presents the code that we must add to the **clsMember** class to accommodate serialization.

```
288        //Purpose: This method is used to serialize the data in an object using a
289        // binary format.
290        //
291        //Parameter list:
292        //myFile clsMember object
293        //
294        //Return value
295        //stringA message to indicate the action taken
296        //
297        public void SerializeMember(clsMember myFile)
298        {
299            IFormatter formatter = new BinaryFormatter();
300            Stream stream = new FileStream("MyFile.bin", FileMode.Create,
                                            FileAccess.Write, FileShare.None);
301            formatter.Serialize(stream, myFile);
302            stream.Close();
303        }
304
305        //Purpose: This method is used to deserialize the data in an object using a
306        // binary format.
307        //
308        //Parameter list:
309        //myFile clsMember object
310        //
311        //Return value
312        //stringA message to indicate the action taken
313        //
314        public void DeserializeMember(clsMember myFile)
```

Figure 14-17 Serialization code for clsMember

14

```
315        {
316            IFormatter formatter = new BinaryFormatter();
317            Stream stream = new FileStream("MyFile.bin", FileMode.Open,
                                    FileAccess.Read, FileShare.Read);
318            myFile = (clsMember) formatter.Deserialize(stream);
319            stream.Close();
320        }
321        // ------------ Helper Methods ------------
322    }
```

Figure 14-17   Serialization code for clsMember (continued)

The first thing to point out is that C# does not assume that you want to **serialize** objects of a class. If you have any thought of serializing a class, you must add the serialize attribute as shown in the line:

```
16 [Serializable]
```

just before the start of the class declaration. (Look at Figure 14-7 to see the location of the statement.) Note that you need to have line 16 in place *before* you compile, because the serialize attribute cannot be added to a class after the file is compiled.

Lines 297 through 303 in Figure 14-17 present the code necessary to serialize an object in a binary format. The advantage of binary serialization is that it is efficient and easy to use. The disadvantage is that, because the data are stored in a binary format, binary serialization does not lend itself easily to use across different platforms and operating systems. If you need to be concerned about sharing data across the Web, for example, you should investigate using the Extensible Markup Language (XML) for serialization.

The call to **BinaryFormatter** in line 299 of Figure 14-17 defines a binary formatter object named **formatter**. The next line creates a new file stream named **stream**, passing in four arguments. The first is the disk file name you wish to give to the serialized data. The second argument says that you wish to create the file, and the third argument says you are opening the file for writing. The final argument states that there is no sharing of the file. (Again, the Bonus section of Chapter 11 presents the details about binary files.)

The code in line 301 is called to actually serialize the object by calling the **Serialize()** method of **formatter**, the binary formatter object. Line 302 closes the stream object, which causes the object's data to be flushed to disk in a binary format. You now have a file named MyFile.bin that holds the state of the **clsMember** object named **myObj**.

Reading the Object

To confirm that you have actually stored the object's state in a disk file, you need to be able to read the data back from the disk. Lines 314 through 320 in Figure 14-17 show how this is done. As you might expect, the code sequence is almost the same as when you stored the object. First, line 316 creates a binary formatter named **formatter**. The next line defines a new object name **stream** by calling the **FileStream** contructor with four arguments: (1) the filename, MyFile.bin, (2) setting the stream's mode for opening the file, (3) setting the stream's access for reading, and (4) permitting shared status for the file.

Line 318 uses the **formatter** object's **Deserialize** method to read the object from disk and store it in **myObj**. The last line simply closes the input stream. After the routine executes, **myObj** contains the state that existed for the object when it was written to disk.

Figure 14-18 shows the new lines that we added to **frmMain** to use the serialization feature of the membership class.

```
711        //Purpose: This method copies the text box data to the appropriate
712        // class members.
713        //
714        //Parameter list:
715        //  clsMember mine    the class object passed in
716        //
717        //Return value
718        //  void
719        //
720        private void TextToClass(clsMember mine)
721        {
722            mine.FirstName = txtFirst.Text;
723            mine.MiddleName = txtMiddle.Text;
724            mine.LastName = txtLast.Text;
725            mine.Addr1 = txtAddr1.Text;
726            mine.Addr2 = txtAddr2.Text;
727            mine.City = txtCity.Text;
728            mine.State = txtState.Text;
729            mine.Zip = txtZip.Text;
730            mine.Spouse = txtSpouse.Text;
731            mine.MemberType = which;
732        }
733
734        //Purpose: This method copies the class data to the appropriate
735        // text boxes on the form.
736        //
737        //Parameter list:
738        //  clsMember newData    the class object passed in
739        //
740        //Return value
741        //  void
742        //
743        public void ClassToText(clsMember newData)
744        {
745            txtFirst.Text=newData.FirstName;
746            txtMiddle.Text=newData.MiddleName;
747            txtLast.Text=newData.LastName;
748            txtAddr1.Text=newData.Addr1;
749            txtAddr2.Text=newData.Addr2;
750            txtCity.Text=newData.City;
751            txtState.Text=newData.State;
752            txtZip.Text=newData.Zip;
753
754            switch (newData.MemberType)
755            {
756                case 0:// Senior
757                    rbSenior.Checked = true;
758                break;
759                case 1:// Regular
760                    rbRegular.Checked = true;
761                break;
762                case 2:// Junior
763                    rbJunior.Checked = true;
```

14

Figure 14-18 Serialization code in frmMain

```
764                    break;
765                case 3://Social
766                    rbSocial.Checked = true;
767                    break;
768            }
769        }
770
771        private void btnSerialize_Click(object sender, System.EventArgs e)
772        {
773            TextToClass(myMember);
774            myMember.SerializeMember(myMember);
775        }
776
777        private void btnDeserialize_Click(object sender, System.EventArgs e)
778        {
779            myMember.DeserializeMember(myMember);
780            ClassToText(myMember);
781        }
782    }
```

Figure 14-18 Serialization code in frmMain (continued)

The click events for the buttons to serialize and deserialize (see Figure 14-13) the data appear between lines 771 and 782 in Figure 14-18. There are two simple routines to move the data from the text boxes into the object, **TextToClass**, and a complementary routine to move the data from the object into the text boxes, **ClassToText**. If you examine the code, you can see how **TextToClass** prepares things for serialization and how deserialization uses **ClassToText** to move the data back into the text boxes.

Binary serialization methods provide a quick and easy way to store the state of an object to disk. Deserializing the data back into an object is equally as easy. Although binary serialization is not the perfect solution because it is not completely portable, it does offer a relatively easy means by which to have good performance whenever you need to store the state of an object.

Summary

Essential Topics

- This chapter expands upon the concepts of inheritance and polymorphism that were touched upon in Chapter 1.

- A base class may be used to hold those data members and methods that are shared in common with each subclass, and the subclasses may add those data members and methods that make it unique.

- Designing a base-subclass relationship must establish an *is a* relationship.

- A public interface must be created to allow users of classes to change the state of an object of that class.

- The **protected** keyword can be used to permit subclasses to have access to the data and methods in the base class while still encapsulating them from other elements of the program.

- Composite formatting can be used to format columnar data in a list box without having to use a **ListView** control.

- The `region` keyword may be used to hide code when viewing sections of code that have already been tested and debugged.

- Method overriding allows you to "replace" a method defined in the base class with a variant defined using the same name in a subclass. Overriding provides a convenient way to have generic, shared behavior in a base class method, but unique behavior in a subclass when it's needed. Method overloading can be used to add flexibility to your classes.

- C# interfaces are an effective means for providing a consistent way for users to interact with your classes and extending them with polymorphic behavior.

Bonus Topics

- Serialization is a way to permanently preserve the state of an object.

- A binary formatter is used to serialize the data of an object so that its state can be stored on disk and retrieved at a later time.

KEY TERMS

Define each of the following terms, as it relates to software application development using C# and Visual Studio .NET:

Essential Terms

- alignment
- base class
- composite formatting of string data
- fixed font
- format item
- format string
- inheritance
- "is a" relationship
- interface
- method overriding
- new (as relates to overriding)
- polymorphism

- program analysis
- proportional font
- **protected**
- public user interface
- stakeholders
- subclass
- Unified Modeling Language (UML)

Bonus Terms

- deserialize
- serialize

14

REVIEW QUESTIONS

Essential Questions

1. Inheritance recognizes that different objects often have common properties and methods. True or false?

2. A base class can be thought of as a grouping of common properties and methods. True or false?

3. An inherited relation exhibits an *is a* relationship with its base class. True or false?

4. A base class exhibits an *is a* relationship with its subclass(es). True or false?

5. One disadvantage of inheritance is that it promotes duplicate code in the subclasses. True or false?

6. Program analysis is primarily concerned with a clear and concise definition of the problems the program is to solve. True or false?

7. If you plan to serialize a class, it's best to use the [Serializable] statement before you compile the class code. True or false?

8. The **protected** keyword prevents property data from being changed anywhere but within the class where the property is declared. True or false?

9. When using composite formatting, a minus sign in the alignment field means the field is right justified. True or false?

10. One reason for using composite formatting is because Windows programs often use proportional fonts, which makes displaying columns of data difficult to align. True or false?

11. In composite formatting, if the data overflows a field width, the data is _____ to fit.

12. _____ permits duplicate method names as long as the signatures are different.

13. _____ is most often used in programs that have inherited relationships.

14. A(an) _____ statement is like a contract in that any class that wishes to implement the interface must provide code for every element declared within the interface declaration.

15. If you need a subclass to access a member in the base class without using a public interface, use the _____ specifier.

16. Under what circumstances would you make a class property public?

17. What is the difference between method overloading and method overriding?

18. List at least three reasons when you would consider using inheritance in a program.

19. Give a brief definition of polymorphism that could be understood by a non-programmer.

20. What benefits does polymorphism have for the programmer?

Bonus Questions

1. Serialization refers to the process of sorting objects into reference arrays. True or false?

2. The use of binary serialization is limited by the fact that it can store only public data. True or false?

3. Binary serialization is ideally suited for Web-based applications. True or false?

4. It is not possible to restore the state of an object without the use of serialization. True or false?

5. Deserialization of an object has the advantage that you do not need to instantiate the object before you deserialize it. True or false?

6. _____ provides a process by which the state of an object can be stored permanently to disk.

7. _____ is normally done in conjunction with a binary formatter and a **Stream** object.

8. As a programmer, how would you decide whether to serialize an object or not in a program?

9. Give several examples of programming problems where you think serialization is desirable.

10. If C# did not support serialization, how would you persist the state of an object?

PROGRAMMING EXERCISES

Essential Exercises

1. Using the membership program as the foundation, add a `clsTennis` member to the program. Tennis members are not allowed to play golf or vote, their dues are $50 per month, and they must spend $50 per month in the restaurant.

2. The registrar's office tracks information about students enrolled in the university. Things like names, addresses, ID numbers, and other demographic information are common to all students. However, graduate students have additional information such as the name of the school where they received their undergraduate degree, teaching assistants' sponsoring faculty member, enrolled hours each semester (these may be limited if they have a teaching assistantship), and so forth. Write a program that manages graduate and undergraduate information.

3. Modify the contact list program from Chapter 11 to provide for two types of people on a mailing list. The group named `Relatives` gets a copy of a family newsletter, whereas another class name, `Friends`, gets a different newsletter.

4. Golf clubs often bill spouses who use locker and driving range facilities. Modify the membership program to accommodate spouses who play golf.

5. Suppose that you are a real estate investor living in Minnesota. You own property where you live, but you just bought a new piece of property in Florida. You wrote your own software package to manage your properties, including an automated phone system that calls each property owner when more than 2 inches of snow falls. Since snow has never been an issue in Florida, modify your code to ignore the snow removal call for Florida properties.

6. After writing your real estate investment program in Exercise 5, you learn that private homes constructed with brick are treated differently for insurance purposes than non-brick homes. Modify your code to account for the construction material.

7. Add a third contact type to the contact list program that is a catchall group that contains contacts (like business contacts) that do not receive any newsletters. However, you do wish to maintain information about why you are keeping the business information in your contact list. (Perhaps the business is the only one in town that sells a certain item you use.)

14

Bonus Exercise

Write a program that uses a class to model a Christmas card list. The list should contain the person's name, mailing address, and provision to note whether a card was sent to and received from that person last year. Use binary serialization to store the data.

C# KEYWORDS

abstract	float	return
as	for	sbyte
base	foreach	sealed
bool	goto	short
break	if	sizeof
byte	implicit	stackalloc
case	in	static
catch	int	string
char	interface	struct
checked	internal	switch
class	is	this
const	lock	throw
continue	long	true
decimal	namespace	try
default	new	typeof
delegate	null	uint
do	object	ulong
double	operator	unchecked
else	out	unsafe
enum	override	ushort
event	params	using
explicit	private	virtual
extern	protected	void
false	public	volatile
finally	readonly	while
fixed	ref	

B

C# CODING STANDARDS AND GUIDELINES

INTRODUCTION

The purpose of coding standards and coding guidelines is to improve productivity and quality. If everyone on a development team follows the same standards, the result is source code that is easier to read by all members of the team because it is written in a consistent style. Code that is easy to read is easier to debug and maintain by all members of the development team. If a standard doesn't exist for the type of code you are writing, then at a minimum you should use a consistent style throughout the program. Source code readability is also the best indication of program quality. If the source code is easy to read, it is probably a good program. If the source code is hard to read, it probably is not.

NAMING CONVENTIONS

This section covers naming conventions for variables, user interface objects, consistent names for data items, method names, and class and source code files.

Variables

The following list outlines guidelines for the use of variables:

- Use meaningful, descriptive, English-like variable names, even if the variable may appear in only a few lines of code.

- Local-scope variables begin with a lowercase letter.

- Private class variables should have an **m** prefix to indicate a private member.

- Public variables should begin with a capital letter.

- Do not use so-called "Hungarian" notation prefixes to indicate a variable's data type (an exception is made for user interface objects created with the Visual Studio Forms Designer).

- Most variable names are created by combining several words, so use capital letters at the start of each word or word segment, and lowercase otherwise. This is sometimes called "camel-back" notation.

For example, do this:

```
int index;

private string mErrorMessage;

public ArrayList GradeList;
```

Not this:

```
int iIndex;

private string strMsg;

public ArrayList ga;
```

User Interface Objects

User interface objects created with the Visual Studio Forms Designer should be named using meaningful, English-like names, with capital letters at the start of each word or word segment, and lowercase in other positions. Unlike variables, user interface objects should be prefixed with the suggested three-character object-type prefix first popularized by Visual Basic developers. Examples are listed in Table B-1.

Table B-1   Prefixes for interface objects

Control type	Prefix
Button	btn
CheckBox	chk
ComboBox	cbo
DateTimePicker	dtp
GroupBox	grp
Label	lbl
ListBox	lst
ListView	lvw
Menus	mnu
NumericUpDown	num
RadioButton	rad
TabControl	tab
TextBox	txt
Timer	tmr
ToolBar	tlb
ToolBarButton	tbb
StatusBar	stb
StatusBarPanel	sbp

Consistency

Data items should be named consistently throughout all parts of a program.

For example, suppose that you are writing a program that processes information about books, and one data item the program uses is the date the book was published. Decide on a name for date published and use that name whenever the data item is used. This includes variable names, user interface object names, and column names in a database. You would only use something different to add a prefix or change the capitalization of the name.

Do this:

```
DateTime datePublished;
...
datePublished = DateTime.Parse(txtDatePublished.Text);
...
mBooksArray[index].DatePublished = datePublished;
...
datePublished = book.DatePublished;
```

Not this:

```
DateTime dtPub;
...
dtPub = DateTime.Parse(txtPubDate.Text);
...
mBooksArray[index].published = dtPub;
...
pubDate = book.DatePublshd;
```

Use consistent abbreviations for the same word. For example, if you decide to abbreviate **Amount** as **Amt**, then it should be abbreviated as **Amt** everywhere it is used.

For example, do this:

```
decimal hourlyPayAmt;
decimal weeklyPayAmt;
decimal taxAmt;
```

Not this:

```
decimal hourlyPayAmount;
decimal weeklyPayAmt;
decimal taxAmnt;
```

Methods

The following list outlines guidelines for writing methods:

- Use meaningful, descriptive, English-like method names.

- Private class methods begin with a lowercase letter.

- Public methods should begin with a capital letter.

- Words within method names should begin with capital letters at the start of each word or word segment, and lowercase in other positions (that is, use camel-back notation).

- Method names generally begin with a verb to indicate action, followed by a noun to indicate what they perform that action on.

- Method names should describe what the method does and not how it does it.

- Methods with return values should have a name describing the value returned.

Here are examples:

```
private void msgOKOnly()
{
...
}
```

```
public decimal CalculateInvoiceTotal()
{
...
}
```

Class and Source Code Files

Class names should begin with a three-character prefix. Use **frm** for form classes and **cls** for all others.

A source code file name should generally be the name of the class it contains. For example, the class **frmMain** should be contained in a file named **frmMain.cs**.

COMMENTS

The following list outlines guidelines for using general comments:

- Comments should be included in source code to indicate what the code does and to break up large sections of code.

- Comments lines should begin with a comment slash pair (//) indented at the same level as the code they are documenting.

- Do not use /* ... */ blocks for comments.

- Indent comments at the same level of indentation as the code you are documenting.

- Source code comments should be written in clear, concise, English with correct spelling and grammar.

- Comments should not include humorous remarks. Your comments may seem funny to you when you type them, but they won't to the person who has to understand and fix your code during a late-night debugging session.

- Comments should not be used to teach the reader how to program. Assume that the reader knows as much about the programming language as you do.

- Comments should not be used to describe obvious code. The purpose of comments is to increase your code's readability. Often using good variable and method names make the code easier to read than using excessive comments.

- Never leave "commented out" code in your programs without also including a description of why you commented it out. If the code isn't necessary, it should be deleted.

- Do not use "clutter" comments (such as an entire line of asterisks) or "draw flower boxes" around comments (using rows of asterisks or other characters). Instead, use a single blank line to create white space to separate comments from code.

METHOD COMMENTS

Methods may be commented in the following manner (note that examining the example that follows as you read this description may be helpful): a comment block that begins with a comment slash pair, one tab space and the word **Purpose:** followed by a single space, and a description of what the method does. After the description is complete, there is one blank comment line, then a comment line with a tab, and the words **Parameter list:**. The next line has a newline and comment, a tab space, then the data type specifier and name of the parameter being passed into the method, and a brief description of the parameter. This sequence is repeated for all parameters. The list is followed by an empty comment line. Another comment line is followed by a tab space and the words `Return value:` and a newline. The next line has a comment followed by a tab space followed by the data type specifier for the method. This is followed by a blank line and then the opening line of the method, for example:

```
//   Purpose: This method copies the text box data to
//        the appropriate class members.
//
//   Parameter list:
//     clsMember mine   the class object passed in
//
//   Return value:
//     void

private void textToClass(clsMember mine)
{
    // method statement block
}
```

PREDEFINED DATA TYPES

Always use C# predefined types rather than aliases in the System namespace.

For example, do this:

```
string firstName;
bool itemFound;
int itemCounter;
```

Not this:

```
String firstName;
Boolean itemFound;
System.Int32 itemCounter;
```

FORMAT

This section presents guidelines for formatting your code to make it easier to read.

White Space

Use a space before and after most operators, and after the comma in the method's parameter list. Exceptions include (++) and (--). Semicolons should immediately follow the last character in the statement.

For example, do this:

```
private void panel_EnabledChanged(object sender, System.EventArgs e)
{
    txtEnabled.Text = sip.Enabled.ToString();
    Rectangle r = sip.VisibleDesktop;
    lblUserName.Location = new Point(0, r.Height - lblUserName.Height - 30);
}
```

Not this:

```
private void panel_EnabledChanged(object sender,System.EventArgs e)
{
    txtEnabled.Text=sip.Enabled.ToString() ;
    Rectangle r=sip.VisibleDesktop ;
    lblUserName.Location=new Point(0,r.Height-lblUserName.Height-30);
}
```

One Statement per Line

Each line of code should not contain more than one statement. Stacking several statements onto one line of code makes your code harder to read.

For example, do this:

```
string address;
string city;
string state;
string zip;
...
address = txtAddress.Text;
city = txtCity.Text;
state = txtState.Text;
zip = txtZip.Text;
```

Not this:

```
string address, city, state, zip;
...
address = txtAddress.Text; city = txtCity.Text; state = txtState.Text; zip =
txtZip.Text;
```

Indenting

You should indent all statements inside classes, methods, loops, **if** statements, **switch** statements, **try/catch** blocks, and so on. Statements should be indented in four-space increments (that is, aligned at columns 1, 5, 9, 13, 17, 21, and so on.).

For example, do this:

```
private bool inZone()
{
    const double latLongDiff = .0003;

    foreach (TourZone tz in mTourZones)
    {
        // Only check if the zone isn't the current one.

        if (tz.ZoneID != mCurrentZone.ZoneID)
        {
            double latDiff = Math.Abs(Math.Abs(tz.Lat) -
                Math.Abs(mCurrentLat));
            double longDiff = Math.Abs(Math.Abs(tz.Long) -
                Math.Abs(mCurrentLong));
```

```
                if (latDiff < latLongDiff
                && longDiff < latLongDiff)
                {
                    // The user is fairly close to the coordinates of this zone.

                    mCurrentZone = tz;
                    return true;
                }
            }
        }
        return false;
    }
```

Not this:

```
    private bool inZone()
    {
     const double latLongDiff = .0003;

     foreach (TourZone tz in mTourZones)
     {
       // Only check if the zone isn't the current one.
       if (tz.ZoneID != mCurrentZone.ZoneID)
     {
         double latDiff = Math.Abs(Math.Abs(tz.Lat) - Math.Abs(mCurrentLat));
         double longDiff = Math.Abs(Math.Abs(tz.Long) - Math.Abs(mCurrentLong));
         if (latDiff < latLongDiff
         && longDiff < latLongDiff)
       {
             // The user is fairly close to the coordinates of this zone.
             mCurrentZone = tz;
           return true;
       }
     }
     }
     return false;
     }
```

Brace Alignment

Align open and close braces vertically where brace pairs align and place them on a line by themselves.

For example, do this:

```
    for (index = 0; index < 100; index++)
    {
        if (totPurchaseAmt < 0)
        {
            ...
        }
    }
```

Not this:

```
for (index = 0; index < 100; index++) {
    if (totPurchaseAmt < 0) {
        ...
    }
}
```

Variable Declaration Placement

All member variables should be declared at the top of the class, followed by a single blank line. Here is an example:

```
private class clsStudent
{
    private int mNumber;
    private string mName;

    public string Serialize()
    {
    ...
    }
}
```

TYPE CONVERSIONS

The .NET Framework contains countless techniques for converting numbers to strings and strings to numbers. As usual when there are many techniques for accomplishing the same thing, it's best to pick a style and stay consistent for the sake of simplicity.

This is the suggested technique for converting strings to numbers: All numeric types have a **Parse** method, which takes a string containing numeric characters and returns the appropriate numeric value. Here is an example:

```
int i = int.Parse("12345");
float f = float.Parse("123.45");
```

The **Parse** method will accept some non-numeric characters by default, including leading and trailing spaces, commas, decimal points, and plus and minus signs. Additional arguments can be passed to the **Parse** method to control what characters are allowed and not allowed. For example, you can tell the **Parse** method to allow a currency symbol ($).

This is the suggested technique for converting numbers to strings: All numeric types have a **ToString** method that returns an unformatted string representation of the number. This allows numbers to be implicitly converted to strings in simple assignment and concatenation statements. Here is an example:

```
int nbrItems = 1234;
decimal totCost = 5678.99M;
string message = "You have purchased "
    + nbrItems
    + " items for a total of "
    + totCost;

// message contains "You have purchased 1234 items for a total of 5678.99".
```

In all other cases, it is suggested that you explicitly pass an argument to the `ToString` method to explicitly indicate how the number should be formatted. Here is an example:

```
int nbrItems = 1234;
decimal totCost = 5678.99M;

string message = "You have purchased "
    + nbrItems.ToString("N0")
    + " items for a total of "
    + totCost.ToString("C");

// message contains "You have purchased 1,234 items for a total of $5,678.99".
```

DECISIONS

The following list outlines guidelines you should use when coding decision statements:

- Always use a curly brace scope in an `if` statement, even if a true condition executes a single statement.

- Always compare the variable or expression to **true** or **false**.

  For example, do this:

  ```
  if (itemFound == true)
  {
      itemCounter++;
  }
  ```

  Not this:

  ```
  if (itemFound)
      itemCounter++;
  ```

- When the logical expressions of a decision statement include more than two expressions, code each condition on a line by itself, and begin the line with the logical operator.

  For example, do this:

  ```
  if (txtID.Text.Length == 5
  && txtFirstName.Text != ""
  && txtLastName.Text != ""
  && txtStartDate.Text != ""
  && txtClass.Text.Length == 2)
  {
      cmdCalculate.Enabled = true;
  }
  ```

  Not this:

  ```
  if (txtID.Text.Length == 5 && txtFirstName.Text != "" && txtLastName.Text !=
  "" && txtStartDate.Text != "" && txtClass.Text.Length == 2)
  {
      cmdCalculate.Enabled = true;
  }
  ```

QUALIFIED TYPE NAMES

The following list outlines guidelines for using qualified type names:

- Use the **using** statement instead of coding fully qualified type names.
- Do not use the **this** operator when referencing an object's own members.

For example, do this:

```
using System.Net

...

IPAddress ipAd = IPAddress.Parse("192.168.0.1");

...

if (mMouseIsDown == false)
{
    return;
}
```

Not this:

```
System.Net.IPAddress ipAd = System.Net.IPAddress.Parse("192.168.0.1");

...

if (this.mMouseIsDown == false)
{
    return;
}
```

C

USING THE VISUAL STUDIO DEBUGGER

Unfortunately, very few programmers write perfect code all the time. Because of this short-coming, Visual Studio comes with a debugger that is built into the Integrated Development Environment (IDE). The purpose of the debugger is to help you to locate, isolate, and correct any errors that may exist in your program.

A debugger is a major development tool for any language. Without a debugger, finding many types of program errors becomes extremely difficult, at best. Fortunately, the Visual Studio debugger is a robust and effective tool to help you isolate and correct program errors.

TYPES OF PROGRAM ERRORS

There are three types of errors a program may contain: (1) syntax errors, (2) semantic errors, and (3) logic errors. Syntax errors occur when your program code fails to follow the rules of the language you are using. The Intellisense feature of Visual Studio catches all the C# syntax errors the programmer is likely to make. Semantic errors occur when your code obeys the syntax rules of the language, but the code is not used in the proper context. This is similar to English, which also has its own set of language rules. The sentence "The dog meowed." obeys the rules for an English sentence in that it has a noun and a verb, but the context is wrong. Dogs don't meow; hence, there is a semantic error in the sentence. This is also true when writing programming statements. You may use a statement incorrectly at a specific point in a program, using it out of context. For example, if you tried to close a file stream object before you opened it, this would generate an error even though the statements might be syntactically correct. A logic error occurs when you have obeyed both the syntax and semantic rules of the language, but the program does not behave as expected. It is in this third type of program error that the debugger is most helpful.

Simply stated, the Visual Studio debugger is your doctor for an ill program. The debugger allows you to examine all of the parts and internals of a program in much the same way that an x-ray machine enables a doctor to see inside a person's body. The debugger allows you to halt the execution of a program and inspect it closely to observe how the data is behaving. Just as a doctor often looks for errant cells that trigger cancer, you use the debugger to track errant data that causes your program to behave incorrectly.

BEFORE YOU USE THE DEBUGGER...

As good as the Visual Studio debugger is, however, it still assumes that you have a basic understanding of the debugging process itself. Far too often, students jump into the debugging process with no clue how to attack the problem. The first step in solving *any* program bug is:

> Be able to reproduce the error condition.

Program bugs that always behave the same (incorrect) way are usually fairly easy to resolve. If a program crashes each time you click the Save button, obviously you start looking at the offending button's click event. With such bugs, you simply trace the program to the point where the bug manifests itself and work backward from that statement to find the cause that leads up to the error condition.

The really nasty bugs are ones that appear to be intermittent—bugs that seem to show up at random intervals. Intermittent bugs are troublesome because they are hard to reproduce on a consistent basis, making it difficult to figure out where things are going wrong. Quite often, intermittent bugs arise only when two (or more) variables have specific values and combine together to produce the error. It is our experience that looking for **if** statements with logical **And** or **Or** statements often helps isolate intermittent bugs. Sometimes adding new **try-catch** blocks around large blocks of code can help narrow down the cause of the error.

The bad news is that, unfortunately, experience is the only way to learn the debugging process and its techniques. The good news is that all of us write enough bad code to get that experience. Every programmer has gone through the FFC process. (FFC is also known as flat forehead code. You know, code in which, upon discovering the error, you slam the heel of your hand into your forehead, while saying: "How could I be so stupid!") Everybody writes code with bugs in it. It's simply part of the process of becoming a programmer. A good debugger, however, can greatly simplify that process, and the Visual Studio debugger is a good debugger.

DISPLAYING THE DEBUG TOOLBAR

You can activate the debugger toolbar by selecting the View → Toolbars → Debug menu sequence. After you do that, the toolbar shown in Figure C-1 appears somewhere near the top of the Visual Studio screen. (Its exact position depends upon what other toolbars are currently being displayed.)

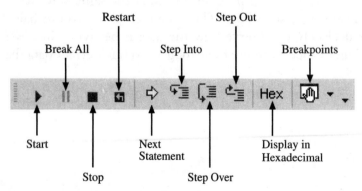

Figure C-1 The debug toolbar

The debug toolbar offers you the following options:

- *Start*—Begin program execution. You can also start to execute a program by pressing the F5 key. There is also a copy of this triangle-shaped blue button to the left of the Debug drop-down list box (usually located just below the Help menu option).

- *Break All*—The debugger stops program execution at the line where the breakpoint has been set and places your program and the debugger in Break mode.

- *Stop*—Suspends the current debug session

- *Restart*—Stops the debugger and restarts the program

- *Next Statement*—Executes the next statement in the program. You can also use the F10 key.

- *Step Into*—If you are on a line that has a method call, the program "steps into" the method and executes the first statement of the method.

- *Step Over*—If you are on a line that has a method call, the code of the method is executed at normal speed, and the program breaks on the first line that it is outside the method that was called. (Usually, this is the line following the method call.)

- *Step Out*—Use this option when you are in a method and you wish to return to the caller. (This provides a means of stepping out of a method without having to step through each statement as it is executed.)

- *Display in Hexadecimal*—Displays all numeric values in hexadecimal

- *Breakpoints*—Shows a listing of the breakpoints that are set

In actual practice, you will likely find that you use only a small subset of these options. The remainder of this appendix discusses those debugger features you are most likely to use.

A SAMPLE PROGRAM TO DEBUG

Many years ago, one of the authors discovered that:

For a given number, N, the sum of N odd positive integers is equal to the square of N.

The author has used this relationship to test the students' ability to implement an algorithm from a one-sentence statement. For example, if N is 3, then:

$$3^2 = 1 + 3 + 5 = 9$$

If N is 4, then:

$$4^2 = 1 + 3 + 5 + 7 = 16$$

Figure C-2 shows the first attempt by a student to provide a test program for the algorithm.

```
  1    using System;
  2    using System.Drawing;
  3    using System.Windows.Forms;
  4
  5    public class frmDebug : System.Windows.Forms.Form
  6    {
  7        private System.Windows.Forms.Label label1;
  8        private System.Windows.Forms.TextBox txtInput;
  9        private System.Windows.Forms.Button btnRun;
 10        private System.Windows.Forms.Label label2;
 11        private System.Windows.Forms.TextBox txtAnswer;
 12        private System.Windows.Forms.Button btnClose;
 13
 14        public frmDebug()
 15        {
 16            InitializeComponent();
 17        }
 18        #region Windows Form Designer generated code

 94
 95        static void Main()
 96        {
 97            frmDebug main = new frmDebug();
 98            Application.Run(main);
 99        }
100
101        private void btnClose_Click(object sender, System.EventArgs e)
102        {
103            Close();
104        }
105
106        private void btnRun_Click(object sender, System.EventArgs e)
107        {
108            int number;
109            int answer;
110
111            number = int.Parse(txtInput.Text);
112            answer = SquareMyNumber(number);
113            txtAnswer.Text = answer.ToString();
114        }
115
116        //Purpose: This method uses an additive method to square a number.
117        //
118        //Parameter list:
119        //    int val        the number to be squared
120        //
121        //Return value:
122        //    int            the square of the number passed in
123        //
124        private int SquareMyNumber(int number)
```

Figure C-2 A program to square a number

```
125        {
126            int i;
127            int sum = 0;
128
129            for (i = 0; i < number; i++)
130            {
131                sum += i;
132            }
133            return sum;
134        }
135    }
```

Figure C-2 A program to square a number (continued)

A sample run of the program as written using the code found in Figure C-2 is shown in Figure C-3.

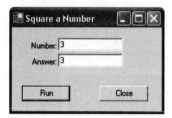

Figure C-3 Sample run of a program

Well, 3 squared is not 3, so we have a program bug. Now what?

SETTING A BREAKPOINT

Obviously, you need to be able to examine the variables that are used in the program while the program is executing. A *breakpoint* is simply a place in your program code where you would like to suspend program execution. If you think you have a good idea of where your program bug is hiding, you set a breakpoint at that line of code so that you can pause the program and inspect the values of the variables. Because breakpoints do not terminate the program but only suspend it, all the variables used in that part of the program retain their values when the breakpoint is reached. This allows you to inspect the values of the variables to help isolate the program bug.

To set a breakpoint, move the cursor to the line of code where you wish to suspend program execution, and press the F9 key. If you press the F9 key again, the breakpoint is removed. When a breakpoint is set on a program statement, that statement is highlighted in red. Because you are not sure where the program bug is, perhaps a good starting point is line 112 in Figure C-2. As you can see in Figure C-4, the breakpoint is on the line where the code is about to call the `SquareMyNumber` method.

```
    private void btnClose_Click(object sender, System.EventArgs e)
    {
      Close();
    }

    private void btnRun_Click(object sender, System.EventArgs e)
    {
      int number;
      int answer;

      number = int.Parse(txtInput.Text);
      answer = SquareMyNumber(number);
      txtAnswer.Text = answer.ToString();
    }

    //   Purpose: This method using an additive method to square a number.
    //
    //   Parameter list:
    //      int val          the number to be square
    //
    //   Return value:
    //      int              the square of the number passed in
    //
    private int SquareMyNumber(int number)
    {
      int i;
      int sum = 0;

      for (i = 0; i < number; i++)
      {
        sum += i;
```

Figure C-4 After setting a breakpoint

You can also set a breakpoint by clicking in the gray area just to the left of the line in the source code window where you want the breakpoint set. (The red dot appears in the gray area of the source code window in Figure C-4.) Clicking on the red dot that appeared when the breakpoint was set removes the breakpoint. You cannot set a breakpoint on a line that does not contain an executable program statement.

When you run the program and the breakpoint statement is reached, that statement is highlighted. Note that when a breakpoint statement is reached, the breakpoint statement *has not* been executed. In other words, when a breakpoint is reached, the program is waiting to execute the breakpoint statement line. You will note that the breakpoint line changes color from red to yellow when it is reached.

If you wanted to execute the breakpoint line, you would need to press the F10 key to execute the breakpoint statement line. Don't press the F10 key right now, however. Instead, hover the cursor over the variable named **number**. You will see a small rectangle open up, revealing the current value of **number**. Hovering the cursor over a variable while program execution is suspended at a breakpoint is a good way to observe the value of a single value-type variable. (Hovering over an object-type variable tells you the object type, but not its value, so hovering over such variables is less informative.)

THE LOCALS WINDOW

While the program's execution is suspended at the breakpoint line (112), it would be nice to inspect the state of all of the variables at this point. Although you could hover over each variable, it's quicker and more informative to let the debugger show you the relevant values of the variables. Recall that local scope is the term applied to all variables that are visible in the method being executed. To open the Locals window, select the Debug → Windows → Locals menu sequence or press the Ctrl+Alt+V keys, and then press the L key. This opens the Locals window near the bottom of the screen, as shown in Figure C-5. As you can see near the bottom of the figure, the variables with local scope have their values displayed in the center column and their type in the third column. Obviously, a key part of tracking down a bug is to observe what happens to the variable values as the program executes. The Locals window provides an easy way to observe the variables that are currently in scope. If a variable has a plus sign before its name, you can click on the plus sign to reveal additional information about the variable. The plus sign appears when reference or object type variables are displayed.

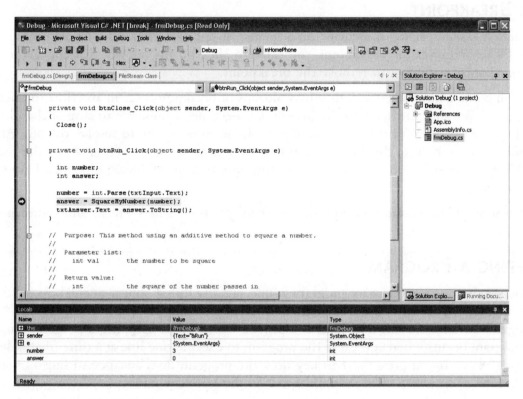

Figure C-5   The Locals window

As you can see, the value of **number** appears to be correct, so everything in the program up to this point seems correct.

There are other debug windows you could inspect at this point, if you wish.

THE AUTOS WINDOW

The Autos window is almost the same as the Locals window in terms of functionality, but it limits the number of variables displayed to those variables that appear in the current breakpoint line or the line immediately above it. Because the Autos window displays fewer variables than would the Locals window (in most cases), there is less scrolling necessary to observe the variables that appear in the window. This is especially useful when you are debugging a block of code that has a large number of variables in scope.

You can invoke the Autos window by selecting the Debug → Windows → Autos menu option or pressing the Ctrl+Alt+V keys and then pressing the "A" key. The output in the Autos window is the same as the Locals window except that there are likely to be fewer variables displayed. Although we elected not to show an example of the Autos window, you might try evoking it here as an experiment to note the difference between it and the Locals window.

Note that most of the debug windows can only be activated after the program has begun execution. (After all, there would be no values to examine if the program isn't running!)

CLEARING A BREAKPOINT

As we stated earlier, placing the cursor on a statement line that contains a breakpoint and pressing the F9 key removes the breakpoint. You can also click on the red dot that appears to the left of the breakpoint statement to remove the breakpoint.

There will come a time when you may have dozens of breakpoints set in an effort to track down a bug. As you progress further into the program, it becomes a nuisance to stop at the old breakpoints because they didn't provide the debug information necessary to resolve the bug. Although you could click on each of these old breakpoints to remove them, it is faster to use the Debug → Clear All Breakpoints menu option. Selecting this option clears all breakpoints that have been set in the program.

If you clear all of the existing breakpoints, don't forget to set a new breakpoint somewhere!

SINGLE-STEPPING A PROGRAM

Thus far, you have suspended your program at line 112 and things appear normal. So, what should you do next? Actually, you have a number of choices available to you. If you press the F10 key, the program advances to line 113. This is a process called single-stepping a program. *Single-stepping* a program occurs when you cause the program to execute one line at a time (that is, by pressing the F10 key). If you press the F10 key now, the program does advance to line 113 and note that the value of **answer** changes from 0 to 3 in the Locals window.

Believe it or not, we now know more than we did before. While we were sitting on line 112, everything looked correct. Single-stepping to line 113 produced a value for a variable that is incorrect. Therefore, because we went from a correct state to an incorrect state, something on line 112 is associated with the bug. You have now isolated the bug to line 112. Congratulations! Isolating a bug is the first step to eradicating the bug. However, when you inspect line 112, you notice that it is the line that calls the **SquareMyNumber** method. Therefore, it is likely that it is the method that contains the bug, not line 112 by itself.

STEP INTO VERSUS STEP OVER

Because the program state is now at line 113 and you know the answer is incorrect, restart the program, keeping the breakpoint at line 112. You can stop the program's execution by pressing the Stop button on the Debug toolbar (see Figure C-1). Now restart the program (press the F5 key).

When the program pauses at the breakpoint, you have several options available. First, you already know that pressing the F10 key causes the program to advance to line 113. That does not serve your purpose, however, because is doesn't pause program execution in the **SquareMyNumber** method where you suspect the problem is. The process of executing a method without pausing in the method is referred to as *stepping over* a method call.

If you press the F11 key, the program advances to line 127 (see Figure C-2). Pressing the F11 key produces what is called a *step into* behavior, because program control advances to the first executable statement in the **SquareMyNumber** method. That is, program control steps "into" the code associated with the method call rather than "over" it, as the F10 key does. This is good stuff, because the program is now paused in the method call that you've isolated as the fertile ground for the bug.

Well, as good as the F11 key is, what's the probability that line 127 contains the error? (Hint: zero!) It seems much more likely that something in the **for** loop starting at line 129 seems a more productive point to advance to than line 127. So, how can you get there (line 129) from here (line 112)?

Stop and restart the program... again. (Sorry, but you need to go through this kind of stuff to learn the debugging options available to you.) When program execution pauses at the breakpoint on line 112, move your cursor to the line you wish to pause on (line 129) and right-click the mouse. You are presented with the pop-up menu shown in Figure C-6. Now select the Run To Cursor menu option. Immediately, program control executes to the first (executable) expression on the line you selected on line 129. (This is probably why it's called Run To Cursor, right?)

Figure C-6 Debug pop-up menu

Obviously, you could have used the F9 key to permanently set a breakpoint at line 129, but the method shown here is a great way to set a temporary breakpoint that doesn't need to be removed at some later time.

Now you can use the F10 key to single-step through the program loop, observing the values of the variables change on each iteration through the loop. If you watch the **sum** variable closely, you can see it is not behaving in a manner that successfully implements the algorithm. Our bug is a logic error in the algorithm's implementation.

THE WATCH WINDOW

Quite often you will sense that it is the state of a particular variable that is likely causing the program error. In those cases, you would like to observe the state of that variable at every stage of program execution. Although you could use the Locals window or Autos window to track its value, the Watch window is frequently a more efficient way to accomplish the same task. One reason is that you can enter the variable's name in the Watch window and not have to scroll to it, as you might have to when using one of the other windows.

You can have up to four separate Watch windows, as shown in Figure C-7. You can open a Watch window using the Debug → Watch → Watch ? menu option, or you can press the Ctrl+Alt+W keys and then press a numeric key (1 through 4). After selecting one of the four Watch windows, the window opens up at the bottom of the screen. See Figure C-7.

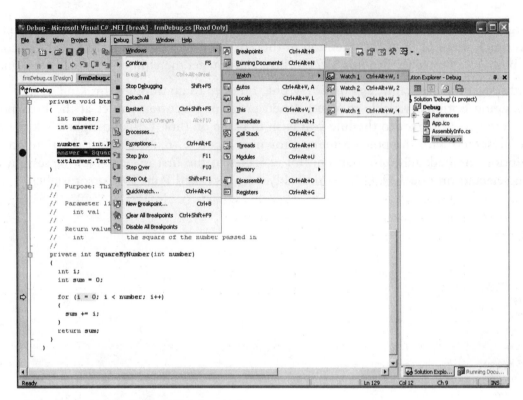

Figure C-7 Activating a Watch window

Now double-click on the name of the variable you wish to track, and press Ctrl+C to copy the variable name to the copy buffer. Now move the cursor to the first line of the Watch window and press Ctrl+V to copy the variable name onto the line. (You can also simply type the name of the variable on the line of the Watch window, or use the mouse to drag the variable of interest from the code window to the Watch window.) Figure C-8 shows an example of what a Watch window entry might look like. You are now ready to watch the state of the variable at all points in the program where it is in scope.

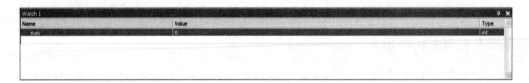

Figure C-8 The Watch window

Why are there four Watch windows? In very complex programs, you may have several different sets of variables that you'd like to switch between at various points in the program rather than trying to watch all of them at once. Multiple Watch windows make this easy to do. Another nice feature of the Watch window is that Visual Studio remembers the Watch windows you've activated for a project and the variables associated with each window. Therefore, if you shut down your system and come back the next day, the state of the Watch window is the same as it was when you shut the system off.

The Command Window

The Command window is used to interact with your code while debugging a program. You activate the Command window using the Debug → Windows → Immediate menu sequence. The Command window appears near the bottom of the screen.

> **Command Mode**
>
> Actually, there are two modes for the Command window. The first is the immediate mode that we discuss in detail here. However, you can also use the Command window in the Command mode, which allows you to issue commands to the Visual Studio environment. Once the Command window is open, you can type > cmd and press Enter, which switches the Command window to the Command mode. (You do need to type the > symbol.) You can now type a command to Visual Studio. For example, if you type the letter E, a drop-down list displays a list of the commands that you may enter, such as Exit. If you type Exit, you are asked if you would like to end the current programming session. Consult the VS.NET Help for additional details.

Once the Command window is activated, you can type a program expression and have Visual Studio execute the expression. A common use is to change the value of a variable while the program is running. For example, if you type:

```
i = 1
```

into the Command window, the value of i changes to 1 at that instant in the program's execution. In other words, the Command window is handy for entering values into the code that you might wish to test without having to hard-code the test value into the program.

Boundary Values

The Command window makes it easy to check values that you think might cause problems in the program. A common area for program bugs is what is called a boundary value. A *boundary value* is the first or last value in a set of values that a variable is expected to acquire during program execution. For example, if you have a **for** loop that is expected to run from 0 to 10,000, the boundary values for the loop are 0 and 10,000. However, perhaps the value 0 doesn't really cause a certain program sequence or value to appear as expected. The value 10,000 may not produce the expected results either. The Command window makes it easy to type in the boundary values and assess their impact on the program.

Although boundary values are not always the culprit for a program error, they are often a good place to start the debugging process. This is especially true in loops that involve array processing.

Beginning students always assume that loops that work on the first couple of values also work on the boundary values. The HLP First Law of Debugging is:

Assumptions are the bane of all programmers.

Never assume anything about the behavior of your code. You should always test every single line of your code, especially boundary values.

OTHER WINDOWS

As you can tell, there are a number of other windows that Visual Studio makes available to you. For example, the Call Stack window may be used to show the name of each method your program calls. If you would like to get a feel for what it would be like to write your program in Assembly language, activate the Disassembly and Registers windows. (If nothing else, looking at the Assembly language window will convince you how easy C# is compared to Assembler!)

While these other windows may be interesting and helpful in certain situations, they are not discussed here. You can always try experimenting with them, using the VS.NET Help to guide your experimentation. At this point, however, you have been exposed to enough debugging features to track down the vast majority of program bugs.

Debugging is almost an art in that it takes practice to become good at it. The best way to learn the art of debugging is to write and test a lot of program code. So, what's the solution to the bug in your program? We're not going to tell you! Your life as a programmer doesn't come with a book that spells out the solutions to all your program problems. Therefore, this is as good a place as any for you to try to figure out how to fix this program bug. Although we do provide the solution to this program, you will learn far more by solving this on your own rather than simply looking at the solution we provide. Dig in and learn! We believe you can learn a good deal from this exercise, and you will get to experience the euphoria that often accompanies eradicating a program bug!

D

SPEED-CODING TIPS AND TRICKS

When you are first learning to write computer programs, you have to learn many things all at once. You have to learn new OOP terminology, you have to learn how to read, write, test, and debug source code, and you have to learn how to use Visual Studio. If you have experience using other Windows applications, we are sure you will quickly learn the basics of VS.NET. However, VS.NET is an integrated development environment (IDE) built for professional software developers and contains many features that aren't obvious. We present some of our favorite tips and tricks in this appendix in the hope that it will help speed up your coding.

For more information, see "Editor Convenience Commands and Features" in the Visual Studio .NET Help.

GENERAL TIPS

Here is a list of useful tips:

- VS.NET is highly customizable. Sometimes too much so. For example, VS.NET windows and toolbars can be resized, moved, hidden, docked, pinned, closed, and made to float over other windows. If you accidentally move or close a toolbar or window and don't know how to get it back, VS.NET lets you reset its layout. From the VS.NET menu bar, choose Tools → Options → General → Reset Window Layout.

- Maximize code editor windows. Source code is easier to comprehend if you aren't scrolling through a small window trying to read code. For the largest possible viewing area, switch VS.NET to full-screen mode using Shift+Alt+Enter.

- Avoid using the mouse for typing code! Reaching for a mouse is always slower than keeping your hands on the keyboard. Instead, use keyboard shortcuts and access keys (Alt+*letter*) when available. For example, use Ctrl+Shift+S or Alt+F1 to save all project files.

- Use Ctrl+Tab to cycle forward and Shift+Ctrl+Tab to cycle backward through all open VS.NET windows.

- Practice touch-typing. You can type code faster if you aren't looking at the keyboard.

- Avoid changing the font used to display source code because proportional fonts make it difficult to determine if statements are correctly indented.

- When typing code in the code window, you can select chunks of text and drag them to the General tab of the toolbox. You can later drag them from the Toolbox to the code window to have that chunk of code inserted into your source code. This trick is a great way to quickly insert code you find yourself typing over and over, for example **try-catch** blocks.

USING DYNAMIC HELP

VS.NET contains a complete Help system that includes references for almost everything about Visual Studio, C#, and the .NET Framework. This is not always a good thing because sometimes it is difficult to find help for exactly what you need. One solution is to use Dynamic Help. From the VS.NET menu bar, select Help → Dynamic Help to display the Dynamic Help window, as shown in Figure D-1. The help links in the Dynamic Help window are context sensitive in that they change to match what you are doing with Visual Studio. This includes using the Forms Designer, selecting controls on the Toolbox, and typing code in the code window. The links displayed in the Dynamic Help window even change to match the code you are typing as you type it.

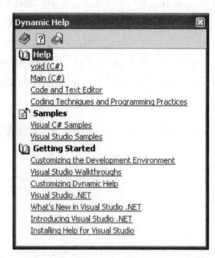

Figure D-1 Visual Studio .NET Dynamic Help window

CODE EDITOR KEYBOARD TRICKS

Here is a list of useful keyboard shortcuts:

- *Home*—Moves the cursor to the beginning of a line.
- *End*—Moves the cursor to the end of a line.
- *Ctrl+Home*—Moves the cursor to the top of a code window.
- *Ctrl+End*—Moves the cursor to the bottom of a code window.
- *Ctrl+Left, Ctrl+Right*—Move the cursor a word at a time.
- *Ctrl+Up, Ctrl+Down*—Vertically scrolls the code window up and down.
- *Ctrl+PageUp, Ctrl+PageDown*—Moves the cursor to the top or bottom of the window.
- *Shift*—Hold the Shift key while moving the cursor to select chunks of code.
- *Ctrl+X, Ctrl+C, Ctrl+V, Delete*—Cuts, copies, pastes, and deletes the selected chunk of code, respectively.
- *Ctrl+Delete*—Deletes a word at a time.
- *Ctrl+Z*—Undoes a previous action.

- *Tab*—Increases the indentation of the selected chunk of code.

- *Shift+Tab*—Decreases the indentation of selected chunk of code.

- *F12*—Navigates to the definition/declaration for the variable, method, or class under the cursor.

- *Ctrl+-*—(Ctrl+dash) Navigates back to the location before F12 was pressed.

- When the Intellisense window pops up, press the Tab or Enter key to select the highlighted method or property.

- Select a chunk of code and then press Ctrl+K+Ctrl+C to turn the selected lines into comments. This is the same as clicking [icon] on the toolbar.

- Select a chunk of code and then press Ctrl+K+Ctrl+U to uncomment the selected code. This is the same as clicking [icon] on the toolbar.

- Select code and then press Ctrl+K+Ctrl+F to correct spacing and indention on the selected code.

E

APPLICATION DEPLOYMENT

Throughout this text, you have learned how to use VS.NET and C# to develop and test Windows applications. Once you are confident that your program is free of errors, you might then want to copy it to other people's computers so they can use it.

Recall from Chapter 2 that when you give your application to others, you don't give them your program source code. Instead, you give them the executable file that is created by the C# compiler. If the other computer has the .NET Framework installed, you can simply copy the executable file to the other computer and run it. If the other computer doesn't have the .NET Framework installed, it can be downloaded and installed free using Windows Update or downloaded directly from the Microsoft Download Center (www.microsoft.com/downloads). However, a better method to get your program on other computers is to create a setup package.

You can use tools within the VS.NET IDE to set up and deploy your application. *Setup* refers to a process that allows you to package your application into an easily deployable format. *Deployment* is the process by which you install your application on other computers, usually by using a setup application. A setup package is a better method for installing your application on another computer because it can be made to automatically create shortcuts for the application and allow the application to be uninstalled using the Windows Control Panel.

The .NET documentation refers to executable files as assemblies. A .NET assembly is a comprehensive, self-describing deployment unit made up of four elements:

- *MSIL (Microsoft Intermediate Language) code*—Your C# source code is compiled into this intermediate common language that can be understood by the common language runtime (CLR).

- *Metadata*—Information about the types, methods, and other elements defined in your source code is included in the metadata.

- *Manifest*—This contains the name, version information, list of included files in the assembly, security information, and so on.

- *Nonexecutable content*—This includes supporting files and resources.

The remainder of this appendix illustrates how to create setup packages that can be used to deploy your C# applications to computers that may not have the .NET Framework installed. For illustration purposes, we have selected the Carpet Cost application from Chapter 2. The general process involves creating a deployment project that includes specific instructions for installing files and components on a target computer. During the process, you will tell VS.NET what to deploy, where to deploy it, and how to deploy it.

CREATING A SETUP PACKAGE USING VS.NET

1. Open the **Carpet Cost** C# application in Visual Studio.

2. Add a setup project to the existing solution by selecting **File** → **Add Project** → **New Project** (see Figure E-1).

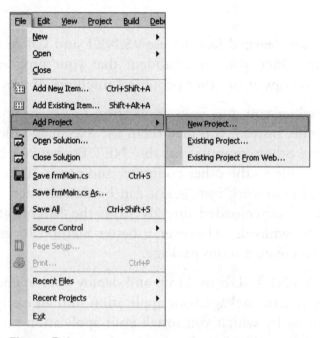

Figure E-1   Menu selections to add a setup project

3. Enter **Carpet Cost Installer** for Name and identify the location where the setup project should reside (see Figure E-2). Click **OK**.

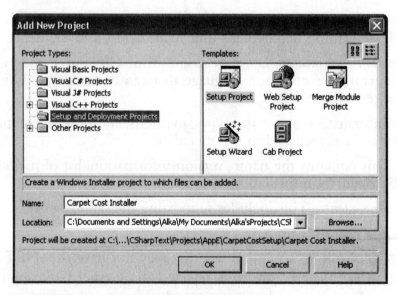

Figure E-2   Adding New Project dialog box

4. Configure the deployment-related properties for the setup project by right-clicking on the **Carpet Cost Installer** project from the Solution Explorer and selecting **Properties** (see Figure E-3).

Figure E-3   Viewing configuration properties for the setup project

5. Select **Build** from the Configuration Properties tree view (see Figure E-4).

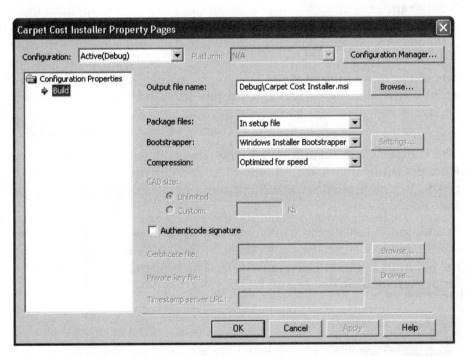

Figure E-4   Application Property Pages dialog box to modify configuration settings

6. Click the **Configuration Manager** button to bring up the Configuration Manager dialog box. If necessary, change the Active Solution Configuration setting from Debug to **Release** for both projects to create a Release build. Also check the **Build** option for the Carpet Cost Installer project (see Figure E-5). Click **Close**.

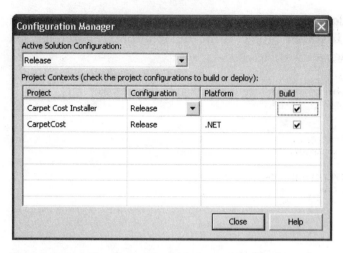

Figure E-5   Configuration Manager dialog box

7. The **Carpet Cost Installer Property Pages** dialog box allows you to select from one of three types of format to use for the packaging. Make sure that **In setup file** is selected so that all files are compressed into a single .msi file. (See Figure E-4)

8. The **Carpet Cost Installer Property Pages** dialog box allows you to also select the **Bootstrapper** setting. When you install the Carpet Cost application, Windows Installer version 1.5 must be present on the target computer. The Windows XP operating system is the first operating system that comes bundled with Windows Installer 1.5. If you deploy your application on earlier systems, you will need to include the bootstrapper as part of the installation program. If you include this option, it increases the file size by about 3 MB. You should select **Windows Installer Bootstrapper** (see Figure E-4) because it is a good idea to include the bootstrapper so that your application can be deployed on PCs with a version of Windows earlier than Windows XP.

9. The **Carpet Cost Installer Property Pages** dialog box also allows you to select a **Compression** option. You should select the **Optimized for speed** option so that the files to be compressed are installed faster. Once all options have been set, click **OK**. (See Figure E-4.)

10. In addition to setting the configuration properties, you should also set the deployment-specific properties for the deployment project. First select **Carpet Cost Installer** from the Solution Explorer (see Figure E-6). The properties are accessed through the Properties window (see Figure E-7).

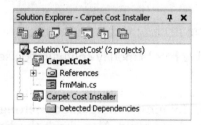

Figure E-6   Selecting setup project in the Solution Explorer

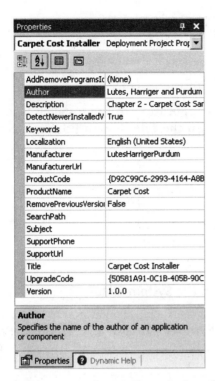

Figure E-7   Properties window for the setup project

The following list describes some of the properties you may wish to change:

- *AddRemoveProgramsIcon*—Specifies the icon to be displayed in the Add/Remove Programs dialog box on the target computer

- *Author*—Specifies the name of the application's author

- *Description*—Specifies the description that is displayed during the installation

- *DetectNewerInstalledVersion*—Specifies whether you want to check for newer versions of the application during the installation

- *Keywords*—Specifies the keywords that can be used to search for an installer on the target machine

- *Localization*—Specifies the locale for string resources and run-time user interface

- *Manufacturer*—Specifies the name of the application's manufacturer

- *ManufacturerUrl*—Specifies the URL of the manufacturer's Web site

- *ProductCode*—Specifies a unique identifier for the application

- *ProductName*—Specifies the public name of the product

- *RemovePreviousVersions*—Specifies whether you want to remove the previous versions of the application during the installation

- *SearchPath*—Specifies the path used to search for assemblies, search for files, or merge modules on the development computer

- *SupportPhone*—Specifies a phone number for application users to receive support information

- *SupportUrl*—Specifies a URL for the Web site that contains support information about the application
- *Title*—Specifies the title for the installer
- *Version*—Specifies the version number of the installer

11. Now you are ready to add the Windows application to the installer. Select **Carpet Cost Installer** in the Solution Explorer. In the File System Editor, select the **Application Folder** node (see Figure E-8).

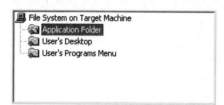

Figure E-8 Selecting Application Folder in File System Editor

12. From the Action menu, select **Add → Project Output** (see Figure E-9).

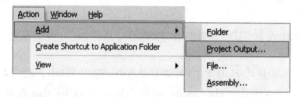

Figure E-9 Menu selections to add Project Output to the setup project

13. In the Add Project Output Group dialog box, select **CarpetCost** from the drop-down list and select **Primary output** from the grouped list (see Figure E-10). Click **OK**.

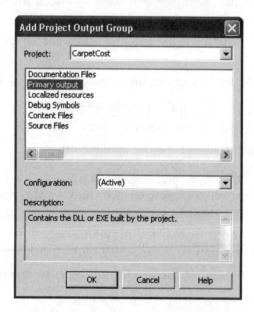

Figure E-10 Adding Project Output Group dialog box

14. To add a shortcut for the application, from the File System Editor, select the **Primary output from CarpetCost** node (see Figure E-11).

Figure E-11 Getting ready to add a shortcut for the application

15. On the **Action** menu, select **Create Shortcut to Primary output from CarpetCost** (see Figure E-12).

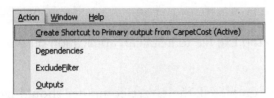

Figure E-12 Menu selection to create an application shortcut

16. This adds a Shortcut to Primary output from Carpet Cost node. Rename it **Shortcut to Carpet Cost**, and drag it to the User's Desktop folder in the left pane.

17. To add a shortcut to the application on the user's program menu, from the File System Editor, select the **Primary output from CarpetCost** node (see Figure E-11). On the Action menu, select **Create Shortcut to Primary output from CarpetCost** (see Figure E-12). Rename it **Carpet Cost**, and drag it to the User's Programs Menu folder in the left pane.

18. On the Build menu, select **Build Carpet Cost Installer** (see Figure E-13).

Figure E-13 Menu selection to build a deployment package assembly

Installing an Application

19. Now that you have all of the necessary files, you may copy the entire contents of the folder to a removable media (diskette, CD, USB drive, and so on.) Insert the removable media on the target computer, and double-click the **Setup.exe** file on the removable media to begin the installation process (see Figure E-14). The user of the target computer must have the necessary permissions to install software to prevent your installation from terminating.

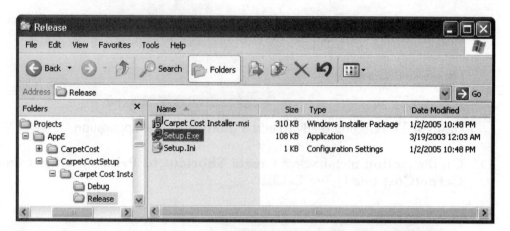

Figure E-14   Double-clicking Setup.Exe file to install an application on the target computer

20. Once the installation has been completed, the target computer should have a shortcut to the application on both the desktop and the program menu.

There are additional options that exist for creating a setup package such as adding conditional deployment and creating a custom installation dialog box. We leave it to the reader to investigate these options using other resources such as those found in the VS.NET help.

Index

Note:
- Page numbers in bold type indicate definitions.
- Page numbers in italic type indicate illustrations.
- Page numbers followed by *tbl* indicate tables.

Symbols

&& (ampersands). *See logical And* operator
* (asterisk): wildcard character, 452, 453
  See also multiplication operator
*=: assignment operator, 87, 87*tbl*
@ (at sign): verbatim string literal symbol, 69
\ (backslash): escape sequence character, 68, 68*tbl*
|| (bars). *See logical Or* operator
: (colon): class delimiter, 512, 517
, (comma): base class–interface delimiter, 517
{} (curly braces):
  statement block delimiters, **18**, 26, 36, 37, 130, 235; alignment styles, 43, 148; omitting in decision statements, 149–150
. (dot): dot operator, 9–**10**, 225
... (dots): one more step symbol (menus), 430
" (double quote):
  displaying/printing, 68
  string delimiter, 67
= (equal sign): assignment operator, **10**, 87, 87*tbl*
== (equal signs). *See equal to* operator
! (exclamation point). *See logical Not* operator
!=. *See not equal to* operator
> (greater than sign). *See greater than* operator
>= (greater than or equal to sign). *See greater than or equal to* operator
< (less than sign). *See less than* operator
<= (less than or equal to sign). *See less than or equal to* operator
− (minus sign):
  hide/collapse region button, 27, 32
  string alignment sign, 507
  See also subtraction operator
−=: assignment operator, 87, 87*tbl*
− (minus signs). *See* decrement operator
() (parentheses): overriding operator precedence with, 86
% (percent sign): wildcard character, 453
  See also modulus operator
. (period): dot operator, 9–**10**, 225
+ (plus sign): show/expand region button, 27, 32
  See also addition operator
+=: assignment operator, 87, 87*tbl*
++ (plus signs). *See* increment operator
; (semicolon): statement terminator, 18
(sharp signs): comment markers, 321

#region statement, 508–509
' (single quote):
  assigning to character variables, 68
  character delimiter, 67
  in SQL statements, 456–458
/ (slash). *See* division operator
/=: assignment operator, 87, 87*tbl*
// (slashes): comment indicator, 36
[] (square brackets): syntax element delimiters, 188, 454
~ (tilde): destructor prefix, 341

A

About form:
  communication with the main form, 426
  constructor, 427
Abs method (absolute value method), 108
Access (Microsoft):
  database engine, 448
  Design View, *451*
  non-textual value formats, 454
Access databases:
  connecting to, 462, 464
  creating programmatically, 482–484
  saving state information to, 470–475
access keys (menus), **397**–398
  indicator, *418*
access specifiers, 312–314
  in class interfaces, 314–316
  default value (on omission), 189, 312–313
  including, 189, 313
  for interfaces, 516
  internal specifier, 516
  for methods, 188–189, 190
  private. *See* **private** access specifier
  protected specifier, **500**–501
  public. *See* **public** access specifier
  types, 312
  which to use, 314–316, 317, 319, 499–500
accessor methods, 315–316
  call operations, 316
  Summary method, 514
  See also property methods
Activate method, 400
Activated event, 399
ActiveX Data Objects. *See* ADO
Add methods, **225**, 283*tbl*, 288, 336, 415
Add/Update form: communication with the main form, 427–429
AddDays method, 107
AddHours method, 107
addition operator (+), 38, 79*tbl*
  precedence, 84*tbl*, 118*tbl*, 128*tbl*
AddMinutes method, 107
AddMonths method, 107
addresses. *See* memory locations
AddYears method, 107

ADO (ActiveX Data Objects), 460, 482
ADO.NET, **459**
  database connectivity using, 459–475
  OLE DB data provider classes, 460–461
  using with C#, 461–469
ADOX, 482
  creating database files with, 482–484
aggregate functions (in SQL), **486**–487, 486*tbl*
aggregate queries, 486–487
alarm escape sequence, 68, 68*tbl*
algorithms (application logic), **18**
  bubble sort, 273
  loop example, 233–234
  sequential search, 270–271
  See also specific program examples
aligning strings, 267, 381, 507–508
Allman style brace alignment, 43, 148
Anchor property, 394–395
And operator. *See logical And* operator
application logic. *See* algorithms
Application.StartupPath
  property, 362
ApplicationException variables, 181
applications. *See* programs
arguments (of method parameters), **196**
  vs. parameters, 195–196
  passing between methods: via **out** parameters, 211–213; by reference, 198–200, 211; as reference data types, 204–206; by value, 196–198, 199
  passing to constructors, 323
  ref arguments, 199
arithmetic expressions, 84–87
  program example, 87–95
  type casting in, 82–83
  See also calculations
arithmetic operators, 38, 78–82, 79–80*tbl*
  assignment operators including, 87, 87*tbl*
  precedence, 84–86, 84*tbl*, 118*tbl*, 128*tbl*; overriding, 86
  See also arithmetic expressions
Array Demo program, 267–268
array elements, **263**
  adding, 271, 281–282
  assigning initial values to, 266
  loops with array element iterators. *See* **foreach** loops
  referencing, 266–267; last element, 268–269, 270, 271–273, 281–282
array indexes (subscripts), **264**
  determining the last valid index, 268–269, 270, 271, 281–282
Array.Copy method, 279
Array.Reverse method, **279**–280
  shortcut notation, 280
Array.Sort method, **278**–279
ArrayList class, 282, 290

`ArrayList` elements:
  accessing, 282
  adding, 283, 287, 288, 336
  displaying in `ListBox`es, 283, 288–289
  removing, 285–286, 336
`ArrayList` Index program, 283–286
`ArrayList` Sort program, 286–290
`ArrayList`s (dynamic arrays), 262, **282**–290
  adding elements to, 283, 287, 288, 336
  clearing, 287
  copying, 289
  defining, 282, 336
  filling, 283, 287
  removing elements from, 285–286, 336
  reversing, 286, 289
  `SortedList`s vs., 304
  sorting, 286–290; in descending order, 290
  vs. static arrays, 282
  usefulness, 282
  See also `ArrayList` elements
arrays, **262**–282, 290–294
  adding elements to, 271, 281–282
  copying, 278–279
  defining: single-dimensional arrays, 266;
    two-dimensional arrays, 291
  dimensionality, 265–**266**
  dynamic. *See* `ArrayList`s
  elements. *See* array elements
  initializing, 266; multidimensional arrays, 291
  jagged arrays, **290**
  `ListBox`es as, 262
  with loops, 263, 264–265
  multidimensional. *See* multidimensional arrays
  one-dimensional. *See* single-dimensional arrays
  parallel. *See* parallel arrays
  rank, **266**
  rectangular. *See* multidimensional arrays
  reversing, 279–280
  searching, 169–173
  size, 266; increasing, 281–282
  sorting, **273**; `Array.Sort` method, 278–279;
    bubble sort, **273**–278; in descending order,
    277, 279–280; parallel arrays, 278–279
  static. *See* static arrays
  terminology, 263–264
  two-dimensional. *See* multidimensional arrays
  useful properties and methods, 266–269
  usefulness, 262–263, 264–265
ArraySortMethod program, 279
ASCII character set, 67
asking users to specify filename and path, 373–377
assemblies (VS.NET), **18**–19, 44
assigning values:
  `null` value to objects, 326, 340–341
  to properties or methods, 9–11
  to variables, 64–65, 70–71; from one reference
    variable to another, 60, 61; from one
    value-type variable to another, 60; special
    characters to character variables, 67–68; string
    variables, 61, 65
assignment operator (=), **10**, 87, 87*tbl*
  vs. *equal to* operator (==), 119
  precedence, 87
assignment operators including arithmetic
  operators, 87, 87*tbl*
  precedence, 87

associativity of operators, 84
  left-associative operations, 84
  right-associative operations, 87
asterisk (*): wildcard character, 452, 453
  See also multiplication operator
at sign (@): verbatim string literal symbol, 69
attributes. *See* properties
automatically generated code:
  avoiding using, 21
  hiding, 27, 32
  inserting, 26–27
Average Item Price program:
  `btnOK_Click` event method, 171
  with general exception handler, 172, *173*
  with nested exception handlers, 174–175, *176*
AVG function (in SQL), 486*tbl*

B

`BackColor` property, 395
backslash (\): escape sequence character, 68, 68*tbl*
backspace: escape sequence, 68*tbl*
base class–interface delimiter (,), 517
base classes, **495**
  purpose, 497
  subclass "is a" relationship with, 495, 497, *497*, 512
beginning-letter case practices, 62–63, 189
`beginPrint` event method, 435, 437, 438
bell escape sequence, 68, 68*tbl*
BETWEEN...AND operators (SQL), 454
binary files:
  advantages over text files, 381–382
  displaying, 385–386
  filename extensions, 357
  hexadecimal format, **386**
  persistence (of objects) using, 381–386
  as random access files, 359
  serialization (of objects) to, 382, 383, 384–385,
    522, 524
  text file advantages over, 357–358
binary formatter objects, 522
binary operations, **85**
binary operators, **80**
binary values: by bit position, 53*tbl*
`BinaryReader` class, 382
`BinaryReader` objects, 382, 383, 384, 385
`BinaryWriter` class, 382
  `Write` method, 385
`BinaryWriter` objects, 382, 383, 384
bits, 53
blank lines (in source code), 36
block scope variables, **192**
blocks. *See* statement blocks
`Bold` property, 395, 433*tbl*
`bool` data type, **58**, 62
  See also Boolean variables
Boolean data type. *See* `bool` data type
Boolean expressions, 37, 116–129
  in decision statements, 130, 131, 148–149
  operands in, 116
  solving complex expressions using substitution,
    128–129, 141
  values. *See* Boolean values
Boolean values, 58, 62, 116
  comparing, 119
  comparing Boolean variables to, 148–149

Boolean variables:
  assigning the value of one to another, 60
  comparing to Boolean values, 148–149
bound controls, **475**, 482
  displaying database tables, 476–482
braces. *See* curly braces
`break` statements:
  in `switch` statements, 147
  in `while` loops, 245–247
breakpoints: setting, 40–41
`btnAddName_Click` event methods, 284–285,
  289, 297, 300
`btnAddNbr_Click` event method, 288
`btnCalc_Click` event methods, 55, 63–64
`btnCalculate_Click` event methods, 35, 36,
  166–167, 204–208, 210–211
`btnClose_Click` event method, 35
`btnLookupHours_Click` event method,
  271, 272
`btnNew_Click` event method, 377
`btnOK_Click` event methods, 171, 292–293
`btnOpen_Click` event method, 376
`btnProcess_Click` event methods, 240,
  245–246
`btnRemove_Click` event methods, 285–286,
  300–301
`btnReverseSortNbr_Click` event
  method, 290
`btnShow_Click` event method, 105
`btnTestFill_Click` event method, 287–289
`btnValidate_Click` event method, 143–144,
  145–146
bubble sort, **273**–276
  algorithm, 273
  Array Sort Demo program, 276–278
bucket memory jogger, 71
buffering, 363
bugs, **2**
  from implicit type conversion, 83
  See also debugging
building applications, 39, 41
buttons (button objects), **30**, 408, *408*
  adding to toolbars, 423–424
  properties and event, 408*tbl*
  See also `btn–_Click` *event methods*
`byte` data type, 53, 53*tbl*, 54
bytecode (Java), 45

C

C language, 4, 8
C++ language, 4, 8
  features not supported in C#, 7
C# compiler, 45
  memory space, *337*
C# language, 4
  advantages, 7–8
  C++ features not supported in, 7, 512
  case sensitivity, 24, 39, 62–63
  code features required, 475
  data type inheritance, 7
  disadvantage, 7
  objects in, 8–12
  portability limitation, 7
  power and flexibility, 310
  using ADO.NET with, 461–469
  variable creation in, 69–72

vs. VB.NET, 8
and VS.NET, 7
C2 argument (in `ToString` methods), 39, 264
calculations (in computer programs):
  displaying the results, 38–39, 91
  storing intermediate results, 86–87, 93–94
calculators: basic math calculator, 78, *79*
call stack (execution call stack), **159**
  catching exceptions with, 159, 182–183, 210–211
  displaying, 159
callback references, 426
calling methods, 191
  options, 216–217
  process of, 214–215
  by UI objects, 474–475
Carpet Cost application:
  processing steps, 20–21; code explanation, 35–39
  project files, 21–26
  source code, 32–34; explanation of, 35–39
  testing, 39–42
  user interface, *21*, 26–31, *31*; production values, 31*tbl*
carriage return: escape sequence, 68*tbl*
carriage return and line feed (CRLF), 360
  `Environment.NewLine` option, 227
  escape sequence, 227
  terminological origins, 361
cascading decisions (`if` statements), 132–134
case:
  beginning-letter case practices, 62–63, 189
  converting strings to uppercase/lowercase, 98–99
case sensitivity, 24, 39, 62–63
`case` statements (in `switch` statements), 147
case-insensitive compares, **124**, 140
case-sensitive compares, **124**
cast operators, **83**
casting. *See* type casting
`Catalog` objects (ADOX), 483
`catch` blocks, **163**–164, 171–173, 210–211
  generalized `catch` block, 177
  for specific exceptions, 177–179
`catch` statements: with `Exception` objects and
  exception variables, 170
catching exceptions, **158**
  with the call stack, 159, 182–183, 210–211
  Contacts List program, 371–373
  general exceptions, 169–176
  specific exceptions, 177–181
  when creating database files, 483–484
`Ceiling` method, 108
change state step (in loops), 234
  `for` loops, 241–242
  `while` loops, 236
`ChangeExtension` method
  (`System.IO.Path`), 356
`char` data type, 67
character delimiter ('), 67
character sets, 67
character variables:
  assigning special characters to, 67–68
  defining, 67
characters (text):
  comparing, 124
  converting numeric values to, 39
  converting to numeric values, 37, 38–39, 151–152
  counting the characters in strings, 97

limiting the characters that can be typed into
  text boxes, 400
sets, 67
storing single characters, 67
string character counts, 96
See also literal constants; special characters;
  strings
check step. *See* state check step (in loops)
`CheckBox` objects, 409, *409*
  properties and event, 409*tbl*
  vs. `RadioButton` objects, 420
`Checked` property, 409*tbl*, 420, 421*tbl*
child classes. *See* subclasses
circles in figures in this book, 7
class constructors. *See* constructors
class delimiter (:), 512, 517
class destructors. *See* destructors
class interfaces, **314**–316
class libraries, 12, 25
  identifying for projects, 22–23
  namespaces for. *See* namespaces
  .NET Framework Class Library, 12
  referencing in DLLs, 23
  using (accessing), 25
Class List Manager program, 230–233
class objects. *See* objects
class property methods. *See* property methods
class scope, 193
  `private` class scope variable names, 193, 271
class templates: avoiding using, 24
classes (of objects), **3**–4
  access specifiers, 312–314
  adding to projects, 310–312
  ADO.NET OLE DB data provider classes,
    460–461
  creating objects from, 8–**9**, 59, 61, 319, 321, 325
  data members. *See* data members (of classes)
  defining, 23–26; with the `private` access
    specifier, 312; with the `public` access
    specifier, 313
  hierarchical relationship between subclasses and
    base classes, 495, 497, *497*
  libraries. *See* class libraries
  naming rules and conventions, 311
  prefix for, 311
  for printing reports, 433–434
  programming-language independence, 12
  source code files, 24
  `System.IO` groups, 352
  user interfaces, **314**–316
`Clear` methods, 228, 283*tbl*, 287
clearing input text boxes, 143
clearing `ListBox`es, 228
`Click` event (click events), 34, 398, 408*tbl*, 419*tbl*
  See also `btn-_Click` *event methods*
`Close` method (`OleDbConnection`
  objects), 463
`Close` method
  (`System.Windows.Forms.Form`), 35–36,
  404*tbl*
closing:
  database connections, 463–464, 471
  files, 373
  forms, 35–36, 143, 362–363, 368, 375

CLR (common language runtime), 45, 337
  managed memory allocations, **339**
  object instantiation process, 325
  object memory reclamation process, 326, 339–340
`cls` prefix, 311
`clsContact`:
  adding (creating), 310–312
  constructors, 321–322, 323–325
  CRUD methods, 472–473
  persistence-related enhancements, 367–371
  user interface, 314–316
`clsContactsListReport`, 435–441
  beginnings, 436
`clsMember`, 497
  `clsSocial` "is a" relationship with, 512
  encapsulated properties, 497–498
  serialization code, 521–522
  source code, 501–506
`clsPhoneNumber`, 336
`clsSocial`:
  "is a" relationship with `clsMember`, 512
  source code, 513–514
Cobol programming language, 377
code:
  intermediate code, 45
  managed code, 339–340
  See also automatically generated code; source code
code checks, **140**–**141**
collection items:
  accessing, 295
  loops with collection item iterators. *See*
    `foreach` loops
collections, **224**–225, **282**
  accessing items in, 295
  items in. *See* collection items
  problems using, 304
  types, 294–295, 304
  See also `ArrayList`s; hash tables; queues;
    stacks
colon (:): class delimiter, 512, 517
`Color` class, 395
column definitions: adding to database tables,
  484–485
column headers, **434**, *434*
  creating, 438, 440
columns (in `ListView` objects): adding, 414–415
columns (in relational database tables), **449**, *449*
`Combine` method (`System.IO.Path`), 356
`ComboBox` objects, 409, *410*
  properties, 410*tbl*
comma (,): base class–interface delimiter, 517
comma-separated value (CSV) files, 359, 360
comments (on source code), **36**
  formatting guidelines, 43
  markers, 321
common language runtime. *See* CLR
communication between forms, 426–429
`Compare` method, 123–124, 416
`CompareTo` method, 276, 277
comparing:
  Boolean values, 119
  Boolean variables to Boolean values, 148–149
  characters, 124
  dates, 119–120
  `ListView` rows, 416–417
  non-numbers, 118–126

numbers (numeric values), 116–118
object references, 121–126
reference variables, 121
strings, 122–126
times, 119–120
comparison operators. *See* relational operators
compile errors. *See* syntax errors
compilers, **19**
C# compiler, 45
composite formatting (of strings), **507–508**
compound conditions in `while` loops, 247–248
computer programs. *See* programs
`Concat` method, 96
concatenation (of strings), 95–96
conditional logical operators, 126–129
conditional statements. *See* decision statements
(`if` statements)
conditions. *See* test conditions (in statements)
connection objects, 476
See also `OleDbConnection` objects
connection strings (for database connections),
464, 483
`ConnectionString` property
(`OleDbConnection` objects), 464
connectivity. *See* database connectivity
consistency checks (cross-field checks), **141–142**,
150–151
`const` keyword, 36, 65, 66
constants, **36**
defining, 36, 65–66
literals. *See* literal constants
reasons for using, 66–67
types, 65
as variables, 66–67
constructors (class constructors), **35, 321–325**
About form constructor, 427
default constructors, 321
explicit constructors, 321–323
`FileStream` constructor, 522
`frmMain` class constructor, 35, 375, 463
initializing data members in, 320–321
initializing properties in, 506
overloaded. *See* overloaded
methods/constructors
overloading, 324, 325
passing arguments to, 323
`return` statement in, 322
rules for, 322
signatures, 324; viewing with Intellisense, 325
writing, 321–322, 323
Contact Info application:
source code, 101
user interface, 99–100
Contacts List program:
adding a class to, 310–312
asking users to specify filename and path,
374–377
catching exceptions, 371–373
creating a new contacts file, 374, 377
opening a contacts file, 374, 376
querying the database, 471–472
removing contact objects, 325–326, 340–341
report design, 434–441
restoring contact objects, 369–371, 383–384

saving contact objects, 367–369
saving state information to an Access database
file, 470–475
source code, 326–335, 471–475; explanation of,
335–336; sample run, *319*
storing contact objects, 336
summary of changes, 425
user interface, 394, 424–425, *425*
`ContainsKey` method, 297–298
context menus, 419
`continue` statement, 253–254
continuous loops. *See* infinite loops
Control box, *402*
Control tray (Form Designer), 418, *419*
controls. *See* user interface objects
converting:
characters to numeric values, 37, 38–39, 151–152
data types, 82–83, 84, 336; changing property
types, 318; data conversion to and from
strings, 357; to SQL format, 458–459
list box objects to class objects, 336
numeric values to characters, 39
source code to executable files, 39
strings: catching exceptions, 164–169; to
lowercase, 98–99; to numeric values, 37,
38–39, 151–152; to uppercase, 98
`Copy` method (arrays), 279
`Copy` method (`System.IO.File`), 355
copying:
`ArrayList`s, 289
arrays, 278–279
leading characters from strings, 97–98, 381
project files, 29
reference variables, 60, 61
value-type variables, 60
COUNT function (in SQL), 486*tbl*
`Count` property, 228–229, 231, 415
counting:
characters in strings, 97
`ListBox` items, 228–229, 231, 238
zero-based counts, 96, 225
counting loops, 235–245, 247–248
See also `for` loops; `foreach` loops; `while`
loops
CPU register, 214
`Create` method (ADOX `Catalog` objects), 483
CREATE TABLE statements (in SQL), 484
`CreateDirectory` method
(`System.IO.Directory`), 353
CRLF. *See* carriage return and line feed
cross-field checks, **141–142**, 150–151
CRUD (common database actions acronym), 450
ADO.NET operations, 461, 463–469
`clsContact` methods, 472–473
.cs files, 24, 45*tbl*, 311
.csproj files, 45*tbl*
.csproj.user files, 45*tbl*
CSV files (comma-separated value files), 359, 360
curly braces ({ }):
statement block delimiters, **18**, 26, 36, 37, 130, 235;
alignment styles, 43, 148; omitting in decision
statements, 149–150
`Current` property (enumerators), 295
cursor: hourglass cursor, 430

D
.dat files, 362
data:
conversion to and from strings, 357
displaying numeric data on forms, 83
importing from fixed-width text files, 378–379,
379–381
manipulating in objects, 77–114
retrieving from database tables, 452–455
retrieving from forms, 83
saving to binary files, 357
saving to text files, 358
sequential file data organization, 359, *359*
storing. *See* storing data
suffixes, 52, 53*tbl*, 54, 56
test data, 160; Carpet Cost application, 40
textual. *See* strings
types of data used in programs, 52, 59. *See also*
data types
data adapters, 476
data declarations, 72
Data Definition Language statements. *See* DDL
statements
data definitions, 72
data hiding. *See* encapsulation
data items:
`lvalue`, 70–71, 197
"out of scope" condition, 338, 340
`rvalue`, 71, 197
See also constants; data members; variables
data members (of classes), **312**
hiding of. *See* encapsulation
initializing, 319–320; in constructors, 320–321
prefix for, 193, 271, 314
`private` members, 312–313; `public` class
user interfaces and, 500
`public` members, 313–314
See also data items; properties
data narrowing, **82**
data states in loop test conditions, 234
`for` loops, 241–242, 266
`while` loops, 235–236
data suffixes, 52, 53*tbl*, 54, 56
data type checks:
in data validation, 138–139
in exception handlers, 164–169
helper methods for, 202–203
data types:
basic types, 52, 59; vs. Access types, 452*tbl*, 484*tbl*;
vs. SQL types, 484*tbl*
cast operators, **83**
checking, 138–139, 164–169
converting (casting), 82–83, 84, 336; changing
property types, 318; data conversion to and
from strings, 357; to SQL format, 458–459
`decimal` type, 36, 39, 52, 56
floating-point types, 52, 56–57
inheritance, 7
integer types, 52–56, 53*tbl*
numeric ranges, 53, 53*tbl*, 57*tbl*
numeric types, 52–57
of operands, 87
pointer type as not supported in C#, 7
reference types, **52**, 59–61

as stored in OOP languages vs. relational databases, 469

unsigned versions, 53*tbl*, 54

value types, **52–58**

which to use, 61–62

data validation, 37–38, 84, 134–142

    btnValidate_Click event method, 143–144, 145–146

    "checking before use" style, 135

    code checks, 140–141

    cross-field (consistency) checks, 141–142, 150–151

    data type checks, 138–139

    data-substitution technique, 135–136

    existence checks, 138

    with **messageBoxOK** method, 190–191

    methods for, 159–160, 206–207

    program example, 142–146

    range checks, 139

    reasonableness checks, 139–140

    restricting input values, 135

    strategy for, 134–135

    in text box events, 135

data widening, **82**

data-substitution technique (for incorrect input values), 135–136

database connections:

    connection strings, **464**

    opening and closing, 463–464, 471

database connectivity:

    acronyms, 460

    using ADO.NET, 459–475

    using bound controls, 475–482

database engines. *See* database management systems (DBMSs)

database files: creating, 482–484

database management systems (DBMSs) (database engines), **448**

    DBMS exceptions, 466

    object-oriented systems, 470

    relational systems, 449, 469

    See also Jet DBMS

database tables:

    adding column definitions to, 484–485

    displaying, 476–482

    See also relational database tables

databases, **448**

    adding table definitions to, 484–485

    common actions acronym. *See* CRUD

    creating database files, 482–484

    relational. *See* Jet databases; relational databases

DataGrid control, 476

dataIsValid method, 206–207

dataset objects, 476

dataValidate method, 159–160

Date property, 106

dates:

    assigning to **DateTime** variables, 104

    comparing, 119–120

    data type, **58**, 62

    DayOfWeek property, 107

    displaying, 104–106

    getting from users, 106–107

    Now property, 104, 106

    parsing, 106

    storing, 104

ToShortDateString method, 105

ToString method, 58, 105

DateTime data type, **58**, 62, 469

    assigning the value of one variable to another, 60

DateTime information:

    displaying, 104–106

    getting from users, 106–107

    standard patterns, 105*tbl*

DateTime methods, 107*tbl*

DateTime properties, 106–107

DateTime variables:

    assigning dates and times to, 104

    defining, 104, 106

DateTime.IsLeapYear method, 107, 214

DateTime.Parse method, 58

DateTimePicker objects, 411, *411*

    properties, 411–412*tbl*

DayOfWeek property, 106, 107

DayOfYear property, 106

DaysInMonth method, 107

DB2 DBMS (IBM), 448, 449

DBMSs. *See* database management systems

DDL statements (Data Definition Language statements), 484

    sending to Jet databases, 485

Deactivated event, 399

debugging, 2, 26, 40–42, 160

    exception handling vs., 161

    introducing logic errors for, 94–95

    methods and, 209

    saving data to text files and, 358

    SQL statements, 464

debugging tools (VS.NET), 19

decimal data type, 36, 39, 52, 56, 62

decimal.Parse method, 37, 38–39, 151–152

decimalTypeCheck method, 202, 203, 210–211, 212–213

    with **TextBox** parameter, 204–206

    with two return values, 211–212

decision statements (**if** statements), 129–134

    cascading decisions, 132–134

    case structure alternative. *See* **switch** statements

    else branches of **if** statements within **while** loops, 247

    else keyword, 130

    indentation (indention) of, 130, 132, 133–134

    nested decisions, **131**–134

    style options, 148–150

    syntax formats, 129–131

    test conditions (Boolean expressions) in, 130, 131, 148–149

    true and false conditions format, 130–131

    true-only condition format, 130, 149–150

declaring: vs. defining, 72

declaring interfaces, 516–517

decrement operator (——), 81–82

    precedence, 84*tbl*, 118*tbl*, 128*tbl*

decrementing numeric values, 81–82

default block (**switch** statement), 147

default constructors, 321

defining: vs. declaring, 72

defining **ArrayList**s, 282

defining arrays:

    single-dimensional arrays, 266

    two-dimensional arrays, 291

defining classes, 23–26

    with the **private** access specifier, 312

    with the **public** access specifier, 313

defining constants, 36, 65–66

defining methods, 188, 189, 200

    with common names, 218–219, 323–325

    shared methods, 216

    void methods, 200

defining regions, 27

defining variables, 63–65

    character variables, 67

    DateTime variables, 104, 106

    vs. declaring variables, 72

    duplicate definition error, 69

    multivariable definition, 65

    numeric variables, 36, 63–65

    reference variables, 59

    shadowing, 193–194

    string variables, 63

    syntax, 63

Delete method (**System.IO.Directory**), 353

Delete method (**System.IO.File**), 355

DELETE statements (in SQL), 455–456, 468–469

deleting. *See* removing

Dequeue method, 300

descending order:

    sorting **ArrayList**s in, 290

    sorting arrays in, 277, 279–280

Deserialize method, 369, 370, 384–385, 522

destructor prefix (~), 341

destructors (class destructors), **341**–342

detail lines, **434**, *434*

dialog boxes:

    modal dialogs, 376, 405

    showing, 376, 404–405

DialogResult property, 428

DictionaryEntry objects, 296

digits of precision, 57

directories (folders), **349**–350

Directory methods (**System.IO**), 353–354

disks, **348**, 349

    partitions, **349**

DivideByZeroExceptions, 158, 161

    catching, 158, 177, 179–180

    error message for, *159*, *162*

    stack trace for, 159

division operator (/), 38, 79*tbl*

    precedence, 84*tbl*, 118*tbl*, 128*tbl*

division program, 54–56

DLLs (Dynamic Link Libraries): referencing class libraries in, 23

Document property, 437

dot operator (.), 9–**10**, 225

dots (...): one more step symbol (menus), 430

double data type, 57*tbl*

    vs. **float** type, 57, 62

double quote ("):

    displaying/printing, 68

    string delimiter, 67

DoubleClick event method, 398

DrawLine method, 440

DrawString method, 440

DROP TABLE statements (in SQL), 484

duplicate definition error, 69

    See also shadowing

dynamic arrays. *See* `ArrayList`s
Dynamic Link Libraries (DLLs): referencing class libraries in, 23

E
early returns, 37, 38, 129, **150–151**
`else` branches of `if` statements within `while` loops, 247
`else` keyword, 130
embedded quotes problem in SQL, 456–458
employee data programs:
  `ArrayList` program, 283–286
  hash table program, 296–299
EmployeeDatabase.mdb file, 450
`Enabled` property, 395, 398, 421*tbl*
encapsulated properties, 495, 497–498
encapsulation, 4–5, 309–345, **310**
  benefits, 310
  bound controls as a violation of, 475
  as represented in figures in this book, 7
  See also inheritance
end-of-file (EOF) condition, 371
`endPrint` event, 436, 437
`Enqueue` method, **300**
`Enter` event, 398, 399
enterprise DBMSs, 448, 449
`enum` data type, 501
enumerators, **295**
`Environment.NewLine` option, 227
EOF condition (end-of-file condition), 371
equal sign (=): assignment operator, **10**, 87, 87*tbl*
equal signs (==): *equal to* operator, **117**
equal to operator (==), **117**
  vs. assignment operator (=), 119
  precedence, 118*tbl*, 128*tbl*
error handlers. *See* exception handlers
error messages:
  design guideline, 430
  displaying, 38, 136–137
  for `DivideByZeroException`s, *159, 162*
  for `FormatException`s, *162*
  IntelliSense messages, 69
  for `OverflowException`s, *162*
  writing, 136
errors. *See* exceptions; program errors
escape sequences, 68, 68*tbl*
Essential ADO.NET text application:
  CRUD operations, 461, 463–469
  user interface, 461, *461*
event methods, **34**
  Carpet Cost application methods, 35–36
  connecting to controls (events), 34–35
events (program events), **34**
  click events, 34, 398, 408*tbl*, 419*tbl*
  common events, 398–400
  connecting event methods to, 34–35
  form event, 404*tbl*
  menu event, 419*tbl*
  `RadioButton` event, 421*tbl*
  `Timer` event, 421*tbl*
  toolbar event, 423*tbl*
`Exception` class, 158, 177
exception handlers (error handlers), **158**
  block combinations for, 164
  `catch` blocks in, 171–173, 177–179

data type checks in, 164–169
existence checks in, 165–166, 167, 174
general exception handlers, 158, 169–173
nested handlers, 174–175
syntax, 163–164; general exception handlers, 170
testing, 174, 180
`try` blocks in, 171–173, 177
when to add, 173–174
writing, 171–173
exception handling: vs. debugging, 161
  See also exception handlers
`Exception` objects, 170
exception variables, 170, 179
  `ApplicationException` variables, 181
exceptions (run-time errors), 40, **158–169**, **161**
  `catch` blocks for specific exceptions, 177–179
  catching, **158**; with the call stack, 159, 182–183, 210–211; Contacts List program, 371–373; general exceptions, 169–176; specific exceptions, 177–181; when creating database files, 483–484
  causes, 161–163
  DBMS exceptions, 466
  identifying specific exceptions, 177–178
  list in Visual Studio, 178
  response options, 163
  throwing, 181–182
  tracing, 159, 182–183
executable files (.exes), **18**–19, 45*tbl*
  converting source code to, 39
`ExecuteNonQuery` method (`OleDbCommand` objects), 464, 468
`ExecuteReader` method (`OleDbCommand` objects), 467, 486
`ExecuteScalar` method (`OleDbCommand` objects), 486
execution call stack. *See* call stack
existence checks, **138**
  in exception handlers, 165–166, 167, 174
`Exists` method (`System.IO.Directory`), 353
`Exists` method (`System.IO.File`), 355, 365
explicit casting, **83**
explicit constructors, 321–323
  reasons for using, 322–323
  writing, 321–322, 323
explicit type conversion, **83**
`expression` (in `foreach` loops), 243
Extensible Markup Language. *See* XML
extensions. *See* filename extensions
external storage, **348**

F
F suffix on numbers, 440
F1 key: getting help, 394
F5 key: debugging programs, 41
F11 key: stepping through source code, 41
factorial methods. *See* `FindFactorial` method
`false` value, 58, 62, 116
  comparing Boolean variables to, 148–149
fields (in database tables). *See* columns
fields (in sequential files), **359**
FIFO (first in, first out) order, 299
figures in this book: encapsulation as represented in, 7
file formats, 350
  sequential file formats, 359–360

File I/O, **361**
file locations: identification information, 352
`File` methods (`System.IO`), 355–356
file processing terminology, 361
file system information: displaying as much as possible, 351
`File.Exists` method, 355, 365
filename extensions, 45*tbl*, **351**
  for binary files, 357
  .txt extension, 357
filenames, 350
  asking users to specify filename and path, 373–377
files, **349**, 350–352
  basic types, 357, 359
  binary. *See* binary files
  closing, 373
  .cs files, 24, 45*tbl*, 311
  .dat files, 362
  .exe. *See* executable files
  extensions. *See* filename extensions
  filtering, 376
  formats. *See* file formats
  HTML files, 358
  names, 350. *See also* filename extensions
  naming rules and conventions, 350
  opening, 374, 376
  processing terminology, 361
  project. *See* project files
  random access files, 359
  saving object state information to. *See* persistence
  sequential files, **359**–360. *See also* text files
  source code files, 24, 45*tbl*, 311
  text. *See* text files
`FileStream` constructor: calling, 522
`FileStream` objects, 382, 383
filling `ArrayList`s, 283, 287
`Filter` property, 376
filtering files, 376
`Finalize` method, 341
`finally` blocks, 163–164, 341, 373
`FindFactorial` method (looping version), 250, 251
`FindFactorial` method (recursive version), 249–250, 251
finding substrings. *See* locating substrings
Fire Alarm Sensor program, 253–254
first in, first out (FIFO) order, 299
fixed fonts, **508**
fixed-point numeric format, 56
fixed-width records:
  reading, 379–381
  writing, 381
fixed-width text files, 359, **377**–381
  format (record layout), 377–378
  importing data from, 378–379, 379–381
  `Parse` methods, 379
  processing, 378
`float` data type, 57*tbl*
  `double` type vs., 57, 62
  number literal F suffix sign, 440
floating-point data types, 52, 56–57
  which to use, 57, 62
floating-point numbers, **56**–57
`Floor` method, 108, 231

`Focus` method, 99, 136, 188, 216, 400
folders (directories), **349**–350
`Font` class (objects), 433*tbl*
`Font` object properties, 395
`Font` property, 395
`for` loops, 241–243
 arrays with, 264–265
 `continue` statement in, 253–254
 data states in test conditions, 241–242, 266
 `FindFactorial` method, 250, 251
 vs. `foreach` loops, 244, 265
 general form, 241
 as infinite loops, 254
 and parallel arrays, 267
 referencing array elements, 266–267; last
  element, 268–269, 270, 271–273, 281–282
 Restaurant Bill Calculator application, 242–243
 as `while` loops, 242
 vs. `while` loops, 243
`for` statements, 241–242
 without parameters, 254
`foreach` loops, **243**–245, 265
 adding `ArrayList` elements, 283, 287
 arrays with, 265
 vs. `for` loops, 244, 265
 general form, 243
 and parallel arrays, 267
 Restaurant Bill Calculator application, 244–245
`ForeColor` property, 394
`Form` class, 25
Form Designer (VS.NET), 19, **26**
 adding menus, 418–419
 connecting event methods to controls
  (events), 34
 Control tray, 418, *419*
 creating the user interface, 26–32
 displaying, 27–28
 experimenting with, 394
 setting the `TabIndex` property, 397
 switching between source code and, 32
form feed escape sequence, 68*tbl*
form properties, 402–404*tbl*
 changing, 27–29
 style types, 405–406*tbl*
form styles, 405
 properties, 405–406*tbl*
format items (`MemberSummary` method):
 syntax, 507
`Format` method (strings), 507
`FormatExceptions`, 161, 164–165
 catching, 177, 179–180
 error message for, *162*
formatting guidelines (for source code), 36, 42–43
`FormBorderStyle` property, 362, 403*tbl*, 432
forms (form objects), 401
 adding menus to, 418–419
 closing, 35–36, 143, 362–363, 368, 375
 communication between, 426–429
 components, *402*
 creating, 25–26, 26–27
 design guidelines, 430
 displaying, 404
 instantiating, 404
 numeric data on: displaying, 83
 placing controls on, 30–31

 properties, 402–404*tbl*; changing, 27–29; style
  types, 405–406*tbl*
 retrieving data entered on, 83
 special effects, 431–432
 state information on: restoring, 364–365, 366;
  saving, 362–364, 366
forward slash (/). *See* division operator
forward slashes (//): comment indicator, 36
freeing object references, 325–326, 340–342
`frmMain` class:
 closing method, 362–363, 368, 375
 constructor, 35, 375, 463
 defining, 23–26
 Essential ADO.NET text application, 462–463
 persistence-related enhancements, 367–371
 serialization code, 521–522
 source code, 25, 32–34, 508–512; explanation of,
  35–39
 source code file, 24
`frmMain` object. *See* main form
`frmMain_Closing` event method, 362–363,
 368, 375

G

garbage collection, **339**–340
garbage collector (CLR), **337**
general exception handlers, 158, 169–173
 syntax, 170
general-purpose objects, 12
generated code. *See* automatically generated code
`get` method, 315–316, 498–499
 call operation, 316
`get-set` method, 499
`GetDirectories` method
 (`System.IO.Directory`), 354
`GetDirectoryName` method
 (`System.IO.Path`), 357
`GetExtension` method
 (`System.IO.Path`), 357
`GetFileName` method (`System.IO.Path`), 357
`GetFileNameWithoutExtension` method
 (`System.IO.Path`), 357
`GetFiles` method
 (`System.IO.Directory`), 354
`getKey` method, 297
getter operations, **11**, 12
getting user input:
 Carpet Cost application, 37
 Restaurant Bill Calculator application, 90
`GetUpperBound` method:
 in single-dimensional arrays, 269, 270, 281–282
 in two-dimensional arrays, 291
 verifying, 271
ghost variables (in property methods), 317
`GotFocus` event. *See* `Enter` event
graphical user interfaces. *See* GUIs
`Graphics` class (objects), 433*tbl*, 438
greater than operator (>), **117**
 precedence, 118*tbl*, 128*tbl*
greater than or equal to operator (>=), **117**
 precedence, 118*tbl*, 128*tbl*
`GroupBox` objects, 412
GUI applications: tools for creating, 7, 19
 See also Windows applications
GUIs (graphical user interfaces): benefit, 429

H

`Handled` property, 400
hard coding, **362**
hard drives, **348**
hash tables, **295**–299
 adding/removing items to/from, 297
 employee data program, 296–299
 iterating through items in, 297
 key values, 295, 296
 `SortedLists` vs., 304
`HasMorePages` property, 438
heap (heap memory), **339**
 reclamation process, 326, 339–340
`Height` property, 396
 saving and restoring, 363, 365
Help system (VS.NET), 394
helper methods, 190–191, 201
 for `ArrayLists`, 283, 288–289
 calling, 216
 for data type checks, 202–203
 `toSQL` methods, 458–459
hexadecimal format, **386**
`Hide` method, 400
hiding:
 automatically generated code, 27, 32
 of data. *See* encapsulation
 regions, 27, 32, 508–509
`HorizontalScrollbar` property, 224
`Hour` property, 58, 106
hourglass cursor, 430
HTML (Hypertext Markup Language), 350
HTML files, 358
Hypertext Markup Language (HTML), 350

I

`IComparable Interfaces`, 289
`Icon` property, 403*tbl*, 426
identifiers, **62**
 naming rules and conventions, 62–63, 63*tbl*, 189,
  311, 325
IDEs (Integrated Development Environments), **19**
 VS.NET, 7, 19–20; settings files, 45*tbl*
`IDictionaryEnumerator`s, 296, 297
`IEnumerator` objects, 301, 303
`if` statements. *See* decision statements
`Image` property, 396, 406*tbl*, 408, 408*tbl*, 423
`ImageAlign` property, 408, 408*tbl*
`ImageIndex` property, 423, 424
`ImageList` control, 422*tbl*, 423–424
`ImageList` property, 422*tbl*, 423, 424
impedance mismatch between relational databases
 and OOP, 469–**470**
implicit type conversion, **82**–83
`importFixedWidthContacts` method,
 380–381
importing data: from fixed-width text files,
 378–379, 379–381
increment operator (++), 80–81
 precedence, 84*tbl*, 118*tbl*, 128*tbl*
incrementing numeric values, 80–81
indentation (indention) (of statement blocks), 130,
 132, 133–134
indexed collections, 294
 See also `ArrayLists`

indexes:
in arrays. *See* array indexes
ListBox item indexes, **225**
IndexOf method, 96
IndexOutOfRangeException, 268, 271
infinite loops, **234**
terminating, 234
when needed, 254
inheritance, **5**, 494–500, **495**
basic concept, 494–495
benefits (advantages), 495–496, 514
data type inheritance in C#, 7
multiple inheritance as not supported in C#, 7, 512
relational databases and, 469
See also encapsulation
initialization step (in computer programs), **18**
Carpet Cost application, 35
Restaurant Bill Calculator application, 89–90
Student Data Validation application, 143
initialization step (in loops). *See* state initialization step (in loops)
InitializeComponent method, 35
initializing:
arrays, 266; multidimensional arrays, 291
controls, 35
data members, 319–320; in constructors, 320–321
properties: in constructors, 506
variables, 64–65
inline code: vs. methods, 202, 208–210, 213–214
See also source code
input. *See* data validation; getting user input
input step in computer programs, **18**
Carpet Cost application, 37–38
Restaurant Bill Calculator application, 90
Insert method (**ArrayList** items), 283*tbl*
Insert method (**ListBox** items), **225**
Insert method (substrings), 102–103
INSERT statements (in SQL), 455, 464
inserting:
automatically generated code, 26–27
database rows, 455, 464–466
substrings, 102–103
instance methods, **216**
instances (of objects), 3, **9**
instantiation (of objects), 8–9, 59, 61, 319, 321, 325
forms, 404
Instruction Register (CPU), 214
int data type, 53*tbl*, 62
int.Parse method, 55, 365
integer data types, 52–56, 53*tbl*
which to use, 62
integers:
data types, 52–56, 53*tbl*
sample program using, 54–56
Integrated Development Environments. *See* IDEs
IntelliSense feature (VS.NET), 25
error messages, 69
red squiggly lines, 40, 69
signature display, 325
interfaces, **515**–521
access specifiers for, 516
advantages, 519
class interfaces, **314**–316

declaring, 516–517
IComparable Interfaces, 289
implementing, 516–519
with properties and methods, 519–521
in subclasses, 515–516
syntax, 516
See also user interfaces (UIs)
interform communication, 426–429
intermediate code, 45
intermediate results: storing, 86–87, 93–94
intermediate variables: storing intermediate results in, 86–87, 93–94
internal access specifier, 516
introducing errors for debugging, 94–95
intTypeCheck method, 202
"is a" relationship of subclasses with base classes, 495, 497, *497*, 512
IsLeapYear method, 107, 214
Italic property, 395, 433*tbl*
Items property, 224, 410*tbl*
Items.Add method, **225**
Items.Clear method, 228
Items.Count property, 228–229, 231, 415
Items.Insert method, **225**
Items.Remove method, 227–228, 415–416
Items.RemoveAt method, 227–228
iteration, **234**
iterationVariable (in **foreach** loops), 243–244

J

jagged arrays, **290**
Java language, 4, 8
bytecode, 45
Java Virtual Machine (JVM), 45
Jet databases:
creating dynamically, 482–484
deleting records from, 469
inserting rows into, 464–466
sending DDL statements to, 485
SQL syntax, 454
updating records in, 468
Jet DBMS (Microsoft), 448, 449
connecting to, 462, 464
non-textual value formats, 454
JIT compiling (Just In Time compiling), 45
Just In Time (JIT) compiling, 45
JVM (Java Virtual Machine), 45

K

K&R style brace alignment, 43, 148
key values (in hash tables), 295, 296
KeyDown event, 399
keyed collections, 295
See also hash tables
KeyPress event, 399–400
KeyUp event, 399

L

labels (label objects), **30**, 406
design guideline, 430
properties, 406*tbl*
languages. *See* OOP languages; programming languages
last in, first out (LIFO) processing order, 302
LastIndexOf method, 102

LeapYear method, 214–215
Leave event, 398–399
Left property, 396
saving and restoring, 363, 365
left-associative operations, 84
Length property (arrays):
referencing array elements, 266–267; last element, 268–269, 270, 271–273, 281–282
Length property (strings), 97
less than operator (<), **117**
precedence, 118*tbl*, 128*tbl*
less than or equal to operator (<=), 37, **117**
precedence, 118*tbl*, 128*tbl*
lifetime (of variables), **64**
LIFO (last in, first out) processing order, 302
Like operator (SQL), 453
line numbers: displaying in the VS.NET text editor, 24
linefeed (newline): escape sequence, 68*tbl*
See also carriage return and line feed
ListBox collections: access syntax, 225
ListBox items:
adding, 225–226
counting, 228–229, 231, 238
determining the items selected, 226–227
indexes, **225**
removing, 227–228
selecting, 229–230
sorting, 229; numbers, 277
ListBoxes (list box objects), **224**–233, *224*, 282
as arrays, 262
Class List Manager program, 230–233
clearing, 228
converting to class objects, 336
displaying **ArrayList** elements in, 283, 288–289
items. *See* **ListBox** items
vs. ListView objects, 412–413
ListView objects vs., 412–413
multiplication table display program, 251–253
usefulness, 224–225
ListView objects, 412–413, *413*
adding columns, 414–415
adding rows, 415
comparing and sorting rows, 416–417
determining the rows selected, 415
vs. **ListBox**es, 412–413
properties, 413–414*tbl*
removing rows, 415–416
ListViewItemSorter property, 414*tbl*, 416
literal constants (literals), **65**
number literal F suffix, 440
verbatim string literals, 68–69
local scope variables, **64**, **192**–193
memory location, 337–338
locating substrings, 96
last match, 102
and parsing, 97–98
Location property, 412
Locked property, 396
locking controls, 396
logic errors, 40, 160
introducing for debugging, 94–95
logical And operator (&&), 126–127
vs. *logical Or* operator, 141
precedence, 128*tbl*

ogical Not operator (!), 127–128
  avoiding using, 128
  precedence, 128*tbl*
ogical Or operator (| |), 127
  vs. *logical And* operator, 141
  precedence, 128*tbl*
ong data type, 53*tbl*, 54
oop body, **235**
oop counter, 235, 236
oop statement blocks, **235**
oops, 233–248, 251–254
  with array or collection element iterators. *See*
    foreach loops
  arrays with, 263, 264–265
  basic algorithm, 233–234
  break statement in, 245–247
  continue statement in, 253–254
  data states in test conditions, 234; **for** loops,
    241–242, 266; **while** loops, 235–236
  infinite loops, 234; when needed, 254
  nested loops, **251–253**
  terminating, 245–247
  well-behaved loop characteristics (conditions),
    234–235
  See also **for** loops; **foreach** loops; **while**
    loops
ostFocus event. *See* **Leave** event
owercase: converting strings to, 98–99
value (of data items), 70–71, 197, 338

M

l prefix, 193, 271, 314, 315
l suffix, 56
L suffix, 56
magic numbers, 66–67, 270
Mail Ballot button click event code, 519
main form (**frmMain** object):
  communication with the About form, 426
  communication with the Add/Update form,
    427–429
Main method, 26, 41
managed code, 339–340
managed execution, **337**
managed heap, 337, *337*, 339–340
managed memory allocations, **339**
manipulating data in objects, 77–114
manipulating strings, 95–104
  methods, 95–99, 102–104
  program example, 99–102
mapping state information to relational database
  tables, 470–475
math calculator, 78, *79*
Math class:
  methods, 57, 108–109, 108*tbl*, 231
  PI property, 107
mathematical expressions, **78**
  See also arithmetic expressions
MAX function (in SQL), 486*tbl*
Max method, 108
mdb filename extension, 448
Membership program: input data, 496*tbl*
MemberSummary method, 507
  code, 505, 514
memory leaks: elimination of, 337

memory locations, 338
  local scope variables, 337–338
  lvalue, 70–71, 197, 338
  references, 59
  swapping the contents of two locations, 274
  See also stack (program stack)
memory management, 337
  garbage collection, **339–340**
  heap memory, **339**
  stack memory, **338**
memory map, *337*
memory reclamation (from the heap), 326,
  339–340
menus (menu objects), 418–419
  adding to forms, 418–419
  properties and event, 419*tbl*
message boxes:
  design guideline, 430
  display method, 190–191
  displaying, 38, 136–137
  source code, 137
  styles, 137
Message property: exception handling use,
  170, 179
messageBoxOK method, 190–191
  as **public** vs. **private**, 428
method body, **189**
method overhead, **213–215**, 338
method overloading. *See* overloading
  methods/constructors
method overriding, 514–515
method parameters. *See* parameters
method signatures. *See* signatures
method statement blocks, **189**
methods (of objects), **3**, 187–222, **188**
  access specifiers for, 188–189, 190
  arguments, **196**; vs. parameters, 195–196
  assigning values to, 9–11
  beginning-letter case, 189
  calling, 191; options, 216–217; process of,
    214–215; by UI objects, 474–475
  catching exceptions in, 159, 182–183, 210–211
  and code changes, 209–210
  common methods, 400–401
  communication between, 192–201
  for data validation, 159–160, 206–207
  DateTime methods, 107*tbl*
  and debugging, 209
  defining, 188, 189, 200; with common names,
    218–219, 323–325; shared methods, 216;
    void methods, 200
  event methods, **34**, 35–36; connecting to
    controls (events), 34–35
  factorial methods. *See* **FindFactorial**
    method
  File methods (**System.IO**), 355–356
  form method, 404*tbl*
  good method characteristics, 201–202
  helper methods, 190–191, 201; for
    ArrayLists, 283, 288–289; calling, 216; for
    data type checks, 202–203; **toSQL** methods,
    458–459
  hiding of. *See* encapsulation
  inheritance of, 5
  vs. inline code, 202, 208–210, 213–214

instance methods, **216**
naming rules and conventions, 189
overhead, **213–215**, 338
overloaded. *See* overloaded
  methods/constructors
overloading, **218–219**, 324, 325
overriding, 514–515
parameters, **189**, 194–200, **196**; vs. arguments,
  195–196
passing arguments between: via **out** parameters,
  211–213; by reference, 198–200, 211; as
  reference data types, 204–206; by value,
  196–198, 199
Path methods (**System.IO**), 356–357
private methods, 188, 189, 190, 312–313
public methods, 188, 189, 313–314, 319,
  428, 499
returnDatatypes, 188
returning values with, 200–201; more than one
  value, 211–213
shared methods, **216–217**
signatures, **217–218**, 324; viewing with
  Intellisense, 325
static methods, **216–217**
string methods, 95–99, 102–104
syntax, 188
Timer methods, 421*tbl*
usefulness, 188
when to use, 208–210
  See also constructors; *and specific methods*
Microsoft Access. *See* Access (Microsoft)
Microsoft ADO Ext. 2000.7 for DDL and
  Security. *See* ADOX
Microsoft Intermediate Language (MSIL), 45
Microsoft Windows. *See* Windows (Microsoft)
MilliSecond property, 106
MIN function (in SQL), 486*tbl*
Min method, 108
minus sign (–):
  hide/collapse region button, 27, 32
  string alignment sign, 507
  See also subtraction operator
minus signs (—). *See* decrement operator
Minute property, 106
modal dialogs, 376, 401, 405
modulus operator (%), 80*tbl*
  precedence, 84*tbl*, 118*tbl*, 128*tbl*
monetary values, 56
Month property, 106
mouse pointer:
  click events, 34, 398, 408*tbl*, 419*tbl*. *See also*
    btn–_Click *event methods*
  displaying the values (contents) of variables, 41
Move method (**System.IO.Directory**), 354
Move method (**System.IO.File**), 356
MoveNext method (enumerators), 295
MP3 format, 350
msadox.dll file, 482
MSIL (Microsoft Intermediate Language), 45
multidimensional arrays, 290–294
  defining two-dimensional arrays, 291
  initializing, 291
  jagged arrays, **290**
  processing the elements of, 291–292
  students program, 291–293

Tip Percent Table program, 293–294
usefulness, 293
MultiExtended property, 230
MultiLine property, 226, 407*tbl*
multiple inheritance: as not supported in C#, 7, 512
multiplication operator (*), 38, 79*tbl*
precedence, 84*tbl*, 118*tbl*, 128*tbl*
multiplication table display program, 251–253
MultiSimple property, 230
multivariable definition, 65
MySQL DBMS (open-source), 448, 449

N

Name property, 30, 396, 406*tbl*, 408*tbl*, 411*tbl*, 421*tbl*, 422*tbl*
named constants (symbolic constants), **65**
defining, 65–66
names:
in arrays: sorting, 276–278
of identifiers: rules and conventions, 62–63, 63*tbl*, 189, 311, 325
namespaces (for class libraries), 12, **25**
System.Collections, 282, 294–295
System.Collections.Specialized, 295
System.Data.OleDb, 460, 483
System.Drawing, 25, 395, 433, 436
System.Drawing.Printing, 436
System.Globalization, 151–152
System.IO. *See* **System.IO** namespace
System.Windows.Forms, 12, 25; controls in, 29–30
naming rules and conventions:
for files, 350
for identifiers, 62–63, 63*tbl*, 189, 311, 325
NaN answer ("not a number" answer), 109
nested decisions (**if** statements), **131–134**
nested exception handlers, 174–175
nested loops, **251–253**
in multidimensional arrays, 291–292
nested **try-catch** blocks, 174–175
.NET Framework Class Library, 12, 361
string methods, 102–104
.NET languages, 12
new operator, 9, 61, 266
method overriding with, 515
newline (linefeed): escape sequence, 68*tbl*
See also carriage return and line feed
non-volatile memory, **348**
"not a number" (**NaN**) answer, 109
not equal to operator (!=), **118**
precedence, 118*tbl*, 128*tbl*
Not operator. *See* logical *Not* operator
Notepad (Windows): displaying text files, 359–360, 369
Now property, 104, 106
null statements, 326
null value, **64**, 319, 469
assigning to objects, 326, 340–341
escape sequence, 68*tbl*
number literals: F suffix on, 440
See also characters
numbers. *See* number literals; numeric values
NumberStyles, 151–152

numeric data types, 52–57
assigning the value of one variable to another, 60
ranges, 53, 53*tbl*, 57*tbl*
which to use, 62
numeric values (numbers):
binary values, 53*tbl*
comparing, 116–118
converting characters to, 37, 38–39, 151–152
converting strings to, 37, 38–39, 151–152
converting to characters, 39
decrementing, 81–82
displaying calculated results, 38–39
displaying on forms, 83
incrementing, 80–81
magic numbers, 66–67, 270
monetary values, 56
precision, 57
See also numeric data types; numeric variables
numeric variables:
assigning the value of one to another, 60
initial values, 64
See also numeric values
NumericUpDown objects, 419–420, *420*
properties, 420*tbl*

O

object instantiation, 8–**9**, 59, 61
Object Linking and Embedding Database. *See* OLE DB
Object list (Properties window), 29
object references:
comparing, 121–126
freeing, 325–326, 340–342
Object.Finalize method, 341
object-oriented database management systems, 470
object-oriented programming. *See* OOP
objects (class objects), **3**
connection objects, 476. *See also* **OleDbConnection** objects
converting list box objects to, 336
creating (instantiation of), 8–**9**, 59, 61, 319, 321, 325
dataset objects, 476
general-purpose objects, 12
hiding of data in. *See* encapsulation
inheritance capability, 5
initial state, 319; changing, 319–321
instances, 3, **9**
manipulating data in, 77–114
memory reclamation process, 326, 339–340
memory space, 339
passing arguments between methods as references to, 204–206
persistence of. *See* persistence
polymorphism, **5**; in method overriding, 515
for printing reports, 433–434
removing, 325–326, 340–342
serialization of. *See* serialization
states. *See* states (of objects)
storing data in, 51–75
StreamWriter objects, 363
See also specific objects
OK message boxes: source code, 137
OLE DB (Object Linking and Embedding Database), 459–460
ADO.NET data provider classes, 460–461

OleDbCommand objects, 461, 464, 466, 467
ExecuteNonQuery method, 464, 468
ExecuteReader method, 467, 486
ExecuteScalar method, 486
OleDbConnection objects, 460, 462
Close method, 463
ConnectionString property, 464
Open method, 463
OleDbDataReader objects, 461, 466, 467
Read method, 467
one more step symbol (menus) (...), 430
OOP (object-oriented programming), **2**
basic concepts, 2, 4–5
classes. *See* classes (of objects)
classes in: *See also* classes (of objects)
goals: vs. relational database goals, 469
historical origins, 2
impedence mismatch between relational databases and, 469–**470**
introduction to, 1–15
objects in, 3. *See also* objects (class objects)
OOP languages, 2, 4, 8
common characteristics (OOP trilogy), 4–5
data types as stored by, 469
.NET languages, 12
See also C# language
OOP trilogy, 4–5
Opacity property, 431–432
Open method (**OleDbConnection** objects), 463
open-source enterprise DBMS, 448
OpenFileDialog class, 373
objects, 376
opening:
database connections, 463–464, 471
files, 374, 376
operands, **78**
in Boolean expressions, 116
data types, 87
type conversion, 55, 82–83
operator precedence, 84–86, 84*tbl*, 87, 118*tbl*, 128*tbl*
overriding, 86
operators, **78**
arithmetic. *See* arithmetic operators
assignment operator (=), **10**, 87, 87*tbl*
assignment operators including arithmetic operators, 87, 87*tbl*
associativity, 84, 87
cast operators, **83**
comparison. *See* relational operators
conditional logical operators, 126–129
new operator, 9, 61, 266; method overriding with, 515
precedence, 84–86, 84*tbl*, 87, 118*tbl*, 128*tbl*; overriding, 86
relational. *See* relational operators
SQL operators, 453*tbl*
typing, 84
Or operator. *See* logical *Or* operator
Oracle DBMS, 448, 449
ORDER BY clauses (in SQL SELECT statements), 454–455
ordered collections, 295
See also queues; stacks
"out of scope" condition (data items), 338, 340

out parameters, **211**
  passing arguments between methods via, 211–213
output step in computer programs, **18**
  Carpet Cost application, 38–39
  Restaurant Bill Calculator application, 91
overflow errors, **84**
OverflowExceptions, 161
  catching, 177
  error message for, *162*
overloaded methods/constructors, 323–325
  signatures, 218, 324; viewing with Intellisense, 325
overloading methods/constructors, **218**–219, 324
  usefulness, 325
overriding methods. *See* method overriding
overriding operator precedence, 86

P

PadLeft method, 267
PadRight method, 267, 381
page footers, **434**, *434*
  creating, 438, 440
page headers, **434**, *434*
  creating, 438, 440
PageSettings property, 438
PageUnit property, 438
parallel arrays, **267**
  adding elements to, 271
  Array Demo program, 267–268
  for loops and, 267
  foreach loops and, 267
  sorting, 278–279
  two-dimensional arrays as, 291
Parameter Details program, 194–195
parameter lists, **189**
  in method/constructor signatures, 218, 324;
    viewing with Intellisense, 325
parameters (of methods), **189**, 194–200, **196**
  vs. arguments, 195–196
parent classes. *See* base classes
parentheses (()): overriding operator precedence
    with, 86
Parse methods, 83, 151, 203
  dates, 58
  decimals, 37, 38–39, 151–152
  as existence checks, 165–166, 167
  fixed-width text files, 379
  integers, 55, 365
  times, 58
  try-catch blocks for, 399
parsing, 97–98, **369**
  dates, 58, 106
  See also Parse methods
partitions (of disks), **349**
passing arguments:
  between methods: via out parameters,
    211–213; by reference, 198–200, 211; as
    reference data types, 204–206; by value,
    196–198, 199
  to constructors, 323
Path methods (System.IO), 356–357
paths:
  asking users to specify filename and path, 373–377
  determining application paths, 362
  hard coded paths, 362
PeekChar method, 383

Pen class (objects), 433*tbl*, 437
percent sign (%): wildcard character, 453
  See also modulus operator
period (.): dot operator, 9–**10**, 225
persistence (of objects), **348**, 350
  asking users to specify filename and path,
    373–377
  restoring state information, 364–365, 366
  saving state information, 362–364; to Access
    databases, 470–475
  using binary data files, 381–386
  using sequential text files, 361–366; program
    example, 366–373
  See also serialization
Person objects, 6–7, 8
  creating, 8–9
PI property, 107
plus sign (+): show/expand region button, 27, 32
  See also addition operator
plus signs (++). *See* increment operator
pointer data type: as not supported in C#, 7
polymorphism, **5**
  in method overriding, 515
  relational databases and, 469
Pop method, **303**
Pop-up menus. *See* context menus
postfix decrement expression, **81**
postfix increment expression, **80**
Pow method (power method), 108
precedence of operators, 84–86, 84*tbl*, 87, 118*tbl*,
    128*tbl*
precision of numbers, 57
prefix decrement expression, **81**
prefixes:
  ~ (tilde), 341
  cls prefix, 311
  destructor prefix (~), 341
  m prefix, 193, 271, 314
  txt prefix, 37
primary key (unique identifier) (in relational
    database tables), *449*, **450**, 465
Print method, 435, 437
printDetailLine method, 438, 440
PrintDocument class (objects), 433*tbl*, 435,
    437, 439
printing reports, 432–441
  classes (objects) for, 433–434
printPage event method, 435–436, 437,
    438, 439
PrintPageEventsArgs class (objects),
    438, 439
printPageHeadersAndFooters method,
    438, 440
PrintPreviewDialog class (objects),
    434*tbl*, 437
PrintReport method, 435, 437
PrintReportWithPreview method,
    435, 437
private access specifier, 188, 189, 190,
    312–313, 500
  in class interfaces, 314–316
  using the public access specifier vs., 314–316,
    317, 319, 499–500
private class scope variable names, 193, 271
private data members, 312–313
  public class user interfaces and, 500

private helper methods. *See* helper methods
private methods, 188, 189, 190, 312–313
  beginning-letter case, 189
  See also helper methods
private properties, 312–313
procedures. *See* methods
processing steps in computer programs, **18**
  Carpet Cost application, 20–21
  processing step proper. *See* calculations
program analysis, **496**
program comments. *See* comments
program design, **497**
program errors:
  duplicate definition error, 69
  logic errors, 40, 160; introducing for debugging,
    94–95
  overflow errors, **84**
  run-time errors. *See* exceptions
  semantic errors, 160
  syntax errors (compile errors), **18**, 39, 160
  types, 39–40, 160–161
  underflow errors, **84**
program events. *See* events
program logic. *See* algorithms
program results:
  displaying calculated values, 38–39, 91
  storing intermediate results, 86–87, 93–94
program stack. *See* stack
program statements. *See* statements
programming: discipline of, 1
programming languages:
  faded languages, 1
  OOP. *See* OOP languages
  RAD languages, 7
  syntax, **18**
programs (applications), **18**
  ArraySortMethod program, 279
  building, 39, 41
  calculations in. *See* calculations
  code. *See* source code
  creating a simple application, 17–49
  debugging. *See* debugging
  division program, 54–56
  Essential ADO.NET text application, 461,
    463–469
  GUI applications tools, 7, 19
  interfaces. *See* interfaces; user interfaces
  logic. *See* algorithms
  memory space, *337*
  path determination, 362
  processing steps, 18; Carpet Cost application
    steps, 20–21
  results. *See* program results
  starting (running), 26, 41
  Student Data Validation application, 142–146
  testing, 39–42, 91–92, 94, 146
  VS.NET file type, 45*tbl*
  See also Average Item Price program; Carpet
    Cost application; Contacts List program;
    Restaurant Bill Calculator application;
    Windows applications
project files (VS.NET), **44**
  adding/removing, 32
  copying, 29
  creating, 21–26
  creating templates from, 29

file types, 44, 45*tbl*
  renaming, 32
project properties: setting, 22
project templates:
  avoiding using, 21
  creating, 29
projects:
  adding classes to, 310–312
  class library identification, 22–23
  property settings, 22
  solutions, **44**
  type selection, 21
  Windows application setting, 22
  See also project files
properties (of objects), **3**
  changing, 28–29
  changing data types for, 318
  changing the defaults as not advisable, 395
  CheckBox properties, 409*tbl*
  ComboBox properties, 410*tbl*
  common properties, 394–398
  creating from existing properties, 318–319
  `DateTime` properties, 106–107
  DateTimePicker properties, 411–412*tbl*
  designing read-/write-only properties, 317–318
  encapsulated properties, 495, 497–498
  executing code on accessing, 318
  form properties, 402–404*tbl*
  hiding of. *See* encapsulation
  inheritance of, 5
  initializing: in constructors, 506
  label properties, 406*tbl*
  `ListBox` properties, 224–230
  ListView properties, 413–414*tbl*, 414–416
  managing: `ListBox` program example, 230–233
  menu properties, 419*tbl*
  `NumericUpDown` properties, 420*tbl*
  passing between methods in reference data
    types, 204–206
  `private` properties, 312–313
  `public` properties, 313–314, 319
  `RadioButton` properties, 421*tbl*
  setting, 9–11, 394; in the Properties window, 29;
    with the `set` method, 315–316, 316–317, 499
  `StatusBar` properties, 424*tbl*
  `StatusBarPanel` properties, 424*tbl*
  text box properties, 407–408*tbl*
  `Timer` properties, 421*tbl*
  toolbar properties, 422*tbl*
  See also specific properties
properties (of projects), 22
Properties list (Properties window), 29
Properties window, **28**, *28*
  changing properties, 28–29
  connecting event methods to controls (events),
    34–35
  elements, 28–29
  experimenting with, 394
  setting properties, 29
property methods (of classes), **315**–316, 500
  ghost variables in, 317
  usefulness, 317
  See also accessor methods
proportional fonts, **508**
`protected` access specifier, **500**–501
  benefits, 501

`public` access specifier, 188, 189, 313–314,
    499, 500
  in class interfaces, 314–316
  for property methods, 315
  using `public` class user interfaces vs., 317,
    499–500
  using the `private` access specifier vs.,
    314–316, 317, 319, 499–500
`public` class user interfaces, **314**–316
  and `private` data members, 500
  using the `public` access specifier vs., 317,
    499–500
`public` data members, 313–314
`public` methods, 188, 189, 313–314, 319, 428,
    499
  beginning-letter case, 189
`public` properties, 313–314, 319
`public` property methods. *See* property methods
`public static void Main` method,
    26, 41
`public` user interfaces. *See* `public` class user
    interfaces
`Push` method, **303**

Q

querying relational databases, 452–455, 466–467
  with SQL aggregate functions, 486–487
querying the Contacts List program database,
    471–472
queues, **299**–302
  adding/removing items to/from, 300–301
  iterating through items in, 301

R

\r\n. *See* carriage return and line feed
RAD languages (Rapid Application Development
    languages), 7
`RadioButton` objects, 420–421, *421*
  properties and event, 421*tbl*
RAM (random access memory), **348**
random access files, 359
random access memory (RAM), **348**
range checks, **139**
Rapid Application Development (RAD)
    languages, 7
RDBMSs (relational database management
    systems), **449**, 469
`Read` method (`OleDbDataReader` objects), 467
read-only properties: designing, 317–318
reading:
  fixed-width records, 379–381
  sequential text files, 361
`ReadLine` method (`StreamWriter` class), 365
`ReadOnly` property, 30, 408*tbl*
reasonableness checks, **139**–140
records (in database tables). *See* rows
records (in sequential files), **359**
  2-byte CRLF end sequence, 360, 361
  layout of fixed-width text files, 377–378
rectangular arrays. *See* multidimensional arrays
recursion, **249**–251
red squiggly lines (IntelliSense), 40, 69
redundancy issue (source code), 469
`ref` arguments, 199
`ref` keyword, 198, 204, 206

reference: passing arguments between methods by,
    198–200, 211
  See also referencing
reference data types, **52**, 59–61
  assigning the value of one variable to another,
    60, 61
  passing arguments between methods as, 204–206
reference variables:
  assigning the value of one to another, 60, 61
  comparing, 121
  defining, 59
  exception variables, 170, 177, 181
referencing: array elements, 266–267; last element,
    268–269, 270, 271–273, 281–282
  See also reference
`Refresh` method, 400–401
`region` statement, 508–509
regions (of source code), **27**
  defining, 27
  hiding/showing, 27, 32, 508–509
relational database management systems
    (RDBMSs), **449**, 469
relational database tables:
  inserting rows, 455, 464–466
  mapping state information to, 470–475
  retrieving rows, 452–455, 466–467
relational databases, 448–450, **449**
  data types as stored in, 469
  goals: vs. OOP goals, 469
  impedence mismatch between OOP and,
    469–**470**
  querying, 452–455, 466–467; with SQL
    aggregate functions, 486–487
  terminology, 449–450
  See also Access databases; Jet databases
relational expressions, 118, 118*tbl*
relational operators (comparison operators), **116**
  for comparing Boolean values, 119
  for comparing dates, 120
  for comparing numbers, 116–118
  for comparing reference variables, 121
  for comparing strings, 122
  for comparing times, 120
  precedence, 118, 118*tbl*, 128*tbl*
`Remove` methods, 103, 227–228, 283*tbl*, 336,
    415–416
`RemoveAt` methods, 227–228, 283*tbl*
removing (deleting):
  `ArrayList` elements, 285–286, 336
  contact objects (Contacts List program),
    325–326, 340–341
  database rows, 455–456
  hash tables, 297
  leading and ending spaces from strings, 103
  `ListBox` items, 227–228
  ListView rows, 415–416
  objects, 325–326, 340–342
  project files, 32
  queue items, 300–301
  stack items, 303
  substrings, 103
`Replace` method, 103–104, 458
replacing substrings, 103–104
reports:
  Contacts List Report design, 434–441
  designing, 434

planning the code, 434–435

printing, 432–441

Reset method (enumerators), 295

resource files:VS.NET file type, 44, 45*tbl*

Restaurant Bill Calculator application:

with data type checks, 166–169; and helper methods for, 202–203

with a for loop, 242–243

with a foreach loop, 244–245

improving, 93–94

source code, 92–93; explanation of, 89–91

with specific exception handlers, 179–181

testing, 91–92, 94

user interface, 88–95

with a while loop, 236–238

restoreContacts method, 370, 371–372, 383–384

restoring contact objects (Contacts List program), 369–371, 383–384

restoring state information, 364–365, 366

results. *See* program results

resx files, 44, 45*tbl*

retrieving data:

from forms, 83

from relational database tables, 452–455, 466–467

return statement, 37, 38, 129

in constructors, 322

early returns, **150**–151

returnDatatypes (of methods), 188

returning values with methods, 200–201

more than one value, 211–213

Reverse method (ArrayLists), 286, 289

Reverse method (arrays), **279**–280

shortcut notation, 280

reversing ArrayLists, 286, 289

reversing arrays, 279–280

right-associative operations, 87

robust data validation. *See* data validation

Round methods, 38, 108

rows (in ListView objects):

adding/removing, 415–416

comparing and sorting, 416–417

rows (in relational database tables), **449**, *449*

deleting, 455–456

getting column values from, 467

inserting, 455, 464–466

retrieving, 452–455, 466–467

updating, 455

run-time errors. *See* exceptions

running applications, 26, 41

rvalue (of data items), 71, 197

S

saveContacts method, 367, 371–372, 382–383

SaveFileDialog class, 373, 377

saving:

contact objects (Contacts List program), 367–369

data: to binary files, 357; to text files, 358

state information, 362–364; to an Access database file, 470–475. *See also* persistence

sbyte data type, 53*tbl*, 54

scientific notation, 57

scope, **192**

types (levels), 69, 192–193

which to use, 193, 194

screen resolution: standard value, 430

scrollbars: HorizontalScrollbar property, 224

searching arrays, 169–173

Second property, 106

SELECT statements (in SQL), 452, 466

ORDER BY clauses in, 454–455

using aggregate functions, 486

WHERE clauses in, 452–454, 468–469

SelectedIndex property, 226, 230, 284

SelectedItem property, 226

SelectedItems.Count property, 415

selecting ListBox items, 229–230

SelectionMode property, 229–230

semantic errors, 160

semicolon (;): statement terminator, 18

SendBallot method, 516, 518

Separator bar (menus), *418*

sequential files (sequential access files), **359**–360

data organization in, 359, *359*

formats, 359–360

See also text files (sequential text files)

sequential search, **269**

algorithm (general logic), 270–271

finding the first match, 269–273

finding the last match, 273

variables needed, 270

[Serializable] attribute, 522

serialization (of objects), **366**–371, 521–524

to binary files, 382, 383, 384–385, 522, 524

to text files, 367, 368

Serialize method, 367, 368, 383, 384–385, 522

set method, 315–316, 317, 498–499

call operation, 316

setter operations, 9–**11**, 11–12

shadowing (of variables), 193–194

See also duplicate definition error

shared methods, **216**–217

sharp signs (###): comment markers, 321

short data type, 53*tbl*

shortcut key indicator (menus), *418*

Show method, 38, 136–137, 400, 404, 437

ShowDialog method, 376, 404–405, 428, 437

showGrades method, 288–289

showList methods, 283, 296–297, 301, 303

sign bit, 53

signatures (of methods/constructors), **217**–218, 324

Intellisense display, 325

significant figures (digits of precision), 57

silent casts, **82**–83

Simula language, 2

single quote ('):

assigning to character variables, 68

character delimiter, 67

displaying/printing, 68

in SQL statements, 456–458

single-dimensional arrays, **265**, **266**–282

adding elements to, 271, 281–282

copying, 278–279

defining, 266

filling ArrayLists from, 283, 287

initializing, 266

ListBoxes as, 262

with loops, 263, 264–265

parallel. *See* parallel arrays

reversing, 279–280

searching, 169–173

size, 266; increasing, 281–282

sorting, **273**; Array.Sort method, 278–279; bubble sort, **273**–278; in descending order, 277, 279–280; parallel arrays, 278–279

useful properties and methods, 266–269

slash (/). *See* division operator

slashes (//): comment indicator, 36

.sln files, 45*tbl*, 351

Smalltalk language, 2

SnapToGrid property, 30, 403*tbl*

software applications. *See* programs

SolidBrush class (objects), 433*tbl*, 437

Solution Explorer (VS.NET), 19, **32**

solutions, **44**

VS.NET file types, 45*tbl*

Sort method (ArrayLists), 286, 289

Sort method (arrays), 278–279

Sort property (ListBoxes), 277

Sorted property, 224, 225, 229, 410*tbl*

SortedLists, 304

sorting:

ArrayLists, 286–290; in descending order, 290

arrays, 273; Array.Sort method, 278–279; bubble sort, **273**–278; in descending order, 277, 279–280; parallel arrays, 278–279

ListBox items, 229; numbers, 277

ListView items, 416–417

source code, **18**

automatically generated code: avoiding using, 21; hiding, 27, 32; inserting, 26–27

blank lines in, 36

Carpet Cost application code, 32–34; explanation of, 35–39

changes in: methods and, 209–210

checks on, **140**–141

clsMember, 501–506

comments on, 36, 43; markers, 321

Contact Info application, 101

converting to executable files, 39

.cs files, 24, 45*tbl*, 311

displaying, 32

formatting styles, 36, 42–43, 148–150, 335; statement block indentation, 130, 132, 133–134; team styles, 335

frmMain class code, 25, 32–34; explanation of, 35–39

hiding, 27, 32

inheritance benefits, 495–496, 514

line width guideline, 86

methods vs. inline code, 202, 208–210, 213–214

redundancy issue, 469

regions, **27**, 32

Restaurant Bill Calculator application code, 92–93; explanation of, 89–91

simplifying, 86

stepping through, 41

Student Data Validation application, 143, 144, 145–146

switching between Form Designer and, 32

VS.NET file type, 24, 45*tbl*

source code files, 24, 45*tbl*, 311

spaces: removing leading and ending spaces from strings, 103

special characters: assigning to character variables, 67–68

spell check feature (VS.NET), 40

`Split` method, 369

SQL (Structured Query Language), **450**–459
 aggregate functions, 486–487
 common statements, 452–456, 484
 converting data types to SQL format, 458–459
 DDL statements, 484
 debugging dynamically created statements, 464
 embedded quotes problem, 456–458
 operators used in WHERE clauses, 453*tbl*
 syntax alternatives, 454

SQL Server DBMS (Microsoft), 448, 449

`Sqrt` method (square root method), 108

square brackets ([]): syntax element delimiters, 188, 454

`SquareParameter` method, 194–195, 196–198

`SquareParameterForever` method, 198–199

squiggly lines (IntelliSense), 40, 69

stack (program stack), **337**–340

stack memory, **338**

stack pointer, **338**

stack trace, **159**
 locating problems with, 182–183, 210–211

stacks, **302**–304
 adding/removing items to/from, 303
 iterating through items in, 303

`StackTrace` property, 170, 183

stakeholders (in program analysis), **496**

starting programs, 26, 41

starting VS.NET, 21

`StartupPath` property, 362

state change step. *See* change state step (in loops)

state check step (in loops), 234
 `for` loops, 241, 242, 266
 `while` loops, 236

state information:
 converting to a stream/string of data. *See* serialization
 encapsulation and, 310
 mapping to relational database tables, 470–475
 restoring, 364–365, 366
 saving, 362–364; to an Access database file, 470–475. *See also* persistence

state initialization step (in loops), 234
 `for` loops, 241
 `while` loops, 235–236

`StatefulForm` project, 361–366
 restoring form state information, 364–365, 366
 saving form state information, 362–364, 366

statement blocks, **18**, 129
 combinations for exception handlers, 164
 curly braces in, 235
 `default` block (`switch` statement), 147
 delimiters ({}), **18**, 26, 36, 37, 130; alignment styles, 43, 148; omitting in decision statements, 149–150
 indentation (indention) of, 130, 132, 133–134
 loop blocks, **235**

method blocks, **189**
 See also `catch` blocks; `finally` blocks; `try` blocks; `try-catch` blocks

statements (in programs), **18**
 first to run, 26, 41
 SQL statements, 452–456, 484
 terminator, 18
 See also specific C# and SQL statements

states (of objects), **6**–7, 8
 changing, 11, 316; initial state, 319–321
 information on. *See* state information
 initial state, 319; changing, 319–321
 writing, 521–522

static arrays, **282**
 See also multidimensional arrays; single-dimensional arrays

`static` keyword, 216

`static` methods, **216**–217

Status bar panels, **424**

`StatusBar` objects, *422*, 424
 properties, 424*tbl*

`StatusBarPanel` properties, 424*tbl*

stepping through source code, 41

storing contact objects (Contacts List program), 336

storing data, 51–75
 dates, 104
 declaring vs. defining, 72
 defining constants, 36, 65–66
 defining variables. *See* defining variables
 intermediate results, 86–87; Restaurant Bill Calculator application, 93–94
 naming rules and conventions, 62–63, 63*tbl*, 189, 311, 325
 using constants, 66–67
 See also data types

`StreamReader` class, 361, 382

`StreamReader` objects, 371

streams, 361, 382
 using with tab-delimited text files, 361

`StreamWriter` class, 361, 382
 `ReadLine` method, 365
 `WriteLine` method, 363, 367

`StreamWriter` objects, 363, 371

`StrikeOut` property, 395, 433*tbl*

`string` class, 61

`string` data type, 61, 62
 See also string variables

string variables:
 assigning values to, 61, 65
 defining, 63
 initial values, 64
 initializing, 65

strings, **39**
 aligning, 267, 381, 507–508
 character counts, 96
 comparing, 122–126
 concatenation of, 95–96
 converting: catching exceptions, 164–169; to lowercase, 98–99; to numeric values, 37, 38–39, 151–152; to uppercase, 98
 converting numeric values to, 39
 copying leading characters from, 97–98, 381
 counting the characters in, 97
 data conversion to and from, 357
 formatting options, 507–508
 inserting substrings, 102–103

`Length` property, 97
 literal constants, **65**
 locating substrings, 96; last match, 102; and parsing, 97–98
 manipulating, 95–104; program example, 99–102
 methods, 95–99, 102–104
 parsing: `Substring` method, 97–98, 379; `TryParse` method, 138–139, 166. *See also* `Parse` methods
 removing leading and ending spaces from, 103
 removing substrings, 103
 replacing substrings, 103–104
 trimming, 103, 379
 verbatim string literals, 68–69
 See also characters; string variables

Stroustrup, Bjarne, 4

structured programming, 150, 151

Structured Query Language. *See* SQL

Student Data Validation application, 142–146
 source code, 143, 144, 145–146
 testing, 146
 user interface, *142*, 143, 143*tbl*

students multidimensional array program, 291–293

styles:
 naming conventions, 62–63, 189, 311, 325
 source code formatting, 36, 42–43, 148–150, 335; statement block indentation, 130, 132, 133–134; team styles, 335

subclasses, **495**
 interfaces in, 515–516
 "is a" relationship with base classes, 495, 497, *497*, 512
 method overriding in, 514–515
 purpose, 497

subfolders, 349

subroutines. *See* methods

subscripts. *See* array indexes

substitution technique: solving complex Boolean expressions using, 128–129, 141

`Substring` method, 97–98, 379, 381

substrings:
 `IndexOf` method, 96
 `Insert` method, 102–103
 inserting, 102–103
 `LastIndexOf` method, 102
 locating, 96; last match, 102; and parsing, 97–98
 removing, 103
 replacing, 103–104

`Subtract` method, 58

subtraction operator (–), 79*tbl*
 precedence, 84*tbl*, 118*tbl*, 128*tbl*

suffixes:
 data suffixes, 52, 53*tbl*, 54, 56
 F suffix on numbers, 440

SUM function (in SQL), 486*tbl*

`Summary` property accessor method, 514

.suo files, 45*tbl*

swapping the contents of two memory locations, 274

`switch` statements, 146–147
 `break` statements in, 147
 syntax, 147

symbol table, **69**–70, 69*tbl*, 70*tbl*, 338

symbolic constants. *See* named constants

symbols. *See* special characters

ntax (in C#):
for decision statements (**if** statements), 129–131
for defining arrays, 266
for defining variables, 63
element delimiters ([]), 188
for exception handlers, 163–164; general exception handlers, 170
format items (**MemberSummary** method), 507
for interfaces, 516
for **ListBox** collection access, 225
for methods, 188
for **switch** statements, 147
for throwing exceptions, 181
ntax (in programming languages), **18**
SQL syntax alternatives, 454
See also syntax (in C#)
ntax errors (compile errors), **18**, 39, 160
ystem namespace (class library), 12
ystem.Collections namespace (class library), 282, 294–295
ystem.Collections.Specialized namespace (class library), 295
ystem.Data.OleDb namespace, 460, 483
ystem.dll: referencing class libraries in, 23
ystem.Drawing namespace (class library), 25, 395, 433, 436
ystem.Drawing.dll: referencing class libraries in, 23
ystem.Drawing.Printing namespace, 436
ystem.Globalization namespace, 151–152
ystem.IO namespace, 352–357
class group functions, 352
Directory methods, 353–354
File methods, 355–356
Path methods, 356–357
ystem.Math class. *See* **Math** class
ystem.Object class, 7, 52, 304
ystem.Windows.Forms namespace (class library), 12, 25
controls in, 29–30
ystem.Windows.Forms.Control class, 394
ystem.Windows.Forms.dll: referencing class libraries in, 23
ystem.Windows.Forms.Form class, 35–36

o: escape sequence, 68*tbl*
o-delimited text files, 359, 360, 366
using streams with, 361
abIndex property, 396–397
ble definitions: adding to databases, 484–485
bles (in relational databases), **449**, *449*
retrieving data from, 452–455
See also rows (in relational database tables)
abStop property, 396–397
am coding styles, 335
mplates:
avoiding using, 21, 24
creating project templates, 29
rminating infinite loops, 234
rmination step in computer programs, **18**
Close method, 35–36

test conditions (in statements):
Boolean expressions in decision statements, 130, 131, 148–149
data states in loop test conditions, 234; **for** loops, 241–242, 266; **while** loops, 235–236
test data, 160
Carpet Cost application, 40
testCondition (in **while** loops), 235–236
testing exception handlers, 174, 180
testing programs, 39–42
Carpet Cost application, 39–42
Restaurant Bill Calculator application, 91–92, 94
Student Data Validation application, 146
See also debugging; exceptions; program errors
text box events: data validation in, 135
text boxes (text box objects), **30**, 406, *407*
clearing input text boxes, 143
Focus method, 99, 136, 188, 400
limiting the characters that can be typed into, 400
passing arguments between methods as references to, 204–206
prefix for, 37
properties, 407–408*tbl*
text characters. *See* characters (text)
text editor (VS.NET), 19
displaying line numbers in, 24
text files (sequential text files), **357**
advantages over binary files, 357–358
binary file advantages over, 381–382
.dat files, 362
displaying, 359–360, 369, 386
persistence (of objects) using, 361–366; program example, 366–373
reading, 361
saving data to, 358
as sequential access files, 359–360
serialization (of objects) to, 367, 368
tab-delimited files, 359, 360, 361, 366
writing, 361
Text property, 37, 164, 204, 397, 406*tbl*, 408*tbl*, 409*tbl*, 410*tbl*, 419*tbl*, 421*tbl*, 424*tbl*, 426
TextAlign property, 397–398, 408*tbl*
TextBox objects. *See* text boxes
textual data. *See* strings
this keyword, 426
throw statement, 181
throwing exceptions, 181–182
tilde (~): destructor prefix, 341
Timer objects, 421
properties, methods, and event, 421*tbl*
times:
assigning to **DateTime** variables, 104
comparing, 119–120
data type, **58**, 62
displaying, 104–106
getting from users, 106–107
Tip Percent Table multidimensional array program, 293–294
Title property, 376
ToLower method, 98–99
toolbars (**ToolBar** objects), 422, *422*, 423
adding buttons to, 423–424
properties and event, 422–423*tbl*
Toolbox (Toolbox window) (VS.NET), 29, 30, 394

ToolTipText property, 423
Top property, 396
saving and restoring, 363, 365
topIndex loop (bubble sort), 274
iterations, 274–276*tbl*
ToShortDateString method, 105
toSQL helper methods, 458–459
ToString methods, 83, 336
C2 argument, 39, 264
dates, 58, 105
decimals, 39
exception handling use, 170
integers, 55–56
times, 58
ToUpper method, 98
tracing exceptions, 159, 182–183
TransparencyKey property, 431–432
tree structures, 349
trilogy (OOP trilogy), 4–5
Trim method, 103
TrimEnd method, 379
trimming strings, 103, 379
true value, 58, 62, 116
comparing Boolean variables to, 148–149
truth tables, 119, 126, 127
try blocks, **163–164**, 171–173, 210–211
for specific exceptions, 177
try-catch blocks, 202
for the **Create** method, 483–484
for database object methods, 466
nested blocks, 174–175
for **Parse** methods, 399
Restaurant Bill Calculator application, 166–167
TryParse method, 138–139, 166
two-dimensional arrays: defining, 291
See also multidimensional arrays
.txt extension, 357
See also text files
txt prefix, 37
type casting/conversion (casting), 82–83, 84, 336
data conversion to and from strings, 357

U

uint data type, 53*tbl*
UIs. *See* user interfaces
ulong data type, 53*tbl*, 54
UML (Unified Modeling Language), **497**
unary operators, **80**
underflow errors, **84**
Underline property, 395, 433*tbl*
Unicode character set, 67
Unified Modeling Language (UML), **497**
unique identifier. *See* primary key
unmanaged memory allocations, **339**
unsigned data type versions, 53*tbl*, 54
UPDATE statements (in SQL), 455, 468–469
updating database rows, 455
uppercase: converting strings to, 98
UseMnemonic property, 397
user input. *See* data validation; getting user input
user interface objects (controls), **29–30**, 393–446
calling methods by, 474–475
class most are derived from, 394
connecting event methods to, 34–35
initializing, 35
listing available controls, 29–30

locking controls, 396
Name property, 30
namespace containing, 394
placing on forms, 30–31
user interfaces (UIs):
    Carpet Cost application interface, *21*, 26–31, *31*;
        production values, 31*tbl*
    class interfaces, 314–316
    Contact Info application, 99–100
    creating, 26–32
    design guidelines, 429–431
    Essential ADO.NET text application, 461, *461*
    GUI benefit, 429
    objects. *See* user interface objects (controls)
    Restaurant Bill Calculator application interface,
        88–95
    Student Data Validation application, *142*, 143,
        143*tbl*
    VS.NET interface, 20
    See also interfaces
users:
    asking to specify filename and path, 373–377
    displaying results to, 38–39
ushort data type, 53*tbl*
using statements (directives), **25**

V

validating user input. *See* data validation
value data types, **52**–58
    assigning the value of one variable to
        another, 60
    vs. reference types, 59–61
    which to use, 61–62
values:
    assigning: null value to objects, 326, 340–341
    assigning to properties or methods, 9–11
    assigning to variables, 64–65, 70–71; from one
        reference variable to another, 60, 61; from one
        value-type variable to another, 60; string
        variables, 61, 65
    monetary, 56
    numeric. *See* numeric values
    passing arguments between methods by value,
        196–198, 199
    returning with methods, 200–201; more than
        one value, 211–213
    for variables: displaying, 41
variables, **36**
    assigning values to, 64–65, 70–71; from one
        reference variable to another, 60, 61; from one
        value-type variable to another, 60; special
        characters to character variables, 67–68; string
        variables, 61, 65
    block scope variables, **192**
    constants as, 66–67
    creation in C#, 69–72
    defining. *See* defining variables
    displaying the values (contents) of, 41
    ghost variables, 317
    initial values, 64
    initializing, 64–65

intermediate variables, 86–87, 93–94
lifetime, **64**
local scope variables, **64**, **192**–193; memory
    location, 337–338
lvalue, 70–71, 197
naming, 62–63, 63, 325
private class scope variable names, 193, 271
rvalue, 71, 197
shadowing of, 193–194
    See also character variables; exception variables;
        numeric variables; objects (class objects);
        reference variables; string variables
VB.NET (Visual Basic .NET), 4
    vs. C#, 8
    perception disadvantage, 8
verbatim string literals, 68–69
vertical tab: escape sequence, 68*tbl*
vertPagePosition variable, 439
View property, 413*tbl*, 414
visibility, **192**
Visible property, 398, 400
Visual Basic: perception disadvantage, 8
Visual Basic .NET. *See* VB.NET
Visual Studio .NET. *See* VS.NET
void keyword, 200
void methods: defining, 200
volatile memory, **348**
Vote interface:
    declaring, 516–517
    source code, 517–518
VoteCounter property, 520
VS.NET (Visual Studio .NET), **19**
    assemblies, **18**–19, 44
    and C#, 7
    displaying binary files, 385–386
    displaying text files, 386
    exceptions list, 178
    Help system, 394
    as IDE, 7, 19–20; settings files, 45*tbl*
    IntelliSense feature, 25; error messages, 69; red
        squiggly lines, 40, 69; signature display, 325
    memory space, *337*
    project file types, 44, 45*tbl*
    spell check feature, 40
    starting, 21
    terminating infinite loops, 234
    text editor, 19; displaying line numbers in, 24
    Toolbox (Toolbox window), 29, *30*, 394
    tools, 19
    user interface, 20
    See also project files (VS.NET)

W

Web page file format, 350
WFS (Windows File System), 349–352
    displaying as much information from as
        possible, 351
    namespace of classes for interacting with. *See*
        System.IO namespace

WHERE clauses (in SQL SELECT statements),
    452–454, 468–469
    operators used in, 453*tbl*
while loops, **235**–241
    break statement in, 245–247
    compound conditions in, 247–248
    data states in test conditions, 236
    else branches of if statements within, 247
    vs. for loops, 243
    for loops as, 242
    general form, 235
    Restaurant Bill Calculator application, 236–238
    testCondition, 235–236
    wish list program, 238–241, 248
wide characters. *See* Unicode character set
Width property, 396
    saving and restoring, 363, 365
wildcard characters, 452, 453
Windows (Microsoft):
    displaying as much file system information as
        possible, 351
    memory space, *337*
Windows applications: setting projects to run
    as, 22
Windows Explorer: configuring to display as
    much file system information as possible, 351
Windows File System. *See* WFS
Windows Forms projects: starting projects
    with, 21
Windows Memory Manager. *See* WMM
WindowState property, 366
wish list program, 238–241, 248
WMM (Windows Memory Manager), 69, 339
    managed memory allocations, **339**
Write method (BinaryWriter class), 385
write-only properties: designing, 318
WriteLine method (StreamWriter class),
    363, 367
writing:
    fixed-width records, 381
    sequential text files, 361
    states (of objects), 521–522

X

XML (Extensible Markup Language), 522
XML files, 44

Y

Year property, 58, 106
Yes or No question message boxes: source
    code, 137

Z

zero-based counts, 96, 225